LOVE AND REVOLUTION: A POLITICAL MEMOIR

x - history
xii - freedom
xv - 80 sns
xvi - fleeing
5 - cultural revolution - the Pandora of culture handle (dancer)
9 - not wanting to work together

New Critical Theory

General Editors:

Patricia Huntington and Martin J. Beck Matuštík

The aim of *New Critical Theory* is to broaden the scope of critical theory beyond its two predominant strains, one generated by the research program of Jürgen Habermas and his students, the other by postmodern cultural studies. The series reinvigorates early critical theory—as developed by Theodor Adorno, Herbert Marcuse, Walter Benjamin, and others—but from more decisive postcolonial and postpatriarchal vantage points. *New Critical Theory* represents theoretical and activist concerns about class, gender, and race, seeking to learn from as well as nourish social liberation movements.

LOVE AND REVOLUTION: A POLITICAL MEMOIR

PEOPLE'S HISTORY OF THE GREENSBORO MASSACRE, ITS SETTING AND AFTERMATH

Signe Waller

ROWMAN & LITTLEFIELD PUBLISHERS, INC.
Lanham • Boulder • New York • Oxford

ROWMAN & LITTLEFIELD PUBLISHERS, INC.

Published in the United States of America
by Rowman & Littlefield Publishers, Inc.
A Member of the Rowman & Littlefield Publishing Group
4720 Boston Way, Lanham, Maryland 20706
www.rowmanlittlefield.com

12 Hid's Copse Road
Cumnor Hill, Oxford OX2 9JJ, England

British Library Cataloguing in Publication Information Available

Library of Congress Cataloging-in-Publication Data

Waller, Signe, 1938–
   Love and revolution : a political memoir : people's history of the
Greensboro massacre, its setting and aftermath / Signe Waller.
      p. cm. — (New critical theory)
Includes bibliographical references (p. 517) and index.
   ISBN 0-7425-1364-5 (alk. paper) — ISBN 0-7425-1365-3 (pbk. : alk.
paper)
 1. Greensboro (N.C.)—History. 2. Riots—North Corolina—Greensboro.
3. Waller, Signe, 1938– 4. Communists—North
Carolina—Greensboro—Biography. 5. Civil rights workers—North
Carolina—Greensboro—Biography. I. Title. II. Series.
   F264.G8 W35 2002
   975.6'62—dc21
                                    2002009974

Printed in the United States of America

♾™ The paper used in this publication meets the minimum requirements of
American National Standard for Information Sciences—Permanence of Paper
for Printed Library Materials, ANSI/NISO Z39.48–1992.

In Memory of

César Vincente Cauce
March 5, 1954–November 3, 1979

Michael Ronald Nathan, M.D.
July 13, 1947–November 5, 1979

William Evan Sampson
January 23, 1948–November 3, 1979

Sandra Neely Smith
December 25, 1950–November 3, 1979

James Michael Waller, M.D.
November 5, 1942–November 3, 1979

Labor's wrath and hope and sorrow
Red the promise, black the threat
Who are we not to remember?
Who are we to dare forget?

—Ralph Chaplin

CONTENTS

PREFACE AND
ACKNOWLEDGMENTS

*L*ove and Revolution: A Political Memoir is a mixed-genre book. It is a memoir, and it is also a history of the people's movement in the United States, with certain geographic and temporal coordinates—the South, North Carolina, Greensboro, the 1970s, and the 1980s. I have sometimes referred to this work as a *documemoir* to capture two of its main aspects, documented history and memoir. To do justice to the astonishing events in this story, I have not been embarrassed to combine many stylistic elements; first person narrative, journalistic essay, philosophical discussion, political analysis, the prosaic, the poetic, the humorous, and the critical.

The book takes in events preceding and leading up to the Greensboro Massacre of November 3, 1979, the massacre itself, and events stemming from the incident. I have included extensive factual details and set the story in its historical context. I have not shied away from causal explanations, analysis, or interpretation.

I must say a few words about my relationship to the book's contents, for this presented a challenge to me, the author, and will do the same, presumably, to you, the reader. I have written about a history in which I participated actively and, at certain moments, centrally. I am inside the story; but because this memoir is framed in a larger people's movement history, I am also outside—both protagonist and historian.

If I were merely an "insider" I might never have attempted this book. My training and experiences as a philosophy teacher, as a social science researcher, and as a press secretary for a political organization have left me with the work habits, if not the confidence, needed to tackle the job. My insider knowledge was acquired as a revolutionary activist over many years with the Workers Viewpoint Organization. WVO sponsored an anti-Klan rally on November 3, 1979, that was attacked by several carloads of Klansmen and Nazis who murdered and maimed demonstrators. I helped to organize the ill-fated anti-Klan rally and participated in it. I survived the attack on the rally by home-grown terrorists and was left widowed. Afterward, I was a press secretary in North Carolina for the WVO (renamed the Communist Workers Party in October 1979). There was a tremendous uphill struggle to extract justice for the murders and injuries incurred in the right-wing attack. Many individuals and organizations took part in that struggle for justice along with the survivors of the attack. I was a plaintiff and witness during six years of litigation that ended in 1985 with an unprecedented legal victory.

To tell this story, I have relied on the memory of what I experienced; on interviews with many friends who experienced these events; on private archives containing numerous unpublished documents relevant to the story; and on published and public documents in various media. As its title suggests, this book is intensely personal and intensely political.

I have made no pretense to being a detached historian, whatever that means; I was an involved participant. I have relied on a factual account backed up by a great deal of documented evidence to tell the story, and not solely on my puny memory. The facts may easily be sorted out from my, or any one else's, opinions. Having presented known relevant facts and having made my own point of view toward these facts as explicit as possible, I hope readers are adequately prepared to form their own judgments and conclusions. My case for being objective rests on explicitness of viewpoint, honesty, and accuracy. The two decades that have elapsed since most of the events I write about occurred perhaps have provided a critical distance from those events. I have sought to incorporate a critical outlook in the book, especially in the final chapter.

My personal relationship to the events discussed in this book is reflected in the way the narrative unfolds, in some emotive passages, and in stylistic effects such as foreshadowing and retrospection. I have tried to be sufficiently clear so that attentive readers are not confused about the sequencing of actual events. The story is a complex one. By rendering many episodes in considerable detail, I hope to reflect that complexity, and to bring out inherent meanings.

A particular challenge has been the use of political language. The book features political activists whose activism was informed by political theories. I have tried to be explanatory for a general reader, but precise enough for those interested in political theory. Above all, I have attempted to make this story accessible to readers who are not political activists or theorists. In explaining the concepts and theories related to Marxism that are relevant to the narrative, my goal has been to define and clarify without diluting or distorting meanings.

I and others who are quoted in this book would not necessarily use the same words today as we did twenty years ago, in speech or in writing. There are various reasons why some of us would say some things differently today. In choosing the most appropriate language, I have tried to be as accurate, accessible, and critical as I could. In order to capture the flavor of the period, I have kept much of the language as we used it. Some terms that I think may not be understood, or may be misleading because they are technical, jargon, or in-group terms, I have rephrased in the interest of better communication. Another issue, however, relates to the repudiation or criticism of a concept or view as it was stated in the past. I have tried to signal, with introductory phrases such as "in retrospect" and in other ways, where a change in language reflects more than the attempt to better communicate with an audience. As youthful disciples of Marx, Lenin, and Mao, we could be, and were at times, overly doctrinaire, though it did not seem that way to us then.

Too many caveats about political language are also not called for. I could not, and have not wished to, free this book of technical Marxist terms, but I do not rely on them to make my case. On the whole, I have tried to use language as it is ordinarily and widely used. Theoretical language is very useful, but a special historical sensitivity is necessary when dealing with politics, perhaps more than with other branches of knowledge.

In sum, I have endeavored to be critical, to explain terms that might be unfamiliar to a general reader, and to say things the way I would say them now, often while also indicating how we said them a decade or two ago. This work was in progress for a long time, and my own outlook was developing further in that period, which certainly also bears on language choices and the manner of the narration.

Just as the manuscript was in the final stages of preparation for submission, the terrorist attacks of September 11, 2001, occurred. Not long afterward came the bombing of Afghanistan by the United States, and a train of still unfolding consequences from all of these actions. These events have cast everything in the world in a different light. "Everything" includes this book. Since the book concerns political revolutionaries working for fundamental social change and is not a book about some delightful and harmless topic such as flower arranging, it almost certainly will be read differently, resonate differently, and be received differently in all quarters of society post–September 11. I have not felt adequately prepared to deal with what is implied in this realization, and I have not thought it necessary to alter the work I offer here that recounts, analyzes, and interprets past events. One thing remains unaltered even after September 11: just as in the Greensboro Massacre and other events recounted in this political memoir, so also in my personal life, I have opposed terrorism, whether enacted by states, sects, or unaffiliated individuals. My life is committed to creating a more just and humane society. Terrorism is not the way.

As some experiences set forth here illustrate, when people speak truth to power, power often talks back by labeling those with courage to speak out as "violent," or "extreme," or "violent extremists," in an effort to cut them off from other people. In a post–September 11 environment, the name-calling is likely to include the words *terrorist* or *supporter of terrorism*. As Marty Nathan said when I interviewed her for this book, "People commit acts of violence. We had never committed an act of violence. The act of violence had been committed against us." Despite stringent rhetoric—and this is one of the criticisms—my friends and I worked for social justice through nonviolent methods of organizing and educating people. During the years it took to write this book, it was *always* my intention to share positive and useful lessons from our experience about *how to organize and how to persist in struggle in a very difficult environment in which people's civil liberties are being attacked.* For those committed to working for a safer and more just, democratic, and peaceful world, I believe that this book, with the amazing slice of history it relates, is of immense and current relevance.

It is particularly important to emphasize that this is not just "my" story but contains many elements of "our" story. To be sure, *Love and Revolution: A Political Memoir* is the fruit of my labor, the work of one white, Jewish woman from a middle-class family in Brooklyn, New York. But it is just as essentially a collective story, and the fruit of collective effort and wisdom. The men and women whose story is told alongside mine represent a diversity of races, ethnic backgrounds, religions, class backgrounds, and other cultural manifestations. It is most significant for every aspect of this story that these people in all their diversity united and acted together. Apart from this, I have no memoir to write. The thoughts, voices, and shared conversation of friends and comrades are in all the best phrases and in any insights of substance you may find here. In a larger sense, the "our" includes the readership of this work, and beyond, in as much as the book is a people's history that revolves around a significant event in U.S. history.

I humbly acknowledge my debts to those whose support and assistance were critical to this project. Several people took the completed manuscript and gave me helpful feedback on the whole thing, challenging me to rethink and rewrite portions of the book, and thereby greatly improving it. Berenice A. Carroll, Professor of Political Science and Women's Studies at Purdue University and Professor Emerita at the University of Illinois at Urbana-Champaign, gave me valuable guidance. She offered specific insights from her vast store of scholarship and activism in the women's movement. I am grateful for her friendship and support. Pauline Lipman, Associate Professor of Social and Cultural Foundations in Education of DePaul University, and Rico Gutstein, Associate Professor of Curriculum and Instruction at the University of Illinois-Chicago, both familiar with the political history covered in the book, made numerous suggestions and criticisms that led me to further reflect on and refine my argument and presentation. Their contribution to the book and their personal support for me were significant factors in any merit the book possesses. (While finishing this book, my floppy disk drive malfunctioned so I could not back up my work. The next day a Fed-Ex package arrived with a gift from Pauline and Rico. It was a new zip drive so that I could happily plug away.) Also reviewing the entire manuscript in its final stage was my sister in struggle, Marty Nathan, M.D., Administrator of the Greensboro Justice Fund and one of the widows in the 1979 Klan/Nazi attack. Marty, too, is familiar with much that is covered in this book, particularly the fight for justice in the post–November 3, 1979, period. Her corrections and suggestions, made with tact and good humor, vastly improved the work.

Other people whose warm friendship I have enjoyed over the years read portions of the final manuscript and helped me hone it further. I am very grateful to Dr. Paul Bermanzohn, Attorney Lewis Pitts, Rev. Nelson Johnson, and Professor Elliot Fratkin, all of whom made specific suggestions and gave me ample encouragement. They are my brothers in struggle and makers of the history I have recorded. A special thanks to Rev. Johnson, for thirty years as my mentor as well as my friend.

I am grateful to several readers of earlier versions of this book. Their feedback and support helped me keep on keeping on. My thanks to Mab Segrest, Dan Eades, Jeffrey Paris, Kenneth Janken, and Marta Rose. Additionally, Clint Fink gave me the benefit of his editorial experience at many junctures. His attention to this book and to articles I have written for the newspaper he edits, the *Community Times*, resulted in improvements in my writing style. Clint believed in the book well before it was clear it would ever be published. I owe much to his assistance and friendship.

Other debts are harder to nail down but just as valid. They are people whose conversation, inspiration, and friendship are invisibly woven into the matrix of the book. Most dear to me are my sisters in struggle, Sally Bermanzohn, Willena Cannon, Floris Cauce Weston, Joyce Johnson, and Dale Sampson-Levin. The entire Board of Directors and Advisory Board of the Greensboro Justice Fund has been a mainstay of support. Some are mentioned in this book, but I hope all, whether mentioned by name or not, understand how much I owe to them. Others who have helped me in ways they may not even be aware of are Rev. Henry Atkins, Fr. Jim Waters, Deanna Pilkenton, Erik Rose, Claire Goldstein, Jane Waller, Myra Schiffman, Michael Yetman, Edward Whitfield, Emily Mann, and Marsha Paludan. They all have my heartfelt thanks. I also acknowledge my debt to Harry Targ and Dena Targ. They and other members of the Committees of Correspondence for Democracy and Socialism have helped to make the Greensboro history that is recounted here more widely known.

Martin Beck Matuštík of Purdue University and Patricia Huntington of Loyola University, the editors of the New Critical Theory series of which this work is a part, saw value in my project when it was in a much rougher form. I am tremendously appreciative of their support, encouragement, and advice and express my warmest thanks to them. For my positive experience with Rowman & Littlefield Publishers, I am grateful to Acquisitions Editor Eve DeVaro and her colleagues.

Helpful with images and with permissions to use photographs were Wayne Lottinville and Marc Green, the latter of the *News & Record* in Greensboro. My thanks to them and also to photographic essayists Fr. Jim Waters and Laura Seel for giving me access to images related to my subject. I have drawn freely on the 1980 documentary *Red November, Black November* for this book and would like to express my appreciation to my friends in the struggle who produced it, Sally Alvarez and Carolyn Jung.

The most valuable prior writings in relation to the Greensboro Massacre have been done by Sally Bermanzohn, Paul Bermanzohn, M.D., Marty Nathan, M.D., and Rev. Nelson Johnson. I incorporated much of their thoughtful analyses in this book as I tried to build upon their excellent contributions.

Finally, my husband, Jim Rose, deserves accolades merely for having married a November Third widow, but he has also earned them for his understanding of the importance of this project in my life and his loving support while I was accomplishing it. My children, Antonia Lilley and Alex Goldstein, have helped sustain me throughout. They have continued to love me in spite of everything that they have gone through (that they would not have gone through if I were not their mother). My parents, Fay and Ted Burke, are also part of this book, and I have tried to honor their loving memory in writing it. The five people killed in Greensboro on November 3, 1979—César Cauce; Michael Nathan, M.D.; William Sampson; Sandra Smith; and James Waller, M.D.—were outstanding in their dedication to the cause of humanity. In revering the example of their lives, I have tried to write a book that honors their everlasting memory.

INTRODUCTION

Only moments before the caravan enters Morningside Homes, anti-Klan demonstrators are standing in a circle singing freedom songs. Rally organizers are checking the sound system on a flatbed truck, distributing posters, and preparing around a hundred people—black and white, young and old—to start a march across town. The atmosphere is almost festive.

When nine cars carrying some three dozen Klansmen and Nazis drive slowly into the black housing project, demonstrators are surprised. People stop what they are doing and line the street. Shouts of "Nigger," "Kike," and "You asked for the Klan, here we are" issue from the caravan. Demonstrators chant back, "Death to the Klan!" A few hit the intruders' cars with picket sticks.

Suddenly, the vehicles halt. From near the front of the caravan, a Klansman fires a long-barreled pistol into the air, leaving a puff of black smoke. The assailants jump out of their vehicles and attack demonstrators who are running for cover or scrambling in an effort to defend people. A brief stick fight and a knife attack ensue. While the first few gunshots, coming from the front of the caravan, draw demonstrators' attention, Klansmen and Nazis in two rear vehicles further up the street are unpacking an arsenal of weapons. They take deadly aim with shotguns, pistols, and an AR 180 semiautomatic rifle. Several people are already on the ground, dead or wounded, when a few demonstrators manage to fire back with handguns, to no avail. The Klan and Nazi ambush lasts eighty-eight seconds, leaving five people dead and ten wounded. Those killed are leaders in their community, known for their opposition to racism. Most are militant trade union leaders as well. Killed on November 3, 1979 are César Vincente Cauce, William Evan Sampson, Sandra Neely Smith, and James Michael Waller, M.D. Mortally wounded and dead two days later is Michael Ronald Nathan, M.D.

There are no police on the scene. Television cameramen, however, record the assault. The assailants return their weapons to the trunk of their vehicle and speed away. A few Klansmen and Nazis, tardy in getting away, are arrested minutes later when police arrive. Police do not pursue fleeing Klansmen and Nazis, but they arrest some of the stunned and wounded demonstrators. Devastated survivors denounce a police setup with the Klan.

The police were not at the crime scene the morning of November 3, 1979, but their fingerprints are all over the Greensboro Massacre, as are those of some other government agencies.

The Greensboro Massacre sliced time into before and after, both flowing to an ugly reference point of officially sanctioned, death-dealing gunfire. On November Third, all possibility for happiness drained from me like the blood that flowed from the bodies of my dead and dying friends. Gone was the dream of growing old with my husband. Ahead was unutterable spiritual desolation, pain, and anger. Personal loss was felt and lived within a public and political context that hardly left time for grieving.

What happened in Greensboro on November 3, 1979, goes beyond personal tragedy. It is part of our political history, especially of a rarely taught people's history, one that aims at democratizing society, insuring civil rights, and realizing social and economic equality. The Greensboro Massacre cannot be understood severed from its context. Like all events, it has a before, a during, and an after; its truest historical meaning emerges from the events before and after the violent assault. November Third is indeed a "reference point" in a larger, significant historical context.

The five people killed at the anti-Klan rally in Greensboro, North Carolina, reached maturity in the 1960s and embodied its activist and idealist spirit. My husband, Jim Waller, who died two days before his thirty-seventh birthday, was the oldest. Though not practicing at the time, he was a medical doctor, trained in pediatrics with a specialty in infectious diseases of children. Bill Sampson, a Phi Beta Kappa student leader and summa cum laude college graduate, had a master's degree from Harvard Divinity School. César Cauce, son of a Cuban emigré who had been an official in the Batista government, graduated from Duke University magna cum laude as a history major. Sandi Smith, the only black person and only woman killed that November day, had been president of the student body at Bennett College. Dr. Michael Nathan was practicing pediatric medicine at a clinic in Durham that served a predominantly black and poor population when he was killed. All five had demonstrated considerable intellectual ability and leadership qualities. They might have had lucrative careers but chose instead to work for racial, social, and economic justice in factories, hospitals, and poor communities.

None of the men who opened fire on the anti-Klan rally, killing five very special people and wounding others, were convicted for their crimes in either of two criminal proceedings, a state and a later federal trial. The shooters' coconspirators and collaborators in the Greensboro Police Department and the United States Government did not even face charges in those trials. In 1985, a civil rights suit by injured victims and survivors of the Greensboro Massacre brought a faint ray of justice: For the first time in various legal proceedings stemming from the violent incident, *some* of the criminals were held liable for *some* of the victims.

The Greensboro Massacre defines endings and beginnings. It broke the momentum we had achieved in our labor organizing and campaigns against racism. It began a new situation in which we were forced to react daily to attacks aimed at discrediting the murder victims and the survivors of November Third. The killings of effective labor leaders froze the progress of the textile workers' unions that those leaders had energized. Before November 3, 1979, we achieved successes in uniting blacks and whites around a revolutionary social agenda, in workplaces and communities in North Carolina. Those manipulating the lives and labor of others felt threatened. After that day, massacre survivors and conscientious citizens embarked on a quest for justice. The survivors worked unremittingly to expose a criminal conspiracy and cover-up. The workplace and community organizing, the massacre, the cover-up of official involvement, and the long aftermath of the violent episode are all essential moments in my story.

This is a tale of government collusion in political assassinations. It is a tale of historically rooted racism in the United States, with its perennial bigots and villains sprouting like weeds each generation. It is also a tale about a home-grown, American variety of communism that rode the crest of the sixties' wave of civil rights and antiwar struggles. And it is a love story. Love gave people courage to challenge the status quo and go forth to change it, in a South that had only recently and very reluctantly discarded its Jim Crow laws—laws that also entrenched a virulent antiunionism.

In speaking about what motivated the murders on November Third and what lay behind the travesty of justice that followed, I deal straightforwardly with the anticommunist and racist scapegoating that served powerful scoundrels as their last refuge. Those who, from the viewpoint of the ruling elite, are the fearsome hordes clamoring at the gates of the republic find a place in my narrative as heroes and heroines. I affirm and celebrate the real power of working people to understand and guide their own destinies.

In the pages that follow, I consider what preceded and precipitated the conspiracy between the government and the right wing that resulted in the November Third massacre. What, specifically, did the City of Greensboro, the Greensboro Police Department, and the U.S. government do to set up the violence, and how did they attempt to cover up their involvement? How could juries acquit defendants seen in live videotapes mounting an assault and shooting people down? What was the political climate in which the struggle for justice was joined? What are the lessons of the Greensboro Massacre for people willing to work for a more socially just and peaceful world?

The philosophical and political implications of November Third continue to haunt me. The Ku Klux Klan and the Nazis appear to be enshrined in the woodwork of Western civilization. How can the government of a supposedly democratic republic aid and abet these racist killers? What does it mean when people, whose actions exemplify the religious and spiritual principles of love and service to humanity that we claim to cherish, can be shot down in the street with impunity? What future is there for a nation that devours the best of its own citizenry? The Greensboro Massacre was a particular incident, but the universal resides in the particular. What do the events surrounding November 3, 1979, tell us about the United States, its culture, and its politics? Were those such times that gentle people had to become revolutionaries? As Dr. Marty Nathan, widowed on November Third, observed at the time: If you truly love people and see how they are oppressed, how can you *not* strive mightily to change the system oppressing them? If that was true then, is it not true now?

I

HEIRS TO THE
RADICAL SIXTIES

1

THE MAKING OF A RADICAL, OR HOW I BECAME ONE OF THEM

THERE BUT FOR THE GRACE OF GOD GO I

Everyone who came of age and became politicized in the sixties has a story. As in a modern-day version of *The Canterbury Tales*, we entertained each other by sharing stories on long trips to protest rallies in Washington, D.C., or New York City. This is the story of my pilgrimage toward revolutionary politics.

Like so many others, I was politicized during the Vietnam War. The crystallizing experience that started me on the road to communism was mundane—having a baby. I was a student in Paris writing a philosophy dissertation for Columbia University when the Gulf of Tonkin incident occurred and provided a rationale for the entry of U.S. troops into Vietnam. One of the American newspapers—I think it was the overseas *Herald Tribune*—ran a photograph of a Vietnamese woman lying on a mined road, her dead baby in her arms. That picture spoke to me about the war. I had just given birth to my first child, Antonia Bess Goldstein, on August 3, 1965, and I felt a wave of sympathy for the woman in the photograph. I could have been that woman. It could have been my baby killed by a mine in the road. I was gripped by the proverbial "there but for the grace of God go I."

It struck me that it was my country doing these horrors *in my name*. Vietnam, a poor peasant country, seemed no threat to the United States. "What are we doing there?" I asked myself. "What did those people do to deserve this? They are a sovereign nation." Thus my political awakening hinged on something so quotidian and apolitical as giving birth. When I returned to the United States in 1966, I was ready to stand up and be counted as one person opposed to the

Vietnam War. If the way had not been prepared by others who took a stand early on and laid the foundations for a protest movement of great magnitude, I would not have had this option, and I don't believe I would have created it. I would have felt powerless. Antiwar protesters set up a power center toward which those with humanitarian concerns could gravitate.

At least ten years would pass between the time I returned with my husband, Carl Goldstein, from France to the United States with our beautiful infant daughter (Tonya then, now Tonie) and my proud self-identification as a communist revolutionary. Having decided, in the early 1960s, on a career of teaching and scholarship, I saw to getting my credentials in order. That meant finishing a doctoral thesis in philosophy of science. As I had resolved while in Paris, once back in the states I attended mass demonstrations against the Vietnam War—protests that grew in size and intensity as the war in Southeast Asia became dirtier and uglier. I marched behind the political heavies who organized such events. Although I felt it imperative to attend these protests whenever I could, I did not attempt to become a leader or organizer. Teaching philosophy and raising two children—Alexander Solomon Goldstein (Shlomo then, now Alex) was born in Rhode Island on March 7, 1968—filled my time.

The liberating currents of the sixties were late to reach me. I only went into action toward the end of the decade—a late bloomer at thirty-something. Philosophy was, at that time, regarded as a masculine pursuit, and women were not particularly encouraged to become philosophers. As a student, then teacher, of philosophy, I took pride in my independence and ability to be unbound by convention, but my pride was individualistic. I might have seen the commonality of my strivings with the women's movement, but actually I had no wish to associate with any political movement.

From childhood, I had determined (rather quixotically) that I would grow up to be a lady and also that I would not respect a dualism of occupations along gender lines. I was determined to do whatever excited my interest and enthusiasm. One activity that consumed many waking hours of my teenage years was learning to play jazz drums in my parents' five-room apartment in Brooklyn. I was also bookish and relished solitude. Life in a convent appeared idyllic. When I found out only Catholics, not Jews, could be nuns, I was a little disappointed.

In the fifties and even in the sixties, there were few established social roles for independent women. I opted for respectability through marriage so I could quietly pursue my love of philosophy, books, learning, and life's adventures.

I was an assistant professor at Southeastern Massachusetts University, in the New Bedford and Fall River area, from 1967 to 1971. While on the faculty, I engaged in *perfectly outrageous behavior*. Those were indeed wild times. There were frequent war protests; the terrible assassinations of Robert Kennedy and Martin Luther King; and urban riots from coast to coast. I had a black student, Paige, who watched his best friend get shot and killed by white teenagers who drove into their neighborhood. Paige came to my philosophy class transformed within days from a boy to a man, a Black Panther with steel in his eyes. During the four years I taught at SMU, not a single semester went by without sit-ins, class boycotts, mass rallies, and such. I reckoned there was one academic year in which I spent more time with students in a courtroom, at rallies, teach-ins, and parties—all in relation to the war protest, the assassination of Dr. Martin Luther King, and other political events—than I did in the classroom.

On campus I joined a faculty-student effort to dump the hawkish president of the university. One evening, at a cocktail party held for faculty, the president told me that if I were a man he would punch me in the nose. I think that on other occasions I have prompted similar feelings in men who heartily despise purposeful, independent women.

Many people saw the mass antiwar and civil rights activity as the sign of a *cultural revolution* happening in the United States. I thought of it that way at the time, and I understood that everything was up for grabs—we could design new ways of living. I stood out from other faculty members because of my close association with the students. I believe that students are the central figures in the education process and not the lowest creatures in a hierarchy.

My ultrademocratic attitude, however, was pressed into service to glorify the life of a libertine. Although married with children, I had become a regular cut-up. A Victorian and a rebel summed up the emotions in my breast. My office door sported a large theatrical poster of a fashionably padded and haughty nineteenth-century actress outside a stage door, with the caption, "Oh, what a wicked woman she must be!" Inside that office—and not necessarily after hours—adoring students gave me gifts from sizable caches of marijuana, which we sometimes smoked together. My marriage to Carl Goldstein was having difficulties in those stormy years. I justified my romantic affairs by convincing myself—in spite of having the worst jealous nature under the sun—that I was polygamous and that polygamy was the intrinsic condition of our tribe and was a fine thing.

At the time, another female philosophy professor, Angela Davis, was a role model for me. I admired her. But she was a communist, and while I had begun to be labeled a radical by others (and to think of myself that way), I was not especially drawn to communism. In this period, I went to a demonstration where I witnessed a small contingent of procommunist protesters attacked ferociously, and without provocation, by club-wielding police on horseback, who seemed to descend out of nowhere. It was a minor turning point. Until then I had thought little about antiwar protesters from the far left. Perhaps I felt it was too bad that they were spoiling things for more respectable, middle-of-the-road dissidents like myself! (If someone had told me then that a decade later I would be standing at the front of an armed funeral march led by communists, and that I would be one of *them*, I might have objected, "Wait, you've picked up the wrong script.")

My ladylike style of sixties protesting—which probably was predictable from my mother's story that as a child I would come in the house and cry every time I got my pinafore dirty—got a jolt by seeing the far-left opponents of the war isolated and abused because of their political views. I began to get a long overdue political education and some understanding of classes in society and other realities. I recall a student who was a Vietnam War vet berating me for *making common cause with the communists*. I must have overcome my bias against communism by that time because, though not yet a communist, I replied, "So be it. If by saying what is true I'm making common cause with the commies, so be it." (That same vet later became an antiwar protester, sought me out, and spoke more kindly to me.)

In the spring semester of 1971, some of my philosophy students drew me into the People's Peace Treaty campaign. It was to unfold at a May Day demonstration in Washington, D.C. The rhetoric inspired me. The people themselves, tired of waiting for their government to get around to it, would declare peace. My students planned to be on the streets of D.C. demonstrating, but I intended to adopt a more dignified posture suitable to a scholar and teacher—that of a nonparticipating observer.

We arrived in town the day before the demonstration along with tens of thousands of other people and had no place to stay overnight. We were picked up off the street by a middle-class white couple. Both government employees, they were cruising around looking for urban guerrillas to host. It was their contribution toward ending a war they too opposed. They took half a dozen of us to their plush suburban home, providing us with food, showers, and comfortable beds.

The next morning I was in the street running with everyone else, the observer idea having proved not merely disingenuous on my part but a patent impossibility in practice. Our strategically preposterous objective was to occupy the Key Bridge. I had a handkerchief that had been dipped in egg. I vaguely remember that the egg was to protect my eyes against mace. We got beat up, gassed with mace, and arrested. My eyes burned so badly that I could not see for hours and thought I had been permanently blinded. Some of my friends were worse off. One young student had his head bashed in by a policeman's nightstick. We had to wait for him to get out of the hospital before we could return to Massachusetts. Another member of our group had her leg bruised purple-black from the top of her thigh to her knee. I was arrested and taken with hundreds of others to Washington's Georgetown Prison. The experience went a long way to consolidating my commitment to political activism and making it clear which side of the barricades I had to be on.

The Georgetown prison hadn't been used for a while and was reopened as an emergency response to other D.C. jails filling up. Each cell was crammed with protesters singing, chanting, and beating on cell bars with their shoes, nonstop. During the fourteen or so hours most of us were there, we talked about what we would do when we got out. The consensus was to go back to our home communities, let people know what our government was doing, and work all the harder to end the war.

The experience of the People's Peace Treaty in D.C. was a catalyst in my political education. I returned from it with a sense of having acquired a mission. "I'm now firmly and irrevocably on the side of the barricades with the people against my warmongering government" is how I might have put it. I felt an obligation to play a more responsible role in working to end the Vietnam War. Around this time too, or somewhat earlier, I read Noam Chomsky's "The Responsibility of Intellectuals" in the *New York Review of Books*. I studied the article, spread out on my kitchen table. It was not enough to revel in erudition. Chomsky's article made me think seriously about how I should *use my education*. His arguments urged me toward commitment.

My husband, daughter, and son were in the foyer to greet me when I returned from Washington. They had made a Welcome Home banner. My husband joked as I walked through the door, "here's your mama, the jailbird." Carl had taken a position in the Art Department at the University of North Carolina in Greensboro, and we were to move south shortly. I went to Greensboro prepared to be an activist in the peace movement. I had no idea what that meant or what I would do. One of my students in Massachusetts, who heard I would be moving south, warned me to watch out. "A person with your views will rile up the Ku Klux Klan," he said. Laughing, I rejoined, "I sure hope so."

MOVING TOWARD A REVOLUTIONARY POLITICS

Shortly after arriving in Greensboro in late spring of 1971, I founded the Greensboro Peace Center in hopes of attracting anti–Vietnam War activists. Some members of the pacifist-oriented American Friends Service Committee

(AFSC) in the Piedmont area joined the small grassroots organization. In slavery times, Quakers who had settled in the North Carolina Piedmont led manumission and abolitionist efforts.[1] Around Guilford College, a spirit of nonviolence and concern for human rights seemed to linger in the memory of the place. Nationally, AFSC produced an impressive body of informational and educational materials for antiwar advocates and activists. This included *The Automated Air War*, a slide show that catalogued some of the gruesome weaponry used against villagers in Southeast Asia, such as antipersonnel and pineapple bombs.[2]

The Greensboro Peace Center became my full-time work. On numerous occasions we followed up a showing of the AFSC slides with discussion about what we could do to end the war. We stood in silent vigil in front of the post office. And we regularly dealt with landlords who threw us out of downtown storefront offices—*after* we'd spent weeks renovating and improving their real estate.

As I became more informed about the causes of the war, I became an ever leftward-moving political animal. The word *imperialism*, for example, was on many lips—a household word, if you walked into the right households. I read Eduardo Galeano's *Open Veins of Latin America*, and I understood that imperialism is not a one-time decision to violate a country's sovereignty, a sort of policy "mistake." It is a historical policy, renewed over time by successive governments, of enforcing economic domination over another country. That book was seminal for me, and I read much, much more.

In the early 1970s, the Venceremos Brigade was sending North Americans to Cuba for short work stints. As the Greensboro Peace Center was phasing itself out at the conclusion of the Vietnam War, I worked with the Venceremos Brigade. Black North American activists returning from visits to Cuba were enthusiastic about the Cubans' success in ridding society of racism. Their reports carried credibility.

Once, in the course of working with the Brigade, I was with a comrade from Durham, Charles Finch, and we were in the home of a young white man in Greensboro who claimed to be interested in going to Cuba on a work brigade. We interviewed him and, on leaving his house, walked around the block to Charles' van. We were followed by a middle-aged man and a woman who materialized just as Charles was about to open the van door. The man hurled angry curses at us and threatened to hang us. He was Ku Klux Klan, he let on, and in case we weren't taking his death threat seriously, he bragged he was also in touch with the FBI.

We had no idea if this lunatic was armed or what he would do if Charles simply unlocked the van and tried to drive away. Finally that is what we did, but at the time it seemed very possible that our stalker would react violently. We learned afterward that the man, George Dorsett, was indeed both a Klansman and an FBI informant. His FBI cover and the Klan infighting that led to his becoming an informant became front-page news a few years after that incident.

The Greensboro Peace Center did not disband immediately when the Vietnam War ended but remained active and monitored the peace accords for a year or two. Along with a few other Peace Center members, I wanted us to mobilize around social justice issues here at home. At the Peace Center, we circulated information about the most notorious of several racist offensives going on in North Carolina at the time—the cases of the Wilmington Ten and the Charlotte Three.[3] In 1973, we invited friends from Charlotte to come to Greensboro to conduct a forum about political prisoners in North Carolina.

In the main, blacks had been marching for civil rights and whites had been marching to end the Vietnam War. The two great movements, however, needed to unite and march together. This was the direction Martin Luther King Jr. was taking when he was assassinated. The ruling class hated to see whites protest and became apoplectic at the mere prospect of blacks organizing. But what they had the least stomach for was *a union of black and white activists striving together toward the same goals, linking up the fight against racism here with anti-imperialist struggles abroad.*

Such sentiments were in my mind the evening several black activists from Charlotte visited our storefront office in Greensboro to talk about black political prisoners from Wilmington and Charlotte. A couple of local black activists were with them. One impressed me immediately with his personality, integrity, and insightful speech. Handsome, with a look of confidence in victory flashing from his eyes, he struck me as a liberated human being, a person of superior intelligence. This man and his wife, after I met her, continued to inspire me with their humanity and wisdom. They were to become two of my most beloved friends. It was my first meeting with Nelson Napoleon Johnson.

In 1974, Nelson, his wife Joyce, and others organized a countywide coalition against the death penalty, and I worked with them. About a year later, I was reading a journal they recommended to me for its political analyses of the issues of the day, like busing and the Equal Rights Amendment. The journal, printed on cheap news pulp, set in broken type, and stapled together, was the *Workers Viewpoint.* I had been searching for truth; a Marxist class analysis made more sense to me than anything I had considered before.

From 1973 to 1975, I taught in the Philosophy and Religion Department at Bennett College, a small school for black women in Greensboro. The college retained much of the atmosphere of a girls' finishing school. Not long before I was there, the "Bennett Belles," as the students were called, were required to attend church wearing white gloves. After two years my contract was not renewed. I was politely told the reason was "economic retrenchment." I supposed the school could not afford the consequences of my political radicalism for financial support from alumni.

The first year I taught there, I invited Owusu Sadauki, a.k.a. Howard Fuller, to speak to my class. The students, mightily impressed, invited him back to address a general assembly, and he agreed. A prominent union organizer and radical political leader in Durham who had the ear of African leaders in the liberation struggle raging in Africa, Owusu delivered a thunderously revolutionary speech. As it turned out, the assembly was held on a recruitment day for the next freshman class and the campus was full of visitors, including alumni. I imagine the Bennett administration was surprised and had some embarrassing moments over this. I knew that my fate at that school was sealed, and I squirmed in my seat, even as I thrilled to Owusu's revolutionary rhetoric. Much later I concluded I was arrogant, racist, and untutored while on the Bennett faculty. I came to understand the odds against survival faced by black institutions and to see how unhelpful were some of my ill-considered actions. In fact, while I was there I did not appreciate the extent to which Bennett College had been a leader in moving Greensboro along democratic and progressive pathways. It was way out in front of better-funded white institutions.

When I returned to Greensboro much later to coordinate the twentieth anniversary of the Greensboro Massacre,[4] the Reverend Nelson Napoleon Johnson, survivor of the Greensboro Massacre and now pastor at the Faith Community Church, spoke at Bennett College. He paid tribute to the school for giving Dr. Martin Luther King Jr. a platform when others in Greensboro were afraid to do so and refused. King was branded as a radical, an outside agitator, and a communist sympathizer.

Bennett, "in the tradition of Sojourner Truth, made the decision that this man needed to be heard in Greensboro," Nelson said. The small, courageous college for black women "opened her doors to Dr. Martin Luther King, Jr. In 1958, this giant of a man stood before this very rostrum and with great eloquence and stirring conviction told the story of how the people of Montgomery, Alabama, pooled their meager resources and stood together against city-sponsored terror to struggle for justice. The struggle of Montgomery, Alabama, belongs to us, in part, because Bennett College helped Dr. King to speak the truth to the people."

Thus spoke Rev. Johnson in 1999, acknowledging that Bennett had opened its doors to us also to tell our story of the Greensboro Massacre.

ORDINARY CATASTROPHES

A train of unusual and disheartening personal and family events accompanied my coming to political maturity. In late 1972, Antonia became afflicted with a rare disease, named (after a physician) Sydenham's Chorea and called in folklore Saint Vitus Dance. The illness is a complication from rheumatic fever and a rheumatic heart, which in turn result from a strep infection. Textbooks promise the chorea will run its course in a few weeks, but Antonia was very sick for the better part of a year. The seven-year-old child was disabled in heartbreaking ways. Her musculature turned to mush. Her nervous system was totally out of control. She was unable even to hold a utensil and bring it to her mouth. When the chorea was at its most severe, she could not talk or swallow food. She was in constant motion, with a frenetic flaying of arms and legs. She twitched, jerked, and flopped about the bed. Carl and I shared the sickbed care and the agony of the prolonged affliction. I began to despair of the full recovery promised by medical books and doctors. Finally, after nine or ten months, Antonia was walking again, swaying like a drunken sailor. It was progress. Ultimately, she regained her beauty and grace, and she fully recovered from the heart murmur, the most serious aspect of this crazy package of bodily disorders.

Following Antonia's illness—she was still wobbly on her feet but mostly recovered—came the deluge. Our house was across from Latham Park, through which ran Buffalo Creek. The area was a flood plain (or had become such from the build-up of paved roads surrounding it). It rained much of the entire month of August 1974. Buffalo Creek swelled and rose with the unrelenting rain until the saturated ground could no longer contain its overflow. Finally, a heavy rainfall turned the waters loose to roam the environs one Sunday evening, September 1, 1974.

I was recovering from a migraine headache and still feeling the effects of Codeine. Carl and I had no sooner greeted a dinner guest and close friend, Alan Brilliant, when Alan noticed that a "lake" was beginning to cross the street. "I think you'd better prepare. Let me help you," he offered.

In the next twenty minutes, I got the children to put on warm clothing and pack some of their favorite things in a bag. Carl and Alan gathered paintings, drawings, and sculptures and stored them in an attic space above the garage. They hoisted couches and chairs onto table tops. I threw some jewelry, my grandmother's afghan, and photograph albums into a suitcase. Still mentally disorganized from my struggle with a migraine, I did not think to remove diaries and journals of the previous fifteen years from a soon-to-be-drenched bottom desk drawer. But Antonia retired to her room where she quickly and methodically sorted all her books, games, and dolls, placing the ones she was fond of on high shelves and everything she didn't like on low shelves or the floor. In overcoming her long bizarre illness, she must have strengthened her determination to be in charge of her fate.

The water appeared totally incongruously from beneath the carpet, climbed up table legs, and went on rising a few more feet. Our four cats went berserk. (Some teenage boys went back to rescue them and fetch our suitcases.) Both children remained calm. In subsequent weeks, as I was despairing over losses, they kept an excellent morale. The actual evacuation remains vivid in my memory not only because it was frightening at the time, but also because I came to see it as a metaphor for my doomed marriage.

We waited until the last possible moment to leave the house. I expected to be wading in water up to my thighs—the level *inside* the house—but outside the water came nearly to my chest, and I had to carry my shoulder bag over my head to keep it dry. Ours was one of three or four houses before a rise at the end of Latham Road. There, above the flood plain, was Wendover Avenue, a main thoroughfare connecting the city with the regional airport. Carl carried Antonia out of the house while Alan had six-year-old Shlomo in his arms. I started walking toward Wendover Avenue, where I could see police cars and emergency vehicles parked. I turned around, assuming Carl was behind me with Antonia, but he was heading in the opposite direction, toward low-lying Northwood, where our parked car was submerged in several feet of water. Through the darkness—by now it was 8:30—I screamed at him, "Follow me! To the high ground! Come heeeeere, this way!" He apparently took it as a contest of wills and stubbornly continued in his own direction with our daughter. I started to feel hysterical, and I continued screaming jabs at him into the night, "Idiot, go to the high ground! Follow me! Wendover, you moron! Hiiiiiiiigh ground!" Several feet behind me stood a perplexed Alan with the baby of the family. Caught in the marital crossfire, he did not know which way to turn. Would Solomon's justice be better served by keeping the siblings together or by making sure that each parent in a warring couple retained one child? In the next few moments, Carl heeded my shrieking instructions and Alan followed. A sarcastic police officer on Wendover Avenue greeted us with "What took you so long, folks? You're the last ones out on the block."

Antonia's illness and the flood occasioned, between Carl and me, moments of conciliation and tenderness while battling a common enemy. But the course of life that inflamed my passions and intellect was strong and not to be circumvented by tricks that patch up some marriages on the rocks. We were going in two separate directions, becoming worst enemies.

The house was cleaned up, repaired, restored, and sold. Tall, stately Susan Clemens, a direct descendent of Mark Twain and a friend who'd helped with childcare before the flood, helped in the cleanup afterward. Alan Brilliant and Teo Savory, founders and publishers of *Unicorn Press*, gave us temporary shelter. I took up Transcendental Meditation for my shattered nerves. Alan joked to Teo, "Susan, the meditator is asking Signe questions about how to go on the Venceremos Brigade, and Signe the brigadista has become a meditator." Carl and I then bought the house on Cypress Street, a large white bungalow with brown trim. I did not imagine that this house would acquire a past more lurid than any flood could confer, or that it would be the most spied-upon house in Greensboro (with the possible exception of Nelson and Joyce Johnsons' Alamance Church Road home).

DEFENDANT SELDOM DOES ANY HOUSEWORK

I fell in love with North Carolina when I moved to Greensboro. Between the mountains and the sea are the plains of the North Carolina Piedmont, in whose bosom sits Greensboro, forming a triangle with High Point to the southwest and Winston-Salem to the west. This triad of small cities manufactured indigo blue denim, fine furniture, and cigarettes in the seventies. A four-hour drive west from Greensboro brings into view breathtakingly beautiful mountains. In roughly the same time, heading east-southeast, red clay soil begins to get sandy. Small farms appear, going nearly up to the sea. An easy day's travel from Greensboro takes you to a jagged coastline and glorious beaches—Atlantic Beach, Wrightsville Beach, and Kitty Hawk.

The blue Carolina sky is captivating. An overcast day is an impertinence, an offense against laws of nature that decree Greensboro be forever green, blue, and caressingly mild. In winter, snowfall of half an inch, though not terribly uncommon, has the city practically on an emergency alert. Classes are canceled, workplaces shut down, and people react as if to the coming of a new ice age. The city didn't own much snow removal equipment, which proves the point: such weather is not supposed to happen.

The house Carl and I bought after the flood was on Cypress Street, at the corner of Yanceyville, in a neighborhood that was racially integrated—to some degree. If you followed Yanceyville north about a mile, you would arrive at Cone Mills White Oak Plant, producer of the indigo blue denim. Not quite a mile south, Yanceyville became Dudley. The change in street name signaled arrival in a black neighborhood, with black churches, a black YMCA, a black university, and a black all women's college. At Market Street, intersecting Dudley, head west and you are downtown in a flash. From Market Street, too, you can easily get on I-85 east to Durham, just an hour's drive away.

On an April morning in 1976 in this green and friendly town, a Guilford County Sheriff's deputy delivered a complaint at the wood-frame house on Cypress Street. My husband was suing me for divorce and claiming I was not fit to have custody of our two children. My alleged unfitness as a parent rested on my having championed communism. In the space of one paragraph, the "c" word is repeated seven times. The complaint read in part:

> Defendant is an unfit and improper person to have the care, custody, and control of the children of the marriage, in that defendant has become a member of a Communist organization, and devotes most of her time and attention to affairs of the organization, and fails and refuses to provide the necessary care, attention, and training for the children. . . . Plaintiff . . . believes . . . that if defendant were given possession of the home place, she would turn it into a Communist headquarters. Defendant seldom does any housework.

I had always been the primary childcare giver in the marriage even while actively involved politically, and the false charge that I had abandoned childcare (which was later retracted) upset me most. I was not a member of any communist organization at that point. Neither Carl Goldstein nor I could know the circumstances up the road that would turn 702 Cypress Street into a virtual communist headquarters. That bit of prophecy and the accusation that I seldom did housework are the only parts of the complaint that could bring a smile to my lips years later. I thought Carl made an unprincipled appeal to prejudice in order to win child custody. In fact, we held different political views; his were more socially acceptable. On a personal level too—respect, affection, passion—the marriage had become pointless.

The complaint left me dumbfounded. If my political views made me an unfit mother, what did that imply for millions of Chinese women? Should they lose their children for being communists? If anticommunism was the text of the complaint, women's oppression was the subtext. I did not know my place, it said. I had gone too far on the road to independence. My activism needed to be curbed, and my husband was the one to set the limits. When the altercation became physical, I went to my lawyer, Jim Rowan. We imagined a landmark custody case going all the way to the Supreme Court—*Can a woman who is a communist be a fit mother?* Never mind that at least one-third of the world wouldn't even understand the question.

The complaint arrived about one week before I was to go to Cuba. Finally, after sending others to Cuba on work tours sponsored by the Venceremos Brigade, I had the chance to be part of one myself. I backed out of the trip, understanding the intolerance I was up against and knowing that leaving the children for a few weeks to visit a communist country would seriously jeopardize my chances of getting custody. I was willing to forfeit the trip to keep Tonya and Shlomo, but I was *not* willing to be false and to renounce communism or deny being a communist. I prepared for a hearing that would be horrible for my children. By adhering to my political principles, it was distinctly possible that I would lose them.

I filed a counterclaim stating that I had had primary responsibility for the children's day-to-day care since their birth and should continue being their primary caregiver. My response pointed out that Carl's professional obligations would interfere with his being a solo parent. It also described two assaults he made on me. "On both occasions," the counterclaim read, "Mrs. Goldstein was forced to leave the house because of the violence of the attack; on the first occasion, she was forcibly ejected from the house."

We were at the dinner table, and the children had finished and left the room, when we had one of our heated altercations over politics. I was defending Cuba with all the facts and arguments in my arsenal. "What do you mean Cuba is not democratic?" I challenged Carl. "Don't the block organizations count, the Committees for the Defense of the Revolution?"

"Stop proselytizing me, you brainwashed bitch," came the angry response. His face reddened and the veins of his neck popped out.

"You believe all the lies you read in the press. Have you been there? What do you know? You don't know shit!" I countered forcefully. "My friends have been there. They've seen the schools, the factories, the farms, the life of ordinary people. They have dignity now. Dignity! What do you know . . . "

At that moment, a corner of the pedestal from the kitchen table jerked up from the floor and I was being flung across the kitchen. He was on his feet, his hands all over my arms and face, pushing me into the hard edges and points of cabinets and appliances. It occurred to me he could kill me if he wanted to. Maybe even if he didn't want to. He was out of control. The scene of the assault soon moved from the kitchen to the living room, then to the foyer. From upstairs the children heard the commotion and were terrified. I heard their cries as he ejected me from the house. The door slammed behind me. I landed on the wood-planked floor of the porch, scraping my hands and knees.

The air felt chilly without a jacket. Otherwise the gentle dampness and cool of an early spring evening might have been soothing. Nursing my bruises, I hurried down the street to a small bungalow on Sullivan Street in a neighborhood of mainly black residents, many of them students or teachers from nearby Agricultural and Technical State University (A & T), the black land grant college that functioned still as part of a largely segregated educational system. Soon I was at the home of Claude Barnes, known to his friends as Abiola.

Abiola had company. He was talking to the young black newspaper editor of the *African World*, Jerry Walker, when, disheveled and shaken, I pounded on his door. He let me in and listened sympathetically to my half-spoken, half-sobbed story.

"Catch you later, man," his friend said, leaving. Abiola took the interruption in stride.

"Take it easy now; you're safe." The situation was common and familiar, he said. "We deal with this all the time. Battered women are among the casualties of capitalism." Then he was on the phone.

"I have a sister here from down the block been knocked around by her old man," flowed out in one smooth, even stream.

Meanwhile, my eyes rested on an issue of *African World*. That anti-imperialist newspaper guided political activists from the Black Power era through Pan-Africanism to the threshold of Marxism-Leninism we were just crossing. Marxism-Leninism consigned the nationalism of Pan-Africanism to the ranks of backward ideologies, calling it narrow nationalism.

"Yeah, that's cool," I heard Abiola continue. I fingered a red, green, and black button with the insignia "February First Movement" on the table with the newspaper. Some of my agitation was ebbing away. I felt protected. Abiola finished his phone conversation. "I'll take you to Nelson's," he said.

The Johnsons gave me their guest room, but I didn't want to stay away from home for more than one night for fear of giving Carl ammunition in a custody battle. Joyce urged me to go downtown to file a complaint with the police and I did. I went on a Friday—the day when domestic violence incidents appear like mushrooms in the woods after the rain—and the police were ho-hum about it.

On University of North Carolina-Greensboro, Department of Art stationary, in a revealing letter dated April 19, 1976, Carl attempted to get my parents, Fay and Ted, to agree with his custody claim.

"This is a shock, I know, so let me tell you more about it," he wrote.

> For some years, as you've known, Signe's main involvement has been with political developments. At first it was in the antiwar movement, but then the war ended and people who had worked to end it went different ways. Some went far to the left as they criticized this country's institutions and Signe went with them. Start-

ing about two years ago, Signe began working with many groups that were communist. She didn't make a commitment to any one of them and her political activity was of a general kind. Signe wanted me to join her in her political activities and I wouldn't, so there was friction between us. . . . This last fall Signe wouldn't stop talking about politics. She said that after thinking for a long time about it, she had become a communist. . . . I had to make scenes to keep her from filling our home with her communist friends, to keep her from filling my head and the heads of the children with propaganda. There was no way that I could reach Signe and finally the only way out seemed to ask for a legal separation with the children assigned to me. Of course, Signe will be able to see them whenever she wishes. But they will live with me and I will see to it that they live normal lives. Had this gone on, incidentally, I might have lost my job.

Signe is very confused. I want her to work out her confusion away from the children. I hope that as their grandparents you'll see that this would be best for them.

It was not confusion, however, that led me to participate in the *People's Coalition against ITT* and to confront Harold Geneen, then CEO of International Telephone and Telegraph, at the company's fifty-fifth annual shareholders meeting in Charlotte in May 1975. The *People's Coalition* was started by the Venceremos Brigade and endorsed by the American Friends Service Committee, the American Committee on Africa, the Southern Africa Committee, the Women's International League for Peace and Freedom, the North Carolina Alliance against Racist and Political Repression, the New American Movement, and the Greensboro chapter of the February First Movement, among others. At the time, ITT met with angry protests in many corners of the globe. Even a *Newsweek* article of 1973 reads like a leftist rag in its recounting of the history of ITT scandals.

Several of us spoke out at the stockholders' meeting. We'd been admitted through ITT's intense security by actually possessing some shares or, in my case, being given a proxy voice by a legitimate shareholder. Once there, we turned the meeting into a forum to try to make ITT account for its subversive role in international politics. The main focus was on ITT's policies in support of apartheid in South Africa and the corporation's illegal intervention in bringing down the Allende government in Chile. The 1973 Pinochet coup, which ITT helped finance, was followed by an incredible bloodbath. These issues were being discussed widely by groups on the left at the time, Allende having been a duly elected Social Democrat who was trying to institute democratic reforms in Chile.

During my turn at the microphone, I hurled my facts and information Geneen's way without trying to imitate the polite palaver of a practiced journalist.

To my surprise, he didn't wing the answer as he had to the other questions, but removed a prepared statement from a sheaf of papers and proceeded to read—to the effect that certain bodies (such as the U.S. Senate Foreign Relations Subcommittee on Multinational Corporations) had already made inquiries and determined that ITT did nothing illegal in Chile.

The *Greensboro Daily News* of May 8, 1975, carried my picture and that of Charles Finch. "Ms. Signe Goldstein, a philosophy professor from Bennett College in Greensboro and a member of the Venceremos Brigade . . . also was walking the picket line but later used her authority as an ITT shareholder to get inside the meeting and lodge her verbal protest." The spirit of the time was still akin to that of the sixties. Even a criminal court judge from New York, a member of the America Committee on Africa, walked the picket line—with a sign protesting Geneen's $800,000 per year salary—and then stepped inside to lodge *his* verbal protest on behalf of blacks in Africa.

Isn't it obvious this sort of activity was making me an unfit mother?

A STUDENT OF DIALECTICS

I became a student of dialectics and participated in several study groups in the mid-1970s. An internal argument accompanied my political readings—Marx's *Manifesto of the Communist Party* and *Wage Labour and Capital*, Engels' *Socialism: Utopian and Scientific*, and Lenin's *The State and Revolution*, to name a few. "This is right. This analysis explains what I see before my eyes," I would think. I wished it were not so. The feeling was liberating but not altogether happy. But then, the claim for truth is that it makes you free: happy is another story.

We took up the *Collected Works* of Mao, especially *On Practice* and *On Contradiction*. At the time, I felt these two essays were more helpful to my understanding of reality than any philosophy I had read before. The study of dialectical and historical materialism led me to do battle with the Platonism I had long nurtured. I struggled to apply dialectical thinking to all problems, political and personal.

Contradiction is inherently part of the dynamic nature of material reality. The smooth and stable surface of reality turns out to be an illusion, taught Mao. Nothing remains static. Change is constant. The key to social change, and indeed to all change, lies in grasping that all processes, natural and social, are dialectical. Opposite qualities coexist in all things, but at any given time there is an aspect that is rising and an opposing aspect in decline. To plot our future actions, we need to figure out the direction of the opposing forces; what is rising and what is declining?

In 1975 and 1976, I participated in study groups led by people in the orbit of the Workers Viewpoint Organization. The WVO called them Study Training Circles, or STCs. In addition to Marx, Lenin, and Mao Zedong,[5] we read articles from the *Workers Viewpoint Journal*, hammering out our differences in an attempt to reach unity in our political views, a unity rooted in a firm stand with the multinational working class. The concept of a multinational working class was central to the politics of the WVO. I knew from several indelible childhood experiences that racism was wrong: now I studied the "National Question," key to understanding racism and how multinational working class unity must be built.

The Workers Viewpoint Organization taught that racism has a deeper historical and class basis than is encompassed by prejudice on account of skin color. The WVO sought the roots of racism in the development of capitalism and the role played by slavery in economic development. The African American people, WVO said, constituted an oppressed nation within the United States, concentrated in the South. As an oppressed nation, African Americans had the right of nations to self-determination, even the right to secede from the United States if they so chose. Eliminating racism and building the unity of the working class required grasping the national question not merely with respect to African Americans, but all national minorities. The WVO criticized the Communist Party USA for dealing with racism solely as discrimination based on skin color and "liquidating" the "National Question." Earlier in the late 1920s, however, Russian communism had developed theories about *national oppression*. Some of the theories found their way into labor organizing in the southern United States in the 1930s via the CPUSA. They were revived and adopted by the WVO in the 1970s. The concept of national oppression as applied to blacks in the United States made sense to me in explaining the systemic and endemic character of racism in this country. It was very unifying in allowing black and white activists to come together and work together in that period, sharing a common scientific understanding of the problem.

By mid-1976, I was an ardent fan of the WVO. I was also applying for membership in the Revolutionary Workers League (RWL). Nelson and Joyce were leading members of the RWL, which was one of two radical organizations in North Carolina from which WVO was seeking recruits; the other one was the Durham Health Collective.[6] RWL had no principle or policy against accepting white members when they took my application—but there weren't any.

Although the Johnsons were several years my junior, I sought them out for advice on all sorts of personal matters: they were so centered and mature. In this period of instructing ourselves about dialectical processes, I recall a conversation I had with Nelson about my rapidly dissolving marriage. All things change into their opposite, we affirmed, even love and hate. It's true—the person you once loved can become the person you now hate if the conditions that nurtured that love erode.

I have since come to understand dialectics as one of the tools of thought, perhaps the single most useful tool, but to be wary of bludgeoning reality with this tool. Reducing real processes to dialectical categories can land you in the same metaphysical boat with Plato's archetypes. Let reality squirm. Let it ooze out the sides of this leaky vessel of our thought patterns. At the time, however, I was not feeling indulgent toward the extradialectical.

While moving forward politically, I was involved in a love affair with a married comrade in Durham. I confided in Joyce, who challenged my thesis that I was just naturally polygamous. Maybe that affair occurred because of important needs in my marriage that were not being fulfilled, she said. She frankly admitted that she had difficulty understanding how I could live with someone who was not political. Political unity in our personal relationships was the ideal we all strove for. Joyce counseled me not to make excuses for my partner in adultery. His actions were male chauvinist and bourgeois, and my own behavior was bourgeois too. My lover's wife, who had been a friend, became an enemy and even threatened to come to Greensboro to dispatch me with an ax.

My impending divorce in 1976 was a potential security issue for my political friends, several of whom were black and members of the RWL. The complaint suggested the custody hearing would have more to do with Communism than Motherhood, and my revolutionary friends might be called as material witnesses, giving the state leverage for future persecutions. Perhaps a white woman fraternizing so blatantly with black men would appear to a racist system of justice as *eo ipso* unfit for motherhood—even if the politics involved were that of the GOP, not communism. A looming court showdown was avoided only due to my Quaker friend Susan Clemens' negotiating skills the night before the scheduled hearing.

"Now, Carl, I know very well you are an excellent father. But will you be able to be home every afternoon when the children get out of school? Can you take time from preparing your Art History lectures to clean the house, do the laundry, cook the meals, go shopping for clothes, and give the children the attention they need? Now, Carl, you know that's a full-time job right there, if we're honest with ourselves," Susan cajoled.

"Sure. I've thought of that, Susan. I plan to have a housekeeper," he replied.

"Well, Signe says she would continue doing those things. Isn't it better to have a parent care for children than a housekeeper? Just think about that, Carl. You don't have to answer me right now." And to me—"You are both in your own ways excellent parents. Couldn't we arrange some kind of joint custody? I think we can get Carl to agree to that."

I finally agreed to a joint custody agreement that allowed the children to continue to live with me at the Cypress Street residence. Carl had liberal visitation rights. We were to consult on any big decisions that affected the children's lives, and neither of us was free to move away from the Piedmont without a new contract being drawn up. It was a conventional enough resolution of an exotic situation.

Of the fallout from that acrimonious divorce, one matter affecting me tremendously was my estrangement from two of my most beloved friends, Alan Brilliant and Teo Savory. When the custody contest was raging, they sided with Carl, believing my acquiescence to his claim would spare our children a horrendous court battle. I saw that as a betrayal and had bitter feelings toward them. Not until 1983, when the pain of crippling arthritis and advancing blindness began to make the last six years of Teo's life hellish, did I pursue reconciliation and become once again her beloved friend and close confidante.

The separation, custody settlement, and pending divorce left me with a feeling of lightness and liberation. In 1976 and 1977, though not formally a WVO member, I was part of a circle of activists who were studying and training to be revolutionaries. I wanted my country to be the democratic land I believed in as a child, where freedom, justice, and equality reigned. I did not know how the road would wind its way to this utopian destination. It was not important to know that. What was important was to plant my feet solidly on that road and take the first steps.

NOTES

1. See John Hope Franklin, "Slaves Virtually Free in Antebellum North Carolina," in *Race and History: Selected Essays 1938–1988* (Baton Rouge: Louisiana State University Press, 1989), 80.

2. This slide show was a project of the American Friends Service Committee called National Action/Research on the Military Industrial Complex (NARMIC) and was produced in 1972.

3. See chapter 6 for more about the Wilmington Ten and the Charlotte Three.

4. For an account of the Greensboro Massacre, see chapter 10 and following chapters. The twentieth anniversary commemoration is discussed in chapter 20.

5. "Mao Zedong" is the contemporary spelling for the Chinese leader. I have used the 1970s spelling, "Mao tse-Tung," when quoting from seventies literature and in the New Communist Movement phrase "MLMTT," used by the Workers Viewpoint Organization and others calling themselves students of MLMTT, i.e., Marx, Lenin, Mao tse-Tung Thought.

6. See chapter 4 for an account of the Durham Health Collective.

2

JIM WALLER, M.D. IN THE NEW COMMUNIST MOVEMENT

"Im Anfang war die Tat!"
"In the beginning was the act."

—Goethe, *Faust*

A BIAS FOR ACTION

The Duke University Hospital physician was out of uniform. Wearing cut-off blue jeans, a T-shirt with holes, and brown leather sandals, he sat on the porch of a woodframe house in a lovely, secluded stretch of woodland in North Carolina's Chatham County. His legs propped on the railing, he was writing on a clipboard decorated with a child's scribbling. Flipping over a hospital form to the blank side, he wrote, "Dearest Jane . . ." It was May 24, 1976.

"My mind and body are bruised and bleeding from the torment of the past weeks," he confessed to his sister. "My life is in crisis right now over what I will do in July. Will I continue being a doctor or is my primary work becoming a professional revolutionary?"

Dr. James Michael Waller had left the ward shortly before. He was outraged. He had just learned that whenever he stopped at a bedside to check on a patient or say a cheery word, the patient was billed. He liked to make frequent rounds, and he chafed at the heartlessness of a system that gave physicians so little latitude in caring for and encouraging patients. It was a system in which children's life chances were set back because their families were poor.

Not far from the house was a stand of delicate pink dogwoods. Sunlight dappled through the cracks in the forest vault, suggesting a holy place. The beauty of nature was in sharp contrast with malignant social arrangements. Jim Waller ached with the contradiction. But years of political activism and intensive study of Marxism were bearing fruit. A resolution of his anxiety was at hand.

Jim had been reading about medicine in China since the 1949 Chinese Revolution. Dr. Joshua Horn's *Away with All Pests* lay on the porch in a pile of magazines and newspapers. He responded to the book's celebration of the heroism of ordinary people—mail carriers, lab technicians, farmers, metal workers, and food servers. Jim was an intense, diligent reader, and the book bore heavy underlining and marginal notations.

Six decades earlier, the Russian Revolution had inspired ordinary people around the world by sweeping away the tyranny of the czars, declaring an end to the exploitation of workers' labor by a privileged few. For Jim, for me, and for many of our friends, the Chinese Revolution led by Mao Zedong was the modern revolution in our lifetime from which we drew inspiration. We looked to China as many in the post–World War I generation had looked to the Soviet Union. We were moved, for example, by the barefoot doctors who went into the countryside to provide health care for a poor population that had never had health care before. For years I had a framed illustration on my wall of a barefoot doctor, a young Chinese woman in pigtails. She was a model for me, a daily reminder that I wanted my life to be about serving people. Jim, like me, was inspired by the accomplishments of the Chinese Revolution. As a result of revolutionary struggle, China was feeding its starving people. Women in China were rising up out of eons-long subservience. Other third world countries around the world looked to the Chinese example, and China supported their efforts to liberate themselves from colonialism and imperialism.

Only a month earlier, Jim's mother, Harriet, had died of a heart attack. He was still grieving for her, but in a sense her death freed him to do what he knew he must do. He knew his mother would have felt hurt and betrayed by the path he was now contemplating. His father, Sidney, a gentle, good-humored, and ethical-minded man, was bound to be more tolerant. Jim attributed his own social conscience to his father's passion for social justice. Sidney might be unsettled by his decision on first hearing it, Jim thought, but his father would understand and support him.

After Harriet's death, Jim returned to Chicago, where he was born and raised, to spend some time with Jane and Sidney. The family was very close. Jane looked up to her older brother, but as he continued writing, he could almost hear her saying, "Jamie, why does it have to be *you*? Let someone else do it. You can contribute without throwing everything overboard?" If he could win her over, it would be easier for Sidney to accept.

"I know this is hard for you to understand," he wrote, "but I have come to see revolution and the construction of a revolutionary communist party as the most important task today. Whereas medicine is work I enjoy and feel is useful, I may give it up, at least temporarily, to devote myself primarily to party building."

Jim's experiences in the preceding decade had brought him to the point of seeing "revolution and the construction of a revolutionary communist party as the most important task." During the Democratic National Convention in Chicago in 1968, he had raced up and down Michigan Avenue and its side streets doctoring anti–Vietnam War demonstrators with broken bones and bleeding heads. They had been beaten by the police. The impression of the state moving against its own dissenting citizens stayed with him.

When the Oglala Sioux at Wounded Knee, South Dakota, were under siege by federal authorities in 1973, Jim organized a medical contingent to help them. He went to Wounded Knee, set up a clinic, and stayed for several weeks, treating patients. A diary he kept describes the tense atmosphere on the reservation. He recorded his participation in a sweat lodge ceremony. The homage paid to "all my relations" struck a very deep chord in him.[1]

Some time later he visited Cuba with other medical workers. They saw that the revolutionary Castro regime was making universal health care and the elimination of racial inequality high priorities.

When we were getting to know one another in 1977, Jim told me, with much amusement, about his earliest political struggle—the "Save Waller's Beard," or "SWAB" campaign as it was dubbed, at the University of Chicago Medical School. Another physician and close friend, Dr. Fitzhugh Mullan, wrote about the SWAB campaign in his account of how medical students were affected by the student rebellions of the sixties.

Jim's swarthy complexion and thick crop of pitch black wavy hair set off a black beard that, by the time I met him, was thicker and coarser than the beard he sported in his days as a medical student. It could no longer be described as a goatee—it was nearly rabbinical. Convinced that his chin beardless would be a huge disappointment to the opposite sex, Jim was never without a beard once the appearance of facial hair permitted it. The SWAB campaign occurred when the medical school administration put pressure on the hirsute student to shave before having regular contact with patients. Beards then were a cultural symbol of defiance and were associated with unwashed hippies. No one on the medical faculty at Chicago had one.

When Jim steadfastly refused to shave his beard, most of his class signed a petition asking the administration to let him keep it. Fitzhugh, then his classmate, wrote later that many students saw SWAB as a political fight for the rights of the individual against the encroachments of the institution, in this case an oppressive and exclusionary medical establishment.[2] It is an indictment of the folly of the age that distinguished men of science were having heated debates over a student's facial hair. According to Dr. Mullan, the matter was laid to rest by the Swiss-German head of internal medicine, the first department Jim was scheduled to work in, with "Beards, schmeards, if the boy knows his medicine he'll pass." Jim kept his beard and passed his courses. Beards soon became commonplace on campus.

Jim did his residency at Lincoln Hospital, one of two hospitals serving over half a million poor people, mostly black and Puerto Rican, in the South Bronx. There he was part of a radical medical collective, the People's Health Center. The collective struggled to expose, and depose, a hospital administration indifferent to the poverty of the surrounding community and apparently comfortable with infant mortality rates as high as any third world country.

In New York, Jim was not merely a serious doctor and political activist. Part of a Bohemian-style collective of health workers and professionals called the *Savage City Nomads*, Jim's exuberance and daring spirit were remarkable even among this nonconforming bunch. When he was courting me, he told me about some of the wild and risky things he had done that, on occasion, included taking LSD. And I wondered that he had survived them.

His closest friend at Lincoln Hospital from 1970 to 1974, Mike Dooley, wrote of Jim after his death, "Jim bought the whole ticket on the trip from student politics to factory organizing." Dooley saw Jim as "beating despair and meaninglessness in a running battle," living his life "as if it was one muscle in the exercise of what he thought and felt," and dying as he lived "in close harmony with his convictions."[3]

When Dooley knew him, Jim was not yet a communist. He was a young doctor with a future in medicine. He was a critic of materialism and consumerism, of a culture and economy built around profit. We are born into a system of exploitation and injustice, he wrote in a diary he kept in 1973, "and most people try to stay afloat and survive in that system. To do it in most cases one has to turn exploiter. So we perpetrate buying and selling useless items, plastic food, shoes that cripple feet. . . . We do not strike out at the monster. We do not know where to begin. We are angry; we know we are being cheated; we know there is more to life."

A month later, Jim wrote in his diary,

> I am so lucky that I have the opportunity to turn my back on it, to go to the
> seashore and let the cold air fill my lungs and dance around my ears, to delight in
> the ever so slowly changing colors and tones of the sun setting, to worship with

the seagulls. And so I have a few moments of peace and beauty. I lose myself in a song, dance an intoxicated dance. I would be lost without the song, without a delight in the goof—sooner or later I will be able to reckon with the more difficult what-is-the-way-to-live-in-this-ugliness and how-do-you-change-it.

In 1975, Dr. Jim Waller was awarded a post-doctorate fellowship by Duke University in pediatric infectious diseases. He moved to North Carolina to become an instructor and researcher at Duke. His friend and lover, Dr. Jean Sharpe (later Chapman), also a pediatrician, went with him. From Alabama originally, she wanted to return to the South to practice medicine.

Finishing the letter to his sister Jane, Jim wrote, "you can't imagine the conflict this has evoked within me and also between me and Jean. I love Jean more than I have ever loved another. But she is not, nor does she intend to become, a communist. Such is my anguish, how to resolve these contradictions, how to move on? Wish me luck and wisdom. Better yet, come down and discuss it with me. I love you. Jim."

Becoming a communist in the middle of the seventies was soul-wrenching. Like Jim Waller, I chose to turn my life around, remold my worldview. It felt like bodily arresting a moving train and reversing its momentum. I could no more function as a college teacher than Jim could as a doctor.

On June 19, 1976, Jim wrote once again, in less distress, to his sister.

I have only another week of work at Duke. After that I will be able to devote more time to political work. It's getting to be that a seven hour meeting is a regular event rather than an ordeal. But there are no two ways about it—the tasks are very demanding. Nonetheless, I feel they are necessary and sometimes even feel exhilarated by the excitement. We will have a new genuine communist party in this country within the next ten years. . . . Tonight I was looking over some documents written six months ago and I'm amazed at how far our theoretical and ideological understanding has grown in that short period. Anyway, you don't need any lectures from me. You admit you are an idealist and isolationist and make no pretenses about wanting to change society. I, on the other hand, do not accept the existing order and want to change it, improve it, revolutionize it. It is within the process of consciously trying to change society that I'm getting a real understanding of it and an understanding of myself.

Very demanding. Necessary. Exhilarated. I do not accept the existing order and want to change it.

For Marxists, it is elementary that you use Marxism to change the world. As we saw it, we had to take on changing ourselves also. We had been shaped by a materialistic, individualist and narcissist society. We rejected those values. Changing ourselves and the course of our lives naturally affected all our personal relationships.

I wasn't acquainted with Dr. Jim Waller in 1975 and 1976 when relations with our respective partners were breaking down. Jim left Duke and his house in the woods, abandoned medicine, and found employment as a textile worker. By the time I met him in April 1977—really met him, unlike the earlier sightings of him—my marriage of fourteen years had dissolved, and Jim had separated from Jean. Jim and I were both participants, he in Durham and I in Greensboro, in Marxist Study Training Circles (STCs) sponsored by the Workers Viewpoint Organization.

In August 1976, Jim Waller became a textile worker at Cone Mills Granite Finishing Plant in Haw River, North Carolina, one of the world's largest corduroy finishing operations. Cone did not know about his medical credentials or suspect his mission. Jim set about organizing his coworkers, aiming to increase the membership and clout of the Amalgamated Clothing and Textile Workers Union (ACTWU), Local 1113 T.

The year of Jim Waller's agony over abandoning medicine was the year Jerry Tung and Phil Thompson brought the Workers Viewpoint Organization to the Duke University campus for a night of discussion and debate. Jim and I sat on opposite sides of the room hardly aware of each other's existence. In this bicentennial year of our country's history, if someone asked me, "What are you doing, Signe Goldstein, née Burke ("Burke" was presumed to be a mistake by an Irish immigration officer with no ear for Russian or Polish), daughter of warm, generous, middle-class, Brooklyn golden-ghetto-Jewish, New Deal-Roosevelt-Democrat parents, Fay and Ted"—and if I thought she'd understand (or want to understand), I might have replied, "Studying to be a communist revolutionary." Jim would have said, "Building the political party of the multinational working class in the United States."

Jim, too, was descended from the tribe of Hebrews. His maternal grandfather, Dr. James Skebelsky, was the first physician to break through the anti-Semitism that kept Jews out of the medical profession in Chicago in the 1920s, a point of persuasion his mother Harriet used freely in influencing her son to become a doctor.

A RADICALIZED GENERATION

The sixties had been an era of consciousness-changing. Many eyes were opened to economic, political, and social injustices. But such progress as there had been in civil rights and in building the Great Society had stalled indefinitely. By committing itself to waging and paying for war in Vietnam and other countries in Southeast Asia, the United States had squandered the national wealth and its moral authority. As Tom Hayden later wrote, "if there had been a national concentration on problems of race and poverty instead of on Vietnam, the outcome might have been different."[4] And for Michael Harrington, "the greatest opportunity for social change since the New Deal was sacrificed to the tragedy in Vietnam."[5] The sensibilities of activists and idealists were pummeled by the war, by government scandals and corruption associated with Watergate, and by other events. The revolutionary seeds of the sixties had not borne fruit.

Countless small Marxist study circles arose in the early seventies. To these flocked a generation of white activists radicalized by participation in the era's great social movements—the civil rights, antiwar, and women's movements. They were joined by activists of all nationalities who saw the need to challenge the root of the problems, the capitalist system, and saw the working class as the engine of social change. An analysis of the class forces in society was on activists' agendas. Political treatises protruded from hip pockets and weighty handbags. The mood was a heady eclecticism, a continuation of the 1960s where any activist or revolutionary had credentials as good as any other. Many strains of antiestablishment and revolutionary thought were investigated and dissected. Major leftist theoreticians of social change around the world—Marx, Engels, Lenin, Luxembourg, Trotsky, Mao, Stalin, Debray, Che Guevara, Nkrumah, Cabral, Fanon, among others—were given a considered reading and a scheduled time for discussion. We sorted through the vast experience of peoples' struggles in Africa, China, and Latin America. Such eclectic searching was the background of many who eventually gravitated to organizations in the New Communist Movement (NCM) of the seventies. By the mid-seventies, political study groups were widespread and were tending toward consolidation into larger organizations. Diverse approaches were congealing into trends, and debates raged.

An important debate for me, and perhaps other white activists coming from a liberal background, was whether society could be changed in piecemeal fashion with reforms or needed a revolutionary transformation—reform versus revolution. Like others who went through the experience of opposing the Vietnam War, and who had studied and grappled with the issue of imperialism, I knew that the same structures and institutions in America that produced war in Vietnam were at the root of racism, poverty, and social injustice here as well. The need to work for fundamental social change in the United States became a given. But how? Do you work inside the system to change it? Or, does the system not allow you to do this, so that you must overthrow the system to change it? Tom Hayden, in his experience as an organizer in Newark, New Jersey, dealing with the city's severe poverty and racism, described the frustrations of someone with revolutionary aspirations trying to work inside the system. There were some gains, he assessed, in federal dollars and in electing people's representatives to City Hall, even in ultimately getting the city's first black mayor, but "there was no permanent redistribution of power to the poor." Staying entirely outside the system, Hayden wrote, left people powerless, "unable to exploit the small but real possibilities of such programs as the war on poverty. Going into the maze of programs, on the other hand, meant being swallowed up in tedious services lacking any political edge."[6] I recall the day I faced the conclusion in my own mind— it must have been in 1972 or 1973—that revolutionary change was needed and that I must contribute to it. Anything else I did with my life would be a cop-out. It was an uncomfortable realization.

THE ROOTS OF THE WORKERS VIEWPOINT ORGANIZATION

The Workers Viewpoint Organization (WVO) was part of the New Communist Movement that flourished in the 1970s. What was *new* about this New Communist Movement? For one thing, its adherents tended to be critical of the Soviet Union and of the Communist Party USA for having abandoned or revised the principles of Marx and Lenin. We viewed ourselves as *antirevisionists*. Those associating themselves with the New Communist Movement looked to the third world, and to China in particular (not to the Soviet Union), as the leader in struggles around the world against capitalism and imperialism, as indeed China then was.

The New Communist Movement (NCM) regarded African American, Chicano, Puerto Rican, and Asian workers, and workers of other oppressed nationalities, as key players within the American working class. Working people of color bore a double yoke in suffering from national oppression as well as class oppression. They experienced exclusion, discrimination, and superexploitation in the capitalist system, and therefore they were motivated toward revolutionary change by the material conditions of their lives.

The New Communist Movement analyzed racism as a systematic manifestation of national oppression. The NCM introduced this analysis into debates about how revolutionary socialism could come about in the United States. Theories on this topic were subsumed under the rubric of the "National Question." Contributing significantly to this discussion was the Asian Study Group, forerunner of the WVO. A member of the Asian Study Group, in reflecting on this history, told me, "We all felt that the white antiwar or even anti-imperialist movements did not address the race and national questions." As activists and Marxist-Leninist revolutionaries of color, the Asian Americans critiqued the American left, and in particular the Communist Party, over a presentation of racism and discrimination that accounted for these phenomena merely in terms of skin color.

The roots of the WVO lay in two small Asian American collectives. In addition to the Asian Study Group, based in New York City, there was Yellow Seeds, a Philadelphia collective. The two groups merged in 1971. The resulting collective had twenty-five members who studied the writings of Marx, Lenin, and Mao together and put out a theoretical journal, called the *Workers Viewpoint*. For want of a better name, the merged group called itself the Workers Viewpoint Organization.

The Asian Study Group authored a position paper on the Asian American National Question, drawing out the thesis that racial discrimination was a manifestation of national oppression and had a deep historical and class basis. The debates over this paper went beyond the Asian American community: the paper was found relevant by revolutionaries of other groups. African Americans, Puerto Ricans, and Chicanos developed their own position papers, and people debated what these theories meant for revolutionary struggle in the United States. China, Zimbabwe, Angola, Mozambique, and Vietnam served as models for revolutionary minded activists from national minority groups, and for some white revolutionaries as well. A related dimension of the New Communist Movement was that the study of Marx, Lenin, and Mao led people to "go to the proletariat." Many quit school to work in their communities or in factories and to organize workers instead of students.

In addition to the initially Asian but then multiracial WVO, the main organizations that were part of the trend called the New Communist Movement were the October League (OL), the Revolutionary Union (RU, later called the Revolutionary Communist Party or RCP), the Black Workers Congress (BWC), the Puerto Rican Revolutionary Workers Organization (PRRWO), the August 29th Movement (ATM), I Wor Kuen (IWK), and the Revolutionary Workers League (RWL). In the mid-1970s, these organizations defined a coherent trend in terms of making a serious effort to build a revolutionary political party to bring about socialism in America. In addition to the above, Marxist activists were part of the Progressive Labor Party (PLP, from which some split to form the Communist Labor Party), the Marxist-Leninist Organizing Committee (MLOC), the Socialist Workers Party (SWP), and many other groups and collectives.[7]

A shared belief that developing a strong Marxist-Leninist theoretical foundation was the central task in building a revolutionary political party brought several of these organizations closer together. The WVO gathered under its banner people from the major Marxist-Leninist groups and from small collectives throughout the country. The culmination of the party-building effort came in October 1979 with the founding of the Communist Workers Party (CWP). The ideological and theoretical underpinning of the WVO/CWP was Marxism-Leninism-Mao-tse-Tung Thought (MLMTT). An outstanding feature of the WVO/CWP was the *strong multiracial composition of its membership*. From an Asian American collective of twenty-five people in 1971, the WVO had grown by 1977 to an organization of white, black, brown, and yellow activists based in twenty cities across the country. Organized by geographic districts, the WVO did not keep a membership count, for security reasons. Probably, at its peak, the organization had between eight hundred and one thousand members, with thousands more supporters around its work. The WVO was not the largest of the groups in the New Communist Movement. That distinction belongs to the Revolutionary Union, or, as it was later called, the Revolutionary Communist Party (RCP).

A STRONG ENOUGH MEDICINE TO COMBAT CAPITALISM

Although its membership was relatively small, the influence of the New Communist Movement was broad among progressive activists during the 1970s. Like a neglected stepchild of the turbulent 1960s, it haunted the next decade. This movement had a considerable role in the surprisingly numerous and vigorous grassroots protests and workers' struggles of the time, but the sixties, cleaned up and repackaged for popular culture, was allowed to eclipse the significant decade that followed.

To those of us who moved toward communism in the early 1970s, poverty and racism were an inevitable and structural part of the capitalist economic system, in which a few people exploit the labor power of many. The self-aggrandizement of the capitalist class was achieved at the expense of the majority of individuals and of society as a whole. Communism—a political theory predicated on eliminating classes in society and using the social wealth accumulated from everyone's labor to satisfy the human needs of all—appeared to be the only medicine strong enough to cure society of the ills of capitalism. Nothing short of a revolutionary transformation of society would get to the root of social and economic problems, capitalism and imperialism. The sounds of sixties' protest were only opening volleys by raw recruits. The goal was victory for the multiracial working class, a basic power shift.

To fight for and win reforms in capitalism along the way was important, but these efforts needed to be directed toward strengthening people's ability to fight for the ultimate goal of socialism, to build a larger social movement, and to build working-class unity. Otherwise, reforms would be used by the capitalist class to co-opt the workers' struggle. The poverty programs of the sixties weakened and divided the forces against capitalism. The ultimate goal was to change the system, not continuously slap band-aids on a rotten, terminally ill system.

It seemed logical to me to assume that capitalism would not be around forever. I had no trouble imagining a system that gave working people real economic and political power. Society is created by human beings and therefore can be changed by them. We can surely change a flawed system that sorts humanity into oppressors and oppressed, leaving the vast majority among the oppressed. The example of China was really compelling and uplifting. The Chinese Revolution fed people in lands that had known frequent famine and starvation under imperialism. China was working toward social equality for women and was bringing health care to people in remote parts of the country. And in Cuba, literacy, health care, race relations, and women's equality were making incredible strides in a short time. We had before us examples of third world revolutions that liberated people from colonialism, countries attempting to build socialist or communist societies, and they were full of promise. My mood, and generally the mood of those who were part of the New Communist Movement, was one of unshakable optimism.

A precept of Mao Zedong is that it is ordinary people like ourselves, not great heroes and generals, who truly change the course of history. I spent some time mulling over the sweeping Maoist doctrine that *the masses make history*. At first I thought it was wishful thinking, not really true. But the massive scale of grassroots activism in the civil rights and antiwar movements did indeed change history. This activism set a standard of social responsibility for future generations. The power of the masses to make history is not always used, but I think the possibility is always there. People often abdicate their power, for lack of leadership or a number of other reasons. Nevertheless, the masses have the capacity to be the makers of history. Believing in the precept and acting on it, I found, went hand in hand. Belief facilitated action, and action confirmed belief.

Long before the New Communist Movement, back in the 1930s and 1940s, there was a fairly strong tradition of communism in the United States. However, it declined after the 1950s, done in by McCarthyism and the internal weaknesses of the Communist Party USA (CPUSA). The party lost many supporters by following Soviet communism under Stalin and lost its claim to the political and moral high ground of the American left. It was widely thought to have sold out, or else to be hiding out in the far reaches of the Democratic Party. Either way it had abandoned its unique mission as an uncompromising opponent of U.S. capitalism. That is how I and my friends felt, even though we studied, learned from, and respected many historical accomplishments of the CPUSA, including its leadership of labor struggles and its stand against racial oppression, especially in the South.

The New Communist Movement rediscovered international communism and set out to construct its American version. The guide for this endeavor was no longer the discredited CPUSA, nor the Soviet Union itself, birthplace of socialism in modern times. For the WVO, as well as other leftist circles and New Communist Movement organizations, the reliable Northern Star bringing light and guidance was China. Mao Zedong provided the theoretical model of people's revolution in a rural, third world country, and we sought to figure out how to apply Maoist doctrine to the industrially more advanced United States. The New Communist Movement retained and nurtured the idealism, revolutionary optimism, and activist mentality that marked the 1960s. We had a bias for action. We wanted new institutions and social relations that respected the dignity of all people and that put political power in the hands of workers.

Another powerful inspiration to revolutionary-minded activists of the seventies was the Black Panther Party (BPP). They were home-grown heroes. In advance of the New Communist Movement, many BPP members embraced revolution, socialism, Marx, Lenin, and Mao, and third world struggles. Many were internationalists, willing to work with whites and other groups of color. They were an important model for us. The BPP took the brunt of the attacks by the FBI's counterintelligence program (COINTELPRO).

By 1971, two-thirds of the American people regarded the Vietnam War as immoral and called for the withdrawal of American troops. Not all, however, saw the war as part of the systemically connected evils of capitalism, or, if they did see it that way, they didn't feel a moral imperative to act on their vision. To act, to organize, to speak truth to power, and to aim ultimately at unseating the abusers of power, all in accordance with the ideal of justice—these are not goals set by a majority of the populace. It is often only a minority of revolutionary-minded workers, students, intellectuals, and peasants who embrace the challenge of changing an unjust social order. Jim Waller was one, and there were many others in the New Communist Movement, who dared to meet the challenge.

Jim had been a member of the leftist Students for a Democratic Society (SDS) during his college days at Ann Arbor in the sixties. In 1974, he was at Puerto Rican Solidarity Day in Madison Square Garden in New York. He was impressed by the WVO and its leader, Jerry Tung, who spoke there. Jim read WVO journals and (after 1976) the *Workers Viewpoint* newspaper. He found in these writings an affinity with his own ideas about social change. After moving to North Carolina, he applied for membership in the Workers Viewpoint Organization. He was not accepted at first. As a doctor from a middle-class background, he was a questionable asset to a working-class party. But in 1977 or 1978, Jim Waller, M.D. was inducted into the WVO. By then he had shown his leadership among the mill workers. In short order, he had major responsibilities within the WVO.

The assumptions my friends and I made in the early 1970s and our attitude toward social change may seem remarkable today in light of many intervening years of rampant conservatism. The grand scheme of redoing society is not usually on the agenda. Even in "interesting times," only a few of the most involved political activists entertain such a goal. And for them it is a calling, a historical mission that includes struggle, pain, errors, dangerous risks, and setbacks. With the sixties' momentum hurling us against the gravity of custom and mores, we had acquired the activist habit of approaching injustice as something not negotiable for accommodation. We assumed that if something is wrong or unjust it should be changed. That's all there is to it. Case closed. Just go ahead and do it.

WE DRIVE WITH JIM TO THE MILL

Imagine you are alongside Jim on his drive to work. With his thick black beard, intense eyes, and large nose; he looks like a rabbi. Most of the mill workers have never seen a rabbi before—or a communist.

Jim shares his outlook with you and, from time to time, turns to look at you as he drives. Words have been forming in his mind, like a mantra—"Build the party on an ideological plane: grasp the key link of political line. Forward to the Dictatorship of the Proletariat."

Here I beg the reader's patience with the terminology. Remember, to millions of people around the world, who had been politicized, "Build the party on an ideological plane" or similar slogans were not the ravings of a lunatic but intelligible slogans concentrating important political truths.

Jim begins with events following the Second World War. It was a period in which, in countries all around the globe, dark-skinned peoples shook loose from the stranglehold of colonialism and strove for independence. In the United States, not only African Americans but also Puerto Ricans, Chicanos, Asian Americans, and others were ready to claim their human and civil rights as national minorities and began organizing accordingly. The African American struggle for liberation was interwoven in this revolutionary tapestry—a major motif. Having fought and died under the credo of U.S. democracy and equality in World War II, blacks were ready to cash in rhetorical chips for reality and demand the same civil rights as other American citizens. The structures of the American body politic were not ready to accommodate them. They came back to the same racist discrimination in housing, jobs, and education as before the war.

Jim emphasizes that the United States emerged from the war not merely victorious, but least damaged in terms of its industry, infrastructure, and land. Vast sources of American wealth were intact and available to restore society to a state of economic and social health much surpassing prewar depression conditions. In the immediate postwar period, the United States was far and away the undisputed world leader in manufacturing, in world trade, and in the commanding heights of finance. Unlike people in Germany, the Soviet Union, Japan, and other theaters of war, the U.S. civilian population came out of the war relatively unscathed. These factors alone warranted high expectations and optimism for our country's future.

To this promising picture, Jim adds another dimension—the moral authority the United States enjoyed as a nation with a long, respected democratic tradition, a leading nation in the defeat of fascism. Thus the blight of Jim Crow, making the United States a virtual apartheid society—not solely in the South—was incongruous and intolerable. Such deep and ever-running historical currents underlay the great movement for civil rights that overflowed the banks of society from the late fifties—currents that flow still. Such courageous initiatives as those of Rosa Parks and of four black students sitting-in at a Greensboro luncheon counter sparked the movement in its early stages: objectively, a hypocritical and contradictory stand on race in the United States made the movement necessary.

As he sketches this tableau of history, Jim arrives at Haw River. His shift is about to begin. Although he has not finished, he must leave you. He walks hurriedly and with a decisive step through the heavy gate in his steel-toed shoes, clutching his security blanket—a black metal lunch box—and committing himself to the noise, dirt, and grease of the textile mill.

VARIOUS ENCOMIUMS

When it was new, he had time (briefly) to write encomiums to factory life—I remind myself he was an English major in college. One poem begins "Sulfurous moonlight pierces August night"—and hardly improves from there.

My encomium to Jim Waller must be based not on his poetry but on his character. After Jim's death, I spent some sad hours sitting in Sidney's kitchen, talking to him and to Jane, trying to get a deeper insight into the character of the man who became my husband. Most characteristic of Jim was his humility. As an adolescent and as a teenager, he won the science fair award for the best project several years running, against the competition in the Chicago school system of the fifties. I never heard of these achievements from Jim himself but had to learn of them from his father and sister. I knew he was interested in biology, chemistry, geology, and astronomy as a student. In fact he was quite gifted in these subjects. He received the grade school commendations quietly, even hid the plaques and medals in his bureau drawer. Harriet accidentally discovered her son's awards. "What's this, Jamie? You got first prize again? Why didn't you tell me about it?"

Jim understood even then that if he stood taller and saw further, it was because he was standing on the shoulders of giants, and he felt his deep affinity with, and dependence upon, the rest of humanity. He took modesty to it furthest implications. In his eyes, he hardly deserved credit for something that others made possible for him to do. He searched for surrogates to whom to assign any merit attributed to him. For his mistakes and failures, on the other hand, he took full responsibility. If he had even the most minor role in something turning out badly, he was constitutionally incapable of blaming others in order to excuse himself. These qualities did nothing for his bardic abilities: they did make him a person of lifelong humility and largeness of spirit.

I think his experience at the Siege of Wounded Knee reinforced the stamp of his character. Jim Waller felt deeply connected—"To all my relations," went the chant, as the sacred pipe was passed from member to member in the sweat lodge. This was a man who, three years after Wounded Knee, made the decision to leave medicine and who, three years after that, confronted the Ku Klux Klan.

The prospects for a bagel-eating Yankee pediatrician to lead a socialist revolution in the Klan-infested black belt South among an undereducated, racially mixed, mostly nonunion bunch of textile workers must have been slim indeed. Jim was succeeding.

NOTES

1. See appendix A, "Diary of Dr. James Waller at the Siege of Wounded Knee," 495.

2. Dr. Fitzhugh Mullan, *White Coat Clenched Fist: The Political Education of an American Physician* (New York: Macmillan Publishing Company, 1976), 22.

3. Mike Dooley, *Jim Waller M.D.*, publication and date unknown.

CHAPTER 2

4. Tom Hayden, *Reunion: A Memoir* (New York: Random House, 1988), 168.

5. Michael Harrington, *The Other America: Poverty in the United States*, revised edition (Baltimore: Penguin, 1971), xx.

6. Hayden, *Reunion*, 168.

7. The BWC and RWL were African American organizations; PRRWO was Puerto Rican and based in New York and Philadelphia; ATM was a Chicano organization in southern California; IWK was Asian and based in Oakland and New York. OL and RU were anti-imperialist groups that followed Marxist-Leninist ideology and had mainly white members.

3

NELSON JOHNSON AND THE POLITICS OF BLACK LIBERATION

INSULTS AND INJURIES

"Very early in my upbringing, the race question thrust itself in the center of my life, and it's been there ever since."[1] I am not surprised that a few seconds into my formal interview with Nelson, he is talking about race.

Nelson Napoleon Johnson was born and grew up on a farm in Halifax County, North Carolina, about a hundred and thirty miles northeast of Greensboro. He, his four brothers, and his four sisters had what he considers a "fairly ordinary Halifax County upbringing." His mother, the daughter of a pastor, was a piano player for the church. His father, a deacon and Sunday school teacher and also President of the NAACP chapter, was very devout. Sundays, at breakfast, they held a miniservice at home. "I was greatly influenced in my early days by the idea of being good and righteous," Nelson declared.

Growing up in eastern North Carolina, seventy-eight years after the Civil War, the African American youth lived amid descendents of former slavemasters. Three miles from his house was a farm supply store run by a white family named Thornes. That was Nelson's mother's maiden name. His family was connected to the white family that had moved to North Carolina shortly after the Civil War when their mill was blown up. They brought with them Nelson's great-grandfather and his grandfather, then a small child. Everyone settled in the community where Nelson was reared.

"Our relationship with the slavemaster families was pretty clear cut. It still is. I can go back and find them. I never have had a decent conversation with any of them, but my mother did, and she thought of them in high terms. It was a cordial slave–master relationship.

"But the younger people, my cousins, would get rowdy on Saturday, and there would be fights, and they would take a racial turn. The sons of the old man who was the head of the plantation would come out with guns. A whole race thing went on. No one ever got killed, but it was very mean-spirited. Finally, people would make up, go to work, and it would be forgotten. My mother talked all the time about the white man—the white man won't give you a loan, the white man this and the white man that. As a very small child, I remember distinctly thinking, 'I don't know why the grown people don't kill all of these mean white people.' I grew up very conscious of race and racism."

In his junior year of high school, Nelson was elected president of the student government and was sent to Gastonia on a school-related trip. It was 1959, five years after the *Brown v. Board of Education* court decision. The incident at Central High in Little Rock, Arkansas, which brought in federal troops, occurred in 1957. Segregation and integration, Dr. Martin Luther King Jr., Montgomery, and racial justice were hot topics of discussion.

"My friend and I rode the bus," Nelson related. "It seemed like an eternity. I had never been on a trip this long—from eastern North Carolina all the way to Charlotte. In Charlotte, when the bus was in the parking lot, we decided to sit in the front seat: it was vacant, and we had been sitting in the back." He paused. "Of course, you sat in the back in those days.

"I got hit up against the head, very hard. A white man held his coat up and just drove his fist against my head. This was after they had thrown paper, trash, and stuff on us and called us niggers, and said, 'niggers don't know how to act.' It was terrifying.

"All the white people on the bus looked out the window like nothing happened. The bus driver acted like nothing happened. The guy who'd hit me went back and sat down in his seat. When people looked at us, it was a stare. Otherwise they looked out the window. I think the people who felt sorry for us looked out the window. The people who were mean toward us looked at us. We got up and went to the back of the bus. We were really crushed."

On returning to his high school, Nelson told the principal what had happened. "I was supposed to give a report to the student body about my trip. A lot happened at the conference I went to, but nothing terribly significant. I wanted to talk about the incident, and my principal refused to allow me to do it. He was probably afraid of what would happen to him. That was the atmosphere in which I grew up."

Life in Halifax County was racially and politically charged. Apartheid was a three-way affair—whites, blacks, and Native Americans all had their own schools. Half of the blacks said they were Indians and went to the Indian school,

Nelson remembered. If that was how you grew up, what else was there? These early experiences conditioned him for "the way I would tend to live my life after that."

Immediately after graduating from high school, Nelson Johnson signed up for the Air Force. Two of his classmates joined him, and they went through basic training together. In the Air Force, he developed a close friendship with a southern white boy from Augusta, but "we had a helluva time trying to talk about race." One day, Nelson was singing an old jingle he'd learned as a child, with words to the effect "we can hear the rebels call, we ain't scared of y'all," when his friend became visibly upset.

"I didn't realize it was a union song and offensive to him," Nelson recounted. "I hadn't thought of it that way. I was just humming the thing. It was a familiar tune." They were never able to discuss the race question, even though "he was my friend and I was his friend. We palled around together. We were simply incapable of overcoming what was put in us," Nelson reflected, "being two southern boys in the context of the time."

Other blacks in the military criticized him for his friendships with whites. When Malcolm X was killed, Nelson, stationed in Europe, found himself in the middle of discussions that pitted the philosophies of Malcolm and King. "My own upbringing as a Christian disposed me toward King. I was impressed with his speech, his eloquence. People ran me down to debate me because I had the minority position: other people liked Malcolm more. I finally said to myself one day that I really could no longer justify turning the other cheek. That's when I became conscious of my drift away from my upbringing."

In 1965, his military duty over, Nelson enrolled as a student at the North Carolina Agricultural and Technical State University (A & T) in Greensboro. That was the true beginning of Nelson Johnson the Organizer and Activist, Nelson Johnson the Community Leader, Nelson Johnson the Most Formidable Opponent of the Bourgeoisie. But in 1965 he was naive and in awe of the campus militants and intellectuals. They quoted Frederick Douglass, of whom he had never heard. They spoke of Nat Turner, leader of a slave rebellion, about whom he knew next to nothing. Knowledge vital to him as a black American had not been part of his previous education. How can one rise to full human stature when the merits and accomplishments of one's collective being are concealed or denied outright? Nelson's student years were times of excitement and discovery. He set about remedying his ignorance, learning the history of African Americans in the United States.

In the spring of 1966, Nelson joined some campus militants demonstrating against ROTC with a sign opposing the Vietnam War. The all-black antiwar protest made the point, he said, that "the people of Vietnam wanted to be free. They weren't doing anything to hurt us. So why were we over there raising the devil like this?"

At A & T, Nelson started studying biology. His father, whom he admired enormously, suggested that he become a doctor, and "I was very much into trying to please my father. I still get a kick out of the good conversation we have about anything." He encountered Lewis Brandon, an African American with a teaching fellowship in biology. A constant and reliable progressive force in the civic affairs of Greensboro, Brandon became a close friend to Nelson. When Nelson married Joyce Hobson and they had two daughters, Akua and Ayodele, Brandon was like an uncle to the girls and a confidant to the Johnson family.

Meanwhile, Nelson, intrigued by discussions around campus of right and wrong, war and peace, and civil rights, abandoned consideration of a medical career and switched his major to political science. He began doing community-organizing work and was part of Youth Educational Services (YES), started by Terry Sanford, then governor of North Carolina. (Jesse Jackson, an A & T graduate a year before Nelson, was the first president of YES). Nelson became a "master organizer" for that white-dominated New Frontier/Great Society project. He visited Fayetteville and other places in the state to coordinate educational services, such as tutoring.

"We started to raise questions," Nelson said. "'What's wrong with the schools?' 'Why do we have to come in and tutor?' The answers were linked to other issues—the kid didn't have lights in the house, his family was poor. That's how I got into the community. It was a beautiful learning experience. I knew I didn't know anything, and I listened a lot. From there I became active in broader community issues. We formed an organization called the Greensboro Association of Poor People."

The Greensboro Association of Poor People, or GAPP, was a community ombudsman that took up the causes of the poorest and most oppressed. Organizers sat down with small groups of people to discuss their problems with them and help them to take action. The problems might relate to poor housing conditions, city redevelopment plans, securing welfare payments, or fighting racism and intimidation by downtown officials or on the job. In a short time, GAPP put down roots in Greensboro's black community and developed solidarity between the community and social justice activists on the city's black campuses.

In response to the leading role Nelson Johnson played in founding the Greensboro Association of Poor People, a newspaper reporter came to him and asked, "Do you know you're a leader?" Nelson told him, "'No, I had no idea.' All I was doing really was listening to people and then discussing in a group what they had discussed with me. That's really all I was doing. GAPP became a significant force."

To Nelson, *Black Power*—a national movement slogan by 1967—meant power obtained through community control. He led GAPP in uniting the black community of Greensboro, speaking at numerous political and social gatherings about how problems in education and housing might be addressed by the community. On the black campuses of A & T and Bennett College, Nelson participated in discussions about what constitutes a *relevant* education. Students asked, "Does this education connect to our people? What does it have to do with freedom or with oppression?"

Owusu Sadauki was the chief community organizer for the Foundation for Community Development, established by Governor Sanford in 1963 to wage the local war on poverty. Owusu and Nelson, among others, made community organizing a radical venture.

Whether community organizing is tame and toothless or wild and woolly is, of course, very much up to the community organizers and the people of the community. If you are organizing people to stand in line, wait their turn, and pick up whatever crumbs happen to be thrown their way, and if people accede to that sort of training, then every politician will be for it—and will consider that folks are behaving very well. If, however, organizers help people empower themselves and bring people together in good working relationships so that each becomes more powerful individually through collective effort, if the group as a whole develops real clout, then the undertaking is far too radical and threatening for most politicians. Empowered people are likely to feel that they can decide what is in their best interest. They are likely to act as if they have a right to remove the obstacles to securing their own well-being. In that sense, GAPP was surely a radical community organization.

Building a coalition between the campuses and the community, Nelson developed skills he retained ever afterward. He could work with and mobilize various classes and strata of blacks, and many whites, too. He came to see the *Black Power* period as "the most relevant and the most mass-based. Thousands of people in the communities were involved, and many participated in a very active way. There was not enough room where we were."

On the floor below the GAPP office was a small barbecue restaurant. The restaurant became an extension of the office. Next door to GAPP, John Marshall Kilimanjaro was just starting a weekly African American newspaper, the *Carolina Peacemaker*. There, and at the nearby NAACP office on Gorrell Street, bordering Bennett College, passionate discussions and debates went on night and day.

"A number of people from A & T and a host of young ladies from Bennett College used to work in the GAPP office, do leaflets and such," Nelson said. "It was a wonderful social setting and work environment," he reminisced. One young woman who frequented GAPP was Sandra Neely (later Sandi Smith). When Nelson mentioned Sandi, I interrupted my interview with him to ask what Sandi was like in those days.

"Very vibrant—she would get the other girls to come down. We'd all pile into my old Volkswagon to go to some meetings at other campuses, Shaw, NCCU. Sandi could be counted on to be a part of that."

As Nelson spoke, I thought of the Sandi I knew—clear-sighted and determined, but also fun-loving and vivacious. Sandi's mother was a school teacher and her father a textile worker at a J. P. Stevens plant. I imagined her childhood and coming of age in Greenville, South Carolina, in the fifties to mid-sixties, where facilities such as restaurants were segregated. White people were served inside, at proper tables and chairs, while blacks were made to line up outside at a coloreds-only take-out window. I could picture Sandi as a teenager, dark and comely, her hair brushed, unsnarled, pomaded, and set in order, her clothes ironed and feminine.

The insults of Jim Crow hurt. They hurt on a daily basis. Why did she and her friends have to stand outdoors at a window to wait for food or be forced to occupy a segregated section of an establishment? Why was there not just one women's bathroom? These questions were as natural as they were painful. A passion for justice burned within Sandra Neely. She followed the mass movement for civil rights as she absorbed the insults, taking note of the marches, sit-ins, and freedom rides. Her parents encouraged Sandra, always a good student, to continue her education and fulfill her dream of becoming a nurse. Mr. and Mrs. Neely were overjoyed when their only child was accepted at Bennett College. Bennett had an excellent reputation as one of the very best finishing schools for young Negro ladies.

But Bennett was not Greensboro's only attraction for Sandi. The decade of the sixties that saw massive civil rights struggles had begun and was roaring to a close *in Greensboro*. From the birth of the movement at a Woolworth's lunch counter in 1960, to the armed police assault on the A & T campus in 1969 (which Sandi followed in the South Carolina newspapers), Greensboro was definitely where the action was. There was a leader there—someone named Nelson Johnson. She read about him in the papers. Sandra Neely arrived in Greensboro in September 1969. She had hardly unpacked her bags and settled in her dormitory room when she attended a Students Organized for Black Unity (SOBU) conference at North Carolina Central University in Durham.

From SOBU, you carried the torch of the Black Liberation Movement into the seventies, writing the history of Greensboro and of America with fire and blood. Your martyrdom on November Third was the gift of your life in the valiant struggle for human and civil rights for the poor, for minorities, for women, and for workers. Do you somehow know that I have wept for you? That Joyce, Nelson, Chekesha, and many others have wept? That Ayo and Akua feel the soft touch of Auntie Sandi as remembrance of you stirs in them? That Sandi Chapman and Sandi Bermanzohn and Sandi Gutstein and all the other Sandis named for you throughout the country study your picture and feel they knew you? That the mill workers even today recall you with a thrill of inspiration? You came in 1969, they conquered your body in 1979, and for ten years in between you spent your soul's coinage relentlessly and selflessly striving toward human liberation. Your spirit holds the promise of decades to come. And the decade that gives us final victory in the struggles for elementary human justice—it belongs to you Sandi, it is yours, it is what you lived and died for, beautiful sister.

Nelson, too, was thinking back to the extraordinary young woman. "One incident that occurs to me now," he said to me, "about Sandi, is the way she insisted we treat the winos like real human beings."

"The winos?"

"The GAPP office was right by the Bennett campus, remember? That was one of the most blighted communities in terms of housing. We were in the middle of that, and a lot of winos used to come around. They would ask the young ladies for money. Well, some of them reacted and raised it with me. Sandi, instead of being fearful and running away, talked to some of the other young ladies, and they called a meeting and invited all the winos up to Bennett. The winos were totally stunned when I told them the young ladies have invited all of y'all to come on up to Bennett. They came to the basement of the dining hall, which functioned as a student union place, and we talked about brotherhood and sisterhood and all standing together. The young ladies came over and hugged them and said how good it was to see them. It turned the whole thing around. After that, when someone would jump up and say, 'Oh baby, you sure are . . . ,' he couldn't even finish the sentence. 'Don't talk like that. That's our black sister. That's our queen.' An old wino would jump in and scold a new wino. And they started to drop in at the office," Nelson remembered.

Speaking of that period, Nelson said, "It was a time of intense being and belonging. 'Beautiful' comes to mind. We didn't appreciate how precious it was. In fact, we let it get away because we didn't appreciate it," he added wistfully. "As we got to theorizing and developing long-term strategies, we tended to pull away from the door-to-door work."

Nelson's tactics, commonsensical and flexible, aimed at developing a multi-class power bloc among blacks, with white allies. He has always been able to lead across the generations. African hairdos and dashikis were "in" by the late 1960s; they were outward trappings of allegiance to Black Power. But for older and more conservative members of the black community, these were not *their* symbols of struggle. Nevertheless, the black community closed ranks under Nelson's leadership. He worked on voter registration with the NAACP and cooperated with black ministers on social welfare projects. When three students who were challenging segregation were killed in February 1968 in the Orangeburg Massacre, a large and largely spontaneous protest ensued: Nelson was out in front of it. (Unlike the killings of white students at Kent State two years later, the deaths and injuries of the black students in South Carolina was a mere whisper in the media.)

In the summer of 1968, Nelson, along with other black activists, formed the Greensboro Association of Poor People (GAPP). In the late 1960s, Nelson successfully rallied the black community behind a series of rent strikes and actions by public school cafeteria workers, by housing tenants fighting the AAA Realty Company, by sanitation workers, and by blind workers in a craft factory. Many years later, in 1996, Nelson's leadership was instrumental in bringing victory to Kmart workers struggling for unionization. From Black Power through Communism to Christianity, much remained constant. The African American leader always sought to unite the community and to help empower people by expanding their understanding of what was happening to them.

When reading William Chafe's *Civilities and Civil Rights*, I was reminded of another constant I associate with Nelson—showing up late for meetings. In the sixties, representatives of the white power structure deemed it a deliberate insult that Nelson did not show up on time for meetings with them. Class and culture gaffe of the highest order. There are far more obstacles in the way of poor people getting to meetings on time than there are for the rich, and hence more obstacles for blacks. My friend Teo Savory, who was a friend of Langston Hughes, said he used to joke about CPT—colored people's time. Perhaps the white power structure would be consoled to know that, even as a communist, Nelson kept his comrades, white and black, waiting for him to start meetings on many occasions. It was certainly not from a lack of respect for his friends. Being on time is not necessarily a virtue in organizers. If he is in the middle of listening to someone's heartfelt story about unjust and wounding treatment, a good organizer does not get up and bolt because there is a meeting across town in ten minutes. Good organizers try to help people develop political awareness, something that does not happen on schedule. Organizing poor people to fight together against injustice is extremely demanding work, precisely because classism and racism make life very difficult. Organizing is messy, behindhand work.

Considering the vast leadership ability of Nelson Napoleon Johnson, it seems altogether appropriate to me that he carries the names of two famous generals and two American presidents.

CIVIL RIGHTS STRUGGLES IN GREENSBORO IN 1968 AND 1969: COURTSHIP AND MARRIAGE IN THOSE WILD TIMES

Five years before Nelson enrolled at A & T, on February 1, 1960, four black A & T students—Franklin McCain, David Richmond, Joseph McNeil, and Ezell Blair Jr.—sat down at a Woolworth lunch counter in Greensboro and launched a wave of sit-ins. Over the course of the next few years, pickets, protests, and mass arrests in Greensboro and elsewhere in North Carolina and in the South made segregation increasingly indefensible as a visible mark of discrimination and in-equality. The mass protests made clearer how much more needed to be done.

The assassination of Rev. Martin Luther King on April 4, 1968, brought frustration and anger to the surface in Greensboro, as in other cities. Hundreds of students marched downtown chanting "Black Power." When some in the crowd threw rocks and bottles, riot police responded with tear gas and shot guns. Things calmed down somewhat, but Mayor Carson Bain requested National Guard units anyway. There was relative calm the next day when Nelson addressed a noon assembly of several hundred students at the courthouse, and during a service for King that was held later at the A & T gymnasium and that drew close to four thousand people. To prevent the situation from becoming more dangerous, A & T president Lewis Dowdy declared an early spring break, returning students to their homes. But several days of campus turmoil followed that involved white snipers, gunfire exchanges between some A & T dormitories and National Guardsmen, the wounding of several policemen, and a curfew called by the mayor, until the violence was ended by a tear gas assault on A & T by police and guardsmen.

At the time, civil rights protests addressed several fundamental issues. The white power structure bypassed black leaders, as if they were children, and de-cided what was in the interest of the black community. In the response to King's murder, black leaders were not even consulted before the city's white elite made the decisions to call in the National Guard and to impose a curfew. Black peo-ple wanted to be represented in policymaking posts in the city. They wanted an open-housing ordinance, an end to police brutality, a ward system of city

government, and a black history curriculum in public schools. In the middle of
the tumult, trying to direct suddenly unleashed energies constructively, was
Nelson Johnson. He was wearing, as Chafe says, the "dual hats of student
leader and founder of the community-action agency." Nelson's ability to rally
people caught the attention of police, government, corporations, and the media. They began to portray him as a dangerous extremist. However, Chafe notes
that Nelson Johnson was "on the scale of radicalism present at A & T in
1968—a relatively moderate figure."[2]

A December 1968 speech by Stokely Carmichael to four thousand students
assembled at the A & T gymnasium had the effect of radicalizing the campus, although student dissent tended to focus on narrow campus issues. Students boycotted classes and then in February 1969 student activists occupied A & T's
central administration building with a set of mostly campus-related demands.
The situation was brought under control by President Dowdy, but things became more confrontational a couple of weeks later when police showed up in the
black community at a memorial service for Malcolm X that was sponsored by
GAPP and attended by hundreds of students. The police blocked sidewalk traffic and provocatively set off a tear gas canister, but organizers of the event maintained control of the crowd.

When, shortly afterward in March 1969, A & T cafeteria workers went out
on strike, they were supported by a student boycott of the dining hall. All over
the state, black cafeteria workers were protesting poverty wages, forced overtime
with no extra pay, and no fringe benefits. The black community in Greensboro
rose to the occasion, old and young, students and merchants, to support
the workers, confirming at a stroke Nelson's success in building a broad
community–campus coalition. With help from churches and merchants, students organized food preparation and distribution for thousands of people. After Nelson announced in a speech that one merchant was being uncooperative
about contributing food, students spontaneously marched to his store to "liberate" the food, and three were arrested. Meanwhile, over two thousand five hundred students marched to President Dowdy's home and rallied in support of the
cafeteria workers. When their rally was over, police faced down students with
gunfire and tear gas. One student was wounded. According to students, police
shot randomly into the crowd, and students responded with rock throwing but
did not retaliate with guns. The cafeteria walkout lasted two days and was settled in negotiations between the workers and the school administration.

Hostility between the police and the black community was escalating. Faced
with a growing solidarity and unity in the black community, the paranoia among
the white city fathers knew no bounds. It cast Nelson Johnson in the role of in-

surgent bent on blowing up buildings and toppling established authority. The Vietcong in our midst! At the very least, part of a Black Panther conspiracy!

In spring 1969, Willie Drake, a leader in the Student Government Association (SGA) at A & T, initiated the Students Organized for Black Unity (SOBU). The founding conference at A & T State University of this national organization drew many black student activists from the eastern part of the United States. In the environment of social turmoil and mass organizing outlined here, the following incident occurred. Claude Barnes (Abiola) was a junior at Dudley High, a black school within Greensboro's still segregated school system. He had been president of his class, was an honor student and a student council member. He was also a member of Youth for the Unity of Black Society (YUBS), which was the youth organization affiliated with GAPP. Abiola was prohibited from running for the office of student council president and accused of being a subversive because of his membership in YUBS. (In essence, all of the local community organizing by GAPP was being branded as subversive.) When the Dudley election was held, Barnes received six hundred write-in votes—four hundred more than the runner-up. Write-in ballots were declared illegal, however, and the runner-up was given the election. Some students began walking out of school in protest, and several Dudley High School students marched over to the A & T campus where the founding conference of SOBU was being held right at that moment. Edward Whitfield, a Cornell University student present at the founding of SOBU, recalled that the Dudley students presented their plight to the gathering of black college student activists. The SOBU conference responded by adjourning in order to march over to Dudley in a show of support for its beleaguered student body. "At that time," said Whitfield, "Nelson Johnson stood on a table and gave a brief speech in support of Claude Barnes' election and in praise of the Dudley students' activism in the community. For exercising his free speech, Nelson was to serve time in prison."[3]

A week later, more students walked out of Dudley to protest officials' highhandedness over the election. They were soon joined by even more Dudley protesters, and by some A & T students. Nelson addressed the protesters in the street. Although a bonafide member of the black community, and someone who was seeking to manage a tense situation rather than to further inflame it, Nelson and others like him were accused of being "outside agitators."

After a real outside agitator, a city-appointed, white public relations director of the schools, quashed all efforts by the black community to resolve things peacefully, the situation at Dudley deteriorated quickly. By the middle of May, verbal controversy had escalated into a paramilitary confrontation. Hundreds of Dudley students boycotted classes, demanding their school president be brought "out of exile." There were several fracases between police and picketing students. Finally, on May 21, 1969, as police riot squads dispensed their mace canisters and descended on a crowd outside Dudley High, many innocent bystanders, including children, became victims of the violence. The venue of conflict then shifted to A & T, when Dudley students went over to that campus. In the evening, as a black insurgency that they themselves had called forth was threatening the white establishment, Mayor Jack Elam requested support from the National Guard. As with the similar request a year earlier, Lewis Dowdy and the black community were not consulted. Late into the night, crowds formed on the A & T campus and were routed by police. An Armored Personnel Carrier was ordered to go to the area. Then came the first report of gunfire from the campus. Another Armored Personnel Carrier was ordered in. Police reported returning sniper fire coming from the campus. Still visible to this day are the police bullets in the walls of Scott Hall. Further dangers on that spring night in 1969 lurked in carloads of white youths who rode through the neighborhood. The violence did not abate until after the tragic shooting death of A & T student Willie Grimes.

According to Nelson, it was common knowledge that Grimes was killed by the Greensboro police. "A man was killed and no one was ever brought to trial. We knew who did it because people saw it. But the police did not even interview eyewitnesses, and we had no capacity to bring them to court." At the time, Nelson said, an enterprising reporter who was part of the liberated student movement was working on the Greensboro newspaper. He wrote an in-depth story contradicting the police version of events. The police claimed that Grimes could not have been killed by a police officer. The reason they gave concerned the size of the bullet that killed the young student. It was not, they said, the same as that used in the standard revolvers issued to police. However, the reporter also learned from some black policemen (who chose to resign from the force so that they would not be compelled to fire on the black community) that most police carried private guns in addition to the ones they were issued. Thus the police claim that the murder bullet did not match those used in police guns came to nothing at all. The incident was not investigated; it was covered up. And the reporter did not stay at the paper long before he was fired.

Students at A & T reacted to the police siege and the killing with another three or four days of semiorganized revolt. Nelson was their public spokesperson. "In terms of the military things that people were doing," he told me, "I had virtually no role. I was being told what was happening. However, the perception of the white power structure was that I had all these people under my personal power. They granted me a lot of front-page space in the newspaper—very negative coverage.

"With the King assassination and the cities in revolt, with the Black Panthers on the scene, with the organized state machinery taking out a lot of militant blacks—blaming, jailing, and killing them—and with the intense confrontation in Greensboro that we call the Dudley–A & T revolt in 1969, those were unforgettable times," he said.

"I had started to think in terms of the strategy and tactics of mass struggle. We were trying to unite Bennett, Dudley, A & T, and the community. And, frankly, we did it. We had six neighborhood organizations under the umbrella of the Greensboro Association of Poor People. They worked closely with students from A & T and Bennett."

In the spring of 1970, the growing unity in the black community was displayed when Students Organized for Black Unity (SOBU) in North Carolina held a "Save Black Schools dinner" at A & T, with principal speeches by A & T President Dowdy, state legislators Henry Frye and Julian Bond, and community leader Nelson Johnson. Speaking of that time, Nelson confessed, "I still did not appreciate political power. I was asked to run for a seat on the city council. It seemed the most absurd thing I'd ever heard."

In the summer of 1970, Nelson was sentenced along with another organizer for their intervention and speechifying at Dudley High School the previous year. Nelson exhausted his appeals and began serving a prison sentence in the spring of 1971. Recalling the support he received from people in Greensboro, he told me, "There was an impressive mobilization by the community. Henry Frye, George Simkins, Rev. Julius Douglas, Rev. Otis Hairston—they all went to Governor Scott to speak in my behalf." Governor Scott granted the organizers an executive pardon a month or two into their two-year sentences.

"I spent some time," Nelson related, "doing road construction. My first daughter, Akua, was born. She was so small, she can't remember, but I have the most vivid memory of her and Joyce coming to visit me in prison. I felt kind of bad. The noble cause thing, eternal optimism of youth, being righteous—these notions helped to keep my chin up. Still, that is not where you want to be when the wife you love and your newborn baby are outside."

Joyce Hobson had enrolled at UNC in Chapel Hill after graduating from Duke University. Nelson met her in early 1969, and they were married three months later.

"I had been meeting people and having a good time. We used to have a lot of parties. I got to the point where I didn't really enjoy the parties anymore. I'd leave and go to Chapel Hill because I enjoyed being with Joyce so much. Joyce and I had some deep and meaningful conversations. They were on a level that I had not experienced with anyone else. Our relationship took off rather rapidly."

It was not a typical courtship. "My apartment was used as an office and a social gathering place," Nelson said. "We worked out of there. We didn't even lock the door. People came in from out of town, pulled up a piece of floor, and went to sleep. I didn't know who would be there when I got in. That was fine with me. People were always decent and respectful. But naturally Joyce and I preferred to spend time together in Chapel Hill."

They did not begin married life the way people usually do. They were married in May 1969, right in the middle of the revolt at A & T. Forget a honeymoon. "Everywhere I went around town, I was followed by a police car," Nelson said. "There was a military jeep parked outside our apartment." After his speech to student protesters outside of Dudley High School, the police really had it in for Nelson. "I had broken no law, and it took the police ten days to figure out how to charge me."

About his marriage to Joyce, Nelson says simply, "We've had a wonderful life together."

A photo of Joyce as a young woman, incredibly beautiful, with a high, proud forehead and her head wrapped in a boldly colored African *gele*, adorned the mantle of their roomy old farmhouse on Alamance Church Road in Greensboro. I always noticed it when I went there. It bore witness to consecutive political forays, to being alive, to struggling fiercely for justice.

"Black power had an appeal for me," Nelson admitted, "and I suspect for a lot of other people who were victims of the color game. It was very affirming. Politically, it talked about unity, about taking control of our community and electing people who would speak for us. If you remember that period, blacks in leadership were almost all handpicked by whites. Selecting our real representatives was part of the Black Power movement.

"Our movement was met with hatred and vengeance by the white population but particularly by those at the top of the social structure. When we used the language of Black Power, they talked about us in very negative terms as people who hate whites. That's all they could see. And to some extent we probably articulated that, but it was largely a reaction."

Attracted by the solidarity of the black community in Greensboro, Howard Fuller (Owusu Sadaukai) moved the Malcolm X Liberation University from Durham to Greensboro. William Chafe sums up: "As the new home of Malcolm X University and the headquarters of the Students Organized for Black Unity, Greensboro had become by 1971 the center of Black Power in the South."[4] Its black population "had achieved a degree of political strength unprecedented in their history."[5] Few conversant with the history of the city would deny that Greensboro's black power was largely due to the organizing efforts and leadership of Nelson Johnson.

WE LEARN A NEW LANGUAGE

When I moved to Greensboro in the spring of 1971, I was virtually ignorant of the tumultuous civil rights struggles that had taken place and what they meant. The struggles and achievements of black citizens were not widely trumpeted by the white city fathers. It took me some time to learn about the situation.

In those days, radical whites and young blacks didn't mix. When I taught at Bennett College in 1973, I had a student, Michelle, who was part of the Malcolm X Liberation University. We liked each other, and I made a bid for her friendship. She seemed to be considering it, but then gently let me know that she could not be my friend because I was a white person. It was the heyday of Pan-Africanism.

History is really too alive, dynamic, organic, and complex to move in categories and simple progressions, but sometimes it is nevertheless helpful to demarcate events somewhat stiffly and mechanically in order to at least get in the ballpark of what you are talking about. So, tripping all over myself with caveats, let me proceed. First there was a civil rights movement (which stressed equality and integration), then there was a Black Power movement (responding to a continued lack of equality and reaching to a deeper level of autonomy and self-determination), then there was Pan-Africanism (which seems to grow naturally out of Black Power in locating a triumphal and empowering perspective from which to view black culture, history, geography, and politics), then there was Marxism (which seeks to transcend race and narrow nationalism and to show the deep source of racism and national oppression in economic determinism, class politics, and Western imperialism).

Casting a critical glance at the early seventies—a time of intense theorizing and flamboyant rhetoric in the movement for black liberation—Nelson commented, "I think we did get turned a few degrees away from the grassroots. We talked about Pan-Africanism and quoted from Nkrumah's *Class Struggle*. It sounded impressive, but it wasn't necessarily an effective instrument to grasp the deep relatedness and mutuality of human existence, or even to advance black unity.

"Rhetoric—the spoken word and the fervor with which people speak—is one of the beautiful things in African American culture," Nelson said. "After a while it gets to be almost a thing unto itself. Take Hubert Brown, the leader of SNCC. We know him as H. Rap Brown. And the 'Rap' was because Brown could rap it down, could just throw that rhetoric down. When that's authentic, it's really great and unifying. But when you get into imitating it and there's a whole culture of people going around rapping at each other, it can lose some of its authenticity."

The concept of Pan-Africanism had been around for a long time, and its appeal is not difficult to understand. In endless discussions about black unity and black control, Nelson heard the same complaint—"we're only 10 percent of the population. All we can do is to go along with the system and work something out." Pan-Africanists, however, could say "we are a minority only in the context of the United States. In the context of the world's people, we are a majority." Pan-Africanism corresponded to a genuine sentiment of black people to take a stand against their own oppression in the United States. It was fairly common for black American leaders to visit Africa for political and cultural purposes. As Nelson saw it, Pan-Africanism quickly got sorted into two wings. One was an escape from reality and from the necessity of struggling in this country. Its litany might go: "We are an African people. We need to reclaim our roots. It's a waste of time to try to build something in the United States. What we need to do is to support liberation movements in Africa." Nelson criticized this interpretation. "If you could get a plane ticket to fly to Africa, you could come back and tell stories about how relevant you were in Africa while being totally irrelevant in your hometown—that was one trend. We recognized and rejected it at the time. The other one was—'we are an African people, and we have to build fraternal ties and support each other everywhere we are. We also must struggle everywhere we are, including in this country.' The leader of that wing in our area was Owusu Sadaukai."

Actually, both tendencies of Pan-Africanism could be found in Malcolm X Liberation University, although the principal stated objective of that independent black school was to train people for nation-building—in Africa. There was an unresolved tension in the school's mission. In the impoverished black communities surrounding Malcolm X Liberation University, people's most pressing needs generally had to do with increasing their wages and combating a variety of injustices that daily kept them and their families down. They may have felt sympathetic toward, and even proud of, MXLU, but clearly its focus was somewhere else.

"Even among those of us who felt we had to do what we could do here, the pull of Pan-Africanism had some detrimental influence. The local struggle became secondary," Nelson attested.

Owusu had been to Africa and talked with Samora Michel, the first president of an independent Mozambique after that country freed itself from colonial Portuguese rule in 1974. Michel, a Marxist, told Owusu what black Americans could do to help the African Liberation struggle. "We don't need any more people," Owusu was told. "Africa's full of people. Our problem is the politics of the United States. We need a voice inside of the United States that can speak to our interest. If you could play a role in that, it would help us much more than sending folks over here who have no idea what they're doing."

"I think Samora Michel was being courteous and honest," Nelson remarked. "Owusu's trip led to a meeting in Greensboro with the biggest Pan-Africanists—Baraka, Don Lee, and others—coming from all around. Something that everyone agreed was very positive came out of that—African Liberation Day.

"We organized the first African Liberation Day in 1972," Nelson said. "People came in huge numbers—considering this thing had been called by a bunch of radical black people. I think there were about 50,000 in Washington. I was on the west coast in 1972, with some 10,000 or 15,000 people. There was a demonstration in Canada. Rosie Douglas led that one. There was one in Grenada. It was led by Maurice Bishop. [Bishop later became prime minister of a revolutionary Grenada.] That's how we got to meet Maurice. African Liberation Day was greater than any of us had hoped. It was such a success that we immediately fell into turmoil about what to do about it."

The Students Organized for Black Unity (SOBU) became Youth Organized for Black Unity (YOBU) and committed itself to supporting the African liberation movement. When visiting this country, representatives of African liberation movements often spoke at programs organized by YOBU. Sandi and Joyce were particularly impressed on hearing Amilcar Cabral, head of the liberation movement in Guinea Bissau. Joyce remembered Cabral told his audience that "our fight was right here. Our most important task was to overthrow U.S. imperialism. Sending support to Africa was only secondary." Cabral challenged his black audience to unite with other people in the United States, like white workers, against U.S. imperialism. White people in general were not the enemy.

Dual tendencies in the Black Liberation Movement (BLM) came to a head in the need to define what African Liberation Day was about. Was it anti-imperialist in character, which meant that it was based on a class analysis? Or was it anti-white, which meant it took race as the fundamental category of analysis and espoused nationalism as its ideology? A major question of orientation confronted the African Liberation Support Committee (ALSC)—the organization that established African Liberation Day (ALD).

In May 1973, local ALD demonstrations were held in over thirty locations and drew over eighty thousand people. There were rallies in twenty-seven cities in the United States (including Houston, Detroit, Philadelphia, Denver, New Haven, Indianapolis, New York, Washington, D.C., Columbus, and Chicago), in three Canadian cities, and on five Caribbean islands. Speaking in Raleigh, North Carolina, ALSC Chairman Owusu Sadaukai said that "because of the efforts of local African Liberation Support Committees, imperialism is no longer an abstract word to many of our people." He talked about the increasing number of black people "who now have some understanding of the relationship between what is happening to Black people in Africa and what is happening to Black people in the western hemisphere."

The path that Nelson, Joyce, and other black activists took to Marxism, unlike the one traveled by most white activists, led through Africa and the liberation struggles on that continent. Throughout the period of his community organizing, Nelson and others deepened their understanding of the theoretical and political questions underlying the struggle of black Americans for full human and civil rights. Always, study informed practice, and practice aided study. In July 1973, shortly after the ALD demonstrations, Nelson presented a paper at a conference in Frogmore, South Carolina. "Who is the enemy of the Afro-American people, *all* white people or the handful of monopoly capitalists?" he asked. "What is the relationship of the black liberation movement to the multinational working class? What is the best way for Afro-Americans to support the struggles on the African continent?" He argued against those in ALSC urging blacks to reject "this 1860 white Marxist bull" and "white ideology of Mao tse-Tung."

It was becoming clearer that the most active and influential organizers within ALSC favored an anti-imperialist stand, one that would put them in the camp of Marxism. In 1974, African Liberation Day was celebrated in Washington, D.C., once again and a major conference was held: "Which Way Forward for the Black Liberation Movement?" Pan-Africanism, represented by Stokely Carmichael, yielded to Marxism and to a determination to base ALSC's program on the concrete reality of the United States, to take up issues of Afro-American oppression, and to unite with other liberation struggles throughout the world. For many activists in the Black Liberation movement, the die was cast at Frogmore, but ALSC decisively turned the corner from Pan-Africanism to Marxism at the 1974 conference.

Roz Pelles (then Roz Bailey) had trained with Owusu in the Foundation for Community Development's program for organizers in the summer of 1968. She had been at A & T, had worked in Greensboro as an organizer, and had been active in GAPP. At the time, she and her husband worked with Nelson and had helped out in YOBU and at the Malcolm X Liberation University. They then moved briefly from Greensboro to Winston-Salem. "There was a point," Roz recalled, "when all the people we knew from the African Liberation period became Marxists. They all went to Frogmore for a conference and came back Marxists, so it seemed. We were shocked. We didn't know what they were doing. I remember I felt betrayed by that. We'd all been into black nationalism together. I spent two years wearing African clothes. I'm with all these people and suddenly, after Frogmore, they put out a paper." She thought about it and added, chuckling, "It was in this new language that I didn't understand."[6]

This *new language*—Marxism—was to become much more widely spoken by Roz and others after 1974. In the meantime, the overall solidarity within the black community held strong even though activists occupied different niches within the developing structure of black liberation. When Roz's second son, Tambaqui, was born, both Marxists and nationalists turned out for a naming ceremony.

At a 1974 ALSC conference with workshops on racism and imperialism, debate centered around resolving the main question—"Which way forward for the Black Liberation Movement?" Represented in panel discussions were Muhammad Ahmad, Saladin Muhammad, and Winston Berry of the All-Africa People's Party; Abdul Alkalimat from People's College; Stokely Carmichael of the All-African People's Revolutionary Party; Kwadwo Akpan of the Pan-African Congress; Imamu Baraka of the Congress of African People; and Owusu Sadaukai of the African Liberation Support Committee. Their positions were set forth in detail in the July 1974 issue of *The African World.*

Joyce Johnson was a panelist in a Women in Struggle workshop that dealt with male supremacist tendencies in the Black Liberation movement. "Though there are clear differences in the conditions and experiences of black people from others, we do not stand unblemished by the pressures of male chauvinism perpetuated by the ruling class," she said. Black women were victims of three types of oppression based on sex, race, and class. Women needed to participate equally with men in the liberation struggle against the ruling class; they did not need to go off by themselves and organize.

We all acknowledged at the time that the struggle against sexism, as against racism, would continue under socialism. We maintained that socialism would provide better conditions for overcoming sexism and racism, both of which we saw as having an existence independent of capitalism. We were not so naive as to think that sexism and racism would immediately or automatically disappear under socialism.

The Marxist trend emerged victorious over nationalism and defined the character of the ALSC in the coming years. Owusu Sadaukai presented a position paper by ALSC. It was an unequivocally Marxist analysis of black liberation and centered around these five points:

1. The principal contradiction in society is a class contradiction between the bourgeoisie and the proletariat, and the national oppression facing black people can only be dealt with through an understanding of the principal contradiction.

2. Marxism-Leninism is the only science of revolution. For the black liberation movement to advance and escape the many traps and pitfalls set for it, black revolutionaries must actively take up the study of Marxism-Leninism and apply it to the conditions in the United States.
3. Individuals, organizations, and the entire black liberation movement must begin to integrate itself with the working class, recognizing that it is the leading social force in the struggle against imperialism.
4. Black revolutionaries, guided by Marxism-Leninism, must take up and lead the day-to-day struggles of black people.
5. Continue the support for anti-imperialist struggles of oppressed people everywhere.

In the pages of *The Black Scholar*, ALSC's Mark Smith mounted a defense of Marxism-Leninism against Haki Madhubuti's (Don Lee's) prior article rejecting Marxism as a white ideology. Speaking for the leading ALSC organizers in the South, Mark repudiated "our former reactionary nationalist-Pan-Africanist position."

In recognizing the enemy as imperialism, a worldwide system of oppression, ALSC committed itself to supporting black people in Africa *and* to tackling the problems of blacks in the United States. The organization adopted an internationalist tone, stressing above all the connection between the millions victimized by apartheid in South Africa and the unequal and oppressed status of blacks in the United States.

Much lively debate back and forth occurred before Nelson settled in the embrace of Marxism. In his circle at the time, Mark Smith was a theoretician of repute and an articulate speaker. Mark played a major part in guiding SOBU toward Marxism. Compared to Mark, Owusu was a shade more nationalist and a little less excited about class unity with white workers, Nelson observed. At first, he confessed, "I didn't know what Mark was talking about. I knew if he went down to Littleton, North Carolina, talking that way, it just wasn't going to play." Sure there were Uncle Toms and sell-outs in the black community, Nelson thought, but there was no real class structure and "this class thing was an invention of white folks to divide us."

Nelson and others in SOBU nevertheless began studying in earnest, reading Samora Michel, Amilcar Cabral, and Nkrumah. "We started meeting increasing numbers of persons from Africa with a sophisticated class assessment," Nelson explained. "I met a young man in New York from Nigeria who laid out this class analysis. We wholeheartedly disagreed with it, but we were determined to be brothers with our brother. We brought him down to Greensboro to a meeting of the leadership council of SOBU and invited our people from all over the country.

He laid out a profound analysis that really rocked our world. As opposed to our convincing him, he started us on this trek. So our movement toward Marxism was really via Africa. It was not via the white movement in this country. We had no contact and nothing to do with them for years. We formed an independent black Marxist organization, the Revolutionary Workers League (RWL), and that was the incubating group for a network of black Marxists around the country."

Nelson talked through his doubts and questions with the leadership of the WVO, then all Asian Americans. In that process, he became surer of Marxism as the road to black liberation.

The RWL, in theory at least, accepted the need for a multinational unity of workers to fulfill the agenda of black liberation. The organization saw black workers as playing a leading role in the struggle to liberate all black people. RWL sent its members into the factories to organize workers. In 1974, Sandra Neely and Mark Smith got jobs at the Cone Mills Revolution Plant (so called after the revolutionary process of textile manufacture when it was built around the turn of the century). Nelson was hired at another Cone textile plant in Greensboro, Proximity Print Works. Two years later, when I went to work at Cone's Revolution Plant, Mark and Sandi were still there. By then there were a dozen or more WVO supporters at that plant and many other workers sympathetic to their views.

NOTES

1. Unless otherwise indicated, quotations by Nelson Johnson are from a taped interview with him on March 2, 1993. In this and other interviews, I have taken minor liberties with grammar, positioning, and cuts in the transcript.

2. William Chafe, *Civilities and Civil Rights: Greensboro, North Carolina and the Black Struggle for Freedom* (New York: Oxford University Press, 1981), 181.

3. In reconstructing the 1968 and 1969 sequence of events, I have used Chafe's excellent account along with the testimonies of Nelson Johnson and Edward Whitfield, both of whom were involved in various aspects of the events. Shortly before publication of this work, Mr. Whitfield provided historical information that filled in certain important details and corrected some inaccuracies in this section of the book. My own experiences in Greensboro subsequent to 1969 allowed me to understand that media distortion of the 1968–1969 events had a significant impact on people's perception, and misperception, of those events, even as it did later in relation to the Greensboro Massacre.

4. Chafe, *Civilities and Civil Rights*, 220.

5. Chafe, *Civilities and Civil Rights*, 219.

6. Unless otherwise indicated, quotations by Roz Pelles are from a taped interview with her on July 3, 1992.

4

DURHAM ACTIVISTS
TELL IT LIKE IT IS

A CERTIFIED ANTI-NAZI

If Dr. Paul Carl Bermanzohn had made a different choice about medical school, he probably would not have met Mike Nathan, who turned out to be his best friend. Nor Sally Avery, who was to become his wife. Perhaps he still would have become a psychiatrist in New York, but it is unlikely he would be practicing his chosen profession with the unique distinction of having caught a bullet in his head from an encounter with Klansmen and Nazis. Much would have happened very differently in Paul's life if the man in the lab coat who showed him around Johns Hopkins one day had not struck him as comical. Paul had his pick of medical schools. The choice came down to Johns Hopkins or Duke University.

"When I visited Hopkins," Paul recalled, "the guy who took me around resembled a cadaver. He looked like he had been locked up in a tower in the backyard of a castle in Transylvania for the last twenty years. He was pale. He was wearing a lab coat, and he had pants that stopped midway down his shins, showing spindly legs and white socks. He looked like he didn't belong in the sunlight. It didn't make a good impression on me." Paul's storytelling and sense of humor remind me of my mother's talents. Like Paul, she understood human foibles well and could render them hilarious, following an oral tradition of Jewish humor that was handed down to her. But Paul did not grow up, as I did, surrounded by grandparents, aunts, uncles, and cousins. Paul Bermanzohn was born in 1949 in Munich, Germany, to parents who were Holocaust survivors and who emigrated to America. He grew up in the South Bronx, in a Yiddish-speaking Jewish

neighborhood, with many other immigrants. His father was silent about his experience in a work camp; his mother, a concentration camp inmate during the
war, talked about it constantly. "I was a certified anti-Nazi by the time I was
three," said Paul.[1] The Bermanzohns wanted their son to blend into the woodwork, to be inconspicuous. "Sei a grueh mensch" ("Be a gray person") was the
frequent watchword of circumspection. They did not want him to *stand out*;
they wanted him to *survive*.

As a student at City College in New York from 1965 to 1969, Paul was as far
from blending into the woodwork as he could be. Of medium build and good-
looking, with a fair complexion, high forehead, and light brown hair, Paul's
attractive features were augmented by a dynamic, charismatic personality and
outstanding scholastic achievements. He was, overall, too outstanding to be inconspicuous, and his fellow students elected him president of the sophomore
class, then president of the student body. He was a student leader during a time
of intense political turmoil, replete with several administration building
takeovers and militant anti–Vietnam War protests. Recalling the antiestablishment sentiment at City, Paul said, "Everything was one big stronghold of opposition to the existing order. The college was so saturated with politics that if you
put out a leaflet, within half an hour you'd have a demonstration with a thousand
people—unless you were careful to hide the leaflet."

Paul's political outlook evolved with events and personal experiences. With
friend and fellow student at City College Allen Blitz, Paul attended his first big
demonstration in 1968, a march on the United Nations led by Martin Luther
King and Benjamin Spock. He watched the state flex its muscles during a
demonstration at City College that ended with hundreds of police massed on
campus. "With their riot gear, they looked like an invading army marching into
the Student Union at night. And I was trying to go back and forth between the
administration and the police leadership and the student demonstrators, late
one night, trying to prevent heads from getting busted. I think we *did* prevent
heads from getting busted. It was very heavy, because it was just a blatant show
of force backed by a college administration that lied to the students, up, down,
and sideways."

As a student leader at City College, Paul also was involved in the tumultuous
events at Columbia University. He was not, however, a leader of any of the rebellions. Paul was critical of many of the leftist campus groups, some of whose
wild and irresponsible actions put him off. He appreciated hearing a speech by
Social Democrat Michael Harrington. "It was the first time I heard Marxism
presented so that it made sense and wasn't obscured by the speaker's bad
mouthing a rival group on the left," Paul acknowledged. His parents, he con-

ceded, had the greatest influence on his political development. "If I was interested in a political group, I asked myself, 'is this something my parents could join?'—the idea being that they were more or less average working-class people."

Paul came to think differently about having publicly criticized, and distanced himself from, some of the leftist campus organizations when he saw the brutality of the police, who were doing the bidding of campus administrators in suppressing the protests. After the assassination of Dr. Martin Luther King, "I adopted a moral imperative right then and there not to hold back," he said. "I kept the *New York Times* clipping of King's last speech in my wallet with a little note to myself that you can't stand apart from struggle."

At City College, Paul Bermanzohn earned enough credits to do graduate work in chemistry, biology, math, physics, or comparative literature: he had majored in practically everything. He was choosing between medical school at Johns Hopkins or Duke when word came over the radio that Duke students had taken over a campus building that served as the living quarters for Duke University president Douglas Knight. That clinched it: Paul opted for Durham, N.C., and Duke University.

SALLY AND MIKE

The day after Martin Luther King was killed, in April 1968, Sally Avery and Michael Nathan, both Duke students, joined a large protest march at the university that ended up outside President Knight's home. Soon, along with a couple of hundred other students, they were *inside* the house. The place, Sally said, "was a symbol of the luxurious decadence of an administration that was paying its service workers 85 cents an hour. One of our demands when we marched was that the wages of Duke's workers be doubled. We also called on the administration to recognize the Duke workers' union, Local 77. They went on strike the day after the takeover."[2]

Durham, in the late 1960s and early 1970s, was alive with campus and grassroots activity. The American Federation of State, County, and Municipal Employees (AFSCME) Local 77, a union of African American service workers on the Duke University campus, was organized in 1965 at the height of the civil rights movement, and began direct action tactics a year later that catalyzed alliances among students and faculty.[3] Local 77 had planned an all-out strike of food service and housekeeping employees during the first week of April 1968. After the King assassination occurred, Sally, Mike, and other students who had been actively supporting the union's demands and other civil rights struggles in

Durham seized the moment to sit-in at the president's house in support of the campus's nonacademic workers. Local 77 activity, led by black service workers (mostly women), galvanized the student population, not the other way around. A coalition of the predominantly minority campus workers with primarily white students and faculty members devoted to civil rights and economic justice was a critical factor in challenging institutional policies at Duke. This powerful coalition shut down the university in the largest demonstration in Duke's history. A "silent vigil" and encampment on the main quadrangle involved thousands of employees, students, and faculty and brought national media attention to Duke. The encampment, the strike by food service workers, and a supportive student boycott of the dining hall showed that Duke workers were a force within an institution trying to marginalize them. Student activism at that time was closely tied to the union movement. The campus vigil was not just a moment when students expressed a moral conscience, but a political act for racial and economic justice, based on an understanding of the interconnectedness of race and class (and, for some, gender) in injustices perpetrated in institutional structures. Nor was the protest "spontaneous": years of coalition building went into it.

Sally and other students were naive enough to think that because their demands were reasonable, Knight would give in. A lot happened over the next few days: none of it included Knight's submission to the occupying student force. Sally recalled their discussion about tactics. She remembered "Mike saying that by actually holding the building, we had some power. We had something under our control, and it would be a real mistake to give it up. We took a vote. It came out something like 200 to 3, against Mike." Although outvoted, Mike Nathan had spoken out bravely and defended his minority view. The students abandoned their occupation and marched back to the campus to build support for the cause.

"Fifteen hundred students came out to support us, and we had a week-long vigil in front of Duke Chapel," Sally said. "We camped on the grass before the chapel. Some of the black restaurants in town provided us with food. The cafeteria workers were out on strike, all the campus workers joined in, and Duke University was shut down for a week." (Subsequently, Duke workers got more money, in line with a new federal minimum wage law that was about to go into effect. Union recognition for the campus service workers came in 1972.)

Sally felt empowered by the occupation of Knight's house. It was the first time she had done something really risky based on her convictions. She believed that if people worked together, they could begin to engage the root causes of injustice. "Yet at the same time as I felt working collectively we could change things, there was the feeling, 'Boy, this is hard. It's really hard to make things change.'"

Sally Avery had moved south in search of the civil rights movement in 1965. "My mother's family could trace their southern roots back to the 1700s," she said. "There were a lot of ministers, teachers, and educated women in the family. My mother always made it clear to me that the family had never owned slaves. She and my grandmother were strongly against segregation, but they thought the only thing to do about it was make some personal gesture."

Sally did not want to be confined to personal gestures. The women's liberation movement aimed to end women's oppression and bring about full equality between the sexes. Even the strong women role models in Sally's family had to struggle in a society that kept women from attaining their full stature. Sally felt intimately connected to the struggle for women's liberation. By 1969, her senior year, when the women's movement hit North Carolina, she joined it enthusiastically. Before that, her commitment to civil rights had brought her into the orbit of Owusu Sadaukai, then director of Operation Breakthrough. She participated in discussions about the civil rights movement that the black leader conducted, in one of the campus religious houses. However, Owusu's cultivation of progressive-minded white Duke students ended rather abruptly in 1967 with the Black Power movement.

In the meantime, while still a student at Duke, Sally moved from campus and lived and worked in Edgemont, one of Durham's poor neighborhoods. She went back to the campus to go to classes, but she was daily involved in community organizing. Her housemate, Michael Nathan, also a student, worked as a community organizer for Operation Breakthrough and was well liked by everyone he worked with. Sally and Mike ended up working together as community organizers in the poverty program. Working among black youth, they started a teen center where dances were held. They formed an African Dance group that toured the state. "Working with very poor kids was a wonderful experience," Sally said. "I did this for three years and got to know them really well. If the mass movement hadn't picked up in 1967 and 1968, I think I would have become a social worker."

It was from Mike that Sally first heard the case for revolution cogently put. "I already knew that blacks and women were discriminated against, workers were exploited, and the Vietnamese were being murdered by the U.S. Army. But I tended to see each thing separately. Mike put it all together for me, showing me how capitalism was the source of all these problems and we would have to overthrow the capitalists to solve them."

Mike and Sally were married shortly before they both graduated in 1969. Mike enrolled at Duke's medical school while Sally continued her community organizing and her involvement in the women's movement. "It was hard on the marriage," she recalled. "We went from spending all our time together as undergraduates to Mike's being in medical school and my supporting the two of us with the very low wages I was getting as a preschool director at a community center."

THE MAMA AND PAPA OF THE MOVEMENT

At Duke, Paul Bermanzohn befriended Michael Nathan, a man with a wry sense of humor and radical political views. The two swapped stories of campus rebellions they had known at Duke University, City College, and Columbia University. Takeovers and shutdowns were very exciting, but both men felt that the nature of American society needed to be addressed: What was going on? Why was it happening? Long term, what could be done about it? How can we get a society that is truly democratic and just? In 1970, Paul and Mike, along with several other medical students, organized a local chapter of the Medical Committee for Human Rights (MCHR). The group's main focus was antiwar activity. When the United States invaded Cambodia, MCHR members shut down Duke Medical School for a day.

By Mike's third year of medical school, his marriage with Sally had come apart. Free love and dope smoking were aspects of the cultural milieu of the sixties. Many of us (myself included) succumbed. Mike and Paul sometimes went to medical classes stoned. Before settling down, Paul had his "Casanova routine." After they were married, Mike was unfaithful to Sally.

Later, the Workers Viewpoint Organization (WVO) would promote what it called "proletarian relationships." It was comforting for insecure partners in a relationship to know that sexual unfaithfulness was frowned upon as unrevolutionary. As I understood it, having extramarital affairs and smoking marijuana were self-centered, petty-bourgeois indulgences that showed a weak stand with the working class. Consequently, we ended up in traditional monogamous relationships that would have brought a smile to the face of the pope, or the modern-day promise keeper. To be real about this, the political work did not leave you any free time in which to be unfaithful: it was all you could do to spend some time with your spouse!

Sally was very hurt by Mike's infidelity. But she was an independent woman, committed to the welfare rights organizing she was doing for Operation Breakthrough. She felt she had sunk roots in Durham. "Mike wanted to go away for his internship," she told me. "And I just couldn't imagine being a medical wife and following him to Texas, not knowing anything or anyone, not being part of a movement. I just couldn't imagine doing that." The couple got a divorce while Mike was doing his internship in Texas.

Meanwhile, Paul interrupted his formal education to do community organizing. With Duke's blessing, he took a leave of absence to work for Operation Breakthrough as a Health Specialist. Paul got to know Sally better. He thought highly of her political work. Together they organized a campaign to change the plans for Durham County General Hospital so that it would better serve public health needs.

"They were building the hospital way out of town," Paul related, "and we wanted it in the center of town. The clinic space was very small. We wanted larger clinic space." Paul led a vigorous campaign around Durham County General Hospital. By the time he returned to medical school from his year's leave, he was a seasoned community organizer. "We spoke in front of every public group that would have us," he said. "We must have spoken to several thousand people directly in the course of a few months. We repeated our set of demands over and over and printed them in a booklet. Many people, black and white, supported us."

Paul put together a flip chart and, with characteristic self-assurance, carried the large display with him onto stages and podiums. His audiences could see that he knew whereof he spoke—and he explained things so that others could easily see the main points. Much to the annoyance of those seeking to line their pockets over the building of a new hospital, the campaign looked at precisely who was going to get what out of the deal and publicized its findings. The newspapers picked up this information. Many of the community demands were ultimately implemented, though not the one about the location of the hospital. "We got more room for the clinic and a much more extensive out-patient program," Paul summed up.

The County Hospital struggle galvanized the left wing of Durham, especially the health care community. Some of the medical students in the MCHR took part in what was, according to Paul's gleeful description, a "subversive network." The students found unorthodox ways to get information about the planned hospital that was not being publicly divulged. Years later, Paul viewed the County Hospital struggle as "a great fight, one of the best fights I was involved in."

In conscious pursuit of clarity, meaning, and direction for their political activism, Paul and Sally formed the Durham Health Collective with other activists. On his return to the Duke campus, Paul and friend Tim McGloin led a campaign against the establishment of Duke Hospital North. "Duke was planning a massive expansion that was slated to cost $92 million plus," he said. "With amortized debt added in, it was a quarter of a billion dollar hospital. Durham already was overbedded, particularly since the Durham County General Hospital had just been built. When we checked into it, we saw that Durham had sixteen times the national average of neurosurgeons per 100,000 population, whereas the city was below average in the number of doctors in family practice, general practice, and the like. The Health Collective showed that the medical needs of the wealthy were being served while those of the poor were being neglected."

Early one morning in 1974, Paul and Sally had breakfast together after distributing some leaflets. Both were having major problems with their partners, and they had a deep heart-to-heart talk. "We both came out of this breakfast saying to ourselves, 'Hmmmm,'" Paul recollected. Soon afterward, clear of all encumbering alliances, the *Mama and Papa of the Durham Health Collective* became an item. Sally and Paul Bermanzohn were central figures in the peoples' movement in Durham in the seventies. All soap operas resemble one another in their fashion, even soap operas of the sublimated leftist variety.

When her ex-husband, Mike, returned from Texas, Sally felt awkward at first at seeing him. But their circle of friends and interests intersected, and they could not avoid running into one another. "Then one day we were at Duke," Sally said. "We began talking to one another, and we became friends again." Meanwhile, Mike got involved with Marty Arthur (later Nathan).

As Sally tells it, "Paul and I got married and we had a baby, Leola. Then Mike and Marty were married and they had a baby, Leah. Of course, I knew Esther, Mike's mother. She used to be my mother-in-law. She came down and was living with Mike and Marty. We didn't live very far away from each other in Durham, and I remember a time when we helped each other paint our houses. We occasionally got together for a big spaghetti dinner at our house—Esther, the two babies, Mike and Marty, Paul and myself. We were becoming very good friends. Things had worked out. Mike and Marty were very happy. I had felt that my marriage with Mike was a casualty of medical school and the women's movement—a lethal combination. I always liked Mike a lot, and it was good to become friends with him again. I was very glad I had found Paul. It all worked out."

FROM THE DURHAM HEALTH
COLLECTIVE TOWARD MARXISM

The Durham Health Collective, drawing activists from the peoples' movements of the late sixties and early seventies, especially the antiwar, civil rights, and women's movements, was the first in a string of groups in that city whose path would ultimately lead to the WVO. Started in 1972 to focus on health-related community issues, the Durham Health Collective became the Durham Organizing Committee after its members began to embrace Marxism. Then, in 1975, it was called the Communist Workers Committee (CWC). A year later, the CWC merged with the WVO, as did the Bolshevik Organizing Collective (BOC) in Greensboro, which was composed of former members of the Revolutionary Workers League (RWL). Thus, the WVO chapter in North Carolina got its principal cadre and organizational character from two major sources: Durham organizers, who had participated in and led a variety of popular social justice movements, and the Greensboro-based Black Liberation Movement.

One night, in the middle of the struggle around the Duke Hospital expansion, Paul, Sally, and fellow activist Lorraine were eating at a local restaurant. They were talking excitedly about how outrageous Duke's plan was and how it was going to be a financial drain on working people. They had already published their information, analysis, and conclusions in the campus paper. Soon their conversation was punctuated with "if people just knew this," and Lorraine was taking notes for a leaflet that would be an exposé and a call to action. They agreed it should be the first in a series of leaflets to inform people, blow-by-blow, about the progress of the opposition. They quickly had it printed and in circulation.

"People picked up the leaflet, read it, and loved it," Paul remembered. "One guy picked it up, read it, and, looking real pleased, started singing, 'tell it like it is, bro, tell it like it is.' After that we started calling the leaflets *Tell It Like It Is*: Number 1, *Tell It Like It Is*: Number 2, and on and on into the high fifties."

The times were changing: 1973 was a pivotal year for the U.S. economy, marking what some economists have described as a u-turn.[4] Weekly wages for American workers and the overall standard of living were adversely affected as corporations and large businesses tried to reduce labor costs in an increasingly competitive global economy. By the decade's end, working people were realizing that all their hard work would not secure the American Dream for their children. The contours of the u-turn—a road leading *away from* prosperity—were becoming ever more visible.

Political changes within activists' circle were also becoming visible. In 1974, Owusu Sadaukai returned to Durham as a Local 77 organizer. AFSCME was trying to bring Duke Hospital's maids and cafeteria workers into the bargaining unit. Much of the energy of members of the Durham Health Collective went into helping the hospital organizing drive: it was ultimately narrowly defeated in 1976. Paul and Sally continued to work closely together, putting out the *Tell It*

Like It Is leaflets at Duke Hospital. In 1975, they got to know César Cauce, one of the leaders in the student movement at Duke. A history major and magna cum laude graduate from Duke University, César was a Cuban immigrant. His father had been a politician in the Batista government before the Cuban Revolution. César wrote articles for *Tell It Like It Is* about the importance of union representation, often including stories of unfair treatment of Duke workers by management. He was one of the leaders of the Duke workers organizing drive. Later he organized community support for striking poultry workers at Durham's Goldkist plant.

By 1975, the Durham Health Collective had become the Durham Organizing Committee and was making its decisive turn toward Marxism and becoming the Communist Workers Committee. Paul, Sally, and then César were part of that evolution. The RWL appeared to be inclining in the direction of the WVO. Owusu, a leader in RWL, had a small study group that included Paul and Sally. "We went very meticulously through some readings by Mao. We acquired the habit of studying things very carefully," Paul said.

LIVING COMMUNALLY IN CHANGING TIMES

Many young people involved in the movement for social change felt inspired to live in a communal way. Among them were some Durham activists important to my story: Lucy Wagner (later Lewis), Sally Ann Munro (later Alvarez), and Tom Clark. All went on to become effective organizers under the auspices of the WVO.

A native of Chapel Hill, Lucy grew up during the civil rights movement. Her mother, Jean Wagner, though overwhelmed with the care of six children, visited jailed civil rights protesters to give them moral encouragement and led her family to boycott segregated places in Durham and Chapel Hill. Jean participated in the Chapel Hill Peace Vigil to stop the Vietnam War. I met Jean in the early seventies when she was an organizer for the Women's International League for Peace and Freedom. Both mother and daughter have always been role models for me.

Lucy entered Duke University in 1969, the year after Sally, Mike, and others sat in at the president's house and massive campus protests occurred. Her first year at Duke was to be her last. It was the time when President Johnson bombed Hanoi, when Haiphong Harbor was mined, and when students at Kent State and Jackson State were killed. In the spring of 1970, Duke students sat down at the traffic circle and tried to bring the campus to a halt. "I participated in that," said Lucy. "I recall how shocked I was when I heard that students at Kent State had been killed. I thought things could not go on in a normal way anymore. How could you be a student when the war kept going on?"[5] She left school to become a full-time political activist, mobilizing against the war and lobbying congressmen.

At the big demonstration in the spring of 1971—the People's Peace Treaty, which was a milestone in my own political commitment—Lucy, one of the organizers of the demonstration, got tear gassed for the second time.

"The police had figured out how to stop everybody even before they got to the bridges and streets," she recollected. "I went with other people to the steps of the capitol to present the peace treaty petition. Ron Dellums and some others came out to receive it. While they were on the steps of the capitol, the police pulled up and arrested everybody. We were taken to an athletic stadium. I was there for four days. They threatened to hold us prisoner for six months if we didn't let ourselves be fingerprinted. We were all women. A lot of people submitted to the fingerprinting and then there were probably a hundred of us left. They opened up a big wing in the stadium. We had a large area to roam around in, but we were obviously behind bars, and they kept the lights on all the time, which made it very disorienting. I met some wonderful, very radical women. We talked about what we were doing with our lives and how we thought we could end the war. It was an important time."

As an itinerant activist, Lucy worked with some Quakers and met students from the University of Pennsylvania who introduced her to a little red book. "We sat around at night in study groups. I was very excited by the idea of looking at the world in a way that pulled all the different pieces together. Prior to that I'd seen U.S. policy in Vietnam as a mistake. I thought people would have to have a lot of education to understand the history of Dien Bien Phu and to see that it wasn't really in the interest of the United States to intervene there, that the United States was making a foreign policy blunder. But after the discussions based on Mao's little red book, I had another way of looking at it. U.S. policy wasn't a blunder or an accident: it served the large corporations."

Her commitment to social justice grew, and Lucy responded to a call to go to Mississippi to work on the Charles Evers campaign. The brother of Medgar Evers, Charles was the first black gubernatorial candidate in Mississippi. "I traveled up and down the coast, between Biloxi, Gulfport, and some other small coast cities, and set up fundraisers," Lucy said. "I did voter registration and ran workshops on how to be poll watchers. We warned people about the tactics they used to intimidate people and keep them from voting. Many people were sensing, for the first time, that they could act as a political force. The Mississippi Freedom Democratic Party had a powerful impact on many people at the time, including me."

The American Friends Service Committee (AFSC) hired her to work on a project called *Indochina Summer*. The job put her in contact with many people, not just Quakers and students, but also typical folks at county fairs. The war in Indochina, she came to see, did not signify that the American people were bad, or somehow responsible. Rather, there was a tremendous amount of ignorance.

"Here I was talking to these farmers, and they were telling me how we had to defeat communism and why it was important to wage the war. These were the people whose kids were getting killed, whose tax dollars were going over there, and it was clear to me that it wasn't because they hated the Vietnamese or wanted to promote imperialism. It was just their false belief that if they didn't do that, somebody was going to come in and take over the United States. I realized then that the potential to organize against the government's policy and to win people over was much broader than I had thought. Responsible activists had to work *with* those people. We didn't need to organize *against* the American people to end the war: *We needed to organize the American people to end the war*."

In 1973, the AFSC in High Point, North Carolina, brought people together from various peace groups in North Carolina to plan an antiwar action at the Military Ocean Terminal at Sunny Point. I was first introduced to Lucy Wagner and Sally Ann Munro at that meeting.

The Military Ocean Terminal at Sunny Point, North Carolina, was the largest munitions shipment port on the east coast. Bombs and other war materiel were sent from there to Southeast Asia, employing a fairly recent technological innovation called containerized shipping. The AFSC in High Point organized a coalition to pay a visit to the ocean terminal: it was known as the MOTSU Project.

On April 16, 1973, I brought my gang of peace activists from Greensboro to Sunny Point for a vigil. Several people had been there since the day before, protesting nonviolently with much praying and singing. They had offered to the authorities an alternative peace shipment of medicine, clothing, and blankets, but their symbolic action was met with unceremonious refusal. Now eight people, having been trained for civil disobedience—they included Lucy and Sally Ann—were prepared to block trucks rolling into the port to prevent them from loading their ordnance onto the ships. It turned out to be an "epiphanal moment" in Sally Ann's political awakening.

"I remember lying down in the road in front of the ammunition truck in Sunny Point," she told me.[6] "And I remember the face of the man, the guard, who came and picked us up off the road and handed us over to be arrested. It occurred to me that the way to make change was not with these symbolic, heroic, moralistic actions that distanced you from people. *It was people like the man who stood guard at the gate at the Sunny Point Ocean Terminal who was going to make change.* If we could convince the guards at the gate, and the man who made the bombs on the line, and the man who drove the truck, and the women who cooked the cafeteria food that fed the people who made the bombs—that was what was going to make change in this country. It wasn't the moralistic praying and singing and chanting sort of stuff that would do it. What that did was put you apart from those people, it made you morally better than them because *you* knew the truth and *they* didn't; they were just ignorant tools.

"I was struck with how elitist much of the peace movement was in disregarding who really makes change. We wouldn't make much difference until we worked with the people who actually produced things and made everything run," she said. "It was so easy for them to haul us out of the road and fine us: we were just little mosquito bites."

Born in Greensboro, North Carolina, and raised in Georgia, Sally Ann was the daughter of a Presbyterian minister with a progressive but unpopular stand on civil rights. He supported, but his church opposed, integration. Congregation members eventually set up segregated Christian schools for their kids. "My father helped the black community start the second Presbyterian Church, which was the Black Presbyterian Church. The Ku Klux Klan threatened to run him out of town. Other people hailed him as a great progressive. Looking back on it," Sally Ann said, "I think many of the supposedly forward looking folks were relieved that they didn't have to integrate the Presbyterian Church."

Sally Ann was a freshman at Duke when she participated in the huge demonstration on campus after King's assassination. She recalled spending several nights on the quad, camped, cramped up, and sleeping under a camellia bush. "We boycotted the cafeteria in support of the striking cafeteria workers, we boycotted classes, and I remember feeling utterly miserable and conflicted. It was the first political activity I was ever in, and I was thinking about commitment. I was coming to the conclusion that if you lived in a society where things were totally messed up, the comforts of privileged people like myself—having a comfortable bed at night and enough to eat—weren't important. To be overly concerned with these comforts was a superficial way to live."

In the spring of 1973, after traveling around for three years and doing civil rights and antiwar organizing, Lucy helped to set up four communal houses in Durham. Inspired by the Movement for a New Society, a Philadelphia-based Quaker group, the members at her house met each week to talk about various issues of the day. In one house, Sally Ann Munro joined Lucy, Chris Lewis, Jim

Wrenn, and three or four others to live collectively and build a community for social change. In these communal houses, social democrats, pacifists, liberals, counterculturalists, and budding Marxists all rubbed elbows.

Jim Wrenn was studying with Progressive Labor (PL), a Marxist-Leninist organization. A housemate who wanted to have a study group, but not with PL, contacted Sally Avery and Paul Bermanzohn. Paul and Sally invited everyone in the house to meet with them to hear about the work of the Durham Health Collective. At the time, the New American Movement (NAM) was a promising formation within the New Left, and the Durham chapter of NAM was basically lodged in the Durham Health Collective.

Soon after the MOTSU project, Sally Ann joined Sally and Paul in the Durham Health Collective. A little later, Lucy also became part of the DHC. They studied Marxism together, and they also organized together, against the Duke hospital expansion project and in support of workers' unionization efforts.

To Duke University in 1969 had come freshman Tom Clark, a beltway hippie and the son of a CIA agent. Tom had grown up with world-class movers and shakers. "My impression of what grown men did when they went to work was that they literally ran the world," he declared.[7] "My dad's job was to read the *Washington Post*, the *New York Times*, and the *Wall Street Journal* cover to cover every day. I think he passed the habit on to me, the habit of keeping up with what is going on all over the world." Coming from that background, there is the little matter of convincing leftists that your allegiance is genuine: Tom turned out to be not only one of us but one of our heroes.

After he graduated, Tom wrote for the *North Carolina Anvil*, an alternative progressive newspaper. Sent to cover a county commissioners' meeting about downtown revitalization, he watched as "Paul Bermanzohn came forward and put a money tree on the commissioner's desk. It was Monopoly money stuck on some twigs. The point was 'you guys want to plant trees downtown so you can grow yourselves some money, not because you really want to do anybody any good.' I thought it was really bold of Paul. I went up to him in the elevator and asked him to tell me more about what they were doing." The next day, over breakfast, "it took Paul and Sally about two seconds to convince me to be in a Marxist-Leninist study group. I'd been reading *Fire in the Lake* by Frances Fitzgerald, an amazing writer. Her father was a CIA guy, too, and was a friend of my father. It was about the war in Vietnam from the point of view of the North Vietnamese people. It described the process of liberating a village. It was to repel or kick out any American presence there and then start study groups to educate people about why this imperialist army was in their little village and was dropping bombs on their rice paddies. I remember putting the book down and thinking that's what liberation means—having an awareness of what's going on, making an assessment of where you are to help you struggle. So when Paul said, 'we have a study group,' I thought, 'that's for me.'"

Music and lively conversation animated the communal house in which Tom lived with five other people. Tom played his guitar, drove a cab in order to earn just enough to pay $27 a month in rent and otherwise get by, and studied Marxism with Sally and Paul. "As the study group progressed and became the Communist Workers Committee, it got more elaborate and more tense," Tom said. "We discussed Marx's dictum that philosophers have *interpreted* the world but the point is to *change* it. That's really true. All my conflicts about my family came out. Here I was, a rich, highly educated college kid. Anybody can have a great time like I'm having now. I've got to get down to some real work."

BEING A DOCTOR IS NOT ENOUGH

By the time Jim Waller arrived in Durham toward the end of 1974, Paul Bermanzohn had graduated from Duke Medical School. Paul was part of Duke's fledgling environmental medicine program. He did research with one of two groups in the country working on byssinosis (or brown lung), an occupational disease caused by inhaling cotton dust, and he published on this topic.

In the early 1970s, another occupational disease, pneumoconiosis (or black lung) was the object of organizing and strikes by coal miners in West Virginia and Kentucky. Labor's strength succeeded in getting into law an improved standard for the permissible level of dust and in setting up a compensation program. The sustained fight for health and safety by miners in the Black Lung Association in the Appalachian coal counties gave impetus to similar organizing efforts around brown lung. Thousands of textile workers in the South suffered from an impairment of lung function caused primarily or partially by working in carding and spinning rooms. In 1971, the North Carolina General Assembly made byssinosis a disease for which disabled textile workers could legally be compensated. But, notwithstanding the passage of a law, labor's organizing muscle was still needed to get owners to clean up the mill, set up clinics in which workers could be tested with impartiality, and compensate disabled workers. The problem was that only a small percentage of textile plants in the South had unions and about 90 percent of southern textile workers were unorganized.

Several groups and organizers were already shaping the brown lung movement when Paul, who was doing his residency in psychiatry at the University of

North Carolina in Chapel Hill, got involved. He met Len Stanley and others from the Southern Institute for Occupational Health, a group funded to do brown lung organizing. He worked with organizer Mike Spaak, who had lost both a father and a grandfather to brown lung; together they set up several brown lung clinics in the Piedmont through South Carolina. While still up north, Jim Waller had heard about the active, progressive forces on the Duke campus. Once at Duke, he joined the brown lung project. He and Paul made plans to screen workers at the clinics.

At the founding meeting of the Carolina Brown Lung Association in Columbia, South Carolina, on April 25, 1975, Jim told workers and others assembled, "I'm a newcomer to the South. I've recently moved to North Carolina from New York where I worked as a children's doctor for the past four years. I have only begun to learn about brown lung since I arrived here. Many of you know more about the disease than I do.

"I do know brown lung is a disease which is preventable by enforcing a low dust standard. It is like the lead poisoning I saw so much of among New York children in that it is not prevented now because of a concern for profit over people's health. . . . I want to join the fight for enforcement of safe standards, for just compensation, and for screening programs not controlled by the companies."

"A sea of coughing gray heads" is how Paul described the 120 retired and disabled textile workers he saw when it was his turn to speak. It was an audience of people with breathing problems. One by one, workers stood up and testified about their lungs, about their sick brothers and fathers.

Jim was overwhelmed by his emotions that day. He saw a sixty-five-year-old man with fifty years in the mill who could not walk across the room without having to stop for loss of wind. He was touched by the older workers imploring their fellow workers to act for the sake of the young people in the mills, not yet beyond help. He and Paul were greatly affected by the words of the president of the Columbia chapter of the new organization, Hub Spires. "I'm here to tell you I'm a victim of bad health and bad circumstances from the mill," Spires said, against a background cacophony of coughing and wheezing. "Out of my life, I worked about thirty-six years in the mill. And I got to where I just couldn't breathe hardly at all. . . . They didn't take any pity on you when you was sick. They expected just as much out of you or more after you got a little age on you and wore out. They put you out to pasture to graze, to fight, and get something to eat the best you can, and I think those companies owes me something for my life and my health that I ruined and run down workin' and makin' them money."

Five days after returning from that meeting, Jim wrote to the head of Occupational Health in the North Carolina Department of Human Resources on behalf of the Medical Committee for Human Rights. I found this letter and other documents from the period while sorting through his papers years after he was killed. He was asking to borrow the department's spirometers, instruments for measuring impaired lung function. "We intend to administer a questionnaire, screen for decreased $FEV_{1.0}$, and counsel the workers over a several day period," he wrote.

The "$FEV_{1.0}$" or the "Forced Expiratory Volume in one second" was the clinical test used to measure the effects of cotton dust on breathing. It measures how much air a person can exhale in one second after having taken in a full breath. Using this test, it had been found that workers in the early stages of brown lung (i.e., occasional Monday morning chest tightness) showed reduced flow rates after exposure to cotton dust for several hours. Those with chronic lung damage showed a constant low $FEV_{1.0}$—their ability to exhale was permanently impaired.

After the screenings, Jim explained the byssinosis test and the results to the workers tested, pointing out the limitations of the procedure. He even included two copies of the test results so that people could keep one and give the other to their family physician. That was so like Jim. How many other professionals would be so concerned and meticulous? Jim realized it would be hard for many workers to get to a copy machine, and he wanted them to be able to use the information from the brown lung testing.

There was much about the South Jim was not yet used to. He strained to decipher the southern dialect. An experience resonated within him—the unbearable steam of the sweat lodge was enveloping his skin, filling his lungs, and Henry Crow Dog was pronouncing with great solemnity *all my relations* and the pipe was being passed to him and *all my relations* was rising with the smoke. The supplicating arms of the tree outside his bedroom at City Island changing its mood and attire with each season. The sea gulls skimming the ocean in Nova Scotia as he and Jean watched with wonder—Jim walked with *all my relations*. *These workers are all my relations.*

It may have been around the brown lung screening project that the story that became part of the legend of the revolutionary doctors began to circulate. "I feel like a doctor who keeps patching up people's broken legs," Jim said. "The doctor is wondering why there are so many broken legs. Then one day he sees a huge hole in the street that people keep falling into. He realizes it makes no sense to be a doctor. He needs to take off his white coat, put on his work clothes, and fill up the hole." That was the kind of thinking that motivated Jim, Paul, and Mike, and that ultimately led Jim into the textile mill. He took off his white coat, put on overalls, and set about filling up the hole.

In 1980, in a pamphlet titled *Being a Doctor Is Not Enough*, the Communist Workers Party paid tribute to its members in the medical profession killed or wounded at the anti–Klan rally the previous year. Mike, Jim, and Paul became revolutionary doctors because they had learned that "a correct diagnosis in itself means nothing to a patient who has to choose between feeding his family and buying his medication."[8] They "came to see that there can never be decent health care in a country controlled by the rich, and in which most hospitals and clinics are part of a massive industry operated solely for profit. . . . These three men were faced with a choice: put a few band-aids on the gaping wounds of America's health care victims, or fight to create a society where the people and their health come first. They chose to fight. This is why Jim, Paul, and Mike began to study Marxism together, and eventually joined in the struggle of the Communist Workers Party. They took the only road that leads to a decent future—to organize for revolution and fight for a socialist America."

On September 27, 1975, after having held screening clinics in several cities, the Carolina Brown Lung Association returned to Columbia, South Carolina. The Southern Institute for Occupational Health and MCHR analyzed and summarized the data obtained from the questionnaires, lung function tests, and examinations. They found that of ninety-seven cotton workers screened, eighty-seven of whom were retired or disabled, thirty-six were found to be totally disabled byssinotics and another thirty-two partially disabled byssinotics. Four totally disabled and thirteen partially disabled people were identified as possible byssinotics. Significantly, the study found thirty-three people with brown lung who never smoked cigarettes and found people with the disease throughout the mills, not just from the preparation areas.

A curious and freelancing local radical, I went to the brown lung screening clinic at the Hope View Presbyterian Church in Greensboro on June 21, 1975. I went because Sandi suggested it. She was working at Cone's Revolution Plant, and Nelson had recently introduced me to her.

The Vietnam War was over and antiwar activists celebrated a moral victory. I recall embracing Chekesha—a student at Bennett College when I taught there. The two of us danced around campus on hearing the news of the U.S. withdrawal. The Vietnam War, a chink in U.S. armor, proved that superior technology, though more deadly, was not necessarily decisive. Historical victories require more than the mere possession of military means. The graphic picture of U.S. military personnel stranded on a Saigon roof and being airlifted out of Southeast Asia in hasty retreat epitomized the shame of U.S. imperialism. Now energies consumed by the divisive Vietnam War could be redirected. The domestic economy could occupy front and center stage: occupational health and safety issues could be spotlighted. And Marxism, the working class, proletarian-ization were in the air breathed by activists. So I went to the Brown Lung Clinic.

I greeted Paul whom I had recently met on the Duke campus. To a question I asked, he responded, "I don't know. Ask Dr. Waller, over there in the suit and black beard." He indicated a dark, tallish, nearly slender figure walking briskly across the room. His gait seemed propelled by a vector of energy streaming from his head through his forward-set torso down to the ground. He walked with au-thority and with a pronounced footfall, as if all the earth were his domain and his concern. When he was pointed out to me, this swarthy-skinned, black-bearded physician, I decided not to approach him with my question after all. Some twenty feet away, too far away to smell, too far away to touch, I mistook his bustling, intense manner for something else, something disagreeable, the self-importance of his profession, the arrogance of doctors. Arrogance was the last thing you could associate with this man, as it turned out.

I was to sight him equally briefly a year later from across a large meeting room and again did not speak to him. Nearly two years passed after that Brown Lung Clinic before I met and spoke to him. Yet I certainly noticed him and retained the image in some remote cells of my brain.

In the spring of 1975, I was in my problem-ridden marriage. I had recently been given walking papers by Bennett College. I was still recovering from the nightmare of the flood and Tonya's pitiable encounter with Chorea. Transcen-dental meditation and tent camping alone at Hagan Stone Park were the pallia-tives of choice for my shattered nerves. The Venceremos Brigade and the study of Marxism occupied many of my waking hours. There was *not* a small voice in me whispering *you will share a little lifespan with the handsome doctor whose bearing now makes you reticent to approach him. You will come to listen for the distinctive signaling of his footfall. You will treasure the imprint of his life on yours beyond anything you can imagine.*

A TIME OF SWEET PROMISE

The Durham Health Collective wanted to form a Marxist-Leninist caucus within the New American Movement. There were discussions about whether social change organizations like NAM should see themselves as preparty forma-tions preparing for the coming of a working-class, that is, Marxist-Leninist, party. It was one of those junctures when people—good people—went their sep-arate ways in disagreement. Harry Boyte, founder of the NAM chapter in Durham, debated Sally, Paul, Lucy, and others in the Health Collective about whether Leninism was democratic. Boyte stopped working with the Health Collective and formed the Peoples Alliance for a Cooperative Commonwealth, which later became the Peoples Alliance in Durham. Critical of NAM's unwillingness to go along with the centrality of class struggle and class analysis on every question, DHC members left NAM. Their keen pursuit of various national organizations in the New Communist Movement with which they might possibly affiliate brought them into contact with the Workers Viewpoint Organization (WVO) and the Revolutionary Union (RU), among other groups.

"We started talking to people in the *Guardian*, and Irwin Silber came down and talked about what he was doing," Lucy told me. "People from the Philadelphia Workers Organizing Collective came down. We sent someone up to Ohio to meet with the October League. One of the issues in the party building discussion was the national question. We were developing a position on black-and-white unity based on seeing class as principal."

The Bermanzohns had followed accounts of the 1974 Which Way Forward conference in *The African World*. By the end of 1975, Durham was a strong center for white revolutionaries while in Greensboro were concentrated prominent black revolutionaries, but there was scant communication between the two groups. The time was ripe for an unprecedented merger. "WVO was appealing to us because it was multinational and multiracial," Sally recalled.

As the Health Collective members—by now calling themselves the Communist Workers Committee—were gaining respect for the WVO, they continued having their own study groups. They also began sending some of their members, including Sally Ann, to get jobs in the textile mills in Greensboro where several RWL members were already working. "We wanted to continue organizing at Duke," Sally Ann said, "but we also really wanted to get into textiles. That was a more central place to be in terms of statewide organizing and organizing in the South. We set up a formal liaison between our collective and the RWL to study certain issues and questions."

I attended many study sessions in Greensboro with some people from the Durham group and local RWL members. We discussed the hot topics of the day: *Is party building our main task? What is the relationship of building the party to building the mass movement?* Everyone acknowledged the need to both build a working-class party and engage in mass organizing, but much about priorities, relationships, and strategies remained over which to argue.

My most vivid recollection of the study group actually had to do with the issue of women's liberation. This was during the period when the RWL was conferencing with the WVO and a merger between the two groups appeared likely. At one of the study meetings, Joyce Johnson, in a very soft-spoken but firm manner, criticized her husband's political line. Here was a woman criticizing her husband *in public* for his political view, arguing confidently and with authority. Furthermore, she was demanding that he deal with the matter in a self-criticism. She was behaving like his equal on the turf they shared—politics. I was flabbergasted that she could raise politics above their marriage, above personalities, as if she were just another comrade to whom Nelson was accountable. Only a *liberated woman* could do this. And only a *liberated man* would accept it and not walk away in disgust, nursing a damaged ego. Joyce served as a tremendous role model for me that day—I already had a deep and abiding admiration for Nelson. A woman's real independence, I thought, has nothing to do with practicing free love but resides in her independence of mind, in her ability to think for herself and state her positions without regard to pleasing or keeping the love interest in her life. At the time, that was a revelation to me.

At one point in this intense period of political learning and growing, Joyce went to the hospital for some minor surgery, and I visited her there. On the stand by her bed, among flowers and cards, was a copy of the latest *Workers Viewpoint Journal*. Though feeling weak, Joyce had talked to some of the hospital staff who were curious. (Our zeal was such that there was hardly an occasion that was off-limits for politics.) After I was in the room a few moments, Nelson arrived. He had not seen his wife since she had had surgery. She got up from the bed in her robe, walked toward him, and husband and wife, unselfconsciously, locked in a warm embrace. I suddenly felt I should not be in the room and stood there awkwardly trying not to be there. It was a highly romantic moment and one that lingered in my imagination.

The WVO wanted to bring under its banner all Marxist-Leninists circles that could be united. WVO had sought out the groups it saw as part of the "revolutionary wing" of the New Communist Movement, such as the Revolutionary Workers League. The "revolutionary wing" was defined by its bedrock agreement that the principal task was to build a revolutionary political party, one founded solidly on the theory of Marxism-Leninism Mao tse-Tung Thought.

A critical juncture was reached on May 30, 1976. There were political differences between the WVO and the RWL, and Jerry Tung, Phil Thompson, and other WVO leaders came to Durham to struggle over them. In a large lecture hall on the Duke campus, a decisive meeting occurred of Marxist activists and revolutionaries, primarily from Greensboro and Durham, with the WVO leadership. It started the evening of May 30 and didn't end until the wee hours of May 31. You can almost assemble the China Grove and November Third rallies of 1979 from the people who went to that meeting. Jim Waller and César Cauce were present. The Bolshevik Organizing Collective was represented by Nelson, Joyce, and others. Paul, Sally, and other members of the Communist Workers Committee were there.

My impressions have dimmed with time, but I recollect some details of the evening. I went to the meeting in one of several carloads from Greensboro. A few textile workers, friends of Nelson or other political activists, were present, and I sat near them. I was surprised by the number of people in the room when we arrived—perhaps a couple hundred. WVO people were stationed at the door. They were friendly but serious, as they frisked people going in. That made a good impression on me. It indicated they were taking responsibility for the security of the crowd. During an intermission everyone stood up to stretch. From across the aisle, a vaguely familiar man with a black beard darted into the periphery of my vision.

The discussion was very theoretical and many terms were unfamiliar to me so that when I thought I understood something, it often reeluded me with the next sentence. For example, talk about "building the communist party on an ideological plane" entered and exited my ear tubes, but not too much processing went on in between. I remember that the phrase "advanced workers" was repeated many times that evening. It sticks in my mind because I was puzzled about what the criteria were for an advanced worker. Were the workers we had brought with us advanced workers? How would I know an advanced worker from an ordinary worker? It had to do with fighting for the working class and being open to Marxism—that much I gathered. But I was still left with the feeling that here was a precise technical term, and I was missing a crucial nuance somewhere. The whole evening went like that. All the same, I was powerfully impressed and inspired that evening. Something *did* come through the elevated Marxist discourse, and that something reached the workers there too. Jerry Tung's thick accent was a further hindrance to comprehension, but, despite it, most of the audience responded appreciatively to the Chinese-born WVO leader.

The format of the meeting was a knock-down, drag-out polemic between the WVO and the RWL. It had the flavor of a horserace or a boxing match. Before the meeting, Owusu was the heavy favorite in that he was so widely known and admired in our region. His oratory power and skill in articulating political positions were universally acknowledged. Owusu spoke easily in an appealing vernacular, and simultaneously, he made good use of his higher education. Well over six feet tall and strikingly handsome, he captured your attention visually as well as with his eloquence. "On the surface, the group from the WVO was less impressive," the Bermanzohns wrote four years later. But, they added, "when Jerry spoke, he gripped the audience like a vise. . . . Getting to the essence of how to build a revolutionary party in the U.S., he described how it must be built in the course of mass struggle, through uniting all the genuine communists and winning the advanced workers."[9]

The polemic raged over RWL's claim that party building was the central *and only* task. Jerry argued that that slogan would hold back building a party because of the critical role played by the relationship of mass organizing to party building. Frankly the polemics are fuzzy to me now; the histrionics were more memorable. Jerry challenged Owusu to defend RWL's "raggedy line." The Bermanzohns wrote: "Sitting in the audience, Owusu looked glum. His charisma crumbling before our eyes, he hesitantly came to the front and read a long statement defending RWL. Then one of RWL's top leaders tried to more vigorously defend RWL. Dressed in a dark leather jacket, dark glasses, and slinky pants, she was all style, no content. Yelling 'Check it out!' she read from RWL's journal, something nearly everyone in the audience had already studied."[10]

So it was. Short, squat, muscular, Socratic-faced Jerry Tung bested the estimable, imposing Owusu, who, that particular evening, projected an uncharacteristic indifference. "In the polemics," Lucy remembered, "I'm waiting for Owusu to blow away Jerry Tung—and he didn't."

Although, at the end of 1975, the RWL had voted to merge with the WVO, the merger never happened. (My application for membership in the RWL was swallowed up in the downward trajectory of that organization.) In a bitter and sometimes violent atmosphere, the RWL disintegrated and members who were WVO sympathizers were driven out. Among those who left the RWL was Mark Smith. He and Sandra Neeley Smith had been married only a short time. It was a painful, confusing, and demoralizing time for Sandi, who tried to remain in the RWL but soon left. She and Mark temporarily withdrew from the movement and from Nelson's and Joyce's lives. Eventually, Sandi rejoined Nelson and Joyce in political organizing, but her marriage to Mark fell apart within a couple of years. Nelson and Joyce broke away from the RWL and formed the Bolshevik Organizing Collective (BOC). Some former RWL members, among them Chekesha, became part of BOC, which looked hopefully to the WVO and earnestly studied WVO journals.

After the forum, the Greensboro and Durham groups decided to merge with the understanding that the new, enlarged circle would apply to join the WVO. Membership in the WVO entailed a process of reaching agreement over major political positions. "The CWC/BOC entered into formal discussion with WVO about where our differences were," Lucy summarized. "Basically, to join the

WVO you had to denounce all your incorrect lines and work through everything to get to the correct line. And we did that. We honestly changed some positions on things or sharpened up positions. But the merger process was not a collaboration. It was very clear that the WVO felt it had the correct line. So, looking back on it, there were some problems. At the time, it was exhilarating to feel that we were finally on the right track and part of a larger national movement."

Association with the WVO provided a training ground in political, organizational, and leadership skills. For Sally Bermanzohn, it was a very exciting period. "I really felt very good about Workers Viewpoint," she said years later. "We consciously and carefully built a multiracial group and carried out some really good community work. I felt we did better organizing once we were communicating with WV."

"I think it was an exciting and principled period," Nelson reflected years later. "We were moving in a principled way to act on our best understanding of how to be a force for good in our society. I think we were able to use the tools of Marxism." Nelson felt grateful to Jerry Tung for "his capacity to grant insights into matters that were otherwise cloudy to me, and for systematic training that remains useful today in understanding large international questions as well as small, concrete, day-to-day questions, lessons like pulling toward a point, the theory that things happen in a tack-right, tack-left fashion and not in a straight line, being focused and paying attention to details.

"It also was the first time," Nelson acknowledged to me, "that I've had deep and principled relations with people who were not of my race. Up to that point, I had not built any relationships that would gradually cause me to see the particularities of the person more than what their race happens to be. Meeting you, Signe, and Paul, struggling over the national question, the black belt South, colonial theories—this entire period of learning was invaluable. I think the notion of drawing together committed people whose commitment can be nurtured to an even deeper level, and people who are willing to learn the structure and operation of their society and to learn how we can work together to bring about change, is one I would not exchange for anything."

I was so inspired by the WVO that the day after the Durham forum I sent a letter to Jerry Tung thanking him for coming to North Carolina. I had found what I wanted—an organization that had an all-encompassing view of the world, an analytical and critical intellectuality, committed and morally principled people, a program, a plan of action, a strategy, and a warm heart to boot. The autumn of 1976 was indeed a time of sweet promise: an era of great organizing lay ahead. Our struggle was multiracial and beautiful. Furnished with the philosophy of historical and dialectical materialism, we were hope for the world. Because we loved our fellow human beings and hated injustice, we were ready to resist. To better resist, we taught each other how to organize and fight.

More radicals and activists, joining their friends in the movement or looking for a center of political activity, moved to North Carolina. They settled in Greensboro or Durham and became active WVO supporters. We set up and ran our study groups with guidance from the WVO. One such study group early on had a formidable group of black and white women. Joyce, Willena, Sally Ann, Dale, Roz, Chekesha, Dori, and Rosella Jarrell from GAPP and I met regularly, some of us with kids in tow. In the beginning, Abiola was part of it too, but he soon dropped out. It must have been unbalancing to be the only male in a sea of female political dynamos.

***

The marriage between the CWC and the BOC was performed by the WVO in whose house the newlyweds came to reside. Within a few short months of the forum and of the BOC/CWC merger, the following events occurred:

Paul Bermanzohn and Sally Avery got married.

Jim Waller, his long agony resolved, left Duke Hospital and went to work at Cone Mills Corduroy Finishing Plant in Haw River.

Nelson and Joyce Johnson brought Sandi Smith back into their lives and their political circle.

I got a job as a mill worker at Cone Mills Revolution Plant in Greensboro.

The BOC/CWC circle liquidated its organizational self in favor of joining and building up the WVO. The WVO, consequently, established a chapter in North Carolina with former BOC/CWC members in its ranks.

Three years of revolutionary activism under the auspices of the WVO followed. We lowered a heavy mantle of responsibility onto our shoulders and became soldiers in the army, marching in stride with liberation struggles around the world. It was the youth of conviction, the flowering of commitment, and the age of comradeship.

NOTES

1. Unless otherwise indicated, quotations by Paul Bermanzohn are from a taped interview with him on June 27, 1990.

2. Unless otherwise indicated, quotations by Sally Bermanzohn are from a taped interview with her on June 27, 1990.

3. See Erik Ludwig, "Closing In on the 'Plantation': Coalition Building and the Role of Black Women's Grievances in Duke University Labor Disputes, 1965–1969," in *Feminist Studies* (Spring 1999) for the labor history of Local 77.

4. For a more detailed discussion of this economic trend, see Barry Bluestone and Bennett Harrison, *The Great U-Turn: Corporate Restructuring and the Polarizing of America* (New York: Basic Books, 1998).

5. Unless otherwise indicated, quotations by Lucy Lewis are from a taped interview with her on June 29, 1990.

6. Unless otherwise indicated, quotations by Sally Ann Alvarez are from a taped interview with her on July 1, 1992.

7. Unless otherwise indicated, quotations by Tom Clark are from a taped interview with him on June 29, 1990.

8. Communist Workers Party, *Medicine and Revolution: Being a Doctor Is Not Enough* (1980), 22.

9. Paul C. Bermanzohn, M.D., and Sally A. Bermanzohn, *The True Story of the Greensboro Massacre* (New York: César Cauce Publishers and Distributors, 1980), 118.

10. Bermanzohn, *The True Story of the Greensboro Massacre*, 119.

II

HOME-GROWN
BOLSHEVIKS

5

ORGANIZE! MAKE A MIGHTY RIVER

NEWCOMERS TO TOWN

The job at Revolution was called "spare help." It was the first blue collar job I ever had and was a real education. I enjoyed being among other workers and looked forward to our chats at break time. Compared to most conversations I'd had with academic types, I thought these more down to earth and interesting. There was dark humor, for example, in talk about how to decide which bill to pay this month—telephone or gas—and the likely consequences of not paying one or the other. Most of the textile workers did not have enough money to meet all their basic expenses in any given month. So sensitive were they to the value of a few pennies that someone borrowing your newspaper at break time offered to pay you for it.

I had spent virtually my whole life being a student or a teacher. The physical demands of the factory job and the noise in the mill were a big adjustment, though I tried to pretend that wasn't so. I spent my day bouncing between hypersensitivity and mesmerization. I primed all my senses to avoid dangers while moving about the plant, and then allowed myself to lapse into a dream state while performing some simple repetitive motions. When Friday evening came, I tore out of the prison-like factory and thought seriously about going to a bar, drinking, and flirting. Going to a bar and drinking would have been completely out of character, but it was a nice fantasy. I usually went home and read the Workers Viewpoint newspaper. On the short ride home there was a hill, a bump, and railroad tracks. As I approached this shocks-challenging stretch, I would speed up as much as I could so that my head hit the ceiling of the car and my bottom bounced back harshly against the seat. I looked forward to this reckless moment of release every day, but especially Fridays. After several months at the mill, some comrades suggested that I seemed out of place and perhaps should look for another job. This hurt me as it seemed to imply I was a failure at becoming proletarianized. I gave notice at the textile plant around February 1977 and was hired at Cone Hospital as an EKG monitor and desk clerk. I worked there almost two years, then had a few more blue collar jobs. I was working in a textile mill outside of Greensboro in 1979 while helping to plan the anti-Klan rally.

Between the time Workers Viewpoint carved out a district in North Carolina in the fall of 1976 until the Greensboro Massacre three years later, Jim Waller and I met, fell in love, got married, and were separated by his death. Until the sudden and violent assault of November Third, our organizing was done mostly away from the greedy lenses of TV cameras. We worked behind the scenes, organizing our forces steadfastly and intensely in opposition to capitalism.

My main political work was with the African Liberation Support Committee. At some point, however, I worked in every local struggle we engaged. I did a lot of the leaflet production, some writing, some organizing, some picketing, and endless support work for whatever the party took on—for the WVO was building itself up to become a full-fledged political party. We focused on the textile industry as a key strategic area for moving forward the whole working-class struggle.

In the summer and fall of 1976, several new people arrived in town. The Cypress Street house was part of their initial itinerary. Allen Blitz from New York City, immediately recognizable to me as a *landsmann* (i.e., a compatriot from the old country), came with his friend Dori Dietz (later Blitz). She was a strong pioneer sort of woman from the Midwest, with roots in Quakerism and family connections to the Daughters of the American Revolution. "What brought you here?" I asked Allen as he opened the back screen door to enter the kitchen. He had been Paul Bermanzohn's friend since their days at City College in New York, and he heard that exciting things were happening in North Carolina. He and Dori meant to settle in the country near Greensboro. They were prepared to hunker down and get some social change going with the Workers Viewpoint.

Through some other newcomers to town I met Dale Deering (later Sampson), a warm and unreservedly gregarious person. She had more close friends all over the country with whom she regularly corresponded than anyone I'd ever met. With her straight, sandy-blond hair and fair, freckled complexion, she looked like the all-American girl you jumped rope with—*"D" my name is Dale Deering and I come from Dover, Delaware.* She was the girl you saw cheerleading the home teams through victory in high school and college. Her typically radiant and shining face lit up even more when she talked about her honey, Bill Sampson, who was to join her soon.

"The second evening Bill and I were together," Dale said, "we were sitting by a fire, drinking wine, and he told me that he considered himself a communist. I was amazed. I had an image of communists as sinister men wearing gray trench coats."[1]

He told her because he wanted her to know who he was and how he looked at the world. At the time he met Dale, Bill was in the October League (OL), one of the organizations in the New Communist Movement. He had joined while in Boston as a Harvard Divinity School student. Radicalized in the antiwar movement, he once thought he could best serve the people's movement as a revolutionary minister. But he faulted the church for not taking a stronger stand for poor people and against the Vietnam War. After getting a master's degree in divinity at Harvard, he switched professions. When Dale met him, he was in his second year of medical school in Charlottesville, Virginia.

In its theoretical journal of the mid-seventies, Workers Viewpoint led a charge against revisionism in Marxism. William Evan Sampson, a serious student of Marxism, read *Workers Viewpoint Journal* articles that critiqued the October League. He also had occasion to hear Jerry Tung and to talk through some political questions with another WVO leader, Phil Thompson. When Bill broke with OL, he wrote a detailed letter to his friends in that organization. Bill believed that by failing to consistently link immediate struggles to the overthrow of capitalism, OL was not providing communist leadership to the mass struggle. He thought American workers would be open to communism and that we should be bold and forthright with out politics and not hide our views.

Dale moved to Greensboro in the summer of 1976, after getting a master's degree in social work from the University of West Virginia. She was following several good friends who, like Bill, had declared they were communists. In fact, her friends and Bill had become acquainted with Sally Bermanzohn when the Communist Workers Committee (CWC), in search of a national organization they could agree with, went to an OL meeting in Ohio. Bill dropped out of medical school shortly before he was to graduate and earn the title of medical doctor. He moved to Greensboro to join Dale and the group of Workers Viewpoint supporters.

"What I really liked about Workers Viewpoint," Dale later said, "was that even though most people in the country were not doing that kind of work anymore—the big movements for social change had dissipated—the people I met in North Carolina were really practicing what they believed. Even though I didn't call myself a communist and Bill did," she said, "how we looked at the world and what we thought had to be done were really the same. I had found a man who was warm and intelligent and who wanted to spend his life trying to right wrongs. That was more magical than everything else." Bill and Dale got married in the backyard of my Cypress Street house in August 1977.

I still vividly recollect the first time I met Dale. We were driving from Greensboro to Roanoke Rapids in September 1976. Along the way we picked up Lucy in Durham. Dale didn't stop asking questions the entire trip. She wanted to know who was doing what with whom, where they came from, how and why this or that was happening with the WV crowd. She was assembling a picture of this new situation she had landed in. Dale reminded me of Miranda in Shakespeare's *The Tempest*—"O, brave new world that has such people in it" was written all over her face. She was so natural and without pretension that it was impossible not to love her.

As we chatted away on the road to Roanoke Rapids, Dale spoke of being a community organizer in Appalachia. She worked with people who were scorned by some as *hillbillies*. "We trained very poor people how to get welfare and food stamps," she told me. "Not just get the things they needed, but to demand that they be treated with respect, like human beings." She helped mountain communities organize against strip mining by coal companies that were poisoning the local water system. She had also been part of the Vista program and worked with inner-city black women in federal prison in Washington, D.C. Disparities of wealth, power, and opportunity are not inevitable, she had concluded: "There is no reason for somebody to eat collard greens every night if somebody else is having steak every night." Dale was searching, as were the rest of us, for ways to act effectively to change blatant injustices. Then why, I thought at the time, had she taken a social worker job in Winston-Salem? Why work within this rotten system? Why would she want to fight using only weapons handed to her by the enemy?

When she mentioned to Lucy and me that she had been a cheerleader in college, we teased her about it. The ex-cheerleader was now part of an activity organized by two communist circles in the process of merging into the WVO. She had in her hand flyers that stated baldly and abstractly: "The CWC/BOC is a communist organization in North Carolina that is part of a nationwide antirevisionist communist movement. This movement is working to build a genuine revolutionary Communist Party that will be able to provide leadership to the working class and the masses in the day to day struggle against capitalist oppression and exploitation and toward the final aim of smashing capitalist rule, establishing the dictatorship of the working class, and building socialism in the U.S."

CAST AWAY ILLUSIONS

We were heading to a J. P. Stevens rally. Workers in the textile plant had won the right to a union two years before, but they did not yet have a contract. The company had been stalling, spreading lies and rumors in the plant to divide the workers. Now the organizing victory was in jeopardy. A huge percentage of workers' electoral victories for union representation never are consummated into negotiated contracts. Companies are adept at union busting. When they fail before the issue is put to a vote, they are not without recourse to prevent the signing of a contract with the union anyway—especially if the union lacks the will to fight through to the end. This particular union victory became, in the late seventies, the subject of the Hollywood film *Norma Rae*. In real life, Norma Rae was Crystal Lee, and our paths were to cross. Though the moment of triumph celebrated in a film may linger in the viewer's mind after the final cut, in real life, triumphs can dissipate or unravel.

The CWC/BOC flyer we brought to Roanoke Rapids was addressed to J. P. Stevens' workers. It had a banner headline reading *Cast Away Illusions! Prepare to Struggle!* The target of its polemics was the Textile Workers Union of America (TWUA). Looking back on our tactics, particularly early on, some were unproductive or even damaging to the workers' cause. At Roanoke Rapids, we were like a bull out of the gate. Though lacking experience with trade unions at that point, we were, in effect, saying to established union organizers, "Hey, we've read the book by Marx, and you guys are doing this all wrong!"

TWUA leaders were promoting a big boycott of J. P. Stevens' products. Our view was that they were not, and should have been, relying primarily on the workers themselves to be organized into strong, fighting unions in all Stevens' plants. "If they can't even organize the 44,000 Stevens' workers, how do they expect to organize 200 million consumers to boycott products you can't even recognize because of the different labels they are sold under?" the flyer admonished the union leadership. We said that the capitalists used officials in the organized labor movement to keep the lid on the only threat to capitalist rule—the anger and militant spirit of an organized working class. Those union officials who played along to keep their high-salaried jobs were not giving leadership to workers. We called them trade union misleaders and referred to them disparagingly with the acronym TUMS. Misleaders in the trade unions, we said, promoted illusions among workers about the National Labor Relations Board (NLRB) and the courts—institutions really designed to perpetuate capitalist rule.

The flyer predicted that "the boycott as the primary strategy will cause the drive to fail" and that to have some positive effect it would have to be based on the strength of the workers' organization. Liberal politicians Andrew Young and John Brooks, invited by the union as featured speakers that day, came in for denunciation along with union leaders as sell-out lackeys of the capitalists. Brooks, the state's labor commissioner, had said that wages in North Carolina were the lowest in the nation *due to neglect*. Instead of appreciating that a government official was publicly, at a workers' rally, highlighting the fact that North Carolina workers had the lowest wages in the country, the commissioner was totally written off. The CWC/BOC flyer countered that it was not *neglect* but the ruthless efforts of the capitalists to smash workers' struggles that kept the state's workers earning poverty wages. As for the boycott, we were not part of the discussion among trade union leaders that arrived at that tactic. We had not walked in the shoes of trade union officials, and yet we dismissed them in a doctrinaire fashion. The point is not whether there was a small, or even a large, grain of truth in our analysis, but whether, with our tactics, we drove a wedge between ourselves and many others who may have had honest differences of opinion, or with whom we needed to talk things out. The question is whether we were building the greatest unity for the workers' cause, as we intended.

At any rate, I did not have such reflections as the above in 1976. As I said, we had read the book by Marx—and we were positively messianic. In the course of the speeches that day there was heckling, and the atmosphere in the hall was charged. Nelson was rudely ushered outside for passing out our flyer. Alarmed, I followed the fracas out to the street. Nelson was surrounded by several policemen. I stood nearby monitoring the situation and trying to make clear by my glances and body language that I would take note of any mistreatment of Nelson. It was the first of several occasions through the years when I felt Nelson was in danger and instinctively moved to protect him.

IN WILLENA'S KITCHEN

From Willena's kitchen came smells of a ham hock cooking on a greasy stove and stale coffee. I sat on a chair that teetered on two good legs and two fractured ones. There wasn't a single good chair in the room. Frequent meetings had left them with splintered surfaces and unwoven cane seats. Every ten to fifteen minutes, one of several children tearing around the house was tugging at his mother, complaining and wanting attention. Willena, from a sharecropper family in South Carolina, was one of several African American women in a group that included Joyce, Rosella, Chekesha, and Roz. The nonblack sister revolutionaries were Dale, Dori, Sally Ann, and me. We all had the latest issue of the *Workers*

Viewpoint and were preparing to celebrate International Working Women's Day on March 8, 1977.

We had studied *Socialism: Utopian and Scientific* at previous meetings, and now we were making our way through *The Origin of the Family, Private Property and the State* by Frederick Engels. We were learning about the origin of monogamy, that "first form of the family based not on natural but on economic conditions, namely, on the victory of private property over original, naturally developed, common ownership. The rule of the man in the family, the procreation of children who could only be his, destined to be the heirs of his wealth—these alone were frankly avowed by the Greeks as the exclusive aims of monogamy. . . . The first class antagonism which appears in history coincides with the development of the antagonism between man and woman in monogamian marriage, and the first class oppression with that of the female sex by the male."[2]

Fundamentally, women's liberation meant our right to be treated as equal to men and not suffer oppression on account of gender. Women's oppression denied women full human stature and made participation in public life difficult. We viewed our struggle as a component part of a proletarian revolution that would liberate all humankind. We talked about women *smashing the double yoke of capitalism and domestic slavery*. Under capitalism, women are a reserve labor force and a source of cheap labor, and thus they are used to depress the wages of workers overall. In our study group, we discussed how the women workers at Farah had won the right to unionize after a twenty-two-month militant strike, thus benefiting all workers. The struggle of women workers for childcare and equal pay for equal work was a rightful concern of the whole working class.

We spoke often about "remolding ourselves"—both women and men set this as a task—in order to become better fighters for the working class. To this end, we engaged one another with criticism and encouragement. I remember much discussion in the women's group about Dale's job as a social worker. Wasn't she fostering illusions that the system could be patched up with reforms? Not quite convinced, Dale nevertheless quit social work and got a job at Cone Mills Print Works plant. I think I was a little more into remolding myself than Dale. I really wanted to adopt the working-class stand, method, and outlook: I was ready to do battle with my "petty-bourgeois" demons.

I had written an elaborate self-criticism, which I titled "on bourgeois love," in an effort to deal with what was holding me back, keeping me from becoming the class fighter I could be. At the time, I was in a relationship that was dragging me down. It felt like the worst personal crisis of my life. In the terms of the time, I could be viewed as, and viewed myself as, a "sexual opportunist" and "petty-bourgeois individualist." I had shown the self-criticism to a couple of comrades, and when asked if it could be shown to a few others, I assented. The account of my inner struggle to become a true member of the proletariat might be helpful to others, I thought. Putting the words on paper had been therapeutic. I was all alone on New Year's Eve 1976, drowning in tears and anxieties, when I wrote it. A few weeks into the new year, during a coffee and donut break in our study meeting, Sally Ann asked me if I had heard anything from a doctor in Durham, a WVO supporter. When I said I hadn't, she replied, "Well, we gave him your self-criticism to read."

Someone in Durham who read my class analysis of love immediately thought that Dr. Waller should read it too. After all, a woman who referred to herself as a "romantic alcoholic" needed to meet a man who called himself a "romantic junkie." When Dr. Waller finished reading the manuscript, he was eager to meet the person who wrote it. "Are you willing to meet him?" I was asked. I agreed but did not give the matter much thought. A campaign to unionize Cone's Revolution Plant was about to be openly and publicly proclaimed. Workers, under WV leadership, had been meeting in secret for several months. Someone suggested that I leaflet Revolution with Jim Waller. Since I had worked at that mill, I could show him where it was.

***

The day hung between chilly traces of winter and springtime's restoring warmth when a tall, black-bearded man rang my doorbell. It did not come into my mind then that I had first seen him nearly two years earlier, but I must have felt that his being there made certain demands on me that I was not prepared to meet. I took him in with my eyes. *He was strong and attractive, but thank heavens he was not my type*, I thought. *He was not my type at all*, I insisted to myself. This inner acknowledgment brought a feeling of relief. I hated all men just then and did not want to be attracted to anyone. I was determined to break free and remain free of all enslaving romantic entanglements. I pulled the stack of flyers from my desk, and we were off.

MAY DAY

Early in 1977, WVO founded the Revolutionary Youth League (RYL) for young workers and college and high school students. WVO was gearing up for two big mobilizations in May. Having become the leading force within the African Liberation Support Committee, the organization was preparing for African Liberation Day. A massive May Day demonstration was also in the works.

On May Day 1977, marchers gathered at Rutgers and East Broadway and at Chatham Square in Chinatown, New York, and proceeded to Tompkins Square Park for a rally with speeches, skits, songs, and poetry. I learned that May Day, a working-class holiday, originated in the United States, not in Russia. This holiday is decidedly different in character from Labor Day in September, which is celebrated generally with harmless, apolitical diversions, like a family picnic. On the first May Day, the 1886 General Strike, 350,000 workers marched through the streets of Chicago and elsewhere in the country for trade unions and the eight-hour day. Inspired by the militancy of the American workers, the Paris Congress (called later the Second International) on the centennial of Bastille Day (July 14, 1889) officially adopted May Day as the International Workers Day.

Before the May Day parade, we talked about the militant mass demonstrations and strikes of the working class, about working-class martyrs, and about the impact of communism on workers in the thirties. The history we discussed was not one we were taught in school. Ordinary people and workers like ourselves cared about justice, fought and sacrificed for it. We were carrying on a legitimate tradition.

May Day 1977 was one of several large WVO demonstrations I attended. Jim Waller boarded the bus with us in Greensboro early in the morning, after working in Haw River at the mill all night. He had volunteered to do childcare. When he tried to catch some sleep on the bus, the casual, crumpled drapery of his body across the seats and aisle amused me and warmed me to him. He marched alongside me that day. We chanted ourselves hoarse.

The march was vintage WVO, extremely tight, brisk, well organized, and disciplined. There were banners in Spanish, English, and Chinese. Thousands of us marched through working-class neighborhoods where curious people peered out of windows, waved, and saluted us with raised fists. A truck equipped with a sound system carried a crew to lead the militant chants while additional marshals with bullhorns ran beside the marchers and kept people chanting. "Workers Viewpoint is the Party! The Party is WV!" we exclaimed triumphantly. "The workers united will never be defeated!" Our steps fell in with the beat of the chant. Young people on bicycles rode around surveying and reporting anything unusual or problematic to designated leadership. What I experienced that day was repeated in all the WV rallies and marches I participated in: the longer I marched and the louder I chanted, the more energized I became. A smooth, steady flow of adrenaline that kept the marchers' fatigue at bay seemed to be part of the overall chemistry of the organizing. Others also experienced this and commented on it.

When we assembled indoors for a meal later, WV cadre were polite and efficient. They seemed to shine. At the rally after the speeches, in order to keep the crowd together and the march orderly, instructions about what to do next and where to go were sung out to the crowd as part of the spirited entertainment. In that way, we got the park cleaned up, filed out without trampling each other, were able to visibly demonstrate our solidarity and sense of purpose, and, very importantly, improved the circumstances relating to the security of the march. My enthusiasm for the WVO and for the dedicated and caring people I met in New York—white, black, Puerto Rican, Chinese, Japanese, Gentile, Jewish—was unbounded after that May Day.

Based in New York and also strong in California, Workers Viewpoint was expanding and setting up chapters in the Midwest and throughout the country. Like a wave gathering the waters and gaining momentum as it rolls to shore, WV was drawing into its ranks small circles of class-conscious workers and revolutionary political activists like those it had won over in Greensboro and Durham. The crest of the wave would come in the fall of 1979 with the convening of the Founding Party Congress. The congress represented the organization's assessment that the WVO had attained the level of political maturity it needed to assume its role among other genuine communist parties in the international scene—parties that were then either vying for state power or attempting to exercise in a responsible way power already achieved. It was at this crest in the organizing fortunes of the Workers Viewpoint Organization/Communist Workers Party that the Greensboro Massacre occurred.

THE REVOLUTION ORGANIZING COMMITTEE

Cosmos I was a black-owned nightclub and restaurant near downtown Greensboro. Along with nearly two hundred other people, I went to kick off the union drive at Revolution one Sunday afternoon. A sense of excitement pervaded the large room as we filed in and took our seats. Most of the people were workers from Revolution, but representatives and supporters from two of Cone's unionized plants, notably White Oak and Granite Finishing, also came to express solidarity with the union drive.

Sandra Smith, chairperson of the Revolution Organizing Committee (ROC), greeted those gathered. "Management had a meeting Friday," she announced. "I'm sure it was about how to stop this union drive." Everyone was listening keenly, nodding assent. Yes, Cone wants to stop this, no doubt about it. "Well, I got news for you fellows," she continued. "You ain't gonna stop this union drive."

The house exploded with applause. Other speakers shared anecdotes about conditions in the mill. The audience heard about the history of struggle at Revolution. Mark Smith, an articulate speaker, represented the Workers Viewpoint. With communist leadership in the present union drive, he emphasized, the ROC would lead the way to a fighting rank-and-file union at Revolution. Having been intellectually prepared, I connected to Mark's speech. However, I imagine it may have been too academic and doctrinaire for many of the workers. A lot was going on that day, and the more down-to-earth speaking style of Sandi and others set the predominant tone.

A worker testified that he had seen other union drives at the plant, but this was the most determined and strongly supported. Applause. Another worker, an elderly white man who had been in the plant since the early thirties and had opposed previous union drives, declared that now his goal was to do all he could to get a union before his retirement. More applause. The issue of communist involvement in the union drive was put out for discussion by a young white worker. "Unions are for workers of all political beliefs," Sandi said. "And I tell you, to fight Cone Mills, we *need* bold communist leadership."

The worker responded, "I was brought up to hate communists. But if this is what communism is about, I'm for it."[3] Loud cheers. Then someone else raised a concern about how having communists on the organizing committee would hurt the union drive. His remarks sparked a lively debate about what kind of union we wanted anyway—a love-our-bosses union or a real union that fights hard in the workers' interest. One worker said he was not willing to sacrifice or put his job on the line for just a love-our-bosses type of union.

The worker who raised the concern about having communists on the organizing committee assured the audience that he was *for* the union. But, maybe, just maybe, we wouldn't be having all these problems getting support from union officials if there weren't communists involved. It was a concern that was shared by others there. The suggestion that Revolution workers would do better to write communists out of the union script was met by jeers and hoots. It was hardly a resolution of this important issue with which people were grappling. One worker jumped into the fray shouting, "Yeah, but look what happened in the last three drives *without* the communists. Do we have a union now?" Enthusiastic applause.

On April 3, 1977, I had no doubt that I was witnessing a union local—nay, the revolution!—being born. The rhetoric, enthusiasm, determination, righteousness, and willpower were infectious. Magic was the act of people gathering. Hands tingling and numb with clapping would surely bring forth the revolution. In fact, months of behind-the-scenes organizing preceded the union drive that surfaced that April day. Sandi, who by then had been at Cone Mills Revolution Plant for three years, was one of its acknowledged leaders, and workers elected her chairperson of the ROC.

Conditions in the southern textile mills were among the most oppressive and exploitative for workers anywhere in the country. Textile workers made far less per hour than other industrial workers. To cope with their poverty and feed their families, they worked long hours of overtime, took second jobs, or continued small-scale farming on top of their mill jobs. Most received few or no health and retirement benefits and no sick pay. At times, workers' fingers or hands were ripped off by machines with exposed gears. They often had to work in areas that were fire hazards. And they were exposed to cotton dust that crippled many for life with brown lung. Black textile workers labored under even worse conditions than their white counterparts. When they finally were able to get jobs in the mills in the mid-1960s, they were hired to do the dirtiest, most dangerous, and lowest paying jobs.

Cone Mills, nationally known for its denim and corduroy, was the fourth largest cotton manufacturing company in the industry. It operated twenty-two plants in four states with a workforce of 14,000 people. Over 43 percent of its productive capability was in the Greensboro area. It was the city of Greensboro's largest single employer, employing 5,000 persons in its several plants. The company had tremendous influence in local politics. The previous mayor had been a corporate lawyer for Cone, and several of the city councilmen were beholden to Cone. The local press reflected the antiunionism of the powerful interests controlling the city.

Over the years, to keep workers divided and to attack striking workers, textile companies used Klan terror, the National Guard, armed goons, and federal troops. A few of the older workers at Revolution still remembered the machine guns Cone placed atop the mill in 1934 when 420,000 textile workers from the Black Belt South and New England were on strike for three weeks. In the nearly all-white old mill towns, the companies held sway over every aspect of the workers' lives. The companies hired ministers who preached sermons about how the union is the devil, they shut off the line of credit in the company store to militant workers, and they evicted strikers and their families from company-owned housing. By the 1970s, these tightly controlled mill villages of the 1920s and 1930s had faded as a visible institutional entity. But the same underlying power relationships still held between individuals in the different classes—with the same consequences.

From the beginning, the ROC wanted to organize an Amalgamated Clothing and Textile Workers Union (ACTWU) local at Revolution and sought ACTWU support. They kept knocking on the door demanding to be let in but kept being rebuffed by union officials. The struggle with the ACTWU occupied at least as much time and energy as the struggle against Cone. That the textile company's interest was opposed to that of the workers was a given. But that the union, which is supposed to be the workers' organization, should oppose the will of the workers needed explaining and certainly needed remedying. The ROC did not give up easily but persevered in making the case for its inclusion in ACTWU and therefore in the larger AFL-CIO family of unions. To survive and grow, the ROC needed the resources, the legitimacy, and the protection the established union offered.

WV supporters did not want to set up a union structure in competition with the main textile workers union. Later on, however, Jim Waller and others who had struggled in vain to get ACTWU to support their union work were seriously considering plans for an independent textile workers union in the South because ACTWU abandoned or tried to sabotage the rank-and-file, communist-led movements in the Cone plants. And there was no rank-and-file movement in the mills at the time except in so far as it was led by communists.

The union drive led by the ROC was actually the fourth attempt in twenty-five years by workers at Revolution to organize their plant. A previous attempt in 1973 was crippled when Cone moved quickly and aggressively to intimidate the workers. "The union will just take your dues and do nothing at all for you," they said. "But never," ROC responded in one of its leaflets:

> did Herman [Cone] tell us the real reason why he didn't want us to have a union. He didn't want us to have control over our working conditions. . . . Never did he admit that by having a strong fighting union we would be able to force him to pay us better, have a better pension, get a grievance procedure, force them to clean up the mill and make it safe. . . . He wants to use us until we are all used up and then put our pictures in the Textorian and send us off to die with a two-bit pension and brown lung. But, this time we are *prepared to struggle and win!*

The ROC was committed to building a militant, democratic, rank-and-file-controlled union, one that would involve all the workers in decision making and would take up the fight for all the workers in the mill, not just union members. As ACTWU officials continued to live in peaceful coexistence with the textile company, the ROC continued to press the union and to hold it accountable for balking at the rank-and-file organizing initiative. Not deterred by a continuing lack of support by ACTWU or by the fact that the union movement was communist led, more and more workers joined the struggle to unionize the mill.

The ROC did not succeed in obtaining official recognition from the prevailing union structure. In the process of trying, however, it assumed those functions genuine unions perform and was a de facto union local, an independent local. "The essence of a union is a broad organization of workers which leads the struggle against the company," wrote Paul and Sally Bermanzohn in their account of the Greensboro Massacre. "Bringing Cone workers together to fight the company, taking up shop floor struggles, educating people about the nature of the company, the ROC did not need ACTWU to be a union."[4]

***

Jim had moved to Greensboro around the time the union drive at Revolution was starting. He had a small rented cottage on Dewey Street, near A & T State University, only a few blocks from me. Soon he was spending more time at my place than his own. I remember visiting him only once on Dewey Street, and on that occasion I almost burned the house down. A leg of lamb I had put in the oven caught fire, and the kitchen and tiny adjoining rooms quickly filled with smoke. Jim put out the fire and didn't make too much of it.

In November 1977, he moved in with me. We were both looking for a "proletarian relationship," and we discussed frankly what that meant to us. We talked about marrying but for a little while could not bring ourselves to make a firm decision. This would be the second time around for both of us, and I had a twelve and a nine year old. There were some self-imposed obstacles spicing up the courtship. I reminded him too much of his mother, he said. Dale and Bill, practically newlyweds themselves, took us out to dinner one night, and Bill argued with Jim that the only decent thing to do, and what he really wanted to do, was to marry me. "All that stuff about your mother is a smoke screen," Bill chided Jim.

Once we were married, the rightness of our union sent me to the stars. For Jim, too, the feelings were deep and sacred. "You are the greatest love I've ever known," we told each other. I felt blessed with good fortune. As I confessed to my mother, if I could have chosen any man in the entire universe, I would have chosen Jim Waller.[5]

Jim and I were intent on our tasks and optimistic about the future. Jim had a scientific and sober approach to the organizing he was doing at Cone's Granite Finishing plant in Haw River. He examined everything that happened and everything he did very closely. He summed up lessons, corrected mistakes, and studied political theory to gain a deeper comprehension. His persistence and dedication were unshakable. We talked often about what he was trying to do at the plant. He spent many of his waking hours trying to figure out how to get the dormant union up and running. "We've been losing ground the past few years because of low participation in the union," Jim told his fellow workers at a meeting of the Haw River local that was held around the same time as Revolution workers rallied at Cosmos I. "The contract is being opened this spring for bargaining on wages and benefits. It's up to us to decide what we need and what demands we will fight for."

THE STRUGGLE TO UNIONIZE REVOLUTION

Workers Viewpoint had followers in four Cone plants in the area that had unions, however weak—White Oak and Proximity Print Works in Greensboro, Granite Finishing in Haw River, and Edna in Reidsville. There were a couple of other Cone plants with weak unions, the Tabardrey and Salisbury plants, but we had no organizers there. Nothing much developed at the Edna plant, as it turned out, and Cone Mills shut down Proximity Print Works that spring, which left White Oak and Granite Finishing. At both of these plants, contracts between the union and the company were due to be renegotiated. The WVO strategy was to bring workers together from both union locals and to come up with a unified set of demands about wages, pensions, and a whole range of other issues, such as dues check-off; an overhaul of the job bidding system; a reduction of the dust, heat, and noise levels in the mills; some restraint on Cone's ability to raise production quotas any time they felt like it; forced overtime and mandatory six- and seven-day work weeks; and the right to strike over unsettled grievances. "We know that we may not win everything we demand," WV activists told the workers, "but if we *ever* hope to have a decent standard of living for our families—if we ever hope to bring textiles out of the basement—we must begin *now* to organize and fight."

Meanwhile at Revolution, momentum from the April 3 organizing meeting carried the ROC forward. The organizing committee put out regular bulletins and distributed them at the plant gate. On April 22, Cone announced that it would close the Proximity Print Works plant in June. The plant was very old, bought by Cone in 1912 and operated ever since, and Cone claimed that a declining demand for printed fabrics and a rise in imports added to its unprofitability. Moreover, Cone Mills had recently been sued by the federal government for continued violation of antipollution laws. The Environmental Protection Agency charged that dye and other chemical waste pollutants at the company's waste disposal operation on North Buffalo Creek were being discharged into the creek in impermissible amounts, and the EPA was seeking a stiff fine against the giant textile firm. (This was the same Buffalo Creek whose waters overflowed into my living room when I lived by Latham Park. Cone had received a permit to discharge a certain level of waste into the creek in June 1974, and the flood carrying Cone's noxious by-products into the homes of Greensboro residents occurred in September of that year.) Faced with more stringent pollution control requirements and possible fines, Cone had another reason to shut down Print Works. What would happen to the six hundred workers who would be out of work when Cone closed the doors of its fabric printing plant? The ROC championed the cause of the soon-to-be-unemployed workers and made one of their demands guaranteed jobs for all Print Works workers.

After the April 3 meeting and another one on April 24, Cone had supervisors poking around the card room, the spinning room, and the weave room trying to intimidate workers away from the ROC. The process of signing union cards was underway and was going well.

On May 22, 1977, the ROC and workers from other Cone Mills rallied outside Cone Headquarters on Fourth and Maple, in front of the central employment office. In a flyer distributed that day, ROC put out its demands: a decent wage increase, jobs for all laid-off Print Works workers with no loss in pay or seniority, ACTWU support for the union organizing drive at Revolution. "The union officials say the workers at Revolution don't want a union, and that if we did, the union would be glad to come in," ROC said. "Cone Mills says we don't want a union. Why is it that the company and the union officials are saying the same thing? How can anyone say we don't want a union . . . when hundreds of us have already signed cards pledging our support to the union? . . . We are trying to build a union that doesn't just collect dues money, but that *fights* for the workers' interests."

It was anticipated that Cone would offer a 9 percent wage increase to all plant workers in response to an announcement by Burlington Industries. Militant workers pushed for a better wage increase: inflation was over 13 percent, and the cost of living had skyrocketed. In contrast to a percentage increase, which would benefit higher-paid workers more than others, ROC demanded an across-the-board increase of seventy-five cents an hour and insisted that Cone stop speeding up workers.

A news report of the rally, titled "Cone, ACTWU Both Opposed to ROC," underscored that the company and union officials were saying the same thing: "'We all suspect their motives,' said the ACTWU's regional organizing director John Kissack of Charlotte. Kissack used almost the same words as Cone in dismissing the organizing drive. 'We think they are a disruptive force that will do more harm than help,' he said."[6]

Having done his research, W. O. Leonard, Cone's vice president, had ascertained that some of the same people who were giving him grief had been part of a group called the Communist Workers Committee/Bolshevik Organizing Collective. "These people are out to do no good for you, your family, your company, or, for that matter, your country," he said in a vacuous appeal to patriotism.

Also part of this same article was a rather revealing statement from ACTWU's Kissack: "'Although they say they want us to help, the control is going to be in their hands. They want the cover of our legitimate reputation. We frankly suspect their motives. We suspect what they are trying to do is infiltrate a legitimate union.'"

If there was anything we communists were *not* good at, it was hiding our motives. We not only spelled out what we wanted from the union (support and membership), from the company (specific demands about wages, benefits, and working conditions), and from the workers (participation in building the union), but our larger political vision was no secret. Our ultimate aim, made explicit, was for power to change hands—from those who exploited workers to the workers.

The term *infiltrate* was used—actually misused—frequently by our detractors. That term implies something covert and deceptive. When you infiltrate an organization, you hide your real identity or allegiance; for example, a reporter who pretends to be a real Klansman for a story, or a KGB agent paid by Great Britain. WV supporters, however, were really textile workers trying to join the Amalgamated Clothing and Textile Workers Union of America, and they weren't in the pay of anyone but Cone Mills. But the word *control* is probably the operative word in Kissack's statement: "the control is going to be in their hands," he complained. The workers actually controlling their own union local—what cheek!

In chorus, the company and the union dismissed the ROC as insignificant and without a following. But as the staff writer for the *Greensboro Daily News* was able to gather and was honest enough to write, "the major criticism of the organizing group from both Cone and the union centers around the ideology of the organizing group: a number of its members admit freely they are communists, others are socialists and others say they just want to organize a union."[7] The ROC dealt with the red-baiting straightforwardly, acknowledging that communists played an active role in building the ROC and fighting for the union. The ROC included people with all kinds of political beliefs, organizers said. Decisions were made democratically, ideas were discussed democratically, and leadership was elected democratically.

I was at the May 22 rally at Cone Headquarters; I listened, chanted, and carried a sign. Also at the rally were several Greensboro police detectives in plainclothes.

One of them had his camera aimed at the line of demonstrators and clicked away as Sandi spoke from a flatbed podium. A WV supporter who worked in the mill with Sandi noticed the surveillance and argued with the plainclothes officer. "Quit trying to intimidate union supporters," he told him. The altercation that developed drew the attention of a young white reporter and photographer, Wayne Lottinville. He was covering the rally for the *Carolina Peacemaker*, and the argument provided the spin for his story, "Workers Rally at Cone as Police Cameras Click." Incensed by the infringement of civil rights in police and FBI spying on American citizens, this reporter confronted the police about the surveillance. For what purpose were they taking pictures of people attending a union rally? He was told the pictures would be studied for future efforts at crowd control.

Despite surveillance by Cone and the police and a rude rebuff by the labor establishment, the ROC forged ahead at full tilt. WV members met regularly to discuss tactical plans to put forth to ROC members. Leaflets written by Sally Ann and by other WV supporters issued from the ROC in a steady stream. Sandi took sexual harassment in the mill very seriously. She is probably responsible for the following flyer, with the headline, "Supervisors, Keep Your Hands to Yourselves":

One big headache for women workers all over the mill is supervisors making passes at them, pestering them to go out with them, etc. Some of these men have even told certain women, "don't worry about making your eight hours here if you'll just . . . " There's a *big difference* between men workers doing this kind of stuff and men *supervisors* doing it, because supervisors always have the threat of harassment or firing to use if women don't go along or at least keep quiet about it. And although this stuff is bad enough with white women, with black women the supervisors are downright *outrageous*. In fact, the same guy in the Card Room who has been calling white union supporters "nigger-lover" is well known for his roaming hands and slimy personal questions to black women! . . .

In the Spinning Room a young woman worker reported to the overseer that one supervisor kept making passes at her. What did the overseer do? He laughed at her! . . .

There is one supervisor in the Card Room . . . [who had] been trying to get next to a young white woman for months, when she finally got fed up and went to the overseer, complained about it, and asked for a transfer to another mill to get away from this creep. She did not get the transfer and she continued in the same spare help job. She finally quit work—but the supervisor is still here doing the same old dirty thing, and the company covered the whole thing up.

WOMEN WORKERS SHOULD NOT HAVE TO PUT UP WITH THIS GARBAGE TO HOLD ON TO THEIR JOBS!!

Women who are getting abused like this should know that it's happening to *lots of people*, not just them. When you get harassed you can stand up and fight it. Tell the ROC and the workers in your department. File a grievance against the supervisor and the ROC will help you push this and organize fighting support for you. It is by all workers uniting behind women who get harassed that we will put a stop to all this junk.[8]

ROC members filed many grievances about unsafe, unhealthy, or inhumane working conditions. They took what had been a sham grievance procedure, from the workers' point of view, and turned it against Cone. By the time the ROC got through massaging that grievance procedure, it no longer resembled anything that any owner or manager of Cone Mills in his right mind would have devised. One grievance that I remember related to the company denying workers information about exactly what chemicals were being used in processing the cloth and what effects they might have.[9] The ROC put muscle into Cone's intentionally flabby grievance system.

A typical issue concerned a mill worker named Mary who became sick on the job. Her supervisor refused to believe her and took his time sending for her husband. Other workers, realizing how sick Mary was, risked their jobs to rush her to the emergency room. She had symptoms compatible with blood clots, and a fifteen-minute delay could have been fatal. Two months before the incident with Mary, a supervisor at Cone's White Oak plant had ignored the pleas of a woman worker in the card room, and by the end of the shift, an ambulance had to be called. The woman had had a heart attack. In Mary's case, when she returned to work with a doctor's note stating that she could work, her boss told her to go home because she was "stirring up the other workers." The company refused to give her a sick leave slip so that she might draw disability benefits, but at the same time, they wouldn't allow her to work, saying that she was sick. Finally they let her work and threatened that if she got sick again, she would be terminated. The ROC helped Mary file a grievance against the company.

On many occasions, it was Sandi who accompanied workers to the grievance hearing and argued for them. Or several workers would appear at one time. From a polite, behind-closed-doors, one-on-one joust between the company and a single worker, the grievance procedure turned into an infantry charge by groups of militant, well-led workers against a mortified opponent. ROC Bulletin #17 shows what things had come to by September 14, 1977: the grievance procedure was used to file a grievance about the grievance procedure!

A group of us went to confront [the] personnel manager ... [who] said that to have workers filing joint grievances "does not follow sound management practice. ..."

Although the grievance system is a sham we must use it the best we can. We went ahead and filed the grievance around short time and around the fact we can't file joint grievances. . . . We asked that the procedures . . . be posted on a bulletin board. . . . We have a right to have these rules publicly posted in that we are the ones who have to suffer under them. . . .

We can't rely on the grievance system. Whenever there is a problem that faces a group of workers the thing to do is to get together and go to the bossman's office—sit the man down, and get some answers and don't leave until you get some. The company can do nothing when we stand firmly united. Cone's grievance procedure that prohibits joint grievances proves this is what they are scared of. It's by . . . uniting as many workers to stand together as possible that our union drive will move ahead.

Meanwhile a WV supporter and mill worker who I will call Craig filed an unfair labor practice complaint against Cone with the National Labor Relations Board on behalf of the ROC. The NLRB ruled that Cone had violated the law by harassing Craig for union activity. Cone refused to accept the ruling and said that they would not post a notice promising to stop their antiunion practices. They even denied that there was a union drive going on at Revolution! The Labor Board announced that it would take the company to court in November. In September, the ROC met again at Cosmos I to discuss the future of the union drive. Then, Cone fired Danny, a militant white worker involved in the drive. Flyer #18, on September 29, 1977, took up the fired worker's cause, demanding that Cone rehire him. "The NLRB could take months or even years to reinstate a worker fired illegally," the flyer said.

At the end of October, Cone fired Craig for using the air hose to blow globs of cotton dust from his clothes at the end of his shift. This was a common practice among the workers, and Cone could have used the same excuse to fire Craig on any previous day. By the middle of November, a total of five workers who supported the ROC had been fired. These firings show how desperate Cone was to get rid of the union drive and subdue the workers' militancy. The NLRB hearing against Cone was postponed at Cone's request until January 30, 1978. The ROC was determined to win back the jobs of all five union supporters.

Sandi led a rally in front of the Cone Revolution Plant employment office to protest Craig's dismissal. As she spoke to the crowd, Craig entered the employment office and, to the accompaniment of demonstrators outside chanting "workers we must stand and fight, organizing is our right," asked to file a grievance over his termination. The company, perhaps fearing Craig would start a worker uprising on the spot, called the police. We later learned that it was Detective Jerry Cooper who went to investigate. The name, had we known it then, would have meant nothing to us; after November 3, 1979, it meant a great deal.

REMINISCENCES OF SANDI

Years later, Sally Ann reminisced about Sandi's leadership to the ROC. "Of all of us," she told me, "Sandi pushed the hardest to get the union in at Revolution. It was really important to her that we become part of the real labor movement, that we bring the ACTWU around and get them to support us. Or she had us consider joining the Teamsters. That was a discussion, too. But somehow we needed to get in somewhere. Her father had been a mill worker in South Carolina. I think she had a more real and profound sense about the whole working-class struggle, was more grounded than the rest of us. We were all committed, but we had more middle-class baggage. Sandi went the extra mile to get us accepted in an established union. She was constantly writing letters to union officials, making phone calls, building the strength of the ROC so that the labor movement would have to take notice." In retrospect, however, Sally Ann was critical of many of the leaflets she and others wrote for ROC. She admitted that the workers reading them may have choked on one too many "Dictatorship of the Proletariats."

"Sandi was less into that longwinded, doctrinaire stuff," she said. "She brought Marxism down to earth, making it part of the everyday lives of American workers, black and white. Sandi was able to really identify with the workers, talk their language. We all made friends in the mill, but Sandi's relationships with the other workers were not just narrowly focused on the mill work, on our filing of grievances or trying to get a union. They were personal, socially satisfying relationships. She became good friends with people, visited their homes, took care of their children, went partying with them on Saturday night. That was not so easy for me," Sally Ann admitted.

"Sandi was one of those people in the struggle I was supposed to look up when I moved to Greensboro," Chekesha recalled.[10] "Even though she was only slightly older than me, she was my mentor." Chekesha became good friends with Sandi when they both worked at Revolution and studied together with the WVO. They had a lot in common. Both black women had parents with expectations for their daughters that were quite different from what these women were actually involved in. Chekesha was supposed to be studying law, redeeming all the sacrifices African Americans had made in the civil rights movement. It was a reasonable expectation for a student who, against the odds, was always put in the class with the white, especially gifted students. Sandi's parents were very pleased when Sandi became president of the student body at Bennett College, and they expected their daughter would do them and their race proud by becoming a fine nurse some day. "Sandi hated to disappoint her parents,"

Chekesha said. "All their hopes were in her. It was almost like she had to lead two lives. She had two sets of clothes. There was the mill uniform—blue jeans and T-shirt—and then there were those nice feminine things her folks liked to see her in. She would wear them every time she went home, to weddings and family events. And she would try to be the person they wanted her to be."

I vividly recall Sandi dressed up when Rand and Lorraine got married in my backyard in 1979. (Yes, my backyard was the scene of several weddings.) Sandi was beautiful in a pastel chiffon décolleté dress with a tight bodice. It was easy to imagine this woman moving in high society—at least in circles of the black bourgeoisie—her vibrant presence a ticket to an allotment of material wealth and security. By that time Sandi and Mark were separated. "Mark wasn't happy. So of course Sandi wasn't happy," Chekesha said, recalling their conversations when they all worked at Revolution. "He wanted to go off and become a doctor, and he did that."

When Sandi, conflicted about whether to follow Mark and a career path of her own, sought advice from her friends, Jim and Paul counseled her with the accepted wisdom in our circle at that time. As Paul later wrote, "Even if she became the best nurse ever, I told her that she wouldn't be able to cure the sickness in this society. Sandi knew that this rotten system is the main hazard to people's health. After a lot of thought, she made her decision, a very difficult one. She would continue to be a full-time revolutionary, regardless of what Mark decided to do."[11]

To the workers at the mill, when they spoke of her after her death, Sandi was "the most motivating factor" in the ROC. They looked to her for leadership and knew they could always rely on her. One black worker said, "If something jumped off that was not close to right, Sandi would be there fightin'. Everybody knew it. Sandi stood for fightin'. We all knew we could count on her."[12]

BITING IN

In September 1977, Jim and I attended a national Trade Union Conference in Chicago sponsored by the WVO. The speeches and cultural activities inspired me enormously. We heard from people who were leaders in their union locals and workplaces. They said that workers were ready to fight over economic, bread-and-butter issues, and that communists must *bite into* these day-to-day struggles. We must not merely *win* the fights for workers' immediate economic gains, but we must simultaneously *broaden the fight* to embrace a fundamental transformation of society. In the course of *biting in*, WV organizers and leaders would educate workers to a deeper understanding of political economy (i.e., how political structures serve the capitalist class) and would win workers over to the fight for a socialist society.

A tremendous spirit infused the conference site—a broken-down school building. The conference was multicultural—primarily in English, but with people of several nationalities participating in different languages. The May Day Singers, a musical group of WV supporters, performed *Organize! Make a Mighty River*—a solid, frenzied half hour of roof-raising with all of us joining in on the chorus. For years afterward, I hounded the May Day Singers to do *Organize!* In response to my display of enthusiasm for their music, Mary Trevor dubbed me the band's groupie. Here are some lines from a song that celebrates working-class strength and solidarity:

> You can't make revolution from the sidelines,
> Or from the outside looking in.
> This is the time—this is the hour
> For the hard work to begin.

As a result of the Trade Union Conference, we took stock of our plans for the textile industry. U.S. imperialism is collapsing, we concluded.

> We see the signs all around us. Food, gas and housing costs are rising. Unemployment is on the rise. Cone Mills has laid off, forced to quit, or fired over 1,000 people in the past year and a half. The bourgeoisie always comes down on the working class to make up for any loss in profits. That results in speedup, rules crackdowns, etc. Because of this, the working class is going to rise up even more angry and determined and this is why we resolved in the Trade Union Conference first and above all to take the lead in these economic struggles. It is the main form of struggle in the working class movement.
>
> This struggle will become increasingly political and revolutionary as the capitalists are pushed to the limit and must resort to outright repression through the police and courts and as we as communists exert our influence and leadership in these struggles.[13]

The ROC Steering Committee prepared a position paper for discussion by the ROC membership. Assessing that "the ROC has been the leading force in creating a sense of movement and energy in the whole textile industry, and we've spearheaded the area-wide efforts to win the textile workers' union (ACTWU) back from the handful of officials that control it," the steering committee suggested that it was not by narrowing but by expanding the struggle that victory would come; the ROC should set its sights on the textile industry as a whole. Textile workers needed an organization that would tie together all the rank-and-file movements in the mills, both the unionized and nonunionized ones. Such an organization would build strong, robust organizations, namely unions, in the course of fighting for a unified program. It would put out an area-wide newsletter and would be in communication with ACTWU locals throughout the country and also with the leadership of rank-and-file movements in plants around the area. This plan aimed to build up ACTWU. Every effort would be made to get ACTWU officials to support it, but it would proceed without their acceptance if necessary. About a year later, this sketch developed into the Trade Union Education League (TUEL).

Toward the end of 1977, ambitious plans were brought to the workers for discussion. The ROC and the White Oak Organizing Committee (WOOC) would work closely together. A joint rally was set for mid-January 1978, and an effort would be made there to get textile workers to support the J. P. Stevens boycott. (We supported it in spite of criticizing it as a poor tactic.) The two organizing committees planned an aggressive campaign around the NLRB case at Revolution and considered how to draw all the Cone locals and the ROC together in active support for the White Oak local in its upcoming contract struggle with Cone. In all the community organizations we worked with, we would seek support for our labor work.

Jim Waller, Sandi Smith, and Bill Sampson, all of whom led textile workers struggles in the period between 1976 and 1979, understood how important the African American liberation struggle was for textile workers, and their leadership reflected this understanding by uniting workers across racial lines. In 1977, the WV supporters who were leading struggles in the mills committed themselves to winning positions in union locals and on the ACTWU Joint Board by 1979. They realized how disabling to workers was the state's Right to Work law, defended by Jesse Helms, and they planned a campaign against it. In a union shop, all permanent workers who receive benefits from a union and union contract must belong to the union. The Right to Work law made a union shop (or closed shop) illegal, thus making it impossible to build a strong union and collect union dues. WVO supporters intended to develop a united front opposing the Right to Work law as part of a massive organizing campaign for the whole textile industry. Since the ACTWU appeared to them to be unwilling or incapable of taking the lead in organizing the whole textile industry, in 1977 Jim and other WVO people planned to establish an organization that textile workers could depend on for militant leadership, the Trade Union Educational League

(TUEL). Some of these plans had materialized and some had not when the Greensboro Massacre broke the momentum of the union organizing and eliminated Jim, Bill, and Sandi, some of the most powerful labor organizers.

The union drive at Revolution, as intense as it was, was not the sole focus of our energies in 1977. WVO supporters were also involved in the issue of police brutality, in mobilizing for African Liberation Day, in political training of its members and supporters, among many other tasks. By the close of 1977, we were looking forward to things becoming *more intense*, not less, as we expected to be even more deeply and thoroughly immersed in the politics of the whole textile industry.

If I had to choose the year when the organizing was at its height, when great numbers of people were waking to our call and a revolutionary current seemed to surge through the mills, the streets, and the places where the people congregate, when our initiative and such wise leadership as we could muster were causing our enemies to become snarled and defensive, it would be 1978. I remember being at an April 1978 ALSC meeting in the Uhuru Bookstore in Greensboro, preparing for African Liberation Day. I remember compiling all my assignments in a notebook—the ones relating to ALSC, the textile union support work, the media work I was to do, and so on. How was I going to get one-tenth of it done, especially since I was so tired all the time, disoriented from working a swing shift at the hospital? But others had even more responsibility than I did. I understood that our engagement was not in this or that *arena* of class struggle but in *all of society*. In North Carolina, the fire at the treetops that lit up the sixties was burning down to the roots in the seventies.

NOTES

1. Unless otherwise indicated, quotations by Dale Sampson Levin are from a taped interview with her on November 5, 1992.

2. Frederick Engels, "The Origin of the Family, Private Property and the State," in *Karl Marx and Frederick Engels: Selected Works in One Volume* (New York: International Publishers, 1968), 502–503.

3. Quoted in Bermanzohn, *The True Story of the Greensboro Massacre*, 122–123.

4. Bermanzohn, *The True Story of the Greensboro Massacre*, 126.

5. See appendix C, "The Personal Is Political," 503.

6. Rick Gray, "Cone, ACTWU Both Opposed to ROC," *Greensboro Daily News*, 22 May 1977, C3.

7. Gray, "Cone, ACTWU," C3.

8. Quoted in Bermanzohn, *The True Story of the Greensboro Massacre*, 123–125.

9. This activity was a forerunner in a later victory in the struggle for right-to-know laws in North Carolina.

10. Unless otherwise indicated, quotations by Frankie Powell (Chekesha) are from a taped interview with her on March 5, 1993.

11. Bermanzohn, *The True Story of the Greensboro Massacre*, 126.

12. From the documentary *Red November, Black November*, 16 mm, 80 min., Reelworks, Inc., coproduced and directed by Sally Alvarez and Carolyn Jung, New York, 1980. Also produced as a videocassette.

13. "Plan for the Textile Industry," Workers Viewpoint in N.C., 22 November 1977, mimeographed.

6

PEOPLE, PEOPLE,
HAVE YOU HEARD?

AFRICAN LIBERATION DAY 1977

The African Liberation Support Committee (ALSC) taught people that the liberation struggles in Africa were closely linked to the struggles of blacks in the United States for economic and social justice: the same system of monopoly capitalism oppressed and exploited people of color here and abroad for the profit of the same ruling class. ALSC in Greensboro and Durham were typical of ALSC chapters around the country and functioned like community organizations. Through ALSC, people were educated about domestic and international events.

Many activities took place around the annual mobilization for African Liberation Day (ALD) in May. In 1977, ALSC held a cultural program for a large audience at the Morningside Homes Auditorium, brought its members to the rally at Cone Mills headquarters to support the union drive at Revolution, and showed a film and held a discussion about Malcolm X at the Peeler Community Center. We had neighborhood fundraising drives—one afternoon I drove back and forth between Morningside Homes and Connie Lane's kitchen carrying plates of fried fish, mashed potatoes, and green beans she had prepared to raise money for chartered buses—and we had air time for ALSC's message on WEAL, the black radio station, and WFMY–TV, the local CBS affiliate.

ALSC remained an active grassroots organization throughout the year with regular meetings, often at the black-owned Uhuru Bookstore on East Market Street. Upon returning from the ALD parade where they demonstrated against apartheid in South Africa, many people worked on local issues affecting blacks, such as police repression and a lack of quality education in the public schools.

After ALD 1977, ALSC held rallies against Burlington Industries and the North Carolina National Bank for buttressing the apartheid regime in South Africa through their investments and financial dealings. ALSC also commemorated the anniversary of the Soweto uprising of June 16, 1976, when the apartheid regime in South Africa slaughtered scores of unarmed young students who were among thousands demonstrating against a law mandating the use of Afrikaans in the schools—the language of the racist white minority rulers and a symbol of colonial oppression.

Membership in ALSC did not necessarily imply agreement with communism or involvement in other parts of the WVO agenda. ALSC was a multiracial organization for everyone who wanted to support African liberation and oppose the oppression of black people anywhere. The Greensboro chapter had black and white members and was led by Joyce Johnson. Nelson Johnson was in the national leadership body of ALSC, as was Owusu Sadaukai, who led the Durham ALSC group. Paul Bermanzohn was a key organizer and one of the local leaders in Durham.

On African Liberation Day 1977, ALSC (as we stated on a flyer) aimed "to express our militant support for the liberation struggles of the peoples of Azania (South Africa), Zimbabwe (Rhodesia), and Namibia (Southwest Africa) against the racist white minority regimes and their imperialist backers." Because of political turmoil and sectarianism leading up to ALD, there were actually three separate mobilizations that year. Along with ALSC (allied with the WVO), Stokely Carmichael's group of black nationalists demonstrated, as did the Revolutionary Communist Party. Each with its own politics and ideology, the three groups stayed apart. The contingent led by the WVO was most remarkable in bringing together racially and nationally diverse groups and individuals.

On the trip to Washington, D.C., for African Liberation Day 1977, I sat next to Bill Sampson, newly arrived in Greensboro. After receiving a master's degree from Harvard Divinity School, Bill had decided that he would become a doctor and was just weeks away from earning a medical degree in Charlottesville, Virginia, when he left for Greensboro. I remember the wonderful conversation we had on the bus. We talked about his college major in philosophy, the difficult decision to leave medical school, and his plan to work at Cone Mills. Bill was practically deaf in one ear, and he kept directing me to his good ear. He and a fellow Divinity School student, Philip Zwerling, had been beaten by police after an antiwar demonstration as they walked back to their car. Bill was hospitalized, lost hearing in one ear, and nearly lost an eye.

At the rally, Joyce, beautiful, held her head high and led a call-and-response chant:

People, People, Have you heard?
  Liberation is the word.
People, People, Ain't it right?
  Liberation is our fight.
Am I right or wrong?
  You're right!
Am I right or wrong?
  You're right!
Am I right or wrong?
  You're right!!!

A song written especially for African Liberation Day, *All Africa's Standing Up*, made its debut in 1977, performed by the May Day Singers. We took it back to our communities and taught it to everyone we knew.

Countries want independence,
That's the way it's gotta be.
Nations want liberation,
They are fighting to be free.
People want revolution,
It's the course of history.
All Africa's Standing Up!
All Africa's Standing Up!
All Africa's Standing Up!
Drive the imperialists to the sea!

WVO literature at the time argued that besides U.S. imperialism, the other main enemy of the African people was Soviet social-imperialism and, of the two, Soviet social-imperialism was more dangerous.[1] A few years later, the WVO dropped this very pro-Chinese take on the Soviet Union. It was undeniable that Cuba and the Soviets were giving assistance to third world countries in Africa struggling for liberation. In the late 1970s, WVO and ALSC won the respect of a number of international dignitaries and nongovernmental organizations (NGOs) in Africa. They were impressed by the multiracial character of our organization and appreciative of the efforts of Dr. Michael Nathan, who had led a campaign that sent substantial medical aid to the liberation struggle in Southern Africa. I and others around Workers Viewpoint in those years felt confident that the WVO would become a party, lead a socialist revolution in the United States, and have diplomatic and cooperative relations with other fledgling socialist countries and national liberation movements around the world.

SOUTHERN JUSTICE EXAMPLE 1: WHITAKERS

Three examples show ALSC's work in confronting racial injustice: the first occurred against a backdrop in which white people could murder blacks with impunity; the second illustrates police brutality against blacks; and the third demonstrates the government's suppression of black leaders in the civil rights struggle. None of these were particularly exotic. All typified what happened or was liable to happen, frequently. However, popular outrage, organized and led by ALSC and others, won a modicum of justice where otherwise there would have been even more injustice and repression.

Whitakers, North Carolina, was typical of many small towns in the Black Belt South. A majority black town, it was controlled by a white oligarchy to which belonged Joseph Judge, a descendent of slavemasters. His family owned land, slum houses, and many of the town's stores. Judge was accustomed to doing as he pleased.

In April 1977, black agricultural worker Charlie Lee was fatally shot by white shopkeeper Joe Judge. Judge had shortchanged Lee, as he had done to many African Americans, and when Lee demanded the right change back, Judge reached for his gun and shot him in the chest. Yet it was a pretty good bet that Judge would not go to jail for the cold-blooded murder: a year before, in the nearby town of Scotland Neck, a relative of his had killed a black man and gotten away with it.

Paul Bermanzohn led the ALSC chapter in Durham in a militant struggle to bring the dangerous and arrogant shopkeeper to justice. Black people in Whitakers were ready to fight back. Immediately after Charlie Lee's funeral, five hundred people staged a protest march through town. The People's Coalition for Justice was formed. That spring, summer, and fall, Paul commuted often between Durham and Whitakers, working with the coalition and helping to organize meetings and rallies.

The People's Coalition for Justice held a people's trial. They tried not only Joe Judge but the courts, the police, and the rich white landowners and factory owners who stood behind the murderer and protected him. The coalition presented testimony from the Lee family and also from farmers, factory workers, and young people who had been victimized by Judge. Though invited to attend the trial, the town's notables, including the mayor and police chief, declined. Instead they followed the organizers around and arrested Paul and another coalition leader, Waldo, an African American man from Whitakers.

More than one hundred people crowded into the Bloomerhill Community Center on highway 301, south of Whitakers, for the people's court. The witnesses testified to Joe Judge's conduct, ranging from the unsavory to the downright criminal. Judge was found guilty of the murder of Charlie Lee. The capitalist judicial and economic system was found guilty of assisting him.

In the "legitimate" trial, Joe Judge was found guilty of the murder of Charlie Lee. He was given a ten year suspended sentence, three years probation, and fined $25,000 to Lee's widow. Paul attributed the outcome "to the tremendous mass struggle carried out under the leadership of the African Liberation Support Committee and the Workers Viewpoint Organization."[2] Grassroots organizing by black people and their allies had brought about the unusual verdict—a defeat for the white power structure. In the long history of vicious lynching of blacks by whites, this was one of the rare instances in which the perpetrator received any punishment at all.

Of interest to some people might be the theoretical ideas that circulated around these events and that were developed by African American theorist Philip Thompson and others. Injustice done to black people is usually subsumed under the rubric of racism, that is, prejudice based on skin color. But the WVO analysis treated racism as also a manifestation of something deeper—a consequence of underlying economic structures and historical developmental relationships. An individual like Joe Judge was not simply an evil man, but an evil man playing a role that is generally rewarded in an evil, racist, and classist society.

WVO maintained that having been forcibly brought to the Americas and oppressed throughout their history here, black people, although originating from different nations and tribes in Africa, constituted a nation in the United States, with a unique historical and cultural identity. Oppression directed against them was *national oppression*.[3] In struggles in the late 1970s, such as that at Whitakers, the WVO upheld the doctrine that black people in the United States constitute a *national minority* and have the *right to self-determination as a nation*. Writing for *Workers Viewpoint*, Paul propagated this theory: the democratic right of black people to secede and form their own country "must be upheld even if the Afro-American people decide not to do so, the same as the right of divorce. . . . Communists must be in the forefront of this struggle against class oppression and national oppression."[4]

WVO attempted to account for how racism arises in the first place. Racism, an ideology or belief system with a behavioral component, was seen as rooted in and sustained by a system of economic exploitation. After-the-fact *rationalizations* for racism abound, such as theories of the biological inferiority of the people who are being exploited. Racism did not *cause* the white plantation owners to have slaves; but it was a convenient, self-serving, after-the-fact justification for slavery. It was in the class interest of the white slaveholders to preach the inferiority of the black slaves and to diffuse racist ideas throughout society.

This is not the place for a definitive discussion of this complex theoretical issue. I will only remark here that if it seems that racism is not entirely accounted for by tracing its roots in a system of economic exploitation, and if it seems that one form or another of xenophobia seems a perennial albatross on the human race, there were nonetheless valuable insights in the WVO's position on racism and national oppression. The WVO explained the apparent independence of racist ideas by pointing out that ideas tend to have a life of their own and to hang around a long time, even after the actual conditions that gave rise to them have changed. Racism—a doctrine that seeks to justify social inequality on the basis of skin color—hung around after the system of chattel slavery was no longer acceptable. Racist ideology, by keeping workers divided and hence more easily exploited, continued its useful life under the wage slavery of capitalism. Such considerations led WVO leaders to go beyond more conventional and well-intentioned sentiments about eliminating racism. Ultimately, said WV, blacks must be free not merely from racial insults and racially motivated murders, like what happened to Charlie Lee and countless others, but free to live as a self-determining nation of people, with full national sovereignty.

SOUTHERN JUSTICE EXAMPLE 2: GERNIE CUMMINGS

In the fall of 1977, an African American woman in Greensboro told her friend in ALSC that her son Gernie Cummings had been beaten up while in a holding cell in the jail. Gernie had sickle cell anemia, and his mother was very worried about him. Our ALSC chapter encouraged the family to speak out. At the end of September, Gernie announced that he had been beaten in jail by three sheriff's deputies.

Gernie Cummings was a passenger in a car that was stopped by two Guilford County sheriff's deputies for a driving violation. The law enforcement men were racist and abusive to him, and he talked back to them. He was arrested and roughed up in the process, his head slammed against a car.

From a cell in the county jail, Gernie demanded his phone call. He was not a quiet, compliant prisoner, and by all accounts, neither captor nor captured had a monopoly on swearing. On his third request to call, a deputy told him, "Tell your black mammy to give you a telephone call." "I'll ask your black daughter for a phone call," the prisoner retorted defiantly. "I don't have a black daughter," the white jailer returned, whereupon he and a fellow deputy entered the holding cell. While two deputies, Richard Belch and Colon Smith, assaulted Cummings with a blackjack and with fists, a third deputy, Larry Canter, witnessed the beating. The deputies then departed from the cell, leaving the prisoner lying face down, unconscious, on the floor. They got in an elevator to go to another part of the jail, congratulating themselves with remarks like "I think we taught him a lesson."

The deputies later went down to check on Cummings—he was still unconscious, lying face down on the floor. They propped him up on a bench in the cell and left again. About an hour afterward, they once again went to the holding cell, this time with their supervisor in order to bring Cummings to his bond hearing. They found him face down on the floor once more, lying in a small pool of blood. The magistrate failed to notice (or pretended not to notice) the blood on Cummings head when he was brought before him. An initial charge of public drunkenness had been changed to resisting arrest and disorderly conduct. Gernie told magistrate Clark that he had been assaulted by the jailers, but the magistrate took no action except to order, "Get him out of here!"

His mother bailed him out on a $500 bond and took him to the hospital, where he was treated for severe wounds on his head, forehead, back, and leg. He was in pain and still had to face an unfair indictment: he was convicted of disorderly conduct and resisting arrest and sentenced to a thirty-day jail term and a year of probation.

Required to file a written report of the incident, the three deputies concocted a story that Cummings had fallen. The Sheriff's Department did an internal investigation (the contents of which they refused to reveal) with the result that two of the three deputies were suspended and then fired shortly after the incident.

Previously, Nelson and Joyce organized against police abuse and sought to establish a citizen review board. By the end of October, the Johnsons had formed a committee with about forty members to look into the Gernie Cummings incident. The Concerned Citizens Committee against Police Brutality included several black preachers, community activists, and ALSC members. Joyce chaired it and wasted no time in getting letters out to the Greensboro Human Relations Commission, the State Bureau of Investigation, and the North Carolina Civil Rights Commission, asking them to conduct a thorough investigation and take appropriate action including indictments where warranted. The local press was notified. This flurry of activity and the promise of more to come put Greensboro Police Chief W. E. Swing and Guilford County Sheriff Paul Gibson on notice that many people, white and black, thought that the firing of two deputies was not enough. These deputies had engaged in criminal acts for which they should be indicted and, if proved guilty, convicted and punished.

Any who participated in or aided the crimes of the two deputies should also be brought to justice: no one is above the law.

Throughout the fall of 1977, meeting at the Shiloh Baptist Church, the Union Memorial United Methodist Church, or the Uhuru Bookstore, the committee continued to put pressure on public officials to follow through in the Gernie Cummings case. On November 18, the group held a press conference to announce that they had requested District Attorney Raymond Alexander to launch a criminal investigation into the September beating of a prisoner at the county jail. "We have been conducting our own investigation into the matter, and we are prepared to turn our findings over to the District Attorney," Nelson told reporters. The committee named the third deputy, who had observed the brutal beating, and two other supervisors or deputies on duty at the jail who knew about the assault but failed to take the proper action. Sheriff Gibson was accused of covering up a criminal act by refusing to make public details of the incident.

Meanwhile the high-profile case of the Wilmington Ten, that I will discuss in more detail below, was making the news. Governor Hunt had just refused to pardon Reverend Ben Chavis and nine other civil rights organizers who were serving lengthy jail terms. Hunt reduced their sentences, making them eligible for parole sooner. But this small concession angered rather than appeased people who knew that the Wilmington Ten were arrested on trumped up charges in order to put a stop to their civil rights activities. In a letter to the Concerned Citizens on January 23, 1978, Joyce called the governor's refusal to pardon or commute the sentences of the ten political prisoners in Wilmington "a slap in the face to all freedom-loving people, especially Black people who are the main victims of the North Carolina 'justice' system." In like manner, District Attorney Alexander of Guilford County had not even responded to the request that he investigate the malicious beating of Gernie Cummings. "However," Joyce wrote, "both Hunt and Alexander underestimate the powerful determination of Black and other oppressed people to seek justice. . . . The people will have justice in the Wilmington Ten case and the Gernie Cummings case!"

***

Six or seven of us strolled down the street in a festive mood. Ahead, Jim was talking and laughing with César, who had come from Durham for a meeting but had some time to celebrate with us first. I walked behind them and got acquainted with César's girlfriend, Floris, another newcomer to North Carolina. From a Panamanian family that settled in Washington, D.C., and became U.S. citizens, Floris was a young black woman with a pretty, round-shaped face. I was telling her about Gernie Cummings. "The response from the community has been tremendous," I said. "We're trying to get the D.A. to prosecute the racist deputies that beat him up." We walked quickly toward a downtown restaurant for breakfast. I clutched my coat against the bite in the air. I had chosen glamour over practicality and wore a light spring jacket that I thought would flatter me. I wanted to look beautiful. It was January 27, 1978, my wedding day.

After breakfast, César and Floris had to leave. Another friend from Durham stayed to witness our wedding. The second witness was Bill Sampson. Bill picked up my son, Shlomo, at school and brought the nine year old to the Guilford County Courthouse. The Justice of the Peace was ready to start. My daughter, Tonya, was still not there. She was on a winter camping trip with her New Garden Friends School class, and the arrangements we made to have her brought back for the wedding had somehow fallen through. We had to go ahead without her. I wanted both children to be there so we could start out immediately being a family. Jim and I exchanged the plain gold bands we'd bought. Thus two communists were joined in matrimony in an uneventful civil ceremony.

In less than two years, I would be wearing our wedding bands on a chain around my neck, as a gesture of mourning and also as a defiant widow's reminder of a shocking tale. But then, everything was forever—old age together, our whole lives together, forever.

Working the night shift and having mountains of political and union responsibilities had exhausted the bridegroom. The bride, due to similar overwhelming pursuits, was not in much better shape. Weary we were, but weariness could not touch our bliss. How right it was for us to be joined together!

***

Soon after Jim and I returned from Galax, Virginia, where we spent our brief honeymoon, we learned that the D.A. was ready to prosecute two ex-deputies on misdemeanor assault-and-battery charges in the Cummings case. The following day, February 1, 1978, members of the Concerned Citizens Committee met with District Attorney Ray Alexander to let him know that people thought the attack on Cummings was a felony crime and were not happy with the misdemeanor charges. The community felt that the third deputy and others in the Sheriff's Department should also have been indicted.

At a rally sponsored by the Concerned Citizens Committee against Police Brutality, on February 4th at the Governmental Plaza in Greensboro, people demonstrated in subfreezing temperatures. They applauded speeches by Rev. Leon White, head of the Virginia–Carolina chapter of the Commission for

Racial Justice of the United Church of Christ, Brenda Wagner of the Black Lawyers Association, Abiola from Greensboro ALSC, and Nelson Johnson, representing the WVO. People went to the rally "to let Gov. Jim Hunt know they haven't forgotten his 'political decision' on the Wilmington Ten, to let the Democractic Party know that black votes cannot be counted on like clockwork anymore, to let local law enforcement officials know some concerned residents want 'justice for Gernie Cummings' and to let the people know that they will take their cause to the streets."[5]

The ex-deputies went on trial on April 6, 1978. The judge was a fair-skinned African American, Joseph Williams, with a reputation for being rigorous. The deputy who witnessed the beating testified that the three deputies involved made up a false report about an apparent fall. Two of the three ultimately retracted the report and admitted the prisoner had been beaten.

On April 7, Judge Williams sentenced the two Greensboro ex-deputies to two years in prison—the maximum sentence for the misdemeanor—with six months to be spent as active time in jail. It was a sweet victory. ALSC's newpaper, *All Africa's Standing Up*, appreciated how unprecedented this turn of events was.

To call Whitakers and the Gernie Cummings case victories does not mean that they resulted in perfect justice. Joe Judge did not even serve jail time for murdering a man. While the conviction of the ex-deputies was upheld, months later on appeal (with a white judge presiding) their penalty was made less harsh with no active jail time. They were nonetheless victories: law enforcement officials who committed racist crimes were met with well-organized and determined opposition. People were making it clear to those in power, at least at the local level, that they could not kill a Charlie Lee or beat up a Gernie Cummings with impunity.

The competency test was another issue taken up by ALSC members. Competency testing was introduced in North Carolina public schools in the late seventies. We saw it as part of a general trend of disinvesting in public education—and subsequent events, sadly, have borne out that view. Alarming information was coming to light about how many Americans were illiterate or functionally illiterate. How could it be that children deposited in the schools for all their prime learning years were coming out almost more ignorant than when they went in? What exactly was happening and what wasn't happening that was supposed to happen, and why? A good faith commitment to remedying the problems implied an extensive investment in public education: instead, Governor Hunt promoted competency testing, which did nothing to improve the educational system but only forced students out of it.

Those who failed the competency test received a piece of paper—not a diploma—that said, basically, that they had muddled through for twelve years only to fail the test. We believed that the real point of the competency test was to cater to the business community and lure investors to the state by sorting out the labor pool for them. Job applicants with a diploma could be assumed to know how to read and write a little, and even do some basic math, while those clearly second-class applicants with the piece of paper proclaiming their minimal achievements would receive minimal wages. A two-tier labor pool with a low bottom would naturally depress wages for all workers. Along with the state's famed high workforce productivity and low unionization rate, low wages for workers would clinch the North Carolina advantage for capitalists searching for a home for their capital.

In December 1977, Durham ALSC led a campaign against the competency test with pickets in front of Hillside High School. Durham ALSC also protested a Durham Police Department initiative to put police officers in the schools. The plan was announced following a demonstration outside Hillside High and ALSC thought it was meant to chill students from organizing against the competency tests. In February 1978, ALSC demonstrated outside Durham High School, drawing twice as many pickets as in December. This time the resistance was opposing both competency testing and police patrols in the schools. "We're interested in quality education," Paul Bermanzohn assured reporters, "but the competency test doesn't accomplish that goal. That goal can be accomplished much better through salary increases for teachers, reducing teacher-student ratios, and providing more educational resources in classrooms. The testing program is really educational cutbacks in disguise."

The campaign against competency testing went on for many months. The Greensboro ALSC chapter took it up, and ultimately we built a statewide coalition against the test. But when Governor Hunt dashed hopes that he would pardon the Wilmington Ten, on January 23, 1978, ALSC chapters in North Carolina joined the United Church of Christ and other organizations in a commitment to the political exposure and mass mobilization necessary to free the ten civil rights activists. Efforts to defeat the competency test program were to resume later.

SOUTHERN JUSTICE EXAMPLE 3:
THE CHARLOTTE THREE AND THE WILMINGTON TEN

To understand what the Charlotte Three and the Wilmington Ten cases were about, one must understand how threatening black civil rights activists and organizers appeared in the eyes of powerful southern whites.

Richard Nixon's "Southern Strategy," when he campaigned for president in 1968, was assisted by his campaign manager John Mitchell and southern organizer Robert Mardian—two crooks of later Watergate infamy. They understood that for southern politicians to support Nixon, they would have to know that Washington would allow them to maintain segregated schools and to break up organizations of blacks demanding equal rights.

Of course attacks on black activists were not new and certainly not limited to North Carolina or the South. The FBI's counterintelligence program, or COINTELPRO, carried out with the help of federal, state, and local police agencies to harass and disable black leaders, resulted in the jailing and assassination of hundreds of Black Panthers and other activists.

Going into the 1970s, African American student activists and community organizers were trying to achieve the equal education guaranteed by the 1954 Supreme Court ruling. The Black Liberation Movement had many leaders. One was Jim Grant. Originally from South Carolina, with an undergraduate degree from the University of Connecticut and a Ph.D. in organic chemistry from Penn State University, Grant was active in the civil rights and antiwar movements. He was among the first Americans to burn his draft card at Sheep Meadow Park in New York. He worked with the American Friends Service Committee, the Southern Christian Leadership Conference, the Southern Conference Educational Fund, and the 1972 Black Political Convention in Gary, Indiana.

Another black leader was Ben Chavis. A native of Oxford, N.C., and a staff member of the United Church of Christ's Commission for Racial Justice, Chavis had been a student at the University of North Carolina in Charlotte, where he established the Black Student Union. He had worked as an organizer for the American Federation of State, County, and Municipal Employees (AFSCME) and for the Southern Christian Leadership Conference. He was a widely respected youth organizer in the South and a supporter of King's philosophy of nonviolence.

Both men were involved in starting an independent political organization when they were indicted in 1971. The witnesses for the prosecution were two black felons, David Washington and Al Hood, who testified that Chavis and Grant had helped them flee the country. Washington and Hood had long records of narcotics dealing and armed assault. They had been arrested during a period of racial unrest and spontaneous rebellion in Oxford, N.C. (occasioned by the familiar scenario of murders of black people by whites going unpunished) and charged with violating the Federal Gun Control Act. They jumped bail, fled to Canada, and were returned on fugitive warrants.

Federal authorities seized the moment to put both Jim Grant and Ben Chavis behind bars by making a deal with Washington and Hood, whose perjury was rewarded with money and with the dropping of all charges against them. The *Charlotte Observer* later revealed that it was Robert Mardian, working out of the U.S. Justice Department under John Mitchell, who handled the payments of thousands of dollars for the Nixon administration. In charge of the case within North Carolina was Stanley Noel, an agent for the U.S. Treasury Department's Bureau of Alcohol, Tobacco, and Firearms (BATF). Chavis and Grant were tried for conspiring to help Hood and Washington escape prosecution, while the escapees were turned free. In a federal court in Raleigh, Chavis was found not guilty. However, solely on the bought testimony of the two felons, Grant was convicted of aiding the fugitives and sentenced to ten years in prison.

North Carolina and federal officials were not finished with Grant or Chavis. Three months after Grant's sentencing, he was tried along with two other civil rights activists, T. J. Reddy and Charles Parker, for burning a riding stable. The three were known as the Charlotte Three. Assistant Attorney General Robert C. Mardian approved a deal giving Hood and Washington cash payments of four thousand dollars each, immunity from prosecution, and federal relocation assistance in return for their testimony.

Parker, an honor student in high school and a dean's list student at college, had been a community youth organizer. T. J. Reddy was a poet and playwright who regularly published and lectured. He graduated from UNC-Charlotte, where he was an editor of the campus arts magazine. Like Parker, Reddy had worked as a youth organizer.

The Charlotte Three case reeks of that racist arrogance and contempt with which the government was attempting to herd leaders of the people's movement into jail. The stable in question had burned down four years prior to the indictments. In October 1967, an integrated group of people, including T. J. Reddy, went to the segregated Lazy B, a public stable, to ride. They were denied admission. The next day they returned with friends. In front of television cameras and reporters, one of the group, Charles Parker, was allowed to ride. The integration of another public facility was accomplished and the incident was considered closed. A year later the stable burned down. An investigation at the time determined that the fire was accidental. There was no mention of arson. Then, four years after the fire, the Charlotte Three were charged with arson at the Lazy B stable. They were tried in July 1972.

I attended part of that trial. There was no evidence linking any of the defendants with the stable fire and no physical evidence at all except for a bottle that police said had been found at the site containing traces of a flammable liquid.

Under cross examination, the police confessed that they did not have the bottle—they had lost it. The fire inspector admitted that the picture of the bottle submitted as evidence was not taken the night of the fire—he had gone back to the stable, put the bottle down, and taken the picture. Nothing linked the elusive bottle with the defendants. Four witnesses for Grant testified that he had been at Penn State University at the time of the burning. While he was in jail, Grant's apartment was ransacked and his bank records were destroyed, eliminating evidence pertaining to his whereabouts on the day of the stable fire.

The Charlotte Three were convicted of burning the Lazy B riding stable based solely on the concocted stories of Washington and Hood, whose testimonies on important particulars were contradictory. Judge Snepp insisted that the trial was not political but an ordinary criminal trial. At the sentencing, the judge lectured the three defendants, saying, "you burned to death fifteen horses in that stable. What you would do to human beings, God only knows." Snepp sentenced Parker to ten years, Reddy to twenty years, and Grant to twenty-five years in jail.

Investigative reporting by the *Charlotte Observer* less than two years later (after appeals for the Charlotte Three had failed) uncovered the extensive federal involvement in what was supposedly a local trial. Of course during the Lazy B trial, defense attorneys did not know that Hood and Washington had already received their first one thousand dollars and that more was to come. After the stable burning trial, Hood was arrested twice—one charge was for murdering a local drug pusher, who, it was thought, was in competition with Hood for control of the heroin trade in Charlotte. The Justice Department had strange bedfellows. With the revelation of secret payments by the federal government, defense attorneys moved for a new trial. In September 1975, Superior Court Judge Sam Ervin III, calling the Mitchell-Mardian secret payoffs "harmless error," ruled that the Charlotte Three were not entitled to a new trial. Just as the Charlotte Three story was not really about a burned down stable in Charlotte, the Wilmington Ten story was not really about a burned down grocery store in Wilmington.

Before the Emancipation Proclamation, Wilmington was the largest slave market in eastern Carolina. During Reconstruction, the city acquired a black mayor and other black and progressive white officials, elected by an alliance of black Republicans and white Populists. There were many black-owned businesses, and Wilmington was becoming one of the South's major seaports. However, after 1877, when the period of Reconstruction ended, African Americans were systematically stripped of many of the rights they had gained. One by one the southern states amended their constitutions to disenfranchise black people at the ballot box, using poll taxes, literacy tests, and other methods. Historian John Hope Franklin notes that "by 1898 the pattern for the constitutional disenfranchisement of the Negro had been completely drawn."[6]

In Wilmington, the showdown came around the elections of 1898. In the 1898 Wilmington Riot, white vigilantes called the redshirts, who were associated with the Democrats, unleashed a reign of terror against blacks. State military forces, sent by the newly elected Democratic governor, sided with a mob that shot down defenseless citizens in the streets of a black community. Scores of people were killed and their bodies dumped into the Cape Fear River. After that incident, the "pacified" city was run under a system of white rule. Efforts by blacks to organize were stymied by economic pressure or outright terror. The area was long a Ku Klux Klan stronghold.

After the civil rights movement of the 1960s, black students in North Carolina and other southern states discovered that court-ordered desegregation often harbored new forms of inequality and persecution. Many blacks saw integration as a cover by Nixon and southern racists to destroy black institutions and enforce a de facto segregation in supposedly integrated schools. Black schools had functioned as centers of community life. Now, as schools were consolidated, black teachers were laid off, with civil rights activists a special target for dismissal. Within a newly "integrated" school system, blacks were being segregated anew, and school discipline was pursued unequally, with harsher penalties for black students than for whites.

In Wilmington, a city of 50,000 residents and a 40 percent black population, organizing efforts by black high school students were met with repression from school authorities and police. Students were demanding a black studies program, more black instructors, and an end to unequal and racist treatment by school authorities. At the end of 1970, black students at Hanover High launched a school boycott around these demands. After the Christmas recess, a white boy assaulted a black girl with a knife. The principal suspended her but did not punish the boy. Adults in the black community dug in and began to organize in support of their children.

Approached by students, Rev. Gene Templeton, a white minister at the Gregory Congregational United Church of Christ in the black community, allowed the use of the church as headquarters for a student boycott. Soon white men in pickup trucks were driving by the church, shouting obscenities, and flashing their guns. Rev. Templeton appealed to the United Church of Christ's Commission for Racial Justice. Field organizer Rev. Ben Chavis and commission head Rev. Leon White went to Wilmington to try to improve a volatile situation. From February 3, 1971, there was sporadic shooting and fires. The two organizers left

Wilmington but, when matters continued worsening, Chavis returned and asked for a curfew and police protection for the community.

The curfew was denied, and the 1971 Siege of Wilmington began in earnest—four days of armed attack by racist vigilantes on black youth who had barricaded themselves inside a church in self-defense. The shooting was almost continuous. Rev. Templeton's home beside the church was shot at repeatedly. Blacks shot back against the white vigilantes to defend themselves and their community. On the third day of the siege, a grocery store near the church burned down. Rev. Chavis was in the church with Rev. Templeton when the two men heard a commotion and ran outside the parsonage. They could see the burning store from the churchyard. That same evening, a nineteen-year-old black youth was shot and killed near the burning store by the police. The bloodshed still did not move the police to impose a curfew or to take any other measures to protect the African American community.

The day after the grocery store fire, a white man was killed. The curfew repeatedly requested by the black community finally was granted. A state of emergency was called, and National Guardsmen came into the area. Armed guards were posted around the church.

Sporadic flare-ups continued for over a year. In this period, black students were beaten, and Rev. Templeton, having received Klan threats on his life, left Wilmington. The Rights of White People (ROWP), a vigilante group in eastern North Carolina, criticized the Klan as too moderate. "If necessary, we'll eliminate the black race," announced career marine and ROWP leader, Leroy Gibson, before an armed rally of supporters. (ROWP was part of the racist coalition that planned the attack in Greensboro eight years later.) Highway billboards at the time, taken out by the United Klans of North Carolina, said, "You are in the heart of Klan country." Motorists were urged to "Help save America from Integration and Communism." I was amazed to see these billboards in the early seventies, shortly after I moved south.

In March 1972, Ben Chavis was arrested and charged with arson. With Chavis were eight youths between the ages of eighteen and twenty—all black and all leaders in the student movement. The tenth was a white woman, Ann Shepard, a community volunteer working on inner-city problems, and one of the few whites in Wilmington known to side with the Black Liberation movement. The Wilmington Ten were convicted and given combined sentences of 282 years, with Chavis receiving the harshest treatment, a thirty-four-year sentence. The prosecution's star witness was a black youth with a criminal record and a history of mental illness, who physically attacked a defense attorney during the trial.

Prior to his 1972 conviction for arson and conspiracy, Chavis was repeatedly arrested and held in jail on ridiculously high bonds. None of the charges stuck. Sometimes he was dragged into court in leg irons and waist chains. Once his car was firebombed, and he narrowly escaped death. When one of the many cases against Chavis was brought to trial in June 1973, a dynamite blast demolished the office of the *Wilmington Journal*, a well-established newspaper serving the black community, and a bomb blasted a big hole in front of Wilmington's B'nai Israel Temple. The Commission for Racial Justice, the Southern Conference Education Fund, and a newly formed National Alliance against Racist and Political Repression, of which Angela Davis was a cochair, called North Carolina a "laboratory for racism and repression" and sought to bring a national spotlight on the state. The same techniques used against Ben Chavis—the state's use of questionable witnesses, high bail, and severe sentencing—were sweeping off to prison many of Chavis' friends and other black citizens. North Carolina was gaining a reputation for, as Representative Ron Dellums put it, its "calculated attacks against the civil rights movement." Meanwhile, Wilmington Ten prosecutor Jay Stroud was promoted by President Nixon to Assistant U.S. Attorney.

By February 1976, all appeals had failed, and the Wilmington Ten began serving their sentences. Chavis insisted the ten were political prisoners. By the end of 1976, the state's conspiracy started unraveling as several witnesses against Ben Chavis began to recant their trial testimonies. Prosecutor Stroud's main witness denied seeing Chavis teach others how to make Molotov cocktails and admitted that he never heard Chavis, or any of the ten prisoners, plan acts of violence or urge others to violence. The witness said he was coerced by Stroud and other officers and threatened with life imprisonment if he did not cooperate. The defense team was able to document their claim that several witnesses for the prosecution were promised early release from prison in exchange for their testimony.

In May 1977, newly appointed U.S. Attorney General Griffin Bell, under pressure from civil rights groups, called for a Federal Grand Jury hearing of the case. The stories of bribed testimony from the prosecution's side, as well as other exculpating evidence, came out at the hearing. But North Carolina Superior Court Judge George M. Fountain refused to grant the Wilmington Ten a new trial. Around this time, President Carter was fussing about human rights and calling attention to the treatment of political dissidents in the Soviet Union. The Soviet Union turned its propaganda arsenal on the United States, pinpointing the Wilmington Ten case as a violation of human rights.

Legal maneuvers continued since Judge Fountain's decision was subject to appeal. It was up to the Justice Department's civil rights division to evaluate if federal legal action was required. Public opinion widely condemned the persecution of the Ten and the corruption of the judicial system. The case received a lot of international attention, none favorable to the U.S. government. When a federal magistrate ruled against granting the Wilmington Ten a new trial in September 1977, supporters of the Wilmington Ten turned to Governor Hunt.

On January 24, 1978, the day after Hunt announced there would be no pardon for the ten prisoners, Chavis and the other nine held a news conference in Central Prison. Present were reporters from East and West Germany, Great Britain, and Sweden. A news crew from the Soviet Union had come over but was said to have been barred from attending by a U.S. State Department order.

Ben Chavis declared the case of the Wilmington Ten a "racially motivated frameup." "The courts of North Carolina are racist to the bone," he told reporters. Prosecutor Jay Stroud committed a heinous crime not merely against the ten people convicted but against the Constitution. Governor Hunt made it clear that there was no longer any opportunity for North Carolina to treat the case fairly. The Wilmington Ten had been declared "prisoners of conscience" by Amnesty International. Chavis told reporters he had a list of 103 political prisoners in the United States. He announced that a mass rally would be held in Washington in March in support of freedom for the Wilmington Ten. African American attorney James Ferguson told the media that he had filed a writ of habeas corpus in federal court seeking immediate release for the ten prisoners and that he was going to ask the Justice Department to file a "friend of the court" brief in support of the writ.

***

Jim Waller embraced parenthood wholeheartedly. He won Antonia over by listening to her and talking over her problems with her, often surprising me by telling me things I had missed. Shlomo's wit and humor were delightful, but his timidity and fearfulness troubled me. Jim introduced the young boy to sports, taking time to teach and encourage him. Soon Shlomo was riding a bicycle, roller skating, doing karate, swimming, and playing ball, though in none of these activities, it was clear, would he ever be an Olympic contender.

One day at supper, Shlomo told us he was being teased at school. "Honeylumps," I cajoled, "tell us just what happened." It had to do with his classmates making fun of his slowness and taunting him by pronouncing his name "Slomo." Jim was sure it was time to wean Alex from the Hebrew name which, though a perfectly good name and intended by me as a term of endearment, was causing him grief. We all discussed the relative merits of "Alexander," "Sander," "Alex," "Solomon"—his middle name from whence Shlomo had been derived—and "Sol."

"Henceforth you shall be known as Alex," Jim announced officially after we arrived at our consensus. "Not Shlomo, not Honey-lumps—except of course on special occasions and Sundays," he quipped. "Is that okay with you, Alex?" he asked, turning to the boy.

"Alex? Is there an Alex here?" the youngster replied, looking around and responding without missing a beat.

Jim laughed.

"That's fine with me," Alex added, looking relieved and grateful.

Once, around that time, Jim was sitting at his desk writing a summary of his last union meeting when I began rubbing his shoulders and neck.

"Wonderful," he said. "Feels wonderful."

I could tell something was troubling him. "I thought we were making some progress," he said. "The guys are beginning to talk about reopening the union contract, making up a wish list. Charles, Ted, Shorty, Glenn, they've all gotten more involved lately. I thought we could have a real fighting force by May."

"What happened to change your mind?" I asked.

"It's much harder than I thought," Jim said. "I have been remiss in not grasping how deep the racism is. It's really crucial to overcome the racist attitudes of the white workers or we'll get nowhere with the union."

He was bleary-eyed. It was already late morning. Jim should have been in bed sleeping since he worked at night, the third shift. He liked to be at the supper table with me and the children whenever he could manage it. Consequently he got very little sleep and was always running a sleep deficit. I, too, was tired, but at least it was my day off. I would be able to get some press releases out about the upcoming Wilmington Ten rally.

In February 1978, the African Liberation Support Committee formed the North Carolina Coalition to Free the Wilmington Ten. The coconveners were Joyce Johnson of ALSC, Rev. Leon White from the United Church of Christ, and Jean Wagner of the Women's International League for Peace and Freedom.

The previous night, Jim had gone to work an hour early to pass out leaflets to second-shift workers leaving the mill and to the third shift going in. The leaflet was from the recently formed North Carolina Coalition to Free the Wilmington Ten. Jim motioned toward a small stack of flyers on his desk. "Glenn came up to me in the cutting room," he said. "He was real angry. He crumpled up the flyer and threw it on the floor. He asked me why I wanted to defend that bunch of niggers. I struggled with him as much as I could in the brief time we had," Jim continued. "He was on his way to another part of the mill. I told him his racism is just helping the bossman screw over all the workers, black and white. He said I'd got that part right and he wouldn't say they weren't screwing all of us over, royally. I told him those ten people were railroaded because they decided to fight and struggle to be treated like human beings, that whether he thought so or not we all were brothers in the same struggle. 'You're just a nigger lover, Jim'—that was his response." Jim paused and then said, "Oh, he thought to try to scare me a little by telling me he'd discussed this matter of the leaflet with a couple of other guys—I wouldn't be surprised if they and he are Klan—and one of them said, 'Waller better watch his back.' That's it, that's all."

"Are you scared?"

"Hell no!" Jim returned quickly. "They're just blowing off. But this racism dividing the workers is a serious problem. I'm sure I can get Glenn and the others to come around and have a different view. But it will take some work. That's what I was trying to figure out now."

March 7, 1978, was Alex's tenth birthday. It was also the day we chose to celebrate our January marriage. With Joyce officiating—Nelson was out of town—we exchanged meaningful vows. In marrying we had a larger purpose than our own happiness and the care of our family. Our union was based on our shared commitment to serve the people. Our parents were there, Fay and Ted and Sidney, and Jim's sister, Jane. I was ecstatic that the two families, meeting for the first time, got along famously. By early morning, with all the guests gone, Jim lay sprawled across a wing-back chair, sauced. His guitar stood upright against the chair, and he had fallen into a contented doze.

WOKE UP THIS MORNING
WITH MY MIND SET TO FREE THE TEN

"The Wilmington Ten case is not closed," said the press release I sent out for ALSC. "On April 1, 1978, thousands of people will march and rally in Raleigh under the sponsorship of the newly formed North Carolina Coalition to Free the Wilmington Ten." The press statement referred to the Gernie Cummings case. "We have shown the people have the power to organize and to fight injustice. We will continue the same hard fight to get justice for the Wilmington Ten and all political prisoners." We demanded unconditional freedom for the Wilmington Ten and the Charlotte Three.

We asked preachers to make Palm Sunday a "Free-the-Wilmington-Ten-and-Charlotte-Three Sunday" and dedicate their sermons accordingly; college and high school students to mobilize their campuses; and community organizations and trade unions to pass supportive resolutions. We invited all these groups to join us in a *Haunt Hunt* campaign—"Governor Hunt and the power structure he represents should see no peace in our state until the Wilmington Ten and the Charlotte Three are freed," we said. The coalition included the North Carolina Alliance against Racist and Political Repression, main planners of the March 18, 1978, demonstration in Washington, the A. Phillip Randolph Institute of North Carolina, and several North Carolina ministerial alliances. It was powerful.

The "Dr. Martin Luther King Jr., Memorial Day Rally to Free the Wilmington Ten" started with a march from Chavis Park in Raleigh and went through the city's black community. We stopped at the Women's Correctional Center and the governor's mansion before proceeding to a rally in Capitol Square. Gathered in Chavis Park were hundreds of students from North Carolina's A & T State University and people from Whitakers, Durham, Charlotte, Henderson, and other towns and cities across the state. More than three thousand people assembled for the three-mile march. Allen Blitz wired the sound system on a flatbed truck. The spirit and militant air of the marchers was excellent as we set out, walking briskly.

As we passed the women's prison, a voice filled with emotion issued from the sound truck. It was Shirley, speaking out for the first time. She had been incarcerated in that prison, and she talked to the marching crowd about the lives of black women in poverty. From the rear of the march, some North Carolina Central University students started chanting, "Fired Up! Won't take it no more!" Miss Fannie, an elderly black lady from Greensboro, took up the chant at the top of her lungs. Soon we were all chanting "Fired Up!" as we proceeded to Governor Jim Hunt's mansion. The governor was preparing a reception for Democratic Party brass that day. Excitement rose, and the chant changed to "Hunt, you dunce! Free the Ten at once!" We were propelled forward as Paul's voice came from the sound truck—"Justice thundering condemnation." I admired his boldness and self-confidence. Banners and signs aloft, we surged ahead. Jim held a "Free the Charlotte Three" sign as he walked alongside Chekesha and carried on an animated conversation with her.

At the capitol, our ranks swelled with elderly people and others who had been unable to march the route. Parade marshals were around the platform getting things in place for the speeches. We played cat and mouse with the police all day, and they served Allen with a summons about the sound system, to get him to shut it down. People reacted by chanting, "Stop the summons! Stop the summons!" The police tried to hustle Allen away quickly, but dozens of demonstrators followed. Meanwhile, as Nelson tried to find out what was going on, the police began manhandling him. Craig jumped in to protect Nelson. The officers took some swipes at Craig, too. I was nearby when this happened, and I saw Nelson and Craig being surrounded and seized by several police. I walked closer still and joined in the melee, pummeling one of the cops with my fists. He just brushed me aside like a fly and carted off his prey to the police station.

The May Day Singers performed a song that they had prepared for the occasion. It had a tune borrowed from a well-known civil rights song, "I woke up this morning with freedom on my mind." The singing reinforced our solidarity. It was the type of music that invites you to invent verses, and the song became a favorite in North Carolina. We sang it a year and a half later at the fateful anti-Klan rally.

> Woke up this morning with my mind
> Set to free the Ten
> Woke up this morning with my mind
> Set to free the Ten
> Woke up this morning with my mind
> Set to free the Ten
> Free the Ten
> Free the Ten
> Free the Ten
> Right now!

Then:

> North Carolina's organizing,
> Set to free the Ten

Then:

> Governor Hunt can't stop us
> We're set to free the Ten.

Then, "Ku Klux Klan can't stop us; Jimmy Carter can't stop us," and so on.

The program went on. At one point, the crowd was about to march down to the police station to demand the release of the arrested demonstrators when Nelson appeared, to great cheers. It was a relief to see him and hear his richly resonant and booming voice, one hardly in need of amplification.

"Brothers and sisters, today is a *great* day," he roared. He proceeded to tell of the courageous struggle of the Wilmington Ten and the Charlotte Three against racist persecution and a government/police frame-up. He linked the

Wilmington Ten case to other oppressive conditions confronting blacks and poor whites in the schools, the jails, and the workplaces. "Let us remember that the Ten were fighting for quality education. Take up the struggle by joining the Durham Coalition for Quality Education and other community groups fighting against the competency test and against federal plans to abolish black schools." His speech touched on oppression in the textile mills and on the "struggle for freedom in South Africa against the very same enemy that has put the Wilmington Ten in shackles." He concluded that "there *will* be no justice, there *will* be no equality, there *will* be no human rights until the people *refuse* to let them lock up these brothers and this sister on trumped up charges, until we *all* join hands and build a new socialist society, a beautiful society where justice and equality and respect for each human being will reign. We say the way to break the back of this lynch justice in the Black Belt South, the only way to end the suffering of our people, and the *only* solution to the problems of national oppression and worker exploitation is socialist revolution." Thunderous applause, hand clasps, and embraces followed Nelson off the podium.

***

Miss Fannie picked up the fly swatter and wham!—fly met formica. A formica table and several chairs with worn plastic upholstery took up about half the kitchen. When standing at her table, and by pivoting around a half turn, you would be in the correct position to cook something on the gas stove. One step from there was the sink. The table was against a wall on which a few items had been scotch-taped: a bill, a housing authority notice, and two birthday cards with loving messages. I had sent her one of the cards several months before. The other was from Sandi. Lorraine, Rand, Sandi, and I were giving Miss Fannie reading lessons in our spare moments. It was a start. Later she took some informal classes in the community and finally, pushing seventy-five or so, learned to read. I loved sitting in this kitchen. Once I obeyed the order to sit down, I found it hard to leave the smell of chicken frying or the sweet scent of angel cake baking in the oven.

A letter from her grandson in jail had just arrived and was on the table. Next to it was a can of bug spray. Next to the can was an ashtray for guests. Would I read the letter aloud? I did and was interrupted by three children from the Florida Street project knocking loudly on her door. Miss Fannie's place was also a candy store. She did her business—one six-cent purchase and another for a quarter—and hustled the children back outside. I looked at my watch. I hadn't planned enough time on this visit for the letter, for the children, for our chat about mutual friends, although I should have. I had come to tell Miss Fannie about the April 23, 1978, meeting of the Coalition to plan the next stage of the strategy to free the Ten and to arrange her transportation if she wanted to go. I had also come to invite her to go fishing with me, Jim, and our children. Miss Fannie pivoted around to turn her chicken pieces in the frying pan. She said yes to both invitations, and she had a piece of advice about the time of day when fish are biting. We took Miss Fannie fishing in the Dan River in Virginia. I don't remember catching any fish—we apparently got there too late—but we all had a good time anyway.

All the organizing around the Wilmington Ten made North Carolina's bourgeoisie defensive. The Greensboro newspaper had to deny that the Wilmington Ten case was a "glaring example of the machinery of justice being deliberately used to punish civil rights activists,"[7] which of course it was. However, the newspaper also had to acknowledge that "the prosecution did offer gifts and favors to its main witnesses of which jury members were not fully aware" and, further, that "all three main prosecution witnesses have since recanted their testimony." It did not play well in the Cold War to impute political repression to the U.S. government. "There is, of course, no legitimate comparison," the *Greensboro Daily News* insisted, "between the Wilmington 10 case and the recent trials of Soviet dissidents. Alexander Ginzburg and Anatoly Shcharansky were tried, with the full force of the Soviet state against them, for expressing views inimical to the Soviet system of government." But in the U.S. South, anyone struggling against racism was expressing a view that was inimical to the system of government. Whether the state put that person in a mental institution or in jail seems a fine point.

The U.S. Justice Department was forced to review the Wilmington Ten case. Finally, in the middle of November 1978, they announced that the fundamental principles of fairness as mandated by the Constitution had been denied the Wilmington Ten, and they petitioned the District Court in Raleigh to set aside the convictions. The Justice Department's request was filed in a friend-of-the-court brief—the first time the Department had ever filed such a brief in behalf of a defendant in a state case. The Justice Department's intervention on behalf of the Wilmington Ten was a tribute to a people's struggle that finally tipped the scale in favor of justice.

The last of the political prisoners in the group known as the Wilmington Ten was not freed until December 14, 1979, with the release of Ben Chavis from prison. Several weeks later, Ben was leading a march in Greensboro and urging that justice be done in the case of the five anti-Klan activists slain on November 3, 1979.

NOTES

1. See "All Out for African Liberation Day!" *Workers Viewpoint*, June 1977.

2. See "Victory in Whitakers: Struggle Cracks Black Belt South 'Justice,'" *Workers Viewpoint*, November 1977, 18.

3. See Signe Waller, "Reconsidering Race and Nation," in *The American Constitutional Experiment*, ed. David M. Speak and Creighton Peden (New York: Edwin Mellen Press, 1991). My essay was inspired by the theoretical work of Phil Thompson, who addressed the issues in writings and speeches for the WVO in 1976 and subsequent years. See "The Afro-American National Question," vol. 2 (New York: Cesar Cauce Publishers & Distributors, no date, but probably 1982). The concept of national oppression was applied by the WVO to other minorities in the United States, e.g., Asian Americans, Puerto Ricans, and Mexican Americans (Chicanos).

4. "Modern-Day Lynching in Black Belt South: Masses Fight Reactionary Killing," *Workers Viewpoint*, July 1977, 16. (This, like almost all articles in *Workers Viewpoint*, was unsigned.)

5. Greg Lewis, "Groups Rally against Hunt," *Greensboro Daily News*, 5 February 1978, B1.

6. John Hope Franklin, *From Slavery to Freedom: A History of Negro Americans*, 4th ed. (New York: Alfred A. Knopf, 1974), 340.

7. Editorial, *Greensboro Daily News*, 26 July 1978.

7

CONE, YOU OWN THE FACTORIES, BUT US YOU DO NOT OWN

THE WHITE OAK ORGANIZING COMMITTEE

Bill Sampson entered White Oak, Cone's largest mill and the world's leading producer of denim, on June 6, 1977. He was assigned to the dye house, an area that was dirty, dangerous, and unbearably hot. Big Man (a.k.a. Thomas Anderson) and other black workers looked closely at the tall, lean man with wavy blond hair wondering if he would pull his weight on the job. They concluded that he would not last long.[1] Yet within a few months, Bill was leading a rank-and-file movement of black and white workers at White Oak.

Nine years earlier, no one, including Bill, would have imagined Bill in this situation. In 1968 and 1969, when the young Augustana College student spent his junior year in Paris, he kept a diary in which he recorded his thoughts about a future vocation. In turn he considered becoming a minister, a philosopher who would write his magnum opus on morals and ethics, a writer, a psychologist, a lawyer, a politician, and even the president of the United States.[2] Bill might have become any of those things: the world was his. He was beautiful, with regular Nordic features, and quite brilliant, capable of mastering many fields of study. Bill had earned every honor that Augustana College could bestow—Phi Beta Kappa, the junior year scholarship for study in Paris, and graduation summa cum laude. While in France, he learned that he had been elected student body president for his senior year. His year abroad coincided with a time of popular upheaval in much of the Western world that included student rebellions in Paris. Bill absorbed the political scene around him; he went to meetings of different organizations on the left to observe, listen, and learn. He was on the Boulevard St.

Michel at a key moment in late April 1969 when wild revelry in the street greeted news of General Charles De Gaulle's removal from power. Later that night, Bill witnessed waves of students challenging the police and the police clubbing demonstrators in response. Repelled by the United States' role in the Vietnam War, he thought his own country had become "grosser, uglier, and sicker" during his year abroad. Back at the Augustana campus in September 1969, new Student Body President Bill Sampson considered himself a "new left radical."[3]

Now he was filing grievances for spinners, doffers,[4] and other workers at White Oak. As at Revolution and Cone's other mills, there was plenty to object to—job overloads, a lack of safety, and the rude treatment of workers. Before Bill arrived, resistance to oppressive supervisors and rules was spontaneous and uncoordinated. Bill won over his coworkers to another approach. By building a strong union local, workers would be able to fight effectively against the boss man and, ultimately, against the powerful forces backing up all boss men. During the two and a half years that Bill worked at the plant, led the White Oak Organizing Committee (WOOC), and actively worked in ACTWU Local 1391, he taught workers to resist dangerous and unfair practices in an organized and effective manner, personally filing numerous grievances and assisting others through the grievance procedure. Bill's conscientiousness about moral values, reflected in his diary from his student days in Paris, was evident in his relations with other workers: he treated everyone with the utmost respect, listening to and considering their views.

Bill believed the union, as the basic organization of workers, should be run democratically. Once, after an unsuccessful attempt to file a grievance, Bill outlined the lesson in the WOOC newsletter. He wrote on October 7, 1977, "Make sure all workers affected by a grievance are informed about all important details of the grievance before it is filed. Make sure all questions are discussed and answered among the workers before the grievance is filed." The workers won almost every grievance Bill filed or helped others to file.

The third-shift shop steward in the dye house was Big Man, an African American worker with many years in the mill and much valued by other workers. Big Man joined Bill in a job action to stop their supervisor from forcing workers to speed up at the end of the shift. Rand Manzella, a new white worker at Cone, was impressed to learn how every single one of the ten workers in the dye house had marched into their boss's office. But within a week, Cone fired Big Man and another active union shop steward. WOOC tried to win back those jobs.

After firing the two shop stewards, Cone sent the workers a letter. "A small group of radical employees is threatening your job security," they wrote—the company view. They promised that they would take good care of all their employees and provide them with job security. The WOOC newsletter of October 17, 1977, responded swiftly to the company—the workers' view—"If Cone really believes it's only a small group of radicals involved, why did they take the time and money to send out 2,300 letters to all of us?" Cone's claim to take care of its workers rang hollow: they had thrown six hundred workers out on the street when they closed Print Works in June; they were eliminating forty-five jobs at Revolution; pending was a shut down of the warp room at Proximity that would idle another thirty-three workers; and several White Oak workers had been fired who, after being denied permission to leave when they felt too sick to work, left anyway.

Outside the weave room at White Oak, Cone had an engraved sign—*The World's Largest Weave Room*. Inside, as some of the world's hardest working weavers ran the denim cloth, their meals, breaks, and bathroom stops were subordinated to the tyranny of the mighty machine. The weavers were production workers, receiving an hourly wage based on the number of picks a loom would run.[5] It was, therefore, of considerable importance whether the looms malfunctioned or broke down. It was not unusual for mechanics, called fixers, to have two or more machines in need of attention at once. The net result of overextended fixers, frantic supervisors, and the company's tricky rules about downtime pay was that the weavers could not make a decent salary: they were paying for the state of disrepair of the looms. Workers sought to address these and other unfair or hazardous conditions in the mill.

North Carolina was a "Right to Work" state. The Right to Work law—Orwellian in nomenclature—does not mean that everyone needing a job has a right to one. Rather this law is just shy of outlawing unions: it is insidious in allowing legal unions while eviscerating them and assuring they remain more or less nominal and very weak. In a union shop, all permanent workers who receive benefits from the union and union contract must belong to the union and pay dues, but the Right to Work law disempowers workers by making a union shop illegal. Even if a union is elected, workers do not have to join it and pay dues, and, in between contract struggles, the locals tend to fall apart. When Bill came to work at White Oak, the union local had only about thirty members actually paying dues among a workforce of over 2,200. However, White Oak workers who did join Local 1391 had to buck the ACTWU bureaucracy as well as the company. Julius Frye, manager of the ACTWU Joint Board, refused to allow union members full use of the union hall. Consequently union meetings often took place at the downtown public library, at Big Man's home, or wherever else space could be found. As more workers were drawn to participate in union meetings, the official union leadership hardened their attitude toward the active workers. Bill wrote to the president of ACTWU Local 1391, Duffie Burke, on November 8, 1977, in behalf of the WOOC:

> It is clear that the company is making an all-out effort to bust our union. Four shop stewards have been unjustly fired in the last two months. Many of us are subjected to harassment for union activity. . . . For months now the membership of Local 1391 has been denied the right to make decisions concerning our local union by you, the General Shop Committee, and the International representative Frye. Many times this has even been done in violation of our own By-laws. There is a lack of democracy in our union because you have consistently refused to go along with majority decisions.[6]

Just as ACTWU discounted the rank-and-file activity at Revolution by failing to support a union drive there, the union International slighted the already unionized White Oak workers. They prohibited departments with small union membership from electing shop stewards, disregarded an overwhelming vote to take up a fight against a Job Performance Rule, and failed to defend the jobs of shop stewards unjustly fired for union activity.

ZIMBABWE LIBERATION DAY

ALSC celebrated November 12, 1977, as a day of solidarity with the people of Zimbabwe—then still known to the world as Rhodesia. In Greensboro, we marched from Windsor Center, past Morningside Homes and A & T State University, and held a rally in the parking lot of the small shopping center, outside of Cosmos I. On October 19, 1977, ALSC had arranged for Tirivafi Kangai, who represented the Zimbabwe African National Union (ZANU) in the United Nations, to speak at A & T State University. The ZANU independence fighters already controlled about one-third of Rhodesia. Kangai appealed for badly needed clothing and medical supplies for the liberation forces.

On November 12, 1965, the United Nations condemned the Universal Declaration of Independence of the Ian Smith regime in Rhodesia and called it an illegal government. The United Nations later called on all countries to stop trading with the apartheid Smith regime—a quarter of a million white settlers exercising fascistic rule over more than six million black Africans. But, in 1971, the U.S. Senate passed the Byrd Amendment, permitting U.S. corporations to continue importing Rhodesian chrome in violation of international sanctions. South Africa was used as a conduit for U.S. investments in Rhodesia. ALSC was proud of the fact that in 1973 and 1974, in an act of international solidarity, it had led longshoremen in Baltimore, Boston, and Louisiana to refuse to unload chrome from the outlawed state.

As part of the Zimbabwe Liberation Day campaign, we picketed in front of the North Carolina National Bank (NCNB)—a supporter of apartheid through its loans—and rallied and leafleted at Claremont Court and other housing projects, drawing in tenant councils and youth at those places. I went to Claremont, talked to people, helped produce flyers, and scheduled radio and TV time for our organizers. I thought that since I worked in a hospital, I should contribute to the medical aid drive for refugees.

The first shift at Cone Hospital got off at 3:00 P.M. Several times, after leaving work, I went to Greensboro's medical establishment, still wearing my white hospital jacket, to beg medicines and medical supplies for Southern Africa. The usual donations were outdated medicines and samples. I also went through the hospital, keeping my eyes and ears open for potential donations. I came up with what I thought was a prize—an operating table. It was no easy matter to arrange for this table's removal from the hospital or to find places to store it while in transit. Like an indigent relative, the table occupied several people's living areas before it ended up, I hope, on another continent. (I later learned that an operating table, because it is bulky and expensive to ship, might create more problems than it would solve. Though useful, it is something that can be much more easily improvised, even in rural conditions, than, say, an X-ray machine.)

A kindly physician, the husband of a lady I knew from the peace movement, agreed to keep the table in his Greensboro home until it could be sent to Durham to the Committee for Medical Aid to Southern Africa, headed by Dr. Michael Nathan. Mike and others sent tens of thousands of dollars in medical supplies to the liberation fighters in Southern Africa. At the time I had heard about the fine work Mike was doing in gathering substantial supplies but had yet to meet Mike or his wife, Marty.

The Greensboro doctor who was storing the operating table invited me to go with him to a professional meeting where, he told me, I could make a short pitch for more aid. I sat by his side at a large banquet table on the stage. However my reputation had preceded me. Naively, I was caught off guard when a doctor in the audience stood up, almost before I opened my mouth, to strenuously denounce me with a red-baiting tirade about the international communist menace and how I'd been sent by Russia. Perhaps I made some verbal response that evening; my best recollection is that I stood there dumbfounded.

My host was embarrassed. I felt bad for him and also felt privately humiliated. At a subsequent ALSC meeting, I mentioned the incident, but no one seemed to attach any importance to it. The fact is that a lot was going on inside me at the time that wasn't *supposed to* be part of the profile of a real working-class revolutionary. In matters of politics and love, I was terribly insecure. Why was I left to deal with a bunch of professional, petty-bourgeois gentlemen? *If only I were more proletarian*, I thought, *I would have responsibility for more important tasks with workers and community people.* Some of my comrades with an aura of proletarianism about them had backgrounds similar to mine, but they had apparently escaped bourgeoisification to the same degree as myself. In retrospect, my thinking at the time reflected political immaturity. In that, I was not alone, but I also think we did not do too badly, despite mistakes, excesses, and immature ways of thinking.

On November 12, I left the Zimbabwe demonstration early to visit with Jim at Cone Hospital, where he had just undergone a hernia operation. A day or so later, when he was discharged, he insisted on walking home, and I went to the hospital to accompany him on the two-mile walk back to Cypress Street. A few months later, he had to have a second hernia repair operation. He used his sick leave to go to Haw River on a cold winter morning in order to open up the union hall and meet with other workers. Jim rarely made any concessions to his state of health. Even in our circle of dedicated revolutionaries where expectations of selflessness ran high, Jim was awe-inspiring.

A RENAISSANCE OF WORKING-CLASS AND GRASSROOTS ACTIVITY

In 1978, strikes both great and small indicated a rising consciousness of the working class. The militancy of 160,000 miners in Appalachia outstripped that of their union leadership in the longest strike in the history of the United Mine Workers of America. During the strike's course, President Carter invoked the Taft–Hartley Act[7] against the miners as they struggled to hold on to gains they had fought for and won in preceding decades. The miners beat back the "stability" clause—designed to allow mine owners to get rid of rank-and-file leaders and thus to weaken the workers' fighting ability—through two attempts by the mine operators and the Carter administration to foist it on them in contract negotiations.

The lesson Workers Viewpoint drew from the miners' strike was that an economic struggle could become more political in character as it progressed. WV viewed the miners as an example to the entire labor movement and approvingly quoted one miner: "I have defied the operators and the union. Now I'm going to defy the President of the United States." Once the government intervened, the labor leaders were forced to respond by coming to the aid of the miners. Autoworkers, steelworkers, and others sent financial support. Farmers ran tractor motorcades through the streets of Washington, D.C., and state capitals across the country in support of the miners. They were demanding 100 percent parity between the cost of producing crops and the income from crops. A mile-long caravan of farmers gathered at Central City, Kentucky, bearing sacks of potatoes and flour and messages of solidarity with the miners.

When Jim and Bill conducted their Marxist study groups, went to union meetings, or talked to other textile workers, a central area of discussion was what the miners' struggle meant for textile workers in the South. Meeting in Florida in March 1978, ACTWU resolved to call upon the southern textile industry to meet its obligation by raising workers' wages substantially and improving fringe benefits. The WVO rank-and-file leaders at the Cone plants wanted some muscle to throw at the industry in case it refused to meet its obligation. To prepare for the coming contract negotiations with Cone, Jim and Bill asked workers what specific demands they wanted to raise.

Workers at the nearby Eno plant, a small corduroy factory owned by Cone, were trying to establish an ACTWU local. Their union drive was supported and encouraged by the White Oak and Granite Finishing locals. On May 14, 1978, a rally was held in Hillsborough as organizers prepared for the union vote. Jim was one of the invited speakers and WOOC also sent a representative. The *Alamance-Orange Enterprise* of May 17, 1978, had a photo of Tom Clark with his guitar leading the gathering in "Solidarity Forever." A few days later, Cone was able to defeat the union campaign by three votes.

In the process of building solidarity and unity in the workers' movement, WVO members resolutely confronted workers' racist attitudes. Throughout the spring and summer of 1978, black and white textile workers were struggling together against their common economic exploitation. That material fact helped to overcome long-standing racist attitudes of some white workers. I accompanied Jim one day to a trailer that housed Ted, a young white textile worker, and his wife and infant son. Ted seemed open to abandoning the racist attitudes of white society, and he wanted to be part of the Wilmington Ten rally. Before that rally, a flyer in support of the Wilmington Ten had evoked a racist response from Glenn and some other Granite workers. After the powerful Raleigh demonstration in April, it no longer looked so smart to be racist. With patience and persistence, Jim talked to many Granite workers. Glenn, who had called Jim a "nigger-lover," began to change his outlook. After a time, he invited Jim and me to a family barbecue, where we had a good time and socialized as friends. I cannot say whether there was subsequent backsliding on the part of some individuals, but at the time we were encouraged and felt that progress was made against racist attitudes.

On May 4, 1978, five active ACTWU locals, including White Oak, presented their wage demands to Cone. WOOC had polled White Oak workers and found out that almost all favored a raise of at least 15 percent. More than half of those responding to the Organizing Committee's survey reported that more work had been added to their jobs in the past year. All ACTWU locals agreed to ask for a 16.6 percent wage increase—a 6.6 percent cost-of-living increase plus a 10 percent raise. Other demands addressed paid holidays, medical coverage, and the pension. Bill pointed out that two top Cone executives each received $262,500 a year, more than most Cone workers made in a lifetime. President Carter helped Cone by declaring that wage increases should be kept below the cost of living.

While awaiting Cone's counteroffer, members of White Oak Local 1391 sent an open letter to Mr. Cone. "We know by the last financial report that the company is making quite a profit, even though the economy looks pretty bad at this time."[8] Workers reminded the company "that we have an ace or two up our sleeves. . . . If we do not accept your final offer on wages and benefits within the next few weeks, we have the full right to strike, walk out of particular departments, slow down, walk off, pull a sick-in, etc. (according to the Union contract with Cone Mills, White Oak Plant, Section XIII, pages 40–41)." In mid-June, Cone came in with an offer of an 8 percent wage increase, a 50 percent pension increase, and no increase in paid holidays or health benefits. Cone would indeed have to contend with a strike, but not at White Oak.

In 1978, the dormant union movement in the South was awakening. In Greensboro, the Revolution Organizing Committee (ROC) was trying to get back the jobs of workers fired for their efforts to organize a union, and the ACTWU was at last *saying* it would give its official blessings to the union drive. In Durham, the Duke Workers Organizing Committee was making a comeback.

North Carolina was in the mood to strike. Auto mechanics at Traders Chevrolet in Greensboro from Operating Engineers Local 465 went on strike in the spring and summer of 1978. After nearly a year of meetings, the company failed to negotiate a contract with the union and was trying to enforce wage cuts. WVO supporters helped staff their strike committee and marched on their picket line. The car dealership was just a few blocks from our house, and Jim and I took our exercise in the lovely spring weather by walking up and down the picket line. Often, Bill, Sandi, Sally Ann, Dori, Allen, Rand, and other friends were already there, walking the line in support of the auto mechanics.

Poultry workers struck in Durham at Goldkist, one of the city's worst sweatshops. They were helped by César Cauce and other WVO supporters. In Morehead City and Wilmington, the International Longshoremen Association, Locals 1850 and 1426A, went out on strike. The Longshoremen opposed the state's Right to Work law and demanded dues check-off—the automatic deduction of union dues from workers' paychecks to insure the locals' solvency. And, very significantly, in terms of worker militancy, there was the strike at Cone's Granite Finishing Plant in Haw River, discussed below, that Jim Waller led in July 1978.

Several union locals in the area sent representatives to meetings of the Trade Union Educational League (TUEL), an organization newly founded by WVO supporters involved in labor organizing. TUEL got support from community organizations, and TUEL gave support to those who were challenging the competency test, calling the test a "knife in labor's back." As the strike wave of 1978 washed over North Carolina, union locals came to each other's mutual aid.

At White Oak, Cone tried very hard to get rid of Bill Sampson, and Bill fought Cone like crazy. As the union steward for the card room,[9] Bill filed grievance after grievance, helping workers resist Cone's attempt to overload their jobs or speed them up. On August 30, 1978, in the morning, fifteen card tenders went into the overseer's office with their steward, Bill, to file a work overload grievance and prevent doffing from being added to their jobs. The overseer ordered all the tenders except Bill to leave. Bill protested that this action was a violation of the union's grievance procedure. The next day the overseer gathered all of the card tenders *except Bill* and told them about the work being added to their jobs. When Bill caught up with the meeting, the overseer ordered him out. Bill replied that it was his duty as shop steward to remain in the meeting and that the contract backed him up, at which point the overseer suspended him. Bill was ordered to leave the plant, but he refused, saying he had violated neither the contract nor any plant rules and meant to continue working. The overseer called the police and Bill was arrested for trespassing. When his case went to trial in October, the district court judge threw it out of court. Back in the mill, Bill picked up the fight against work overload right where he left off.

The key to the victory in court against Cone Mills, "with its stable of high-paid lawyers and its political pull in Greensboro," stated an October 20, 1978, WOOC newsletter, was that "one hundred percent of the card tenders involved stood firmly together behind their shop steward and maintained they wanted him in that meeting as shop steward. . . . They upheld the principle 'United we stand, divided we fall.'" WOOC fought for all the workers in the plant, union and nonunion alike. Cone eventually had to hire back some of the union supporters they had fired. Shop steward Rand Manzella went back to the mill with full backpay for the three months he'd been out and with full seniority and benefits. Rand attributed that to the unity and fighting spirit of the workers who supported him.

Jim and Bill tried to insure that all the departments in Cone's unionized plants elected shop stewards, that the stewards were trained to be good worker representatives, and that workers knew who represented them. I typed a long manual used to prepare shop stewards to carry out their functions. We did not have to reinvent the wheel: the stewards' manual was compiled from a standard AFL-CIO booklet in use for many years.

The trespassing arrest was not all Bill endured at Cone Mills. One day he was injured when machinery malfunctioned, snatched him up, and dangled him precariously over the machine works. He was alone when it happened, but owing to the entry and quick thinking of another worker, who quickly stopped the line and extricated him, Bill got away with only minor bruises. With mere suspicions but no evidence, neither Bill nor anyone I spoke to about this was willing to say that the incident was contrived and malicious, rather than merely an accident. Malfunctioning machinery and accidents, even horrible ones, were not uncommon in the textile industry.

Carelessness about health and safety by the company was demonstrated dramatically in the middle of 1979 when a chemical fire broke out in the dye house near the boilers. A WOOC newsletter of July 26, 1979, described it this way: "dangerous chemical fumes started to spread. The fire department came out. A fireman said to stay back from the doors. Meanwhile several workers in the Finishing room started throwing up from breathing the fumes. Naturally, many of these workers wanted to go home. The fireman suggested evacuating the whole area. But the supervisor . . . said 'If you value your job you better get back to work!' He refused to let people off, accusing folks of just wanting to be off because it was Saturday. The fireman was heard saying, 'This is the poorest supervision I've ever seen anywhere.'"

In the summer of 1979, one of Bill's brothers was dying of testicular cancer. That rare form of cancer is associated with radiation poisoning. Bill felt certain that the cancer arose from his brother's prenatal radiation exposure when both his parents worked at Oak Ridge doing atomic research. (At the time the government assured workers they had nothing to worry about.) In any case, although Bill received Cone's permission to leave the plant and visit his brother, Cone tried to fire him when he returned to work.

TRUE LOVE AND CLASS STRUGGLE

"Are you ready to go?" Jim asked.

"I am, but I forgot the camera," I answered, dashing back into the house.

"What do you need a camera for? We're going to pick tobacco."

"I want to take pictures of everyone, all your friends," I replied.

"Oh," Jim moaned, "do you really think that's a good idea?"

"Well, why not?" I was already rummaging around my solid oak desk, as big as a piano. Camera in hand, I was back out the door. "Why not?" I repeated.

"It might be embarrassing to have you standing around taking pictures. We'll look like a couple of tourists. I work with these guys."

I had the camera over my shoulder as we walked toward the car. I assured Jim that I would only take pictures if doing so met with everyone's approval, and he let the matter drop. Later he said he was glad that we had several pictures of the tobacco harvest. The farmers, his buddies at the mill on third shift, all wanted copies.

Many families in North Carolina at the time had small farms. They couldn't make it on mill wages or by farming alone. They constituted a "semiproletariat" with one foot in agriculture and the other in industry. We spent the better part of that day in the rural outskirts of Mebane. After two hours, my back was burning from stooping to pick tobacco leaves. Others were halfway down their rows when I had progressed only a few feet. The large, floppy elephantine tobacco leaves, already turning yellowish-brown, were packed at least three feet high atop flatbed trailers for removal to the barn for curing.

Jim and I were invited to share a supper of beans cooked in fatback until limp, biscuits, meat and gravy, slaw and corn. This occasion, in the fall of 1977, was not the first time Jim volunteered to help someone bring in the harvest or do building construction. He took the opportunity to socialize, talk union and politics while helping: moreover, Jim relished hard work. A coworker of his (whose name I have forgotten and will call Pete) stood slouched against a porch rail smoking and expounding his views to Blackbeard, as Jim was fondly called. They were talking about Ken Crawford's recent injury in the cutting department. Pete was saying that it was a terrible thing, but it might light a fire under the union president, an old African American worker who did little or nothing to build the union. They talked about the last union meeting and what they might do next.

One of the men called Jim aside. He was one of the few who knew about Jim's medical background, and he wanted to discuss a problem in the family involving a baby born with a serious birth defect. Jim later consulted with the baby's family over the phone and even visited them and examined the infant. When I heard and saw Jim helping others in these ways, the love I felt for him welled up in me mightily.

We were not yet married when we helped harvest tobacco. We were falling more and more deeply in love. We were not perfect. We fought, and the courtship had its rocky moments. I had been to Chicago to meet Jim's father, Sidney, during the summer before the harvest. Since I met Jim, I had experienced magical things.

In the late spring of 1977, shortly before we went to Chicago, we became lovers. Before that, a self-conscious touch on the shoulder or arm was all we permitted ourselves. Before we slept together, we had a serious discussion about it. We wanted to know what our respective hopes were, and how this relationship, once cemented, would serve the class struggle. We spoke about it just that way. The personal and political were intertwined; for us it could not be otherwise. I remember we sat at my kitchen table, discussing the topic that was on our minds. Present but invisible were our hormones, entities with a definite stake in the outcome of our decision. "Are you quite finished now?" they whispered insistently, as we pretended not to notice. Their annoyance dissolved immediately in a burst of gladness as two bodies, having united their minds and souls, flowed into the next room to consummate the approved union.

After he was killed, I remembered the look of love that streamed from Jim's eyes the first time we made love. *So this is what it is really about*, I had thought right afterward: *It is about the magic that someone who knows how to love creates with his being. If I live through a hundred winters, I will never forget the look of love.*

In early fall of 1977, I brought Jim to Latham Park and told him the story of the flood. It was still warm as we lay beside one another in the grass. He told me many things. I don't know how long we lie there, for we both lost track of time. Maybe we had been there for years, talking in the fading sun. Everything around us simply stopped. Then, in a perfectly natural way, there came a moment when the world returned, and we both knew it was time to get up and go on. We remarked to one another how interesting it was that time could stand perfectly still for those in a relationship with magic in it. To accommodate us, our stories, our gazing deeply into each other's eyes, time had slowed down to a lazy crawl and then receded altogether. We were in a timeless space that only true lovers know.

WE ARE MET ON A GREAT BATTLEFIELD

By the fall of 1977, Jim had been at Granite Finishing for more than a year. He went from being an oddity to a leader in the mill. In mid-August 1977, a worker, Ken Crawford, was seriously injured on the job while handling, lifting, and flipping heavy bolts of cloth. This was the injury discussed a few weeks later at the tobacco harvest. Crawford required an operation and a long period of recovery, but Cone denied him workman's compensation even though his injury occurred while he was doing what his job required—flipping heavy bundles of cloth onto a flat truck. Jim investigated the history of the incident and wrote this flyer that circulated to Granite Finishing workers in August 1977:

> About a year ago the cutters were able to avoid flipping the cloth by running it onto a flat truck. But after 6 months of this the company took the trucks away, saying they didn't have enough to go around. This is nonsense! . . .
>
> There are many cutters who have been hurt flipping cloth, but the company says there is nothing they can do about it. This is the same attitude they had last year when a man in the warehouse complained his crane wasn't working. Since they were planning to tear the crane down in a few days, they told him to run it anyway. The next day the cable slipped and he fell, crushing both ankles. This is the same attitude that resulted in motor lifts having bad brakes and leaking oil over the floor, why the air in the dye house is hard to breathe, why there are fires in Preparation, why we sweat in 110 degree temperatures. There are many examples of bad safety conditions, all of which point to why we need to get together and fight—we need to build up our union!
>
> What is the cause of the accidents? The company keeps telling us that . . . we just come in and "carelessly" rupture ourselves and crush our ankles. They give us $25 a month for the best safety slogan, promise us a safety dinner, and have even formed a token safety committee. What hypocrites!!! Why don't they get more trucks, fix the machinery, improve the ventilation?
>
> *The truth is that the company cares more about their profits than the health and safety of the workers.* . . . They use us like any other tool—when we rust or break they throw us away for another.
>
> We don't know which of us will be hurt next. It's our unity and our organization which is our source of strength. . . . We need to fight every abuse workers in the mill suffer. We need a strong organization—OUR UNION! Through building a strong, democratically controlled union we can fight for a decent contract, better wages and working conditions. . . . We can fight against wage cuts and speed ups. *COME TO THE UNION MEETING SATURDAY, AUGUST 27, AT 3:00 PM.* Let's help KEN. Let's deal with health and safety questions as well as other problems in the plant.

The cutting room workers took around a petition demanding the return of the trucks, an end to having to flip cloth, and full compensation for the injured cutter. Jim led workers through the grievance process and, in a leaflet dated September 7, 1977, reported on the results. Nearly every worker in the cutting department signed the petition. Eight workers took the petition to management and were told by the plant manager that workers could have the trucks if they wanted them but that they would still have to flip the cloth (as opposed to running it right onto the truck). The reason he gave for continuing the injurious practice was that flipping the cloth improved its quality. Not only would those who were already flipping cloth have to continue, but other workers running sixty-inch cloth who hadn't been required to flip it in the past two years would now be required to do so, too. Once again, a group of workers marched into the plant manager's office to express their ire at the new plan. Management came up with a thirty-day trial period to "see how it works out." They want "to wear us down and make us give up," Jim warned.

Although most of the workers were of a mind to fight the company on the issue, a few cutters started fighting among themselves and blamed other workers for stirring up trouble. In the same September 7 flyer, Jim said that Cone wanted to divide the workers, just as they try "to split blacks and whites, union and non-union, young and old. . . . The cutters who run 60-inch cloth put their jobs on the line so no one should have to flip cloth! That was correct! All workers should stand together. That's how we are strong, and that's how we will win better working conditions!" He added that "the company's retaliation is an admission of our strength. If we get together and are clear on this issue, they haven't got a chance. Their only hope is to keep us divided and confused."

Jim helped workers file grievances whenever situations arose demanding it. Workers took the company to task for the defective trucks used to move the cloth in the cutting department. Some of the trucks had wheels that wouldn't turn, thus forcing the workers to drag heavy loads that put undue strain on their backs and legs. Each grievance Jim filed was precise in stating the details of the situation, the section of the union contract that it violated, and what was needed to resolve it. Workers also fought the company's attempt to reduce its labor costs by eliminating some positions and padding the job descriptions of remaining workers.

The union locals had begun negotiating wages with Cone in mid-March 1978. No agreement about wages was reached in the sixty-day period set aside for this part of the negotiation process. Meanwhile, in the warehouse another faulty crane cable snapped and put another worker in the hospital with multiple breaks in his leg and back. It was the third time in a year and a half that a worker has been seriously injured on a crane, and there were many near misses. More demands issued from the Granite workers to help insure workers' safety around the crane.

In the spring of 1978, Cone hired an industrial engineer to do production studies at Granite Finishing. Workers at that plant were familiar with the wage cuts—euphemistically called "wage adjustments" by Cone—that typically followed these production studies. On Sunday, June 25, 1978, there was a special union meeting. Workers were ready to take action for, indeed, their pay was being cut. Earlier that week, cutters staged a work slowdown that led to a walkout. The slowdown and walkout by the cutters soon led to a strike throughout the mill. The union hall stayed open. Jim, now a shop steward, practically lived there. He focused on signing up workers to the union.

The union is the workers' weapon against the companies. However, the Right to Work law, combined with other conditions of the workers in the South, made the few unions that existed practically ineffectual. Every fight had to begin and end with a fight to hone the main instrument in the workers' arsenal. Beyond the engagement of the moment, workers needed the ability to sustain a struggle through their organization, and so the fundamental task was to build and consolidate the workers' organization for the long haul. How well that task was done gave the true yardstick for success.

It is one thing to talk about war, another to be at war. *ON STRIKE!* announced ACTWU Local 1113 T at Cone Mills Granite Finishing Plant in Haw River, North Carolina. It was official, at least as far as the Haw River local was concerned, by June 29, 1978. Within a day or so of that date, the strike committee circulated a flyer that stated, "If Cone can cut the cutters' pay, they can cut everyone's pay next. We are on strike to demand an end to these starvation wages." The workers listed their demands:

16.6% pay increase
Three more paid holidays
100% paid medical insurance
$5 per year worked/per month pension
No more pay cuts

The other Cone plants, including White Oak, accepted the company's offer of an 8 percent pay raise, one more paid holiday—Thanksgiving—and a tiny bit more money in the pension plan. It's not enough, Bill told his fellow workers, but it's the best we can do right now. We will build up our union so that we can fight for something better next time.

In the little town of Haw River, by the mill, a crude, home-made sign was planted in the road across from the union hall. *The workers united will never be defeated* scrawled on weathered cardboard and attached to a three-foot picket stick remained in the road a long time. It thrilled me to see it each time I drove to Haw River to be a part of the strike support effort.

Two years later, a white worker, Charles Reaves, one of the Haw River strikers, vividly recalled the conditions in the mill, the workers' feelings, and Blackbeard's role in preparing for and leading the strike.

> What I remember, it was May of '78. Inflation was hittin' us hard, and all the mills around were getting a raise, and it was time we're gettin' a raise, and they post it on the board—pay cuts! Oh Lord. Everybody lookin' for a raise, they come up with pay cuts.
>
> So Jim was down there, and he had been doin' a lot of union work, tryin' to build the union up. So we went to talk to him about this pay cut. And he said the onliest way we could stop it was strike. At first we were on a work slowdown, and that just tore 'em up. We wouldn't do nothin'; I bet they weren't gettin' a third of the cloth they'd been gettin'. Wouldn't nobody work, wouldn't nobody listen to his supervisor, to the plant manager. The whole third shift would go outside and sleep, maybe a couple of hours, you know, just have a good time. We weren't makin' no money, but we was havin' a good time. And we were on strike. We'd just gather around him, and he kinda told each one what we needed to do and how to do it. And he didn't get up and do it hisself. He just told us how we should do it, and we just took the ball and run with it. He didn't want no glory out of it, he was just showin' us how, trainin' us, in other words, how we could do this thing on our own. So everybody gathered at the gates—first strike I'd ever been in, and I didn't know what to expect.
>
> We had the thing goin' pretty good until they come out with this injunction. We was on the sidewalk protesting with a sign and here comes highway patrolmen and sheriffs and deputies and says, "We understand what y'all fightin' for, but y'all can't be on the side of the highway like this. If somebody has an accident y'all gonna be to blame. I'm gonna have to lock all of ya up." So that didn't work. We went back down to the union hall. We talked and discussed everything.[10]

The North Carolina Trade Union Education League (TUEL) helped the strikers form a Granite Strike Relief Committee. Sally Bermanzohn, then leader of TUEL, gathered information about food stamps, how to defer payments of utility bills, and other tips to help the strikers. Into the dirty, musty, turn-of-the-century Haw River union hall, Sally went nearly every day of the strike to personally assist in the filling out of forms preliminary to receiving what meager help was available. She arrived laden with infant paraphernalia for her daughter Leola, a few months old, and she plunked Leola's portable playpen with toys on the wooden floor. The infant's vocal prowess soon became legendary but did not altogether drown out strike support efforts. Sally and another WVO member from North Carolina worked closely with Jim. They constantly analyzed new developments and consulted with the strikers.

The strike went on for twelve days. It was an unforgettable experience for many workers, not because wage and other demands were met—they were not—but because of the gain in human dignity. Like my love affair with Jim, here, too, was magic—the magic of breaking out of an oppressive mold, standing in sunlight, grasping for the first time that the bars that seemed to stand between you and your destiny were never there, and that your destiny has been in your strong hands, in your heart, and in your mind all along. "Today we are met on a great battlefield which involves the people and the company," wrote a worker in the log book kept by the strikers in the summer of 1978.

Much that happened, in hindsight, seems predictable: there were few surprises in this never officially authorized or wildcat strike. Cone got a court injunction restricting the number of picketing strikers to two at each gate and making it illegal to park where strikers would need to park their cars. The sheriff assisted Cone by putting some strikers in jail for overstepping a line in the road or blowing a whistle. Someone ran a car almost into the picket line, even grazing a striker. Outside the union hall, Brunswick stew was served to raise strike funds, while speeches and words of encouragement came from other union locals to buoy the strikers' spirits. Cone sent a letter to workers on strike in an effort to woo them, and a rumor circulated that the strike was over when it was not—it was announced on the radio—and then another false rumor circulated that it was only the cutters who were on strike.

When the strike started, ACTWU negotiator Julius Frye was on summer vacation, and as we later learned, the union big-wig happened to be taking his vacation at the same time and on the same Caribbean island as company big-wig Red Leonard.

Jim and I had been married only five months at the beginning of the Granite strike. During that time, we succumbed to the stresses in our lives more than once. At the end of June, our marriage was challenged. Jim hardly had a chance to be at home and was exhausted all the time from meetings. I was on a swing shift at the hospital, and my schedule, working from seven in the morning to three in the afternoon for half the week and from eleven at night to seven in the morning the other half of the week, was making me crazy. I nearly self-destructed. One night I became hysterical while Jim was meeting in his upstairs study with Chekesha's husband and went screaming through the house. When Jim and I finally had a few minutes to take a walk and talk to one another, things seemed so bad that we both acknowledged that we were probably headed for divorce. I remember feeling that both options, continuing to live with Jim and divorcing him, were equally inconceivable to me. During the week of the slowdown that preceded the strike, Jim's full attention was on the mounting crisis at work. The first night that pickets were out in force, June 30, was like a glorious premier—and I missed it. I don't remember if I had to work that night or if I just couldn't bring myself to go. I went the next night.

The front of the mill was swarming with strikers and their supporters, since the injunction limiting the pickets to two had not yet been granted. It was very exciting. Workers, black and white, marched together; by their side were many WVO supporters from Durham, Greensboro, and the surrounding area. I recall Jim teasing me for wearing a frilly cotton sundress that left my shoulders bare. Other pickets were in T-shirts and blue jeans or shorts. I was conspicuously overdressed and looked like I might have been on my way to a garden party. When, two years after the strike and after Jim and the others were assassinated, I was arrested for disrupting a city council meeting, I had on that same sundress. I spent several days in jail feeling half naked and horribly chilled, having, once again, failed to dress for the occasion.

A series of strike bulletins were issued during the brief workers' revolt. On July 11, 1978, Strike Bulletin #3 of ACTWU Local 1113 T read: "Fellow workers, we need to continue to stick together. Those who have been going to work need to give this matter serious thought. As long as a few people dribble in steadily, Cone will continue to hold out and offer us nothing new. But if we stay out and even more workers become strikers, we can force Cone to negotiate a much more favorable contract which will insure a better living standard for all of us and our families."

Cone was hurt by the strike. The warehouse with finished cloth was emptied, as there was no one left in the plant to cut the grooves in the corduroy and re-stock it. The warehouses with uncut cloth became full. Some strikers observed that Cone had turned away tractor-trailers of uncut cloth for a lack of storage space. Nevertheless, against Cone, the workers were toddlers facing a titan. The corporation had daunting power and no scruples to restrain its use.

Inevitably the dehumanizing aspects of class warfare entered the strike: people tend to be reduced to icons representing a class, to bloodless abstractions. Early on, a few workers scabbed on the strike. This could have been anticipated in light of how unions had to fight so hard in the South just to exist. However one instance of scabbing was especially upsetting to us. Preston, a Granite worker at the time, was the boyfriend of Crystal Lee, and Crystal Lee was the real-life heroine of the J. P. Stevens' strike, as immortalized in the movie *Norma Rae*. Jim considered Crystal to be his friend. They had spent time together going over some *Workers Viewpoint* articles. Jim had invited her to the trade union conference in Chicago the year before the Granite strike, and Crystal considered going but could not get away from her family. When Jim talked to me about Crystal, it was usually to comment sympathetically about how her personal life was dragging her down and preventing her from being a more effective fighter for the working class. I think he idealized her as the proletarian heroine par excellence and was unable to appreciate who she really was and where she was politically. On a few occasions, we had socialized with Crystal and Preston. We went to a dinner club together once, and they attended our wedding celebration a few months before the strike. I had loaned Preston a small handgun I owned, a .38 caliber pistol. He said that he needed it because Crystal's personal entanglements from her failed marriage posed some danger to the couple. When Preston walked back into the mill as a strikebreaker, apparently with Crystal's full approval, we were shocked. As I now recall, Jim's efforts to discuss matters with Crystal were rebuffed.

When the dribble back to work by workers with scant economic reserves threatened to become a flow, Jim called the workers together. They discussed ending the strike, and Jim argued passionately that this was the right decision to make under the circumstances. With increasing numbers of workers beginning to drift back to the plant, some hard feelings were developing among people on one side or the other. Jim was afraid that prolonging the strike in the face of this drift could result in destroying all that they had worked for. True, they did not get their 16.6 percent pay raise, or their 100 percent paid medical insurance, or other things they had asked for, but it was time to make an orderly retreat with the idea of fighting another day when they would be better prepared and better organized. If they stayed out one more week, they risked shattering the strength of the union. The union was the real winner in this whole struggle. The last two strikes, in 1951 and in 1964, almost destroyed the union, Jim pointed out. This strike raised union membership from about forty to nearly two hundred workers. There were two objectives in striking, he said. First "there are our demands, and it looks like there we have to give in. But the most important objective has been achieved—a long-term building of the union and its strength. We were successful in that."

Jim urged all of the workers to remain active and to keep building up the local. In a year they could be in a stronger position than ever. If they walked back in the plant tomorrow, united as one body, he said, they could all hold their heads high. They were neither defeated nor broken. "Retreat," he counseled, "but do not surrender." This was voted on and most agreed with Jim. The workers voted to accept Cone's wage offer. Not exactly jubilant but very far from crushed, the striking workers returned—united, heads held high. A couple of weeks later, they elected Jim Waller vice president of their union local.

Cone had helped to provide a fringe benefit of which they were probably not aware: the tide of racism receded. Working together during the strike to build the union democratically had a salutary effect on the workers. Looking back at that time, Jim's friend and fellow striker Charles Reaves remarked:

> Up there at the mill . . . blacks and whites wasn't near as close as they are. When we'd go to eat, the blacks would go over to one side and we'd go over to the other side. And now, after the strike and everything, everybody just sort of mixes it up and nobody tries to act better than the next guy. Jim made people see that we was actually workin' for nothing. And the man at the top was gettin' it all. Main thing about him, it looked like everything he'd say would come true. I don't know whether he could see the future . . . it seemed like every time he'd tell me something, whether I believed it or not, that's the way it would happen.[11]

By going back when and how they did, with their local intact, the workers were able to extract some promises from Cone. "The Company agrees that all employees will return to their respective jobs and shifts without reprisal," said a Memorandum of Agreement, signed on July 10, 1978, by Leonard for the Company and Frye (now back from vacation) for ACTWU. At the end of July, Cone closed all its plants for the customary week of summer vacation. Jim, Tonya, Alex, and I went to the Outer Banks of North Carolina.

The vacation week was filled with the comings and goings of many close friends including Bill and Dale. There was Tonya's adolescent rebellion, expressed in tantrums and in poetry, and there were some sweet moments of family togetherness and respite. Jim's mood was very heavy. He tried hard not to appear weighted down, but really he was, and it showed. When we returned, Cone was ready to deal with Jim. They fired him. No puerile, boy scout type consideration, such as the promise to the strikers that there would be no reprisals, gave them pause. After all, this was the real world of class struggle.

The strike had left behind its poetry. Bill, who might have passed for the handsome bard of a medieval romance with his guitar in hand, composed and performed *The Ballad of the Granite Strike*. It was sung to the tune of Woody Guthrie's *Buffalo Skinner*. The genre is perhaps best described as "contrived archaic," but it is nevertheless worthwhile repeating a few of the verses.

> It started with the cutters in the spring of seventy-eight
> When Cone said to the cutters, your raise will have to wait.
> You'll have to take my offer, I cannot pay you more.
> The workers said to Mr. Cone: You know that this means war. . . .
> When they called a meeting, down at the union hall
> Came o'er a hundred workers, a strike vote now to call.
> They all discussed the matter, much courage did they show.

They voted then to shut it down, hit Cone a mighty blow.
Support rolled in like thunder, 'cross Carolina land,
Came many union locals, to lend a helping hand,
To help build up the strike fund, and man the picket line.
They said: Brother this is your fight, but also it is mine.
Then old man Cone responded, like all those of his kind.
This "great friend of the working class" attacked the picket line
With cops and courts and scabs, all at his beck and call
They carried out Cone's harsh command: My profits shall not fall! . . .
And now Cone's fired Blackbeard, strong leader of our men.
They think that by this tactic they'll make our union bend.
It only makes us stronger, it's this Cone has to face:
He'd trained already hosts of men to take his fighting place.
And so with these brave strikers, we know that they are right.
They set a strong example, they show us how to fight.
And Cone you own the factories, but us you do not own,
Before our struggle's ended, you'll surely lose your throne!

**

It was Saturday morning in the middle of August, and Tonya, Alex, and I were trying to keep the poster board from curling. I had a yardstick and pencil and was making lines every which way, but I made signs the same way I cooked. I knew the letters would no more end up in their allotted spaces than the recipes I prepared ended up using the required ingredients.

"I don't want to do another 'Workers United Will Never Be Defeated' one," I told the kids. "What else can we say? Something about getting Jim's job back. . . ."

"I know," Antonia piped, "How about 'Dr. Waller is not a scab.'"

"Yeah, so he should get his job back," Alex said indignantly.

I grinned. "Close. Wait, how about 'Don't pick those scabs?'"

"Who shouldn't pick scabs? You're always telling me not to pick scabs," Alex complained.

"I got it." I chuckled with enjoyment. "'Dr. Waller says, "Cone, Don't Pick Those Scabs!"' with a little Rx symbol at the top."

"Hey, yeah" from both. They got it. It didn't matter if the letters were out of alignment after that because we went on enjoying our joke as we worked on the poster. Jim loved it, too. Cone's pretext for firing him was that they had suddenly discovered he was a medical doctor and had falsified his job application by lying about his education.

The next day, Sunday, August 13, 1978, Local 1113 T marched to the Haw River Bridge and held a rally at the union hall to protest the firing of Jim Waller.[12]

About a hundred workers came out, and several spoke at the rally. Glenn told how in the preceding week third-shift workers had refused to begin work until management answered their questions about Jim's termination. The workers were told to get to work within fifteen minutes or the company was going to sign warrants on them. Cone management had to call the sheriff's department and four deputies went to the plant. Threatened with immediate arrest, the men finally got to work. "It wasn't right," Glenn said. "Anything they say do, we're supposed to go along with it. If a man goes to showing progress, they got to get rid of him. They knew Waller was going to be the next president of the union."

After Jim was fired, he spent as much time as before, if not more, meeting with workers and taking care of union business. His teaching and influence were vital to what went on in the mill day to day. The ties among Blackbeard and the other workers were growing stronger. So was our marriage. We had weathered the storm of the strike and Jim's being fired. We decided that we had come through all of our difficult moments and reached a higher level of unity as man and wife. As a result of our struggles, we were even better able to serve the working class. If this rhetoric seems out of place in a love story, it was quite understandable at the time—it was how communists made love in the seventies.

NOTES

1. See Bermanzohn, *The True Story of the Greensboro Massacre*, 137–139, for a description of Bill's entry in the mill.

2. Diary of Bill Sampson, made available to me by Dale Sampson Levin. It is written in French.

3. Diary of Bill Sampson, 2 September 1969.

4. Doffers remove full bobbins or cones of yarn from machines and replace them with empty ones.

5. Number of passes the yarn makes running in a horizontal or crosswise direction in a woven fabric.

6. This letter formed the content of a WOOC newsletter on November 9, 1977.

7. The Taft–Hartley Act, passed in 1947, gives employers legal means to break strikes (such as court injunctions, fines, and limiting pickets) and to refuse to bargain collectively with union representatives.

8. The letter was printed in a WOOC newsletter in May 1978.

9. The card room is where fibers are separated, cleaned, and laid parallel.

10. Interview of Charles Reaves by Sally Ann Alvarez in *Red November, Black November*.

11. Interview of Charles Reaves.

12. See appendix B, "Blackbeard's Speech to Union Local 1113 T," 499.

8

SOMETHING'S RISING IN
THE NATION

THAT CAN'T BE OUR DOCTOR

Things changed after the Haw River strike and the firing of Blackbeard in the
summer of 1978. The strike, though seemingly just a little local skirmish,
upped the ante. Even then, I had the sense that the struggle was intensifying as
workers were taking the initiative. In our conversations with one another and
with the people we worked among, we used the term *bourgeoisie* to talk about the
small elite group that runs society for its own benefit, takes all the wealth, and
makes all the decisions. *Bourgeoisie*, while not exactly au courant, was becoming
a meaningful term to many workers and community people with whom we had
contact. We shared our analysis of society and our belief in the possibility of
democratic social change, and people were receptive.

Many workers closed ranks around Jim as he fought to get his job back at
Granite Finishing. Workers went to hearings to testify on Jim's behalf, signed petitions and sworn testimonies, collected money, wrote letters, and confronted
management. They were preparing to elect Blackbeard as president of the local
at the next union election.

Jim first challenged the Employment Securities Commission to grant him unemployment insurance. Next there was arbitration between the union and the
company. Finally he took his case against Cone to the National Labor Relations
Board claiming that his termination was an unfair labor practice. The National
Labor Relations Act states that the fact that a lawful reason for discharging an employee may exist does not entitle an employer to discharge him when the true reason for the discharge is the employee's union activities that are protected by law.

Cone maintained that Jim was fired for not stating his true education level and the fact that he was a medical doctor on his job application. If a worker does not do his job satisfactorily or blatantly violates plant rules, a company has grounds for termination: companies do not usually terminate employees for omitting or falsifying information on a job application. Cone also justified dismissing Jim by pointing out that while he was employed in the mill, he wrote medical excuses for employees at other Cone plants.

Later, when Dale and I were in mourning, we had occasion to see a xeroxed page of doctor's excuses that Cone had submitted to the arbitration proceeding, and it afforded us some much-needed moments of laughter and levity. Here was the union firebrand and strike leader who was daily agitating the workers, turning the mill upside down, putting the company in a tailspin, and, under their very noses, writing medical excuses for other union troublemakers in their sister plants! It had been going on for months, even during the period of union negotiations, before Cone figured it out. It seemed that Dale, when she was a shop steward at White Oak, was often in need of a doctor's excuse. Most of Jim's notes were excusing her—"I have seen Dale Sampson repeatedly over the last 2 months for complaints of upper respiratory and gastrointestinal illness. She should be excused for May 7th, 9th, and 10th. I am suggesting she take a two week leave of absence to recuperate. James Waller, M.D. FAAP." One time, Bill wanted a doctor's excuse so he could attend an important meeting, and Jim was nowhere to be found. I took Jim's prescription pad and wrote it myself. Looking at the xeroxed sheet on which were laid out, side-by-side, four notes from the same prescription pad, I knew Cone did not need a handwriting expert to establish that one of the four notes was written in a different hand from the other three. Next to Jim's semilegible and slantless scrawl, executed with heavy pressure, was my light and arty, right-leaning penmanship.

The real reason that he was fired, Jim maintained in the grievance he filed, had nothing to do with his application for employment and everything to do with his union activities and his role in leading the strike. The firing violated the contractual agreement after the strike and was also an unfair labor practice. Redress of the grievance called for immediate reinstatement in the plant with full backpay and seniority. Workers from all departments signed a petition supporting Jim's grievance and redress demand.

To the Employment Securities Commission (in both the adjudication and appeal), it was an open-and-shut case—unemployment benefits denied. The commission did not care that this employee was being singled out for his union work or that the firing was a violation of a contract the employer had signed.

I remember well the appeal hearing on September 18, 1978. It had the air of a three-ring circus. Nine of Jim's union buddies came down to Greensboro to testify for him, but their testimony was written off as merely their opinions. Looking at the transcript of the Employment Securities Commission years later, I vividly recalled the camaraderie and mirth we shared—it was a case of the people versus the bureaucracy.

Appeals referee to worker: Do you have personal knowledge of Mr. Waller's discharge?[1]

Worker: I think it's true he was fired for the simple reason of what he was doing in the strike.

Appeals referee: We're not here to take personal opinions. Do you have some knowledge of a Cone Mills official discharging him due to his involvement in the strike?

(Interruption. Referee tries to quiet people down.)

Worker: After the strike was over, why, they come up and said Mr. Waller was fired.

Appeals referee to another witness: How do you testify?

Another worker: A supervisor on second shift said to a cutter that the plant manager had told him they knew way back in the spring that Waller might have falsified his application when he come to work. They knew like months before the strike.

Appeals referee: Did the plant manager say this to you? Do you have personal knowledge?

Another worker: No, but he leads the strike and they fire him for that.

Appeals referee: That is your opinion.

(Interruptions. Referee tries to quiet people down.)

. . .

Appeals referee to Jim: Mr. Waller, you may not question the company's attorney. You may question their witness only. Of course, your witnesses may not question anyone, Mr. Waller. Now do you understand?

Jim Waller: Yes, I think you should have laid that out to us before. If I knew I would have questioned their witness while I had the opportunity.

Appeals referee to Jim: You have not had the opportunity. He has not testified yet, Mr. Waller. You can question him after he has testified.

. . .

Personnel manager to appeals referee: We heard a rumor in, I think, May. The company nurse from another plant called. Do you know a Dr. James Waller? Some employees are coming in with excuses he wrote. I told her that can't be *our* doctor.

Appeals referee: You mean your employee.

Personnel manager: Er, yes, employee.

(Uproarious laughter.)

Appeals referee to workers: Be quiet. Listen to me. I'm going to adjourn this hearing.

(Noise fades.)

Jim Waller: Why was nothing done about this "rumor" at the time?

Personnel manager: We took it lightly, joked about it, couldn't imagine it was *our* doctor.

(Laughter. Interruptions.)

Personnel manager: We couldn't imagine it was the same James Waller.

Jim Waller: Those medical excuses were written on my prescription pad with my name, my address, and my signature on them. I mean, I don't understand. They knew exactly where I lived, what my phone number was. And this was before the strike. Don't you think you could have established whether this rumor.

. . .

(Interruption. Threats from referee to adjourn hearing.)

Personnel manager: We didn't really know until about July 14th.

Jim Waller: That was right after the strike. I went back to the plant. You waited until August 7th to fire me. Why?

Personnel manager: We needed to verify it.

. . .

Signe Waller: I got on the phone to the Medical Board. It took exactly one minute to verify James Waller is a doctor. The company could have verified it in one minute even prior to the strike by making a phone call.

Personnel manager: We wanted to be sure and took a picture to the Medical Examiner's Office in Raleigh in July to verify it.

Jim Waller: Why didn't you try to verify it by the address and phone number on the prescription pad?

Appeals referee: Mr. Waller, you're not here to argue as a lawyer.

Jim Waller: I watch Perry Mason.

(Interruptions. Laughter.)

. . .

Company lawyer to Jim Waller: Mr. Waller, you said previously you *did* falsify the information on your application. What was your reason for doing so again, please?

Jim Waller: People don't hire doctors to work in mills. There was no way I would get hired putting that down.

Company lawyer to personnel manager: Would you have hired him if you had known?

Personnel manager: If we had known he was a doctor and wanted to come to work for us we would have found a better corporate slot for him.

Company lawyer to Jim Waller: Well, you admit then you falsified your application at the mill in order to get a job in the capacity that you evidently got one and that was your reason for falsification; that had the truth been known you wouldn't have gotten the job and so you felt it necessary to falsify the application to get the job.

Jim Waller: Yeah, that's what I've said. I admit I falsified the application. No one would hire a doctor as a mill hand. Just like people don't hire someone with a criminal record.

(Laughter. Noise. Intervention from the referee.)

Company lawyer to Jim Waller: It is your position, then, that you falsified your application because you knew if you did not falsify your application and the truth were known about your background, you would not have gotten the job that you were applying for?

Jim Waller to appeals referee, exasperated: Why does he keep harping on the same point?

Much later, I took a sociological interest in this hearing. I was intrigued by the reaction of the company's representatives to a severe violation of social norms about what people in certain professions may or may not do. From the company's point of view, Jim's union work was an attack on them. But also, from their point of view, it is not permissible for a medical doctor to swap a white coat for a blue collar. Doctors are not supposed to put themselves and their careers on the line to organize for democratic trade unions and for socialism. Perhaps the impropriety was the *real reason* behind the real reason for the firing. In fact, as we later learned, someone from Cone *did* drive by our Cypress Street home, the same address on Dr. Waller's prescription pad. From the rundown exterior of the bungalow and the fact that it was located in a racially mixed, working- and middle-class neighborhood, that person simply concluded it could not be a doctor's residence and left it at that. Doctors are supposed to live only in certain kinds of neighborhoods and houses. Jim violated social norms and rules of propriety about doctors. That was shocking. Or perhaps, from the workers' point of view, it was liberating.

The second floor of our house had a huge closet under the eaves in which we kept a serviceable and sturdy Roneo mimeograph machine. There I printed a good portion of the trade union and community flyers circulated by WVO supporters in Greensboro. The *Granite Workers Update* continued through seven issues, the last of which was printed in March 1979. Granite workers contributed articles and poems, and Jim wrote a column on labor history. In October 1978, he wrote about the Right to Work law. A month later, he added a second installment on the topic, stressing that it is a mistake for workers to rely mainly on lobbying by organized labor and on Congress.

What we need to defeat the "Right to Work" laws is a movement of trade unions and other progressive people. Workers can only win victories in congress and state legislatures when we are organized, stand together and fight. This is the way the National Labor Relations Act was passed in 1935, as discussed last month. Similarly, miners in West Virginia got Black Lung legislation passed ten years ago only after they solidly organized rank and file miners in the Black Lung Association and led a three week strike which forced the legislature into a three day emergency session. This is how we must wage our campaign against the "Right to Work" laws. . . .

The big corporations, especially textiles, have Governor Hunt firmly in their corner. Nonetheless, this summer, dockworkers in Wilmington and Morehead City heroically set an example for workers across the state in their four week strike for a union shop, which was a direct attack against the "Right to Work" laws. Similarly, city workers in Rocky Mount, Asheville, Durham and Charlotte are organizing and fighting for better wages and benefits in defiance of the "Right to Work" laws.[2]

The *Granite Workers Update* was a morale booster and a nurturer of class consciousness. In the first issue, begun in September 1978 after Jim was fired, ten workers signed a letter of solidarity with the mechanics in Local 465 of the Brotherhood of Operating Engineers, who had been striking against Trader Chevrolet for over two months. "As we have just recently ended a strike against Cone Mills, Granite Finishing Plant, we know every bit of encouragement helps," they wrote. "Our message to our brothers at Traders is to keep fighting and stick together. As long as there is not a union contract at Traders, we will not do business there."[3] This is not what the bourgeoisie had in mind when Cone removed Jim from the mill. The education and organization of workers at Granite seemed to be just beginning.

On October 7 and 8, 1978, Jim joined Sally, Paul, César, and several hundred workers from around the country for the founding convention of the Trade Union Educational League (TUEL) in Pittsburgh. Initiated by the WVO, TUEL was a national organization of active and militant workers committed to building a strong democratic trade union movement. Local chapters, including the North Carolina chapter, had already been organized and were active. With many workers' struggles being led by militant workers, and with both authorized and wild-cat strikes occurring in many places, TUEL was potentially quite significant. The organization aimed to unite labor struggles across the boundaries of states, industries, nationalities, generations, and all other divides.

The meeting in Pittsburgh showed that there were particular features to workers' struggles in different regions of the country. A Chicano speaker emphasized that TUEL must regard undocumented workers as part of the working class of this country and fight for their rights. Chicano workers in the Southwest faced sexism and prejudice from other workers both inside and outside of unions. The ruling class used issues involving undocumented workers as a wedge to split the working class. Deportation was used as a weapon in union elections and strikes. In the Southwest, TUEL would be confronted with the labor issue and immigration issue tied together.

In the South, when sanitation workers in Rocky Mount, North Carolina, walked off the job, they were aided by organizations in the black community. The African Liberation Support Committee and the Southern Christian Leadership Conference helped the city workers organize well-attended rallies and marches. Sally Bermanzohn, who led the North Carolina delegation to the TUEL conference, summarized the lessons for organizing the unorganized in the black belt South. "It was not an economic strike at all," she said. "Those guys went out four times in one month over an issue of national oppression [historically rooted, systemic oppression of African Americans]. It was the national movement [the movement occasioned by national oppression] that came out and supported them, not the trade unions." The sanitation workers walked off the job because they were treated with a lack of dignity and respect; the rest of the African American community was able to identify with the workers and rally behind their cause. To be sure, various classes and strata within the black community gave their stamp to the struggle; the workers in Rocky Mount wanted the voices of those most oppressed, that is, workers and the poor, to be heard. The main point, Sally emphasized, was "how we have to organize the South. If TUEL came down there, or anybody else went to Rocky Mount talking trade union, trade union, trade union, people would look in the other direction. Trade unions are not a reality down there. But by taking up this bigger struggle against national oppression, the Rocky Mount city workers are going to get unionized," she declared to big applause.[4]

Jim spoke of the Granite strike and argued passionately about the need to make trade unions more democratic by building the shop steward system and getting workers involved in the local. Jim maintained that unless the rank-and-file really understood what was going on and were involved in decision making even though victories might be won, they would embody the seeds of future defeat. The Granite strike might outwardly appear to be a defeat because the workers went back to work without gaining their full demands, but because the strike involved many more workers in union activities and decisions, defeat carried the seeds of future victory.

Two months after returning from the TUEL conference, Jim had his arbitration hearing between Cone and the union. Once again, a group of Granite workers accompanied him to the hearing. One wrote in the January 1979 *Granite Workers Update*, "Most of us had never been to an arbitration hearing before and in the eight hours we spent there, we learned a lot." The workers thought that the union lawyer "made the case we all know is true, that the company did not have just cause to fire Waller and that they fired him for his union activity. Waller worked there for two years. Having too much education didn't stop him from doing his job. The company knew about his background before, but only decided to do something about it when they saw him helping to build up the union. . . . No matter what the decision, as Waller said at the arbitration, we have again shown how we can stick together and fight the company. And we will continue the fight to build the union if we lose this decision. We have already filed a Labor Board suit and that will be the next step."[5] Another worker later wrote, "Jim Waller lost his arbitration and I regret it very much. But it didn't surprise me at all, because I know Cone Mills thinks without Jim Waller, we'll fall apart and be their little dumb slaves again. But it won't happen unless we let it happen. Jim isn't finished yet. . . . But with or without Jim, we can still fight. He has educated a lot of us."[6]

Having struck out twice, Jim's last and best shot was the National Labor Relations Board. To my knowledge, nothing came of the NLRB charges, and the case was still pending, months later, when he was killed.

STOP THE TEST!

At the TUEL conference, César Cauce argued vigorously that TUEL should take clear positions on the issues facing workers and the trade union movement, and that the organization should strive to unite people around pro-working-class positions. Jim and the rest of the Executive Committee of the North Carolina chapter of TUEL resolved to educate workers on the need to build the labor movement, on labor history and traditions, and on issues such as the Right to Work law and statewide competency testing, both seen as anathema to workers' welfare. Mandated by the state legislature in mid-1977, competency testing fit neatly with Hunt's strategies for wooing industry into North Carolina with a cheap and abundant labor force—namely, workers who, with a measly certificate of attendance in lieu of a high school diploma, would have to work any job at any wage.

For almost two years after the Hillside picket launched the Campaign for Quality Education in Durham, the challenge to competency testing, among other education issues, was an important part of WVO activities in North Carolina. In a continuous history of struggle, black people fought against segregation and to uphold their own institutions—institutions they had been forced to create as a result of being denied full participation in white ones. Sandi and Nelson did much of the research and organizing work in a "Save Black Colleges" fight. Durham College in Durham and Shaw University in Raleigh were in financial distress. Other state-run black universities, Agricultural and Technical State University in Greensboro and North Carolina Central University in

SOMETHING'S RISING IN THE NATION

Durham, were facing major cutbacks. The Housing, Education, and Welfare Department (HEW) and the University of North Carolina (UNC) decided to get rid of duplication by closing certain programs in the black schools. Blacks faced a two-pronged attack—the diminishing of already impoverished black colleges and the denial of credentials to thousands of black youth to attend college. These were blatant moves, in the post–civil rights era, to rob African Americans of educational resources and opportunities for which they had fought.

In February 1978, North Carolina did a trial run with 88,000 high school juniors of the competency test planned for later in the year. The failure rate was horrendous. The socioeconomic statistics of the high school juniors tested were striking: 86 percent of all those whose family income was less than $5,000 failed the test. On the reading portion, about half of the students whose family income was less than $5,000 made below the passing score of 70 percent, but only 5 percent of the students from families with an income of over $15,000 did that poorly on reading. Striking too was the racial disparity: 9 percent of white students across all income ranges failed the reading test compared to a 40 percent failure rate for the black juniors. When it came to the math portion, white students who took the test had a 38 percent failure rate compared to an 85 percent failure rate for black students.

It is interesting that, historically, the median family income of whites runs about twice that of the median family income of blacks. Similar is the unconscionable poverty rate of children in our society that has worsened considerably since the seventies. In the late 1970s and 1980s, approximately one of every four white children was struggling in a family below the poverty line. That is bad enough, but for black children approximately one of every two lived below the official poverty line. There has been no pronounced departure from this racist situation—there is *at least twice as much* poverty, misery, reduced life chances, unemployment, and so on for blacks as for whites today. That the results of educational testing in a racist and classist society are linked to race and class is not startling or unexpected. The students who did best came from families with some degree of economic security—annual incomes above $15,000—and had parents with a better than high school education. And there was a far higher proportion of such students among whites than among historically oppressed people of color.

In Durham—where around two-thirds of the students failed the trial test at Hillside and Durham high schools—ALSC joined with the local NAACP, a ministers alliance, and several neighborhood community organizations to form the Durham Coalition for Quality Education. In Greensboro, we organized a picket in front of the school administration building in July 1978. At the picket, Willena Cannon, longtime community organizer in issues affecting African Americans, told reporters about our newly formed Greensboro Coalition for Quality Education. We already had hundreds of signatures on our petition demanding that the test be stopped and that our tax dollars be spent in ways that would truly further a quality education for all children. Hardly a day passed in the summer of 1978 that articles and views about competency testing did not appear in the newspapers. The competency test was not at all popular in North Carolina, and it was an issue in other states as well at the time.

On August 12, 1978, the Durham Coalition sponsored an all-day statewide meeting at Durham College. Over two hundred educators, students, and parents attended from eighteen cities and left with plans to maintain a North Carolina Coalition for Quality Education with local branches all over the state. A distinguished roster of speakers included the president of Durham College, Rev. Leon White of the United Church of Christ's Commission on Racial Justice, Rev. Grady Davis of the Union Baptist Church in Durham, and U.S. Attorney Mickey Michaux. When competency testing was passed into law, Michaux was in the state legislature and was one of only three representatives to vote against it. Representing the Workers Viewpoint Organization, Nelson argued that the HEW–UNC agreement recognized no specialized mission for traditionally black institutions that happen to be geographically proximate to traditionally white institutions. It was an agreement that would kill black colleges. We have, said Nelson, "on the one hand massive educational cutbacks, elimination of teachers' jobs, a large pool of cheap labor, and an increase in the conflict between the races. And on the other hand, [we have] absolutely nothing to push forward the educational process. . . . In whose interest is this? Is this by accident? Is it an accident that this test will have an oppressive effect on blacks, Indians, poor and working-class youth of all races? Are teachers, parents, or students getting anything good out of this test? There is only one group that will get something good out of this. It's the capitalist class, the industrial barons, the rulers of this society, like the Burlingtons, the R. J. Reynolds, the J. P. Stevens, the Dukes, the Cones. . . . They will hire us for little or nothing, and use the test to keep unions out. In the meantime, their children will keep going to good schools." Nelson doubted that the legislature would heed the growing opposition to a test that "has a provision to put you out of school and no provision to teach you anything."

The statewide conference resolved to save black schools against the incursions of HEW; to support teachers in their fight to keep their jobs, improve their working conditions, and increase their wages; and to hold a statewide demonstration to oppose competency testing. With people organizing in Durham, Guilford, Washington, Pitt, Martin, Edgecombe, Halifax, and Chatham counties, politicians and education officials were jolted out of complacency. The

Durham City School Board, when they met two days after the August 12 conference, strongly criticized the competency test. A week later the State Board of Education voted to seek millions of dollars more for remedial aid. One of the strongest grassroots coalitions formed in that period was the Chatham County Committee on Human Rights. Several weeks before the statewide coalition in August, rural Chatham County had a very well-attended mass meeting, at which Rev. Leon White stirred people's passions. Jean Sharpe, living in Pittsboro and a practicing pediatrician, was an organizer and spokesperson for the Chatham County Committee on Human Rights. The group added considerable clout to the state fight against the competency test and was a force for improving race relations in the county.

With the first high school competency tests scheduled for November, the Greensboro coalition packed the room at a school board meeting on September 19, 1978. Sandi Smith urged the School Board to come out against competency testing. "It punishes youth who are already economically deprived and racially oppressed for the weaknesses of the school system," she said. In October, I drove to Charlotte with Miss Fanny for a State Board of Education meeting at which the passing scores for the soon to be administered competency tests were to be decided. It was a wild evening and one, I confess, that I relished. The board, sitting on a stage amid awesome statistical charts on easels, barely managed to set their cut-off scores. Nearly a hundred black and white, adult and high school student demonstrators, wearing "Stop the Test" buttons and carrying picket signs, chanted, "Stop the test, stand and fight, education is our right." Unable to silence the comments and chants from the audience, the board members abbreviated their meeting and hastily left the stage, seeking the nearest side exit. They were at pains to vacate the building as quickly as possible. We were in the corridors, on the stairs, all over the place, and we drummed them away with unrelenting chanting. Their retreat appeared ignominious, as if they had been expelled for bad behavior.

Later that month, the overwhelming majority of those who spoke at a public hearing in Raleigh voiced strong opposition to the competency test. On October 21, several hundred people, also opposing the test, rallied at the state capitol.

Nelson Johnson and Rev. Leon White, the two coconveners of the North Carolina Coalition for Quality Education, prepared the coalition to continue its efforts in defeating the competency test after the first round of testing. The state has the responsibility to educate all children, Nelson and Rev. White asserted, and that job requires a massive input of funds as well as a reorientation toward the undertaking. Community groups and private tutoring programs could not do the work of the broader school system. The competency test had to be staunchly opposed with or without Hunt's offer of remedial aid money. The Coalition encouraged a boycott of the test at the grassroots, but it did not happen. When tests scores were announced a couple of months later, the results, though somewhat better overall than on the trial run, once again showed, predictably, that wealthier students scored higher on the test than poor or working-class students. Speaking to the press, Nelson refused to concede that protests against the test had been a failure. From competency testing to attacks on black colleges, people were much more aware of education issues than if the campaign had never been fought. And the struggle for quality public education for all children would continue.

The Steering Committee of the statewide coalition met at the Union Baptist Church in Durham on November 5, 1978, to take stock of the situation. There were people prepared to set up new local chapters in Bladen County and in Charlotte. A strategy for meeting with legislators to get legislation revoking the competency test was discussed, as was the status of the Coalition's legal case against the test with the law firm of Chambers, Ferguson, Becton, and Stein. Students present suggested that the Coalition look at curriculum questions to see if courses on the cultural heritage of African Americans, Native Americans, and working-class white people could be introduced.

On November 11, 1978, at a demonstration in Washington, D.C., to demand the cutting of diplomatic ties with South Africa, we carried the banner of the North Carolina Coalition for Quality Education. As we marched to Lafayette Park, across from the White House, our chants related far-away liberation struggles to those nearer home. *Same Struggle: Many Fronts* read the headline of a flyer I designed. Helms and Smith both represented the interests of monopoly capitalists, we said, who profited from workers earning nothing or nearly nothing.

The statewide Coalition met again in Greensboro that December. To some extent, people's attention was focused away from competency testing when the city Board of Education began announcing the closing of some local schools and the redrawing of school attendance zones. Parents affected by these changes came forth to protest, and we joined them. The cutbacks in education, being effected in several ways, signaled a bigger onslaught on the public sector to take place in the eighties.

We continued to campaign around education into 1979, fighting the school closings and raising the ongoing issue of saving black schools. A broad spectrum of the population participated in these struggles and in the opposition to the competency test. In a sense, progressive politics were becoming mainstream politics through the campaign in education. In March 1979, the first (of only a few issues) of the North Carolina Coalition for Quality Education newsletters came out and was distributed around the state. Member groups were skirmishing here and there: The Chapel Hill–Carrboro Coalition won a reinstatement for a local high school student who complained of harassment; the Greensboro Coalition was fighting the imposition of school fees it had earlier taken up; in Chatham County, students protested the dismissal of a black coach. However, a decisive victory of quality education for all children has yet to be won. Issues similar to those we engaged in 1977–1979 were still on the agenda of activists in Greensboro in 2000 and 2001, as in many other places. In early 1979, WVO organizers in North Carolina had little choice but to put the campaign around education on the back burner in order to respond to increasing threats against the work in the trade unions.

MY LIFE AT HOME AND AT WORK

On New Years Eve, 1978, we stood on the porch of the Cypress Street bungalow at midnight with some workers from White Oak and fired a shotgun in the air to welcome in 1979. This would be the year WVO would give birth to the Communist Workers Party. Inside, couples danced to soul music. We were Emma Goldmann's dream communists, and we were not going to make the revolution without dancing. To set the example, Jim and I danced with utter abandon and enjoyment. Jim threw himself, heart and soul, into the music, moving expressively and exuberantly. Everyone stopped dancing to watch us. Friends conversant with that Hollywood era dubbed us Fred and Ginger—said with a wink. Fred and Ginger dipping and swinging, stepping and stomping to motown no less. It was zany and contagious. We were so awful that we were good.

Except for the simple pleasures of our parties, we carried the world on our shoulders. I quit my job at Cone Hospital that winter and went to work for the Binswanger Glass Company, putting together prefabricated doors. I was the lone woman in the shop, and I felt constantly isolated and oppressed. Almost no one thought twice about making sexist jokes at my expense. Only one worker, a Native American named Donny, patiently and consistently tried to help me with various machinery and tools in this hardhat job.

Jim was proud of me for doing a hard job and thought I would benefit from its physical demands. He felt my back and swore that I was getting stronger. After many attempts, I managed to lift and carry the nearly one-hundred-pound patio doors that I had assembled back to the rack without asking for help. When I had worked there a few months, the company gave me glass delivery runs. With the truck loaded with huge sheets of plate glass on its sides, off I went for the day into the mountains of North Carolina and Virginia. On every run, some glass would break. I was told that was normal. I felt much freer driving the truck than working in the shop. I often managed, especially if the weather was pleasant, to stop en route at a picnic site for a long siesta, to lie in the grass and take a nap, or to sit at the table and read. I remember reading *Fascism and Social Revolution* by R. Palme Dutt during that period. I timed it so that I was back in the shop shortly before quitting time.

One day all of the workers were told to attend a slide show about caulking. The shop emptied, and I went with them. Whoever put together the slide show decided to spice up the subject matter by interspersing slides about caulking with briefly flashing pictures of naked women. I was the only woman in the room, and it made me feel sick. I told my supervisor that I would not tolerate this indignity, and I walked out. I returned to the deserted shop and stayed there until quitting time, doing whatever busywork there was. No one said anything to me about it.

Jim and I celebrated our first wedding anniversary in January 1979. After a year, we felt ourselves more in love, and we affirmed as much to each other, allowing ourselves tremendous joy in the realization. We frequently stopped in the middle of some mundane kitchen chores to share a great, loving hug. And when Alex popped up we teased tenderly, "Don't look, Alex." This happened more than once, and "Don't look, Alex" became the stock remark of feigned embarrassment over a normal and desirable display of marital affection.

Supper was our time to be together as a family. There were often five of us. Antonia had a friend, Mandy, who virtually took up residence with us, eating many meals and sleeping over. Dinner did not lack playfulness. At the end of a meal, we sometimes played a version of "Simple Simon," in which you pound the table twice, clap your hands twice and then make up another hand, foot, or body motion and perform it twice. The next person repeats the sequence and adds his or her own motion, maintaining the rhythm. As you go around the table the sequence gets longer and harder to remember, fumbles develop, and laughter ensues. As each fumbler is eliminated, the contestants narrow until one is left who has managed to perform the entire sequence perfectly up to that point. This was an enjoyable, if somewhat obnoxious, way to end a meal, and we all had a good time with it.

Supper was also a time when friends and comrades stopped by with children in need of a medical examination. On those occasions, the game playing stopped, the table was quickly cleared of dishes, and the kitchen was converted to a people's clinic. A work buddy from my days at the hospital, Sheryl, used to come by with her two children. Coo Coo, her daughter, was plopped on a kitchen stool while Jim tested her reflexes and peered into her eyes, ears, and throat. A few feet away, I washed dinner dishes. Sheryl walked out with a diagnosis and, if needed, a prescription. Jim never charged anyone. If the family was poor, he even paid for the medicine.

Sheryl, like so many other African American women, was in a real bind. She had a regular relationship with the man with whom she'd had two children. But marriage was an impossible dream, about as unlikely as winning the lottery. Her man was in and out of prison all the time. Sheryl's situation, I learned, was not exceptional. An alarming proportion of black men were in prison, or on parole, or out of work, or somehow disqualified from being in a long-term, stable and economically viable relationship. In the following decades, the plight of African American males received more attention, at least from scholars. In the late seventies, civil rights progress seemed dead in the water. As the economic fabric of the country deteriorated, and America's perennial racism continued, black males were treated as a superfluous and disposable part of the population.

GROUNDS FOR OPTIMISM

That winter, in mid-January, the Shah of Iran was overthrown. A client of the U.S. government, the Shah ruled in a brutal and repressive way. His secret police, SAVAK, arrested and tortured the democratic political opposition. Now images of millions of people celebrating in Iran, thronging the streets, appeared on our little black-and-white TV in the kitchen. Jim and I waltzed around the kitchen to the children's delight. Then Jim got out his guitar and plunked away at *All Africa's Standing Up*. We felt connected to people around the world who were breaking the shackles of imperialism.

The Iranian revolution was the biggest defeat for U.S. imperialism since the Vietnam War. U.S. rulers viewed it as an unmitigated disaster, and one that caught most by surprise. The *Washington Post*, in an editorial dated January 14, 1979, called Iran "a region of almost incalculable political and economic importance to American national security." What would happen next, they asked, in this region "where once there was a familiar, reliable and influential ally, tightly tied to the United States by treaties, defense commitments and commercial arrangements." However, from the people's point of view, said WVO supporters, the Iranian revolution was a fine thing.

As we looked about us, there seemed to be grounds for optimism everywhere. People striving for decent lives, for social and economic justice, were sweeping away oppressive, oligarchic, or brutal regimes. The fall of the Shah in Iran was followed by the success of the revolutionary movement in less strategic Grenada, in the Caribbean off the coast of Venezuela. The New Jewel Movement seized power in the middle of March 1979 from the dictatorial Gairey regime with its infamous Mongoose Gang, police thugs that beat and killed Gairey's opponents. Maurice Bishop was the head of the New Revolutionary Government. He was a former member of the African Liberation Support Committee who had worked with Nelson Johnson in establishing African Liberation Day. "The revolution is for work, for food, for decent housing and health services, and for a bright future for our children and great-grandchildren," Bishop proclaimed. "Let me assure the people of Grenada that all democratic freedoms, including freedom of elections, religious and political opinions, will be fully restored to the people," he announced.

In June 1979, the Sandinistas embarked on a final offensive to liberate Nicaragua. Then, on July 19, 1979, thousands of Nicaraguan people poured into the streets of Managua. Truckloads of young guerrillas drove around the city, waving the red and black Sandinista flag, and firing shots into the air. They were celebrating the end of forty years of dictatorship by the Somoza family and seventy years of U.S. imperial domination. The people tore down the statue of Anastasio Somoza Garcia, the overthrown dictator's father. The jail doors were opened, freeing hundreds of political prisoners. With the victory of the Sandinistas, a genuine peoples' government had come to power in Nicaragua.

Revolt and militant challenges to the status quo were not merely the province of distant third world countries. A massive antinuclear movement was gathering momentum in Europe and, on a somewhat lesser scale, in the United States. Against a background of inflation and President Carter's imposition of wage controls, militant workers' strikes flared up. Around the country, protests of the Bakke and Weber so-called reverse discrimination cases heralded that the progress of the civil rights era would not be easily foiled. Popular movements striving leftward were commonplace in the late seventies, and the WVO led or participated in many of them.

Our experiences in the mills encouraged us and fed our optimism. Jim still had some hope of returning to Granite, but even if he did not, he was determined to fight the good fight from outside, and many Granite workers supported him. Each time the company fired workers for union activism at Revolution, White Oak, and Granite, workers fought to get their jobs back. They often succeeded, and Cone was put on the defensive. Even the trade union hierarchy seemed to be changing their tune. By the fall of 1978, ACTWU agreed to support the union drive at Revolution, and the union workers at White Oak were allowed to hold meetings in their own union hall.

At the beginning of 1979, things looked good for the workers' cause. At White Oak and at Granite, union elections were around the corner. Every indication suggested that WVO supporters would gain official positions of leadership and authority. At White Oak, where Bill was running for president of the local, there was an entire slate of candidates—about a dozen—who were activists. Many were WVO supporters, and all were at least open to working with the WVO. The slate led by Sampson was a "shoe in," everyone agreed. Although the arbitration between the union and Cone over the charge of Jim's unjust firing was against Jim, he was still technically a union member since his NLRB suit was alive, and Cone might yet be forced to take him back in the mill. Jim was running for president of his union local. He clearly and overwhelmingly was the person union members wanted to lead the local.

THE ADMINISTRATORSHIP

On February 14, 1979, we were caught by surprise when the International of the ACTWU put all five of its Cone locals into an administratorship (also called a receivership) and canceled all elections. An International vice president, David Harris, was appointed administrator over the five Cone Mills locals in Greensboro or its vicinity. The administrator reappointed all the old officers and stewards. Since the contract was going to be reopened in the spring, and the negotiating team was chosen from the locals' officers, that meant that the old guard would again be in the position of negotiating the contract with the company. At a union-sponsored hearing, on May 10, 1979, at a hotel in downtown Greensboro, ACTWU's regional director and international vice president, Scott Hoyman, and manager of the Central North Carolina Joint Board, George Justice, sought to justify the receivership by saying it was needed to build up the membership and increase participation within the locals.

Bill and Jim, joined by some coworkers, were spokespersons for their locals at that May hearing. (The other three locals did not even have a slate of candidates to run for union offices.) Speaking for White Oak Local 1391, Bill pointed out that in the year prior to the administratorship, the present union officers had made no attempt to build up membership or increase participation in the local. The new slate of candidates, on the other hand, were active members within the local who were processing grievances, recruiting new members, and promoting the participation of union members in the local's affairs. In the past year, these activist candidates had elected six new shop stewards—more than were elected or appointed in the five previous years. On the premise they would be able to unseat the incumbent officers, the activist candidates had signed up twenty more union members at their January meeting. Bill contended that the administrator-ship was imposed for the sole purpose of blocking the upcoming union elections and preventing new leadership from unseating the old.

True to their wildcat spirit in the Strike of 1978, the workers at Granite Finishing Plant defied the union's administratorship. Shortly after it was announced in mid-February, they went ahead with the election of union officers. Although his firing by Cone happened months before the election, Jim was elected president of the local, and the other slots were filled too. It was as President of Local 1113 T that Jim testified passionately at the May 1979 hearing about the effect the administratorship would have on the Granite local. In the past year, Jim said, a solid core of dues-paying members had been built within the local. For the first time in years, employees at Granite were beginning to show support for the union. Training sessions had been held for stewards and officers, fundraising events had increased the local's treasury, and workers were participating in a new newsletter. The strike of the preceding summer was the largest display of strength in the local in years. All these things taken together, Jim asserted, were proof that the local was beginning to be built up through collective action by its members. In imposing the receivership, the International was destroying workers' faith in the union. Already the level of union activity had started to decline. The administratorship was a blatant violation of the principle of union democracy, Jim charged. Not surprisingly, the union-appointed hearing officer upheld the administratorship. The situation was to be reviewed in a year.

Although now president of Local 1113 T, Jim was still in limbo about his status in the plant; he was neither outside nor inside. The company tried to discredit him, and he could not ignore their attacks. In the March 1979 issue of the *Granite Workers Update*, Jim wrote:

The focus should not be put on me. The focus has been and still is *how to build the union.* I've never hidden my motives and views from the workers. I have stood and continue to stand shoulder to shoulder in our fight for more money and better working conditions. In the course of giving leadership to these fights I am working to raise the organization and consciousness for the workers. In other words, how to fight, when to advance, when to retreat, who our friends and who our enemies are, what we are up against, and what are the short and long-term goals and interests of the working class. But at each point, it is the workers themselves who must decide what to do and carry it out. . . .

The workers in Local 1113 T are the union and no one else. The workers must run the union democratically—that is the lifeblood of the union and the road forward. . . . There is no question the company has lots of weapons. . . . But when it comes down to it we are much much stronger, that is, when we stick together. Cone wants to bust our union because they are still stinging from the strike and they for sure don't want another one. But how do you think Cone would fill all their orders for this year without us?

The meeting next Sunday is an important one because we are at a turning point in our struggle. We are looking forward to wage negotiations this spring. There is no way we can get a raise to keep up with the twelve and a half percent inflation without organizing the workers. . . . We must all move in the same direction. We must decide that direction together and carry it out together.

Jim and Bill counted on the rank-and-file and not on the federal court to advance workers' struggles. Bill and the thwarted slate of activist candidates at White Oak continued to file grievances and to battle Cone. The active workers in Revolution went on functioning as a de facto union and skirmishing with the company. To my knowledge, nothing came of the promise eventually extracted from the ACTWU to support their union drive. Such support would certainly have been incongruous anyway in light of the administratorship over the union locals. Jim continued to meet with Granite workers and tried to help inexperienced workers run the local.

It was time to reassess the whole issue of union building in the South. A new discussion was in the air. Jim, Bill, and those who worked with them in the mills were talking about forming an independent textile workers union in the South. The General Secretary of the WVO, Jerry Tung, after hearing reports from Jim and other WVO members who were trade union leaders around the country, agreed with the idea.

In the spring of 1979, Jim was elected president of the Trade Union Educational League by the WVO's National Executive Committee, taking over from Sally Bermanzohn. Jim studied William Z. Foster's writings on the history of the trade unions. He learned from and critiqued Foster, a labor leader and head of the Communist Party USA for many years. In the 1920s and 1930s, the CPUSA was a revolutionary party that stood for achieving socialism. Jim felt that despite his important work in building a mass labor movement and bringing the trade unions into the American Federation of Labor (AFL), Foster had lost sight of the main goal—working-class revolution. In September 1979, Jim completed a paper, "The Party and the Trade Unions," in which he made a case for building an independent union in the South.

Foster had warned of the danger of weakening the union movement through dual unionism, that is, splitting off the more progressive workers into a new organization and leaving the rest to reactionary leadership. Dual unionism was not desirable, Jim agreed. However, workers were rejecting trade unions with reactionary or stagnant leadership anyway, and Jim believed that they were looking for new leadership. More dangerous than dual unionism was the lack of an organization to struggle for workers' real and long-term interests. The long-term goal was not mere unionism, but breaking the chains of wage slavery altogether so that the working class is empowered to run society. Jim's experiences with trade union organizing had been brief but very concentrated and rich in lessons. He worked through the theoretical questions pertaining to dual unionism and the relationship between a revolutionary party and the trade unions. It was not an academic exercise. The WVO meant to establish a revolutionary party of the working class and was looking forward to the Founding Congress of this new political party in the fall of 1979. Jim's position paper was a contribution to that effort.

We could not afford for Jim to be a full-time organizer for the party. Alex and Antonia were both at different points in that difficult stage of growth known as adolescence. I did not make enough money at Binswanger to support our family and pay the mortgage. We had no investments and only a few hundred dollars in savings. After looking for a job for a few months without success, Jim was finally hired at the sewage treatment plant. He was told to start work at the beginning of May. Jim's new employer was the City of Greensboro.

For what my speculation is worth, it is inconceivable to me that the City of Greensboro did not know whom it was hiring. Jim testified openly about the administratorship at the hearing in May, discussed above, and that was shortly after he had started his new job. But even before he was hired, Cone Mills—a company so tight with those who governed Greensboro—would have warned City employment officials about a man whom Cone must have regarded as constituting a bizarre threat to their corporate welfare. The City—that is, the human agents who were making decisions for the whole city—may have felt it useful to have Jim at the sewage treatment plant, where they could keep tabs on him and where he worked virtually alone. (There were very few other employees there for him to "contaminate" with his radical views. He saw one or two other workers at the shift change, but that was all.)

The job itself required that Jim monitor instruments showing the flow of sewage through various channels and reservoirs. Jim loved science and actually enjoyed being involved in the technical aspects of waste management. There was a considerable amount of idle time—often an hour or two at a stretch—when no duties were required to be performed. The sewage treatment plant became a customary place for WVO leaders in the district and region to meet. Aware the place might be bugged, they played the radio when meeting as background noise to confound any eavesdropping devices.

More prominent in our consciousness over auditory sensations were olfactory ones. Once, Bill came to the door, and my nose immediately informed me that he had been at the treatment plant, so I knew that the District Committee had just met. It must have been on the way to (as opposed to coming from) his job that Jim made a particular doctor's visit, which Willena later reminisced about—otherwise, my smelly husband could not have made such a positive impression. Willena suspected that her youngest child, Kwale, had foot and mouth disease. "One of the teachers in the nursery called me," Willena said.[7] "She was afraid Kwale would be spreading stuff all over. So I left word that the doctor would be there." Willena paused to laugh heartily before continuing. "They said, 'who does she think she is that a doctor's gonna come, a pediatrician's gonna come, to the day care center?' My sister Annette was around and she told me that. So Jim went there with his doctor's bag and the clothes he was working in—I think it was a blue or a khaki shirt that was the city worker's uniform. Annette told me later all the women in there was going crazy over this doctor. They said he was so good-looking. They didn't actually believe he was a doctor because he wasn't acting like he was all important, and he was so gentle with the children."

I BRING YOU REVOLUTIONARY GREETINGS

In Jim's new position as president of the Trade Union Educational League, he was asked to address the African Liberation Day rally on May 12, 1979. I can't do that, he protested at first, anxious at the prospect of speaking before thousands of people. He rehearsed his speech at home many times and was nervous on the bus ride to Washington, D.C. We went our separate ways for most of the day, fulfilling different duties. To relieve him of having to carry his doctor's bag around when he soon had to get on the podium to speak, I offered to take it. It was an ancient brown leather bag that he regularly used on house calls or at demonstrations. It looked like a relic from the nineteenth century and may have been his grandfather's. Jim gave his speech and was terrific. Once on the stage, he brought his nervousness under control. In a voice that turned from soft to husky whenever he tried to speak loudly, he belted out, "Brothers and sisters, I bring you revolutionary greetings from the Trade Union Educational League."

During the day, I circulated ALSC and party literature. At one point, I helped someone whom I didn't know by selling oranges for their fundraiser. When Jim and I got together later in the day to return to Greensboro, I had sad news—"I don't have your doctor's bag." It had disappeared somehow while I was submerged in oranges. We filed a stolen property report with the D.C. police. Jim never saw the bag again. During the years of litigation stemming from the November Third murders, the Washington police sent me a letter saying that they had recovered the doctor's bag from a drug addict who had stolen it. They claimed that they had been trying to locate the person to return it to. Was I the right person and did I want it back? I didn't believe the letter. "*You took it, you bastards!*" I thought. "Yes," I wrote to them, "I want it back." Jim's prescription pad, his stethoscope, and some other items he used for examinations were in the bag when it was mailed to me, his widow.

Another clear recollection I have of May 12, 1979, is that the march was so fast-paced that it could more aptly be described as a trot. WVO was consciously trying to upgrade its level of militancy, to become more adept at combining legal and illegal tactics. Someone, probably with WVO's blessing, hurled a brick through the storefront of a big dealer of the Krugerrand, the gold currency that financed the apartheid regime of South Africa. If WVO was to be the party of the proletariat and lead American workers in making socialist revolution and in establishing a government run by the working class, it had to promote boldness—both in rhetoric and in deed. In the spring of 1979, looking forward to transforming the organization into a revolutionary political party, WVO members and supporters assumed a posture of boldness more and more. Revolution is not for wimps. It is, as Mao had said, not a tea party.

THE UNITED STATES' JOY RIDE WITH CHEAP ENERGY

In 1979, the United States' joy ride with cheap energy was again threatened. As in 1974, the oil producing nations demanded decent prices for their resources, and people in the United States were confronted with purported gas shortages. The price of diesel fuel rose. Independent truckers were being squeezed by government regulations and bled dry by rising fuel prices. It looked like they would be the next sacrificial lambs on the altar of monopoly capitalism.

In May and June, independent truck owners and operators went on strike all around the country. For this group of latter-day cowboys and cowgirls, mavericks outside the giants of the trucking industry and truck drivers' unions, it was important to maintain their sense of independence, freedom, and individualism. That's why many became independents to begin with. Their multiple regional organizations, some would insist, were not unions but associations. Most were from working-class backgrounds—having their own rig was their ticket out. In the recession of 1973–1974, many owner-operators lost their rigs. In 1979, they were going bankrupt by the thousands. They were struggling for their very survival. Their strike was a protest against government regulations on weight loads and hauling rates that were cutting into their profits or forcing them to operate at a loss. They wanted a guarantee for their allocation of diesel fuel, and they wanted its price reduced. They needed, they said, higher freight rates to compensate for ballooning fuel costs.

The issue of regulation versus deregulation can be confusing. Many of the strikers stated that they wanted government deregulation, and they wanted it now. But they were asking the government to set standard weight and length limits on trucks, to raise the maximum hours per day of driving, to change the speed limit back to sixty-five miles per hour, to prohibit loading and unloading fees common in large cities, and to institute a national truck licensing system. Did they want deregulation or nationalization?

What they actually wanted was a chance to be competitive with the big trucking companies. Many truckers failed to appreciate that deregulation would destroy competition even faster, further centralization and work to the advantage of the large carrier companies. For weeks the truckers' strike, combined with other features of the economy, disrupted daily life. Farmers lost perishable crops that they could not move quickly enough to markets. In some places, gas and food were rationed. To call attention to their plight, truckers tried to jam the flow of commerce. In suburban Levittown, outside of Philadelphia, independent truckers blockaded the main intersection to their town. For three nights of fiery skirmishing in June, working people and youths (mainly whites) in Levittown took to the streets, set cars on fire, and fought police. Many people were hurt and arrested. Not all fingers pointed blame at the Arabs or the truckers. Many shared the view of a worker quoted by WVO, who said, "The hell with the oil companies, and the hell with the government. The fuel companies control it."[8]

In Greensboro we assembled a coalition to support the truckers' strike. We recruited people to go to the tank farm on West Market Street near the Greensboro–Winston-Salem–High Point Regional Airport. On the evening of June 27, 1979, just a few days after the Levittown riot, I dropped Jim off with a sleeping bag, sandwiches, and a thermos of coffee at the fuel terminal. In the morning, when I returned to pick him up beside the giant cylindrical storage tanks that squatted by the dozens along a stretch of Highway 421, I was surprised to see National Guardsmen all over the place. They had been dispatched to that terminal, and to one in Charlotte, by Governor Hunt during the night, to the chagrin of the truckers who were picketing peacefully.

Jim hadn't slept, but he was ebullient. I wanted to hear about what he accomplished in the way of political education. He had spent the night swapping stories with the truckers and passing around a six-pack—they were great guys, he told me. Even some of the National Guard were friendly and were fraternizing with the pickets. I concluded that very little political education and lots of male bonding had gone on.

MY BLACK EYE

An attitude many of us shared was that we needed to be bold. We knew what we were doing was politically risky and becoming ever riskier. Boldness would somehow minimize the risks, or somehow prepare us for them. Our organizing and outspokenness constituted a *political* offensive, not a military one. Some WVO members and supporters, in the various chapters around the country, had training with weapons in the usual ways, that is, by serving in the U.S. military or (like Bill) by growing up in the country and learning to use hunting rifles. In North Carolina, not very many of those around the WVO had experience with guns or, for that matter, other means of self-defense. I went to the woods on two or three occasions with Jim, Bill, and a few other people, and we shot at targets for about fifteen minutes. We thought it was right to defend ourselves if we were attacked, but we did very little that indicated we took seriously the possibility that we would be attacked and would have to defend ourselves. For me the need to defend myself or others was just a scary thought in the back of my mind that would probably never happen. I dismissed it so that I would not stay scared.

One morning in the spring of 1979, I was selling the Workers Viewpoint newspaper at one of the White Oak gates before the early morning shift change, as I had done many times before. First shift at Binswanger began later than first shift at the textile mill, and I would be able to get to work on time. On this particular morning, I had competition—a man was selling the newspaper of the Revolutionary Communist Party (RCP). The RCP, an organization in the New Communist Movement, alienated the people they were organizing to such an extent that we had to explain to people that although they called themselves communists, we had nothing to do with them. What happened next made me sure the man was not a genuine communist but some sort of anticommunist agent.

Somehow I got into an argument with the person claiming to be an RCP member, and he became extremely nasty. Of average size but powerfully built, he told me he was a Vietnam War veteran. Although various communist groups had different positions on issues, I knew no communist worthy of the name who advocated the inferiority of women. However, I was subjected to a vicious tirade against women. The man with the RCP papers angrily assailed me for not being home in the kitchen—it was that crude. I don't remember who grabbed the other's stack of papers first, but a shoving match developed. Then the vet brought around the full force of his fist and punched me squarely in my right eye.

We stood confronting one another for a moment. I had never physically fought someone in earnest. I didn't know the first thing about the techniques of fighting and how to defend myself. The punch had been shattering. He had hit me as hard as he possibly could. I should have felt fear, but instead I felt supremely angry and glared at him for all I was worth. At being stared down, he seemed dumbfounded. He probably expected me to run away or withdraw; instead, I started advancing on him. I must have looked as savage and menacing as I felt. As I advanced, instead of engaging me again, he retreated. I ran after him as if I was prepared to trounce him to smithereens, and, indeed, I *was* prepared to *try*. I was going to fight, because giving in was out of the question.

As he ran down the street, and I pursued him, bloody-eyed, I noticed a metal rod sticking up from the cement, a post that once held a street sign. In some primitive center of my brain, it flashed on me that I needed that metal stick to defend myself. The fact that I was not entirely rational was something that I concluded later in considering the several seconds I spent trying to lift the piece of urban hardware out of the cement. My attempt was naturally unsuccessful and gave my attacker time to get further away. When I realized that it was futile to continue struggling in order to dislodge the steel from the cement, I continued my pursuit. First-shift workers were beginning to stream into the mill through the main gate. My attacker ran toward them. From a distance down the street, I saw Rand and Bill about to go into the mill, and I shouted out to them to stop the RCP man. Then Bill, Rand, and a few other workers fought with my attacker and some other RCP men. An old-fashioned fist fight was in progress. When I caught up with them, I saw that Rand was pinned to the ground by my RCP assailant, who was bent down over him. I grabbed the assailant's hair and pulled with all my might. That allowed Rand to work his way loose. Soon the RCP group began fleeing, outnumbered as workers ran to Rand and Bill's defense. Only after it was over, and the first shift, including Bill and Rand, were sucked into the plant and "making eight," did I have time to feel shaken. I rushed back to my car, aware of my heart pounding loudly. My hands were tightly clenched around the substantial clumps of hair that I had extracted in payment for my black eye.

I got back to the house just as Antonia and Alex were leaving for school and Jim was preparing to go to work. "Mama, what happened?" the children cried out. I assured everyone that I was all right. Jim disinfected my wound and made me sit down with an icepack over my eye. I was beginning to get a headache. The children were sent on to school, and Jim listened to my story and calmed me down. He assured me that my black eye would be avenged and suggested that I stay home and rest. But I didn't want to admit defeat. I called my workplace to say I would be late.

At this point in my job as a glass factory worker, I was with a crew performing outdoor work on a scaffold. It was work that I really could not handle, and my employer knew this when he assigned me to the job. My black, blue, and purple eye was the hottest topic of conversation for several days, drawing quips about what my "old man" did to me. My comrades, on the other hand, treated me as a hero and knew enough not to pin my injury on Jim. Still, I quickly tired of having to explain my black eye and just wished it weren't so visible for so long.

A series of scuffles ensued between the WVO and the RCP. Jim went to the mill with several comrades that very afternoon. According to the tales of triumph in our camp, we whipped them soundly. Jim hurt his hand in the process. A short time later, Rand, Bill, and some other White Oak workers were attacked by the RCP as they entered the plant. They had to be treated at Cone Hospital for minor cuts and abrasions. There was also a fight between the WVO and the RCP in Durham.

Dale, as I interviewed her, reminded me of the time when she was in charge of a leafleting crew at a housing project in the fall of 1979. With her was Big Al, a strong Jamaican who was on the ill-fated union slate with Bill, and two pregnant women, Chekesha and Rand's wife, Lorraine. (A few weeks later, Chekesha, still pregnant, was wounded in the Klan and Nazi attack.) As the crew was preparing to carry flyers door to door in the project, Dale received information that some RCP cadre had arrived from out of town and were in the project armed with pipes and spoiling for a fight. Dale called off the leafleting and sent everyone home. When she told Jim about this, his reaction was, "What do you mean you called it off? Be bold, comrade, be bold!" In relating this, I must say that I do not now believe it was Jim's sanest and finest hour. "Jim had me backed up against the refrigerator in your kitchen," Dale told me later, "and we just stood there arguing fiercely over this. He was telling me I should have been bold enough to complete this assignment even at the risk of pregnant women and the rest of us getting our heads bashed in, that I wasn't carrying out the party's line. I wouldn't give in to him. No, this was crazy. No way."

Although each one of us was responsible for his or her own actions, we all were influenced to some extent by the party's *boldness line*. For me, being bold meant standing my ground when attacked by someone who was capable of pulverizing me. For Jim, it meant being willing to put oneself in harm's way for the revolution. But Dale and a few other people responded to a palpably more dangerous environment more appropriately, without falling prey to the delusion that boldness is everything and that boldness will invariably win the day.

NOTES

1. See Employment Security Office, Greensboro, N.C., Docket No. VIII–UI–1549, transcript of testimony from appeal hearing on September 18, 1978.

2. *Granite Workers Update* (November 1978).

3. *Granite Workers Update* (September 1978).

4. Audio tape of Trade Union Educational League conference (8 October 1978).

5. *Granite Workers Update* (January 1979).

6. *Granite Workers Update* (March 1979).

7. Unless otherwise indicated, quotations by Willena Cannon are from a taped interview with her on March 3, 1993.

8. "Desperate Truckers Gunning for More Gas," *Workers Viewpoint*, July 1979, 1.

9

CHINA GROVE AND THE PREPARATIONS FOR NOVEMBER THIRD

COMING OUT OF THE WOODWORK

It was Saturday, June 30, 1979. Jim, Nelson, Paul, and Sally were meeting in our backyard. On one of my trips there, with a tray of sandwiches and a pitcher of lemonade, I handed Jim the Greensboro newspaper, pointing out a small notice: The Ku Klux Klan was planning to show the film *Birth of a Nation* in the town hall of China Grove on July 8. The film, a technical triumph of early filmmaking, is also a rabidly racist glorification of the Ku Klux Klan. The Klan used this film to recruit members to its organization.

In the ensuing discussion, the four WVO leaders agreed on the need for action. We were all familiar with the Klan's history of murdering and terrorizing African Americans, their primary target. We knew, moreover, that the Klan's racism and racist violence was inimical to the interests of people of all races and ethnic backgrounds. Our organizing work in various workplaces and communities was gathering momentum. WVO supporters who were open communists had become respected leaders. They were building trust and overcoming racial barriers to workers' unity. Along its bloody pathway, the Klan, a destroyer of working-class unity, had targeted union leaders on many occasions. It was categorically imperative to protect black people against the murder and mayhem brought by the Klan, and furthermore, it would not be possible to build a strong trade union movement while ignoring the Klan. Groups of Klan were openly marching and conducting recruiting drives on the streets of small and medium-sized southern towns. In 1978 and 1979, as at other historical intervals, the Klan was coming out of the woodwork.

Some further background to the action we took at China Grove is helpful here. There were several confrontations between the Klan and groups of workers and antiracist activists in the South, and WVO supporters from North Carolina participated in some of these. Two instances, one in Tupelo, Mississippi, and the other in Decatur, Alabama, illustrate Klan and anti-Klan activity of the period.

Tupelo is in an area maintained by the Tennessee Valley Authority. A supply of cheap labor and antiunion laws had drawn multinational corporations there, like Rockwell International and General Motors. A grassroots civil rights organization called the United League, founded by Skip Robinson, was having an impact on Tupelo and the surrounding area: people were organizing against the injustices that were diminishing their lives. The Ku Klux Klan attacked United League members in beatings and shootings, and a young black prisoner was murdered in jail by a sheriff's deputy who was an avowed Klansman. With no redress from local authorities forthcoming, people planned a civil rights march with wide support from outside the town. Thousands marched in Tupelo in November 1978, and WVO supporters were among them.

Answering the United League's call for help and marching in Tupelo in 1978 was Yonni Chapman, a WVO supporter from Chapel Hill. He recalled that the civil rights march was also an act of solidarity with a workers' struggle for unionization. "There was a local group of striking poultry factory workers marching with us," he said.[1]

> Black women workers mostly, some men. We stopped at the poultry plant and there were speeches. The poultry factory workers were the spark plugs of the march. They had a tremendous amount of energy, singing as we went along, doing a syncopated clapping as we marched. . . . As we got into downtown Tupelo, people started yelling, "There's the Klan!" The Klan had a little counterdemonstration a few blocks away from us. They were standing around the U.S. post office dressed in their robes—maybe thirty or forty of them. They had clubs and guns. People from Tupelo were talking about the connection between the Klan and the police.

In Decatur, Alabama, in 1978, police arrested a severely retarded black man and charged him with raping three white women and stealing money. A prison psychologist tested the prisoner and declared him mentally incapable of committing the sex act, but the charges stuck.[2] On the eve of the trial, the Southern Christian Leadership Conference (SCLC) led a march from Decatur to Cullman County, where the trial had been moved after threats by the Klan. They were turned back at the county line by two hundred angry whites, some in sheets. The SCLC again tried to march and again was taunted by a Klan-led mob. In August 1978, an all-white jury convicted the retarded man and sentenced him to thirty years in prison.

On May 26, 1979, SCLC and others marched in Decatur. The march was approaching the main street in downtown Decatur when some hundred Klansmen with ax handles and lead pipes blocked the path of about seventy-five black demonstrators. Two Klansmen and two black demonstrators were wounded that day—local police joined the KKK in shooting at the crowd. As a result of the May 26 violence, the City of Decatur outlawed firearms near demonstrations, but the Klan rode through the streets anyway toting Thompson machine guns and M-16's in open defiance of the ordinance. Imperial Wizard Bill Wilkinson declared that the Klan would stop blacks from marching again, but people vowed they would march again. Decatur became a cause célèbre to civil rights activists. On June 9, 1979, in a tension-charged march, three thousand people joined SCLC to confront the southern justice system.

In Durham, on the evening of June 8, 1979, WVO supporters held an emergency meeting at the Break the Chains Bookstore. Several people from Durham and Chapel Hill went to Decatur, including Paul Bermanzohn, Roz Pelles, and Jean (Sharpe) Chapman.[3] Arriving in Decatur in the wee hours of the morning, the Durham contingent was met and warmly welcomed by an armed community patrol. They were on their feet the next day marching and holding up a long red-and-black Workers Viewpoint banner with the bold inscription "BREAK THE CHAINS OF WAGE SLAVERY AND NATIONAL OPPRESSION!"

Leading the march were U.S. Congressman Walter Fauntroy and SCLC notables R. B. Cottonreader and Joseph Lowery. Their following was singing "We Shall Overcome." More militant people, among them the WVO supporters and local demonstrators, were critical of an SCLC attempt, in a church prior to the march, to disarm the demonstrators. For its part, SCLC was not happy about some of the marchers agitating into the faces of the police and the National Guard. Different philosophies and levels of militancy marched side by side through the streets of Decatur: that was typical at the time. Everyone who marched was met with armed police on rooftops, state troopers lining the streets, confederate flag-waving Klan, and the battle-ready U.S. Army with tanks. Local people joined the militant chanting of the WVO—"Fired up, gonna smash the KKK!" Some older black people said that the march was the biggest thing they had seen in Decatur since the Scottsboro Boys' case forty years earlier.

Monitoring Klan activity, the Anti-Defamation League of B'nai B'rith observed that Klan membership was on the rise again after dying down in the early 1970s. A political climate of official inertia and backtracking on civil rights was an inducement to the Klan to disrupt further civil rights progress. The WVO maintained that the Klan's reappearance had a great deal to do with the economic downturn of the late 1970s. Historically, the white supremacist Klan provided the race card to the ruling class to use to divide workers and to close down resistance to an unjust social and economic system by blacks and by poor and working people of all races.

Now, just three weeks after the June 9, 1979, Decatur protest, we made plans to confront the Klan in China Grove, North Carolina. There was only a week to organize for the July 8th event. Rand and I went to China Grove to try to find out what was happening. We learned that there was something of a debate going on. Some people had written letters to the editor in the daily paper opposing the Klan's use of town property to show their film. But we were no wiser about what the black residents of China Grove were up to.

Another visit to the town of China Grove, this time by Nelson, Paul, and Willena, quickly followed. They talked to quite a few local people in the segregated black community. The protest letters in the newspaper were written mainly by white liberals; the mood among some of the town's black residents was angrier and more militant. The black community of China Grove *did* plan to protest, the visitors were told. Furthermore, people did not mind having some help from the WVO. Paul, Willena, and Nelson hardly needed to be outside agitators—if anything, they were counseling restraint! Some black China Grove vets, with ordnance left over from the Vietnam War, wanted to do something severe against the Klan—like explode the town hall with the Klan inside. The WVO visitors discouraged the proposed violence. Others in China Grove wanted the counterdemonstration held safely on the other side of town from where the KKK would be gathering. "We pushed the idea of having a demonstration right up there with the Klan," Paul said. "We wanted to confront the Klan directly."

An alliance was formed between the black community in China Grove and the North Carolina region of the WVO. Each group brought roughly equal numbers to the protest march, and a few local white liberals and leftists also showed up on the day of the march.

In the 1979 anti-Klan campaign, from China Grove through November 3, Paul, Nelson, and Jim wrote most of the flyers, news releases, and other public literature. We always put out the WVO analysis about the Klan. I worked fairly closely with Sandi on the anti-Klan campaign, and we produced some flyers together. I think this one, used to get people to go to China Grove with us, was written by Sandi and me.

> Who are these dogs? For a hundred years they have beaten, murdered and raped while the cops protected them. They have lynched or shot thousands of black people. They have flogged, tarred and feathered union organizers, black and white—union organizers trying to unite people against the rich. They are cowardly nightriders who shoot into the homes of defenseless people.

Today, gas prices and everything else are too high to afford. And the Klan tells white people that blacks are the enemy. The Klan is trying to recruit people who are fed up with the situation today. There are some honest white people who have been misled into supporting the Klan. Don't be misled by the Klan! The Klan is a blood-soaked, tiny, vicious circle of agents for the capitalist class—the rich. They are paid by the FBI and supported by sheriffs and local police. The KKK lies saying they're fighting for white people. But these dogs serve only the rich ruling class—the enemy of black and white workers. This class pays the Klan to split us up, just at a time when unity between black and white workers is rising. That's who the Klan is!

The day before going to China Grove, Jim and I talked seriously about what might lie ahead. Jim said the bourgeoisie would throw the Klan in our faces every time we were successful in organizing workers. They would use the Klan to stop the momentum of our new drive for a worker-controlled trade union movement. We had to confront the Klan, and we had to expose their secret supporters. I felt strongly about the anti-Klan campaign: I was part of it, heart and soul. But I also had trepidations. China Grove would be different from previous demonstrations. We knew we were going out to meet a bunch of Klansmen. Jim agreed this was a different situation.

The conversation between us was even more personal. We had talked about having a baby together. Now we were conscious of new risks in our lives. We had to acknowledge to one another that we did not know where we would be the following evening, nor what condition we would be in. "It's altogether possible," I told Jim, "that one or both of us will be in jail. Or in the hospital, hurt. Or worse." We could not control the outcome of this thing. Jim did not dispute what I said. As he saw it, by boldly going ahead, by making the most militant stand we possibly could against the Klan, we would *minimize* danger, not only to ourselves, but to others as well. The Klan's signature was beatings, torture, and murder. For all we knew, others might be spared those horrors if we took a strong stand at China Grove, whatever our personal fate turned out to be. I agreeded but continued to grapple with my emotions. I loved Jim so much, I could not bear the thought of anything happening to him. I was afraid for myself, too. My response to the RCP assailant had been unthinking and spontaneous. A truly courageous action, I thought, is undertaken only when one is fully aware of the danger. In standing my ground at White Oak, I had acted impetuously. I had been surprised and reacted on the spur of the moment. Courage was not involved. The China Grove demonstration felt different: a calculation of the danger lay just below the surface of consciousness. Jim and I made plans to go to the beach, following China Grove, for a few days—*if* the demonstration there went without a hitch. I was relieved that Tonya and Alex were in New York on summer vacation with their father.

THE CHINA GROVE CONFRONTATION

With the summer's heat already hanging in the early morning air, WVO supporters assembled to confront the Ku Klux Klan. On no other occasion that I
can recall was our gathering so punctual. Never before had our departure for an
out-of-town event been on time, as it was that morning. We were usually plagued
with missed or misinterpreted communications, vehicles breaking down, and
mothers canceling at the last moment because of sick children. On July 8, 1979,
we connected like clockwork. The residents of the black housing projects who
joined us showed up, or were picked up, on time. The chronically late among us
were on time. Absolutely every adrenaline-driven body was on time. No one's
car broke down. We left when we said we would. We left with a consciousness of
going off to battle.

To the twenty-five or thirty people from Greensboro were added roughly that
number from Durham. The nervousness typical before a demonstration was
augmented before this one—a planned confrontation with a group with a long
history of responding violently to even mild actions for equality and civil rights.
We headed directly to the Westside Community Center in the heart of China
Grove's black neighborhood. There, people suited up in what can only be described as substandard attire for combat readiness. Photographs taken that day
show a weird assortment of hats—riding hats, football helmets, and construction
hard hats among them. Jim was wearing a hard hat to which was attached a big
plate of scratched-up plastic. The plastic was a welding shield designed to protect the eyes. Jim had horrible vision. The first thing he did on waking each day
was to grope for his thick corrective glasses. I'm sure the welding gear turned
him into a blind person at China Grove.

We armed ourselves. A few people were designated to carry concealed handguns and to defend the marchers, if the occasion demanded it. The rest of us
took whatever was at hand for protection: rocks, broken bottles, pieces of pipe,
sticks. I talked to Sally Bermanzohn. She was nervous. She had found a broken
bottle, and she gave it to me for self-defense. The local protesters also armed
themselves with such primitive weapons as were available: metal pipes, wooden
sticks, and broken glass. Probably, some carried concealed guns.

Around noon we sprung into action and marched toward the China Grove
town hall to the cadence of "Black and white must unite, Death to the Klan!"
Then we marched right, left, right, left, with brisk rhythmic steps to "The
people united will never be defeated!" and "El pueblo unido jamas sera ven-
cido." Militant voices roared out "Death to the Klan!" We kept our ranks
tight. Clutching sticks, rocks, and bottles in one hand and picket signs in the

CHINA GROVE AND THE PREPARATIONS FOR NOVEMBER THIRD

other, the crowd surged forward, with rising intensity, steadily increasing its pace.

At one point, as if for comic relief, the march halted temporarily. Paul was in one of a few cars at the rear of the march, placed there for medical and security needs. I learned later from him what it was that held up the march. "This thing was being led by these radical communist types—overthrow the government, whatever, whatever," he recalled, "and we were sitting for fifteen minutes in the hot sun with a stalled march. It was a *very* hot day," he added emphatically. "Then it got back to us what the matter was: the march stopped before a turn in the street because otherwise it would have been going the wrong way down a one-way street. They stopped to debate about whether to go down the street because it had arrows pointing the other way," he said. "So I started screaming, 'What the fuck is going on here? This is a revolutionary march. A fucking one-way sign is gonna stop the revolution?!'"

Whether Paul's spirited upbraiding helped to resolve the quandary about breaking the one-way-street law I do not know, but the march resumed and approached the town hall. By the time Paul's vehicle arrived at the town hall, the marchers were all there, consisting of about 100 to 150 people milling around on the large, grassy front lawn. Facing the noisy crowd, in front of the building, stood fifteen to twenty white men, some young, others middle-aged, and a few police officers. One man wore a T-shirt imprinted with the words "White Power" and a Nazi insignia. His gut dropped over his belt, and he struck a fierce pose as if to say he was ready to take on all comers. This was Roland Wayne Wood. There was a crazy assortment of uniforms that day. In a group of four men standing together, one had on the white Klansman habit, hood and all; another, evidently a neo-Nazi, wore the stiff brown uniform of a German storm trooper; a third, Gorrell Pierce, dapper in a dark suit, looked like a small-town mayor about to receive a gold watch in honor of retirement; and completing this excrescence of humanity was a boy in blue from the local police force. However, it wasn't funny. The tension in the air was tangible. The Klan and Nazis stood there with their rifles pointed at us. They had moved away from the demonstrators toward the porch of the town hall, where several of them now stood. Paul saw a man with what looked like a semiautomatic rifle, an M-16, and thought, "Holy Shit!"

I was weaving through the crowd, shooting a role of black-and-white film. Paul, standing close to the porch, watched as a policeman walked between his fellow officers and Gorrell Pierce. The noise level throughout the whole area was incredible. Paul could not hear what was said, and he noted that the police emissary had to talk directly into Pierce's ear to be heard above the din.

CHAPTER 9

There was shouting back and forth and it was getting angrier by the minute. Against the rhythmic roar of the anti-Klan chants, some marchers pulsed their way toward the porch. A cluster of protesters, Jim among them, reached the porch and, with sticks and pipes, began whacking at its wooden columns. Everyone gripped his or her weapon more tightly in readiness for whatever would come. The entire scene resembled the crescendo of a cacophonous symphony. Layers of hot summer air were rising more and more slowly, mired in a fever pitch of anger, hostility, and fear. As the combined passions approached a top pitch beyond which the ceiling of the world would surely shatter, time moved so slowly that it seemed to stop. For a moment that only metaphorically can even be called a moment, past and future parted, leaving only a disjointed reality awaiting definition by humans, a terrible unknown out of the hands of any single knowing human being. Anything was possible. The surface of time was hammered flat; any design might be imposed on it—by gunfire about to erupt, by bodies floating uncertainly as if already dead, by spirits seeking revenge. The roar of insults in a moment when both sheaths of time, the once-was and the not-yet, were rent apart felt to me like a deathly silence. When the continuum was restored, the police were ushering the Klan and Nazis into the building. The demonstrators took the withdrawal of the racists into the building as an indication of a retreat and as evidence of their inherent cowardice. That is how we represented what happened at China Grove at the time and for long afterward.

The Klan and Nazis were holed up in the building and were looking out through the windows, their guns at the ready. "Once they were inside the building," Paul admitted, "we were presented with a dilemma. We didn't have a clear plan what to do." There was general approval for capping the victory by taking and burning the confederate flag. "The most difficult problem," recalled Paul, "was getting somebody whose hands weren't shaking too much to light a match." The emblem of southern secession from the union ended up in the hands of Charles Finch. About Charles, Paul said, "he was the most Aryan looking person in our group—to my mind perfect for the role." A southerner, born and bred, from Thomasville, North Carolina, Charles spoke with a thick southern drawl. Even a college education had not purged his formal writing of "y'all." Cheered on by the demonstrators, this traitor to the confederacy now lit the confederate flag and ceremoniously held it up as it burned, in full view of the Klansmen inside the building. Simultaneously, Charles was making the TV news that evening across the state, to the dismay of some of his relatives.

This wild, crazy scene went on a bit longer until the demonstrators marched once around the town hall and then back to the Westside Community Center. There was much jubilation and celebration. In addition, there was concern about possible retaliation by the Klan. I photographed Sandi and others standing guard with rifles.

We had the most recent issue of the Workers Viewpoint newspaper, and we distributed copies. I talked to a lot of China Grove residents that day. They were interested because they could see that we were serious about what we said. I remember explaining to several people that the capitalists want people to think there is no alternative, or that the alternatives would all be more oppressive and totalitarian than what we now have. But things do not have to be this way, I said. In some places working people have taken over their governments. They may not be running things perfectly, but at least the main obstacle is lifted and all people may strive to reach their full humanity. A black teenager listened eagerly, then grabbed a cardboard sign that read "the only solution is socialist revolution" and displayed it on the front of his motorcycle.

We held a little rally right then and there. Durham's Black Belt Singers performed several songs, among them *Women Hold Up Half the Sky*. There were speeches by local community leaders and by members of the WVO. Nelson gave a revolutionary speech that met with great approval. "Tell it, brother," he was urged on. Someone from the community had taken away a piece of the burnt confederate flag as a souvenir. I asked him to repeat the flag burning so that I could photograph it. Smiling, he held up and burned the flag fragment as I clicked my camera. We did not know it at the time, but in the other camp Joe Grady was also holding up a piece of tattered, burnt confederate flag to show to the media as his fellow Klansmen smoldered with revenge.

I had seen little of Jim the whole day. With the confrontational part of the action past, we briefly made contact, assuring one another that we were fine. We hugged, talked for a minute or two, and went back to our tasks. Before leaving China Grove, WVO leaders arranged for some people to stay behind overnight to help insure people's safety. Driving back, we were alert, especially when we stopped at a gas station along Route 85. I could imagine Klansmen on CBs telling gas station attendants along the route, "They're headed your way; blast the nigger-lovin' commies." Our safe haven was back in Greensboro.

ROMANTIC INTERLUDE

In bed the next morning, Jim and I nursed taut nerves and weary spirits. We were thankful that it was vacation time; we would be able to relax and bask in the sun for a few days. When we planned to start our vacation early the next morning after the return from China Grove, we had underestimated the raw nerves factor. We couldn't get ourselves to move from the house until four in the afternoon.

The trip was punctuated by two stops. Jim wanted me to meet Marty Nathan. We stopped at Mike and Marty's house on the way to the beach. Mike wasn't home when we arrived, but Marty was. Jim introduced me to a woman with black hair, an exceptionally pretty face, and a warm, appealing personality. Marty was in medical school at Duke when Jim was on the staff. Both had been part of the Medical Committee for Human Rights. I could not guess then the unspeakably sad and heavy events that would cement strong bonds of friendship between us.

The other stop was at a phone booth on the highway. I called my kids who were vacationing in New York with their father. I tried to explain how magnificent, how scary, how significant the China Grove demonstration had been, while assuring them that Jim and I were fine. There was no residual feeling of loose ends, of future threats. It was done. We were triumphant against the Klan! Somehow the words that came out of my mouth did not convey what I meant or felt. In the end, I gave my children no more information than a hello, an I love you, and an I miss you. I had meant to distinguish the China Grove event from everything we had done before—all the workplace struggles they had heard us discuss. I left the phone booth feeling that my words were flat. I knew I hadn't communicated to them what China Grove was about—I hadn't communicated it yet to myself.

Jim used to tease me about my poor planning for vacations. I was so consumed in political work that when I planned a family vacation, my family found themselves in some ridiculous situation. One time we arrived at our hotel two days early, and we slept on the beach the first night, where we were chewed up by mosquitoes and other insects. On this occasion, I booked Jim and me at a hotel outside of Atlantic Beach, North Carolina. Somewhere I had seen a circular with a picture of the hotel, and it looked good. The dream hotel turned out to be a semiabandoned place on a peninsula that was closing permanently at the end of the season. We parked on some bumpy grass because the hotel had never had an asphalt parking lot. We asked the young manager if we could have a room overlooking the water, and he told us to take any room we pleased; we were the only guests. So we selected our "honeymoon" room. (We called all our vacations together "honeymoons.") The TV didn't work and there was no hot water. We went downstairs and made a barbecue in the back of the hotel. The property had a marina, but there was no real beach. We walked along the rocks that swept out toward the ocean. A mangy dog was hanging around, its presence altogether in keeping with the forlorn aspect of the hotel. Jim roughhoused with it. Then we ate our barbecued dinner and stayed out until dark.

Returning to our room, we decided to make something of the full moon. We rearranged the furniture so that, as we lay in bed, the moonlight would be streaming in upon us. This appealed to our super-romantic mood at the time. We shifted things around, displacing bed, chairs, and tables until the bed captured the strongest beam of moonlight at just the right angle. The next day, agreeing that we did not like the isolation of this haunt, or the fact that there was no proper beach and no direct access to the ocean for swimming, we decided to look for another hotel.

"No heat, no TV, you can't seriously ask twenty-two dollars for this room," I said to the manager.

"Didn't know about the TV," he said. "Sorry about the heat."

"I'll give you sixteen dollars," I offered. He took it immediately.

I told Jim in the car as we drove away, "I bet he would have taken twelve. What a jerk I was to offer him sixteen dollars."

"That's okay," Jim said. "He has furniture to move. Remember?"

"We bathed it in moonlight for him," I said, dreamily.

"Bathed in moonlight, baptized with nookie, he's still got to move it, no? Don't worry that you gave him too much," he said, adding, "the place was a gem right out of a Vincent Price movie. Where did you say you found that circular?"

I laughed. We both laughed. One more day at the beach and we would have to return to Greensboro. Our lives were large and full of meaning. And we were happy.

I JOIN THE PARTY

I was fired from Binswanger on account of my ineptitude on a scaffold. A short time later, I was hired as a spinner at a Collins and Aikman yarn mill in Graham, about a half hour drive from Greensboro. More memorable and meaningful to me than starting a new job was my formal induction into the Workers Viewpoint Organization on September 16, 1979. Jim and I had intense discussions leading up to this event. He encouraged me along, telling me several times that I was becoming a better communist and had developed a stronger working-class stand— words that were music to my ears.

Bill Sampson was one of my sponsors. When he interviewed me, he asked me a question about the forms of transition to socialism. I panicked for a moment as I realized that for all my hours of studying and organizing, I really had no surefire recipe for getting there from here. I imagined aloud a scenario that included local enclaves that modeled the new society. These small experiments would gradually catch on and spread. Factory nuclei would play a big role in their propagation. I cited the homosexual culture in San Francisco as a positive example emphasizing that if you organize and mass your forces properly, you change the character and conditions of a place. Bill thought about my response and admitted that he did not have any clearer ideas than I did about the forms of transition to socialism. He complimented me with, "Signe, you are a traitor to your class," meaning that I was now a genuine force for working-class revolution and no longer stuck with my petty-bourgeois credentials. Bill recommended that I be admitted to the Workers Viewpoint Organization, and another member, knowing how long I had been an ardent and hardworking WVO supporter, said that it was high time. Jim presided over my induction, which was a simple ceremony at the home of another party member. Jim's little speech remains sharp in my memory. "The comrade has three outstanding attributes," he said. "She is good at learning, good at learning, and good at learning." It is still the highest praise anyone has ever given me.

In the fall of 1979, between late September and mid-October, the WVO held its founding party congress. I heard from Jim and others afterward what transpired in the course of several sessions. The name Workers Viewpoint Organization was abandoned. The organization, henceforth, was called the Communist Workers Party (CWP). At the Founding Congress of the CWP, Jim was elected to the party's Central Committee. Warnings—perhaps premonitions—of the difficult period ahead and the amount of dedication and sacrifice that would be required issued from Jerry Tung, general secretary of the CWP. Many people definitely felt that we had raised the ante of class struggle, and that the bourgeoisie would be forced to strike out at the Communist Workers Party. The CWP was not some vague threat of creeping socialism; it was the vigorous exercise of getting there at a gallop.

THE ANTI-KLAN CAMPAIGN IN THE FALL OF 1979

Wherever we went around the state that summer and fall, we boasted of the victory of China Grove. Faced with the wrath of the people, the Klan turned tail and ran—that's how we played it. The North Carolina leadership of the WVO decided to build on the victory and use it to boost the trade union work. As Paul recalled, a plan was developed for an anti-Klan march with an educational conference at the conclusion of the march on November 3, 1979, "to talk about the Klan's role in breaking up workers' movements over the preceding hundred years, since the period of Reconstruction. We had a lot of ideas and people to make speeches. It was going to be a major educational and organizing event." Paul had strong feelings about the anti-Klan march: because of his parents' experiences as Holocaust survivors, antifascist politics was the name of the game for him.

A main propaganda piece used in the anti-Klan rally was an "open letter" to some Klansmen. Its inflammatory rhetoric would return to haunt us. The intention, however, was to tap the anti-Klan sentiments of workers and the poor and to draw them to the march and conference. Although addressed to Joe Grady and Gorrell Pierce, among others, the letter was a device to get the public's attention. It was an Orson Wells-type bit of realism, if you will. No one ever discussed delivering the letter to Grady, Pierce, or any other Klansman, much less did anyone attempt to do so. Dated October 22, 1979, the letter was written in the rush of organizing by Paul, with input from Nelson. It was signed by Nelson for the WVO.

AN OPEN LETTER TO JOE GRADY, GORRELL PIERCE, AND ALL KKK MEMBERS AND SYMPATHIZERS

The KKK is one of the most treacherous scum elements produced by the dying system of capitalism. . . . Your program is based on lies and is being promoted to fan racial and national prejudices. It is used to turn worker against worker, white against black, Indian, or Chicano, Protestant against Catholic or Jew. The Klan is being promoted to make it harder to fight this capitalist system which is the real source of the problems of the American people.

Grady and Pierce, . . . you are nothing but a bunch of racist cowards. Your militant front is calculated to attract whites and particularly white youths who are being crushed daily by this system and who are mad and are looking for someone to fight. You hope to frighten and terrify blacks, Jews, and anyone who fights against this system. You don your hoods and run around with guns spreading your poison. But, as we showed in China Grove, the Klan is a bunch of cowards.

We are having a march and conference on November 3, 1979 to further expose your cowardice, why the Klan is so consciously being promoted, and to organize to physically smash the racist KKK wherever it rears its ugly head. Yes, we challenged you to attend our November 3rd rally in Greensboro. . . . You were quoted in the AP press release as saying that "if the communists think they are going to get me to attack them, they are crazy as hell." No Grady and Pierce—we are not crazy. We are very clear on what you are doing and that you and the KKK are a bunch of two-bit cowards. You "invited" us to show up at Klan rallies. *Grady and Pierce, we accept! Where in the hell are you holding your scum rallies?* You cowards manage to keep the location of your rallies a secret. We challenge you to say in public where and when you hold your rallies so that the people can organize to chase you off the face of the earth.

What you do is disorganize the people and make it difficult for workers and op-pressed people of all races and national backgrounds to unite and fight together against the daily abuses of the capitalist system. But, in spite of your treacherous-ness, the Klan will be smashed physically. Grady and Pierce, all Klanspeople, and your Nazi friends—you are a temporary pest and obstruction in our fight to end all exploitation and oppression. But we take you seriously and we will show you no mercy.

To announce our anti-Klan march and conference, we called the media to Kannapolis, a working-class mill town near China Grove. Some months earlier, Sandi, along with a couple of former White Oak workers, moved to Kannapolis. Sandi was working at Cannon Mills, training to be a textile machinery mechanic. She may have been the first woman fixer anyone ever heard of there. Almost def-initely, she was the first black woman.

"There were union victories in textile mills in the western part of the state, and they were moving eastward little by little toward the China Grove-Kannapolis area," Paul said, in recalling the context of our anti-Klan work. "Kannapolis, a large unincorporated town, was the ultimate company town, with some thirty to forty thousand ununionized textile workers in the Can-non Mills Corporation. Having made strong inroads at Cone Mills, we felt we were in position to expand our textile work."

In sum, the anti-Klan campaign was not a diversion from the WVO's labor work, nor an admission of failure in its labor organizing, as newspapers sub-servient to capitalist interests were to state later. A thesis in this book is that the capitalist class deployed the Klan when it was threatened by a potentially pow-erful and united workers movement *and* out of fear of African American activists linking up with communists who were outspokenly promoting socialist revolu-tion. The activities of the WVO in the mills and at China Grove certainly at-tracted the notice of stakeholders in a system with gross economic disparity and needless poverty. The "threats" from blacks and workers grew and merged, set-ting off an alarm button to the stakeholders that their race and class domination might not be forever—a terrible thing from their point of view.

There is no denying that what happened in China Grove on July 8, 1979, is linked to what happened in Greensboro on November 3, 1979. News stories de-signed to cover up the facts said simply that the Klan came to Greensboro for re-venge. While there is no doubt that the Klan was lusting for revenge after China Grove, the Klan's desire for revenge does *not* account for how or why the Greensboro Massacre happened, or why it happened as it did. More essential to the explanation of that event is that *shortly after China Grove*, some government official notified Bernard Butkovich, an agent in Cleveland, Ohio, for the U.S. Bureau of Alcohol, Tobacco, and Firearms (BATF) and gave him an assignment in North Carolina. At this point in my story, the BATF was not even on our radar screen. For now it is good to keep in mind that what China Grove set in motion was not merely a vengeful right wing and a pumped up left wing, but agencies working behind the scene, as will be discussed more fully later.

WVO's Kannapolis press statement of October 12, 1979, became part of an Associated Press wire story. The *Charlotte Observer* headline read, "Group Seeks Confrontation with Klan." In a *Durham Morning Herald* article, "Anti-Klan Rally Scheduled," Paul mentions that we had applied for a parade permit. In fact, Nelson had been downtown trying to secure the parade permit several weeks before the scheduled November 3 march and conference, but his request was ignored.

Newspapers alluded to the confrontation and potential violence at the Ku Klux Klan rally at China Grove in July and quoted from the WVO press release—"We invite these cowards to come out from under their rocks on Nov. 3 . . . to come out and face the wrath of the people."[4] The WVO press statement at Kannapolis, Paul later conceded, was "gratuitously inflammatory. We did it on the fly, at the last minute." Contacted by a reporter, Winston-Salem Klan leader Joe Grady said Klansmen would not confront Bermanzohn's group in Greensboro and that Klan detractors should show up at Klan rallies. "They might catch us on the defensive one time too many there," he said.[5]

Although I was at Kannapolis on October 12, 1979, did media work, and helped provide security for the WVO, I had forgotten it. When I interviewed Paul, I recollected the role I played that day. I remembered sitting in the cottage Sandi had rented with some friends and stuffing envelopes with press releases to mail to the majority of the media that had not shown up at the press conference an hour earlier. I also remembered being one of several lookouts on a street corner to watch for potential disruptions as Paul and Nelson talked to the media.

To make a point about how disorganized he and Nelson were that day, Paul related this anecdote of the Kannapolis press conference. "Big Al came with us to provide security with a rifle Nelson had in his house. It was one of these things with a clip. When we got to Kannapolis we did this bold press conference and everything was fine, except that Nelson had forgotten the clip for the rifle. So our security person was walking around with what was essentially a club in the shape of a high-powered rifle. We realized it only on the way back because while we were there we were too busy grandstanding to realize everything that was going on. Big Al told us when we stopped at a fast food joint on the way back from Kannapolis."

After the Kannapolis press conference, we leafleted in Greensboro and Durham, using the open letter and other flyers. When I handed out leaflets to public housing residents at Ray Warren Homes, some people raised a concern about the possibility of the Klan interfering with the rally. I assured people that the Klan would not be there. That was my honest belief. None of us tried to discern if Grady's remark to the press meant anything at all, or if he was even speaking for all Klan members since other Klan factions were at odds with his. In Durham's black community, also, there was uneasiness and anxiety over the leaflets.

Mike Nathan had participated in China Grove and was horrified by how narrowly a violent and bloody outcome was avoided. Mike interpreted what the WVO was calling boldness as something more akin to insanity. He and Marty argued about it. His criticisms notwithstanding, Mike would be there on November 3. Sally Bermanzohn attempted to get the attention of the top WVO leadership in New York and to persuade them that there was a dangerous situation in North Carolina since China Grove. But her well-founded worries were merely brushed aside. Sally would be there on November 3, too—pregnant.

One night, Big Man dropped by to speak with Jim. The three of us sat around the kitchen table talking and drinking. Jim and Big Man had enough to drink for some earnest conversation. Big Man got out what was on his mind. "With your education, bein' a doctor, an' white—now what you doin' this for? You know you're crazy; you don't have to be doin' this." Jim tried to explain, but then came the sequel to Big Man's thought—"You can *stop* doin' this any time you get ready to *stop* doin' it; you can quit fightin' the Klan. We black folks have no choice. They won't let us be." Big Man was trying to understand why Jim didn't want a big house, a comfortable life, lots of money. "Walk out on this now an' ain't nobody gonna say nothin,'" Big Man pointed out.

Jim argued with Big Man that he wasn't being a do-gooder; he'd had privileges and opportunities, Jim said, but the fight against the Klan was his fight, too. Jim insisted that the Klan is really against the interests of white people and of all workers, whatever their race, religion, or nationality. Yet nothing Big Man said was false. In fact, it was profoundly true that white people could (usually) escape or ignore the Klan's wrath, but black people could not. The Klan was aimed at them, as were the institutions that allowed, protected, and promoted the Klan. The Klan did more than just wreck the unity of the working class; it destroyed the lives of a portion of humanity. The WVO spoke of *national oppression* of African Americans on account of a historical and systemic practice of attacking human lives and rights; the Klan was an explicit expression of this. I think Jim didn't really answer Big Man. Jim was in the fight because he hated injustice, oppression, and exploitation; because his father had a big social conscience and taught him well; because he was Jewish and sensitive to race hatred; and because he was Jim. I think that there is something in human beings that hates injustice, no matter to whom it is directed: we built a culture that actively nurtured and reinforced this sentiment.

If Jim had the option of ignoring the Klan, Big Man did not. Nor Willena. Nor other African Americans. Willena had memories of Klan terror from her South Carolina childhood. In her small town of Mullens, an interracial couple in a mutually consenting relationship were attacked by a mob. The white woman was stoned but got away. The man was locked in a barn, and the barn was set afire. Called to the scene, the local sheriff did nothing but let the black man burn to death. "His screamin' and hollerin' went on in my nightmares for a long time," Willena said. In the 1940s, Big Man fought the Klan in South Carolina. He told Jim about lynchings that he had witnessed. He saw a man dragged from a car and killed. Another time he witnessed a man hung and then shot until nothing was left but the rope.

FOREWARNINGS IGNORED

The Klan did not interfere with our preparations for November Third, but the police did. In Greensboro, when Willena and Joyce put up posters around town announcing the November Third anti-Klan march and conference, they were harassed by the police, and many of the posters were torn down.

Possible forewarnings went unheeded. Once, Sandi was going through the Greensboro–Winston-Salem–High Point airport when she was stopped by the police and her suitcase was confiscated. No charges were brought against her, and the incident was never explained. The encounters we had with the RCP might have been, in actuality, police harassment against the WVO. Again, very shortly before November 3, an automatic teller machine swallowed Jim's bankcard. He never got it back. In the context of what was happening in our lives, I think it may not have been a fluke. Even the fact that the City of Greensboro so readily hired Jim came to seem, in retrospect, ominous. One of Jim's coworkers was Rex Stevenson, a large man very fond of alcohol. He took a great interest in Jim and drew him into long conversations on political and historical topics (which, admittedly, was not hard to do). At his request, Jim loaned his coworker *The Bolsheviks in the Tsarist Duma*—an unlikely read for an inveterate drunk. Stevenson surfaced at the Klan trial after the murders and was a defense witness for Klan lawyers. His gratuitous lies at the trial suggested the possibility that he was a police agent when he became chummy with Jim.

One night some weeks prior to November 3, the police burst into the home of our friends Ed and Claire, who lived just around the corner from us. Ed worked at White Oak and was an active trade unionist. His wife was an activist, and both were WVO supporters. The police said that they were looking for an escaped felon and gave a name. It happened that a man giving that name, whom Ed and Claire had never met before, appeared at their door moments before and then left. The police proceeded to look for the purported felon by turning the couple's home upside down. One officer stood with his weapon pointed squarely at Claire, who had her tiny infant daughter in her arms all the while. They ransacked the whole house, opening closets, pulling out bureau drawers, and rifling through books and papers on shelves. Not long before, I had moved the Roneo from our house to Ed's, which I felt was a more secure location. My whole printing operation was set up at Ed's house at the time, and, unable to think of anything better, I moved it back to my house.

(The incident that befell Ed and Claire triggered a memory from my antiwar days. Late one night, we were meeting at the downtown storefront that housed the Greensboro Peace Center. We were planning a protest demonstration to greet then-President Nixon at the Greensboro airport the next day. Earlier in the day, some men dressed as plumbers had torn apart the bathroom facilities on one pretext or another. That evening the police rushed in on the meeting announcing that they were looking for an escaped felon.)

Of all the indications that should have been warnings to us, one is most firmly implanted in my memory. I was in the habit of combing the newspapers regularly for information—in that way I caught the notice of the Klan's recruitment rally in China Grove. In mid or late September of 1979, I saw a small article in the Greensboro paper stating that the Klan and other right-wing groups met and formed a coalition that they called the "United Racist Front." I was going over to Nelson's house, and I took the clipping with me and showed it around. There were several people in the room, but the only one I remember clearly other than Nelson is César. I said to everyone, "These guys have had a meeting. I bet they have our pictures up on a tree and they're doing target practice on them right now." I said that almost nonchalantly—it was just a passing comment. There was no discussion about it.

Given our mindset at the time, I am not sure what we would have done with that information. I shared the heady feeling that we could accomplish anything. I believed in us with a confidence that gave the lie to our vulnerability. It has haunted me for years that I might have acted more responsibly that day and *insisted* that the leadership of our organization come to terms with a potential threat. In retrospect, the scenario I mentioned probably was taking place and perhaps, as later information suggested, with pictures supplied by the FBI! On the other hand, how could we have guessed or anticipated the depth of the conspiracy that was actually afoot?

THE PARADE PERMIT

Securing the parade permit, on November 1, 1979, provided the occasion for a final press conference. That morning Nelson was told by Captain Trevor Hampton that the permit was ready and that Sergeant Comer would meet him at 11:30 on the morning of the march at the corner of Everitt and Carver, the starting point of the march. Nelson and Paul held the news conference at Greensboro's Governmental Plaza in front of the police department. As a party leader, spokesperson, and the main Greensboro organizer for the march and rally—not to mention as a black man who had long dared to struggle for civil rights—Nelson was the person most entangled with the Greensboro cops. After some weeks of not responding to Nelson's request for a parade permit, the police issued the permit two days before the march and conference were to take place. Furthermore they made Nelson agree to a condition before they would grant the permit—*the marchers must not have any arms that day*. This condition entailed suspension of the legal right of North Carolinians to bear arms openly in public and may have been unconstitutional. The police, in effect, told us that we could march if we disarmed ourselves; otherwise we could not march. When the police demanded a ban on weapons, Nelson expressed his concern about the safety and security of the march. Captain L. S. Gibson looked him in the eye and assured him that the police would protect the march.

Since several incidents had occurred by then in which the police harassed citizens who were advertising the November 3 assembly, Nelson lambasted the police to the media. "We fully expect the police to continue their slimy tactics," Nelson announced at the WVO/CWP press conference. "We say to [Mayor] Jim Melvin and the police, stay out of our way. The march will go on. The police hate us—we know it—and they are out to get us. But the people of Greensboro are intent on driving out the scum KKK."[6]

On the periphery of that press conference stood a few spectators. A man whom neither Nelson nor Paul had ever seen before entered into conversation with Paul, saying he was surprised to hear that the Klan was still around and was a threat. It occurred to Paul then, or soon after, that there was something fishy about this man. If he was, as he seemed to be, a small businessman, it was odd that he lacked awareness of the continuing presence of the Klan.

CHAPTER 9

The spectator was Klansman Edward Dawson. Before standing on the side-lines at the press conference and having an amiable chat with Paul and Nelson, Dawson had been inside the police station. Unknown to Paul and Nelson, Dawson was instructed by Detective Jerry Cooper to request a copy of the parade permit. He did so, and he had it in his pocket when he was feigning ignorance about the Klan. The police were familiar with Dawson when they gave him a copy of the permit. They knew Dawson was a Klansman. *They were paying him to be their agent!* Two days later Dawson would lead a caravan of cars filled with Klan and Nazis to the anti-Klan rally in order to murder people.

On the permit was the information that Nelson had agreed to a weapons ban. The permit stated the starting point of the march—Everitt Street and Carver Drive. That intersection, in the heart of the black housing project known as Morningside Homes, was precisely where the police arranged to meet Nelson at 11:30, a half hour before the march was scheduled to begin. The permit detailed, as well, the entire parade route. Nelson had gone over the parade route with the police. The information on the permit was never altered. In view of the fact that the police later on would profess confusion about the starting point of the march, it is important to present these details.

A second gathering place at Windsor Community Center was described on the permit filed with the police. Windsor Center was along the march route. It was on a main thoroughfare and easy for out-of-towners to find. Hence, Windsor Center was printed on the posters plastered around town as the gathering place for those wanting to march. March organizers and party leadership, who attended to many details in order to get the day off to a good start, were expected at the intersection of Everitt and Carver, the actual starting point as stated on the permit. We would march the short distance—about a half mile—from Everitt and Carver to the Windsor Community Center and join with the main body of march participants. We would all proceed together in a militant and spirited march through town. It would be a marvelous prelude to the educational forum planned for the afternoon. We considered the anti-Klan conference, with analysis and lessons from interesting speakers and a discussion open to all, as the main feature of the event, the part that would make a lasting impression on people.

A BEEHIVE OF ACTIVITY

My living room on the evening of November 2, 1979, was a beehive of activity. At the last minute, important details were attended to in a rush. Dot and her daughter, Doris, longtime friends of the Johnsons from the days of the Greensboro Association of Poor People, now sat on the mahogany-veneered Empire couch in my living room. They and other women from the black community were sewing the new Revolutionary Youth League uniforms, which some of their children, Alex, the Johnson's daughters Akua and Ayo, and Willena's son Kwame would wear the next day. In the course of the evening, Nelson dropped by, as did Big Man, Rand, Lorraine, Dale, Bill, and others. Sandi was there for most of the evening. As the sewing group in the living room plied needle and thread, others scurried around the house trying to deal with loose ends. We filled up the big eight-room house with our comings and goings, and we electrified it with sparks of animated conversation and debate.

Small groups of people were sequestered in Jim's study upstairs. Others sat around the kitchen table, absorbed in planning the march and forum. A heated discussion took place about the security of the march. Fragments of the conversation spilled out from the kitchen and dining room to the living room. Someone raced downstairs from Jim's study with questions, answers, suggestions. At one point the imposing figure of Big Man was there, greeting Jim, Bill, and Sandi—he was particularly close to the three of them. Nelson and Big Man had a lively debate. Big Man was on the program after the march and was slated to talk about his experience fighting the Klan years before—in his bootlegging days. Now he stated his strong reservations about what he perceived to be inadequate security and a failure to appreciate fully the threat posed by the Klan.

Someone suggested urging the residents of Morningside Homes to be on their porches with weapons at the ready for self-defense and to defend the marchers in case the Klan showed up. Or, with the residents' permission, we could stand on their porches with weapons. At some point this proposal was evidently in the hopper because we actually produced flyers intended for the residents of Morningside Homes. I have them—printed on blue paper. I do not think any were distributed.

On Saturday, Nov. 3rd, the "Death to the Klan" march will come along this route. . . . The Police Department of Greensboro . . . has made a special rule that says we can't have any weapons to defend ourselves. . . . The police say they will protect us. . . . Nothing could be further from the truth. The police are more dangerous to us than the Klan. They can murder us legally. . . . The police . . . protect the property and wealth of the rich and try to smash the struggles of the people. Any strike that we have, the police show up for harassment. . . .

We, the working class people, have to defend ourselves and depend on each other. We should not depend on the police. So, on Saturday, we want you . . . to sit on your porch or stand in your yard with your gun. This is the best way to defend the march. Our only real strength is the people—Black and White united!

Any plan that might have taken seriously Big Man's prophetic reservations was checked. Morningside residents on their front porches, at attention and flashing guns to defend the anti-Klan march, was a nonevent. It was one of an infinite number of what-ifs in mulling over the outcome of November 3. Whether the spectacle of an armed, prepared community would have given the Klan and Nazis pause before unpacking their own arsenal, whether it would have deterred, or only deferred, their assassination plans, or whether (as Nelson believed) it would have brought the police down on our heads, must be left solely to one's imagination and sense of history.

Nelson thought it "not at all likely that the Klan would come to Greensboro into an African American community, into a hostile situation with people who they believe may have weapons." He was more worried about the Greensboro Police being a source of disruption. When I interviewed Nelson many years later, his recounting jogged my memory. Suddenly I could see him standing in the middle of my living room on the night of November 2, 1979, facing women who were sewing uniforms. They listen and continue sewing.

"The police want to attack this march, and they intend to use the issue of weapons as the basis to do it," he told the group assembled. "They've set up a situation where there's a ban, and they have invited us to violate the ban. And as soon as we do, there'll be a police riot headed at us. I have a meeting arranged with the police a half hour before the march starts. I intend to talk clearly to them and tell them—'Listen, we do not want any trouble with you all today. We don't trust you. We know you're up to no good, but we don't want any trouble.'"

His voice dropped to barely a whisper in the retelling. This was a painful subject for him. I prodded him gently. I tried to remember to tell all my friends that I interviewed to pretend that I was an ignorant journalist hearing the story for the first time and to explain everything.

"We frankly did not believe or expect the Klan to come," Nelson continued. "I did not. And I said so the night before. When the city required us to have no arms on that day, I reluctantly agreed with it, and I led the effort to persuade our organization that we should not have any public arms available. I did not think we should give the police an excuse to lock people up because we were violating their ban on weapons. So we went to some lengths over some opposition," he explained, "to make sure there were no public weapons present."

Nelson argued, "in a lawyerly fashion, to our folks," about what he thought the most likely source of disruption to the march. Someone planted in the march might suddenly pull a weapon. Or the person's coat would swing open, revealing a weapon, in order to provoke a response.

"The provocateur would wait until the march to attack the people," he conjectured. "Our natural instinct would be to respond to the provocation. If we did, we would have a police riot. We agreed that if anyone should come into the march with a weapon, that person is either just an innocent person with a gun or a provocateur, and more likely it's a provocateur. Our strategy was to immediately pull away from the person and leave him alone, and let the police take him, and then we would accuse the police of planting the person. Our marshals would isolate anyone trying to start such an incident from the crowd and would see to it that the marchers remained disciplined. That way we would avoid the thing. We would not be baited into responding to violence with violence. That's how I had thought this whole thing out."

None of us, Nelson included, anticipated collusion between the Klan and the police. Nelson constructed his scenario "from all the indications I was getting—from the unwillingness of the police to give a parade permit, which they declined to give right up until we had a press conference and forced it out of them; from the fact that their operative, a lady who worked in their office, was communicating with the pastor of the church where we were to have the afternoon conference and telling him about bombs and stuff. The police succeeded in taking away the church and made us scramble to find another place. All the harassment I was getting was coming from the Greensboro Police. *They* were the people who it seemed to me were in a position to destroy this march, and ultimately, I think that's exactly what they did." He paused. "I don't think they did it the way I thought they would do it." Focusing on one scenario, Nelson missed the actual set up, but he didn't miss the point about the police.

As Nelson spoke, I pictured the young man I first met at the Greensboro Peace Center some twenty years earlier. In place of the flashing, triumphant smile that saw only victory ahead, there was a warm and welcoming smile on a face touched with the sadness and realism of life. Nelson is not lavish in showing emotion, just genuine. I still regard him as my mentor and have never ceased to admire him. No one who has ever met Nelson Johnson can forget him—certainly no one who has heard him speak. To be able to say hateful things about him, his enemies have to substitute a stereotype from their own diseased and bigoted imaginations. All but his enemies quickly see that he is a very rare person, one with a superior intellect and moral character.

Because he was sure the police were looking for an opening to destroy the march, Nelson argued against the plan of asking the people of Morningside to be on their porches, or allowing us to be on their porches, with weapons. "We would have had the problem of getting to their porches with the weapons or, if we got there before the police got there, we'd have to stay there. Once we left their porches and went to the street, we would immediately be in violation of the ban. 'So forget the whole thing,' I advised, 'and let's just go with the march and have a great time. The Klan isn't coming and if one or two people with weapons show up and try to disrupt things, we have a plan to deal with that by isolating them.' And that's the way that it went down," he concluded.

In the aftermath of the brutal murders, Nelson was indicted and was under attack. "The media put out the speculation that I was in the FBI and set the whole thing up," Nelson said. "Any way I went there was a scenario they were going to play back on me. So, to the media and at the trials, we basically stated our position that we were not seeking an armed confrontation, didn't expect one to occur, were unprepared for one, and we left it at that. That is the basic truth. There was no need to go into all the details of who said what and what scenario we expected."

None of us ever imagined the police would *not be there*, that they would arrange to stay away. We had declared the Klan too cowardly to commit their crimes in broad daylight: on this we were not entirely wrong. *We overlooked government and police complicity with the Klan.* We knew from our study of history that police arranged to give the Klan time to beat freedom riders in the sixties, but we failed to *apply* the lessons about police complicity with the Klan and to *grasp their relevance to our own situation.* We knew about COINTELPRO, but in no way, before November Third, were we prepared to grasp *its* relevance to our own situation. We were not inclined to see conspiracies lurking on every corner; we did not think in terms of grand conspiracies.

The thesis of official complicity with the Klan remained too abstract for us to imagine its concrete transposition to our own case. Was it that the police are not supposed to do this sort of thing in a democratic society? In one of those third world dictatorships maybe, where the police collaborate with civilian death squads, but not in the democratic United States. And so, although we were students of history, our democratic illusions disarmed us figuratively, so that the police could do so literally. Big Man's warnings and the premonitions of people in Greensboro and Durham went unheeded. The march security came down to a half dozen parade marshals who met among themselves and agreed on tactics, including the disposition of the few concealed weapons we would bring in spite of the ban.

NOTES

1. Unless otherwise indicated, quotations by Yonni Chapman are from a taped interview with him on April 7, 1990.

2. See Ted Quant and John Slaughter, "We Won't Go Back! The Rise of the Ku Klux Klan and the Southern Struggle for Equality," *Southern Equal Rights Congress*, Mobile, Alabama, 1980, 25.

3. Ironically, Jean's father had been in the Klan. Jim had a World War II carbine rifle, given to him by Jean, that he brought with him into our house after we were together. Jean received it from her father, the Klansman.

4. Associated Press, "Group Seeks Confrontation with Klan," *Charlotte Observer*, 12 October 1979.

5. Associated Press, "Anti-Klan Rally Scheduled," *Durham Morning Herald*, 12 October 1979, 12A.

6. Nelson Johnson, "Press Release," *Workers Viewpoint Organization*, 1 November 1979.

10

LIKE THE WOLF
ON THE FOLD: THE
GREENSBORO MASSACRE

"The Assyrian came down like the wolf on the fold."

—Lord Byron, *The Destruction of Sennacherib*

"It was a turkey shoot."

—Michael Schlosser, District Attorney

The meetings were over. Everyone was gone. It was long past midnight when we went to bed. Suddenly, without knowing why, I was sobbing profusely. "Darling, don't do this to yourself," Jim chided gently. The next morning, before the day's demands were upon us, we held each other in a long embrace. In the following years, my tears, his tender consolation, our long embrace, assumed their rightful part in the story as our leave-taking. A leave-taking conveyed without our knowledge, without our consent. It was our last night together for all eternity.

***

Many out-of-towners attending the anti-Klan rally were sent to the Waller's house on Cypress Street for directions to Morningside Homes. First to appear was Allen Blitz, who was to assemble a rented sound system on a truckbed for the march across town. Another early arrival, Nelson, breakfasted with Jim in the kitchen. Dori Blitz came with a carload of friends from Martinsville, Virginia. Soon Jim Wrenn, Kate White, Roz and Don Pelles, the Bermanzohns, and others from Durham were at the door.

At another rendezvous house, in another part of town, our enemies were meeting and identifying a route to Morningside. Downtown, law enforcement officials were meeting. We were blissfully unaware of all that was going on that morning.

"I'm always anxious around these demonstrations, about things not going right," Nelson later confessed to me. "I was that morning, too, not related to the Klan but simply to organization. The sound truck, placards, music, leaflets, song leaders, marshals, people showing up on time—I was concerned about all those things."

Nelson was shuttling people to Windsor Center where a big crowd was expected to gather. He had already dropped Joyce off there before coming to Cypress Street. His two daughters, Ayo and Akua, were going with him to Morningside. "I was anxious also about whether we were going to get the numbers," he admitted. "And about the weather. It was overcast. But around ten o'clock it began clearing up. One of the last things I said to Jim was how beautiful the day was turning out."

We had many bundles of the party's newspaper, *Workers Viewpoint.* I was responsible for seeing to the distribution of the newspapers and other printed materials during the day. There were stacks of placards announcing the founding of the Communist Workers Party (CWP). The anti-Klan rally in Greensboro was the CWP's debut as a serious national revolutionary political organization. Much of the large assortment of posters, flyers, and song-and-chant sheets were produced locally. I designed an attention-grabbing poster announcing the "ANTI-KLAN MARCH AND CONFERENCE." On top of the poster was our bold slogan, "DEATH TO THE KLAN." The poster bore a photo, framed in jagged lines that suggested a broken window, of people on the march in China Grove. Just below the jagged-framed photo was a smaller picture depicting the burning of the confederate flag at China Grove. A place, an assembly time for both the march and the conference, and the sponsor, the Workers Viewpoint Organization were printed on the poster. For the march, the public was asked to assemble in the parking lot of the Windsor Community Center at 11:00 A.M. The conference was to start at 2:00 P.M. across town.

It was about ten o'clock when I loaded all the flyers, posters, and newspapers into our beat-up Dodge and left for Morningside Homes. Jim and I did not leave together. He, Jim Wrenn, and Paul Bermanzohn stopped at a drugstore on the way to Morningside to get batteries for walkie-talkies. Jim briefly left Morningside Homes to go to Windsor Center. There he told Mike and Marty Nathan that the march would soon begin at Morningside and asked that one of them go there with the first-aid van, a standard accompaniment to our public rallies.

At Morningside Homes, the air rang with an old church hymn. Strumming his guitar, Tom Clark led us in song. "We shall not, we shall not be moved. We shall not, we shall not be moved," we sang as we stood in a wide circle near the intersection of Everitt and Carver Streets. "Just like a tree that's standing by the water, we shall not be moved. . . . Black and White together, we shall not be moved." Some Morningside residents wandered over and joined the circle. "The masses are behind us, we shall not be moved," we sang on gaily. "We'll build a fighting party, we shall not be moved." Someone held up an effigy of the Klan for ridicule. We sang as we mocked the effigy, "We'll smash the Ku Klux Klan. We shall not be moved."

For what seemed like a long while, we entertained ourselves with songs and chants. "Woke up this morning with my mind set on freedom" was another tune borrowed from the civil rights movement for the occasion. As we had at other protests, we made up verses. "The Ku Klux Klan won't stop us; Set on freedom," we sang. Similarly, we named the police, the bourgeoisie, Governor Hunt, Mayor Melvin; none of them would stop us from realizing "freedom now, freedom now, freedom now, right now!"

A festive atmosphere was developing. "It really would have been a great march," Nelson observed. "The way we planned it, weaving through the neighborhoods, we would have drawn hundreds, maybe thousands of people to it. That was already happening. People were drifting toward it. They had to. It had charisma."

Meanwhile at Windsor Community Center, less than a mile away, a few dozen people had assembled. Many people there were aware of the police harassment that occurred leading up to November Third. The church announced on the posters for the afternoon conference was no longer available because the preacher, at the instigation of the police, had withdrawn permission for its use. We had to find another site, and we arranged to use a dinner club in a small shopping mall near the church. Before going to Morningside, Bill and Dale went to the dinner club to set up chairs for the afternoon conference, deemed the most significant session in the day's activities. When a couple of police officers turned up at Windsor Center, the crowd, in a militant spirit, responded viscerally to their brief presence with "Pigs, stay away; Pigs, stay back" and "Cops for the rich, jails for the poor; we ain't gonna take this no more!"

The march organizers at Morningside had a lot to do. As demonstrators Roz and Chekesha arrived, they saw Sally Bermanzohn help Mike get the first-aid vehicle ready, César unload party placards that were tacked to picket sticks, and Dale and Lacie attach posters to the sides of the sound truck.

A few people noticed that there were no police officers present. Roz and Chekesha talked about how weird it was that no policemen were there, and they wondered what was going on. "We'd been to a zillion demonstrations between the two of us," Roz later commented, "and we'd never been to one where there were no cops. But then we just dismissed it and set about doing what we were doing," she said.

Sandi also noticed the absence of police after she arrived at Morningside and commented about it to Paul. "I took a look around and she was right," Paul said. "We had organized hundreds of demonstrations in North Carolina. It was highly unusual to have no police in the immediate vicinity. They would usually be telling us to quiet down, trying to gather us in a set area, or going over the march route. And we'd just had this press conference two days before on the steps of the police station. So I agreed with Sandi that the lack of a police presence was very bizarre."

At 10:40 that morning, roughly the same time Paul and Sandi were having their conversation, police officers of the Tactical Unit assigned to the march concluded a meeting downtown at police headquarters. They were told that they did not need to be at their posts until 11:30 A.M. and were sent to an early lunch.

That morning I was more preoccupied with the media than with the police. Several TV crews had arrived at Morningside Homes and had their cameras set up and rolling by midmorning. The rally was no mere media event or photo opportunity, and I did not expect much of the mainstream media. Why would they report fairly about the anti-Klan rally when they virtually ignored our organizing work in poor and black neighborhoods and in the plants? But now we were denouncing the Klan, and so we became newsworthy—just like the ever-newsworthy Klan. My disdain for the bourgeois media was expressed when I got into a tiff with a reporter from one of the area TV stations. She thought that I should give her, rather than sell her, a copy of *Workers Viewpoint*. Of course the argument was not about the twenty-five cents. I antagonized that reporter without even trying. I would be reminded of that later.

As the morning wore on and the sun emerged from behind clouds, spirits rose higher. The morning's chill vanished and pleasant autumnal warmth enveloped everyone. The tensions I felt the previous evening were gone. I was into it. I relished what we were doing. By daring to take a stand against the Klan, we were advancing the struggle toward a bright future for all humanity. Willena, who traveled back and forth between Morningside Homes and Windsor Center, trying to seal a childcare arrangement, spotted Sandi and spoke to her. Sandi was in an upbeat mood, too. The march would start out soon, she told Willena, and things were looking really good.

In the circle of singers with me were about a dozen children. They looked sharp in their Revolutionary Youth League uniforms, sewn the evening before. Alex, fair-skinned and blond, then eleven years old, stood out in the sea of youthful African American faces. They were all beautiful. Leaving the group for a minute, Alex crossed the street to complain to Jim about a sore on his mouth. Earlier in the morning, he had shown it to one of the other doctors who said it was probably impetigo. "Jim was busy with placards and bullhorns," Alex remembered. "He said he would take care of me once the rally was over."[1] Alex crossed back to the group. Ten-year-old Kwame, Willena's oldest child, handed him a sign to carry on the march.

It was now about a quarter past eleven, and we readied ourselves to march out at half past. We planned to march to, and to merge with, the contingent at Windsor. Then everyone would continue westward across town for the forum, picking up more people en route. Our security people were patrolling with walkie-talkies. I thought someone near me said that he picked up a Klan message on a CB. Whatever he heard failed to alert me. I was in a triumphant frame of mind and smiling brightly when the Klan caravan rolled in a moment later.

The cameras of four television stations were recording as cars drove very slowly down Everitt Street. People stopped what they were doing and lined the sidewalk. I heard Rand's voice among others chanting insistently, "Death to the Klan." Epithets and insults were being flung back and forth. "Nigger!" "Kike!" "You asked for the Klan, you got it!" spewed forth from the occupants of the caravan. The words "China Grove" issued from one of the caravan riders. A couple of demonstrators hit the passing cars with sticks. "Get out! Get out!" shouted a Morningside resident to the vehicles' occupants, and he gestured to the intruders to get out of their cars. "Just the presence of the Ku Klux Klan in a black community was a calculated provocation," Paul and Sally wrote afterward in their account of the incident.[2]

I was quite close to the vehicles as they inched down the street. My attention was drawn to a man in one of the cars, middle-aged, graying, and nattily dressed in a sport jacket. Then, or shortly afterward, I concluded—erroneously as it turned out—that he was George Dorsett, the Klansman who had detained and threatened to kill me and Charles Finch five years earlier and who was subsequently exposed in the papers as an FBI agent while in the Klan.

Nelson watched the caravan drive in from across the street, where he was busy with the sound truck. He heard someone say "the Klan is here," and he saw the confederate flag on the front vehicle. Immediately he crossed the street, passing between a couple of cars in the caravan. Nelson was certainly not alone among us in having thoughts or responses that day which, in a calmer, more knowing aftermath, could appear as regrettable or inappropriate.

"Let me see if I can say this in a way that's really honest," he said to me much later. "I want to affirm that I didn't expect the Klan. When they came I wasn't frightened by it. I didn't feel the threat of it. I was thinking that this really makes this thing relevant now. That was a thought that occurred in my head. And I've regretted that thought. But I had it as I was crossing the street, because all of a sudden it was not just an abstract march against the Klan. A lot of people were saying 'there ain't no Klan been in Greensboro recently,' and here they were. Little did I realize the dastardly and tragic action that would take place."

Paul peered into the cars as they traced a slow path down the street. "There was this guy I had just seen at the press conference two days before, who I now know to be Eddie Dawson, the Klansman who was given our parade permit by the police without our being notified. He yelled out at me, 'You communist son of a bitch!' I knew I knew the guy from someplace, but I couldn't place him. Then I think I placed him as the guy who was fishy at the press conference. But by this time all hell was breaking loose. So it wasn't the time to say, 'Don't I know you from somewhere?' That would have been a little inappropriate, maybe better for a high school reunion."

In just a few moments, most of the caravan was past the area around the intersection of Carver and Everitt, where the crowd was concentrated, but some vehicles in the rear hung back. Suddenly, all the vehicles halted. At the front of the caravan, down the street, a man with a long-barreled pistol leaned out of the window of a pick-up truck and fired a shot in the air. Nelson, crossing the street, saw the shot fired from the window of the pick-up. "I have a vivid memory of it imprinted on my mind," he said. "And I was also aware of the movement of the people away from that gunshot." The shot seemed to signal the rest of the caravan: immediately, men jumped out of the vehicles. "What I remember most is hearing car doors slam," Roz told me. "That's when I knew we were in trouble."

The children near me began running back into the housing project. I hesitated. I wanted to investigate what was happening and almost ran toward the gunfire to do so. Most likely, I heard Sandi's voice shouting, "Get the children to safety!" I don't remember it now at all, but I told everyone about it right afterward. While I was making up my mind whether to run away from or toward the source of the tumult, my hesitation seemed to affect Alex; he didn't flee immediately with the other children. Maybe Sandi's strong command was what ended my indecisiveness; or maybe seeing Alex finally join the others and run; or maybe the primordial instinct to survive. In any case, I, too, fled.

I ran after my son, away from the street and into the heart of the housing project. Alex was behind all the other children. He seemed to be running so slowly; my inner reflexes and muscles were urging him to go faster. I stayed behind him deliberately so that I could keep him in my vision and perhaps shield him with my body, for now there was a whole barrage of gunfire behind us as we ran.

The terrain seemed boundless, and the run had the feel of a marathon that would never end. Seconds seemed to dilate into hours. I felt I would be running and hearing gunshots forever. Time was crawling so that no matter how fast I ran, endless stretches would still remain. Then doors opened up to us. We were sucked inside, into small houses that became sanctuaries out of harm's way. Later the place where we rallied and the field where we ran shrunk to their actual size—a small space—and the gunshots to their real time span—eighty-eight seconds.

The assailants poured out of their cars and began attacking people with sticks. The gunfire sent most of the marchers and news people scrambling for cover. The initial shot, fired from the front of the caravan, had the effect of making people retreat up Carver Drive, a small, partially enclosed space, more like a courtyard or alley than a street. The same shot also drove people toward the rear of the caravan further down Everitt Street. There, within seconds, Klansmen and Nazis were unpacking an arsenal of lethal weapons.

TV videotapes captured much of the action of this ambush. Even as the caravan was approaching the demonstrators, a camera picked up the motions of one of the attackers loading a pistol from the passenger seat of a slowly moving vehicle. When viewing the tapes, one is struck by the casual, unhurried manner in which firearms are removed from the trunk of a rear vehicle and distributed. The assailants give no indication of being concerned about possible retaliation from those attacked or about police interference with their actions. They do not bother to take cover, and they do not look behind. Striking, too, is the cigarette dangling all the while from the mouth of one of the shooters. About a half dozen of the armed intruders continued to fire on people as they ran for cover or tried to ward off the attackers with sticks.

Two people who wrote about this have described what they saw in the videotapes: "Klansmen calmly walk to the trunks of the rear cars, open them, and take out and distribute rifles and handguns. A shot rings out and demonstrators run for cover. Armed Klansmen walk about, carefully select victims, fire and reload. . . . They seem like casual participants at a skeet shoot. One of them methodically pumps bullets into the body of a fallen protester. Another shoots with a lit cigarette dangling from his mouth. . . . The gunmen calmly pack their weapons in the cars and slowly drive off."[3] Another writer who viewed the videotapes closely notes, similarly, that "half a dozen Klansmen and Nazis stand in the middle of Everitt Street and methodically begin to shoot people." When the gunfire stops, "Klansmen and Nazis calmly put their guns away. . . . The man firing the M-15 never drops the lit cigarette from his mouth. The caravan moves on."[4]

When the men jumped out of their cars, they went after Sandi, Dale recalled, "even though I was closer to them." Sandi was clubbed on the back of her head. She fell down, bleeding. Dale helped her back to her feet. Sandi then herded children out of the street and directed others to safety before going for cover herself. She steered her friend, Claire, who was disoriented, away from danger. Running for cover, Claire was shot and wounded, though only slightly. She and Sandi huddled together on the porch of the community building, just out of the line of fire. Claire poked her head out and saw a man with a gun aimed right at her. Pulling back, she warned Sandi. But Sandi wanted to make sure that there were no children still in the open. She stuck her head out for an instant to look. The marksman who had passed over the white woman took aim at the black one. Sandi Smith was shot between the eyes.

Jim Waller rushed toward the assailants. He made his way to a pick-up truck where he knew there were a couple of rifles stowed away—now barely accessible in the moment of need.

"It's a moment of truth," Jim Wrenn later told Sally.[5] "What are you going to do in a situation like that? . . . I remember realizing we were under attack and stopping to see what other people were doing." He saw a few people moving forward to meet the attack and took courage from that. He saw Jim Waller struggling with some Klansmen. He ran across the street and "I got involved in that fight and was thrown on the ground. Then I realized they had guns, and they started shooting, and I ran behind a car."

Klansmen were all over Jim Waller, who managed to get hold of the rifle brought by Tom Clark. When he could not repel the attackers and Clark's rifle ended up in the hands of a Klansman, Jim, disarmed, ran for cover. The killers shot him in the back as he fled.

Jim Wrenn was running for cover when he spotted Floris Cauce and his girlfriend, Kate White, pulling a wounded demonstrator to safety behind a car. Chekesha, eight months pregnant, had been shot. Wrenn saw Paul waving a stick, bravely trying to fight back. At some point, after taking cover, he saw Mike Nathan, bloody, lying in the street. He went to help Mike, and he, too, was shot. He managed to crawl back behind the car where he had secured himself only seconds before. Now he was bleeding from the head and could feel that he had lost his teeth. Later, at the hospital, he realized the extent of his injuries. "I had two wounds to my head, but the most serious was the one to my chest that grazed my lungs. That caused me a lot of problems during the first couple of days, and I didn't know if I was going to make it or not."[6]

When the Klan and Nazis opened fire, Bill Sampson and Rand Manzella took cover behind a car. Bill evidently tried to fire back with a handgun. He was shot in the heart. Mortally wounded, Bill passed his pistol to Rand, his friend and coworker in the mill, and told him to keep on shooting to defend the demonstrators.

Of all the brave attempts to protect people and to fight back with whatever was at hand, most conspicuous in the eye of a recording video camera was César Cauce's. He stood boldly before the intersection of Carver and Everitt facing off armed assailants with only a picket stick. Behind him, people ducked for cover. Paul was rushing back into the housing project with the crowd, but he stopped when he saw César. "What kind of way is this for a member of the Communist Workers Party to behave?" he asked himself. "We need to defend the community and the demonstrators." He saw César blocking and returning the Klan's blows. Then César was struck on the head and shoulders and knocked down. Paul, stick in hand, started toward his fallen comrade. As César struggled to get up, he was gunned down and killed by a Klansman who lurched down the street firing, a pistol in each hand. At nearly the same instant, Paul was hit.

"It really felt like nothing, like a blast of air, just a force with no mass. . . . I was suddenly knocked off my feet." He did not lose consciousness and remembered seeing Dori Blitz in a yellow slicker crouched down, firing back. She made him think of Annie Oakley. "I tried to get up to continue moving toward César, and I couldn't. I mean I could move, but it was more wriggling than any kind of useful, purposive action. Then I had what may well have been a death-in-life type experience," Paul told me. "I felt very peaceful, very calm. I was no longer responsible for any human. It was kind of a draining of guilt, if you will. And I figured what's gonna happen is gonna happen."

Mike Nathan was shot squarely in the face in the exposed stretch of Carver Street toward which the gunmen converged. He was probably going to help César, Paul, or Jim when he was killed. Notwithstanding his reservations about the Greensboro anti-Klan rally after having been to China Grove, Mike believed it was right to take a stand against the Klan. He risked and gave his life trying to save his friends. That was his moment of truth.

Several people had taken cover behind a station wagon parked on Carver Street that belonged to Channel WXII, one of four TV stations at the march. That vehicle was peppered all over with gunshots by the attackers. As she crouched behind the station wagon, Kate White was in a state of disbelief. She cradled Chekesha's head in her lap and leaned over the pregnant woman's belly in an attempt to protect her baby. Chekesha's legs had been sprayed with bird shot. The wounds were not serious, but the shots had caused her to fall against a car door and cut her head.

Kate White talked to Chekesha, trying to reassure her, "patting her head in the middle of all this. And then Mike Nathan got shot right beside that car," Kate said.[7] She was aware that Jim Wrenn, who had somehow ended up behind her, "saw Mike and crawled out to pull Mike back. He was shot by the same person that had shot Mike. . . . Then to my right . . . Claire's screaming, 'Sandi's been shot.' . . . I centered on this one thing—to listen for when the shooting stopped and get an ambulance." As Kate was waiting in terror for the shooting to end, a "funny" thought struck her—"I was thinking in rapid succession of every single country in the world, of where you could go and live, where there wouldn't be any violence."

The sole victim to be attacked with a knife, Nelson, was assaulted as he crossed the street after becoming aware of the Klan's presence. Though many of his memories are fuzzy—"I've had so many discussions about them I don't know whether I'm talking about what I've discussed or what I remember"—one or two things remained clear. "And that is that a man was coming after me with a long knife. I wasn't frightened then," Nelson told me. "I really felt that I could handle this." He used to box regularly.

"A stick was thrown to me by Lacie Russell. That's one of the pictures that was used in the paper right afterward—me with a stick. The way the picture was used suggested that I was menacing, that I was one of the attackers. The media supplied no context about why this stick was thrown to me. Lacie probably saved me from serious injury, if not saved my life. This fellow from the Klan caravan really lashed at me. I had the stick, and he was coming upward toward my rib cage, and I blocked it with my arm—that's the only thing I could do—and the knife went right through the fleshy part of my left arm. He slashed across and got my hand, across here," Nelson told me, displaying the wound. "So there was a cut and blood. I swung at him. The fellow ducked, and I went over his head. I was really rather embarrassed that I missed this guy."

Nelson kept swinging. "But I never really got a lick on him," he said. "He dropped to his knees and came up cutting, and I jumped back. We squared off again. At this point I really felt that I was going to get a good lick on him. And I probably would have 'cause this dropping to your knees thing, you can't do that but one time." But then, abruptly, Nelson's assailant turned and fled, leaving Nelson still holding the stick and bleeding badly. Nelson's next recollection is of being crouched down behind a car, beside Sally, and hearing the shooting.

"My military training was helpful then—whenever there's shooting, get low. That's the first thing you do because otherwise you're a bigger target." He didn't know where the shots were coming from. He guessed he was not behind the car for very long. At the trial later, a newspaper reporter recalled that Nelson had taken cover near him, but Nelson was unaware of the reporter's presence. By the time Nelson had a sense of where the shooting was coming from, "it was over. People were moving away. I raced back across the street. I still had the stick in my hand. And when I came back across, I was stunned—that was the first time I realized that anyone had been hit."

Lying on the ground barely conscious, Paul noticed it had suddenly become very quiet. He heard someone yell for a doctor. "I tried to respond," Paul said, "but an unspeakable fatigue prevented me. I figured Mike or Jim could handle it." It didn't occur to him that he was losing four or five pints of blood from a gunshot wound to the head and that he might be dying. "I saw blood on the grass around me and figured it was mine, but I wasn't sure." He was aware of Sally kneeling beside him, comforting him. "My vision was blurry, but I was relieved to hear her voice and to know she was okay. She was pregnant with our second child at the time."

People came out of hiding when the gunfire stopped. A dazed reporter wandered around pleading, "let me do something." It was moments after the shootings, and police were not yet on the scene, when Dori Blitz looked into a TV camera and stated unequivocally: "Five people are dead! The Klan and the State got together and planned this. That's why there are no policemen here. Do you hear me? The State protects the Klan and this makes it clear. They came through and they opened fire on us. They opened fire on us. And we fired back to protect ourselves."

When Sally saw that people were hurt, she looked around frantically for a doctor—Mike or Jim or Paul. "Then I recognized Paul in his black raincoat, lying in a heap on his side facing the wall of the Morningside housing project. My heart stood still. I ran to him and knelt down, calling his name. He groaned in response. He was alive! When I rolled him over, there was a huge bloody gash across his forehead. He had been shot in the head. He opened his eyes and looked at me, dazed. His eyelids were swelling up with blood. He could hardly open his right eye. But he recognized me and called my name.

"I looked through his pockets for something to stop the bleeding, finding only his old fake leather glove. I put it over his forehead. Should I press hard or just lay it on top? I had never had any desire to be a nurse or a doctor until that moment. Paul and others needed help and I felt helpless. Paul opened up his left eye and looked at me. 'Our first armed confrontation,' he whispered. 'And man, do we have a lot to learn.'

"That's Paul, I thought, shot in the head, but still talking politics. The last thing I felt like at that point was a political discussion, but his words comforted me. He did not think he was dying; he wanted to keep learning."[8]

The house where I had taken refuge was crowded and full of nervous chatter. Adults were trying to calm fearful children. Dot was there with the children from her household. Alex, Dale, Roz, and others were in that house. A couple of minutes after we no longer heard gunfire, Dale said to me, "I can't stand the suspense any longer, Signe. I'm going back." Some women promised to look after the children, and I went with Dale.

My heart was pumping fast as we walked quickly back to Everitt and Carver. What image did I have in my head then? I had heard the gunshots and knew them to be gunshots. I pictured the Klan firing into the air over people's heads, to frighten us. I think I had been carrying that image around like a talisman all the while.

Later I beat myself up over this. How could I forgive myself for being so stupid and naive, so slow to comprehend? Some experiences are *unrecognizable* when they happen for the first time, for instance, giving birth. Being in a war and being deliberately targeted by an enemy for slaughter was like nothing I had ever experienced—it was unrecognizable. People the world over know that an enemy really does try to kill you, and does not merely shoot over your head to frighten you. For all the years I spent in school, I had not learned that simple lesson. My soul resonated to Beethoven's Ninth Symphony with Schiller's *Ode to Joy*, which exalts a universal love binding together all humanity, a love that signals an all-powerful creator. Too many years the sage, the dreamer, the idealist had not prepared me for the incomparable experience of war and death.

The place where, minutes before, we had been milling about and singing came into view. It was a battlefield. Bodies were strewn around in the grass. The police had just arrived, and they were cordoning off certain areas. They tried to stop us, but Dale and I went inside the cordoned-off area anyway.

Nelson discovered Jim lying face down and still breathing. He saw the bullet holes in his back. Jim was on the lawn of a house fronting Carver Street. "I turned him over," Nelson told me when I interviewed him many years later. "He was laboring. He was not conscious when I turned him but was breathing heavily. And I think he expired in the next few seconds, right there as I was kneeling beside him. I think I had his head in my hand. I was conscious of the fact that he stopped breathing. At that point you came. I don't know what I said to you."

When I found Jim, Nelson was kneeling over him. Very softly, he said, "He's gone." When I said nothing, he added, "Just a moment ago." Then Nelson left. I felt a wild sensation, a determination to go on at all costs. I also felt certain that my life was over. I wanted to embrace Jim, but I understood that he was dead. There was nothing left of his life but that for which he lived. I wanted the world to know that Jim's death and the other deaths I saw as I looked around were not in vain. Our cause would triumph. I made this announcement to the world at large, over Jim's body. With my fist raised, I shouted, "Long live the Communist Workers Party! And long live the working class! And in spite of you goddamned cops, we will make socialist revolution." Getting up, I walked away from Jim's body into the crowd. The police now were everywhere, in full riot gear. I shouted at them, "You protect the capitalists! You protect the Klan!"[9]

Across Carver Street, watching her husband die as a policeman and a wounded Tom Clark worked unsuccessfully to bring him around, Dale heard me through her agony. "Tell it, Signe," she called back. A TV camera caught her screaming curses at the Klan. Someone must have tried to quiet her. "I'm not going to hush, this is my husband," she answered; and then, in an anguished voice, asked, "Where are the ambulances?"

My mood alternated; when anger and sheer defiant determination were spent, grief overwhelmed me. I fell into the arms of Allen Blitz, saying over and over, "I can't live without Jim, I can't go on without him." Dale and Floris kept returning to their husbands' bodies as if to reestablish the conclusion. We were in a place too sullied for humanity, too cruel and unjust to bear, a place of eternal torment. The drama swirling around me of other lives and other deaths magnified my own loss a million times. I recall wondering right then "How many widows have they made today?" Nothing made sense anymore in terms other than political ones: It was a *political assassination* that would never have occurred without this particular cast of political players—the Klan and the police, their political motives exactly at odds with our own.

All of us came independently and swiftly to the same inevitable conclusion—we'd been set up by the police. Across Everitt Street, Ed, one of the White Oak union leaders, spoke in measured tones, telling the media what had happened. The Klan drove in and fired at the thickest concentration of people. They seemed to be aiming at particular people. "One way or another," he said, "the cops did this."

The police did not pursue the departing Klan. Nine out of ten vehicles in the caravan got away. The last vehicle, a van tardy in leaving, was stopped by police some minutes after the attack, and its twelve occupants were apprehended. Those arrests were fortuitous—the arresting officers were not supposed to be in the area.

Very soon after their arrival, police took Nelson, Rand, and Willena into custody. As soon as the police arrived, they saw Rand standing over César's body. Rand, stunned, was at a loss for how to help César. He still had Bill's gun in his hand. A policeman ordered Rand to get down. "To hell with this—get an ambulance," responded the young textile worker. He was among the protesters wounded that day.

CHAPTER 10

"One pointed his gun at me. I got down. Another took the gun that Bill gave me and handcuffed me," Rand said. "At that point, Nelson Johnson and Willena Cannon ran over and told the cops I was one of the demonstrators, not one of the Klan." He was arrested anyway for being "armed to the terror of the people" and taken downtown.

Morningside residents were riled up. Many had gathered and were talking excitedly to one another. They felt solidarity with the demonstrators. A whiff of urban rebellion was abroad. To these people, Nelson's voice came thundering like a mighty storm breaking over the land: "The police organized this," he bellowed. "They allowed our people to be murdered. To be muuurrdered! It's Jim Melvin," Nelson's voice boomed, pinpointing the mayor of Greensboro, "and it's the capitalist class. And so we declare war against them. Waaaarr! Our people lay dyin' on the ground, because these dogs, these pigs, these representatives of the imperialists. . . ." he continued in mounting fervor. "It's gonna be war, it's gonna be war," came a response from the crowd. "I'm on your side," another onlooker called back to Nelson.

Nelson's speech was interrupted by the police. As they moved to apprehend him, Willena clung to him in an effort to protect him. Then, in a flash, Nelson, his left arm and hand still bleeding, was on the ground trying to hang on to an iron, chain-link fence above him while police around him tugged at his limbs. At one point, a black officer had his boot on Nelson's hand and arm. This was Lieutenant S. Daughtry, Commanding Officer of the Tactical Unit, who would in later years become Greensboro's Chief of Police. Nelson was charged with "inciting to riot" and hauled away. Willena followed, protesting Nelson's arrest. "Take her on to jail," she heard one of the cops say. "What charge?" came back. "I don't know. We'll find something," riposted the first. She, too, was arrested.

At the sight of Nelson being dragged away, the crowd made an incipient movement of surging forth against the police. But this collective impulse was checked when some officers abruptly turned their guns around and pointed them directly at the Morningside Homes residents. Their neighborhood had just been invaded and shot up. Some still-rolling television cameras recorded the random conversations that took place. There was solidarity with the demonstrators and, above all, a concern with self-preservation.

"Sticking together. That's the main thing. They stuck together, those vans that came in and did what they wanted to do. There's more of us than there is of them."

"It could have been your sister, or your mama, or your wife, or your girlfriend. You see what I'm sayin'? Go home and get your gun. I'm gonna get mine."

Meanwhile, at the Windsor Community Center, the assembled crowd watched police cars with flashers fly by. Joyce gathered people together and brought them to the Cypress Street house. Then she asked Marty to come with her. "We went over to Morningside, and I still didn't know what happened," Marty told me, "just that there was an attack and some people were down."[10]

Years later, when I interviewed her, Marty sorted through the jumble of painful memories. She recalled walking through the crowd at Morningside. She had not yet learned about Mike, but she was crying. Sally came up to her and told her to stop. Sally, too, recalled berating Marty for crying.

"I saw boots being put on a stretcher—boots attached to some person—and into an ambulance, with the face covered," Marty told me. "And Floris was crying, 'Let me kiss him goodbye, let me kiss him goodbye.' I said to the ambulance man, 'did you hear her? I'm a doctor and I tell you that she's to kiss him goodbye!'" Marty broke off her narrative and laughed sadly.

"Maybe that's when I started crying and maybe that's when I saw Sally," Marty pieced together. "She was doing agit-prop,[11] telling people that the police did this. She saw me crying and told me to shut up, to stop crying. I'd been wandering around trying to figure out what was going on, and I ran into Kate. I hadn't thought about Michael before—it was an off-the-cuff question—and I said 'Where's Mike?' She said, 'he's been shot.' And she suddenly froze because it was obvious she didn't want to tell me. I said, 'is it bad?' She answered, 'I don't know. He looked pretty bad. They took him away.'"

I asked Marty if she felt any resentment over how she had been talked to, or not talked to, on November Third. We have all been friends over many years, so her answer did not surprise me.

"Oh, no, no, no. It was chaos. It was a dream. I wasn't resentful at all, not even toward Sally. Later she told me why she said those things. But she didn't have to tell me. I understood it. Just like I understood why you stood up over Jim's body—it all made perfect sense." Marty paused and laughed sadly. "It made as much sense as anything else did."

A friend went with her across Everitt Street to a laundromat with a telephone. They made some phone calls to find out where the dead and the wounded had been taken. "And I remember curling up on the floor, on the cement floor, and just pounding my head against the floor and crying and crying and crying and crying," Marty said. "Then I went out and I started doing agit-prop. I was yelling at the police they were responsible for these murders when this cop shoved his rifle in my face and told me he was going to arrest me. A young black woman from Morningside got in front of me, between me and the gun, and told the cop, 'You shut up, buddy. She's with me.'"

Once again, Marty's tears made way for sorrowful laughter. "If I'd had the emotional strength, I would have hugged her. But I didn't have it, and I never found out who she was."

Marty went to Moses Cone Hospital and stayed with her husband for the next two days, until he died. "My mother-in-law blamed me for Michael's death, and we had a six-month-old baby. Leah was weaned on November Third because I couldn't get back to her. In the hospital, I had to run hot water over my breasts so they wouldn't hurt as bad as they did," she said. The anguish of those days returned as she said in a flat voice, "I waited for Michael to die. Then came home. Faced my mother-in-law. Took care of my baby. Went back to work. Went to every demonstration possible. Talked about government complicity. Talked about the role of the police. Worked with friends and loved ones for justice."

In the Greensboro hospital where he was admitted, Paul's life hung in the balance. "I was fortunate," he later judged, "because the best neurosurgeon in the area happened to be in his scrub suit in the emergency room, having just finished a procedure, when I arrived." Looking at Paul's X-rays, Sally saw the bullet in his brain and the fragments in the right side of his head. An operation that should have taken an hour or two, lasted over five hours. Paul's condition was critical when Sally went into the Intensive Care Unit to see him.

"There was my beloved husband, with tubes and machines connected to every part of his body. His whole face was puffy, his eyes black and blue and swollen shut. Tubes ran down his nose and throat, bandages covered most of his head. 'Speak to him,' the nurse told me. 'Squeeze his right hand and see if he responds.' I bent down near him and whispered, 'Paul, this is Sally. Can you hear me?' He squeezed my hand so hard it hurt."[12] Dr. Paul Bermanzohn, son of Holocaust survivors, would survive.

Roz passed the stadium on the way to the Cypress Street house, where she was going to tell the Windsor Center group what she knew about the attack at Morningside. "There was a football game at the stadium," she told me. "It was the first time I realized that nothing stopped because of this." She knew, at that point, that her husband Don had been hurt but did not know where he was. She knew several people were dead, "and this football game continued. It just blew me away that the world didn't stop. But it didn't, it went on, and it kept going on."

Lucy Lewis took charge at my house that day, I learned. In the aftermath of the attack, the party was organized and disciplined. Naturally, consciousness of security was very high. Lucy's mother, Jean Wagner, was one of the people waiting at Windsor Center for the march to begin. She related to me, with awe and respect in her voice, what a tremendous spirit prevailed among the shocked demonstrators. People reviewed why they were a part of the struggle and expressed their willingness to continue and to make sacrifices if called upon. It was a time of recommitment, not fear and abandonment. Jean was sent, with several other people, to another house that was thought to be safer. The people brought there were required to follow certain precautions about using the telephone and were dismissed to go home in some pattern presumed consistent with everyone's maximum safety. Jean didn't know whose apartment she was in, but the hostess, pregnant and still bloody from being wounded in the attack, prepared food for everyone. Of course it was Chekesha's place. That night, upon returning to Durham, Jean did not stay with her husband. She babysat Mike and Marty's infant daughter, Leah, and kept Mike's mother company.

Back at Morningside, after arresting him, the police took Nelson to the hospital. "I was bleeding and a young intern from Duke sewed me up. She was talking to another doctor like I wasn't there. Of course, I was a prisoner. Police were at the door, talking about what happened, about the Klan, the communists. My arm was stitched up. I was given pain medicine and taken to jail. I really did not know the fullness of what had happened. At that point, I assumed Paul Bermanzohn was dead, because I thought he was when I saw him. I knew Jim was, and I felt Sandi was."

For all Willena knew, her son Kwame, or Ayo, or any number of the other kids who were in the area, had been killed. This was the impression fostered by the police as they drove downtown after her arrest. "That freaked me out. I never experienced nothing like that," Willena told me. She was taken to a tiny basement room with a table and some chairs and questioned.

"Willena, how are we gonna find your children if you won't cooperate with us?"

Willena had to struggle to maintain control and not respond to the provocative interrogation. She focused on her childhood, growing up in South Carolina, because she "didn't want to get into what the police were saying, get mad, and start hollering." She knew for sure that Jim and César were dead. But what had happened to the children?

The next thing she recalled was lifting her head from the table and trying to get her bearings. "There was no one in the room but me. My mind had shut down. I couldn't deal with all of that and not holler—I was like numb. They came back in and told me they were taking me over to where I could make bond." It was around five o'clock. Her sister, Annette, had been trying to get Willena out of jail all afternoon.

"I was brought down to a small room, some kind of holding room," Nelson told me. "A man who introduced himself as the FBI and a detective from the police department came in and talked rough to me and wanted me to tell them everything. There really wasn't much to tell. But I wasn't talking, period, to anybody. I said, 'I have nothing to say to you, to any of you all.'"

"You best talk to us," they told him, "because your name is mud; your life isn't worth a nickel; your name is on the lips of every Klansman out there." They threatened to tear the bandages off his arm and to put salt on his wounds.

"I said, 'well, do what you need to do—I'm not talking to you all.' So this went on for a while and they left." He later reported how he had been threatened but "it was just one of many things that got swept aside."

Nelson spent an agonizing night in jail. "I wasn't able to sleep. I was just worried about everything. I had the same bloody clothes on." On his release the next morning, he walked into a bevy of reporters. Their questions, cameras, and microphones were shoved his way. He was unprepared for the magnitude of press coverage that had already developed around the incident. "For the next week, until the burial, I was on automatic pilot—every day responding to crises, helping to think through what to do, meeting with the NAACP and this one and that one."

I did not return to my house on the night of November Third. I have a vivid memory of sitting in Big Man's living room with many other people. His house was a couple of blocks from the Morningside project. As the afternoon sun went down, I watched papers go up in flames in the fireplace. Jim was a meticulous note-taker, and his office was full of his writings, political documents, and trade union records. Someone decided to destroy his files immediately to protect the activists and workers who were in any way involved with us. Considering that we were under attack at that moment, and that it was not clear how long the attack would last or who would be dragged into it, that was not an unreasonable decision. Unfortunately, most of Jim's and my love letters and poems to one another were destroyed, inadvertently. Only a small part of our personal correspondence was spared.

The loss of the letters and poems devastated me out of all proportion. How could I care so much about mere pieces of paper with written words when the husband I loved more than anyone in the world and comrades who were my dearest friends had forfeited their very lives? During this period, I was swept into a spiral of guilt and psychological self-flagellation. Among ourselves, such intense feelings were expressed and discussed; we seldom, if ever, aired them in public.

That night I went to WFMY-TV, the CBS affiliate in Greensboro, with Joyce, Willena, and Larry Little, former head of the Black Panther Party in North Carolina. When I interviewed Willena for this book, she filled in the holes in my memory. My son was there in the TV studio too—I hadn't remembered that.

"Alex was there, too?" I asked Willena, surprised.

"Alex spoke," Willena said. "He said something like 'no matter what they do—they killed my stepdad—and I'm taking his place.' To me that was so baaaad . . . he was what . . . eleven years old." She chuckled. Some memory synapses in me came alive, and I suddenly recalled Alex's presence at the TV studio. Alluding to the fond nickname his fellow workers had given Jim, Alex said, "just call me 'Blackbeard Junior.'"

When she joined us at WFMY, Willena had been released from jail only hours earlier, but Nelson was still inside. We were very worried about him. We knew that there were people downtown who wished Nelson Johnson dead.

Susan Kidd, a black news anchor for WFMY, interviewed Sandi some months before, when Sandi led busloads of antiapartheid protesters to Washington, D.C. Somehow Susan managed to get us on television the very night of the murders, and she allowed us to talk freely for quite a while. Moments before the broadcast, Willena recalled, "Susan took us into a room and told us whatever kind of way we wanted to do it, she wanted to do it that way. And if they tried to do it different, then she would stop it and protest it, even if she ended up losing her job."

Joyce announced that a wounded Nelson Johnson was in jail. "We hold the police accountable for his safety," she declared. I warned, "we're watching what you do with our brother Nelson."

Willena summed up our TV appearance. "We put out our views about the government. The FBI had to be involved. They knew who the organizers were. We said the government was responsible for Nelson's safety in jail and for the murders of our comrades." Our posture was not one of victims—it never was. We vowed to make the November Third assassinations *the costliest mistake the bourgeoisie ever made*. Susan asked us if we were afraid. Such a personal question struck me, at the time, as a distracting irrelevance. We responded, in all honesty, that we were not. Emotions more powerful than fear ruled us.

***

A marriage ceremony was in progress when news about Greensboro reached Baltimore. Gathered there on November 3, 1979, were about fifty CWP supporters from Washington, Philadelphia, and Baltimore. Instantly and spontaneously, a wedding was transformed into a political rally. Stunned, tearful, and angry wedding guests raised their fists in the air and vowed the murders would be avenged. A spontaneous sentiment of get-your-guns-and-prepare-for-war reigned. People declared that they were ready to do whatever the party asked of them.[13] In the following days, weeks, months, and years, volunteers to go to Greensboro to help were not in short supply.

In Chicago, on the morning of November 3, Jane Waller carried two airplane tickets to Greensboro in her purse. Her brother's 37th birthday, on November 5, was to be the occasion for a family reunion. She and her father planned to fly south that evening. Then Jane heard the first sketchy report on a car radio, and she knew.

"I remember having this heavy feeling in my chest."[14] Her brother "had an image of himself as the hulk, impervious to bullets. He had always been handsome and intelligent and successful and he was able to do whatever he wanted. I think he felt so right in what he was doing he thought nobody could stop him. He was courageous. Immediately, I had this feeling he was in the front lines trying to shield everybody, trying to right all the wrongs of the world that morning."

I was in Big Man's house when I finally could gather the strength to make a few phone calls. I called Jane.

"Signe's voice was—ah, it was heavy, it was like doom, like a death knell. 'Jim has been shot,' she said, 'killed.'"

It was time to pick up her father at his art-framing shop and to go to the airport. A friend drove Jane to the Waller Art Gallery. Sidney Waller was listening to a Beethoven symphony on the radio while helping some customers get their pictures framed.

"He was conducting, like he often did, lightly with his hands. He looked at me, and he knew something was wrong, but he said, 'I know we have to go to the airport. I'm not ready yet. I have to finish conducting Beethoven.' He could see I had been crying and asked what was wrong. I started stammering. He said, 'You know, I heard something on the radio about Greensboro. Was Jamie involved in that?' And I said, 'Daddy, Jamie was shot and killed.'

"He started screaming. I ushered everybody out of the gallery and locked the door. People still wanted to have their pictures framed in the middle of all this. I said, 'Listen, you'll have to come back because Mr. Waller can't help you now.' My father went running around the downstairs of the shop from room to room, screaming, crying, and tearing his hair out. He was wild, incoherent. He was talking, but there was no sense in what he said. I wanted to fall apart, but I couldn't because I had to hold him together."

Nighttime of November Third found Jane and Sidney Waller inside the city limits of Greensboro, in a war zone. They were grieving to the depths of their souls.

As a result of the violent attack by right-wing extremists, abetted by the police, five people were cut down in the prime of their lives. Killed on November

3, 1979, were Dr. James Waller, 36; William Sampson, 31; César Cauce, 25; and Sandra Smith, 28. Dr. Michael Nathan, 32, died on November 5. Of ten people wounded, eight were anti-Klan demonstrators, two of whom were wounded seriously. Paul Bermanzohn was left partially paralyzed for life. Another two people, a TV cameraman and a Klansman, were hurt. The right-wing extremists, who accidentally shot one of their own men, inflicted all of the deaths and all of the injuries.

We knew the police and Klan acted in complicity. We had no doubt of further government involvement, such as the FBI. We had the main outline right, but none of the factual details were known to us on the day of the violent assault. Soon to unfold were a conspiracy and cover-up that involved, at the very least, factions of the Ku Klux Klan; American Nazis; the Greensboro Police Department; Greensboro's elected and appointed officials; the North Carolina State Bureau of Investigation; the Federal Bureau of Alcohol, Tobacco, and Firearms; and the Federal Bureau of Investigation.

The story drummed into people by the media bore little resemblance, with respect to plot or character, to the real story. The ultimate strategy of the cover-up was to sidestep the guilt of the perpetrators by making the victims into the criminals. Even as we buried our loved ones and mourned their untimely and unnatural deaths, we had to respond to attacks on their character and motives. As we grieved, we fought attempts to cut us off from all potential support.

NOTES

1. Unless otherwise indicated, quotations by Alex Goldstein are from a taped interview with him on March 2, 1993.

2. Bermanzohn, *The True Story of the Greensboro Massacre*, 18.

3. Wyn Craig Wade, *The Fiery Cross: The Ku Klux Klan in America* (New York: Simon & Schuster, 1987), 381.

4. Blanche McCrary Boyd, "Ambush: An Inquiry into the Holy War in Greensboro," *The Village Voice*, 26 May 1980, 13–14.

5. Sally Avery Bermanzohn, "Survivors of the 1979 Greensboro Massacre: A Study of the Long Term Impact of Protest Movements on the Political Socialization of Radical Activists" (presubmission draft copy of Ph.D. diss., City University of New York, 1994), 303–304.

6. Bermanzohn, "Survivors of the 1979 Greensboro Massacre," 304.

7. Bermanzohn, "Survivors of the 1979 Greensboro Massacre," 305–306.

8. Bermanzohn, *The True Story of the Greensboro Massacre*, 23–24.

9. This and some other dialogue reported here was captured on TV videotapes.

10. Unless otherwise indicated, quotations by Marty Nathan are from a taped interview with her on November 1, 1992.

11. Political, extemporaneous public speaking meant to instruct and motivate people.

12. Bermanzohn, *The True Story of the Greensboro Massacre*, 29–30.

13. From a taped interview with Elliot Fratkin on November 2, 1992. Elliot Fratkin was the bridegroom at this wedding. The marriage did not last long. Fratkin later married Dr. Marty Nathan.

14. Unless otherwise indicated, quotations by Jane Waller are from a taped interview with her on November 19, 1993.

HOME-GROWN
FASCISTS

11

THIS PRECIPITOUS HOUR

Mein Leben ist nicht diese steile Stunde,
darin du mich so eilen siehst.
Ich bin ein Baum vor meinem Hintergrunde,
Ich bin nur einer meiner vielen Munde
und jener, welcher sich am fruehsten schliesst.

—*The Book of Hours*, Rainer Maria Rilke

No, my life is not this precipitous hour
through which you see me passing at a run.
I stand before my background like a tree.
Of all my many mouths I am but one,
And that which soonest chooses to be dumb.

—Translation by Babette Deutsch

GRIEF

When my next-door neighbor ventured outside to gather up his morning paper a couple of days after November 3, he saw a twelve-foot-long red cloth banner with large black letters streaming across the porch of the Waller home. Hoisted high and facing the street, it proclaimed to all passersby: "COMMITTEE TO AVENGE THE COMMUNIST WORKERS PARTY 5!"

My house had become party headquarters. I thought it would be a museum of the revolution some day. I would show everyone the upstairs study where Jim wrote his trade union papers, the closet with the low slanted ceiling that housed the Roneo mimeograph machine used to produce our flyers, and the kitchen that sometimes served as a free clinic for the poor.

As a security measure, I was directed away from 702 Cypress Street. For a while, I stayed with Dale. The soul of the departed lingered: Jim did not want to leave me. The first night, I was aware of his distinctive masculine scent. Some of the warmth of his body was still present in the universe, and it clung to me, his nearest companion in this world. I sensed his touch, his strong, sensitive, slightly polio-stricken fingers. I could still feel his arms embracing me. Too soon, those consoling traces of physicality eluded me, first smell, then touch, even visual memory. Longest resident in memory was his voice, the unique and faithful registrar of the intelligence and personality that was Jim Waller when he walked this earth with his decisive footfall.

As I lay in bed next to Dale, our tears flowed spontaneously toward one another and back inside ourselves. The sensation of sinking into the earth was intense. My body was being pulled into the bed, through it, then through the floor and through the ground, deep, deep into the earth. I lay on my stomach succumbing to the pull. Somewhere deep down in the depths of the earth was a balm for my soul.

"My whole body is aching. I can't imagine how I'm going to get through even one week, Signe. I can't imagine one day without Bill," Dale confided. "I feel as if someone has taken my heart out of my chest and lacerated it and rendered it into thousands of bloody bits," I confessed to her.

I was surprised that grief was so corporeal. I felt as if anyone might view my mangled and lacerated heart protruding from my chest. The image haunted me for years. Talking to Marty, I discovered that our physical metaphors were similar. The four widows formed a sort of sorority. The CWP stands for the Communist Widows Party, Floris remarked, in a black humor reference to our solidarity.

A "VERY COMMENDABLE" POLICE PERFORMANCE

After the murders, the police were forced to give an accounting to the news media and the general public. The information supplied by the police in press conferences immediately following the killings, and the official Greensboro Police Department (GPD) report released on November 26, 1979, damned the police.

Chief of Police, William E. Swing, acknowledged on the day after the massacre that the police had kept the Klan caravan "under surveillance from the time it arrived at the city limits" and that "police officers followed the vehicles from the intersection of Interstate 85 and U.S. 220 to near the scene of the shooting."[1] The police report reveals that the police knew that the caravan's occupants were armed and dangerous and that there was a potential for violence in any confrontation between the Klan and the demonstrators.[2]

At ten o'clock on the morning of November 3, 1979, a police briefing was conducted for members of the Tactical Support Unit (also called the Tact Unit). The police report reads:

> Detective Cooper advised the officers that according to intelligence information received that morning, an undetermined number of Klan members would be coming to Greensboro. Detective Cooper further advised some Klan members were already meeting at an individual's residence on Randleman Road. The officers were further advised by Cooper that some Klan members had handguns. Detective Cooper indicated that based upon information received, the Klan members plan to follow the parade route and heckle the marchers. The officers were told by Detective Cooper that if any confrontation happened, it would probably occur at the end of the parade around Freeman Mill Road and Florida Street.[3]

Omitted from the official police report is the source of Detective Cooper's intelligence. As we would soon learn, Cooper received a phone call before the police briefing from Klansman Eddie Dawson, whom the Greensboro Police Department had hired and paid to be its agent. Dawson's role in organizing the Klan and Nazi factions into the deadly caravan and ensuring that the caravan arrived at its destination was a crucial one. Detective Cooper (nicknamed "Rooster") was Dawson's control agent. The omission of the fact that they had a paid informant in the Klan speaks to the GPD's attempt to cover up their complicity in the Klan/Nazi crimes.

Most of the twenty-six persons assigned by the GPD to the march activity were present at the police briefing on the morning of November 3. In addition to Detective Cooper, the commanding officer of the Tactical Section, Lieutenant S. Daughtry, the tactical sergeant of Squad A, T. L. Burke, and the tactical sergeant of Squad B, J. L. Hightower, were at the briefing, along with the tactical officers in their squads. The executive officer of District II, Lieutenant P. W. Spoon, was there. According to the police's administrative report, the commander of District II, Captain T. A. Hampton, had put Spoon in charge of the march. Present also was a police attorney, M. A. Cawn, who discussed the laws and ordinances that might come into play if some enforcement action became necessary.

> Lieutenant Daughtry then made assignment to Tactical Squads A and B. Both squads were instructed to be on their post by 11:30 A.M. The Tact officers were

granted permission to get something to eat as it was uncertain how long they would be involved with the march assignment. This permission was conditional in that it did not interfere with their being on assignments at 11:30 A.M.[4]

Having been told that the Klan was already gathering at a Greensboro residence and planning to ride the parade route, that some Klan members were armed, and that this information was considered "reliable and up-to-date," the Tactical Section officers, who "would provide back-up and support if needed"[5] for the security of the march, were sent to an early lunch. Around 10:40 A.M., when the briefing ended, they went to restaurants in the Randleman Road area. Police had until 11:30 to get to their posts; the shootings occurred at 11:23.

After the briefing, Detective Cooper and a special investigator from the Police Crime Lab, J. T. Matthews, were sent to "locate suspected Klan vehicles which might move into the area of the march route."[6] Cooper "proceeded to the general area of U.S. 220 and I-85."[7] Eddie Dawson and the Klansmen, having assembled near Randleman Road at the home of Klan member Brent Fletcher, were forming their caravan while the police were being briefed. Dawson, as later trial testimony revealed, urged his fellow Klansmen to hurry it up. By 11:05 A.M., a caravan of vehicles was poised at the entrance ramp of I-85, approximately ten minutes from the march starting point; Cooper and Matthews photographed the caravan and then followed it as it proceeded to Everitt Street and Carver Drive. They hung back about a block and a half from the crime scene.

Cooper's radio transmissions, as he followed the caravan to the murder scene, were reported in the press a few days afterward. They seem like a play-by-play sportscast rather than the transmissions of a law enforcement officer trying to protect citizens under imminent threat as they exercise their legal right of assembly. To Tactical Sergeant Burke, Cooper says at 11:06 A.M., "Okay, you got 8 vehicles parked and loaded on the ramp from down where we went this morning. They're on the ramp of 85 and 220. It looks like about 30 or 35 people, maybe not that many in the vehicles. They're just sitting on the ramp there waiting, all in the vehicles. So, we're gonna stand by here and kinda monitor them, see what they do."[8] And then at 11:11 A.M. to District II Sergeant W. D. Comer, "information only, we got about 8 vehicles the opposite side parked on the ramp at 85 and 220, headed your direction. However, they're stationary at this time. We'll have further if they move in."[9]

District II Sergeant W. D. Comer, said in the report to have primary responsibility for the march, told District II officers Williams and Johnson to be at Everitt Street and Carver Drive at 11:30 A.M., the time police had arranged to meet with Nelson Johnson. That arrangement, as noted earlier, was made on November 1 when Nelson and Paul had a press conference in downtown Greensboro and picked up the parade permit. Also on November 1, police had at least two meetings to set plans for the march and make assignments about deployment of their forces.[10]

Sergeant Comer claimed that he checked Everitt and Carver, looking for Nelson, at 10:15, but no one had arrived there yet. Comer then drove to the Windsor Community Center where he observed "a racially mixed group of approximately 40–50 persons." The crowd was hostile and was chanting, according to the police report, "Death to the pigs, death to the Klan, and pigs stay away."[11] Comer did not return to Everitt and Carver but spent the next hour going back and forth between the Windsor Community Center and nearby Washington Street School. At the school, he saw his officers who were to escort the march. He returned to the Windsor Community Center at about 10:36 with Officer Williams "to try to locate Nelson Johnson and inform him the police would lead the march to make sure the march was not disrupted. Neither Sergeant Comer nor Officer Williams knew Nelson Johnson by sight."[12]

Each time Comer returned to Windsor Center, he was met with expressions of disdain by the crowd. Comer, nevertheless, was able to explain that "officers would be there for protection and to prevent disruption of the march. The group was informed by Sergeant Comer that one police car would lead the march and one police car would follow the march. The group was further informed that officers would control traffic at street intersections for the safety of the group."[13]

Around 11:00 A.M., Sergeant Comer radioed to District II Executive Officer P. W. Spoon that he was unable to locate Nelson Johnson, and Spoon told him to keep trying. Comer and Williams parked on a street adjacent to the Windsor Community Center parking lot waiting for Nelson Johnson to show up and observing the group at Windsor continue to grow. Remember that they claimed not to know what Nelson looked like, but nevertheless they waited for him to show up among a rapidly growing crowd. The police report states that Comer "planned to go to the Everitt Street and Carver Drive area at 11:30 A.M. if Nelson Johnson did not arrive at Windsor Community Center prior to that time."[14] Neither Lieutenant Spoon nor anyone else suggested to Comer that he might return to Everitt and Carver, the intersection Nelson named on the parade permit as the origin of the march and the agreed-upon meeting place with the police.

At 11:11 A.M., Detective Cooper radioed to Comer that the vehicles parked on the ramp at 85 and 220 were "headed your direction."[15] At 11:13 A.M., Cooper told Tactical Sergeant Burke, "We're rolling now, headed that direction from this location. There's a total now of 9 vehicles."[16] At 11:14 A.M., when

Burke responded to Cooper with "Dave [Comer] called a minute ago and said the bunch where he's at is real hostile and belligerent," Cooper said, "Ah, we're gonna have to wait and see. They're definitely headed in that direction."[17] Cooper's transmissions seem to be deliberately vague with regard to directions.

A critical turn for the caravan was on Lee Street. It is a two-way street going east and west, and the Everitt and Carver intersection is to the east of Windsor Center. Until the caravan turned east on Lee, it could have been headed for either site. Once it turned east, it was within a couple of blocks of Everitt and Carver. Cooper, in his transmissions to Comer and Burke, seems to be implying that the caravan is going to Windsor Center, where Comer was.

At 11:15 A.M., the Tact Squads were still out to lunch. Sergeant Comer was sitting tight at Windsor Center and making no effort to check on activities at Morningside. A weapons-laden caravan was headed in a direction that could take it to either of two sites where crowds of unsuspecting people were gathering. The police knew the caravan vehicles contained weapons. At this moment, Sergeant Burke reported to the officer in charge of the Tactical Units, Lieutenant Daughtry, about his two recent communications, one from Comer and the other from Cooper. Daughtry asked Burke at 11:16, in response to the information about the Klan caravan's movements, "they headed in the direction of the starting point?" and Burke answered, "that's what Jerry [Cooper] said. He's been keeping me advised." Lieutenant Daughtry then told Sergeant Burke (who was stationed quite far, about a ten-minute drive, from either of the gathering sites), "Be alert to shift over that way if we give you a call."[18]

The biding of time, vagueness of directions, and banter about the belligerence of the group at Windsor Center over Frequencies 1 and 3 that morning seem calculated to distract from the main point—the avoidance by the police of the starting point of the march as stated on the permit. At 11:17 A.M., Detective Cooper transmitted to Lt. Daughtry, "just made the turnoff onto Lee Street."[19] Up to this point, the caravan might have gone with equal ease to either of the two gathering sites, separated by less than a mile. When the Klan vehicles turned east on Lee Street, it was very clear that they were heading away from Windsor Community Center and toward Everitt and Carver. But Cooper makes no effort to clarify his hitherto ambiguous descriptions. In fact, taken in the context of his previous transmissions that seem to be referenced on Comer's location, the "turnoff onto Lee Street" could easily be understood as a turn to the west, to Windsor. Bear in mind that Cooper followed the caravan even as it turned onto Lee. He knew whether he and the caravan were going east or west and certainly could have rectified his previous ambiguous descriptions at this point with a clear report.

Nearly two minutes later, at 11:18 A.M., Cooper radioed, "turning on Willow Road now."[20] It is clear that the turn onto Lee Street was to the east, not to the west—or the caravan would not have arrived at Willow Road. The turn onto Willow Road, going north from Lee Street, put the caravan in a direct route to the starting point of the march at Everitt and Carver, only a couple of blocks away. But aside from Lt. Daughtry (commander of the distantly stationed Tactical Squads) reminding his officers to finish lunch and get into position, there is no attempt to move units to a probable confrontation site. At 11:20 A.M., Cooper radioed to Daughtry, "part of them should be there by now almost," and then several seconds later, "they're parking up on Everitt Street at Willow Road."[21]

What the GPD did *not* do that morning is as interesting as what they did. Cooper did *not* let Sergeant Comer, over at Windsor Community Center, know of the caravan's route after the transmission of 11:11 A.M., when Cooper told Comer the vehicles were parked on the highway ramp and "headed your direction." By 11:20 A.M., when Cooper, still following the Klan, radioed "they're parking up on Everitt Street at Willow Road," his transmission was to Daughtry, not to nearby Comer. Daughtry then radioed Lt. Spoon. (Spoon was intent on meeting with Daughtry to let him know that the preacher on the other side of town, whose church originally was to be the termination point of the march and site of the afternoon conference, called to say that he did not want the marchers to come to his church. This, the police report claims, was significant because of Cooper's earlier intelligence that if trouble developed it would likely be at the end of the march. Be that as it may, in the context of the known movements of the Klan caravan occurring that very moment, it was just another sideshow for reporters to stumble over.)

Of all the police units scattered hither and yon (and in restaurants), Comer and Williams, parked less than a mile from Everitt and Carver, were among the closest to the impending confrontation. They could have been at Everitt and Carver within a minute from the time Cooper reported that Klan vehicles were parking on Everitt at Willow Road—*before* the deadly fusillade, as could officers stationed even closer to Everitt and Carver than Comer. But instead of relaying this critical information to Comer or other nearby officers, or intercepting the Klan vehicles himself, Cooper continued his radio transmission to Daughtry, saying at 11:22 A.M., "they're now at the formation point."[22]

Another minute and a half went by in which Cooper made no attempt to have the Klan vehicles intercepted, but continued his sportscast. From 11:22 A.M. to 11:23 A.M., he announced, "Ok, we got about 9 or 10 cars on the opposite side has now arrived at the formation point for the parade and it appears as though they're heckling at this time, driving on by, uh, they're definitely creating attention and some of the parade members are, uh . . . " After a brief break in transmission, Cooper's voice is heard: "they're scattering. . . ." Another interruption of several seconds and again Cooper with, "We've got a 10-10 [fight in progress] down here, you better get some units in here."[23]

Some twenty seconds later, when the firing became heavy, Cooper radioed, "shots fired, sounds like . . . ," and only then did Lt. Spoon give the command, "Move the [District II] cars into the area."[24] Cooper is next heard on the radio saying "heavy gunfire." A few seconds later, Lt. Spoon ordered, "pull all available cars in the city to the area of . . . *the Windsor Community Center.* Don't all come to the area, I'll advise further when I arrive on the scene."[25]

It was 11:24:02 A.M., according to the police administrative report, and heavy gunfire was underway and had just been reported when Lt. Spoon sent the message directing police *away from* Everitt and Carver. The lieutenant was not confused about where the shooting was. The police report "explains" (but does not explain) his response. "Spoon was en route to Everitt Street and Carver Drive at the time, but did not want all the police units in the city to rush into the area of Everitt and Carver. So, he directed the cars to head towards Windsor Community Center until he could arrive at Everitt Street and Carver Drive to advise further on the situation."[26]

At 11:24:29 A.M., Cooper, still stationed a block away, reported that "most of the fire is coming from the yellow van" and "they're now leaving the scene."[27] The rest of his transmission is obscured by telephone calls from people at Morningside reporting the incident. The police called for ambulances. The next noteworthy transmission in the police report was at 11:25 A.M. Two tactical officers report, "we got the van on Everitt, get some help."[28]

The interception of the van at that point led to the arrest of its twelve Klan and Nazi occupants. However, this interception was totally unbidden and largely accidental. It appears that the yellow van, the last in the Klan and Nazi convoy to leave the scene, was delayed waiting for stragglers. As police officers A. A. League and S. A. Bryant were to testify, they rushed to Everitt and Carver when they heard Cooper's radio report about gunfire there and heard him say that a yellow van was involved. They positioned themselves to intercept the van. "Both [League and Bryant] said the driver looked startled, halted, and then accelerated," but the two officers managed to stop the van before it made its getaway.[29] They had not been *ordered* to go to Everitt and Carver.

"If all the cops had gone where they were told, every single killer would have been able to escape," Paul and Sally Bermanzohn commented in their account of the attack.[30] Nowhere in the entire police report can any command be found to

stop any of the vehicles fleeing from the scene of the shooting. In fact, only one transmission even makes reference to stopping the Klan vehicles, and that one comes to zilch.

"You want to try to stop some of those other cars that were leaving, the other members?" Sergeant Burke asked Lieutenant Daughtry over Frequency 3 at 11:27 A.M.[31] "Daughtry did not hear this message because he was outside his vehicle assisting with the arrest of the suspects in the van," the police administrative report says,[32] and that was the end of it. Sergeant Burke, the commander of one of the two tactical units that day, did not attempt to pursue any of the fleeing vehicles; nor did he order any of the four cars under his command to do so.

Journalists, lawyers, and others who read the police report noted discrepancies and raised questions regarding police statements about response time. The surviving victims of a police conspiracy understood that the police were *not trying to* stop a crime and *not trying to* get to the scene quickly enough to arrest the perpetrators. Cover up was the order of the day, and fig leafs were in short supply.

Two days after the murders, Police Chief Swing told the media, "the fact that the cars went to Everitt and Carver indicates that they had information" about where the rally was. But, Swing lied, "how they got that information, I do not know."[33] On November 7, 1979, police spokesman Captain C. W. Hilliard told the press that a man requesting the parade permit, who identified himself as Ed Dawson and a Klansman, was given a copy of the permit by the police two days before the march because a parade permit is a public record.[34] That the police did not inform us of this before our rally—particularly in light of their insistence that we be unarmed—speaks volumes.

At the press conference, Captain Hilliard told of Klansman Dawson getting the permit, and the police still did not let on that they had any special arrangement with Dawson. It later came to light that the police approached Dawson in October 1979 and asked him to be an informant. When Dawson called Detective Rooster Cooper shortly before the 10:00 A.M. police briefing on November 3 and reported that more than a dozen armed Klansmen were brandishing weapons at a meeting place on Randleman Road, he was fulfilling his police assignment.[35]

The public and the media wanted to know why the police had not stopped the Klan vehicles to search for weapons. This obvious question was raised at the earliest press conferences, even before Swing admitted the police *knew for certain* that caravan members were armed. In fact, during those long minutes when Cooper was monitoring the Klan on the ramp of I-85 and 220, the caravan halted. When a light blue Ford Fairlaine arrived, it was positioned by Dawson so that it was the next to last vehicle in the caravan, right in front of the yellow van. The Ford Fairlane contained the weapons used to kill demonstrators. The van behind it carried the men who used those weapons. Chief Swing mendaciously declared to the press that the police did not stop the caravan vehicles before the shootings because "we had not seen weapons at that point. There had been no law violated."[36] In the eyes of the public and of legal experts alike, police knowledge of the prevailing situation and its distinct potential for violence warranted some level of intervention before allowing the caravan to proceed to the rally.

The police were pressed by civil rights leaders. Rev. Joseph Lowery, president of the Southern Christian Leadership Conference, and Steve Suitts, executive director of the Southern Regional Council, pointed out that those killed would not have been killed had their assailants not "thought they could get away with it."[37] Similarly, Dr. George Simkins, president of the Greensboro chapter of the National Association for the Advancement of Colored People, observed "this never would have happened if the police had done their job." Swing lied when he said, "we had no indications that there were guns in the car; there's no way we could have known."[38]

While Rev. Leon White of the United Church of Christ and George Gardner, director of the North Carolina Civil Liberties Union, made separate statements calling for an independent investigation of police conduct,[39] Greensboro mayor Jim Melvin called the actions of the police "very commendable."[40] Not surprisingly, the police sided with the mayor, asserting that, in all details, the officers "assigned to the march performed their duty in a professional and reasonable manner."[41]

The police cited a desire to maintain a "low-visibility position" and "to avoid promoting confrontation between marchers and police" to justify their actions.[42] (Most ludicrous was an oft-repeated police excuse that Nelson and others had told them to stay away: were they suddenly taking their orders from Nelson Johnson and the CWP?) There is much specific background information about the Workers Viewpoint Organization in the Administrative Report that indicates that the police not only harassed people trying to leaflet for the rally but also monitored the WVO closely during the month of October.

In their report, the police attribute their being in the wrong place at the wrong time to "confusion" created by "having groups at two locations simultaneously" and to "confusion . . . further created by the early movement of the Klan caravan."[43]

The salient fact here is that when Nelson first applied to the police for the parade permit on October 19, he specified Everitt Street and Carver Drive in Morningside Homes as the beginning of the march. Nelson signed off on this information and never changed it. It is plainly written on the permit handed to Nelson (and to Ed Dawson) on November 1, 1979. The police were not confused when they agreed to meet Nelson at Everitt and Carver prior to the march at 11:30 A.M. Four TV crews and several reporters managed to locate the march origin at Everitt and Carver without even seeing a copy of the parade permit. It simply does not wash that two assembly points "confused" the police and that was why they were not present at Morningside Homes. How difficult would it have been to protect both sites or, at least, to have been present? The police avoidance of Everitt and Carver cannot be justified by a disingenuous appeal to a low-visibility strategy, nor to confusion about the starting location of the march. Their evasion can only have been for the purpose of letting something happen.

Even though the correct time and place for the start of the march was on the permit filed with the police and police themselves had arranged to meet Nelson at the specified march origin of Everitt and Carver at 11:30, the media never conveyed this essential information clearly to the public. Instead, the media repeated ad nauseam the lie that the police were confused about the starting point of the march.

MEDIA PORTRAITS

An honest and independent press would have explored the issue of police complicity with the terrorist attack on citizens who were exercising their right of free speech on November 3, 1979. Instead, outright lies on the part of a city's police chief invited scant or no scrutiny by the media. Instead, the media focused on the politics and characters of the massacre victims. Media calumny against the murder victims and devastated survivors, based on prejudice and stereotyping, was ubiquitous. The subservient posture assumed by the media allowed those responsible for crimes to divert attention from their actions by appealing to anticommunist prejudice. Once the cover-up stories were in circulation, few reporters had the courage, will, or means to break the iteration. In an atmosphere of official propaganda and intimidation, a fear factor was operating. Many people were afraid to express doubt or dissent. Perhaps more insidious was people's failure to *think* outside of the official canon, a failure fostered by the absence of a critical and independent media.

Of course there was some resistance to media control and manipulation. I was told by a friend who worked for WFMY that on the afternoon of November 3, 1979, Police Chief William Swing and Director of Public Safety Hewitt

Lovelace went to see the news director of that television station, Gary Curtis. They tried to pressure him not to show all the video his cameraman, Jim Waters, had shot earlier in the day. Curtis refused their request and aired video footage that clearly shows the Klan attacking the demonstrators. After November 3, several of the media people at the scene, including Waters, were harassed.[44] But despite efforts by some exceptional media workers, official control over mass media, along with self-policing by reporters and editors, provided the public with news stories that covered up and distorted what happened on November 3, 1979, as well as how and why it happened.[45]

The headline in the evening edition of the Greensboro paper on November 3, 1979, reads, "Klan Ambush Kills 4 WVO People." The article leads off with: "At least four members of a communist protest group were shot to death late this morning in east Greensboro after an ambush at the corner of Everitt and Carver streets." It refers to the "people who were riding in the ambush van."[46] But the term *ambush* disappeared from Greensboro's morning paper and was not used again. On November 4, 1979, the headline read, "Four Die in Klan-Leftist Shootout in SE Greensboro."[47] An *ambush* was repackaged as a *shootout*.

The dramatic video footage taken by black cameraman Ed Boyd of WTVD-TV captures an *ambush* in progress. It is an *ambush* that is described by several media persons who immediately gave their vivid eyewitness accounts.[48] It was not less of an ambush because a couple of people, surprised by the attack, nevertheless managed to respond by firing back—without effect, as it happened. An *ambush* is a snare, a trap, or an unexpected attack. A *shooting* is an act of discharging a firearm. A *shootout*, a slang expression, connotes a gun battle: the term evokes an image of cops and robbers or of gang warfare over drug turf. These terms mean different things and resonate differently.

In an ambush, people are surprised, not prepared. An ambush does not just happen spontaneously—in fact, the claim that spontaneous shooting *broke out* was at the heart of the Klan's defense. An ambush is *laid, set up in advance*. That definition raises all sorts of questions about prior intelligence, complicit individuals or institutions, or whatever else is required to set up the ambush scene in advance. It was not mere happenstance that the word *ambush* was not used in the mass media after the first few hours—the incident was framed in a certain way to manipulate public opinion.

A *shootout* served Greensboro's elite far better. A shootout can erupt spontaneously as an ambush does not. Tabloid usage makes shootouts seemingly self-contained events whose sordid nature does not and could not possibly mix with lofty political goals—for instance, blood running in gutters, not workers' unity. That the gunfight was lopsided due to the victims' utter surprise and lack of preparation was not part of the official storyline of a shootout. Nor were other relevant facts. The shootout version of the events of November 3, endorsed by officialdom, was repeated so much that many of our friends and well-wishers used it without being aware of the implications.

The focus shifted from "the worst Klan-associated violence in this country since the 1960s when the civil rights movement was at its peak" to "the shootout confrontation between radical rightists and leftist groups."[49] In actuality, the November 3 rally was very much within the tradition of the entire civil rights movement. But our detractors had to sever that connection. Our rally was not to be confused with "legitimate peaceful demonstrations by those who feel aggrieved," warned one editorial. It was not "a direct descendant of the Greensboro sit-ins, which were carried out in the non-violent civil rights spirit. Peaceful assembly is a right that must be protected."[50] The implication was that ours was not a peaceful assembly, and that we did not have rights that had to be protected.

So that they would not invoke the public's sympathy, the November Third victims were dehumanized, set beyond the pale: others must not see their own humanity or their own possible fate in them. Several stories appeared that interpreted the positive characteristics of the massacre victims, making them look like monsters. An Associated Press article described Bill Sampson: He had a "beautiful face," and "the kind of awesome intellect heaven grants to maybe one in a million." The article went on to mention Bill's successes and honors at Augustana College and his Masters Degree in Divinity at Harvard. But when, instead of finishing medical school, Bill went to work in a textile mill, "somewhere, something went wrong."[51] The story ends with a sensationalistic, demeaning account of Bill's final moments, one suggesting a monster gone amok. "It was not what went wrong," Dale responded, "it was what went right. It was a continuation of a path Bill had taken from an early age to really struggle to find out what the source of the injustice and oppression was, in this country and around the world, and how to fight it."[52]

The major manufacturers of public opinion did not interview people who worked with Bill in the mill. The omission of authentic voices of black and white workers from the officially ratified narrative of events about November Third is an example of an inherent media bias. Shortly after the murders, WVO supporter and documentary producer Sally Alvarez talked to white worker Bill Johnson (a.k.a. Big Bill) and his wife Virginia in their small cottage in Greensboro. They reminisced about Bill Sampson: "His interest in the welfare of other people is what really led to his death," Big Bill said. "He was concerned about others more than he was concerned about himself. That's what really done it.

And there's no better way to die than a man concerned—even the Bible says that—being concerned to give up his life for a brother."[53]

Big Bill regarded Bill Sampson as a hero who was "really out to help the oppressed." Cone Mills "just couldn't cope with Bill. He'd take a grievance, where it looked like it was impossible to win, and come out on top," Bill Johnson said in tribute to his friend. In spite of ever-present anticommunist propaganda, Big Bill noted that many people around the world, "real, down-to-earth people," believed in Marxism-Leninism, and "there's a lot of people catching on to it and supporting it—you might say, like a wild prairie fire." He suspected that Cone Mills, the Police Department, the FBI, and the CIA all had a hand in what happened on November 3, 1979. His activist friends were "a thorn in Cone's side. . . . They got hurt the most by people such as Bill Sampson, Jim Waller, Sandi Smith." He thought November Third was a set-up, involving paid assassins.[54]

A black worker interviewed by Sally Alvarez said, "if I wasn't sure about a certain situation, I would always go to Bill and ask him, 'What do you think about this?' Well, if he didn't know off hand, he would pull out his little contract book. We'd sit down and reexamine everything and talk about it, and then we would strategically map out what we should do. . . . We used to sit back, me and Bill, and laugh. We knew we had Cone on the run."[55] Also interviewed by Alvarez was a black woman who worked with Bill at White Oak. Her comments show that Bill's communism was not an insuperable barrier for the workers. "All of the working-class people, includin' myself, we're all for the same thing that Bill's for," she said.[56]

Big Bill and other workers give the lie to a key element in the official media version of the Greensboro Massacre—that the reason WVO organizers waged an anti-Klan campaign was that they failed to gain adherents in the mills.[57] According to this cynical fiction, repeated endlessly, WVO organizers went into black communities to get the support of poor blacks after failing to get a positive response from mill workers. In truth, WVO/CWP supporters opposed the Klan because they were opposed to racism. Bill witnessed a cross burning as a child in South Carolina and had been deeply offended by the desecration of a religious symbol that stands for love, not hatred. The official version is also racist in implying that black people in a housing project could be *easily manipulated* to become adherents of the WVO/CWP (i.e., they are not bright enough to determine their own self-interest), and that the activists (many of them black) were *using* black people for some selfish gain. If one acknowledges that WVO organizers were actually remarkably successful in uniting black and white workers around an antiracist and anti-imperialist agenda, the motivation behind the assassinations becomes clear: the powers-that-be did not want such an example to catch on more widely or to go any further. Hence the media distortions.

With the media's help, the victims of the massacre were slandered in ways that tormented their widows. Evidently, no one could be found to say anything bad about Dr. Michael Nathan. "A very caring physician who was always willing to go beyond what was just enough," "a very sensitive and devoted physician," "a kind, caring person," "his loss is to the community of children he served," "a very effective teacher," "a highly competent physician," were some of the ways those who had worked with Mike, supervised him, or known him well described him.[58] However, someone attributed to Mike Nathan "some kind of death wish."[59] That piece of spite, or random speculation, was a good fit for the police and government cover-up, and it was injected into the official narrative. Marty Nathan was livid. Although Mike had a daughter who was only six months old, a wife whom he dearly loved, and an invalid mother whom he cared for devotedly, he could now be dismissed as just a crazy man with a "death wish."

Another cruel slander and blame-the-victim-for-the-crime tactic that surfaced within days after November Third attributed a martyrdom plan to Jim and me. The boozing coworker, Rex Stevenson, whom Jim befriended at the sewage treatment plant, claimed that Jim and I thought the party needed martyrs and national publicity and that Jim plotted to get himself and a few others killed to further the cause of the CWP! Character assassination, following physical assassination, was hard to bear.

AT THE HIGHEST LEVEL

On Sunday, November 4, 1979, we held a press conference at the Cypress Street house. Nelson, just released from jail, sat in the middle of my massive Empire couch, flanked on either side by two heavy-hearted widows, Dale and myself, and joined by Sally Bermanzohn. Gesturing with bandaged arms and hands, Nelson described the sequence of events of the previous day. He called the attack a military maneuver, a planned ambush that trapped and then picked off CWP leaders.

The vehicles drove up to Everitt Street and past the marchers gathered at the Community Center on Everitt and Carver, Nelson told reporters. When the first car was about 175 yards from Gillespie Street (the next cross street), it halted. By the time all of the cars had come to a standstill, the assassins had prepared their weapons for the attack. The only purpose of the gunmen in the lead car was to fire in the air to scatter people toward the last car carrying the marksmen, Nelson asserted. The assassins *knew* whom to pick out of the crowd, he insisted. From a crowd of roughly one hundred people, there were about twenty-five who were in the party and six who were leaders in the organization. Four of those six were killed.

"Then why did they spare you?" Nelson was asked. He speculated that in any pictures the Klan might have seen before November 3, he was not wearing a hat, but he wore a hat on November 3. Then again, perhaps while he was defending himself against a knife attack by a Klansman, he was not easily identifiable.

"This was a high-level assassination plot," Sally charged. "People are rising up and so they bring out the Klan in an attempt to wipe out the leadership of this rising movement." Sally's outspokenness and ardor were not subdued by the multiple burdens she carried in the aftermath of the shootings. Her husband Paul and her ex-husband Mike were both in the hospital, their lives hanging in balance. Mike was clearly about to die and Paul was critically injured and had just undergone lengthy brain surgery. If he survived, it would be with permanent handicaps the extent of which was not known. At the moment she was charging our enemies with their heinous crimes, Sally had a toddler to care for and was several months pregnant with her second child.

To the skepticism expressed by one of the reporters upon hearing Nelson Johnson assert that CWP leaders were singled out for assassination, Dale responded passionately, "Bill got shot right in the heart. You don't just blindly fire into a crowd and somebody gets hit in the heart and in the head. . . . That is marksmanship. That is planned. They had singled out who they were firing at."

The reporter wanted to make sure she got it all. "You're saying your husband and your husband . . . "

"Were murdered," Sally cut in sharply.

" . . . were intended targets?" finished the reporter.

"Absolutely," said Dale.

"'Cause how can you have the leadership—her husband," Sally cried out, pointing to Dale, "who leads the rank-and-file movement at the White Oak mill, right? Her husband," she went on, pointing to me, "who leads the workers' struggle at the Granite Mill, Sandi Smith leading the workers' struggle at Revolution Mill, and César Cauce leading the struggle at Duke Hospital—those four leaders seen at all their places where they work by all the workers there as leaders—they were murdered right then, right on the spot."[60]

As this press conference took place, Marty Nathan was in the hospital with her dying husband, Mike. At some point, Dr. Mike Nathan, a longtime friend and supporter of the WVO/CWP, was inducted into the party—a sort of last rite. Mike's death the following day, November 5, brought the fatality total of the Greensboro Massacre to five. (That day also happened to be Jim's birthday: he would have been thirty-seven, the oldest of the five victims.)

We knew the federal government had a role in the horrible crimes. The FBI was quick to deny that they had any involvement. "Today the FBI said the Greensboro violence caught it completely by surprise," Susan Kidd reported on Channel 2. Cut to FBI Agent Cecil Moses: "We had no evidence that the Klan was actively engaged, or any other organization for that matter, was actively engaged in any violent activities. . . . We have not tried to penetrate or to direct any informants to the group because that's not within the guidelines to do so. And so we had no advance knowledge at all that we could pass on to the local authorities that there might be that kind of situation brewing."[61]

On November 6, 1979, while Greensboro's Chief Swing was still trying to explain away police actions, Moses' denial was contradicted by another FBI agent. We learned that the FBI had been watching us prior to the murders: "Since Oct. 23, the FBI has been investigating the Communist Workers Party to which the demonstrators belonged, according to a federal official. Andrew Pelczar, supervisor of the Greensboro FBI office, said the investigation was begun because of the group's frequent advocacy of the use of violence to achieve political ends."[62] Pelczar told the press that FBI Director William Webster "has taken a very personal interest in this case."[63]

By Monday, November 5, 1979, the FBI began dispatching agents to Greensboro. The official purpose of the Justice Department's Community Relations Service (CRS) agents, sent by President Carter, was to expand the investigation of the murders of anti-Klan demonstrators. What they actually did, according to lawyer Gayle Korotkin, however, was to work with "city officials, the city and state human relations offices, the police, the North Carolina State Bureau of Investigation, and the FBI to keep the lid on the situation and shift attention to the CWP. They relied on half-truths, rumor mongering, red-baiting, and innuendo, and manipulated the existing tension between disparate groups."[64] The federal agencies seized evidence and assisted with a cover-up in progress.

In an interview with a Winston-Salem reporter on November 5, Nelson restated that "this was a SWAT-team-like assassination crew; it was not the act of a few crazy Klansmen. The guns were trained on people who were active in trying to organize workers across the state."[65] The state's chief medical examiner confirmed that all those killed were shot in the head and upper body. Nelson pointed out that the gunmen must have fired with tremendous accuracy to kill so quickly.

The same reporter talked to Klansman Joe Grady and reported, "He [Grady] said that one person, who is not a Klansman and whom he did not name, brought most of the weapons to Greensboro. Grady said that Raeford Milano Caudle, who was charged with conspiracy to commit murder in the incident, told him that the man was not supposed to go to the rally point but knew who was to be shot."[66]

The reader may recall that Joe Grady and Gorrell Pierce were Klansmen present at China Grove the previous July. The open letter of October 22 was addressed to them. Neither was in the caravan on November 3. Grady split with the Federated Knights of the Ku Klux Klan after Pierce attended the rally in Louisburg in September at which Klan and Nazis formed a United Racist Front. Historically, Klan and Nazis rarely joined forces: Many Klansmen retained a World War II aversion to Nazis as America's enemy. By November 3, Grady was leading another Klan sect. Both Grady and Pierce denied that their groups had anything to do with the attack at Morningside, and Grady told United Press International, "It was not the Ku Klux Klan over there. They were damned Nazis."[67]

In July 1980, we would learn the identity of a government agent who seemed to fit the description given by Grady—someone not a Klansman who brought most of the weapons to Greensboro, who was not supposed to go to the rally point, but who knew who was to be shot.

WE GRIEVE AND WE FIGHT BACK UNDER SIEGE

Among the crop of new faces in Greensboro was a very short person with straight blond hair quietly functioning as the nerve center in my house where volunteers stayed. Gayle Korotkin, a lawyer friend of CWP head Jerry Tung from New York and an unassuming, self-effacing person, volunteered to stay in Greensboro indefinitely to do whatever necessary for justice in our case. Over the next six years, she lived, slept, ate, spoke, wrote, and dreamed Greensboro. She was a tireless grunt as well as a brilliant analyst and intellectual. No task was beneath her, and none was too large or complicated for her to handle. I leaned on Gayle for support. I could speak out, and I could fight back, and I did those things. But grief incapacitated me in serious ways. Gayle, and later Lewis Pitts, Katie Green, Earle Tockman, and many others, were enormously supportive to me. In the months-that-stretched-into-years of being under siege, the leadership of Nelson Johnson was also a prime factor in holding me together. What was left of the North Carolina leadership body communicated frequently with the party's leadership in New York. Shortly after November 3, I agreed to be a press secretary for the CWP in North Carolina. The CWP leadership did all that it could to ease our hardships and to keep the political struggle moving forward.

Surveillance and wiretapping were part of the landscape. We knew it was going on. At my house one day, the phone rang, and when I picked up, I realized that something funny was happening: It seemed to be ringing somewhere else, too. A voice said, "SBI, oops!" Then the call was cut off. Gayle and I laughed about this botched wiretapping job, presumably by the State Bureau of Investigation. The police and government surveillance did little to deter CWP members and supporters. But routinely implemented harassment and surveillance of those who appeared to be sympathetic to us had the effect of frightening people and keeping them away, thus depriving us of potential support that we needed so badly.

Right after the murders, it looked like the mills might erupt. Cone shut down White Oak Mill early the next day and called in state troopers to guard the plant gates. Foremen on the shop floor carried shotguns. At Revolution, Cone had security guards at the gates and police patrolling the streets around the mill. A friend of Sandi's described it as "intense harassment—they sort of monitored your every move."[68] Other workers shared her suspicion that Cone had something to do with the killings. Right after November Third, with police surrounding the area, "it was really a weird feeling," she said. "It scared a lot of people. I think that was their basic tactic. If there's gonna be an uprising, we've got the guns already outside the gate, so we'll put a stop to that before you start it."[69]

Nevertheless, even in North Carolina, where attempts to intimidate CWP supporters and allies were most intense, people were not cowed into passivity. Many attended demonstrations, vigils, and memorial services. In public squares in the Triangle Area—Raleigh, Durham, and Chapel Hill—silent vigils and assemblies were held. At one vigil, over four hundred people stood before the capitol building in Raleigh. Spokesman Chuck Eppinette said that the vigil was intended "to send a message to everyone in Raleigh to quit thinking that the Klan has no base in North Carolina and that racism will go away without anyone doing anything about it."[70]

In Durham, police with binoculars peered down from the rooftop of a nearby building at some two hundred people. The group included, among others, the pacifist War Resisters League, church groups, and some Durham City Council members.[71] Addressing a group of concerned people who stayed on after the Durham vigil were widows Marty Nathan and Floris Cauce. Marty told them that her husband hated violence and went to Greensboro unarmed on November 3. Floris called the killing of César and the other demonstrators a drop in an ocean of blood that the Klan has spilled for over a hundred years. César died trying to defend his comrades, she said. Wave upon wave of others would come to take his place in the struggle.

In New York, soon after the murders, over a hundred of Jim's former colleagues and friends from his medical days in the South Bronx gathered to commemorate him. A virtual media blackout, however, kept New Yorkers in the dark about ongoing developments in Greensboro. To locate the Greensboro Massacre on a trajectory of history, recall that on November 4, 1979, Iranians took over the American Embassy. Iran became the central focus of the national news media in the United States for a long time. International events, and the jingoism that ensued, conveniently eclipsed coverage about the significant violence in Greensboro, perpetrated by home-grown American terrorists. But while the Greensboro story was ignored in the national press, local and state media covered it for years, day after day. Instead of ignoring it, they managed it.

WE SEEK TO AVENGE THE MURDERS AND
A GAGGLE OF ASSORTED FASCISTS OPPOSE US

We announced that we would have a funeral march to bury our dead with honor. In the week following the massacre, there were tense back-and-forth negotiations about the funeral march between the CWP and the City. In New York, party spokesman Mike Young promised that we would avenge the brutal assassinations of the CWP 5. "We're going to turn the country upside down," he said. We guaranteed that we would be armed for the funeral march, but we made it clear that bloodletting was not part of avenging the deaths of our comrades. "We're defending ourselves. We're not chasing anybody. We're not out to hunt down these killers," Young told reporters.[72]

The shape of the November 11 funeral march jelled: we would march through the streets of Greensboro carrying the caskets of our slain comrades. Since it was a funeral procession, we would not need a parade permit. From downtown we would go to Maplewood Cemetery where four of the five were to be buried. (Sandi's parents chose for her body to be sent back to South Carolina.)

Meanwhile, downtown, a dozen Klan and Nazis, arrested when the van was stopped and charged with first-degree murder and conspiracy, were in police custody at the Guilford County jail. Most of them were Klan from Catawba and Lincoln Counties in western North Carolina. But, two days after the murders, the state leader of the Nazi Party, Harold Covington, told reporters that one of those arrested, Roland Wayne Wood of Winston-Salem, was a Nazi unit leader in Forsyth County. Covington openly exulted in the cooperation of the Klan and Nazis as a revival of "white supremacy." He said that he had given the Nazis permission to participate in what he called a "peaceful rally" against the WVO.[73]

"Many of these men are Vietnam veterans who have fought against the Communists. The idea that the Communists would march on American soil did not sit well with them," Covington told the press.[74] Covington's crude anticommunism was reinforced by District Attorney Mike Schlosser. We knew what zeal Schlosser would bring to his job of prosecuting the killers when, prior to the state trial, he told the press that most people in Greensboro felt the communists got about what they deserved, making it clear that he agreed with the sentiment.

In the period right after the murders, before the well-orchestrated cover-up was quite ready, the Greensboro police were on the defensive. They had a jailful of unpredictable, bond-deprived, *Onward Christian Soldiers*-singing, and God-bless-America right-wingers, with whom they had partnered in crime. We had exposed their game. Prominent civil rights leaders were asking why the police were not at the site of the bloodshed to prevent it. The police indicated that they were looking for other suspects, including Virgil Griffin, head of the Invisible Empire, Knights of the Ku Klux Klan in North Carolina, and one of the leaders in the formation of a political alliance between Klan and Nazi groups. On November 4, the Greensboro police arrested two more people on conspiracy to commit murder charges. They were Nazi Raeford Milano Caudle and his sixteen-year-old stepson, also a professed Nazi.

Tuesday night, November 6, 1979, police impounded the light blue Ford that carried the murder weapons and the hit men. The car was owned by Caudle, in custody since Sunday night. Police had a murder and conspiracy warrant out for Jack Fowler, the driver of the Ford. They were still seeking Klan leader and caravan participant Virgil Griffin for questioning.

On November 7, 1979, a funeral service was held for Sandra Smith in the South Carolina mill town of Piedmont. That same day, the CWP held a press conference in Winston-Salem. We announced that we would file suit in federal court against the FBI, the SBI, the City of Greensboro, and the Police Department.[75]

Investigative reporting by the *Charlotte Observer* established the dates and places of three Klan meetings following a KKK rally in Lincolnton, North Carolina, on October 20, 1979. It was at these meetings, on the nights of October 20, October 28, and November 2, that plans were made to go to Greensboro.[76] Neither the prosecuting D.A. nor anyone else in law enforcement made much of this information. When Klansman Virgil Griffin came out from hiding on November 11 and turned himself over to the FBI, he was merely questioned and let go; they did not arrest him. The district attorney's repeated insistence that anyone aiding and abetting the murders would be prosecuted, and not only those who pulled the triggers, was exposed as sheer hypocrisy and media hype.[77]

In preparation for our funeral march, the media told people what to think and what to do about us. By turning grief into strength, we were said to be manipulating a tragedy to further our own ends. People were cautioned to stay away from us and not to contribute to a memorial fund that we had set up: "People . . . who believe in decency and a society of laws will no more contribute to this cause than they would to the Klan or Nazis."[78]

Klansmen and Nazis were portrayed as family men, God-fearing Christian patriots for whom "the destruction of communism was as high a priority as the Klan's familiar position of white supremacy."[79] White supremacy, however, was (politely) hardly discussed. In the official accounts of what happened in Greensboro, it was standard to mention the communist's inflammatory rhetoric. In contrast, the fact that several planning meetings were conducted by Klansmen and Nazis for the purpose of organizing a death squad was not generally mentioned. The stereotype of violent revolutionaries looking for martyrs left no column inches for the real violence of white supremacists.

THE FUNERAL MARCH

At my house-turned-headquarters, as I awaited the arrival of a reporter from Chicago, someone came in to say that a couple of white guys at the door, strangers, were offering to take out the Klan for us. We turned them away. We were not looking for any hired guns or even volunteer ones. We made it clear that we wanted nothing to do with terrorism or violent retaliation. Neither were we about to give up the revolutionary struggle for socialism. We meant to continue to organize and to speak out. We would defend ourselves if we were attacked. We described this stance as political offense, military defense. "The house teemed with activity," the Chicago reporter wrote. "Party members discussed plans for the funeral and a lawsuit against the police department and FBI for not protecting the marchers. Several workers had pistols stuffed inside their belts."[80]

The *Chicago Tribune* reporter was at Cypress Street for a story about the bizarre fate of one of their own. Jim Waller grew up in Hyde Park and graduated from the University of Chicago medical school. Jim's father, Sidney, still owned an art-framing shop in the city. Reporter Michael Hirsley now found himself facing Jim's widow.

> She sat at a small table in the front room of the white frame house where she and Jim had lived since their marriage Jan. 27, 1978, with two children from her previous marriage, Alex, 11 and Antonia, 13. Venetian blinds on the window were

drawn shut. Her eyes reflected sorrow, but her speech did not. "We will turn our grief into strength," she said. "We won't let them die in vain. We will accomplish the whole struggle they were involved in. . . . My husband died a hero," Signe Waller said. "His most extraordinary quality was his selflessness."[81]

Downtown Greensboro prepared for the funeral march. Chief Swing announced that he would call in five hundred National Guard troops in addition to another four hundred on-duty law enforcement officers. Anyone armed at the procession, marcher or bystander, would be arrested, City Attorney Jesse Warren warned. Busloads of people were expected from cities around the nation, from New York to San Francisco.

In editorials and public announcements, on radio, television, and in the press, Greensboro officials urged people to stay away from the funeral procession. That the events of November 3 had besmirched the city's reputation was one of the most oft-repeated themes following the massacre. "Last Saturday's violence may have occurred here, but geography is its only meaningful connection to Greensboro. It was imposed on the community by tiny fringe elements seeking a confrontation. . . . The most helpful response . . . will be to stay away."[82] And a Durham newspaper, upon learning that a prayer vigil was being planned in Duke Chapel by Duke's Divinity School students, set forth guidelines for the prayerful. "We should save our indignation and our vigils for innocent victims of real tragedies," they countenanced.[83]

The City of Greensboro set up a rumor control center. Mayor Melvin (just reelected) disappeared and was thought to be suffering from a nervous breakdown. Chief Swing pleaded with the CWP to tell him the exact route of the funeral procession, while City Manager Osborne drew up a route that he said would be the easiest to protect and announced all other routes would be cordoned off. Federal agents fanned out into the black community, knocking on doors, warning people to stay away from us. A & T State University was shut down, and the students were sent home.

By Friday, the state's Guard commander, Major General William Ingram, activated about five hundred members of the 2nd Battalion of the 120th Infantry for duty on Sunday. It was the same unit that had been sent to put down the student rebellion at A & T State University ten years earlier.[84] And it came, incidentally, from the same area, Hickory, as most of the Klan charged in the deaths of our comrades.[85] On Saturday, as National Guard troops began arriving to join 250 state highway patrolmen and 175 local police, Mayor Melvin proclaimed a state of emergency in the city.[86] Five hundred National Guard troops camped at Grimsley High School on Saturday night. On Sunday, before assuming their positions for the march, they were issued live ammunition and briefed on "force options"—when to load their weapons and when to put bayonets on their rifles.[87]

The police and the city had been in almost continuous planning sessions for several days, and CWP representatives were negotiating with city officials. An agreement was finally reached that we could have honor guards bearing unloaded weapons accompanying each of the caskets, but the city refused to lift the state of emergency so that people might feel free to join the procession. Chief Swing reiterated that anyone seen with a weapon would be arrested on the spot. "We seek no confrontation," Nelson told city officials, but, "if we are attacked, we will be prepared to defend ourselves and we will defend ourselves."[88]

A final round of poison pen editorials and articles appeared in an attempt to crank up public hatred and mistrust toward the funeral participants. The confrontation on November 3 "fell far outside the scope of racial politics," wrote the editor of the *Greensboro Daily News* and *Record*.[89] The "Klan is considered no present danger," reassured a *New York Times* headline, "despite recent membership gains, widening popular support and an increased use of violence."[90] An editorial in the *New York Times* blamed the CWP for provoking the violence by calling the Klan "racist cowards" and other like epithets.[91] By embroidering around that theme, Anthony Lewis and others could ignore the facts pointing to a preplanned attack. In a last minute blitz to isolate the massacre victims, the local paper published the disinformation that the police were "nearly certain the first shot, and possibly the second, was fired by a marcher in the 'Death to the Klan' rally."[92] One day later, when the funeral march was over, the police and FBI denied that they had any information to the effect that demonstrators had fired first.

On the day of the funeral march, the 2nd Battalion of the 120th Infantry from Hickory was equipped with rifles, bayonets, flak jackets, gas masks, and batons. The commanders and officers had live ammunition that could be quickly and easily distributed. The decision about distribution rested on the shoulders of Col. Kenneth Newbold, commander of the guardsmen, who was also at that time the superintendent of Greensboro Schools. For back-up, sheriff's deputies were stationed on the outskirts of the city. Local hospitals had emergency personnel on standby. State liquor stores were closed. The state of emergency gave law enforcement officials sweeping powers to set up roadblocks, to restrict access to the march at any point, and to stop and search any vehicle for weapons and explosives.[93] It was the tightest security in the city's history.

Police stopped and searched vehicles trying to enter the city. They set up roadblocks on all streets approaching the main march route of East Market between downtown and the cemetery. They frisked people who tried to enter through these barricades. Reporters from local, state, national, and international media were searched. Clusters of National Guardsmen were stationed at every street entrance, and state police in cars and on foot were spread throughout the area. The state's guns that accompanied the march were pointed *at the marchers.* Three battle-ready armored personnel carriers and two helicopters were in evidence. The helicopters hovered above all day.

Despite energetic efforts to scare people away, some five to eight hundred people forced their way past roadblocks and barricades in order to join the procession. People came from Detroit, New York, Atlanta, Chicago, Norfolk, Baltimore, and elsewhere. Some thirty-five people were arrested—the weapons they carried would not have produced arrests without the state of emergency, lawyers noted. Tom Clark, wounded on November 3, and Charles Finch, visible in press conferences about the massacre, were among those arrested when a convoy of cars from Durham was followed and stopped.

My memories of that day are mixed with those newspaper photos in which I am standing beside Dale, both of us holding rifles and preparing to be part of the Honor Guard. The march was supposed to start at 1:00 P.M. at the Cosmos I restaurant, but it did not get underway until 3:00. Milling around anxiously, we talked and embraced. We were blacks, whites, Asians, Latinos—people from everywhere. I felt like I was with my family at a family reunion.

The city tried to renege on their agreement about the guns of the Honor Guard. We did not let them. I handed my rifle to a guardsman who inspected it to make sure that it was not loaded. Instinctively and with feeling, I raised the rifle high as I was somehow ejected like a comet out of the Cosmos. I took my place in an Honor Guard of ten. Behind us was a banner with white lettering on black cloth—"Textile Workers Loved Bill, Jim & Sandi, Fight On! Long Live the Invincible Communist Spirit of the CWP 5!" The crowd chanted, "We won't run, we'll stand our ground, we'll turn this country upside down." Shivering, I chanted, too. It was a cold, wet day.

In the documentary film *Red November, Black November*, I am marching at the head of a procession of several hundred people, cradling a rifle, walking solemnly before a rolling bier containing a casket draped in crimson cloth. I wear a poster with a large black-and-white photograph of Jim on my shiny, green, down-quilted jacket. The size of the funeral crowd is doubled by the armed presence of the state. The camera pans to a couple of armored tanks. Guardsmen wearing helmets with protective shields walk along in file. Some police have bandoleers of ammunition across their chests.

The march was slow, raw, and disjointed. Everyone seemed to have lead in his feet, even the armed presence. The armed presence was flanking the marchers so closely that they were its adhesion: from space, looking down at planet Earth, the locomotive would have appeared like a single being, with cells of different types (some had hardware appendages), but the nuclei of facial expressions were not very different. The procession seemed eerily quiet as if all the songs and chants, militant though they are, could hardly touch the silence—the container was too vast, what filled it too puny. Yet, in another sense, it was very noisy—the drone of helicopters above was, spitefully, trying to drown out the martial hymn that set the rhythm of the march. We marched to a Negro spiritual for which we made verses about each of our five fallen martyrs. The chorus went like this:

We are soldiers in the army
We've got to fight though some fall at our side
We've got to hold up the bloodstained banner
New fighters joining us to seize the time.

The march felt endless. At each moment I was unsure whether my legs would support me for one more step. I was numb. I had to keep telling myself that I must not faint. My greatest fear was that, if I did not keep on keeping on, history might become what the lies of the bourgeoisie were trying to make it. We were not the villains. Through this awful nightmare, we had to redeem ourselves and liberate the American people. The issue was not settled: the powerful might yet succeed in smothering and subduing the truth with their lies. Their lies would cover the whole Earth, like an ice age. So I kept putting one foot in front of the other on that bone-chilling day, propelled by a sense of history, determined that the lies of powerful people would not prevail over the truth. A composite account of the funeral march taken from different media follows.

"Before and during the procession, the CWP sympathizers charged, 'The whole world is watching, avenge the CWP 5' and joined in choruses of songs by the May Day Singers. . . . Periodically as they marched they raised clenched fists."[94]

"The cortege headed down East Market Street toward Maplewood Cemetery with a cadre of policemen and newsmen in the lead. Flanking the marchers were two lines of policemen, some carrying loaded shotguns.

"Some of the marchers carried signs and placards dedicated to the five—César Vincente Cauce, Michael Nathan, William E. Sampson, Sandi Smith, and James M. Waller—and, as they marched, they eulogized their dead.

"As the procession moved past side streets, National Guard troops stood ready with bayonets fixed; police with shotguns also stood guard along the railroad tracks that run along the road on some high ground about 100 feet from the street."[95]

At the head of the march, two people carried a 7-foot high picture of Jim Waller, "Central Committee member of the Communist Workers Party, National Chairman of the Trade Union Educational League, President of Local 1113 T, ACTWU, and a communist folk hero among the North Carolina workers."[96]

The rain fell continuously and temperatures dipped down to the forties.

"Her face streaked with tears and rain, Waller's widow released her two-handed grip on a shotgun only to salute spectators with a clenched fist.

"She chanted with the other mourners and sang songs in tribute to the dead men."[97]

Media people darted about getting interviews: "Many of those in the procession were young and refused to talk to reporters about their reasons for being there.

"However, Anne Braden, fifty-five, of Louisville, spoke freely.

"'I've been in the civil rights movement for years,' she said. 'When people are murdered by the Klan, I go to protest.'"[98]

As we neared the cemetery, close to Morningside Homes, "the streets were lined with people who greeted the march as if it were an army of liberation."[99] On the rooftop of one cottage, seven men stood in a clenched-fist salute of silent tribute as the marchers went by.

"This is the single largest assassination of communists in this country's history," said Phillip Thompson, of the CWP's Central Committee, delivering the eulogy at the cemetery. "The CWP 5 were not only fighting against the Klan and Nazis," Thompson proclaimed, "they were fighting to destroy the entire capitalist system which is the root source of racism and national oppression and daily and constantly breeds Klan and Nazis." He called the five "the first communist martyrs since Saco and Vanzetti and the Rosenbergs." We thought we were on the verge of a revolutionary period. People could not continue living in the old way, and they wanted change. The oppressing class would not be able to hold back the revolutionary tide to come. We would lead people in seizing state power for the working class. To avenge the CWP 5 was a "clarion call to the whole world and especially to the U.S. people."[100]

It grew dark quickly, and the speeches at the cemetery were shortened. When we were through, it seemed dangerous for the mourners at the cemetery to ride back in the Duke Power buses allotted by the city. Thoroughly exhausted, wet, and cold, we marched back. People later recalled this as the scariest part of the day and said that they felt like walking targets. One man who had traveled from afar said that he did not expect to see his family again.

My parents and Jim's father participated in the procession from the inside of a conventional black hearse, the sort associated with normal funerals. I was relieved to know that they were there. Direct exposure to the ambiance of the street, the whir of the helicopters, phalanxes of armed soldiers, and angry fist-raising chants of the marchers was surely a different experience from being in the sound-retarding, protective interior of a coach. That night, Fay and Ted stayed with me in a motel room. I collapsed on the bed and lay on my back, down jacket and boots still on. I gave myself to my parents' loving ministrations. My mother removed my tight boots. In the warmth of their love, I drifted off to sleep.

My state of mind the day of the funeral march is recalled by what I wrote two weeks later when I went to Chicago to stay with Jim's father for a few days.

"Today, November 26, 1979, I'm sitting in Sidney's apartment looking out at Grant Park. My heart aches so, I want to die. It has been extremely painful to return here, but equally painful at home. The next task is to somehow overcome this mountain of grief."

I eulogized Jim: "He struggled for consciousness over spontaneity. The way this struggle was unfolding, toward the end of his life, he was acquiring greatness at a rapid pace. His humility was increasing, his love for the masses growing, his selflessness becoming truly exemplary. . . . He was a folk hero, a national hero. His spirit will be embodied in millions of people who will consciously try to live like him, like he lived in the last five years, when he was a communist and following the leadership of the Communist Workers Party.

"Jim was buried on November 11, 1979, under a thousand bayonets. If he could have perceived it, he would have relished every minute of that cold, rainy day of fierce and uncompromising class struggle, of a moment in history when his communist spirit was becoming a material force—on the grim, determined faces of the masses, in the hopeful, suffering hearts of the workers and fighters for justice!

"Beloved comrade husband Jim, we will avenge you! We will go forward to workers rule in the United States!"

The state of emergency was lifted Monday, November 12, but the City of Greensboro was to have no respite. On Tuesday, November 13, newly formed community groups announced a rally to be held on November 18 at Governmental Plaza and a church service on the same day that would be an "interfaith, interracial expression of commitment and concern" about the deplorable violence on November Third.[101]

NOTES

1. Charles Babington, "Police Near Scene Not Told Klan Was Approaching," *Greensboro Daily News*, 4 November 1979.

2. William E. Swing, Chief of Police, "An Administrative Report of the Anti-Klan Rally, Greensboro, North Carolina, November 3, 1979," Greensboro Police Department, 19 November 1979.

3. Swing, "An Administrative Report," 26.

4. Swing, "An Administrative Report," 27.

5. Swing, "An Administrative Report," 9.

6. Swing, "An Administrative Report," 10.

7. Swing, "An Administrative Report," 11.

8. Swing, "An Administrative Report," 66.

9. Swing, "An Administrative Report," 67.

10. Swing, "An Administrative Report," 3–4.

11. Swing, "An Administrative Report," 11.

12. Swing, "An Administrative Report," 12.

13. Swing, "An Administrative Report," 12.

14. Swing, "An Administrative Report," 14.

15. Swing, "An Administrative Report," 67.

16. Swing, "An Administrative Report," 68.

17. Swing, "An Administrative Report," 68.

18. Swing, "An Administrative Report," 69.

19. Swing, "An Administrative Report," 70.

20. Swing, "An Administrative Report," 70.

21. Swing, "An Administrative Report," 71.

22. Swing, "An Administrative Report," 72.

23. Swing, "An Administrative Report," 72.

24. Swing, "An Administrative Report," 72. The ellipsis after "sounds like" is in the original police report.

25. Swing, "An Administrative Report," 73. The ellipsis and faulty punctuation are in the original police report; italics are my emphasis.

26. Swing, "An Administrative Report," 20.

27. Swing, "An Administrative Report," 73.

28. Swing, "An Administrative Report," 76.

29. Jim Wicker, "Prosecutors Begin Attack on Smith Defense Strategy," *Greensboro Record*, 6 August 1980, A2.

30. Bermanzohn, *The True Story of the Greensboro Massacre*, 45.

31. Swing, "An Administrative Report," 77.

32. Swing, "An Administrative Report," 22.

33. Ken Allen, "Killers Seemed to Know Rally Details, Police Say," *Charlotte Observer*, 6 November 1979, 1A.

34. Associated Press, "Police Gave Site of Rally to Man 'Who Was in Klan,'" *Durham Morning Herald*, 8 November 1979, 1A.

35. See Bob Hiles, "Informant Believes Shooting Avoidable," *Greensboro Daily News*, 3 October 1981.

36. Babington, "Police Near Scene," A7.

37. Associated Press, "Klan 'Thought They Could Get Away with It,'" *High Point Enterprise*, 5 November 1979, 9A.

38. Howard Troxler, "Police Arouse Anger in Wake of Shootout," (Raleigh) *News & Observer*, 5 November 1979, 7.

39. Troxler, "Police Arouse Anger," 7.

40. William M. Welch, "Causes of Violence Not Easy to Pinpoint," *Durham Sun*, 6 November 1979.

41. Swing, "An Administrative Report," 40.

42. Swing, "An Administrative Report," 39.

43. Swing, "An Administrative Report," 39.

44. The information about WFMY-TV was told to me by Father Jim Waters, who was working for WFMY at the time as a cameraman and who photographed the Klan/Nazi attack.

45. The FBI relied on friendly contacts in the media. Two of these contacts, named in FBI documents released in the mid seventies, happened to be editors at the Greensboro paper during and after the massacre. See Gayle Korotkin, "The Campaign for Justice in Greensboro" (unpublished summary report, 1985), 25.

46. See "Klan Ambush Kills 4 WVO People," *Greensboro Record*, 3 November 1979. See also "Four Shot to Death at Anti-Klan March: Ambush at a North Carolina Rally Starts Gunfight with Leftists," *New York Times*, 4 November 1979, 1.

47. See Jack Scism, "Four Die in Klan-Leftist Shootout in SE Greensboro," *Greensboro Daily News*, 4 November 1979, A1.

48. See, for example, the account of newsman Charles Travis of WGHP-TV in "Shooting at Anti-Klan Rally Leaves 5 Dead, 9 Hurt," *Richmond Times-Dispatch*, 4 November 1979.

49. Scism, "Four Die in Klan-Leftist Shootout in SE Greensboro"; and William D. Snider, editor, *Daily News & Record*, "Healing a Community's Wounds," *Greensboro Daily News*, 7 November 1979.

50. Editorial, "This Newspaper's Opinion: The Folly of Extremism," (Raleigh) *News & Observer*, 6 November 1979.

51. See Wayne Slater, "Shootout Was Finale to Life of Promise Gone Sour," (Raleigh) *News & Observer*, 20 November 1979, 25; and "Sampson: Did Early Promise Go Wrong?" *Greensboro Daily News*, 20 November 1979. The two titles head an identical piece written by Slater that went out over the AP wire.

52. Alvarez and Jung, *Red November, Black November*.

53. Alvarez and Jung, *Red November, Black November*.

54. Alvarez and Jung, *Red November, Black November*.

55. Alvarez and Jung, *Red November, Black November*.

56. Alvarez and Jung, *Red November, Black November*.

57. See "Shootout Was Finale." See also Snider, "Healing a Community's Wounds," in which he says, completely misleadingly, that the CWP "had been trying, unsuccessfully, to infiltrate workers' groups at local textile mills for months." This version of events was repeated countless times.

58. Henry Wefing, "Friends Call Nathan Death 'Waste,'" *Durham Morning Herald*, 7 November 1979.

59. "Zeal for Union Was Trademark for Activists," (Raleigh) *News & Observer*, 5 November 1979.

60. Part of the press conference on November 4, 1979, is shown in the documentary by Alvarez and Jung, *Red November, Black November*.

61. Reproduced in Alvarez and Jung, *Red November, Black November*.

62. Charles Rowe, "Durham Police to Probe Shooting in Greensboro," *Durham Sun*, 6 November 1979, 1A.

63. See Associated Press writer Monte Plott, "Court Hearings Opened in Greensboro Slayings," *High Point Enterprise*, 5 November 1979, 5A.

64. Korotkin, "The Campaign for Justice," 20.

65. Bob Raissman, "Organizer Says Victims Were Marked," *Winston-Salem Journal*, 6 November 1979, 2.

66. Raissman, "Organizer Says Victims Were Marked," 2.

67. Bob Kolin and Steve Levin, "Nazi, Klan Members Suspected," (Raleigh) *News & Observer*, 5 November 1979, 7.

68. Alvarez and Jung, *Red November, Black November*.

69. Alvarez and Jung, *Red November, Black November*.

70. "400 Mourn Slain Men in Silence," (Raleigh) *News and Observer*, 8 November 1979, 60.

71. Henry Wefing, "Police Surveillance Heavy during Durham Vigil," *Durham Morning Herald*, 8 November 1979.

72. "Group 'To Be Armed,'" *Durham Morning Herald*, 5 November 1979.

73. Kolin and Levin, "Nazi, Klan Members Suspected," 7.

74. Kolin and Levin, "Nazi, Klan Members Suspected," 7.

75. See Michael P. Massoglia, "Leftist Group to Sue for $500 Million," *Winston-Salem Journal*, 8 November 1979, 16.

76. "Seeds of Confrontation," *Charlotte Observer*, 9 November 1979.

77. Associated Press, "D.A. Plans to Use Abetting Theory," *Durham Morning Herald*, 7 November 1979.

78. "Manipulating a Tragedy," *Durham Morning Herald*, 7 November 1979.

79. See Brent Hackney, "Klan Activity Up throughout South," *Greensboro Daily News*, 4 November 1979.

80. Michael Hirsley, "A National Disgrace Puts City in Spotlight," *Chicago Tribune*, 11 November 1979, 1, Sec. 3.

81. Hirsley, "A National Disgrace," 1, Sec. 3.

82. "Let It Pass," *Greensboro Daily News*, 9 November 1979, 4A.

83. "Unworthy Causes," *Durham Sun*, 9 November 1979.

84. "Rhetoric Fuels Marchers through Soggy Day," *Greensboro Daily News*, 12 November 1979, A4.

85. Associated Press, "National Guard Prepare for Duty in Greensboro," *Thomasville Times*, 10 November 1979, 1.

86. Michael P. Massoglia, "Troops Enter Greensboro," *Winston-Salem Journal*, 11 November 1979, A1.

87. UPI, "Guardsmen Are Ready to Assist in Greensboro," (Roanoke Rapids, N.C.) *Sunday Herald*, 11 November 1979, 10.

88. Jack Scism, "City Sets State of Emergency for Funeral March," *Greensboro Daily News*, 11 November 1979, A1.

89. William D. Snider, "Is Greensboro's Image Distorted?" *Greensboro Daily News*, 11 November 1979, G3.

90. Robert McG. Thomas Jr., "Klan Is Considered No Present Danger," *New York Times*, 11 November 1979.

91. Anthony Lewis, "Free Speech and Provocation Can Be Hard to Separate," *New York Times*, 11 November 1979, 6E.

92. Lindsey Gruson, "Police Suspect WVO Fired First Shot," *Greensboro Daily News*, 11 November 1979, A1.

93. Scism, "City Sets State of Emergency for Funeral March," A1, A4.

94. Jack Scism, "Funeral March Is Peaceful," *Greensboro Daily News*, 12 November 1979, A5.

95. Michael P. Massoglia, "CWP Procession Ends Peacefully," *Winston-Salem Journal*, 12 November 1979, 2.

96. "'Hold Up the Bloodstained Banner, New Fighters Joining Us to Seize the Time . . . ,'" *Workers Viewpoint*, 19 November 1979.

97. Bill McKelway, "Greensboro Funeral March Uneventful," *Richmond Times Dispatch*, 12 November 1979, 1.

98. Bob Drogin, Marion A. Ellis, and Ken Allen, "Greensboro March Nonviolent," *Charlotte Observer*, 12 November 1979, 5A.

99. "'Hold Up the Bloodstained Banner.'"

100. "'Hold Up the Bloodstained Banner.'"

101. Kenneth Campbell, "Rally Set to Deplore Shootings," *Greensboro Daily News*, 13 November 1979, B1.

Jim and Signe Waller, fall 1979.

Jim and Signe with Alex and Antonia, summer 1979.

Michael and Marty Nathan, wedding day, 1978 (courtesy of Marty Nathan.)

César and Floris Cauce, wedding day, 1979 (courtesy of Floris Cauce Weston.)

Sandi Smith with Mike and Marty Nathan's newborn, Leah.

Bill and Dale Sampson, 1978. (courtesy of Dale Sampson Levin.)

Strike support for Traders Chevrolet mechanics. Bill Sampson with guitar; next to him, Dori Blitz, 1978.

Jim Waller outside Cone's Revolution Plant, rally for fired workers, fall 1977. In foreground, L to R, Sandi Smith, Kwame Cannon. (courtesy of Joe Rodriguez, Greensboro News & Record.)

Klan and Nazis attack anti-Klan rally, November 3, 1979, Morningside Homes, Greensboro, NC. (courtesy of Don Davis, Greensboro News & Record.)

Police arrest bleeding demonstrator Nelson Johnson at anti-Klan rally.

Funeral March on November 11, 1979, Greensboro, NC; Signe Waller on right with rifle.

Greensboro 6 give press conference after being charged with felony riot, May 1980; from L to R, Allen Blitz, Dori Blitz, Rand Manzella, Nelson Johnson, Willena Cannon (earlier charged; then charges dropped), and Lacie Russell. Percy Sims, part of the Greensboro 6 and a Morningside resident, is absent from the photo.

Nelson Johnson is released from jail after a 20-day hunger strike, summer 1981; pictured with his wife, Joyce. (Copyrighted by Wayne Michael Lottinville.)

Some plaintiffs in the civil rights suit at press conference in Winston-Salem, 1985; from R to L, Dr. Paul Bermanzohn, Signe Waller, Dale Simpson, and Floris Cauce. (Copyrighted by Wayne Michael Lottinville.)

Premier of documentary Red November, Black November in Greensboro, March 1, 1981; from L to R, Joyce Johnson, Dale Simpson, Sally Bermanzohn, Paul Bermanzohn, Marty Nathan holding Leah, Nelson Johnson, Signe Waller, and film director Sally Alvarez (Courtesy of John Rottet, News & Observer, Raleigh, NC.)

12

RESISTING UPSIDE DOWN JUSTICE: THE CIVIL RIGHTS MOVEMENT REAWAKENED

THE ATMOSPHERE IN GREENSBORO

In the aftermath of the killings, groups of people sought to come together for discussion and action. It was very difficult for such groups to operate freely. On every occasion, they were subjected to interference meant to frighten and intimidate them. The religious service and rally announced for November 18, 1979, for example, did not happen on that day. When it did happen, its character was totally changed.

The involvement of black ministers was crucial to the planned November 18 service and rally, wrote Gayle Korotkin in her summary of the campaign for justice in Greensboro.

> "But as soon as the ministers began planning, they began receiving clandestine phone calls and unsolicited advice from city officials saying their efforts might result in violence. Two churches of ministers involved in the effort were broken into. At least one received a call from the downtown (white) bank which held the church's mortgage, suggesting the church would suffer if he participated. Rev. George Gay began receiving threats against his life. Anonymous phone calls from alleged 'leftists' threatening violence scared off another minister. The ministers finally canceled the service altogether. A service in December with the participation of city officials was not a memorial for the victims but a 'let's get this behind us' rally. It was four years, November 1983, before Greensboro ministers, black and white, were able to hold a memorial for the victims."[1]

Ervin Brisbon, a Morningside Homes resident and community leader, testified to the Greensboro Human Relations Committee that the shootings left the black community shaken. "The psychological effect of small black children witnessing dead bodies blown away by automatic weapons fire and the psychological effect of living in fear knowing that such groups as the KKK can legally exist in the community must be addressed," he said.[2]

In December, much of Greensboro's black community came together for the postponed interfaith and interracial service to honor the dead and deplore the violence of November Third. Mayor Jim Melvin spoke at the gathering at the Bethel AME Church. Trying hard to lay to rest the November Third issue, a villainous mayor told those congregated, "I don't know if we'll ever know the answer to why such an incident occurred in Greensboro."[3]

Ann and Ed Whitfield, both deeply rooted in community struggles, reacted to the presence of the mayor and other city notables "who had the audacity to come into our community and condone the actions of the Greensboro police in their total failure to protect black lives and property."[4] They warned that the gains of the civil rights and black liberation movements to bring about changes in society for blacks could be snatched away in the 1980s. A group of black Greensboro citizens demanded that the city council suspend the police chief pending an investigation by a people's commission into police actions surrounding the November attack. Mayor Melvin's response was to get the council to adopt a resolution *commending* the police on their actions that day. It was a slap in the face of the entire black community.

LETTER FROM "A DANGEROUS MAN" TO A NUMBER OF UPSTANDING CITIZENS IN GREENSBORO

A letter written by Nelson Johnson, dated December 23, 1979, and sent to friends and community leaders is revealing about what we were up against in our struggle for justice. Before I quote from the letter, I will flash back to June 1979, when Mayor Melvin called Nelson "a dangerous man with a proven police record."[5]

That June, workers and community folks heard the Workers Viewpoint Organization deny that OPEC or the Iranian people were the cause of a gas shortage: they heard the oil monopolies' greed and drive for profit faulted instead. On a different evening that month, people came to a WVO forum at the All Nations Pentacostal Holiness Church—the one originally scheduled to host the November 3 forum—to hear Nelson's reflections on "which way forward for the black liberation movement." The occasion was the tenth anniversary of the student revolt at A & T State University. Nelson spoke about the Bakke and Weber cases of so-called reverse discrimination and exposed the capitalist tactic of dividing black and white workers while attacking the living standards of all workers. At that assembly, he also took note of the rise of the KKK in nearby Winston-Salem, in Decatur, and elsewhere and declared that behind the revival of the Klan was the rotten system of monopoly capitalism and its need to sow divisions among workers. When Nelson, a charismatic black liberationist, talked about uniting the entire multinational working class to fight capitalism, people listened and learned.

These forums and meetings happened before November Third, even before the confrontation at China Grove. Earlier that spring, police ransacked the home of a trade union steward, as told in chapter 9. Nelson and several of us went to a city council meeting in June to support the union steward's demand that the incident be investigated. At this council meeting, the mayor called Nelson "a dangerous man with a proven police record" and treated him rudely. In connection with his 1960s civil rights activities, Nelson was sentenced on a misdemeanor charge, and he served some weeks in prison when his sentence was commuted by then-governor Bob Scott. This did not make him dangerous, although it did prove he had a police record. To be truthful, the mayor should have said that Nelson Johnson was a dangerous man *to Greensboro's ruling elite* and that Nelson was a *proven leader*, respected by broad segments of both black and white communities. For example, Sol Jacobs, an elderly white owner of a standing-room-only Jewish delicatessen and a former mayoral candidate, knew Nelson since Nelson's student days at A & T. Liberal and outspoken on civil rights issues, Sol once remarked that Nelson had "one of the greatest potentials for leadership I've ever seen."[6] Black businessman B. J. Battle, a bank manager, stated that "Nelson Johnson has contributed much to the welfare of this community" and "was one of the few people who could rally black people across the spectrum."[7]

Now, in the wake of the Greensboro Massacre, Nelson needed to counter the propaganda that threatened to drive a wedge between him and his former friends and allies. "Dear friends," he wrote in December 1979:

> The reality of November 3 is still reverberating throughout the Greensboro community, the state and the country. The brutal daylight assassination of five members of our Party while preparing for a march against the Klan is unprecedented in the history of this country. In the wake of the avalanche of anti-communist hysteria since November 3, many honest people have lost sight of the basic facts surrounding the November 3 murders. That is why the Communist Workers Party (CWP) is communicating with you directly. . . . We will start with several basic points which we should not forget.

A. While we were preparing for a legally called march (exercising our constitutional rights), we were attacked without warning by the Klan and Nazis. Five people were selectively murdered. *It was not a shootout!*

B. The attack on us by the Klan and Nazis was a surprise that we were neither expecting nor prepared to deal with. Most of us had our families present, including children. *It was not a shootout!*

C. The Greensboro police department did not fire a single shot to defend us as we were murdered. This occurred despite the fact that the police department knew in advance that the Klan and Nazis were armed and planned to be at our march. *It was not a shootout!* . . .

You probably did not know Jim, Bill, Sandi, Cesar or Mike. These five people were murdered. They were not plastic faceless reflections of ideology. They were fine, dedicated, hardworking, selfless people. All of them had their families and loved ones just as you do. Far from the impression given by the press that these comrades were a "little off," all of them had a comprehensive understanding of the social forces that underlie the current crisis in this country. They understood deeply the forces giving rise to the Klan and Nazis and the interests which these racist groups served. Most importantly, all of them had the courage to act on their convictions. That's why we were all in Morningside on November 3rd.

I know that what I have just described is not the picture that you have been getting from the media. The basic facts of what happened are being lost in a growing hysterical atmosphere. In fact, things are being turned upside down. Our Party is actually being seen by some people as the cause of the assassinations. Coverage by the press, particularly the Greensboro press, has been scandalous. . . . It eventually reached a point where the *Greensboro Record* permitted a story essentially saying that we planned the murder of our beloved Party members in order to have martyrs because our work was not going well! You really have to step back and think hard in order to appreciate how deep that charge is. Frankly, the massive attack on the CWP, the work it has been doing and our members, both dead and alive, are unequaled in recent times. . . .

We stated in our first official press statement after the November 3 assassinations that the attack on the CWP was an attack against all the workers and oppressed people, be they black, brown, white or yellow or red. The Palmer raids, the McCarthy era, and the attack against the Black Panther Party are pale in comparison to this new wave of attacks in the coming period. We must be prepared . . . to beat back these systematic attacks.

Six weeks after the assassinations, the McCarthy era atmosphere is very apparent. Not only have CWP members and supporters been fired from their jobs but now the families and friends of Party members are also threatened with being fired and are harassed by the SBI and FBI. Some people are actually afraid to talk with us because of fear of *guilt by association*. The *witch hunt* is on! Anyone familiar with history knows that it will not stop with the CWP. Next it could be trade union leaders, progressive professors, Black leaders generally, outspoken clergymen. That is the inevitable path this repressive pattern will take if it is not checked. . . . Some well-intentioned people, especially members of the clergy, have come out to oppose violence in general. . . . The stand of just being against violence in general, while it might be popular, avoids the hard question of what is happening in the country daily. It avoids dealing with the fundamental source of violence, which is this oppressive system. . . . The stand of just being against violence opens the door to equate those of us who have been struggling for equality, justice and an end to exploitation to the notorious violence of the Klan and Nazis. That's what it means when what happened on November 3 is described as the *extreme right* vs. the *extreme left*. . . .

The view that some people are just bent on violence . . . does not explain why the Klan and Nazis have been so actively promoted over the last 18 months. It draws no relationship between the rise of the Klan and the economic crisis, which the entire country is in. . . . In the last analysis, the stand of simply being against violence in general without addressing the question of justice and the source of violence aids further repression and violence. We can see that happening as Governor Hunt calls for the infiltration of "extremist groups" which actually translates into whoever speaks the truth about the nature and essence of this system.

The current situation requires of us that we unite to struggle against the vicious injustices in relationship to November 3. Police collaboration with Klan-Nazi terror must be our point of unity. The CWP wants to work cooperatively with anyone in building support against the Klan/Nazis' murder and terror. . . . We think that it is both possible and necessary for us to unite in our opposition to the obviously premeditated murders of November 3rd, even if there are a number of other questions on which we disagree.

FIRINGS AND ATTEMPTED FIRINGS

On the Monday following the funeral march, I returned to my job at a Collins and Aikman yarn mill. On seeing me, my coworkers were friendly and offered condolences. "We're glad you're back," one woman told me. Exactly at the start of the 7:00 A.M. shift, a company representative came to the shop floor to inform me I was relieved of my job as a spinner. Prior to November 3, I finished an eight-week training period with praise for doing a good job. I demanded to know why I was being fired. "We think you are incompatible with the workforce here," I was told. I responded angrily that their problem was that I was too compatible with the workforce.

Before leaving the plant, I went to the women's restroom where the scene resembled a minirally. One woman was irate at how upside down things were—"They have Klans working here and they don't fire them, but they fire you!" Then we talked about the conditions at the plant—for example, the deplorable state of the women's bathroom in the spinning department. After that, I left and drove back to Greensboro from Graham.

Driving back, I was absorbed in the sad reverie of a conversation I'd had with Jim not long before he was killed. I was telling him how hard it was to keep up with the broken-down machinery, with strands of yarn breaking off or getting tangled every other second. Jim listened to my dizzying account of the calisthenics I had to perform—bending, angling, reaching, snatching, stretching to tie knots, stopping and starting one machine after another. He laughed when I acted out the scene and kept commenting, "terrific, terrific."

"What?" I asked, laughing in spite of myself. "I'm killing myself there. What's so funny?"

"The verbs," he said, still laughing. "You're cracking me up. I never had so many verbs slung at me . . . "

"*Slung?*" I cut in.

"Well," he teased, "you can't be doing such a fine job if you have to stretch five yards to the ceiling. And anyway that part of the machine is not called the 'what-cha-ma-call-it-bobbin.'" We both laughed.

"You don't like my verbs?" I asked. "Now, let's get this straight, what is it you don't like, my verbs or my nouns?"

"Oh, the verbs, no question," he shot back.

"Well, in that case I will *fling* myself at you." Still laughing, we embraced.

The day after I was fired, I returned to the mill to leaflet. My brother, Jay Burke, had come south for a few days to be with me. Although a loving and sympathetic brother, Jay did not share his sister's causes or radical lifestyle. He was a good sport though, and he helped me pass out a flyer that I had produced about my dismissal, the November 3 attack, and a few other things.

The leaflet was a parting shot: I decided not to try to regain my job. Instead I would work full time to get justice for the Greensboro Massacre by being responsible for the party's media work in North Carolina. Upon hiring me, Collins and Aikman announced bluntly, in a briefing for new employees, that they would not tolerate union organizing. I mentioned that illegal intimidation in the flyer. I also said that we must overthrow capitalism and racism and establish socialism. In a parenthetical remark, I talked about the women's bathroom. I wrote: " (The workers keep it as clean as they can, but it's a pigsty with no place to sit down if you are falling off your feet except a torn-up floor.) Under socialism the economy is run to satisfy people's needs, not for the profit of a few vultures. . . . Workers and the majority of people will have political power and can change what they don't like."

Apparently, this diatribe about bathrooms under capitalism and socialism had some effect: a coworker I bumped into later told me that the day after I leafleted, the company had a work crew in the women's bathroom. They fixed the broken toilets and sinks, repaired the floor, and made it altogether more pleasant. A minor coup. I was reminded of that incident years later. My daughter Antonia hung on her bathroom wall in Durham an old advertisement from the 1930s, a classic, in which business establishments are urged to stock Scott's toilet tissue—"Is Your Bathroom Breeding Bolsheviks?" asks the ad. A sneering, contemptuous employee, presumably deprived of Scott paper products and as a result ready to switch to socialism in an eye-blink, is the sell.

Dale was fired by Burlington Mills after the anti-Klan rally. Her priorities, like mine, were in the struggle for justice, and she did not contest the firing. But many of our friends successfully resisted the attempt to dismiss them or else won back their jobs after putting up a fight.

Dr. Jean Sharpe Chapman, under pressure to resign her staff position with Orange-Chatham Comprehensive Health Services at a federally funded health clinic in Moncure, North Carolina, staunchly refused and kept the job. Over two hundred people in the community signed a petition saying, "she is a fine doctor, respected by both patients and co-workers, and as long as she continues to care wholeheartedly for the patients at OCCHS we don't think anyone has a right to threaten her job."[8] With her husband, Yonni, and an African American friend in the civil rights movement by her side, Jean held a press conference in which she revealed that Jesse Helms had put pressure on the clinic to fire her.

Tom Clark was fired from a job he had held for five years as a patient care assistant in the emergency room at Durham County General Hospital. He successfully fought both a weapons charge (for having a gun the day of the funeral march in violation of the state of emergency) and the job dismissal. When the *Durham Sun* editorialized that his reinstatement at the hospital showed how well the system worked, Tom countered, "the reason I got the job back is because we fought the system, not because the system worked."[9] He refuted the newspaper's claim that his dismissal had nothing to do with his political beliefs. "As my work record is excellent," he wrote, "the only possible motive for my dismissal is not only my political beliefs, but the action I have taken to organize workers based on these beliefs, and my outspoken support for the CWP."[10]

Immediately after November 3, Cone Mills suspended White Oak shop steward Rand Manzella. Later in the month, they fired him. The picture of Rand, dazed and wounded, kneeling over the lifeless body of César with Bill's gun still in his hand, was much reproduced in the local media. While the police allowed the assailants to leave the scene of the crime without pursuing them, they charged Rand with "going about armed to the terror of the people"—a provision made originally to curtail Klan activity!—and carted him off to jail. Cone said that they fired Rand because "he is a dangerous employee who is engaged in dangerous activities."[11] A few months later, Earle Tockman filed an unfair labor practice charge with the National Labor Relations Board on Rand's behalf. He claimed that the firing was illegal and that the "dangerous activities" were Rand's legally protected union organizing efforts.[12]

Two other workers, both black, were dismissed by Cone for fabricated reasons. They were Al Richardson, Bill Sampson's running mate in the White Oak union election that was shut down by ACTWU, and Shirley Clark, who had been on the Organizing Committee with Sandi Smith at Revolution Plant and who distributed an anti-Klan leaflet at the plant gate after the murders.[13] Another CWP supporter, Dori Blitz, a Teamster and a shop steward at the Budd Company in Martinsville, Virginia, was already in a heated struggle with the tractor-trailer company when she went to Greensboro with some of her coworkers for the anti-Klan rally. After November 3, that skirmish became a full-fledged battle, and Dori was fired.[14]

The wave of firings and harassment of organizers was not confined to North Carolina or the South. Many CWP activists leading worker struggles in Pittsburgh, Boston, New York, Philadelphia, Washington, D.C., Detroit, Chicago, Los Angeles, San Diego, the Bay Area, Houston, Wichita, West Virginia, and Hawaii were under attack.[15]

CONSPIRACY CHARGES ARE DROPPED

One day in winter, several weeks after the killings, a writer for *The Village Voice* swaggered into the Cypress Street house and straight away offered me a drink from a flask of whiskey that she carried in her knapsack. This was my introduction to Blanche McCrary Boyd. She came armed for her writing assignment. Before leaving New York, she'd had weapons practice: it was clear to her that guns were a very important part of life in North Carolina. She did a good piece of investigative journalism, grappling with and anguishing over the story.

On the day of the funeral march, when Klansman Virgil Griffin came out of hiding and turned himself in to the FBI, he also appeared on WSOC-TV in Charlotte. He admitted to the TV station that he was involved in planning the caravan to Greensboro.[16] Blanche McCrary Boyd talked to Griffin. She wrote:

The Klan's humiliation at China Grove was bitter. If Gorrell Pierce began to flirt with the Nazis, Griffin took more decisive action. He allied his group, the Invisible Knights of the KKK, with the Nazis and the National States Rights Party. The new alliance was called the United Racist Front. . . .

At a Klan meeting that preceded the November killings by only a few weeks, the *Charlotte Observer* reported that Griffin said, "If you cared about your children you'd go out and kill 100 niggers and leave them dead in the streets." After November 3, Griffin told the *Observer*, "The Communist Party has always been our main goal. . . . If there was no Communist Party, there would be no problem with niggers."

The FBI questioned Griffin for a few hours about the shootings, then released him. He has since been arrested for cross-burning.[17]

Where was Schlosser going with the prosecution when he failed to indict Griffin, a ringleader in the murderous expedition to Greensboro, and Dawson, who (it had meanwhile come to light) made fiery speeches at Klan rallies urging the Klan to go to Greensboro and then led the caravan with out-of-town Klansmen and Nazis to Morningside Homes? Nor were these the only conspicuously missing indictments: Brent Fletcher, whose home was a rendezvous point for men and weaponry en route to the rally, was photographed as such by the police and was not indicted. More than twenty-five participants in the caravan were not indicted, even though the police and the FBI claimed all were identified. Nazi leader Harold Covington, who indicated that he had given Wood and other Nazis permission to go to Greensboro, was not indicted or even questioned. Nor was any action ever taken to bring criminal charges against anyone for the ten people injured on November 3. Yet the district attorney would later boast that his was a prosecution that left no stone unturned.

When Nazi Jack Wilson Fowler Jr. of Winston-Salem, driver of the car with the murder weapons, surrendered to the FBI in mid-November, the police said that he was the last person sought. There was a fugitive warrant against him, but the federal charge of illegal flight to avoid prosecution was dropped. As the Klan and Nazis were released from jail on bond (none higher than $52,000), Schlosser continued to pursue the prosecution of three demonstrators, Nelson, Willena, and Rand, for their alleged offenses arising from November Third.

Most revealing of the prosecutor's biased intention was *the dropping of all conspiracy to commit murder charges* against the fifteen Klansmen and Nazis in custody. This decision was fraught with legal implications, all entirely favorable to the Klan/Nazi defense. The dropping of conspiracy charges, despite knowledge of at least three planning meetings by Klansmen and Nazis before November Third, narrowed the scope of the investigation and trial to only the Klan and

Nazis visible in the videotapes attacking demonstrators. Evidence relating to complicity between law enforcement and the Klan/Nazis, or the cover-up of that complicity, would be ruled out. The prosecution was supporting the defense contention that violence erupted spontaneously and that the Klan/Nazis merely reacted to provocation by the demonstrators and fired in self-defense. This scenario, consequently, set up a series of felony charges against six demonstrators. *The dropping of all the conspiracy charges against the Klan/Nazis in mid-December and the felony riot charges against demonstrators led to our decision to boycott the state trial as sham justice.*

"When I asked Schlosser about dropping the conspiracy charges," Blanche McCrary Boyd wrote, "he said, 'Conspiracy is hard to prove. Where is the evidence of conspiracy?' I told Schlosser how uncomfortable I'd been, watching the Channel 11 videos. I remarked about how calm several of the Klansmen and Nazis seemed, unworried about returned fire or fire from behind them, that is, from the police. Schlosser must have misunderstood what I meant to imply, because he said, 'Oh, yes, it was like a turkey shoot.'"[18]

The dropping of all conspiracy charges included those against Raeford Caudle, the Nazi caravan participant who owned several of the murder weapons and the car that carried them. Fourteen indictments were handed down on December 12, 1979, by a special grand jury session requested by Guilford County District Attorney Michael Schlosser. Eleven of those were charged with five counts of murder and engaging in a riot. The other three were charged only with engaging in a riot. On December 14, the *Greensboro Record* noted that "The grand jury did not return any indictments for conspiracy against the defendants even though all had previously been charged with that."[19] Schlosser told the press that more indictments against other persons would be presented to subsequent grand juries.[20] We wondered if he meant the other killers or us.

In February, Judge James Long denied without a hearing our motion that the court appoint a private prosecutor to assist the prosecution. William Kunstler had agreed to serve in this role. In the motion, we cited Schlosser's public remarks—his apparent agreement with the opinion that the communists got what they deserved and a reference to his military service in Vietnam in which he said, "and you know who my adversaries were then."[21] Such unnecessary public statements injected communism as an issue in the investigation and led us to think that the D.A.'s actual agenda was to railroad communists, not punish criminals.

The demand for a private prosecutor was not a major rallying point among the public, but Duke University Professor Sydney Nathans appreciated its importance. He wrote: "Unfortunately we know from the recent past that dissenters are not only harassed by vigilante groups that go beyond the law. They have been harassed as well by those who hold power legitimately—the FBI, the police, employers—and shunned by one-time friends who fear 'guilt by association.' We simply cannot let this happen as it did in the era of Joseph McCarthy and as it did again under the reign of J. Edgar Hoover."[22]

Schlosser called the cases stemming from the shootings "the most complicated in the history of Guilford County."[23] We said the complexities were exacerbated by the simultaneous prosecutions, pending or threatened, of CWP members and supporters. By prosecuting the victims, the D.A. was restricting his access to all possible witnesses. Demonstrators would have to wonder how, and against whom, their testimony would be used. We thought the D.A. was setting the stage to blame the CWP for his purported problems producing evidence against Klansmen and Nazis charged with crimes.[24] We figured that he would scapegoat us if his prosecution of the Klan and Nazis was unsuccessful, and we said so in the petition for a special prosecutor. And he did.

A U.S. government–assisted fascist attack on activist American citizens was being framed in the local media as a shootout between right-wing and left-wing extremists. The hostage crisis on November 4, 1979, supplied a pretext for national media to ignore North Carolina altogether. Distant terrorism by people of a foreign country was a more comfortable subject for the ruling class than its own terrorism at home. Besides frequent press conferences, street demonstrations, and public forums—that inevitably met with obstacles as the further narrative will show—some CWP supporters threw eggs and tomatoes at politicians in cities around the country. These were not mere pranks. We urgently needed to get people's attention to keep the struggle for justice in Greensboro alive and to keep the November Third murders from becoming legally sanctioned government assassinations.

THE WIDOWS' TOUR

The CWP arranged a "National Tour to Avenge the Communist Workers Party 5." The program usually featured one or more of the four widows along with a leading CWP member and some local organizers. In North Carolina, we called the National Tour the "Widows' Tour." Dale and Floris launched the series at the All Soul's Church in Washington, D.C., on November 20. They were joined by Central Committee member Phil Thompson, who took aim at "the provocation line" that blames communists for police terror. "This is a fascist lie and covers up the fact that the state is the greatest perpetrator of violence against the masses," Phil said.[25]

I went to New York, Chicago, Houston, and Charleston, West Virginia. Floris and I spoke in New York on December 1, 1979. Something odd happened even before I got to New York. I was traveling alone on an Amtrak train at night. A man in his thirties or forties sat down opposite me and tried hard to engage me in conversation. I tried equally hard to ignore him. He quickly let me know that he worked in Langley. Did I know what was in Langley? I did not let on that I knew. The CIA was in Langley and he worked for the CIA, he said. I thought, *Why is he telling me that? This could just be some dude who thinks working for the CIA is a great line to use on a woman traveling alone. If this guy* really *works for the CIA, why is he letting me know.* The mystery was never solved, and I dismissed it from my mind, only puzzled. Another unsolved mystery, but more harrowing, occurred on my return from another city on the tour. Nelson met me at the airport. On the way back to Greensboro, the driver of a large furniture company truck tried to run us off the road. Nelson's quick thinking and superior driving skills saved us. We were both shaken afterward by what was clearly a deliberate attempt to force us to crash.

Throughout this book, I am combining the memory of events with their public documentation. This form might be called a *documemoir*. I do not have an extraordinarily good memory. It needs all the help it can get from documentation. Many of the public events and rallies I attended after November Third are a blur—even if I recollect *who* spoke, remembering *what they said* is another matter. The forum in New York was in an auditorium at Long Island University. Attorney Stuart Kwoh from California, who spent some time in Greensboro helping us file the petition for a private prosecutor, introduced the main speaker that night, attorney William Kunstler. Kunstler's clients included Fred Hampton and members of the Black Panther Party, the Chicago Seven, the brothers from the Attica Prison takeover, and the Native Americans at Wounded Knee. "You can murder a revolutionary," the powerful attorney asserted, "but you can't murder the revolution."[26]

Also noteworthy on the program was Dr. Michio Kaku, an eminent physicist and a leader in the antinuclear movement. "The chauvinist hysteria over Iranians and the murderous terror against the Communist Workers Party 5 remind me of the same scapegoat tactics they used against Japanese Americans during World War II. At that time they came for my family and took them to Tule Lake concentration camp," he told the audience. Dr. Kaku appealed to the antinuclear movement to support the CWP 5 campaign. The CWP 5 were murdered and then said to have provoked their own deaths for the same reason Karen Silkwood was murdered and said to have poisoned herself with plutonium: these are attempts to destroy the people's movement by eliminating the leaders, he charged.[27] Scapegoat politics was also a theme in the last talk that night by Phil Thompson, who denied that the CWP 5 caused their own deaths by provoking the Klan with violent rhetoric.

Floris and I stayed in New York for several days after the forum to give interviews. The major newspapers and TV networks ignored us, but alternative media, such as radio stations WLIB and WBAI, gave us a good deal of time and space to tell our story.

UHURU

In Greensboro and in other cities, we postered. It was strictly a late night activity, a cat-and-mouse game, just this side of legality. A half dozen of us would gather at Willena's house, or at Dale's, and brew a paste made of cornstarch and water. Any adhesion made with this concoction was invincible and permanent. I had an ancient, bucket-style stock pot to which I had a sentimental attachment. It came from my grandmother Bess' kitchen, and I used it all the time for cooking. It was ideal to hold paste for postering since it had a handle, and so I loaned it for that purpose. Unfortunately, one night I got a call very early in the morning to go downtown and post bond. Dale, Rand, and a couple of friends from out-of-town had been arrested. They were caught in the act and charged with illegally postering advertising material. The police confiscated the evidence. I never saw my grandmother's pot again. The "advertising material" demanded that charges against the Greensboro Three be dropped, denounced Klan and police complicity, and announced a CWP-sponsored December 13 forum at the Uhuru Bookstore.

Lewis Brandon, manager of the Uhuru Bookstore, was asked by a reporter why he was allowing the local chapter of the CWP to use the place. "The word *uhuru* means freedom," he responded. "There has to be some means of giving the Communist Workers Party the opportunity to air what they are trying to do. Other groups have been intimidated from giving them this opportunity."

Larry Little arrived at the forum late, with boxes of files from the FBI's COINTEL program, the evidence of the government's attempt to destroy black leaders in the sixties and seventies. He had come to our aid even though some of his friends advised him against it. "It's those people who want to play it safe who create a world of insecurity," he said. "You have to speak out."

Nelson presided over the forum at the Uhuru Bookstore and gave the main address, an impassioned narration of all that had happened. It was an evening packed with many presentations. Willena's ten-year-old son Kwame and my eleven-year-old Alex recited in unison "Good Morning Revolution" by Langston Hughes. *Greensboro Record* staff writer Martha Woodall, who covered many aspects of the November Third story over several years, wrote about the December 13 forum at the Uhuru Bookstore:

> A racially mixed audience of about 80 people turned out for speeches from CWP members and sympathizers and for a slide presentation about the five slain CWP members.
>
> No police were in evidence, but security-conscious CWP members demanded to see reporters' press cards and two members with walkie-talkies took up positions at the front and rear of the store.
>
> It was an unusual evening of politics and emotion.
>
> Flanked by volumes of leftist literature and displays of Afro-American greeting cards, speakers addressed the audience from behind tables covered with frayed, red paper table cloths and photographs of slain CWP members.
>
> Speakers included Dale Sampson and Signe Waller whose husbands were killed Nov. 3.
>
> The women's wedding rings were hanging from thin chains around their necks. Mrs. Waller strode purposefully through the gathering. A handgun was holstered at her hip.
>
> The evening featured speeches by Willie Drake, a former student body president at North Carolina A & T State University and now a political science professor at a small college in upstate New York; Winston-Salem Alderman Larry Little; and Michio Kaku, a physicist at City College of New York and a leader in the anti-nuclear power movement.
>
> Little, who expressed solidarity with the CWP, gave accounts of the political harassment he underwent during his days coordinating the state's Black Panther Party.
>
> Drake described the sympathy and support for the CWP that is growing on campuses across the country and Kaku asserted: "an attack on one (progressive political group) is an attack on all."
>
> The program included a sophisticated slide presentation the CWP had prepared about the five CWP members who were killed and a description of the CWP's work.
>
> The words to the song written to commemorate the slain CWP members for the Nov. 11 funeral march were printed on the back of the forum program.
>
> The audience stood and sang along with the recorded music that closed the slide show.[28]

The very next day, Nelson left Greensboro early in the morning for Atlanta to attend a conference called by the Southern Christian Leadership Conference (SCLC) and the Interreligious Foundation for Community Organization

(IFCO) about strategies to counter KKK activity. Events in our city had added a sense of urgency to thoughts already in the air about how to respond to the recent wave of Klan organizing and violence.

Within the civil rights movement, there were inertial tendencies to bow to anticommunism and to isolate the CWP. We wanted people to understand that as long as they did anything terribly inconvenient to the power structure—like organize and struggle for equal rights—they, too, could be painted red. Not everyone had the political maturity to grasp the lesson in a familiar saying, "united we stand, divided we fall." Despite contradictions and disagreements, all anti-Klan and civil rights forces needed to strengthen their fragile unity and work together.

More than four hundred clergy, civil rights leaders, lawyers, trade unionists, and political activists, who went to Atlanta in the middle of December for the founding of the National Anti-Klan Network (NAKN) and represented approximately forty organizations, thought the moment was ripe for a national effort to fight the Ku Klux Klan. The group reached a decision to march in Greensboro on February 2, 1980. The march would protest the shooting of the five CWP members at the anti-Klan rally on November 3. At the same time, it would celebrate the twentieth anniversary of the sit-ins in Greensboro that helped to launch the civil rights movement and renew the struggle for civil rights.

The National Anti-Klan Network arose from an SCLC meeting in August 1979 in Norfolk. As noted earlier, the Klan attacked demonstrators in Decatur, Alabama, in May 1979. The incident engendered the June 1979 demonstration led by SCLC to which a couple of thousand protesters flocked, including a lively bunch of CWP people from Durham and elsewhere. During the summer, SCLC and IFCO agreed to host a conference drawing together all anti-Klan forces to respond to the growing presence and danger of the KKK and to hold the conference in Atlanta during the coming winter. In the meantime, November Third happened.

According to reporters at the *Carolina Peacemaker*—who told the behind-the-scenes story because they thought many people had the false impression that the February 2 march was the CWP's brainchild (it wasn't!) and that this erroneous impression was damaging mobilization efforts—the Atlanta meeting was regarded as more urgent after November Third. The date was moved ahead to December and the call to attend was broadened.[29] The *Peacemaker* credits Anne Braden of the Southern Organizing Committee for Economic and Social Justice (SOC) with being the mover and shaker who promoted the idea of going to Greensboro.

Anne, a renegade white southern lady who eschewed her expected role to become instead one of the most estimable figures in the civil rights movement, was upset at the lack of response to the November Third incident by progressives. Anne wrote to Dr. Joseph Lowery on November 25 and, in a much circulated letter, suggested that the failure to respond to the Greensboro killings was a major blow to the civil rights movement. She thought there needed to be an effort to go back to Greensboro and that February 1 would be an appropriate time, since it marked the twentieth anniversary of the sit-in movement. The closest Saturday to that date was February 2. The Klan must not be allowed to run progressive people out of Greensboro, Anne stressed, and it was high time to renew the commitment to struggle for civil and human rights. By the time of the Atlanta conference, Anne's initiative had buzzed around the country, and those who came to the Atlanta meeting in December were prepared to act.

"In no way do we agree ideologically with the Communist Workers Party and the overthrow of the government," Lowery said. "We asked for a meeting of all groups opposed to the Klan. There is no way to exclude the CWP who lost five people to the gun of the Klan." "Sure we have political differences," Nelson acknowledged, "but we'll have to accept that and work together."[30]

AN EXCITING CROSSROADS

In the tense and red-baited environment in Greensboro, coalition leaders attempted to force the CWP to assume a low profile. It was not the greatest model for an organizational response to red-baiting. There were guidelines for organizational behavior that were violated by the organizations that set forth the guidelines. But if some of the February 2 march organizers failed to embrace warmly their brothers and sisters in the civil rights movement who happened to be communists, another group that was preparing to celebrate the birth of that movement on the twentieth anniversary of the sit-ins went further. The sit-in anniversary crowd went to great lengths to completely disassociate themselves from the February 2 march.

The problem of strengthening the unity of civil rights advocates and activists was aggravated by the federal Community Relations Service that worked to divide the people and organizations involved in the February 2 rally. They helped float a rumor through the North Carolina media that the SCLC and NAACP were not going to participate in the march. SCLC remained a cosponsor and participated fully, and the Greensboro NAACP endorsed the action. Most of the people in the coalition sincerely tried to work together with others to respond to the right-wing threat, but it was very difficult to do, and doing it drew on more than good will.

A local group arranged to commemorate the first sit-in at Woolworth's in downtown Greensboro on February 1, 1960, with a historical marker. The rogues of an earlier time, arrested and spat upon, were now to be lionized by city officials, the Chamber of Commerce, and potentates previously responsible for the spitting and arresting. This was all the more remarkable as the original icons were not even safely dead. When Rev. Lucius Walker of New York–based IFCO arrived in Greensboro to plan the national mobilization for the February 2 march, the historical marker folks announced that they would change their plans and conclude their activities by February 1. They apparently did not wish to be associated or confused with those marching the next day. Ironically, the February 2 marchers were telling the world that the struggle for equal rights and human decency was still ongoing. Greensboro was an exciting and crowded crossroads.

A "February Second" mobilization office was established in a poor neighborhood of the city. Rev. Lucius Walker was in Greensboro on January 1, 1980. With codirector C. T. Vivian of Atlanta, a just-retired executive director of the SCLC and associate of Martin Luther King Jr., Walker was prepared to work full time organizing the February 2 march. "The gathering of civil rights, religious, labor, legal, political and educational groups is projected as a beginning for a new decade of civil rights activity. The march will protest the Ku Klux Klan massacre of five demonstrators, and it will commence work on the unfinished civil rights agenda of the nation," Walker told the press.[31]

Walker and Vivian were joined by other civil rights groups that sent organizers to Greensboro, including Phil Gardner from the National Anti-Racist Organizing Committee in New York and Lynn Wells of the Southern Conference Educational Fund (SCEF) in Atlanta. The CWP in New York sent Dwight Hopkins, and the party mobilized around the country. Also participating in the planning and organizing was the Chicago-based Equal Rights Congress. The Center for Constitutional Rights in New York sponsored the rally and sent William Kunstler and some other top-notch civil rights lawyers to Greensboro to give legal assistance to the event at critical points. Anne Braden of Louisville, Kentucky, and many other seasoned organizers helped line up the buses and get the bodies to the event. In Greensboro, the Concerned Citizens against the Klan did heavy-duty organizing for the February 2 rally as did the Triangle Vigil Committee in the Durham–Chapel Hill–Raleigh area.

At the beginning of the year, some city officials tried to change the parade permit ordinance. Groups applying for a permit would have to post bond in advance if the city manager thought extraordinary police protection would be needed. Marchers would have to declare how many participants they expected from outside the county: if more people showed up than were estimated on the permit application, the excess number of persons would not be allowed to participate in the parade. The proposed ordinance would have banned "weapons disguised as signs." It called for keeping the parade route away from residential areas.[32] On January 3, 1980, I spoke at a city council meeting against the proposed changes, and I returned to challenge the ordinance when the mayor decided to delay the vote. I objected that if demonstrators had to post bond or foot a security bill, it meant that people who had nothing but the streets on which to exercise their free speech would be silenced. The decree was so blatantly unconstitutional that I had plenty of company in arguing against it—everyone from politicians and ACLU lawyers to high school students.[33] When a new parade ordinance was passed two months hence, it was stripped of some of the objectionable amendments but was more restrictive than the ordinance it replaced.

It was not long before Walker, Wells, and other organizers tasted the insidious and hostile milieu of Greensboro at that moment. Wells applied for the permit on behalf of the February Second Mobilization Committee on January 2, 1980—just as amending the parade permit ordinance became an urgent priority. City Attorney Jesse Warren warned Wells that new stringent regulations could be in effect for the February 2 parade. The permit application indicated an expected crowd of 5,000 to 10,000 marchers and specified a route to the Greensboro Coliseum. The marchers planned to gather inside the coliseum for speeches.[34] When the permit was requested, the city mumbled something about the coliseum being booked on February 2. Meanwhile, Wells and Walker were prepared to go to court with ACLU Director George Gardner to file suit against Greensboro's proposed ordinance if the city council had not delayed the vote on it.

On Monday, January 6, 1980, City Manager Tom Osborne denied the permit, declaring that the coliseum where the march would end was under option for February 2. "I'm telling Ms. Wells that, if the other group doesn't exercise its option, then we would be glad to talk with her group again," Osborne said.[35]

Randolph McLaughlin, an attorney with the Center for Constitutional Rights, answered the telephone at the mobilization center in Greensboro and told reporters that what was happening was a "classic confrontation between constitutional rights and economic and political interests."[36] Simultaneously, the rumor that SCLC was on the verge of bailing out was being bandied around, and the February 1 historical marker group reiterated categorically that they had nothing to do with the organizations seeking to march on February 2.

The February Second Mobilization Committee hung tough. "The city can't deny us our constitutional rights," Lynn Wells said. "The march is on. The city will have to change its position."[37] Mark Smith, also a spokesperson for the Mobilization Committee (and a medical student at UNC-Chapel Hill and the estranged widower of Sandi), told reporters, "We are confident we can get a permit, we think the Coliseum can be had and we will fight for it."[38]

Meanwhile, a hapless rhythm and blues concert promoter in Danville, Virginia, who held the option, was caught off guard. When informed of developments in Greensboro, he indicated that he might reconsider his claim on the contested coliseum. He did not have his act together anyway—literally speaking.

That same week, the Greensboro Human Relations Commission, which had just appointed twelve citizens to review the conditions leading up to November Third, intervened. "In light of the dispute over the Coliseum and the fact that the demonstration has become confused with the Feb. 1 observances of the 20th anniversary of the Woolworth lunch counter sit-ins that ushered in the country's civil rights movement, the HRC Wednesday decided to ask the Feb. 2 group to consider delaying the march."[39] The February Second Mobilization Committee didn't bite.

On January 11, 1980 (ignoring a bomb threat to "blow those communists to pieces"), the civil rights organizers held a press conference at which they reaffirmed their commitment to February 2 and announced the organizations that had endorsed the march thus far. These included the National Lawyers Guild, the Institute for Southern Studies, the Women's International League for Peace and Freedom, the Martin Luther King Movement of Atlanta, the National Conference of Black Lawyers, the Texas Farm Workers Union, the state of West Virginia Human Rights Commission, the Gray Panthers of Jackson, Mississippi, and politicians from various and sundry places—an assortment of county commissioners, city councilmen, and a congressman or two. SCLC was onboard for sure, ending the rumors that one of the original two cosponsors was about to drop out.[40] The thirty-member board of the Greensboro branch of the NAACP endorsed the February 2 march, with the group's president, Dr. George Simkins Jr., making the disclaimer for the record that endorsement must not be taken to imply ideological unity with other marchers.[41] The local NAACP endorsement, caveat and all, was significant in the prevailing atmosphere of intimidation. The Pulpit Forum, consisting of local black ministers, did not follow suit. But endorsements continued to come in from religious and other organizations around the country including, in North Carolina, the Raleigh Ministerial Union.

The mobilization workers complained that they were being harassed and spied on by the police and that their phones were being tapped. In one ludicrous incident, two police officers were exposed as spies when they infiltrated a gathering and signed in as members of the Baptist Coalition, a nonexistent organization. Public Safety Director Hewitt Lovelace admitted that the officer should have signed in as an officer from the Greensboro Police Department, but he "apparently felt he would not be allowed to tape-record the entire conference if he identified himself as a police officer."[42] Probably not! Lovelace said that the city would continue to monitor developments leading to the march, and the media finely sifted every endorsement for organizational rifts, disclaimers, and innuendoes.

On January 15, the Virginia promoter announced that he would go ahead with his concert on Feb. 2 and the march mobilization committee still did not have a permit to march.

The state was keeping tabs on the CWP and made no secret of the fact that it was devoting resources and manpower to that task. The Greensboro police set up a six-man special intelligence unit, headed by Captain D. C. Williams, to "gather all the information possible about participants in the planned march."[43] They were in contact with "law enforcement agencies in cities and states where known chapters of the Ku Klux Klan, Nazi Party, and Communist Workers Party exist," Captain Williams said. Police efforts clearly were focused on counteracting the CWP. The pattern of lumping the CWP (a group with a history of nonviolent labor and civil rights organizing) together with the Klan and Nazis under the rubric of "groups with a history of violence" was repeated like a mantra. In truth, our claim to "a history of violence" would have to be established on the sole basis that five of our people had been murdered!

Captain Williams' red squad, with its broad powers of spying on citizens, had Governor Hunt's blessings. Illustrative of the widening net of police repression against citizens in the 1980s, Williams' intelligence unit had a purpose extending past February 2. I would have my own personal encounter with the unit's activities in July. In general, when the media repeated the police phrases about *potentially violent groups* or *extremist groups with violent tendencies*, this was a coded way of referring to the CWP. The Klan was not fooled. Hunt was put in an embarrassing position when Virgil Griffin announced that the Invisible Empire of the KKK endorsed Hunt for reelection and called Hunt the best governor the state ever had. The racists understood very well at whom the state's fire was aimed, and it was not at them. "'We welcome all police in the Klan as long as they are white,' Griffin said in response to Hunt's remarks about infiltration. 'We don't hold that against Hunt. He couldn't single out one organization but had to include all in his remarks.'"[44]

A cloud hung over Greensboro. It was seeded with the police tracking and spying on dissenting citizens, the sham Klan prosecution, and attempts to sabotage the February 2 civil rights event.

Two weeks before the march, organizers were still without a parade permit. Then the news broke that *the City of Greensboro was underwriting the concert that was preventing marchers from getting the coliseum!*

After denying the parade permit and claiming that the coliseum was already booked, city officials signed a contract with the Danville promoter to shore up his rhythm and blues concert. It was the first time that the city ever copromoted a rhythm and blues concert. The contract committed the city to share the expenses and profits (or losses) of the concert with the promoter. Moreover, the promoter already owed the coliseum over six thousand dollars from a previous concert. Rev. Lucius Walker charged the city with trying to block the civil rights group from ending its march at the coliseum and holding an indoor rally.[45]

Apologists for the City of Greensboro need not have troubled to put a good face on things by explaining that the city was copromoting the concert to help a fledgling black-owned business—a stretch that qualified them to become the show's comedy act. Contacted about what was going on in Greensboro, the African American rhythm and blues artist Roy Ayers expressed solidarity with the civil rights marchers and regrets that he could not get out of the booking without risking a breach of contract suit.

The fallout for Greensboro from the news that the city was behind the booking of the coliseum was considerable. Critical of the city for using taxpayer money to sponsor a rhythm and blues concert, some people pointed out that on February 2, A & T was scheduled to play basketball in Winston-Salem with Winston-Salem State University. Thus the city would be competing with North Carolina black universities for gate receipts—eight to ten thousand people typically went to those games—and would probably lose the taxpayers' money invested in the concert.[46] As more facts came to light, the city became surrounded by a bad odor. It appeared city officials tried to conceal the deal, the payments to performers were higher than normal, and local black promoters came forward saying that they had never benefited from a largesse that the city was now bestowing on a Virginia promoter. It was too much even for the conservative press. The morning paper raised the question on everyone's mind—"Did the city somehow help arrange the concert to block the marchers' use of the building? If not, why is the city risking its own money—at least $14,150 so far—through the unusual co-sponsorship of a concert that may be unprofitable?"[47] And the evening paper called the city "dumb" for ruining Greensboro's progressive image.[48]

On January 21, 1980, the February Second Mobilization Committee applied once more for a parade permit. City Manager Tom Osborne again cited the rental of the coliseum as the reason for denying it. (He offered the marchers an outdoor stadium for the February rally.) Simultaneously, the news broke that the city had just paid deposits to the rhythm and blues acts. Mobilization Committee lawyers filed a civil suit against the city and asked the U.S. District Court to void the contract between the coliseum and the Virginia promoter and to make the coliseum available to the civil rights marchers. An affidavit from an Atlanta concert promoter stated that on January 3, right after the city denied the application for a parade permit to the civil rights group, ostensibly because the coliseum was already booked, she called the coliseum and was told the building was available for rental on February 2.[49] An irate mayor called the civil suit "without substance" and expressed his displeasure with the newspapers for making it seem that city hall was trying to pull something! The Human Relations Commission had an emergency meeting with the city council. Forced to give an accounting, the city only further exposed its duplicitous dealings.[50] By January 23, some of the performers were working on disengaging from the concert; the main act, Ayers, reaffirmed that he did not want to be in conflict with a civil rights event.

From Washington, the recently pardoned Rev. Ben Chavis of the Wilmington Ten warmly endorsed the march. Earlier, Jesse Jackson, then director of Chicago-based Operation Push, had backed the march. Around the country, buses were being chartered and people were rearranging their work and childcare schedules in order to march in Greensboro on February 2. The march was gaining momentum and things were coming to a head in Greensboro. Public skepticism about the city's motives was rampant. Finally, January 25, the city backed down and moved the rhythm and blues concert to February 3, making the coliseum available to the marchers on February 2. (The city lost over $32,000 on the delayed concert.) Even after the coliseum site was opened up, however, paying the large rental fee demanded by the city was not easy. Finding an insurance company to issue the mandatory property and personal injury coverage proved even harder. These preconditions to obtaining the parade permit and using the coliseum were almost not met. The permit was issued one day before the march.

The last week in January, I was in Chicago and in Gary, Indiana, speaking at forums on the Widows' Tour. I kept abreast of events connected to the February 2 mobilization—including various cabals. Two days after the victory over the coliseum, the Mobilization Committee expelled the CWP for refusing to pledge to march unarmed.[51] The issue was one that everyone had agreed was not to be made an issue lest it become divisive. The CWP had declared itself united with the goal of conducting a peaceful civil rights march. There was not supposed to be an *official* position—a declaration either supporting or prohibiting armed self-defense—imposed on the coalition as a whole since no organization was authorized to speak for the coalition on that issue. But some mobilization spokespersons abrogated that rule, declaring an official position—theirs—and then expelled the CWP. The CWP refused to be expelled. We said that we would play an active role on February 2 and that we would "never, never be disarmed or ask the masses to disarm themselves."[52]

The CWP was not being expelled because it was a communist organization, Rev. Walker assured people. "We reiterate our demand that charges against CWP members, and specifically charges against Nelson Johnson, be dropped," he told the press. Nor did the expulsion imply acceptance of the government interpretation of the Nov. 3 massacre that blamed the victims for the crime. The Mobilization Committee upheld the view that the Ku Klux Klan *and* agents of the city, state, and federal governments were responsible for the five deaths.[53]

At the Atlanta meeting of the new National Anti-Klan Network in December, Phil Thompson and Nelson Johnson established a strong presence for the CWP. Throughout the organizing process for the march, CWP provided a lot of leadership. The attempts to expel the CWP or force it to play a low profile role were resoundingly unsuccessful, and the coalition was not reduced to impotence. But the factionalism and sectarianism of which many (including the CWP) were guilty might have doomed it. In the end, by working together, coalition participants succeeded in rekindling the flame of the civil rights struggle. Positive effects for the people's movement endured over succeeding years of the decade.

The increased civil rights activity and the crack in the city's façade over the coliseum fiasco allowed some of Greensboro's leaders in the black community to reraise their agenda for treatment of blacks as full-fledged citizens within a democracy. African American businessman Alfred S. Webb, a former chairman of the Greensboro Human Relations Commission, reminded people that Greensboro had some real issues related to race that were not resolved after the Dudley and A & T rebellion. Webb wanted specific reforms of local government. Recent events in the city demonstrated "the urgent need for a change in the method of electing members to our City Council," he told the press.[54] Webb endorsed the February 2 march—with the usual and by now apparently obligatory disclaimer that his signature did not mean endorsement of the ideologies of any participating groups.

On January 30, 1980, William Kunstler made his first trip back to Greensboro since he had offered legal assistance to the students sitting in at the Woolworth lunch counter twenty years earlier. He had come to file additional affidavits in a federal court suit charging the State Bureau of Investigation with attempting to undermine the February 2 civil rights march.[55] The suit, prepared by lawyers from the Center for Constitutional Rights, claimed that SBI agents went to college campuses to intimidate students who might participate in the march and, to that end, "launched a systematic campaign of rumor-mongering and insinuation of violence at the Feb. 2 march."[56] Among those filing affidavits were the Student Government Association president from A & T State University and a student government officer at North Carolina Central University. They described encounters with SBI agents. Such SBI activity had a chilling effect on student mobilization at both black institutions, the students maintained.

Other affidavits attached to the suit asserted that the SBI tried to intimidate bus companies into refusing to lease vehicles to groups planning to attend the protest march.[57] The Mobilization Committee failed to get an injunction restraining the SBI and North Carolina attorney general Rufus Edmisten's office from interfering further with people's right to march. Nevertheless, matters could have been worse without the legal initiatives.

In the meantime, the family squabble among coalition groups continued. "Today, CWP leader Nelson Johnson repeated that the CWP members will participate in Saturday's march," reported the *Greensboro Record*. "He said the CWP does not intend to provoke violence but believes in the right to bear arms for protection."[58] Nelson felt that to pledge that we would be unarmed was "an open invitation for an attack."[59]

All of these events polarized the people of Greensboro. Black or white, you had to have a position about the march. You could not remain indifferent. Andrew Young, in Greensboro at A & T on February 1 to speak at the ceremony honoring the twentieth anniversary of the sit-ins, was forced to either endorse or—conspicuously—fail to endorse the next day's march. He endorsed it.[60] The politically charged atmosphere created a dilemma for some who wanted to affirm the civil rights struggle but avoid affirming the organizers. Did they not see that struggle requires people on the front lines, and it is quixotic or hypocritical to dismiss them while honoring the cause for which they take risks and make sacrifices? Many people, whether they marched or not, signed a paid political newspaper ad on February 2, 1980, welcoming people of good will who were coming to Greensboro, opposing the resurgence of a violent Ku Klux Klan, and reaffirming a commitment to racial and economic justice.[61]

FEBRUARY SECOND

The first line of the march was wide. It became even wider as we widows made our way into the line alongside the IFCO and SCLC leaders. I linked arms with Rev. Ben Chavis. It was an extremely cold day with a biting wind. The repeat of a limited state of emergency by the city gave the day a déjà vu feeling. But I felt less isolated than at the funeral march. We were over seven thousand strong as we marched nearly four miles from the War Memorial Stadium at Yanceyville and Lindsey, down Dudley Street, past the A & T campus to Market Street, and on to the coliseum.

Reverend Chavis received death threats shortly before he spoke; his security personnel stayed close to him. "I want to say in the memory of the Reverend Dr. Martin Luther King Jr.—in his memory—I want to dedicate my remarks to Jim Waller, to Bill Sampson, to Sandi Smith, to Cesar Cauce, to Michael Nathan," Chavis said. "Because the fact of the matter is that those four brothers and that sister have put down their lives that we may live. It matters not what their political ideology was. It matters that they have given their lives for everybody in this building, for everybody in Greensboro, for everybody in the world today. And that must be said."[62]

A main theme of the day, addressed by Rev. Fred Shuttlesworth and Dr. Joseph Lowery, was reclaiming the ground taken in the civil rights movement of the 1950s and 1960s. *How* to reclaim this ground was, I felt, more concretely addressed by other speakers. Reverend Iberius Hacker of the Urban Appalachian Coalition issued strong words of challenge to whites to do something about racism. To recruit, he said, the Klan goes to "unemployed white workers; it goes to unemployed white youths; it goes to the disaffected and the confused. That is where these parasites attach themselves and draw out the life-blood of our unions, our communities, and our churches. We must now go wherever the Klan goes and, with every particle of our spirit and our intelligence, demonstrate that racism is not only the enemy of black people; it is the enemy of poor working people of any race."

Anne Braden of the Southern Organizing Committee was impressive. "The men who pulled the triggers that killed five people here on the streets of Greensboro are dangerous men who must be brought to justice," she said:

> But they are not the cause of our problems; they are the result. The real danger today comes from the people in high places, from the halls of Congress to the board rooms of our big corporations. Those people who are telling the white people in this country that if they are having overwhelming problems today trying to survive, it is black people who are causing those problems. The people in high places are telling white people that if their taxes are eating up their paychecks, it's not because of our bloated military budget, but because of government programs that benefit black people. Those people in high places are telling white people that if young whites are unemployed, it's because blacks are getting all the jobs. Our problem is the people in power who are creating a scapegoat mentality among white people. That is what is creating the climate in which the Klan can grow in this country and that is what is creating the danger of a fascist movement in the 1980s in America.

Before Phil Thompson spoke, he called on the widows to come forward. Floris, Marty, Dale, and I stood beside him on stage as he delivered an electrifying speech. Phil challenged everyone in this audience of progressives, whether they liked us or not, to recognize the role the CWP was playing within the movement and to understand and resist the forces trying to destroy the movement. Phil received a thunderous ovation. The final crescendo of his speech is captured in the documentary *Red November, Black November.* "To attack the people, the government must first attack the leadership of the people," he said:

> The Communist Workers Party Five were killed precisely because they were educating people not to blame the Arabs for high oil prices, not to blame blacks for unemployment and inflation, but put the blame on the millionaire monopoly capitalists. That's who to blame. They were killed precisely because they were respected leaders of the workers at Cone Mills and Duke Hospital . . . because they forced the city of Greensboro to fire two police officers for beating up Gernie Cummings, a black youth in Greensboro; because they defended the Wilmington 10; and because they dared to struggle and fight and organize against the Ku Klux Klan. These are the *crimes* which they were guilty of and this is why they were assassinated.
>
> If the ruling class can have the CWP 5 killed in cold blood, in broad daylight, on TV cameras, where one half of the murderers are not even arrested, and can get away with it, then the ruling class will definitely step up violent attacks on all progressive people. They will impose fascism. . . .
>
> That's why we say the struggle to avenge the CWP 5 is the focal point to beat back a new wave of violent repression and fascism in this country. We can not allow ourselves to go back. We know we can not go back to the days when a black person speaking up for his rights could be strung up from the nearest tree for being uppity. We will not go back to the days when to be a communist meant you were a traitor and you could be electrocuted or sent to jail. We will not go back to the days when our leaders were timid yes men, uncle toms, or lackeys for the ruling class. But when five people are murdered by Klan and Nazis, and you don't do anything about it because they're communists, you're back already!

NOTES

1. Korotkin, "The Campaign for Justice," 22–23.
2. Quoted in Dwight F. Cunningham, "Human Relations Group Plans Citizens Study of Police Action," *Greensboro Daily News*, 6 December 1979, B1.
3. Associated Press, "Rally Deaths Service Held in Greensboro," *Durham Morning Herald*, 4 December 1979, 9A.

4. Ann Whitfield, "Interfaith Services Spirit Marred?" *Carolina Peacemaker*, 15 December 1979.

5. Robert Spruill, "Mayor Calls Johnson 'a Dangerous Man,'" *Carolina Peacemaker*, 23 June 1979.

6. Mae Israel and Dwight Cunningham, "Johnson Traces Struggles from Equality for Blacks to Battling Capitalism," *Greensboro Daily News*, 9 December 1979, A12.

7. Israel and Cunningham, "Johnson Traces Struggles," A12.

8. "Doctor to Fight for Job," (North Carolina) *Chatham County Herald*, 20 November 1979, 12A.

9. Tom Clark, Opinion Exchange, "Editorial Stance 'Pathetic Apology,'" *Durham Sun*, 10 May 1980, 4A.

10. Clark, "Editorial Stance 'Pathetic Apology,'" 4A.

11. Cited in Earle Tockman, "Labor Cases Arising out of the Greensboro Massacre" (unpublished report, 1980).

12. Stan Swofford, "CWP Files Complaint over Firing," *Greensboro Daily News*, 29 April 1980.

13. See "Greensboro: Cone Mills Seizes the Time," *Labor Update*, May 1980, 7.

14. See chapter 15 for more about Dori Blitz.

15. See "Kansas Aircraft Machinists Ground Red-Baiting Attacks," *Workers Viewpoint*, 26 December 1979 and "Chrysler Fires Comrade Fighting Klan," *Workers Viewpoint*, 9 January 1980.

16. See John York, "Klan Leader Plans Fund Raising for Defense of Shooting Suspects," *Charlotte Observer*, 13 November 1979, 2B, and also "Greensboro Lifts Emergency Status," (Raleigh) *News & Observer*, 13 November 1979, 32.

17. Boyd, "Ambush: An Inquiry, 17. See also York, "Klan Leader Plans Fund Raising." The FBI told the *Charlotte Observer* that they did not anticipate filing any charges against Virgil Griffin.

18. Boyd, "Ambush: An Inquiry," 17.

19. Rick Steward and Jim Schlosser, "Nov. 3 Deaths: Arrest Orders for 9 Expected," *Greensboro Record*, 14 December 1979, C1.

20. Associated Press, "Grand Jury Indicts 14 in Greensboro Rally Case," *Durham Morning Herald*, 14 December 1979, 1A.

21. "Petition for Appointment of a Private Prosecutor," filed in State of North Carolina, County of Guilford, Superior Court Division, 23 January 1980.

22. Letter to the editor by Sydney Nathans, "Case Deserves Special Prosecutor," *Greensboro Daily News*, 12 December 1979.

23. "Petition for Appointment of a Private Prosecutor."

24. See Associated Press, "Rally Deaths: Prosecutor 'in a No-Win Situation,'" (Thomasville, N.C.) *Times*, 10 December 1979.

25. See "Tide of Support for CWP 5 Organized from Every Walk of Life," *Workers Viewpoint*, 30 November 1979.

26. "New York Forum on CWP 5: Progressive People Rally to Fight KKK/Nazis," *Workers Viewpoint*, 10 December 1979.

27. "New York Forum on CWP 5."

28. Martha Woodall, "CWP to Aid State in Case," *Greensboro Record*, 14 December 1979, C1, C3.

29. "Behind the Feb. 2 March," *Carolina Peacemaker*, 2 February 1980, 4.

30. Vanessa Gallman, "Rights Activists Urge Greensboro Anti-Klan March," *Charlotte Observer*, 17 December 1979, 1B.

31. Katherine Fulton and Martha Woodall, "Feb. 2 March Planned: Civil Rights Activists Seek to Clarify Aims," *Greensboro Record*, 3 January 1980, B1.

32. William March, "Parade Law Provisions Questioned," *Greensboro Daily News*, 6 January 1980.

33. Martha Woodall, "Council Decides Parade Law Needs Further Study," *Greensboro Record*, 18 January 1980.

34. Martha Woodall, "Planned Parade Law Challenged," *Greensboro Record*, 4 January 1980.

35. Jo Spivey and Rick Stewart, "City Manager Denies Permit for Feb. 2 Anti-Klan March," *Greensboro Record*, 7 January 1980.

36. Spivey and Stewart, "City Manager Denies Permit," B9.

37. "March Roadblock May Be Cleared," *Greensboro Daily News*, 8 January 1980, B7.

38. Jo Spivey, "Coliseum Use Becomes Marchers' Aim," *Greensboro Record*, 8 January 1980, B1

39. Martha Woodall and Jo Spivey, "Officials Decline Request to Change Date of March," *Greensboro Record*, 10 January 1980, B1.

40. Martha Woodall and Jo Spivey, "Organizers of March Say Effort Gaining Supporters," *Greensboro Record*, 11 January 1980.

41. Jo Spivey and Martha Woodall, "NAACP Executive Board Back March," *Greensboro Record*, 9 January 1980, D1.

42. Lindsey Gruson, "March Organizers Cite Unity," *Greensboro Daily News*, 12 January 1980, B1.

43. Christopher Simpson, "Police Trying to Find Out Who's Coming," *Greensboro Record*, 15 January 1980.

44. "Grand Dragon Says Klan Endorsing Hunt Re-Election," *Greensboro Daily News*, 7 January 1980.

45. Martha Woodall, "March Dispute Touches Artists," *Greensboro Record*, 19 January 1980, B4.

46. "Group Scores City Role in Concert," *Greensboro Daily News*, 20 January 1980.

47. William March, "City's Role in Concert Raises Complex Questions," *Greensboro Daily News*, 22 January 1980, A1.

48. Editorial, "Greensboro and the March," *Greensboro Record*, 22 January 1980.

49. William March, "Judge Denies Fast Hearing on Coliseum," *Greensboro Daily News*, 23 January 1980, D14.

50. See Martha Woodall, "Co-sponsor Move Shifts Attention," *Greensboro Record*, 23 January 1980, B1–B2.

51. Lindsey Gruson and Kenneth Campbell, "CWP Expelled from City March," *Greensboro Daily News*, 29 January 1980, A1.

52. Gruson and Campbell, "CWP Expelled."

53. Gruson and Campbell, "CWP Expelled," A10.

54. Jo Spivey, "Webb Lends Support to March," *Greensboro Record*, 26 January 1980.

55. Martha Woodall, "Kunstler: Governments Undermining March," *Greensboro Record*, 30 January 1980, A1.

56. Woodall, "Kunstler: Governments Undermining March," A2.

57. Martha Woodall, "Bus Troubles May Reduce March Ranks," *Greensboro Record*, 1 February 1980, B1.

58. Martha Woodall, "City Gives Assistance: March Committee Looks for Insurer," *Greensboro Record*, 31 January 1980, B1.

59. Lindsey Gruson, "March Organizers Say Insurance Bought," *Greensboro Daily News*, 1 February 1980, A18.

60. For Young's nuanced endorsement, see Jim Schlosser, "Young: Leaders with Racist Bent in Office," *Greensboro Record*, 1 February 1980, A1, A7.

61. See the paid political advertisement in the *Greensboro Daily News*, 2 February 1980; see also Jim Schlosser, "March Viewpoint Mixed among Residents," *Greensboro Record*, 30 January 1980, B1.

62. Quotations from speeches on February 2, 1980, are transcribed from Alvarez and Jung, *Red November, Black November*.

A LESSER CRIME TO KILL
A COMMUNIST

SPRING OF 1980: THE COMING POLICE STATE

Harold Covington, leader of the National Socialist Party of America (a.k.a. the American Nazi Party), might have been North Carolina's attorney general in 1980. Covington ran in the Republican Party primary. A vocal defender of the indicted Klan and Nazi murderers and "well-known in the state by publicly espousing his party's white-supremacy line," he got 43 percent of the vote, over 56,000 votes.[1] A stunned GOP accounted for the Nazi's near victory by surmising that the electorate did not know for whom it was voting!

In scapegoating the victims for the crime, District Attorney Schlosser's utterances were consonant with the Nazis' jarring tune. Nazism was the resident evil spirit of the Klan prosecution: Covington offered the full-strength message straight from the fountainhead. In the spring of 1980, as the Klan/Nazi trial approached, the brouhaha around Covington perhaps made the threat of wholesale repression of civil liberties more palpable.

Although the general public may not have been keenly aware of the threat of fascism in the United States, to the CWP, as a current target of repression, the situation seemed to be one of *galloping* fascism. After outright murder, party members and supporters sustained job firings, interference with public assembly, character assassinations, police surveillance, and unfounded criminal indictments. Time and again we were denied facilities as behind-the-scenes pressure was put on the people whose permission we needed to secure a meeting place.

We thought what was happening to us was being done on an early way station to fascism. As long as our adversaries could manage the fallout from our press conferences, we could talk to the media. True, we had Captain Williams' Intelligence

Unit taking pictures at our press conferences and sharpshooters on roofs with their guns sighted on us, but at least we could speak out. We did not yet, as in the prototypically totalitarian state, have to pretend to be strangers when passing on the street. We could not be arrested *easily* for nothing, or shot without causing a tumult. But we were being pushed, prodded, and corralled to such a place.

To manage and mold public opinion, Greensboro's elite needed reports and awards attesting to its splendid performance. At the end of April, the U.S. Justice Department announced the result of their review of the police, done at the city's request. Assistant U.S. Attorney General Drew Days III informed Congressman Richardson Preyer that the Justice Department found "no basis for liability under the federal criminal civil rights statutes on the part of any member of the Greensboro Police Department."[2] The Justice Department has "put its stamp of approval on the assassination by saying the police were not guilty of conspiracy and denial of civil rights," Nelson charged at a press conference we called to announce a rally on May 3.[3]

The Justice Department's bare bones judgment that the Greensboro police had not broken any laws did not appease the city fathers who wanted to hear, in the words of one booster, that they'd done a "heck of a good job" protecting anti-Klan demonstrators. The city contracted with a private consulting firm for an "independent" evaluation of the police's performance on November 3—and the hoped for accolades. The McManis report of May 30, 1980, was another whitewash. In only one particular did the report's authors criticize the police: the police might have stopped and searched the Klan caravan en route to the rally. "Certainly police officers . . . are not obliged to stand by and wait for the crime to be committed when they have a reasonable basis for believing one may be committed."[4] Although the McManis report found everything else in the police performance fine and dandy, this one comment bothered officials. A few months later they came back with a riposte from the North Carolina attorney general's office insisting that the police had no grounds on which to stop and search vehicles even though they knew the Klan and Nazis had brought guns that they intended to take to the rally.[5]

The rally announced for May 3, 1980, was two days before Nelson, Rand, and Willena—the Greensboro 3—were to stand trial on misdemeanor charges stemming from November Third. However, picket signs reading "Defend the Greensboro 3" were out-of-date before May 3. When District Attorney Mike Schlosser emerged from behind the closed doors of a special session of the Guilford County Grand Jury on Friday, May 2, 1980, eight more persons were indicted on felony rioting charges. Only two were Klansmen; the rest were anti-Klan demonstrators.[6]

FROM THE GREENSBORO THREE TO THE
GREENSBORO SIX: FROM MISDEMEANOR TO FELONY

The misdemeanor charges against the Greensboro 3 had been dropped for more serious felony charges against six demonstrators. Blame-the-victim innuendo was now officially sanctioned. Schlosser paved the way, legally and in public opinion, for the Klan/Nazi defense. Here was the D.A., responsible for prosecuting the Klan and Nazi assailants for the state, simultaneously engaged in prosecuting the assailants' victims. How strenuous a case could he make against the Klan and Nazis if he maintained that there was legal justification for prosecuting their victims? The Klan/Nazi defense team got the hint. After the felony indictments of six demonstrators, the Klan/Nazi lawyers asked the judge to order the prosecution to turn over to them evidence that would exonerate their clients, since it was obvious the prosecution saw culpability on the other side.[7] The indicting of demonstrators was legal hostage-taking, a blatant play for the Klan's acquittal.

The three blacks and three whites indicted, now to be known as the Greensboro 6, included a black youth, Percy Sims, from the housing project who was not associated with the CWP prior to November Third. He is seen in videotapes responding viscerally to the intimidating entry of the Klan vehicles by gesturing with his arms for the Klan to get out of their cars. Of the original three arrested, Nelson and Rand were still under arrest. Charged with felony rioting along with them were now Lacie Russell of Greensboro and Dori and Allen Blitz of Martinsville, Virginia. The indictments alleged that the six demonstrators used utterances and gestures likely to provoke violent retaliation and that Rand Manzella and the Blitzes were armed with pistols and Lacie and Nelson with sticks. The police watched as the indicted demonstrators returned to Morningside Homes for a press conference.

At the May 3, 1980, rally at Greensboro's Governmental Plaza, representatives from the Charlotte clergy, the Black Student Union of UNC-Charlotte, the United Church of Christ, and the National Lawyers Guild, among others, spoke against the frame-up of the Greensboro 6. Supporting us then and throughout those turbulent years was Anne Braden, cochair of the Southern Organizing Committee for Economic and Social Justice with Rev. Ben Chavis. Their letter to D.A. Schlosser and Governor Hunt put the indictments of the Greensboro 6 in context:

> We are outraged anew at the efforts of official Greensboro and North Carolina to blame the victims for the crime that occurred in Greensboro on November 3, 1979.

The new indictments of anti-Klan demonstrators on felony charges are a disgrace to this state, to this nation, and to humanity. People are shot down in cold blood, and you say in effect that their friends are to blame . . .

After the international disgrace that came upon North Carolina as a result of the cases of the Wilmington 10 and the Charlotte 3, it is appalling that you are deliberately creating another situation that will bring similar condemnation. The parallels between the Greensboro situation and the Wilmington 10 case are startling. In Wilmington too the Klan and other racist groups shot at innocent people, and criminal charges were brought against the victims. The world condemned this state for this atrocity, and ultimately it will condemn it even more strongly for your persecution of anti-Klan demonstrators in Greensboro. We see these false charges against Communist Workers Party members and supporters as an attack on the entire people's movement in the United States—just at a moment when the spirit that activated the civil rights movement is having a revival all across our land. . . . We call on you to stop this outrage now. Drop the charges against the anti-Klan demonstrators, proceed to arrest all those who took part in the massacre, admit the complicity of the police in the murders, and uncover what people everywhere suspect—that the FBI was also involved. And proceed to prosecute all the guilty parties fully and vigorously.[8]

A WORLD IN GREAT DISORDER

A couple of weeks after the indictments of the Greensboro 6, Miami erupted. Rioting started after four white policemen were acquitted on May 17, 1980, by an all-white jury in the brutal murder of a black insurance man, Arthur McDuffie. The acquittal verdict was the last straw for the black community of Miami and Dade County, Florida. It sparked a rebellion lasting three days. At least fifteen people were killed, three hundred injured, and a thousand arrested. Burning, looting, and violent assaults raged on. Troops were sent to Miami to quell civil disorder. Insurance companies calculated the losses and thought the total would surpass the 1965 Watts uprising.

While the Miami Rebellion was taking place, Mount Saint Helen's volcano was spewing acrid gray ash in the northwest. It was the most violent volcanic eruption on the U.S. mainland in recorded history. However, the death toll was higher in the man-made disaster than in the natural one. No one would be in denial over the causes of a volcanic eruption. But commenting on the verdict in the McDuffie murder case, the white jury foreman declared that race was not an issue!

Everywhere were signs of a world in great disorder, of people resisting oppression. In 1980, it seemed that the profit-driven, white supremacist system of monopoly capitalism was doomed. In Africa, after fourteen years of armed struggle, Zimbabwe was liberated from white Rhodesian colonial rule. The new government of Zimbabwe set out to build a multiracial nation free of the apartheid and racism of the old Rhodesia. In Central America, a struggle for national liberation in El Salvador was gaining momentum. When Archbishop Romero, a champion of the poor, was assassinated and, a week later, forty people were massacred at his funeral service, many North American activists and church leaders built a movement in solidarity with the people of Central America.

In the course of the CWP's active resistance to the right wing in the early 1980s, the organization built and led a coalition in the Midwest that staged a militant anti-Klan demonstration in Kokomo, Indiana, on April 26, 1980. Party supporters and members, helmeted and brandishing sticks for self-defense, took the front line of the march and faced off with helmeted, stick-wielding, uniformed police. In California, the CWP played a major role in keeping Nazis from mass organizing in San Francisco and helped curb the Klan in Oceanside. In North Carolina, the CWP was active in deterring the Nazis from a planned motorcade in Raleigh on Hitler's birthday.

A couple of weeks after he was indicted for felony rioting, Nelson announced that he would be a write-in candidate in November for governor of North Carolina. The gubernatorial campaign was housed in a mobile van, from which party members went into the communities to talk with citizens. Finding a van that did not break down frequently was difficult in the moneyless circles in which we moved. Dale was Nelson's campaign manager and running mate, seeking election as lieutenant governor. The campaign was not realistic in that it lacked financial backing, but it seriously put forth alternatives to people. Nelson's platform called for a guaranteed job for all who wanted to work, an end to racism, universal education through college, decent housing, and equal pay for equal work for women.[9]

THE DECISION NOT TO TESTIFY

When the horse trading around the state criminal trial was over, Schlosser, Superior Court Judge James M. Long, and defense attorneys agreed to separate the indicted Klan and Nazis into two groups. First to be brought to trial would be the group with seemingly greater culpability. It consisted of six Klansmen and Nazis, some seen in videotapes shooting people down: David Wayne Matthews, Roland Wayne Wood, Jerry Paul Smith, Lawrence Gene Morgan, Coleman Blair Pridmore, and Jack Wilson Fowler Jr. All were indigent and were represented by court appointed lawyers. Judge Long ruled in a finding of fact that shots were fired by both defendants and anti-Klan demonstrators, and that the first shot was fired by someone in the Klan-Nazi caravan. The pool of potential jurors to be summoned for the high-profile trial was the largest in the history of the county and possibly the state.

The arraignments for the Greensboro 6 coincided with the first day of official court proceedings in the Klan murder trial, that is, the beginning of jury selection. Having six criminal perpetrators and six of their victims face proceedings against them on the same day was, I thought, Schlosser's warped conception of "even-handed" justice.

"Through prosecuting both the Klan/Nazis and the CWP at the same time," said the CWP, "the state wants to make it look like a shootout between 'two fringe groups' and cover up the leading role of the FBI in planning and guiding the Klan/Nazi assassination."[10]

We anticipated a witch hunt in which *we* would be the ones on trial for our political beliefs and organizing activities. Our resistance took the form of boycotting the trial. If we took part in the trial as if it were a normal process, we would be giving legitimacy to a sham process. We all agreed that if called to testify, we would refuse. However, not just moral but legal principles influenced our decision: our lawyers could not advise us to testify against the Klan when our testimony might be used against our own comrades who were under indictment. A short time into jury selection, Schlosser read the names of 273 potential prosecution witnesses.[11] Jerry Tung was on the list, confirming our fears of a witch hunt. The CWP leader in New York had nothing to do with the decision to have an anti-Klan rally or with its planning, and he was nowhere near North Carolina on November 3. Why would he be called as a prosecution witness against the Klan?

On the eve of jury selection, Marty, speaking for the widows and injured demonstrators, told the press that we expected no justice in the courts. "It is obvious to all who know the facts that November 3 was an assassination conspiracy involving local and federal officials," she said. The murder trial of the Klan and Nazis would be used to continue the cover-up and to go on blaming and persecuting the victims rather than to prosecute the murderers.[12]

The CWP vowed to "put the courts, the FBI, and the entire judicial system that has fostered the Klan/Nazis growth on trial" and to "put the whole damn capitalist system on trial at the Democratic Convention in New York City" the coming summer.[13]

To put our refusal to testify in perspective, one should consider that the case against the caravan participants was overwhelming. There were videotapes documenting the assault as it unfolded. There were numerous potential witnesses ranging from the residents of the housing project to reporters who were willing to testify. Many of these people did testify. *Our testimony was not needed in order to convict the criminals.* We took a principled stand and refused to take part in a travesty of justice. Our refusal did not sabotage the prosecution: the prosecution sabotaged the prosecution. This was a prosecution that referred to people who were murdered as "alleged victims."

Although we did not legitimize the trial by speaking inside the courtroom, we spoke freely and did our truth-telling outside. Like Socrates hanging around the marketplace, we stationed ourselves at every conceivable venue and engaged all comers with our oratory.[14]

ALL HELL BREAKS LOOSE ON JUNE 16, 1980

Yellowing newsprint refreshes my mind on the details of June 16, but the zaniness of the day is unforgettable. "Just as many court observers feared, there was more action outside the courtroom than inside at this morning's start of the Klan-Nazi trial," was the shrewd lead to the story.[15]

My arms were full of press releases. Looking up, I could see the SWAT teams with binoculars and weapons stationed on the rooftops of buildings in the concrete and steel Guilford County governmental complex. They watched as protesters with pickets walked up and down the street. City police, plainclothesmen, and sheriff's men stood on street corners and patrolled inside the buildings. Everyone who tried to enter the trial courtroom was searched and scanned with metal detectors. The rules were geared to keeping people out. There were many empty seats inside the courtroom, but people trying to get in were discouraged from entering.

We marched downtown that morning and held a press conference on the front steps of the courthouse. Nelson, surrounded by the four widows and joined by Anne Braden and Rev. Leon White, declared the trial about to begin "part of the cover-up of the single largest political assassination in the history of the United States."[16] Anne Braden spoke to the press as one of several observers from organizations monitoring the trial in the anti-Klan network. Rev. White was red-baited by a reporter who asked if his presence meant that the United Church of Christ was now endorsing communism. White responded that the United Church of Christ endorses only Jesus Christ but believes in protecting the rights of all citizens no matter what their political views.[17] We entered the courthouse and Nelson repeated his press statement for the benefit of new media arrivals.

Then he disappeared into Guilford County Superior Court Judge Charles Kivett's courtroom to be arraigned on felony riot charges.

I stood outside the third-floor courtroom watching people enter. I noticed that some of the female kin or spouses of the Klan/Nazi defendants seemed terrified. Along with the other widows and demonstrators, I made my way toward the door, but police and sheriff's deputies tried to stop us from entering. Tom Clark was pushing Paul's wheelchair down the corridor toward the courtroom door when a deputy intercepted him. "I got shot at by the Klan and you are going to let me in," Tom protested. "I have a bullet in my head. You're not going to keep me out of this courtroom," Paul said determinedly.

We were told that we could have two observers. The widows of Michael Nathan and César Cauce got permission to enter the courtroom. "You killed my husband. Out of my way," Floris said as she brushed past the deputies.[18]

Judge James Long, hearing about a fracas or an impending one, gave orders to clear the hallways and admit no one else into the courtroom until order was restored. More police arrived to back up the sheriff's deputies.

The charge was led by Paul from his wheelchair. The melee that followed turned the hallways of the courthouse into a wild west saloon. Pushing, shoving, and fighting lasted for twenty minutes. Out of shape cops chased youthful revolutionaries down the hall. Occasionally, a CWP member was caught, clobbered, and carried kicking and screaming into custody. A few people were collared, put on elevators, and told to leave the courthouse—the equivalent of being ushered out the saloon door and being told to leave town by sundown.

I saw Paul's wheelchair careening down a hallway with the battle-ready Paul in it. Nearby, trying to protect the wheelchair and its occupant, was Tom Clark. Sally and others encircled Paul protectively in the confrontation with law enforcement.

They won't let us into the courtroom, people were explaining to those newly arriving. TV cameramen, photographers, and reporters crowded into the narrow hall. They jostled for position, adding to the confusion. "They tried to muscle me out of my wheelchair," Paul told reporters.

An Associated Press photo shows a pretzel of arms: one police officer has his arm locked around Tom's neck, while another is pulling Tom's arms behind his back in an attempt to wrest his grip from the wheelchair. Simultaneously, an officer appears to be trying to perform a choke hold on Paul. But since Paul is seated in a wheelchair and is lower to the ground, the maneuver ends up scrunching his head, to which he responds with a grimace of pain. In the same photo, Willena stands a couple of feet behind Tom and Paul, her eyes narrowly fixed on the scene before her and her face expressing horror and disbelief. Some

moments after this picture was taken, Willena really wrestled with law enforcement. She fought like a tiger and was again arrested.

Meanwhile, in a courtroom adjacent to that of the Klan/Nazi proceedings,
November Third demonstrators charged with felony riot were vocally protesting their arraignment. Judge Kivett ordered them to speak only through their
court-appointed attorneys but could not silence them. District Attorney
Schlosser personally read the indictments instead of assigning the task to one of
his assistants. "'Do you realize that Bill Sampson was my best friend and the best
man at my wedding?' Manzella charged angrily as Schlosser accused him of engaging in the violence which led to his friend's death. Still shouting, Manzella
was pulled from the courtroom by bailiffs. Similar angry protests were raised by
Johnson and the Blitzes. Each was removed after the charges were read."[19]

When the dust settled on the hallway melee, four CWP supporters had been
arrested, including Tom Clark and Willena Cannon. Our lawyer, Earle Tockman, planned to file charges on our behalf against the police and deputies. He
watched a TV videotape of the courthouse disturbance. Laughing, he told us
that Willena was whipping the cops so badly that he was afraid the tape might
be more useful to the other side.

Earle Tockman, a Jewish man with a small frame and handsome Semitic features framed by locks of dark curly hair, had been a judge and a labor lawyer in
Chicago. I first met him when he came to North Carolina early in 1979 to help
Jim file a complaint against Cone with the National Labor Relations Board. In
Greensboro, Earle fell in love with Valeria, an African American mill worker and
friend of Sandi Smith. He married Valeria and became a father to her nine-year-
old son, Phillip. The whole family came to Greensboro after the massacre and
lived in the Cypress Street house. Earle and Valeria were in a large upstairs bedroom that had been Antonia's before she moved out to live with her father,
shortly after November 3. (While Earle and Valeria were there, the Klan, or
someone, drove by shooting at my house.) Alex stayed with us at Cypress Street
for a while, bunking with Phillip. Finally, he moved from the besieged house and
joined his father and sister. We all were under duress and none of us were saints.
From upstairs came the screams of marital fights. Earle and Valeria were drinking a lot. There were cigarette burns in the carpet. I was too steeped in my own
grief to pay much attention to the shouting, fighting, and drinking under my
roof. In any case, *political* sobriety usually reigned—except for Earle's rare lapse
at the courthouse on June 16.

In the midst of all the tumult of that day, when he was unable to get to a bathroom, Earle took a leak outside the courthouse between two parked cars. A policeman caught him and threatened arrest for indecent exposure. "Do you see all

these people demonstrating?" Earle said to the officer. "I'm their lawyer. If you arrest me they're going to riot." The policeman called his captain who said not to arrest Earle. Later Dale teased, "Earle, how would 'CWP lawyer flashes' look on the front page of the *Greensboro Daily News*?" We were social pariahs already, so Earle's slip, smacking of old-world peasantry, could not have further damaged our collective reputation.

JURY SELECTION

Potential jurors were exposed to a case that was portrayed by the prosecution, the defense, Greensboro officials, and mainstream media as, at once, a shootout between two extremist groups *and* a contest of ideologies. The front-page headline in the *Washington Post* of June 22, 1980, read "Klansmen vs. Communists: Their Battle of Beliefs in Greensboro Led Inexorably to Violence, Bloodshed."[20] And calculatingly dishonest was a short article in *Time*. "Who fired first remains unclear and a key issue at the trial, but when police had finally restored order," begins one sentence.[21] Since the videotapes clearly show the first shot coming from the Klan caravan and the fact was never in dispute, no conscientious writer, editor, or magazine could have made such an error.

Racists took refuge in anticommunism. Shortly before the June 16 start of the trial, defendant Coleman Pridmore attended a Klan rally in Walkertown at which a twenty-foot cross was burned and shots were fired at four black men. Pridmore told the crowd that he was confident of acquittal in the Klan trial, but, if found guilty and sentenced to die, he would consider his death penalty as dying for his country in the fight against communism.[22] Column inches that might have been devoted to the Klan's long history of terrorizing, torturing, and murdering people were used instead to reinforce anticommunism. The Klan and Nazis became standard bearers for the "correct" ideology. In one news photo, they are shown picnicking on the plaza, piously bowing their heads and saying grace at table during the lunch recess of court proceedings.[23]Allowed to float on this ideological plane, the Klan and Nazis faced nothing so mundane as a trial for murder. The trial was not about the cold-blooded shooting of human beings, and both sides in the litigation were careful to seat a jury that would stick with the program.

Patricia MacKay, a private investigator from California, covered the trial for some alternative media including the *Guardian*, *Liberation News Service*, and *the North Carolina Anvil*. Unlike the mainstream media, MacKay brought a rich factual background into her narrative, exposed the conflict between the official story and the facts, and asked significant questions about the case. "It remains to be seen whether people can be gunned down for their political beliefs only to have the killers go free," she wrote presciently at the start of the trial.[24]

It took two weeks to seat four jurors. By the third week of jury selection, 2,250 Guilford County residents had been summoned by Superior Court Judge Long. MacKay wrote:

> The prosecutors, District Attorneys Mike Schlosser, Rick Greeson and Jim Coman, ask each prospective juror if "the fact that the alleged victims were communists who held views which are anti-American and repugnant to all of us would make it difficult for you to find the defendants guilty." Or the D.A. asks, "Would the fact the alleged victims tried to organize labor unions and wanted to overthrow the government make it impossible for you to convict defendants."
>
> Since voir dire or questioning of the jury is traditionally the time to educate the jurors as to how they should look at the case, it appears that the prosecution is not seriously trying to convict the defendants....
>
> A true advocate for the victims probably would ask jurors, "Would the fact that you saw people murdered in cold blood on TV cause you to find the defendants guilty?"[25]

MacKay figured that the prosecution had given up on capital punishment when the D.A. selected jurors who said that they would be unable to impose the death penalty in the sentencing phase of the trial. She wondered if the D.A. was seriously trying to get any murder convictions at all when he selected a juror who stated the defendants were not guilty of murder and the fact that the victims were communists would make it hard for him to be open-minded. Prosecutors asked prospective jurors whether they or any members of their immediate family fought against the Communists in Vietnam: if so, would they be unable to convict defendants for killing communists in Greensboro.[26]

A prosecution team acting in good faith would never have admitted jurors who were frank about their prejudices against communists and their sympathy for the defendants. With many of the allotted eighty-four peremptory challenges still remaining, prosecutors accepted:

> a woman who said "I do not think the six defendants did it" and whose view of communists was "they don't believe in God" and "they're against the concepts of what I believe."[27]
>
> a man who told the court he had been the next-door neighbor to Joe Grady when he was a youngster growing up in Winston-Salem.[28] (Grady was a prominent Klansmen and an associate of some of the Klan and Nazis who went to Greensboro on November 3.)

a man who expressed his belief that "it is a lesser crime to kill a communist than to kill other people."[29]

a refugee from the Cuban revolution who said of the CWP, "they need publicity and a martyr and they need to project that they have many more people than they actually have." Calling the Ku Klux Klan "patriotic" and the Nazis "strongly patriotic," this potential juror went on to become foreman of the jury.[30]

Three of the above four actually ended up on the jury. The "lesser crime" theorist did not sit on the jury, but his philosophy certainly prevailed.

Defense attorneys selected only white people and only whites with conservative political beliefs; nearly all had less than a college education. Defense lawyers denied rejecting blacks out of hand, but that is what they did.

All these years I have wondered about the supposedly random jury pool in this ideologically charged trial. Juror number six was Octavio R. Manduley, an expatriated Cuban, who was selling heavy machinery in 1959 when Castro came to power, and was part of the counterrevolutionary group, the 20th of May.[31] He continued his anti-Castro and anticommunist work with the 20th of May for four years after emigrating to Florida in 1960.[32] That organization was involved in the CIA-sponsored Bay of Pigs invasion, and Manduley, a U.S. army veteran, may have participated in the assault. How convenient it was in the propaganda war to have an educated anticommunist diehard, one implicated in anticommunist forays conducted by the U.S. government, lead an all-white jury selected for its anticommunist views.

On July 13, 1980, against this backdrop of strident anticommunism, we held a forum at the Fairview Recreation Center with CWP leader Jerry Tung as the main speaker. Jerry's appearance in Greensboro occasioned careful security preparations by us. As one reporter described, "all persons attending the forum were searched and scanned with a metal detector. CWP members equipped with two-way radios were on patrol outside while members armed with large wooded poles and nightsticks kept watch inside. . . . CWP members also patrolled the streets leading to the center to give advance warning of any persons believed by the CWP to be potential troublemakers."[33]

A STUNNING REVELATION

In the middle of jury selection, on July 14 (my forty-second birthday) came stunning revelations from *Greensboro Record* reporter Martha Woodall, who talked to the Klan and Nazis and investigated several matters. The U.S. Bureau of Alcohol, Tobacco and Firearms (BATF) had an undercover agent operating in the

Nazi Party in Winston-Salem for four months prior to November 3.[34] The agent, Bernard Butkovich, knew at least two days in advance about the planned Klan/Nazi caravan. According to Wood and other Nazis in his unit, Butkovich was at a November 1 planning session in Wood's garage. He "listened for most of the meeting and left shortly after former Forsyth County leader Roland Wayne Wood decided that his group would participate in the Klan-Nazi demonstration planned to counter the CWP's 'Death to the Klan' rally."[35] Butkovich returned the following evening to make sure the Nazis would be in the caravan to Greensboro the next day. "Although Wood said Butkovich told him that he would go with the group he did not appear the morning of Nov. 3."[36]

Among those at the meeting in Wood's garage on November 1, 1979, were Harold Covington, head of the U.S. Nazi party; Gorrell Pierce, from the Federated Knights of the Ku Klux Klan; and a representative of Virgil Griffin's Invisible Empire. Early in the evening, the press heard talk about rival Klansman Joe Grady's criticism of the Klan/Nazi alliance. When TV crews and reporters had left, the November 3 motorcade was planned.

Butkovich, normally assigned to an ATF office in Cleveland, made contact with Covington at a White Power rally in Parma, Ohio, the previous June. After the rally, Butkovich earned Covington's approval by helping the Nazis fight militant Jewish protesters who stormed into a Nazi press conference and disrupted it. Covington put Butkovich in touch with Wood. By the middle of July, shortly after China Grove, Butkovich, posing as a truck driver transferred by his company to Winston-Salem, became a functioning part of Wood's unit, albeit with erratic attendance and suspicion-arousing behavior. Butkovich took part in the formation of the United Racist Front on September 22, 1979, in Louisburg, North Carolina.[37] A pact to attack the CWP was made at that meeting.

The Nazis claimed Butkovich repeatedly urged them to do illegal acts. Before November 3, Butkovich urged the Nazis to get special selector switches to convert their guns from semiautomatic to automatic, offered to procure explosives, including hand grenades, and proposed to train the Nazis in bomb making and assassination techniques. He pushed for killing Klan rival Joe Grady.

Right after the killings on November 3, 1979, Butkovich tried to get Nazi R. L. Shannon, who was not in the caravan, to harbor and transport to safety Caudle, Fowler, and McBride, participants in the attack who were being sought by the police. Caudle claimed that he saw Butkovich the afternoon of November 3 at the home of his stepson, Claude McBride Jr. At that time, both Caudle and McBride were fugitives. Butkovich was looking for another fugitive, Jack Fowler, and told Caudle that he wanted to take Fowler to a farm in Ohio to hide out. Caudle and McBride subsequently turned themselves in. Although all charges were dropped against Caudle, his sixteen-year-old stepson was indicted and faced trial. (As it turned out, the youth was put with a group of indicted Klan and Nazis who were not tried.) Several days after Butkovich's keen concern about Fowler, Fowler surrendered to FBI agents in Chicago.

More of Butkovich's dealings soon came to light. On November 4, 1979, when Roland Wayne Wood, arrested immediately after the murders, was in police custody, an officer led Butkovich to an interview room with Wood and left them alone. The officer told Wood that he did not know who the man was but that he claimed to be in Wood's unit. Wood alleged that "Butkovich asked him if he should burn down Wood's house and make the CWP appear responsible."[38] Butkovich was trying to get him to issue orders, Wood said, by telling him Caudle, McBride, and Fowler awaited his orders. Later that afternoon, Wood was interrogated by Police Detective H. G. Belvin and Special FBI Agent Thomas Brereton. Wood's brother Rodger was present at the session. Rodger said that his brother pointed out Butkovich in a picture and told his interrogators, "This is the guy who came to see me." Both brothers insisted Wood mentioned Butkovich's name more than once during a long interrogation. Butkovich's name does not appear in any police transcripts of interviews conducted with Wood.[39]

After his appearance at the Greensboro Police Department on November 4, Butkovich vanished.[40] He went back to work at the Cleveland BATF office and, when called by reporters, declined comment. Though they would not discuss his assignment, the FBI and the BATF acknowledged Butkovich was an ATF agent who operated in Winston-Salem and Greensboro in the summer and fall of 1979. The BATF said that their policies forbade provocation or entrapment, that they monitored Butkovich closely, and that he did nothing improper.[41]

Butkovich's role in the crimes of November 3 implicated the BATF for whom he worked and strongly suggested a compromised FBI because of the routine coordination between these two branches. Indeed, the relationship between the BATF and the FBI was "as good as it's ever been," according to the BATF's top official.[42]

The worms clamber out of the can—in denial. The Greensboro police said that Butkovich did not inform them of the planned Klan/Nazi caravan after the November 1 Nazi meeting and denied knowing about Butkovich's undercover assignment until after the shootings. Schlosser, after a day of "no comment," denied knowing about Butkovich's infiltration of the Forsyth County unit of the National Socialist Party or of the agent's attendance at the November 1 meeting until "shortly after the shootings."[43] Schlosser did not intend to call Butkovich as a witness in the state trial. Captain B. L. Thomas, in charge of the homicide investigation for the GPD, stated that he had not heard about the ATF infiltration of the Nazis until November 3. He told the press that he did not believe a transcript was made of Butkovich's interview with Wood on November 4.[44] Police Chief Swing, claiming to be one of the last to learn of the federal agent's contact with the Nazis, commented, "If they had thought it was important, they would have told me."[45] U.S. Attorney H. M. Michaux denied that he was aware of Butkovich until informed about him by a reporter some days before the matter was published. Director of the FBI in North Carolina, Robert Pence, denied his bureau knew of the infiltration.[46]

I remember several of us met in an effort to figure out what was going on when we read Woodall's story on July 14. We discussed a press statement for the following day. We thought the information about Butkovich may have surfaced because of a falling out of thieves: each villain, under some pressure, was out to save his own skin and ready to rat on his comrades. The government used right-wing groups covertly but was ready to slap them back if they became too feisty or threatened to expose the game. Some Klan and Nazis indeed might receive a "slap on the wrist" in the state trial, we said. A small punishment could serve the larger cover-up and would remind the Klan and Nazis about who really held the reins of power. We predicted the Klan and Nazis either would go absolutely free or else receive mild, token punishment.

Two weeks after the Butkovich story broke, then-ATF director G. R. Dickerson talked to the press about his bureau's policies. Deep undercover operations such as Butkovich's were very rare, he said. Butkovich was authorized from the top and was closely monitored by the BATF. Authorization is not given just for general intelligence-gathering purposes, the bureau chief claimed, but only when there is good information of a specific violation of gun control laws.[47] The official BATF line was "public safety is paramount. We make an arrest at the earliest possible moment."[48] It is difficult to square this assertion with the fact that "Butkovich made no arrests during the time he was involved with the Nazis in Winston-Salem."[49] Supposedly, ATF agents were barred from participating in illegal acts and were sworn to observe high ethical and moral standards.[50] The BATF claimed everything Butkovich did in North Carolina was legal.

The denials of foreknowledge by local and state authorities were contradicted by statements by ATF agents. Woodall wrote that Dickerson told her that "when the ATF undertakes a major undercover operation, the bureau notifies the U.S. attorney, FBI, the prosecutor and police in the area."[51] From ATF's Office of Criminal Enforcement, Assistant Director Miles Keathley told Woodall that the bureau's instructions called for notifying those agencies before the start of an investigation.[52] The FBI, which had conducted its own investigation of the CWP shortly before November 3, was certainly apprised of BATF agent Butkovich's penetration of the Nazis. The truth is that each agency knew what the other was doing, but the public did not know what either was doing.

Important information suggesting government complicity with and cover up of crimes was unearthed. We felt, however, that if we did not call attention to its significance, it would be buried and rendered useless. We followed up the revelations about the BATF with protests and acts of civil disobedience. On July 23, 1980, party supporters coordinated a series of demonstrations at ATF offices in New York, Chicago, Denver, San Francisco, Los Angeles, Baltimore, Charlotte, Detroit, Philadelphia, and Washington.[53] Some of these were merely pickets, but in New York, as people marched outside, seven people took over a BATF office, barricaded themselves in, and were arrested after several hours. Five demonstrators were arrested in Chicago. The police attacked them when they got off the elevator of the floor housing the Treasury Department.[54] In North Carolina, Marty and others demonstrated at the main ATF office in Charlotte, targeting John Westra, the special agent in charge of that office, in their protest. Attorney H. M. Michaux was greeted with accusations as he entered his office at the federal courthouse in Greensboro. In Raleigh, Dale and Nelson interrupted Governor Hunt's news conference, accused him of involvement in the Greensboro killings, and called him a murderer.

DALE TEARS UP A REPORT, THE DISTRICT ATTORNEY GOES AFTER NELSON, AND MARTY IS GAGGED

On July 31, 1980, the CWP staged an action at a Greensboro City Council meeting to denounce the police report, the McManis report, and the entire official cover-up. Nelson, Willena, Dale, myself, and about a dozen others marched into the chambers ceremoniously. A few people stationed themselves at the back of the room where they unfurled a large CWP banner—a brooding conscience—to hover over the proceedings. At one point, when either Nelson or the chorus behind him said something, the mayor ordered Nelson to shut up. Hardly had council members resumed their business when Dale and I rushed forward like two furies—"Mayor Melvin, you have the blood of our husbands on your hands. This council is covering up the truth about the November 3rd murders. What about Dawson? What about Butkovich?" we said. Dale picked up some copies of the McManis report before the mayor and began tearing them up saying, "this is a whitewash and a bunch of lies." We were both in the council's face with our accusations, and then the police were all over us. Captain L. S. Gibson twisted my arm behind my back. I cried out, "Let go of my arm, you bastard." Still resisting, Dale and I were removed from the chamber.

We spent the next few days in the county jail. The metal springs of the cots could be felt through a tissue-thin mattress, making it too uncomfortable to sleep at night. Although it was summer, I was chilled and shivered constantly. I was arrested wearing a cotton sundress that bared my shoulders, and the jail was cold and damp. The day after our arrests, news reached me and Dale in jail that Nelson and Marty had been arrested in Governmental Plaza. Both were charged with disorderly conduct—Nelson with resisting arrest, and Marty with carrying a concealed weapon. With opening arguments and testimony in the Klan trial about to begin, the district attorney's office was going after Nelson with a vengeance. Schlosser tried to raise Nelson's bond from $15,000 to $100,000 on the felonious riot charge stemming from November Third. The arrest in the plaza came about, essentially, because Nelson made a speech. Shortly after this latest arrest, at the hearing about raising his bond, Nelson *again* was charged— this time for allegedly assaulting a deputy sheriff with his elbow when he was taken from the courtroom. At one point, Nelson had a possible $200,000 in bail as a contingency over his release. Judge Elreta Alexander-Ralston, who had known Nelson since he was a student at A & T in the late sixties, reduced one ridiculous $100,000 bond (for the elbow assault charge) to $200. Superior Court Judge D. Marsh McLelland, later in the week, denied Schlosser's request to raise the felonious riot charge bond to $100,000.

Proceedings on August 4, 1980, the day of opening arguments in the Klan trial, were scarcely underway when Marty Nathan rose and declared, "This trial is a sham and a farce. The U.S. government conspired with the Klan and the Nazis to kill five members of the Communist Workers Party and to murder my husband."[55] Judge James Long rapped his gavel and told Marty to be quiet. When she refused, the judge ordered her gagged. She continued speaking out until three bailiffs closed her mouth with white adhesive tape. Long then told her that she was in contempt of court and had the gag removed to allow Marty to speak in her defense before he imposed the sentence. "My defense is that my husband was murdered on November Third and that this trial is a sham," she responded.[56] She continued in that vein: the court was not fair and impartial, the D.A. made statements damaging to the prosecution, the jurors were sympathetic to the defendants, CWP supporters were being harassed, etc. The judge again ordered Marty to be gagged. "When she spoke through the tape across her mouth," Patricia MacKay wrote, "a bailiff clamped his hand over her mouth, while she was held by two other bailiffs. She was sentenced to thirty days in jail. As soon as she was dragged off to jail, Floris

Cauce, widow of César Cauce, stood up and restated what Nathan had said. . . . She was also sentenced to thirty days."[57]

A few weeks later, Tom Clark was dragged into court after failing to comply with a subpoena. He defied the judge and adamantly refused to testify.[58] Asked by the judge if he had anything to say in his defense before he was to be sentenced for contempt of court, Tom replied that he had nothing but contempt for the court, and was sentenced to thirty days in jail. Marty and Floris were nearing the end of their sentence when they learned that Tom had just been locked up. All three served the full thirty days on contempt of court charges.

The charges from this period leading to the start of the Klan trial were resolved as follows: Nelson was acquitted of the elbowing assault charge when Judge Alexander-Ralston heard the case in September.[59] In October, she not only dismissed all charges against Nelson and Marty from the Governmental Plaza incident, but questioned the arrest procedure. "Alexander-Ralston ruled that the arrests on disorderly conduct charges were prompted solely by the fact that police objected to the content of Johnson's speech. The judge also dismissed a concealed weapons charge against Nathan on the grounds the gun was found during an illegal search of Nathan's handbag."[60]

Dale and I were found guilty of disrupting the city council meeting in July. Mayor Melvin and Captain Gibson (the same Gibson who gave Dawson the parade permit and then assured Nelson of the security of the anti-Klan march) testified against us. We said that we were emotionally upset at the city government's cover-up of the conspiracy to kill our husbands and wanted the city council to acknowledge the truth. The judge told us not to discuss our politics in our defense.[61] Judge Alexander-Ralston gave us a sixty-day deferred sentence and said the convictions would be removed from our records if we promised not to disrupt any public meetings in the interim: we refused to promise. The judge lectured, "these revolutionary movements must be ready to pay the cost."[62] Two months and many struggles later, a sentencing judge ordered us to pay court costs plus a $25 fine.[63] Charges arising from the opening of jury selection in June were also disposed of that fall. Three demonstrators, Tom Clark, James Mapp, and Willena Cannon, were found guilty of behaving in a rude and riotous way outside the courtroom. The highest fine went to Willena who paid $25 plus court costs.[64]

DAWSON'S ROLE UNCOVERED

In August 1980, there were further revelations about Edward Dawson. The reader may recall that within days after the assault, police admitted that they showed a copy of the parade permit to a man who identified himself as a Klans-men and gave his name as Edward Dawson. The police administrative report, written a few weeks after the murders, mentions a ten o'clock briefing on the morning of November 3 at which Cooper advised police that armed Klansmen were gathering on Randleman Road and planned to follow the parade route. But the source of Cooper's information is not mentioned in the police report.[65] Now, as the state murder trial was to begin, it was established that Klansman Eddie Dawson was "both a police informant and a participant in planning and pro-moting the Klan's presence at the demonstration."[66] Dawson was the source of Cooper's intelligence information at the police briefing on the morning of No-vember 3, 1979.

A New Jersey native and longtime Greensboro resident with a general con-tractor business, Dawson had been active in the North Carolina Klan for nearly two decades. He served a nine-month prison sentence for shooting into a black community in neighboring Alamance County in 1967. Along the way, in his ca-reer as a Klansman, he had worked as a paid informant for the FBI.

Dawson's role in the events of November 3, 1979, was key, according to his own statements and those of several Klansmen. He was a leader in planning and organizing the caravan's mission, and he directed it on the fatal morning. At an October rally in Lincolnton County, Dawson made a fiery half-hour speech urg-ing members of the Invisible Empire to come to the CWP's "Death to the Klan" rally to confront the communists.[67]

Dawson met with Griffin and Pridmore in a predawn meeting on November 3, only hours before the murders. He drove them to the Florida Street Shopping Center, near the site listed on the parade permit as the termination of the CWP demonstration.[68]

At 8:30 on the morning of the rally, Dawson made contact with his control agent, Detective Jerry Cooper. He was at the Klan and Nazi gathering place at the house of Klansman Brent Fletcher on Randleman Road, but he left temporarily a little before 10:00 A.M., saying that he was expecting a phone call and needed to get some pills for a back problem. He again reported to Cooper, who shared the "reli-able and up-to-date" information about the Klan's movements at the 10:00 A.M. po-lice briefing. Dawson was back at Fletcher's house somewhat after 10:00 A.M. He admitted that the Klan and Nazis discussed the caravan's route and destination around the kitchen table on the morning of November 3.[69] "Several Klansmen at the house said Dawson continually rushed them. 'He kept looking at his watch. He kept telling us to hurry and rushing us around.'"[70] When an eight-car caravan fi-nally left the rendezvous point at about 10:30 A.M., Dawson was in the lead car. The caravan stopped for a few moments shortly after 11:00 A.M. on a highway exit ramp—I-85 and U.S. 220—to pick up a car of Klansmen who had gone to breakfast. Detective Cooper, following the caravan, took pictures of it. Dawson ordered the car, "which contained a trunkload of weapons, moved from the rear of the caravan further forward, Griffin and other Klansmen said."[71] All these movements were tracked by the police who claimed to be surprised the Klansmen were "moving before we anticipated."[72] With Dawson still in the lead, the now nine-car caravan turned the corner on to Lee Street at 11:17 A.M. and arrived within moments at the unprotected Everitt and Carver intersection.

Dawson assembled and delivered the hit squad. The police failed to intervene, in spite of the intelligence given to them by their informant, because they were colluding with the Klan and Nazis.

Neither prosecution nor defense lawyers called Dawson as a witness in the state trial. (Dawson would later say that he was illegally pressured by police not to testify.) If the jury would not get to entertain any questions about a scenario in which Dawson, lead Klansman and police informant, had a key role on November Third, then you have to ask what the Klan trial could really be about. "Dawson is the second person to be identified publicly as either a police informant or agent among the rightists during preparations for the November confrontation," said *Greensboro Daily News* reporter Lindsey Gruson, referring also to BATF agent Butkovich, planted among the Nazis "supposedly to check on firearms violations."[73]

THE GARDEN BOMB THROWER

Dale and I planned to go to New York to take part in a *Serve Notice* campaign around the Democratic National Convention at Madison Square Garden in August. The CWP was serving notice on the capitalist system and warned that it would crash the Garden party. Our friends in North Carolina advised us to lend our moral authority to the campaign but to avoid arrest. I agreed with that advice. Shortly after arriving in New York, I phoned my parents.

"What are you doing? Signe, Dad and I are worried sick about you."

"Look, Ma, please don't be," I tried to reassure her. "I'm not going to get in trouble. I won't get arrested. Everyone's looking out for me."

"What, your party is looking out for you? It's ruining your life. I'm sick about it, just sick. You're my child."

"I'm not a child, Ma."

"You're not a child, I didn't say you were a child, but you're *my* child, you'll *always* be *my* child. How can I not be worried sick when my child is widowed and jailed and goes around screaming like a lunatic. I just don't want they should hurt you or arrest you. I want you to promise me you'll stay out of it. Whatever you're planning to do, don't do it," my mother's anguished voice poured out over the phone. "I don't know what you're planning to do, but please, my darling, stay out of it."

"There's some protesting going on and I have to take part in it," I admitted. "But I'm not planning to do anything illegal, honestly, Mother. You have to try not to worry about me, please. We've all agreed that Dale and I should not get arrested again."

I was not planning to take part in civil disobedience. I would just be a face in the crowd of demonstrators. I tried to reassure my mother, and I arranged to meet my parents at the home of a Brooklyn comrade in a few days. "Goodbye, Ma," I said, "I'll see you very soon."

"I hope you'll see me very soon," my mother said as her parting shot, still very agitated. "I hope I'll see you very soon, too. I hope I'll see you in the flesh, my own flesh and blood. The next time I see you I want to see *you* and not your picture in the newspaper. I don't want to pick up the *Post* and see my daughter's picture on the front page. That's not how I want to see my Signe, the sweetest girl in the world, on the front page of the *New York Post* the first thing when I open my eyes in the morning."

My mother definitely had a flare for melodrama. To think that she would next see my face on the front page of the morning edition, or any edition, of a rag like the *New York Post*—it was her exaggerated way of expressing her concern for me, under no circumstances a real possibility.

The headline of the *New York Post* on August 15, 1980, read, "Here she is: the Garden 'bomb-thrower.'" The face of Fay Burke's daughter was splashed across the front page. I am holding a rifle and look, in my field jacket and floppy hat, like something from a Hemingway novel. The picture was taken from the funeral procession a week after November Third, but the caption said it was from the anti-Klan rally (when, in truth, the anti-Klan rally found me standing in a circle singing, weaponless. Oh well, why should a newspaper bother with such details?) Another mug shot, identifying me as a "gun-totin' widow," showed me being nearly strangled by Secret Service men at Madison Square Garden. My mother could see how "security personnel grab Signe Waller by the neck, seconds after she exploded firecrackers only feet away from the President." To this fate had come Signe Burke, the sweet little girl sitting on a stoop in Brooklyn. "Nini Beep"—my name for myself as a child just learning to talk—had turned into a bomb thrower in quotes. The quotes were necessary because the bomb was actually a firecracker, which does not generate nearly as much interest on a front page headline.

I did not try to deceive Fay and Ted. In the excitement and confusion of all the protest activity, a disjunction developed between what North Carolina and New York comrades expected of Dale and me. Once there, I wanted to go with the flow. The moral authority of the widows was undeniable. Who better to challenge the news blackout and get the national media to put the spotlight on Greensboro and the cover-up of officially sanctioned murder there? Going from protest to protest, I somehow became available for the big mission—it was unthinkable not to be.

I have the most unnewsworthy memories associated with that New York trip: Dale and me staying with Asian American comrades—a family with several small kids and both parents were active party members—in a crowded apartment with toys all over a varnished parquet floor, half-washed diapers in one sink, dirty dishes in another, sheer havoc and frustration for the parents, surely a marriage at risk. We bopped in and out of that apartment, the last place in the world we wanted to go to rest after marching, chanting, and running all over New York— sleep? shower? Forget it.

I remember how I loved and admired Shelley Wong of the Greensboro Justice Fund as I watched her—a beautiful, gentle, and unassuming person—take the lead one time in doing agit-prop with a bullhorn. How Dale and I laughed when we were accidentally separated from our CWP-assigned bodyguard in the subway. I remember the campus of Columbia University, where a bunch of us sat on the grass after one of the protest actions—was it the one at Cartiers, Tavern on the Green, or the Plaza Hotel? We sat outside Avery Library summing up the day's activities. My first husband, Carl, studied art history at Avery, and I spent many hours reading there. How very strange it felt to be revisiting—not as an academic but as a rebel—the institution that awarded me a doctorate in philosophy eleven years earlier. Did the students walking by recognize that I had been one of them? Would their graduate education lead them to the conclusion that capitalism must be overthrown?

I also recall mad trips all over Brooklyn with six or seven other people in the car, for reasons now forgotten, and wondering how, with wrecked nerves, I was designated the driver over unfamiliar and deserted streets and freeways of an urban netherworld at 3:00 A.M., where to get out of the car probably meant dying and to remain in the car certainly meant tormenting the bladder beyond endurance.

Near the Garden, on a street lined with protesting groups, I was helped onto a flatbed truck by punks in tight black clothes with safety pins in their ears. I accepted their invitation to make an impromptu speech at a Rock Against Racism rally and shouted over the din of the street about Greensboro and about how we must resist being led into world war or fascism. I remember the sleazy detective, after I was taken to jail, fuming cynically about the vile human excrement around him—never suspecting that he himself might be a prime example. I remember well my release from jail. I was cast out into the dark New York night and walked the streets not knowing where I was, terrified that I would be mugged. Then, in-comprehensibly, an hour later, I was at party headquarters. More pleasurable moments followed. Hyper and exhausted, I dined in Chinatown at four o'clock in the morning with the CWP press officer and Blanche McCrary Boyd. We were all excited, intense, and hungry.

"GREENSBORO, MIAMI, PAYBACK TIME!" was the main slogan for the series of CWP protests over several days. Thousands of people were involved in one aspect or another. North Carolina Attorney General Rufus Edmisten, one of the security chiefs for the Democratic National Convention, admitted that secu-rity personnel were more worried about the CWP than any other group.[74] Be-cause Hunt announced that he planned to infiltrate any group deemed "extrem-ist," and because the North Carolina governor was recently embarrassed by the CWP, Dale and I knew the Secret Service were keeping tabs on us. One time we were protesting inside the Plaza Hotel in a crowded area, and I found myself nose to nose with a Secret Service agent. I had taken care to disguise my ap-pearance with makeup and an upswept hairdo. I could have passed for an ele-gant hotel guest. The agent stared at me blankly and went about his business. I resumed agitating in another spot.

I was very nervous in the hours before "crashing the garden party." I was to set off firecrackers at an appropriate moment. A party comrade had gone to some trouble to find firecrackers that would be loud and reliable, but the technical specs were lost on me. Dale and I had press passes that allowed us to enter Madison Square Garden—the first hurdle. Once in, I spent a long time trying to position myself as close to the stage as I could. I pretended to be an enthusiastic Democratic Party supporter and cheered on the speakers. It was a real challenge: in a brief teenage phase, my heart had been set on becoming an actress. Now I was thinking how hard it is to be someone else. I kept up this facade until it was Carter's turn to speak, and by that time, I was within fifty feet of the stage. My hands were trembling and my heart was thumping as I prepared to set off the firecrackers with a lit cigarette. A nonsmoker, I had to appear casual about smok-ing. People were jammed together, and I wanted to take some safety precautions. Despite hands shaking so badly that I could hardly light a match, I managed to get a cigarette going and used its light on a string of high velocity firecrackers in a plastic film canister that I was carrying. I quickly placed the canister under a nearby chair so that the sparks would be contained and not injure anyone. The firecracker went off. I shouted, "The U.S. Government helped the Klan and Nazis kill my husband and four other members of the Communist Workers Party." In the middle of his speech, President Carter, momentarily dismayed by the terrific noise, reacted by referring to "the late, former Vice President 'Hubert Horatio Hornblower—er, Humphrey.'"[75]

In no time at all, I was wrestled to the ground by the Secret Service. I was grabbed around the neck (something I might have forgotten without the graphic news photo) and brought elsewhere in the building to be searched by a female police officer. I was detained inside the Garden for what seemed a very long time, and, when finally I was led outside to be taken to the police station, I made the noisiest exit I could, shouting to curious bystanders about the government's complicity in the Greensboro Massacre.

In another part of the arena, minutes after I set off the firecracker, Dale stood up on a news desk, held up a portrait of Bill, and screamed, "Avenge the murders of the Communist Workers Party 5!" Somehow she managed to get away by landing on top of the Secret Service agent who tussled with her. She went to another part of the Garden and held a six-minute press conference, after which she walked out onto the street and disappeared. Another comrade who unfurled a huge *Greensboro, Miami, Payback Time* banner inside the Garden also avoided arrest. That I ended up in police custody was, I suppose, *my* payback for the anguish I caused my parents.

Outside the Garden on 34th Street and 8th Avenue, shortly before I set off the firecrackers, the CWP was battling the New York police. The CWP sent at least nineteen policemen to the hospital as a result of the street fight.[76] The police managed to arrest seventeen people and took them to the Midtown South precinct. I think that is where I was taken to be booked also, and, if so, I was there while the police took bloody revenge on their prisoners in some secluded chamber of the precinct. At the time, I was not aware of what was going on.

ENTER A BATTLE GRAVELY AND CONDUCT YOUR TRIUMPH LIKE A FUNERAL

In 1992, while gathering interviews for this book, I talked to Elliot Fratkin (married by then to Marty Nathan). We were in Elliot's study in a country house in central Pennsylvania. Around us were artifacts of his trips to Kenya, his anthropology research, a computer. His book, *Surviving Drought and Development: Ariaal Pastoralists of Northern Kenya*—part of a Conflict and Social Change Series—is on a table in view. Leah Nathan, an infant when her father was killed, was now a tall, lanky teenager with a passion for horses. She was about to engage her equestrian skills and dropped into the room briefly to say something to Elliot. She left and I listened to Elliot's story.

Living in Baltimore in 1980, Elliot organized people to go to New York to serve notice with the CWP at the Democratic National Convention. "I was one of the people who was arrested and tortured for eight hours that night," he said. "We all knew that we would militantly march up to the Garden where the convention was being held, shout, make our case about the November Third murders—we knew that there would be people inside making our case for the publicity. And then we would disperse. But just as we did that, and the cops stood their line as we shouted, I also noticed that we had security people—not myself—with helmets and sticks, and somebody—one of us—threw a brick through a window, and that unleashed a police riot," Elliot said.[77] "It was deliberate and it was foolish of the party not to tell us, because I had brought young people, teenagers, who had never been to a demonstration before.

"I had a bullhorn—a big, expensive thing—and I didn't want to drop it. So I couldn't run. I turned around and I saw this cop running at me like a samurai, with a big stick in the air. I stopped and said, 'Okay, you got me.' He clubbed me so hard I'm amazed I didn't go unconscious. I was covered with blood. They threw me in a police car, handcuffed me to another guy, and took us to the Midtown South station. For the next eight hours they tortured us.

"I was standing near the door. So every time the police came in—and we had to stand—they would hit me on the head as they came in, kind of getting ready for everybody else. If you were black, you were in particular trouble. A comrade from Washington—a black guy—was standing next to me. I was standing by a wall. It was a chain fence wall and I was handcuffed to it, I couldn't move. And they started clubbing his head in. And I put my leg out to cover his head, kind of leaned over as much as I could to take the blows. And they said, 'Oh, you want some of this, you can have some of this.' And then they started on me. I had a Jewish policeman come up to me and say, 'If you think just cause you're Jewish I'm not gonna hit you, you're wrong,'" Elliot recalled. "One guy I was handcuffed to for a while had a broken wrist in his handcuffs—they just kept at him until I thought his wrist was going to fall off. People had fractured ribs and broken hands and broken heads. I'm amazed nobody died. And I think the police probably are very skilled at this. The more I think about it, the more I'm sure this is a routine thing that happens in police stations. They know how to beat you without killing you, and they do a very good job," he added, laughing softly. "And sometimes they *do* beat you to death.

"About 3:30 in the morning a medic came in, a Puerto Rican medic, and they stopped for a while. I said to him, 'Listen, they're killing us in here. You've got to stop this.' He didn't say a word. And he certainly didn't treat us.

"At four o'clock a new shift came in. These guys were all fresh. 'Are these the shits that sent our guys to the hospital?' they said, because, mind you, during that riot, we had kids who were beating up cops with lead pipes. So they started in again for another three hours. It was light out when they took us to the hospital, to the police section of Bellevue. But they didn't stop then. There was a black guy, Frankie, in front of me. Two cops came in and started moving him into a room. I thought they would kill him. But, fortunately, a nurse saw this, a white nurse, and said, 'Not in my hospital, you're not going to do that.' She told the cops to get out, and that saved Frankie. I got sutured. They gave me seven great big stitches where they could have given me forty-five, and no anesthetic. They didn't numb it, just stitched it. I have holes in my head from this. I had post-traumatic shock just like war veterans. If I heard a car door slam, I'd get very nervous. And I'd wake up screaming in the middle of the night.

"In any case, when we got out we were party heroes. We had a lot of support from our comrades. And I'll tell you, that was very important, as it must have been for you," Elliot said, looking at me, "that so many people helped you in so many ways and gave you what you needed. That was a very nice thing about the organization.

"But two weeks later, damned if the party hadn't organized another demonstration in Brooklyn to take on the police over the murder of a fourteen-year-old. I was in that march. And then in Philadelphia two weeks later. We were marching on police stations all over the place, and I was becoming more and more apprehensive about things."

Looking at the DNC and subsequent events retrospectively, Elliot concluded that the DNC was the party's revenge. "I think it was guilt that the New York people had about Greensboro—you have suffered so much; we have to suffer too. We were lashing out in frustration and anger," he said, "targeting the police and showing how tough we were. In a way, we had to stand up or the cops and the state would have unleashed more Greensboro's. But it also spelled the beginning of the end for us as an organization. We lost jobs in the mills and elsewhere, and we also gave up a lot of our grassroots work. In a few more years, we ceased being a militant working-class organization altogether, and more and more party members entered the mainstream, including myself. I am proud of my work with the party. I feel like a combat veteran. But that doesn't mean I can't be critical," he concluded.

I returned to Greensboro, after the Democratic National Convention, to the mockery of justice that was the Klan/Nazi trial. The firecracker incident added something to my widow-heroine image. I was far from the Lao Tzu's maxim that one ought to enter a battle gravely and conduct one's triumph like a funeral. The actual trial was anticlimactic, but because the outcome of the 1980 state trial contributed to a political climate tolerant of hate crimes and acts of sociopathic violence, I tell the story in the following chapter. The state trial in 1980 aided the growth and respectability of the right wing in the eighties and nineties. It sanctioned right-wing terror—including (ironically) terror ostensibly targeting the government, like the 1995 Oklahoma City bombing, but actually bringing death and suffering to countless innocent human beings. Moreover, we were asked repeatedly how the people photographed, in broad daylight and in the act of committing murder, could be acquitted. Many people saw the television videotapes. They were used as a station signature on the nightly news. Consequently, I address the ignominious judicial event, anticlimactic though it may seem to me, for the benefit of the genuinely perplexed.

NOTES

1. Associated Press, "Covington's Strong Vote Stuns GOP," *Greensboro Record*, 8 May 1980, A1.
2. William March, "Justice Clears Police of Criminal Wrongdoing," *Greensboro Daily News*, 30 April 1980, A1.
3. "CWP Renews Cover-Up Charges," *Greensboro Daily News*, 1 May 1980.
4. McManis Associates, Inc., "Assessment of Planning and Operations of Greensboro, North Carolina Police Department for Demonstration of November 3, 1979" (Washington, D.C., May 1980), 10–11.
5. See William March, "Opinion: No Right to Halt Klan Nov. 3," *Greensboro Daily News*, 25 July 1980.
6. See Steve Berry, "6 CWP Members, 2 Klansmen Indicted on Rioting Charges," *Greensboro Daily News*, 3 May 1980; and "Eighth Held on Rioting Charges," *Greensboro Daily News*, 7 May 1980.
7. "Klan, Nazis Ask Evidence to Help Their Defense," *Greensboro Daily News*, 15 May 1980.
8. "Group Blasts Riot Counts against CWP Members," *Greensboro Daily News*, 14 May 1980; and "New Charges Said Disgraceful," *Carolina Peacemaker*, 17 May 1980, 1.
9. "CWP Head Plans Write-in Candidacy for Governor," *Greensboro Daily News*, 17 May 1980, A13. See also Jim Wicker, "CWP Leader Announces Bid for Governor," *Greensboro Record*, 16 May 1980.
10. "CWP Indicts Capitalist Judicial System," *Workers Viewpoint*, 23 June 1980.
11. See Patricia MacKay, "Political Ideology on Trial in Greensboro," *North Carolina Anvil*, 4 July 1980, 1.

12. Mark Pinsky, "6 Men Going on Trial in N.C. Klan Shooting," *Washington Star*, 15 June 1980.

13. "CWP Indicts Capitalist Judicial System," *Workers Viewpoint*, 23 June 1980.

14. See Associated Press, "Communists Say Influence Is Spreading," *Wilmington Morningstar*, 8 July 1980.

15. Jim Schlosser and Rick Stewart, "CWP Stirs Up Battle outside Courtroom," *Greensboro Record*, 16 June 1980.

16. Martha Woodall, "5 Communists Hear Arraignment Counts," *Greensboro Record*, 16 June 1980.

17. Patricia MacKay, "What's Behind Jury Selection Questions in Murder Trials," *North Carolina Anvil*, 27 June 1980, 5.

18. Schlosser and Stewart, "CWP Stirs Up Battle."

19. Woodall, "5 Communists Hear Arraignments Counts."

20. Nicholas Lemann, "Klansmen vs. Communists: Their Battle of Beliefs in Greensboro Led Inexorably to Violence, Bloodshed," *Washington Post*, 22 June 1980, A1.

21. "A Dare That Ignited a Slaugter," *Time*, 30 June 1980, 25.

22. "Shots Fired at Rally for Klansmen," (Raleigh) *News & Observer*, 16 June 1980.

23. See Rick Steward, "Picnics Brighten Days for Trial Defendants," *Greensboro Record*, 12 July 1980, front page, staff photo by Dave Nicholson. See also Martha Woodall, "Deaths Detour Wood in His Cause Pursuit," *Greensboro Record*, 25 March 1980. Wood told Woodall, "What I done wasn't a racial thing . . . it was communism versus freedom." In a previous statement to the reporter, Wood talked about killing "niggers and jews."

24. Patricia MacKay, "Klan/Nazi Murder Trial Starts Monday," *North Carolina Anvil*, 13 June 1980, 11.

25. MacKay, "What's Behind Jury Selection," 1.

26. MacKay, "What's Behind Jury Selection," 1.

27. Sylvia Johnson, "Parade of Jurors Favor Klan's Anti-communism," (Burlington, N.C.) *Times-News*, 2 July 1980.

28. Sylvia Johnson, "Trial Jury Search at Half-way Mark," (Burlington, N.C.) *Times-News*, 11 July 1980, 1B.

29. Johnson, "Parade of Jurors."

30. See Jim Wicker, "Man Who Fled Cuba in 1960 Is 6th Juror," *Greensboro Record*, 10 July 1980.

31. Wicker, "Man Who Fled Cuba."

32. Steve Berry, "Selection of Jury at Halfway Point," *Greensboro Daily News*, 11 July 1980, C2.

33. Eddie Marks, "Photographer at CWP Talk Forced Out," *Greensboro Daily News*, 14 July 1980, B5.

34. Martha Woodall, "Nazis Say Federal Agent Infiltrated Unit, Knew of Plans for Nov. 3 Motorcade," *Greensboro Record*, 14 July 1980, A1.

35. Woodall, "Nazis Say Federal Agent Infiltrated," A1.

36. Woodall, "Nazis Say Federal Agent Infiltrated," A1.

37. Woodall, "Nazis Say Federal Agent Infiltrated," A2.

38. Woodall, "Nazis Say Federal Agent Infiltrated," A2.

39. Woodall, "Nazis Say Federal Agent Infiltrated," A2.

40. Woodall, "Nazis Say Federal Agent Infiltrated," A2.

41. Martha Woodall, "Rules Differ for AFT Agents Involved in Undercover Work," *Greensboro Record*, 14 July 1980, A1, A3.

42. Martha Woodall, "Top ATF Officials Gave Infiltration OK," *Greensboro Record*, 28 July 1980, A2.

43. Martha Woodall, "Undercover Agent Gave Report to District Attorney," *Greensboro Record*, 15 July 1980, A1.

44. Woodall, "Undercover Agent Gave Report," A2.

45. Woodall, "Undercover Agent Gave Report," A2.

46. Stan Swofford and Steve Berry, "Police, FBI Said Unaware Nazis Infiltrated by Feds," *Greensboro Daily News*, 15 July 1980, A1, A9.

47. Woodall, "Top ATF Officials," A2.

48. Quoted here from Woodall, "Top ATF Officials," A2.

49. Woodall, "Top ATF Officials," A2.

50. Woodall, "Top ATF Officials," A2.

51. Woodall, "Top ATF Officials," A2.

52. Woodall, "Top ATF Officials," A2.

53. Rick Stewart, "CWP Staging Protests to Expose Agent's Role," *Greensboro Record*, 24 July 1980, B1.

54. See "Communists Arrested in 2 Cities," *Greensboro Record*, 24 July 1980, B1. This article says that the five arrested in Chicago were arrested "after a scuffle" with the police, but one of the five people who demonstrated and was arrested in the federal building that day told me that police attacked the group as they got off of the elevator.

55. Michael P. Massoglia, "Detective Says Nazi Fired Rifle," *Winston-Salem Journal*, 5 August 1980.

56. Quoted in Massoglia "Detective Says Nazi Fired Rifle."

57. Patricia MacKay, "Surprises Mark Opening Days of Murder Trial," *North Carolina Anvil*, 8 August 1980, 4.

58. See Steve Berry, "Defendant's 'Admission' Recounted," *Greensboro Daily News*, 29 August 1980, C2.

59. "CWP Leader Is Acquitted," *Greensboro Daily News*, 27 September 1980.

60. Martha Woodall, "Defense Questions Arrest Procedure in CWP Incident," *Greensboro Record*, 6 October 1980, B2.

61. Winston Cavin, "Judge Delays Sentencing," *Greensboro Daily News*, 7 October 1980.

62. Michael P. Massoglia, "Man Says He Doesn't Remember Firing Gun," *Winston-Salem Journal*, 7 October 1980; and "CWP's Sentences Postponed Monday," (Thomasville, N.C.) *Times*, 7 October 1980.

63. See "Waller and Sampson Are Handed Fines," *Greensboro Record*, 5 December 1980.

64. Stan Swofford, "CWP Members Fined for Trial Disruption," *Greensboro Daily News*, 15 October 1980, B3.

65. Swing, "An Administrative Report," 26.

66. Lindsey Gruson, "Klan Rally Planners Included Police Informant," *Greensboro Daily News*, 3 August 1980, A1.

67. Gruson, "Klan Rally Planners," A9.

68. Gruson, "Klan Rally Planners," A9.

69. Gruson, "Klan Rally Planners," A9.

70. Gruson, "Klan Rally Planners," A9.

71. Gruson, "Klan Rally Planners," A9.

72. Gruson, "Klan Rally Planners," A9.

73. Gruson, "Klan Rally Planners," A9.

74. Edmisten's remark was made to the *Greensboro Record*. It is quoted in "Payback," *Workers Viewpoint*, 25–31 August 1980. See that issue for other details about the convention protests.

75. Cy Egan, Barbara Ross, and Eli Teiber, "It's Mayhem at Madison Sq.," *New York Post*, 15 August 1980.

76. See Barbara Ross and Eli Teiber, "19 Seized after Battle of 8th Av." *New York Post*, 15 August 1980. See also "19 Officers Hurt Battling Communist Worker Groups," *New York Times*, 15 August 1980. The *New York Times* mentions that six officers were injured outside the Plaza Hotel on Central Park South earlier that day when the CWP protested at the Democratic Party victory banquet. The *Workers Viewpoint*, in "We Salute You, Heroic Fighters!" 25–31 August 1980, boasts of injuring twenty-six police.

77. Unless otherwise indicated, quotations by Elliot Fratkin are from a taped interview with him on November 2, 1992.

14

GREEN LIGHT FOR REACTIONARY VIOLENCE: THE STATE TRIAL IN 1980

THE PROSECUTION'S CASE

The prosecution's case against the Klan and Nazis was underway when I returned from New York. It included seven weeks of eyewitness testimony by police officers, cameramen, and journalists—altogether, nearly one hundred witnesses for the prosecution. The district attorney presented videotape and ballistic evidence.

The jury was shown the Klan/Nazi arsenal—shotguns, pistols, brass knuckles, and clubs.[1] Additionally, over three thousand rounds of ammunition, four long-barreled rifles and shotguns, a swastika armband, a tear gas mask, and gun clips were found by the SBI and Greensboro police in Raeford Caudle's home and in his car, the blue Ford Fairlane. The D.A. had dropped conspiracy charges against Nazi caravan participant Caudle even though Caudle's Fairlane, used by Jack Fowler in his escape after November 3, contained most of the weapons used to shoot and kill the demonstrators.[2] The weapon used by Fowler belonged to Caudle: an Armalite AR-180 that looks like an M-16. It elicited "gasps and frightened looks from the jury" when brought into the courtroom.[3]

Detective Jerry H. Cooper and a photographer followed the caravan in an unmarked car to within 245 feet of the murder scene and photographed it. Cooper testified that he saw Jack Fowler fire an automatic rifle. Cooper also confirmed under oath that Dawson was a police informant on and prior to November 3.[4] As mentioned earlier, Dawson was not called to testify in the Klan/Nazi trial. Neither was BATF agent Bernard Burkovich.

The testimony of the police officers responsible for arresting the twelve men in the van—after they heard a radio transmission about the shooting and rushed to the scene unbidden—undermined Nazi Jerry Paul Smith's defense of temporary amnesia. Smith did not appear ill or injured, they said; nor did he complain of his health after being taken into custody.[5] Other aspects of these officers' testimony contradicted the defense claim that the Klan/Nazis were *glad* to see the police because they feared a communist attack. The officers testified that their reaction was just the opposite, surprise at seeing the police and an attempt to get away.

Valuable testimony for the prosecution was given by members of the news media—trained observers. News photographers and reporters at the scene all agreed that the opening shots came from the front of the Klan caravan. They were in agreement about the most heavily concentrated gunfire: it came from around the 1962 Ford Fairlane and the van (alternately described as a yellow or tan van). These two vehicles at the rear of the caravan carried the six defendants and other Klan/Nazis scheduled to be tried later. In testimony, the Klan and Nazis on trial were identified as firing weapons. No one saw any of the defendants fired upon by the people at whom they were shooting. Consistently, the demonstrators were described as scattering and running for cover.

Winston Cavin, covering the rally for the *Greensboro Daily News*, talked about the caravan's approach. Occupants from the first two cars were shouting threats and profanity, saying things like "Nigger, we're going to get your ass." Cavin noticed the behavior of the occupants in the third car was different: they looked bewildered. When Cavin saw that the men in the fourth car had pistols, he decided to go across the street. He saw some demonstrators kick and hit the Klan cars, and he heard a popping sound. Then he saw a white man standing outside one of the Klan cars pointing a long-barreled pistol and two or three demonstrators pulling out handguns. Cavin identified Coleman Pridmore as one of several men who got out of the blue Ford and the van and "were just standing there in the street blasting away" at demonstrators running for cover, including Nelson Johnson, who joined Cavin sheltered behind a parked car.[6]

In his testimony, George Vaughn, a cameraman for WGHP-TV in High Point, identified the first shots as coming from a vehicle at the front of the caravan.[7] Vaughn saw a man get out of the driver's side of that vehicle, start screaming something, and then fire several shots in the air. When he sought cover, Vaughn was behind the same car as Nelson Johnson and another demonstrator. He witnessed a man club César on the head and watched the assailant run toward the Klan/Nazi caravan. He saw Jerry Paul Smith running down the street pointing his pistol. Prosecutor Greeson had already introduced into evidence the .22-caliber pistol found in the van—the only pistol of that caliber—and .22-caliber shells were found in Smith's pocket when he was arrested. Cameraman Vaughn witnessed a demonstrator's attempt to return the Klan's fire: he testified that as he crouched behind a car, his camera still running, he saw a hand holding a derringer pistol.

Laura Blumenthal, a reporter for WXII-TV, crawled under the station's car to hide. From there she saw Bill Sampson stagger after being shot. She testified that Bill called out for a gun, someone nearby threw him a pistol, and he fired one shot before collapsing.[8] The FBI hypnotized Blumenthal to help her recall the day's events. The hypnotizing of Blumenthal and another state's witness—by an investigator with a background of performing magic tricks at parties—created a little eddy of controversy. The jury was shown a tape of Blumenthal's hypnosis session.[9]

Another prosecution witness, Beulah Taylor, was riding in a pick up truck midway in the caravan. Dawson's speech at a Klan rally in Lincolnton brought her to Greensboro that day, she testified. At the Randleman Road house, Dawson told Taylor and her companion that they were going to the shopping center where the CWP rally was to end, and they said nothing about violence. After the first shot was fired, the pickup truck Taylor was in moved down the street and was half a block away when Taylor heard a barrage of gunfire erupt behind her.[10] She passed safely through the boisterous crowd of demonstrators after a momentary traffic jam. Her testimony contradicted the defense claim that the Klan and Nazis were blocked from escaping the area and were forced to shoot in self-defense. Later in the trial, two local black women, accidentally caught up in the caravan, testified that when they saw the cars in front of them hit with sticks and heard shots, they became frightened, turned their car around, and headed in the opposite direction.[11] Their testimony also made the point that escape from the street was not blocked. The defendants, who were several cars behind the two local women, had the option of turning around and leaving the scene.

In her testimony, Taylor also mentioned the repositioning of vehicles on Randleman Road. Initially, Taylor's truck was behind the van, but the van pulled out, Taylor testified, and she never saw it again. The van, with the shooters, was placed at the rear behind the Fairlane with the weapons.[12]

Witness for the prosecution Jim Waters, a WFMY-TV photojournalist, identified Jack Fowler as the man he saw in the street calmly firing a weapon he knew to be an AR-180 rifle. Waters saw César being killed when "a man came running from a blue car with a revolver in each hand . . . firing just as fast as he could."[13] The TV cameraman described how Smith ran in a crouched position while shooting at César, how César ran a few yards after being shot, and how César was then hit in the back of the head with a stick by another assailant. César fell, tried to rise once more, but finally fell face down, motionless, said Waters.

Jim Waters ran across the street, his camera still rolling. He was standing in the open, exposed to the gunfire with a camera on his shoulder, when he realized that a demonstrator next to him had a small gun—a derringer. Terrified that Jack Fowler, who was firing a "military-like rifle," would return the fire, Waters pleaded with the man not to fire the derringer. The demonstrator "appeared to be in a daze," Waters said. He ignored his pleas and tried three times to return the Klan's fire, but each time the derringer would not fire.[14]

WTVD in Durham sent reporter Matthew Sinclair and photographer Ed Boyd to cover the march and rally. Sinclair saw the approach of the caravan and was only a few feet away when he heard a man in one of the lead cars call out "China Grove" and heard something like "you wanted the Klan, here they are."[15] From behind a car on the south side of Everitt Street where he had run for safety, Sinclair witnessed demonstrators running for cover. He saw some men from the caravan in a hand-to-hand stick fight with some of the demonstrators at the Carver and Everitt intersection. He also witnessed Smith running down the street firing two weapons, watched César get hit on the head and fall, and saw Paul Bermanzohn "go down."[16] This reporter witnessed the one Klan injury that occurred that day. Klansman Harold Flowers was shot in the arm, presumably by another caravan participant—an assumption never contested by the police or anyone else.

Matt Sinclair met and interviewed Paul before November 3, when Paul went to the Durham TV station complaining about news coverage of the Klan. Sinclair testified that Paul said that armed self-defense was the only way to deal with the Klan. Paul Bermanzohn did not have a gun on November 3, he told the court. Sinclair did not see any demonstrator fire on the caravan of Klansmen and Nazis as it approached the rally site. The first shot came from the caravan, he affirmed. He saw one CWP demonstrator with a gun that would not fire.[17] In the brief stick fight Sinclair witnessed, he saw Paul swinging a two-by-two-inch stick wildly. "I don't know who he was swinging at, there was nobody close enough for him to hit," the reporter testified.[18]

Ed Boyd's WTVD videotape was the most vivid of the four television stations. Testifying for the prosecution early in September, Boyd was an observant witness who was able to identify Smith, Wood, Pridmore, and Morgan as men from the caravan he saw firing guns. Though he did not identify Fowler and Matthews, he gave descriptions of them holding long-barreled weapons that matched descriptions of the two defendants. Boyd saw Smith, a gun in each hand, shoot César "at point-blank range." The photographer's clear recollection of Pridmore aiming and firing a shotgun contradicted a defense claim that Pridmore did not fire his gun but only emptied shells on the ground. When gunfire erupted, Boyd said, demonstrators "were dropping like flies."[19]

Boyd saw and heard the first shot from the front of the caravan. He testified that he did not see any demonstrator fire on Klansmen and Nazis as the caravan rolled into the rally.[20] As he was filming from the south side of Everitt Street, where he had fled on hearing the gunfire, Boyd saw a demonstrator with a derringer. Like Waters, he was afraid that if the derringer were fired it would provoke return fire, and he went into the WTVD car for cover. About forty seconds later, Boyd estimated, he heard screeching tires and realized vehicles were leaving.

UPSETTING DETAILS

I was not in the courtroom for most of the Klan trial, but I was steeped in it nevertheless. I read all of the news reports, talked to people who were there, and constantly discussed matters with comrades and friends. On August 27, 1980, I called my parents to wish them a happy wedding anniversary. I remember that because of what was in the news—my entire personal life was punctuated by it. A pathologist from the state medical examiner's office testified about the fatal wounds of November Third. Sandi had been first hit on the back of the head and then shot in the forehead just above her right eye. Jim was shot in the back, César through the lungs, Mike in the head, and Bill in the chest.[21] The state's chief medical examiner found "James Waller, thirty-seven, of Greensboro, was turned away from his attackers when large buckshot fired from fifteen to twenty feet away entered his lower back, traveled upward and penetrated his heart."[22] The fatal buckshot penetrated several organs before hitting his heart because he was running stooped over when he was hit. He also had several other buckshot wounds in his back and side as well as many smaller birdshot wounds to his chest and midsection from a second weapon. Because Jim was shot while running away, and since all five victims were unarmed when they were shot, the Klan/Nazis' claim of self-defense seems to be discredited. But let us not forget who was really on trial in Greensboro.

I had not pursued the details of how Jim was killed. I think I tried to avoid knowing about it, except in generalities, but that was impossible. I needed to have all available information to do a responsible job as a CWP press secretary. The painful memories I tried to suppress haunted me for years, and still do.

In a recurrent nightmare of November Third, Jim is still alive, but he is grotesquely disabled by wounds and is no longer a person. These bad dreams tease me with a vision of a man and a lover who is no longer accessible to me, who is neither alive nor dead, though alive in some ghostly way. Either some harsh necessity has pulled him from my life, or he willfully wants nothing to do with me. In one version of this dream, his withdrawal is a token of his love; he would not afflict me. We share a tender moment in the dream before he must take away his presence, but it is enough for me to wake up with a fleeting sense of joy—I have been reminded of his love for me in that evaporating instant, definite though elusive. In another version, he has deliberately abandoned me and may even, in his altered state, be living with another woman. In all versions, he is physically and mentally demolished, irreversibly so. His body is riddled with holes. He belongs to a separate world, not the human one, and he must return there. In that world, he lives with mortal wounds that are beyond imagining, and in that world I can *never* reach him, though I am condemned by my longing to try to reach him and to make him part of my human world. The dream is a desperate scheme to bring him back to my world, to live with him in spite of his fantastic wounds and in spite of the impossibility of communicating with a creature of his otherworldness. I am wrung out and aching in the morning.

***

Three weeks into the prosecution's case, at a news conference in a hallway near the courtroom, we again pointed to the failure to indict Dawson, Butkovich, and Caudle. "In a three-ring circus–kangaroo court, complete with magic acts and hypnosis to befuddle everyone's mind, the district attorney has continued to attack the CWP and lay the groundwork for the Klan-Nazi defense," I said.[23] A week later, after refusing to testify when dragged into court, November 3 demonstrator Tom Clark was jailed.[24] Dale and I were scheduled to testify the same day as Tom, and other demonstrators had also received subpoenas. Each of us made it clear that we would not obey them, and Schlossler did not call us to the stand.[25] From jail, Marty and Floris, finishing their contempt of court sentences, held a press conference and said that they would call for a special meeting of the Greensboro City Council to examine why city police were exonerated for murder when Klansman Eddie Dawson was working for the police as an informer.

"They can't hang me for all of them—I only got three of them," one of the killers confessed. Sheriff's Deputy Coy Jarrett testified that the statement was made, unsolicited, by David Wayne Matthews on November 4, when he was escorting the prisoner to his cell block.[26] Medical testimony established that everyone except César—who was killed by the .357 magnum fired by Jerry

Smith—died from shotgun wounds.[27] Defendants Matthews, Wood, and Pridmore, all Vietnam-era veterans, were seen by various witnesses firing shotguns at demonstrators.[28]

At least thirty-seven shots were fired on November 3, federal firearms specialists verified, and nearly all shots came from weapons linked to the defendants. An FBI ballistics expert said that the lead in the bullet that killed César was the same as that in ammunition confiscated from the home of Raeford Caudle.[29] The bullet, the kind used with a .357, matched a weapon fired by Jerry Smith, who was seen by witnesses and videotaped shooting César. A .357 magnum pistol, registered to Caudle, was found in the van with Smith right after the murders. The chemical makeup of slugs fired from the .357 and live cartridges in the pistol Smith fired were identical. Not much more can be asked for by way of a smoking gun or a closed evidentiary loop. But wait, Smith will be acquitted.

The FBI chemists linked metal fragments taken from the bodies of Jim, Bill, Mike, and Sandi with weapons fired by Matthews, Pridmore, and Fowler.[30] The ballistics evidence established that Bill, Sandi, and Jim were killed by David Matthews. It was possible that Mike, too, was killed by Matthews (thus invalidating his boast that he only got three). Also consistent with the evidence was the possibility that Pridmore fired the bullet fatal to Mike.

Jim took bullets from more than one source on November 3. Besides the double ought buckshot shells, fatal to both him and Sandi, and linked to Matthews' gun through firing pin impressions made in the process of ejection, Jim had number six birdshot pellets in his body that matched those used by Roland Wood. Other nonfatal pellets found in Jim were thought to have come from Tom Clark's shotgun fired by a Klansman.[31] A plausible scenario is that Jim, rushing forward on hearing the Klan's first shots or seeing the stick fight, managed to get his hands on Tom's shotgun, stowed away in a truck. If the defense's story is right, the gun was wrested from Jim by Roy Toney, a Klansman in the second batch of defendants. Then several Klan/Nazis shot at Jim when, unarmed, he ran for cover.

Under the felony murder rule used in the trial, it was not necessary to tie the fatal shots to any single defendant: if convicted of a felony in which a murder was committed, each defendant could be found guilty of murder and given the death penalty. Thus the strong evidence showing Smith and Matthews responsible for specific deaths was enough to convict all six defendants of first degree murder, especially if they were found guilty as charged of rioting (even if some of the six fired no fatal bullets or did not fire at all). A district attorney who really wanted a conviction should have had little difficulty, with or without testimony from demonstrators.

Jurors viewed all of the videotapes (at first only admissible to illustrate witnesses' testimony, but later allowed as substantive evidence), breaking with traditions in the state's court system.[32] Schlosser talked about taking the jury to the crime scene: "It's such a small, tight place—it was like shooting fish in a barrel."[33] That visit didn't happen.

THE DEFENSE CASE (OR LACK THEREOF)

In the middle of September, when the prosecution rested its case, Joe Grady, imperial wizard of the White Knights of Liberty, was at the courthouse to announce a Klan rally to raise money for the defendants.[34] The Klan held their rally on September 13 in Lincolnton, passed the hat for the Klan/Nazi defendants, and burned a forty-foot cross. Griffin was there on work-release from jail. A lot of handguns, shotguns, and some semiautomatic rifles were carried about openly; it was a family day with children and police not far away.

"Klud" Reverend Clyde Jones of United Klansmen of America, a preacher at a Baptist church near Greensboro, gave an opening convocation calling on white Americans to defend the country against communism. Matthews, Smith, and Pridmore, dressed in black, red, and white robes, respectively—black for security, red for kluds or ministers, and white for members—were the stars of the show.

"I have my white race," Jerry Smith said, "and I'll stand and fight for it even if it means the gas chamber." He hated that his kids had to go to school with blacks and Cubans. "When the races start dating it's too late to fight," said César's murderer. The Klan helped the country in 1865, he told the crowd, and "we can do it in the 1980s. What happened in Greensboro is nothing compared to what's to come. We fought for you in the streets of Greensboro; now it's time for you to fight for us."

Grady, the emcee, after reading an antiabortion poem, introduced John Howard, a national Klan organizer from the Georgia Knights of the Ku Klux Klan. Communists have infiltrated the federal government, and the government is infringing on the rights of white Americans and right-wing organizations, Howard claimed. A coalition of the right wing devoted to the "great holy cause" was in the works, he said. All major right-wing groups, even the Nazis, would be included.

Grady, quoting from a speech by Anne Braden in which she said, "the new South cannot emerge as long as we have the Klan," took the line to mean that the Klan was powerful and communism could not take over as long as the Klan prevented it. Grady introduced a black robed and masked man holding a shotgun. "This man is a murderer," he said. "He killed some communists in Vietnam. They gave him a medal." One speaker said, "If the government tries to send us overseas to fight communists, we won't go. We'll stay right here and fight them." And the "n word" was much in evidence too—"You put a thousand dollar fence around your dog but put your kids on a bus with niggers," and "A communist is a nigger turned inside out."

A CWP supporter at the rally reported these things to us. Also featured at this rally was a display by Jerry Smith of a scrapbook with autopsy photographs of the slain November Third victims. The flaunting of the nude autopsy pictures with graphic depiction of the victims' bullet wounds did not remain a secret. When it came time for Smith to testify, prosecutors tried, unsuccessfully, to get the judge to let them raise the issue to the jury.[35]

The defense case started on Monday, September 22, 1980. Having neither the facts nor the law on their side, defense lawyers relied on hermeneutics and the inexhaustible mother lodes of anticommunism and racism.

Wood, first defendant to take the stand, was in the Klan before he became a Nazi unit leader. He maintained that he went to the anti-Klan rally to shout the communists down by singing "My Country 'Tis of Thee." He claimed that he went for his gun out of fear and that he shot over the heads of CWP members.[36] Wood's lawyer, Robert Cahoon, sought to dispel the bad odor of Nazism around his client by arguing that Wood did not know what Hitler had done to the Jews in Germany because Hitler came to power before Wood was born. All Wood knew about the American Nazi Party, the jury was to believe, was that it was against communism, and that was why he joined the party.[37] Defense attorneys "seldom missed an opportunity to emphasize to the all-white conservative jury the defendants' avowed patriotism and strong anticommunist sentiment."[38]

In his testimony, Wood confirmed the presence of Caudle, Fowler, Smith, and Pridmore at the November 1 meeting at his home, where a confrontation with anti-Klan demonstrators was planned. Wood also mentioned Bernard Butkovich as present at that meeting. The federal agent's role, however, was not scrutinized. I have to wonder whether any juror ever thought it should have been. Wood could not explain why, if the Nazi plan was for a nonviolent counterdemonstration, Caudle had an automatic rifle in his car when Wood met him on the morning of November 3. And did Wood need a canister of tear gas and a shotgun for a rendition of "My Country 'Tis of Thee" if, as he claimed, he went to the rally to sing patriotic songs?[39] Wood said under oath that on November 3 he was defending himself against gunshots from the community center of the housing project. But ballistics evidence indicated that the sixth, nineth, tenth, and thirteenth shots came from Wood and that the only gunfire from the community center came five seconds after Wood's last shot.[40] Similarly unbelievable was Wood's story about firing in the air and not "shooting at nobody," when, in fact, the number six birdshot that he fired turned up not only in Jim but also in other demonstrators wounded or killed that day, as well as in wounded cameraman David Dalton.

Wood's actions are preserved for posterity on videotape: he is shown with a cigarette dangling from his lips, standing in a group of men who are removing weapons from a car trunk. This occurs, as if on signal, just moments after the gunshot from the front of the caravan. Wood advances on the fleeing demonstrators, firing his shotgun. No testimony or evidence, videotaped or otherwise, supported Wood's contention that demonstrators fired at him and caused him to be scared.

Several defendants told the court that they got out of their cars and took up weapons to protect the women in the caravan. But Mrs. Hartsoe, a Klan member who was riding with two other women and three men, testified that she never saw any of the defendants rushing to her aid and that the men in her car got out and took part in the fist and club fight with the demonstrators. When they returned to her car, all drove away unmolested.[41]

Defense witness Carl Nappier heard Griffin and Dawson speak at Klan rallies. Nappier said that Dawson asked for volunteers to go to Greensboro to stop the communists from destroying the U.S. government. Dawson told people that the communists were larger in body size than anyone in the building and that there would be six or seven hundred of them.[42] Nappier, who said that he went to the rally to heckle and out-shout the communists, testified that, since November 3, he had quit the Klan out of disgust.

At the rendezvous house in Greensboro, according to Nappier, Caudle showed off his semiautomatic AR-180—the weapon used shortly afterward by Jack Fowler—and bragged that he could buy them for $287.[43] Fowler, seen on videotape shooting a high-powered rifle, fled after November Third and then turned himself in. He was being held without bond in the county jail. (Other defendants were granted bail shortly after their arrests but were returned to jail around trial times for security reasons. In jail they were treated as honored guests.) Like Wood, Fowler was a Nazi who had formerly been a Klansman. Fowler testified that fear caused him to shoot on November 3. He claimed to have seen demonstrators shooting at a time when the defense team's audio expert said there was no gunfire. The same contradiction had caught Wood.[44]

In the video footage taken of the anti-Klan rally, Jerry Paul Smith is running down the street with guns in both hands firing at César Cauce. Smith pleaded amnesia. He said that he was clubbed on the head during the stick fight and didn't remember doing what the tapes show him doing. Smith admitted that he never told the arresting officer or any other policeman about having received a blow on the head.[45] (The obliging amnesia began right when Smith reached in the trunk for a gun and ended when the van drove away from the area.) Like other defendants, Smith claimed that he didn't fire at anyone who wasn't firing at him (just in case the amnesia story didn't work). The jury was not allowed to learn about the autopsy photos that Smith brought to the Klan rally a couple of weeks earlier or the racist speech he gave.[46] Not that these bits of evidence, had they been admitted, would have made a difference in the verdict.

Defendant Lawrence Gene Morgan, part of Griffin's Klan unit, stated that he only went to the anti-Klan rally to heckle the communists. Armed with an eight-inch buck knife, he claimed that he never used it on anyone.[47] Morgan testified that Dawson asked him to drive his van and to turn his CB to Channel 11 for radio contact.[48] He related how Dawson saw to the positioning of the vehicles when the caravan stopped on the ramp at I-85. Morgan's van was placed at the rear of the caravan, and the Ford Fairlaine was put immediately before it, while Dawson took his spot in the first car and led the others to the scene.[49]

The last two defendants to testify were David Matthews and Coleman Pridmore. The ballistic evidence showed that Matthews was responsible for some of the deaths, but the killer insisted that he went to the rally only to heckle. Matthews said that he fired his shotgun in self-defense at three black men who were pointing shotguns at him. But no black males were shot. In fact, there is no evidence of any black male demonstrators holding or firing guns that day. The videotapes, shown to the jury in slow motion, contradicted Matthews' story.[50] The black men threatening him were a figment of his vulgar white supremacist imagination. Matthews admitted to telling another Klansman shortly after the killings that he thought he got "two or three of them." He added, "niggers were falling. . . . I thought that I hit them. I could have been wrong, it could have been somebody else."[51] Overall, Matthews' testimony was inconsistent with that of other defendants and with statements that he had given the police after his arrest.[52]

Pridmore, an "exalted cyclops," also claimed the Klan and Nazis were under attack and acted in self-defense. He said that he never actually fired his weapon. According to him, the pump action on his shotgun failed, and he only ejected some unspent shells onto the ground.[53] However, chemical evidence and witness testimony indicated that Pridmore probably fired his gun and may even have fired the shots that killed one or more people.

TOMBSTONE CENSORSHIP

Four of our five beloved comrades are laid to rest at Maplewood Cemetery, a city cemetery not far from where the murders took place. (They were, as far as we knew, the only white people buried there—we had integrated the cemetery.) In the middle of the defendants' testimonies in the state trial, the City of Greensboro said that it would not allow our proposed inscription on the tombstone and cited a brand new ordinance prohibiting political inscriptions on monuments in city cemeteries. We said that any regulation of the political content of a monument inscription was blatantly unconstitutional. Others agreed with us, and the city was quickly isolated in its stance.

Dale and I had arranged to be on the city council meeting agenda on October 2, 1980. This time our appearance at the city council occasioned a hushed pause, not an arrest. I called the attempt to censor the message on our monument, about the "meaning and purpose" of the lives of those killed, "a despicable act." I reviewed how we had "consistently exposed to the light of day the role of the federal and city government" in the conspiracy to murder our friends and how the mayor, city council, and city officials used whitewashing reports to cover up the truth. Now they did not want the truth to be told *even on a tombstone.* Some council members fidgeted in their seats as I spoke. "Nonsense," the mayor muttered; "You're coming close to libel," a council member blurted out loud.

Dale went to the podium, her eyes stained with tears. She said, "These people meant a great deal to their wives and their friends and their families. And I'd like you to think about that."[54] It is amazing that we had to go out of our way to establish our credentials, and those of five murdered people, as *human beings!*

North Carolina American Civil Liberties Union attorney Norman Smith wrote to the superintendent of cemeteries. Our political beliefs, he said, had the same meaning for us "that religious expressions have for non-Communists. . . . To prohibit the Communist Workers Party members from expressing their conscientious convictions on grave markers is to discriminate against them on the basis of religion and conscientious belief.

"Moreover, the prohibition of political expressions on grave markers would appear to be an unconstitutional deprivation of free speech, since it cannot be demonstrated that these expressions would create a clear and present danger to the public order, if they were not suppressed."[55]

The City backed down.[56] I sent a letter to Norman Smith thanking him—he had been my ex-husband Carl's lawyer in our divorce proceedings a few years earlier—for his "timely help in defeating the City of Greensboro's attempts to censor the monument of our loved ones because they disapproved of its political content."[57]

The message on the tombstone is a partisan and political manifesto. Each time I return to the cemetery and reread the inscription, I have thought it deeply relevant and moving. The particular political idiom may be dated, but the words still have the ring of truth and pack the thrill of a call to action founded on virtue. On one side of the monument is chiseled: "LONG LIVE THE COMMUNIST WORKERS PARTY 5," and below this heading runs the following text:

> On November 3, 1979, the criminal monopoly capitalist class murdered Jim Waller, César Cauce, Mike Nathan, Bill Sampson, and Sandi Smith with government agents, Klan, and Nazis. Heroically defending the people, the 5 charged gunfire with bare fists and sticks. We vow this assassination will be the costliest mistake the capitalists have ever made, and the turning point of class struggle in the U.S.
>
> The CWP 5 were among the strongest leaders of their times. Their deaths marked an end to capitalist stabilization (1950s–1970s) when American workers suffered untold misery, yet as a whole remained dormant for lack of its own leaders. In 1980, the deepest capitalist crisis began. The working class was awakening. The CWP 5 lived and died for all workers, minorities, and poor; for a world where exploitation and oppression will be eliminated, and all mankind freed; for the noble goal of communism. Their deaths, a tremendous loss to the CWP and to their families, are a clarion call to the U.S. people to fight for workers' rule. In their footsteps, waves of revolutionaries will rise and join our ranks.
>
> We will overthrow the criminal rule of the monopoly capitalist class! Victory will be ours!
>
> November 3, 1980   Central Committee, CWP, USA
> FIGHT FOR REVOLUTIONARY SOCIALISM AND WORKERS' RULE

THE LAST DEFENSE WITNESS

The last witness for the defense was its most valuable one. Rex Stephenson, Jim's coworker at Greensboro's South Buffalo Water Treatment Plant, told the jury that we were looking for martyrs so that we would receive national media attention and recruit people to the party.[58] Stephenson, an anticommunist army veteran who fought in Korea and did two tours in Vietnam, told a twisted story that was just what the jury needed in order to blame the victims. The jury, selected for its anticommunist proclivities, was willing to believe any cynical lie about communists. It must have been with great sympathy that the jury heard

Stephenson tell them that he tried to convert Waller from atheism to Christianity (probably unaware that Jim was Jewish). The newspaper account seems to be gloating in reporting that "the entire jury laughed and one even applauded when Stephenson said he once told Waller he would pay Waller's fare to Russia if Waller would go there to see what communism is like."[59]

As the trial wound down to its final hours, suddenly it was Jim Waller who was on trial for his political beliefs. Under cross-examination, Stephenson admitted that he did not think Jim was a violent person. Jim never mentioned plans for the CWP's "Death to the Klan" march, the witness said, and he did not know about it. Nonetheless, the jury bought the sensational tale of a planned martyrdom. One of the defense attorneys later admitted that Stephenson was their "most important" witness, their "most powerful" witness, their "star witness," who gave the "best supporting evidence that their clients acted in self-defense as claimed."[60]

The prosecution did not challenge Stephenson's lying testimony. There was no sympathetic, realistic, or respectful portrayal by prosecutors of the young people who were killed so brutally and suddenly. A lawyer might ask why the judge even allowed Stephenson's testimony, since Stephenson admitted that he had no knowledge of the CWP's November 3 plans. But the judge deemed it important "to show Waller's state of mind" prior to the rally, even though he had been unwilling to admit that Jerry Paul Smith's state of mind afterward, when he boasted of his criminal deeds by showing off the autopsy photos, had any evidential bearing on those prior deeds.[61]

When all is said and done, how could the jury delude itself that the Klan and Nazis were not guilty of murder? The hermeneutics employed must not be too far removed from those operating when medieval onlookers to the ritual of burning women alive convinced themselves that they were freeing the world of witches. They were led to see things that way, of course, by others far more educated and powerful than they, the agents of the Inquisition whose interest was served by the persecution and its underlying mythology.

To rationalize the acquittal verdict, one must ignore the fact that the killers were never threatened by people hitting cars or by any attack on their persons. Since the first two shots came from the Klan caravan, these had to be viewed, in order to rationalize the verdict, as harmless and nonthreatening. No definitive evidence was presented to show the exact source of shots three, four, and five. Thus, jurors were free to interpret shots three, four, and five as the first *hostile* fire, and they could, as directed by the defense, resolve the question of their origin by simply assigning them to the CWP. The evidence simply was ignored— in particular, the TV videotapes and the consistent accounts by media people.

Absent from the warped, false narrative was the role of government agents, informers, and complicit officials. The hermeneutic icing on this cake was the slander about the CWP planning and embracing its martyrdom: the jurors seem to have paid most attention to it.

The acquittal of the Klan and Nazis came on November 17, 1980, a little more than a year after the murders. The shock waves rippling out from Greensboro undulate in its civic space to this day.

REACTION TO THE VERDICT

The acquittals were "a green light for reactionary violence" said a CWP spokesperson at a press conference immediately after the announcement. To a reporter's accusation that we had brought on the not guilty verdict ourselves by not testifying, I replied, "where do you have another case that has the amount of damning evidence that this one has? The evidence was overwhelming whether we testified or not."[62] Then, for two days, I withdrew from the world, letting Durham press officer Charles Finch handle phone calls and press releases. The curtains were drawn to keep out light that was excruciatingly painful. My head throbbed with a sickening pain. Nausea had taken up residence in my head. I went in and out of sleep, hallucinated, ate nothing, and threw up. It was one of the worst migraines I'd ever had.

The morning after a jury acquitted six Ku Klux Klansmen and Nazis of killing five Communist Workers Party members, this woman's reaction was typical—"What went wrong? I saw a man with two pistols shoot someone. Why isn't he in jail?"[63] "Six killers are back out on the street. They killed five people and got away scot-free," said a Morningside Homes resident who had witnessed the murders and testified for the prosecution.[64]

Senator Henry Frye, the first black person elected to the state legislature since Reconstruction, was stunned. "A lot of people said they were going to turn them lose and I took the position, no way. I'm wrong," Frye said. "It makes me want to reevaluate . . . my approach to things."[65]

The Greensboro Justice Fund (GJF), established as a nonprofit organization for education and fundraising in connection with the events of November 3, 1979, held a press conference at which Nelson spoke on the day after the verdict. Students from Duke University and UNC-Charlotte joined him in solidarity. There were spontaneous protests at the grassroots within a few days of the verdict. Several thousand people in Greensboro, Durham, and Chapel Hill marched, rallied, and held vigils and press conferences. In Greensboro, people held a silent vigil in front of the federal building protesting the acquittals.[66] In Durham, Marty denounced the verdict to the media, while a couple hundred Duke University students gathered at the west campus quad for a vigil, the first of a series of protest events and open discussion there.

On November 20, 1980, seven hundred black and white demonstrators, including many students, marched two miles in silence to Greensboro's Guilford County Courthouse in protest of the blatantly unjust verdict. The march was sponsored by a coalition of groups that included the local NAACP and the student government at A & T State. NAACP head Dr. George Simkins, an early civil rights activist who was jailed in 1965, was satisfied with the turnout, saying, "We didn't call anyone and ask them to come; they just came."[67] Carrying signs such as "The Wheels of Justice Do Not Turn in Greensboro" and "We will never go back," the marchers beckoned to onlookers to join them, and many did. The march had the air of a civil rights revival. "We cannot allow the gigantic civil rights victories of the '60s to be swept under a carpet of injustice," declared A & T student leader Aubrey Eatmon.[68] Putting Greensboro in the context of the time, he said, "Innocent children are shot down in Atlanta, our brothers are mangled in Buffalo, there's injustice in Miami, and now a not guilty verdict in our beloved city of Greensboro."[69] City Manager Tom Osborne was handed a petition demanding that the city urge the U.S. Justice Department to investigate the handling of the Klan/Nazi trial.[70]

A couple of days after the verdict, a speech by Julian Bond on the history of the civil rights movement to students at North Carolina Central University in Durham turned into a mass protest march as several hundred students and faculty members, led by Bond, marched to the downtown post office.[71] There, former Wilmington Ten defendant Ann Shepard joined November Third widow Marty Nathan in demanding that justice be served. Bond urged the students to persuade authorities to try Klansmen and Nazis again on federal charges of civil rights violations.

At a public hearing in Greensboro's City Council chambers days after the verdict, Joyce Johnson and I were joined by ministers, students, civic activists, and representatives from community agencies in urging the Greensboro Human Relations Commission to push for a federal investigation into the handling of the Klan/Nazi trial. Several speakers insisted on knowing why Dawson and Butkovich had not been called to testify.[72]

The North Carolina Student Legislature meeting in Charlotte, with over one hundred students who represented colleges around the state, called on President Carter, President-elect Reagan, and U.S. Attorney General Civiletti to pursue criminal civil rights charges against the acquitted Klan/Nazi defendants.[73]

In its post-verdict coverage, the national media ignored the expressions of unrest, dismay, and protest at the grassroots in North Carolina, focusing instead on quotations by the mayor or other public officials, who desired nothing so much as to distance themselves with the speed of light from everything relating to November Third. The media best served those seeking to cover up illegal and unseemly deeds, repair their tainted reputations by discrediting the CWP, and rehabilitate Greensboro's image as a pleasant, enlightened southern city.

After the acquittal of murderers who were seen on TV shooting people down, the issue clearly was not communism but justice, or the lack thereof. The CWP gained credibility: people who were shocked at the jury's acceptance of the Klan/Nazi self-defense argument told us that they now understood what we were telling them all along. Many commentators who did not uphold communist ideology or politics found themselves agreeing with much of the CWP's analysis. The CWP's claim that the verdict was sealed with jury selection was echoed in the *News & Observer* of Raleigh—no fellow travelers they. In an editorial, they found it "relevant to point out that this jury had as a foreman a Cuban immigrant who had previously taken part in militant anticommunist activities in Miami."[74] None of the other jurors had college degrees, they noted, in a case in which highly educated radicals were killed. An editorial in the *New York Amsterdam News* affirmed that the acquittals "may quite easily be interpreted as a form of license for both the Klan and the Nazis to become even bolder in spreading their vileness and violence."[75]

"The Communists' prediction that all the defendants would walk out of the courtroom as free men—inflammatory rhetoric notwithstanding—seems, with hindsight, to have been especially prescient," commented Durham freelance writer Mark Pinsky.[76] The Klan/Nazis' self-defense argument prevailed, he summarized, in spite of "abundant 'neutral' eyewitness testimony by journalists and innocent bystanders, ballistic analysts, four sets of color videotapes of the shootings from different angles, plus scores of black and white still photographs—all taken by news professionals." Some of his northern friends, Pinsky said, "have been dusting off the old lynch-law stereotypes of the South, such as the trial of the Scottsboro Boys."[77] The jury might at least have found some or all of the defendants guilty of lesser charges, the journalist noted, such as second-degree murder, voluntary manslaughter, or involuntary manslaughter. They might have rendered a guilty verdict if they thought the Klan and Nazis had used more force than necessary, especially deadly force, to protect themselves. He guessed that hard economic times and an increasingly conservative mood in the country were factors in the acquittal. "As Communists, as union organizers, the members of the Communist Workers Party simply stepped beyond the pale of acceptable political behavior in North Carolina," Pinsky concluded, "and thus outside the protection of the U.S. Constitution and the Greensboro Police Department. Yet in this respect, Greensboro could have been anywhere."[78]

Such coverage was rare. The vast majority of articles and editorials carried the line of officialdom. On many occasions I spoke to groups of people in their homes and to college students. I could see how people were influenced by what they read and heard in the media. I was most piqued by the suggestion that we communists should be grateful for our freedom in America, such as free speech. When people pointed out, in their patriotic fashion, that we were able to hold a rally and express our views on November 3, and that we therefore were free, I knew immediately that they were logically challenged. Such people forgot something—we were shot down with official impunity. Did we have *free* speech, or did we have speech paid for in blood and suffering? And in light of how attempt after attempt was made to shut down our free speech after November Third, I know that we would have had none had we not struggled for every word.

Virulent and officially endorsed anticommunism sent a clear message to people that they must not give us their sympathy or support—or they, too, would be beyond the pale and treated accordingly. That made it all the more remarkable that great numbers of people joined our protests or started their own, gave us money toward a civil suit, spoke out with us in public, held press conferences, wrote letters, signed petitions, lobbied their congressmen, and personally supported us behind the scenes. It was not a majority but a very significant minority.[79] Concerned and enlightened citizens overcame calculated scare tactics and intimidation to step out of comfortable lives, take the initiative, and push forward the fight for justice. Two groups that sprang up around the verdict were the Citizens for Justice and Unity and the Concerned Citizens about the November Third Incident.

Nearly a hundred people met at a Friends Meeting House in an affluent, predominantly white section of Greensboro to form the Citizens for Justice and Unity. The group immediately pressed for a Justice Department investigation into the roles of Dawson and Butkovich.[80] Rumblings from the grassroots reached Washington, and Deputy Attorney General Drew S. Days III, the black head of the Justice Department's Civil Rights Division, responded by saying that his department would see if there were grounds for a federal prosecution and would examine the roles played by Dawson and Butkovich in the November 3, 1979, attack.[81] He did not say when.

NO STONE UNTURNED

District Attorney Michael Schlosser boasted that he "left no stone unturned" in preparing the prosecution's case. About a week after the acquittal verdicts, Schlosser dropped all charges against a second group of Klansmen and Nazis who were in the caravan and were to stand trial for first
degree murder or felony riot. He argued that the state's strongest case had
been against the six men already tried. Of those, five had guns and advanced
toward the intersection with their weapons. He called them the "gunslingers." All five were acquitted, as was a sixth person who drove the van
and exited knife in hand. Those who remained to be tried only had two-by-
two sticks, Schlosser said, and the pathology report indicated that no one
was killed with a stick. "The 'gunslingers' have been acquitted. No meaningful purpose will be served in proceeding in the prosecution of the 'stick
people,'" Schlosser concluded.[82] Simultaneous with the dropping of first degree murder and felony riot charges against the remaining Klan/Nazis,
Schlosser released his legal hostages, the Greensboro 6, by dropping the
felony riot charges against the six demonstrators. Within hours of the acquittal announcement, a couple of fire bombings and fires occurred in Greensboro's black community, causing minor property damage. Schlosser tried to
link these acts with the CWP and charged seven African Americans initially,
then eight, with conspiracy and acting as an accessory to a crime.[83] Among
those charged was Willena Cannon. The group came to be known as the
Greensboro 8.

The Greensboro 8 case was resolved several months later with a plea bargain
after Schlosser reduced the charges from felony burning to a misdemeanor. The
indictments against the Greensboro 8 were brought only days before a "Conference on Government Repression of Human Rights and the Rise of the Klan and
Nazis," planned by the CWP and other progressive groups for December 5 and
6, 1980. Ironically but not surprisingly, the powers in the city tried to prevent organizers from obtaining a site for that conference.

The hypocrisy of the indictments of the Greensboro 8 was conveyed by
Leila Mae Jenkins, the mother of one of those indicted and a lay preacher.
Rev. Jenkins subsequently played an active role in the Concerned Citizens
about the November Third Incident. In her moving statement after the acquittals and the indictments of her son and seven other African Americans,
she spoke out courageously against the galling double standard of justice. "If
my son was a Klan, if he was a Nazi, if he was a white racist, and if he had shot

people down in the street in cold blood, I probably wouldn't be standing here," she said.

The police knew all about the Klan going to Morningside to murder people. . . . They watched the Klan head to the rally, followed them from the highway to the rally. . . . But they said they couldn't stop any of the cars they knew were loaded with weapons. Yet they could stop my son all right on Nov. 17th, the night the acquittal verdict came down. They weren't worried about violating *his* constitutional rights. If my son were a Klansman on his way to murder someone, the police would protect his "right" to kill and then cover up and lie about it. I guess they would because that is what they did.

My son and the others have conspiracy charges on them. Now, this federal agent Butkovich went and planned Nov. 3rd with the Nazis. Greensboro police informer and FBI agent Ed Dawson went and planned Nov. 3rd with the police. And they had their plans worked out of who they were going to kill and how. So, if that's not a conspiracy, what is? But the D.A. Mike Schlosser dropped all the conspiracy charges in spite of all the evidence. But let a group of Black folks be riding around on the streets Nov. 17th when they let the Klan and Nazis go free and you get conspiracy charges on them and on people who weren't even with them. So this is rotten upside down justice. . . .

They're trying to do to my son and seven other Black people what they did to the Wilmington 10 and Charlotte 3. . . . We will fight for our loved ones to stay out of jail. . . . This could be your son out there. The way things are going, with this double standard of justice, if your son is honest and hates injustice like my son, it will be your son next.[84]

NOTES

1. Steve Berry, "Jury Is Shown Nov. 3 Arsenal," *Greensboro Daily News*, 7 August 1980, D1.

2. Patricia MacKay, "Prosecution Piles Up Evidence in Klan Trial," *North Carolina Anvil*, 5 September 1980. See also Associated Press, "Klan-Nazi Trial Shown Arsenal," *Charlotte Observer*, 30 August 1980, 1B.

3. Patricia MacKay, "Klan/Nazi Murder Trial," *North Carolina Anvil*, 29 August 1980, 4.

4. See Jim Wicker, "Agent's Testimony Sought," *Greensboro Record*, 5 August 1980, A2.

5. Jim Wicker, "Prosecutors Begin Attack on Smith Defense Strategy," *Greensboro Record*, 6 August 1980, A1.

6. Jim Wicker, "Reporter: Klan-Nazis Fired First," *Greensboro Record*, 8 August 1980, B2.

7. See Steve Berry, "Cameraman: First Shots from Caravan," *Greensboro Daily News*, 8 August 1980, A1, A12. This article contains details of Vaughn's testimony.

8. Jim Wicker, "Demonstrator Didn't Know of CWP Tie," *Greensboro Record*, 12 August 1980.

9. See Steve Berry, "Jurors View Videotape of Witness under Hypnosis," *Greensboro Daily News*, 20 August 1980, A1.

10. Steve Berry, "Testimony Contradicts Self-Defense," *Greensboro Daily News*, 14 August 1980, B1, B10.

11. Jim Wicker, "Women Accidentally in Motorcade Testify," *Greensboro Record*, 4 September 1980. See also Patricia MacKay, "Videotape Shows Defendant Shoot César Cauce," *North Carolina Anvil*, 12 September 1980.

12. Berry, "Testimony Contradicts Self-Defense," B1.

13. Quoted in Steve Berry, "Witness Links Defendant to CWP Member's Death," *Greensboro Daily News*, 22 August 1980.

14. Berry, "Witness Links Defendent."

15. Jim Wicker, "Klan Fire May Have Hit Mate," *Greensboro Record*, 25 August 1980, A1.

16. Wicker, "Klan Fire May Have Hit Mate," A2.

17. Steve Berry, "Testimony: Arms Urged by Leftists," *Greensboro Daily News*, 26 August 1980, B1.

18. Wicker, "Klan Fire May Have Hit Mate," A2.

19. Jim Wicker, "Witness Says He Saw 4 Fire," *Greensboro Record*, 3 September 1980. See also Wicker, "Women Accidentally;" and Steve Berry, "Testimony: All Six Fired," *Greensboro Daily News*, 4 September 1980.

20. Berry, "Testimony: All Six Fired," A1, A2.

21. Jim Wicker, "Doctor Testified on Fatal Wound," *Greensboro Record*, 26 August 1980, A1; see also Jim Wicker, "Doctor Says Pistol Shot Killed Leftist," *Greensboro Record*, 27 August 1980, B1.

22. Steve Berry, "Leftist Shot in Back, Jury Told," *Greensboro Daily News*, 27 August 1980.

23. Jim Wicker, "Two Defendants Named in Court," *Greensboro Record*, 22 August 1980.

24. See Wicker, "Two Defendants Named in Court," D2. See also Jim Wicker, "Guns Taken from Home Shown Jury," *Greensboro Record*, 29 August 1980.

25. See Jim Wicker, "Photos of Shootings Scene Admitted as Evidence," *Greensboro Record*, 2 September 1980. "The CWP can put up or shut up," Schlosser told reporters.

26. Jim Wicker, "Jailer: Killings Admitted," *Greensboro Record*, 28 August 1980, A1.

27. See Michael P. Massoglia, "Jailer Testifies Matthews Told Him, 'I Got Three,'" *Winston-Salem Journal*, 29 August 1980, 2.

28. MacKay, "Prosecution Piles Up Evidence."

29. Jim Wicker, "Fatal Bullet Tied to Others in Testimony," *Greensboro Record*, 11 September 1980.

30. Steve Berry, "Testimony Links Pellets with Defendants' Guns," *Greensboro Daily News*, 16 September 1980; and Jim Wicker, "Jury Gets Close Look at Pellets," *Greensboro Record*, 16 September 1980.

31. Wicker, "Jury Gets Close Look at Pellets"; and Massoglia, "Defense Attacks."

32. Jim Wicker, "Showing of Two Films Is Delayed," *Greensboro Record*, 10 September 1980.

33. Jim Wicker, "Defense Attempts to Discredit Expert," *Greensboro Record*, 15 September 1980, B2.

34. Associated Press, "FBI Agent Says Lead in Bullets Matches," *Durham Morning Herald*, 12 September 1980.

35. See Michael P. Massoglia, "Smith's Scrapbook Withheld from Jury," *Winston-Salem Journal*, 3 October 1980, 9.

36. Steve Berry, "Wood: 'I Didn't Want to Kill,'" *Greensboro Daily News*, 30 September 1980, A1, A13.

37. Associated Press, "Nazi Says He Didn't Shoot CWP Demonstrators," *Durham Morning Herald*, 30 September 1980, 13A.

38. Berry, "Wood: 'I Didn't Want to Kill,'" A1.

39. Michael P. Massoglia, "Forsyth Nazi Testifies He Fired in Self-Defense," *Winston-Salem Journal*, 30 September 1980, 14.

40. Massoglia, "Forsyth Nazi Testifies," 14.

41. Patricia MacKay, "Klan/Nazi Defendants Claim Self-Defense," *North Carolina Anvil*, 3 October 1980, 10.

42. MacKay, "Klan/Nazi Defendents Claim Self-Defense," 10.

43. MacKay, "Klan/Nazi Defendents Claim Self-Defense," 10.

44. Steve Berry, "Didn't Speak about Shots, Fowler Says," *Greensboro Daily News*, 2 October 1980, D1.

45. See Rick Stewart, "Smith Can't Remember," *Greensboro Record*, 2 October 1980.

46. "Judge Refuses to Hear Speech," *Durham Morning Herald*, 7 October 1980.

47. Michael P. Massoglia, "Anti-Klan Rally: 'World War III,'" *Winston-Salem Journal*, 8 October 1980.

48. Associated Press, "Police Informant Lead Caravan," *Durham Morning Herald*, 8 October 1980, 9A.

49. Jim Wicker, "Informant Led Klan to Rally," *Greensboro Record*, 7 October 1980, A2.

50. See Jim Wicker, "Prosecution Says Matthews Alters Story," *Greensboro Record*, 9 October 1980, A1, A2. See also Jim Wicker, "Klansman Pridmore Says He Didn't Fire His Weapon," *Greensboro Record*, 10 October 1980, A2.

51. Stefan Bechtel, "Klansman Admits Earlier Confession," (Burlington) *Times-News*, 10 October 1980, B1.

52. Steve Berry, "Tapes, Testimony Not in Agreement," *Greensboro Daily News*, 10 October 1980, C1, C2.

53. Wicker, "Klansman Pridmore Says He Didn't Fire His Weapon," A2.

54. See William March, "City Disallows CWP Message on Tombstone," *Greensboro Daily News*, 3 October 1980, C2; and "Widows Threaten Legal Action," *Durham Morning Herald*, 4 October 1980, 5A.

55. Attorney Norman B. Smith to Mr. Thomas P. Ravenel, Greensboro, 29 September 1980.

56. Blanche Alston, "City to Allow Political Wording on Tombstones," *Greensboro Record*, 17 October 1980.

57. Signe Waller to Norman B. Smith, Greensboro, 13 November 1980.

58. Steve Berry, "Witness Says Waller Wanted 'Martyr,'" *Greensboro Daily News*, 14 October 1980, B1.

59. Berry, "Witness Says Waller Wanted 'Martyr,'" B1.

60. Lindsey Gruson, "Prosecutors Relied on Media Evidence," *Greensboro Daily News*, 18 November 1980, A5.

61. Jim Wicker, "Shot Klansman Testimony Topic," *Greensboro Record*, 14 October 1980, B2.

62. Rick Steward, "Defense Beat State Effort," *Greensboro Record*, 18 November 1980, A17.

63. Steward, "Defense Beat State Effort," A17.

64. "Anger, Shock, Hopelessness, Fear Expressed; Some Distrust Justice," *Greensboro Daily News*, 19 November 1980, B1.

65. Quoted in Scott Shane, "City Officials Appeal for 'Peace, Tranquility,'" *Greensboro Daily News*, 18 November 1980, A13.

66. "Frye Gathers Groups in Post-Verdict Effort," *Greensboro Record*, 19 November 1980, B1.

67. Jim Schlosser, "Silent March, Singing Reflect '60s Protests," *Greensboro Record*, 21 November 1980, D2.

68. Associated Press, "Greensboro March Held to Protest Trial Verdict," *Durham Morning Herald*, 21 November 1980, 7A.

69. Quoted in Bob Hiles and Stan Swofford, "NAACP Calls for 'Period of Shame,'" *Greensboro Daily News*, 21 November 1980, A10.

70. Schlosser, "Silent March," D2.

71. Paul Brown, "Bond Leads Protest by NCCU Students," *Durham Morning Herald*, 21 November 1980, 1A.

72. Flontina Miller, "HRC Told Seek Federal Probe of Schlosser's Klan-Nazi Case," *Greensboro Record*, 22 November 1980.

73. Robin Clark, "Students Ask U.S. Probe in 5 Killings," *Charlotte Observer*, 24 November 1980.

74. "Judging the Jury," (Raleigh) *News & Observer*, 23 November 1980.

75. "Sheets and Swastikas," *New York Amsterdam News*, 22 November 1980, 16.

76. Mark I. Pinsky, "More Anguish in Greensboro," *Virginian-Pilot and The Ledger-Star*, 23 November 1980. This article was originally written as an opinion piece for *Commentary*. A version of it was published in the January 1981 issue of *The Progressive*.

77. Pinsky, "More Anguish."

78. Pinsky, "More Anguish."

79. See, for example, Elizabeth Swaringen, "Governor to Listen to Verdict Concerns," *Durham Sun*, 24 November 1980.

80. William March, "City to Combat Bias, May Hold Vote on Wards," *Greensboro Daily News*, 27 November 1980, B5.

81. Simon Anekwe, "KKK Acquitted in N.C.," *New York Amsterdam News*, 22 November 1980, 69.

82. See Associated Press, "13 Shootout Defendants Are Cleared," (Burlington, N.C.) *Times-News*, 27 November 1980, 1A, 2A.

83. See Eddie Marks, "Seven Indicted on Arson Charges," *Greensboro Daily News*, 2 December 1980.

84. Leila Mae Jenkins, "Greensboro 8 Defense Committee Statement," 5 January 1981.

15

THE BLITZ AMENDMENT
AND OTHER
McCARTHYISMS

RED-BAITING IS FASHIONABLE, FASCISM
ACCEPTABLE IN RULING CIRCLES

In the fall of 1980, a member of the Durham Human Relations Commission presented a position paper on subversive groups. The commission staff should collect information on CWP membership and activities, it recommended, and report to the Durham City Council so that city government could take "appropriate action."[1] The paper was rejected at a commission meeting in which CWP supporters and others concerned with civil liberties stood up to oppose it. Ann Finch, a trade unionist and the wife of Charles Finch, spoke out against it, saying, "Fascism doesn't come like a tank down the street, but in smaller, subtler steps like this position paper."[2] Marty Nathan urged the commission to reject the position paper, calling it a "further attack on people who fight back against the system" and a "resolution to spy upon the CWP."[3]

A witch-hunting atmosphere enveloped all attempts by the Greensboro Justice Fund to raise money for civil rights litigation. With the Klan/Nazi trial going on, the *Durham Morning Herald* published a "naming names" article about medical doctors who were supporting the fund. The article identified seven physicians and researchers on the GJF Advisory Board, along with their positions at the University of North Carolina and Duke University. "Their names appear on the brochure along with such well-known left-wing activists as Ben Chavis, Father Philip Berrigan, former Catholic nun Elizabeth McAlister, and Dr. Harvey Cox of the Harvard School of Divinity."[4] Reporters tracked down several of the academics to find out if they had ties to the CWP. One physician, declaring himself a registered Republican, said that he taught Marty Nathan in medical school. Others were concerned that the rights to free speech and assembly were being compromised and that the facts behind the massacre were being suppressed.

The executive director of the Greensboro Justice Fund, Dr. Neil S. Prose, had worked with Dr. Michael Nathan obtaining medical aid for antiapartheid refugees in Southern Africa. Prose responded to the *Durham Morning Herald* in a letter. "The Greensboro Justice Fund is an independent tax-exempt non-profit corporation which was formed in December, 1979, in response to the brutal massacre in Greensboro," he wrote. "The Greensboro Justice Fund is proud to count both communists and non-communists among its many supporters."[5]

In Greensboro, similar red-baiting tactics were used on attorney John Kernodle when he tried to host a wine and cheese party to raise funds for the Greensboro Justice Fund. Kernodle did not back down, held the fundraising event, and took the risks to his promising career in law and public life.

If a campaign of intimidation greeted contributors to the Greensboro Justice Fund and deterred potential contributors, Nazi fundraising functions seem not to have been similarly disrupted. While others condemned the violence in Greensboro and sought to bring about meaningful change in order to rid society of racism, Nazi Party leader Harold Covington was "incredibly overjoyed" by the jury's not-guilty verdict. He announced plans to create a "Carolina Free State," a home for racists off-limits to nonwhites.[6] He called the Greensboro killings "the first shots of the Second American Revolution." To gain acceptance for their racist state, he said, the Nazis would downplay the swastika symbol and adopt the Confederate flag.[7] No one in local or state government made a fuss over Covington's racist hate-mongering or raised public questions about *his* source of funding.

The resurgence of right-wing forces in a variety of guises and the revival of old-fashioned witch-hunting was met with a spirit of resistance and revived civil rights activity. Many people spoke out, met, marched, and acted to restrain what they saw as a step toward fascism.[8] Vigorous grassroots efforts in the early 1980s undoubtedly inhibited the reactionary violence that was already out of the gate. On the same day Covington boasted that Carolina was the promised land of white supremacy, the streets were full of protesters appalled by the Klan/Nazi verdict.

A coalition of lawyers, politicians, students, grassroots anti-Klan groups, university professors, ministers, blacks, Jewish, and antiwar organizations, socialist and communist parties, and others were part of an antifascist assembly that continued what anti-Klan forces meeting in Atlanta the previous December had begun. The CWP and the Greensboro Justice Fund played leadership roles in the coalition and in a December 1980 *Conference on Government Repression of Human Rights and the Rise of the Klan and Nazis.*

PEOPLE UNITED

Attorney Lewis Pitts, a South Carolinian with a pronounced regional dialect, moved to the Triad with his friend Katie Greene some months after November Third and connected with the Greensboro Justice Fund. An outstanding people's lawyer, Pitts learned about Greensboro while he was working with the Christic Institute in Washington, D.C. Greensboro seemed a likely place to invest time and energy after fighting a nuclear power company in the victorious Karen Silkwood case. He was exactly the kind of lawyer we needed to lead the legal fight for justice in our civil rights suit. A skilled legal strategist, Lewis understood the relationship between political activism and the courts. He was deeply committed to democratic processes and to people at the grassroots. Katie, an attractive, outgoing, and enthusiastic woman—later to marry Lewis— was one of the main organizers of antifascist activities in North Carolina. For years both were leaders in the grassroots movement for justice in the Greensboro Massacre.

The December 1980 conference was almost derailed for want of a meeting place. We would be offered an appropriate meeting facility, but then the would-be host would be alerted, with the result that we were denied the accommodation. Interference with the democratic right of assembly of people trying to meet together to discuss the danger of impending fascism was ironic, to say the least. On the eve of the conference, as participants were disembarking from planes, the site for conference registrants was canceled, this time by a nervous priest who had been told that the coalition was just a communist front. Tired and shivering travelers joined organizers in the street for an end-of-a-long-day press conference. I remember it well. Speaking for the coalition, People United against Government Repression and the Klan and Nazis, Lewis Pitts announced that the Red Velvet Club and Lounge had just agreed to host the conference.[9] A poorly lit and unheated nightclub, its parking lot a haven for winos and drug dealers, was home for over three hundred action-oriented antifascist political organizers for two days.

The media reported the speakers' theme as *racial unrest.* But conference participants came to discuss *government* repression and were in accord that the government was promoting, aiding, and covering up an increasing number of fascist attacks. The media treated this message as if it was in a foreign idiom and could not be translated—as if *racial unrest* was the closest translation into English. The opening panel compared Germany in the 1930s with the United States in the 1980s. Tema Bermanzohn, Paul's mother and a Holocaust survivor of the Maidanek Camp, gave a moving speech. I knew that Paul's parents did not desire political activism—for their children or themselves. This was understandable in light of what they had suffered. But that evening, Tema Bermanzohn publicly and fearlessly spoke the words in her heart. "Hitler started by killing small groups, intellectuals, and ended up killing six million Jews. I came to America for freedom," she said, "but five people are shot down dead in the street like dogs."[10] She did not think it could happen here. She never imagined that in America they could shoot and cripple her son and let the murderers walk away. The parallels to Germany of the 1930s were frightening.

Also inspiring was Anne Braden, a victim of the McCarthy era. She reminded people that fascism must have a mass base to take hold. In the 1950s, the public was told that the Russians were going to drop bombs on us: thirty years later the scapegoat was closer to home—black people were portrayed as the reason for crime in the streets and for unemployment among whites. Anne was optimistic that the government line—equated with the views of the "Moral Majority"—would not hold sway. "They call themselves the Moral Majority, but they're not moral, and they're not the majority. People who want to live together in justice and peace, they're the majority," she said.[11]

The conference brought together Leo Harris, a militant black leader in the Miami uprising and a labor activist in Teamsters' Local 769, with Rev. Phil Zwerling of the First Unitarian Church of Los Angeles and Sol Jacobs, Greensboro business man and civil rights advocate. The National Anti-Klan Network, representing many church and civil rights groups, contributed a solidarity statement read to the gathering.[12] "Combating Anti-Jewish Racism," "Responsible Journalism," "Survival of Black Colleges," "Women's Workshop," and "Government Funding of Klan/Nazis/Paramilitary Groups" were the titles of some of the workshop sessions. Ohio attorney Jim McNamara of Those United to Fight Fascism (TUFF) led a "What to do if the Klan rallies in your neighborhood" workshop.[13]

The coalition, its name abbreviated to People United, helped to direct and sustain grassroots resistance to government-sponsored repression. Katie Greene served as organizer/spokesperson in North Carolina, and Rene Dubose was a cochair from Washington. The group was instrumental in bringing pressure to bear on the Justice Department to prosecute the Klan and Nazis.

RACISM AND REACTION ENCLOSING THE GLOBE

If Harold Covington was salivating over the prospect of founding a racist state in the Carolinas, he was not merely a local anomaly. Xenophobic and terrorist right-wing organizations were becoming more vocal and visible in Western Europe. As in the United States, they enjoyed an alarming degree of official support. And they were beginning to network with American fascists.[14] A neo-Nazi bomb attack at Oktoberfest in Germany in the fall of 1980 killed twelve people and injured more than two hundred. Although officially banned, Nazis were holding outdoor rallies in the style of Hitler's National Socialist Party.[15] A wave of anti-Semitic violence and explosions at synagogues hit Paris in the fall of 1980. Within a three-month period, there were forty attacks in France alone by neo-Nazis. In one assault, four people were killed and seven were seriously injured by a bomb placed near a synagogue.[16]

France's "New Right" had its intellectuals, such as Alain de Benoist, whose writings justified "an intelligent racism." France's interior minister had a list of 150 members of a banned fascist organization, and thirty of them were policemen.[17] The French people responded with vigor. In one demonstration on October 7, 1980, unequaled since World War II, over 100,000 people lined the boulevards of Paris near the Place de la Bastille. The marchers stretched for miles and many carried banners that said "We are all French Jews."[18]

Also responding with vigor to a resurgence of Nazism were thousands of demonstrators in Evanston, Illinois, including many Holocaust survivors. They prevented a Nazi rally. The small contingent of Nazis lasted only five minutes under a hail of rocks, eggs, and tomatoes, accompanied by chants of "Death to the Nazis."[19]

The Klan and other white supremacist groups were operating paramilitary camps with virtually no interference from the government. An Alabama KKK paramilitary camp, modeled after the Green Beret "Special Forces" and named after Lt. William Calley (who wiped out a civilian village in Vietnam), conducted guerrilla warfare training with M-16s in preparation for a "race war."[20] Bill Wilkinson's Invisible Empire of the Ku Klux Klan was the main Klan faction involved in the Alabama camp. (Interestingly, it emerged that Wilkinson was an active FBI informant.) The Invisible Empire was the violent group that fired on black demonstrators in Decatur, Alabama, in 1979, and it was also the Klan faction to which Virgil Griffin belonged. Previously, Bill Wilkinson had been David Duke's chief lieutenant in the New Orleans Knights of the Ku Klux Klan. They went their separate ways, with Duke forming the National Association for the Advancement of White People and embarking on a career in electoral politics.[21]

The regrouping of individuals on the right to better position themselves in a newly more favorable climate included a switch-over by Nazi party member and Greensboro Massacre caravan participant Glenn Miller to become the leader of a new Klan faction formed with his help, the Carolina Knights of the Ku Klux Klan. A former Special Forces soldier, Miller turned over his Johnston County farm, located twenty-eight miles south of Raleigh, to a variety of white supremacist groups to use as a military training camp.[22]

Representative John Conyers, Black Congressional Caucus member, chairing a House Subcommittee investigating whether any governmental bodies were linked to violence-prone organizations such as the Klan and Neo-Nazis, learned that the Klan had paramilitary and psychological training camps in Alabama, California, Connecticut, Illinois, North Carolina, and Texas. Klan Youth Corps camps were operating in San Diego, San Bernardino, and Los Angeles, California; Peoria and Chicago, Illinois; Jeffersonville, Indiana; Oklahoma City, Oklahoma; Denver and Hillsborough, Colorado; and Birmingham, Tuscumbia, Tuscaloosa, and Decatur, Alabama.[23]

In Houston, Texas, under cover of the Boy Scouts and the Civil Air Patrol, a Ku Klux Klansman and a convicted felon were teaching youths how to strangle people, decapitate enemies with a machete, and fire semiautomatic weapons.[24] In another Texas paramilitary training camp in the Houston area, Klan Grand Dragon Louis Beam gave instruction in the techniques of killing and terror.[25] Beam became a main figure in the antigovernment, white supremacist militia movement, and a theorist whose views about guerrilla warfare and leaderless resistance were embodied in such acts of terror as the 1995 Oklahoma City bombing. In a 1998 TV documentary, Morris Dees of the Southern Poverty Law Center called Beam "the bridge between the Klan of the past and the extremist, domestic terrorists of the present and the future . . . the militia, so-called patriot movement in America today." Dees, said that Beam, "had as many as three thousand armed people training in five separate training camps in Texas for the day that there would be a revolution, a race war."[26] Hiding behind patriotism, anticommunism, and opposition to gun laws, a right-wing movement of terrorists was allowed to flourish in the 1980s. In contrast, consider for how many minutes a known left-wing paramilitary operation would be ignored and tolerated by the powers that be.

The 1980 election of Ronald Reagan to the presidency was a victory for right-wing extremists. Many of their positions were made rhetorically more palatable and were actually adopted by representatives of *both* major parties. California Klan leader, Tom Metzger, his campaign built on scapegoating immigrants, ran on a Democratic Party ticket in the 43rd Congressional District in

California. He lost the election but obtained over 45,000 votes.[27] In the course of Metzger's campaign, leftist organizations opposing him were attacked. In Los Angeles, the headquarters of the Communist Party was bombed and an explosive device was found at the back door of the office of the Socialist Workers Party.[28] In Michigan, Gerald Carlson, a former Nazi and Klansman campaigning in support of all-white cities, won the Republican nomination for a congressional district in a Detroit suburb. He lost also, but earned 53,000 votes to his rival's 113,000.[29] And I have already mentioned Harold Covington's bid for North Carolina attorney general.

Official tolerance of right-wing ideology was surely linked to a number of murders and acts of terror that bore a Klan/Nazi imprimatur. Only the Red Summer of 1919, when hundreds of blacks were lynched and sometimes even publicly burned, outdistanced the acts of racist terror and violence in 1980, said African American syndicated columnist Manning Marable.[30] Most sinister were events in Buffalo and Atlanta.

In Buffalo in September 1980, a black fourteen-year-old boy was sitting in a parked car when a lone gunman shot him in the head. Within thirty-six hours, three other black males were executed similarly. Two vehicles with whites invaded the first victim's funeral screaming racial epithets in front of a black church. A few weeks later, two more bodies of black men were discovered, one stabbed and the other bludgeoned to death, both with their hearts cut out. Then a black surgery patient in a local hospital narrowly escaped being strangled to death when a white man entered his room and started choking him, shouting "I hate niggers!" The description of the assailant given to police by eyewitnesses was similar to descriptions of the gunman in the earlier murders, but local authorities apparently did next to nothing to find the killer. In a demonstration sponsored by two hundred religious, educational, socialist, and labor groups at Buffalo's city hall on October 19, 1980, five thousand people, blacks and whites, urged U.S. Attorney Civiletti in Washington to take charge of an investigation.[31] Continuing attacks on black males were endorsed by the Nazi Party that was trying to establish a foothold in western New York. A couple of thousand anti-Nazi demonstrators confronted the few Nazis who rallied in Buffalo on Martin Luther King's birthday.[32]

In Atlanta, a string of child killings in which all the victims were black and poor began in July 1979 and continued into 1981.[33] After eighteen months with as many missing children, seventeen of whom turned up later as corpses, police reported their first lead in the cases—matching fibers on several bodies suggested the same killer for those victims. In the middle of this genocide, an explosion at a day care center killed four preschoolers and a teacher. A disbelieving black community rejected officials' report of a faulty furnace and speculated that the Klan was involved in the deaths.[34] With their childrens' murders unsolved, and little happening to prevent future murders, tenants in Atlanta's Techwood Homes housing project organized to protect their community. But city officials discouraged this initiative: police challenged the residents' right to an armed patrol and arrested two on patrol.[35]

Scholar, activist, and columnist Manning Marable connected the lawless violence to lawmaking strategies for dismantling the Civil Rights Act of 1964. Quoting U.S. Commission on Civil Rights chair Arthur Flemming, Marable suggested segregationists were attaching a series of riders on appropriation bills that would, added together, annihilate the gains of civil rights legislation. In the black experience, Marable summarized, "the turbulent events of 1980 amounted to another periodic rejection by whites of the historical demands of black people for political equality and economic opportunity."[36]

CAUSE AND EFFECT

A Klan resurgence was underway when the Greensboro Massacre occurred, and that event was but a dramatic example of it. The massacre itself, and especially the acquittals a year later, moreover, provided an indisputable impetus for future terrorism by the right. Legally the November Third killers were exculpated: in Klan circles they were venerated. Summarizing the year 1980, Manning Marable wrote, "Motivated by what they perceive as a major victory in Greensboro, N.C., American Nazis are increasingly joining forces with the Klan."[37]

The acquittal of Klansmen who shot four black women in Chattanooga, the acquittal of police who murdered Arthur McDuffie in Miami, the Klan/Nazi acquittals, and the government's blind eye to armed training camps run by the Klan to fight a race war signaled to many that "fascism in America is no longer a remote possibility; it is actually being implemented."[38] To this list can be added the conviction of a black man in Decatur, Alabama—Curtis Robinson—who wounded a Klansman in May 1979 while defending himself and his family against attack. The Klansmen who shot and beat demonstrators at the same rally were not even arrested, proving an oft repeated adage of black people that justice in the United States meant "just us."[39]

Against such a background, one may better appreciate the significance of a federal appeals court decision to overturn the Wilmington 10 convictions, thus vindicating the persecuted civil rights activists.[40] The nine-year legal battle came to a victorious end immediately preceding the Greensboro "Conference on

Government Repression of Human Rights and the Rise of the Klan and Nazis." Anne Braden rejoiced that "such victories can be won in the face of tremendous odds." She took note of "*how*" such victories are won and how they advance the entire people's movement. . . . It takes a combination of mass political action and good legal work to win." Braden described how the Wilmington 10 campaign was built from the ground up during the Nixon years when the black liberation movement was under assault everywhere. Beginning with efforts by the United Church of Christ's Commission for Racial Justice and followed by sustained and committed organizing by the National Alliance against Racist and Political Repression and others, people were drawn into the case, and many became part of a movement for social justice because of it. Thus a defense against repression can become a political offensive. Mass movements do not appear by magic, she emphasized. "They develop because people, in the face of overwhelming obstacles, do the long and sometimes tedious work that it takes to build them."[41]

Oppression breeds resistance: signs of growing racism and anti-Semitism spurred the formation of new groups ready to resist oppression and to fight for a progressive agenda of democratic rights for all people. For example, the New Jewish Agenda, an activist organization for progressive Jews, was founded in the early 1980s. The Supreme Court's Bakke decision, recognized as a historic reversal of hard-won rights of minorities and women, engendered resistance. More than eight thousand students from predominantly black colleges marched in Washington for financial support to educate black youth and maintain black colleges.[42] An active grassroots movement helped Morris Dees and the Southern Poverty Law Center launch "Klanwatch."[43] A thousand people convening in Philadelphia in the fall of 1980, among them Nelson and Joyce Johnson, established the National Black Independent Political Party (NBIPP). Concerned by the election of Ronald Reagan, the Greensboro acquittals, and the economic exploitation of black youths, NBIPP reminded Americans of what the country's priorities should be. Dr. Manning Marable, one of the organizers, described the new organization as "not socialist, but . . . clearly and unequivocally anti-capitalist."[44]

THE BLITZ AMENDMENT

In the 1980s, Reagan presided over the shredding of the safety net in an orgy of budget cutting. In the redistribution of wealth that marked the decade of the eighties, wealth flowed from those who had little to begin with into the coffers of the already wealthy. Rationales by the ruling class were not lacking: the poor were undeserving welfare cheats; the social welfare budget had to be slashed to unburden Americans of big government; minorities and immigrants were to blame for America's economic woes and were lording it over everyone else. After the 1979 murders in Greensboro, the recession in the textile industry worsened, adding to a gloomy economic picture.[45] To accomplish the redirecting of wealth upward and the reordering of national priorities, people had to be persuaded of the merits of discarding existing social programs—or at least keep their mouths shut about it. An oligarchic political will emanating from Washington found ways to dismantle the welfare state. It is in this context that I view, and invite the reader to view, the little known episode of the Blitz Amendment.

Allen and Dori Blitz were unpretentious folks whose conversation was full of sparkle, humor, and instruction. Allen was from a working-class Jewish family in the Bronx; Dori was from a Quaker family in Indiana (not the Nixon variety of Quakerism, she was careful to explain). Both of Dori's grandmothers qualified for membership in the Daughters of the American Revolution, and one was actually a member. In 1978, the Blitzes moved from Greensboro to Martinsville, Virginia, an hour's drive to the north. Jim and I stayed in touch with them, and they continued to participate in WVO activities. They were at the anti-Klan rally on November 3.

Allen set up the sound system that day. Dori, who had passed out flyers about the anti-Klan rally at her workplace, brought some coworkers with her. She agreed to help with security and had my .38 caliber handgun, given to her by Jim, in her raincoat pocket. When the Klan and Nazis started shooting, she fired back in an attempt to defend the marchers. Shocked by the attack, untrained in weapons, and philosophically pacifistic, Dori hit no one. Allen was the person behind the nonperforming Derringer. But the story of the Blitz Amendment begins *after* the rally, when the Blitzes returned to Martinsville.

A former elementary school teacher with an advanced degree in recreation administration, Dori was working at the Budd Company trailer plant in Ridgeway, Virginia, before the anti-Klan rally. She was a union member and shop steward in Teamsters Local 22. The union was passive when Dori first came to Budd. She shook things up, filing eighteen grievances in 1978 and seventy-two in 1979. Dori started a newsletter, organized a Shop Stewards' Committee, and was leading a rank-and-file movement for trade union democracy and safe working conditions at Budd.

Dori's situation was similar to that of the murdered CWP union leaders and brings out the union-busting motive that was a prime aspect of the November Third attack. Her success in organizing the rank-and-file of an established union drove fear into the hearts of the company and bureaucratic union officials alike.

Neither wanted a union that they could not control. Dori was already struggling with Teamster officials before November 3. The union activism that she ignited died with the death of Dori's friends, the CWP 5. One of Dori's coworkers told interviewer John Hubner that at first it made no difference that Dori was a communist. Workers agreed with what she was saying and doing about the union, and supported her. After the Greensboro Massacre, fear drove many workers away from Dori, and support for the union disappeared.

The Budd Company posted a picture in the break room of the five slain in Greensboro. A caption scrawled below it read, "This is what happens to communists." Dozens of workers signed a petition to remove Dori as shop steward. Returning from Greensboro, Dori faced a full-fledged attempt to oust her from her union position. A week after the anti-Klan rally, the union hall at which her stewardship was to be discussed was surrounded by over one hundred state troopers, FBI agents, and local police. Henry County and the City of Martinsville declared a state of emergency. A rumor mill threw out fear-arousing suggestions of a violent confrontation. Workers both for and against Dori, determined to meet anyway, went to the union hall. They found a locked building and a sign canceling the meeting. Dori went to the union hall but left upon seeing the meeting canceled.[46] The evening before, the FBI paid a visit to her home and warned her husband that his wife's life would be in danger if she went to the union meeting. But Dori wanted the chance to speak to union members and to explain that Budd was whipping up anticommunism to divert employees' attention from impending layoffs. (As it happened, within a year, the plant closed, putting five hundred people out of work.) "I am still under a threat for my life," Dori told reporters, "but I shall continue to fight for the oppressed and against all attacks by the capitalists on the working class."[47]

Subsequently—and behind closed doors—Local 22 leaders eased Dori out of her shop stewardship, Budd fired her, and the NLRB, though presented with workers' testimony that the company harassed Dori in response to her building a rank-and-file movement, refused to engage its legal mission of protecting workers' right to organize. Allen's jobless fate unfolded less dramatically: the local furniture company where he worked fired him immediately after the November 3 rally. The Blitzes, parents of toddler Kendra, were unemployed. In April 1980, both qualified for and enrolled in the CETA (Comprehensive Employment Training Act) program. They were learning carpentry and masonry at a local community college and receiving the allotted minimum wage while in training.

I visited the Blitzes in Martinsville one day in the early fall of 1980 at the handyman's special they were trying, with their labor, to transform into their dream house. Some dilapidated houses have rustic charm, but this one did not immediately announce its possibilities to me through the missing pieces of flooring and walls. The kitchen, nevertheless, was cozy, and my friends looked at photos that I had brought of a camping trip Jim and I enjoyed the year before. We reminisced about Jim, Bill, and Sandi with funny stories that let their essences settle back upon us amid light, healing laughter. Dori showed me her latest flyer, rallying the citizens of Henry County to resist the Public Service Authority's mandatory water hook-up fees. Dori, a true daughter of the American Revolution, was reviled by the conservative establishment of Martinsville but had the support of many of the town's poorer residents.

Enter the villain of the piece—5th District representative, Democrat W. C. "Dan" Daniel. The former national commander of the American Legion discovered the Blitzes (as one might discover the location of a hornet nest) when it looked like their sting could adversely affect local capitalists. Enraged that communists in his district were participating in a federally funded program, Daniel went on the warpath to oust the Blitzes from CETA. As the Blitzes were in scrupulous conformity with all the rules of eligibility, removing them threatened the loss of CETA funds to Martinsville. Daniel took the Blitzes' inclusion in the program as "another example of the federal government browbeating localities into submission."[48]

The Blitzes blitzed back—"Yes, we stand on our position that there must be a revolution in the United States." Daniel, they said,

"would strip us of our political freedom, deprive us of our livelihood. If he had his way, he would jail us, just as Russia jails political dissenters. We are unemployed, indeed, and that unemployment is precisely because of the attack on us designed by Budd and the FBI. . . . Over the past year, we and other supporters of the Communist Workers Party have been harassed, slandered, fired from jobs, falsely charged by law enforcement agencies, and, in the case of Greensboro, assassinated. Congressman Daniel's remarks are one more attempt to prevent us from taking a stand against the government imposing fascism and World War."[49]

Naming the Blitzes on the House floor, Daniel introduced a bill in Congress to amend CETA. "No person who publicly advocates the violent overthrow of the U.S. government or has advocated such a course of action within the past five years shall be permitted to participate in any program authorized by this act," went the language.[50]

CETA workers, perhaps intuiting their program was headed for the chopping block, closed ranks. A local citizen defended the Blitzes' right as taxpayers to the same benefits as other jobless persons who may not belong to a political party or voice their opinions.[51] Dori agreed. "We've fed the hand that feeds us for years," she told the *Washington Post*. "We paid our taxes . . . and we are entitled to this program."[52] Allen admitted that "the CETA money we earn keeps us going. Without it, we couldn't present our point of view. Even communists have to eat."[53]

In a letter to the local paper, the Blitzes clarified their views. The U.S. government does not serve the interests of the majority of Americans and must be overthrown, they declared. "But only the American people will be able to overthrow the government . . . the American people will revolt because they have no other choice." The Soviet Union, the countries of Eastern Europe, and China labeled themselves communist, but they were hypocrites just as some people who call themselves Christians are hypocrites—"only if you fight in the interests of the vast majority of the people, and consistently act in those interests, are you Communist."[54] Daniel was attacking the freedom of speech and political belief of all Americans. He was launching a fascist attack through "legal" channels.

Less than two weeks later, the CETA issue came before the Senate, presented by Senator Hollings of South Carolina on behalf of himself and Senator Harry Byrd of Virginia. Hollings asked for unanimous consent for adding "a little language" to the CETA bill. How could anyone object, he asked, to inserting at the end of the bill "No funds appropriated under this act will be expended to provide employment or training to any person who publicly advocates the violent overthrow of the United States Government?"[55] Senator William Proxmire of Wisconsin, known liberal, responded with "Mr. President, I do not know how anybody could possibly object to this amendment."[56] No one did object. Press clips from the Blitzes' various statements asserting the need for revolution were inserted into the Congressional Record. Unanimously approved, the resolution was returned to the House where it passed in an expanded version recommended by Daniel—not merely CETA, but *all* federally funded programs were to deny dollars to people like the Blitzes, who were of the wrong political persuasion. The full spending resolution, of which the Blitz Amendment was a part, then traveled back to the Senate for final approval. That would have been a done deed, but in the pre-Christmas rush to conclude the business of the 96th Congress, legislators haggling over their pay raises had to drop the Blitz Amendment and many other amendments from the spending measure in order to pass it quickly.[57] Congressman Dan Daniel crowed that "total success was almost achieved."[58] He anticipated no difficulty in passing the amendment when the new Congress convened.

In the next year and a half, during which the Blitz Amendment was treading water or swimming through legal channels, the Blitzes stayed active politically and Dori gave birth to their second daughter, Megan. She continued to be outspoken on various issues affecting low-income citizens and ran, though unsuccessfully, for a seat on the Martinsville city council. Allen fought the Virginia Parks and Recreation Department of Henry County when he was sent home on the first day of a job that he had secured through CETA. The Equal Employment Opportunity Commission in the U. S. Department of Labor found Henry County in violation of the 1964 Civil Rights Act. Allen declared it "a small victory" and warned that if the county failed to comply with the EEO officer, he would go to federal court. "We must use the laws and agencies that afford us some measure of civil liberties while such protection still exists. Under the present administration and mood of Congress, both Civil Rights and liberties are rapidly becoming 'endangered species,'" he said.[59]

In their home in Martinsville, the Blitzes' courage in standing up to attack won them, in the words of one local resident, "affectionate tolerance." The red-baiting did not catch on: perhaps people were too busy dealing with survival issues. A local Vietnam War veteran described the deterioration of the textile and furniture town in words that fit many a small town, USA, in the 1980s.

> "We're on the decline. In the last ten years since I got out of the service . . . the population is declining. Lots of people go South, some North or to the coastal areas to get work. Or they go in the service. . . . Most people are poor like me. I don't have no electricity or plumbing. I just got some property here I inherited. Most Vietnam vets here are messed up. Most feel like I do—more radical. They're out to screw the government and fake out Uncle Sam. . . . People here can't understand why they can't keep a job, why wages are so bad. It drives people to drinking and drugs."[60]

Right after the 96th Congress, the nearly passed Blitz Amendment engendered controversy. Civil liberties attorney Joseph Rauh, leader of Americans for Democratic Action, thought "the defeat of McCarthyism in the '50s inoculated this country against this sort of thing," but feared "that the inoculation appears to be wearing off."[61]

Richard Cohen, in a *Washington Post* editorial titled "Want U.S. Job? Check Your Political Views," found it objectionable that belief, and not action or deeds, could be made a condition of training or employment. The Blitz Amendment would tell poor people to keep their mouths shut or starve. Cohen saw it as a return to the spirit of the 1950s when "people were asked what they thought and when they thought it and whether they would be willing, just to prove their patriotism, to think it no more and to inform on those who did."[62]

Similar objections were registered in *The Nation* magazine. After CETA, there were food stamps, welfare, veterans' benefits, and maybe even personal income tax exemptions. What kinds of tests could establish who should be barred from these benefits? "Loyalty oaths come most readily to mind, and the Federal Bureau of Investigation and its pack of informers would have to be set loose again. Congress would also need some sort of oversight committee—say, H.U.A.C., or the new Senate Judiciary Subcommittee on Security and Terrorism—to monitor Federal programs for compliance."[63]

Journalist John Hubner quoted Bob Brauer, special council to Representative Ron Dellums: "We've got to dig our trenches in front of the Blitzes." Brauer recalled the famous lines of German pastor Martin Niemoller—"'First the Nazis came for the communists, and I said nothing. Then they came for the Jews, and I said nothing. By the time they came for me, there was no one left to speak for anyone.' The right in America is coming for the communists. The defense of justice at the first point of attack is the only practical defense."[64]

Senator Strom Thurmond, new head of the Senate Judiciary Committee, proposed a Subcommittee on Internal Security and Terrorism. In early 1981, the subcommittee, chaired by Senator Jeremiah Denton, was ready to go into action. Congressman Larry McDonald was preparing legislation to bring back H.U.A.C. as the House Committee on Internal Security. John Rees, an editor for *Western Goals*, and Bill Poole, of the *Heritage Foundation*, both ultraconservative foundations, expected the CWP would be one of the first groups the new committee would investigate.

Hubner observed that "the extreme right doesn't seem as concerned about the CWP's activities as it does about the party's ideology." He quotes Rees as saying of the CWP, "I don't think their economic analysis is far wrong."[65] Rees predicted, "The first two years of the Reagan free-enterprise administration are going to create many more disasters than the average Joe anticipates. Government programs like CETA are going to end, causing heavy unemployment. . . . The hard times ahead are going to create a climate for extremism. Some people in hardship will go to the CWP. Others will ride with the Klan."[66]

What the right feared, I believe, was that the CWP had the potential to recruit workers like the disaffected Martinsville Vietnam vet who had no future under capitalism, and the CWP had a proven track record in uniting workers across race and nationality: the party posed a "threat" of socialist revolution that had to be taken seriously.

The Blitz Amendment, wrote Jerry Tung in an editorial on the new McCarthyism, reflected the desperation of the ruling class. The capitalists wanted to cut social welfare programs drastically and needed to divert people's attention away from the budget cuts. Tung reminded people that only one of every four eligible voters chose Reagan: the president did not have a mandate from the electorate for government repression. Tung also saw in the Reagan victory "a conscious shift in tactics of the capitalist class as a whole in order to stream-line their rule to meet the crisis ahead." The tactical shift accomplished with Reagan gave play to the reactionary "Neanderthal" elements, Tung thought. In the past these reactionary elements represented the interests of smaller mo-nopolies. They were now the political henchmen picked to serve the biggest monopoly capitalists and help them "get out from under the '80s [economic] crisis at the expense of smaller monopolies and the American people."[67]

The danger of a new McCarthyism, Victor Navasky of *The Nation* said of the Denton subcommittee on terrorism, did not lie in a repeat of the history of the 1950s. Rather, it was a matter of the "lateral encouragement" the Reagan ad-ministration was possibly offering to state and local Red squads, to private vigi-lante groups like the Klan and Omega-7, and to such respectable-seeming groups as the Heritage Foundation and the American Security Council. The new repressive arrangements sponsored by the government would "legitimize the illegitimate" and "make respectable that which was previously done only un-dercover because it was fundamentally shameful."[68]

Many progressive opinion-makers from around the country joined in de-nouncing the Blitz Amendment and its attack on first amendment rights. How-ever, left and progressive forces must have been nodding off when, toward the end of 1981, in something resembling a sneak attack, Daniel succeeded in pass-ing the Blitz Amendment as part of a Labor, Health, and Human Services ap-propriations bill. No media attention and no debate in Congress accompanied the event. The next signs of protest heard came after December 15, 1981, *the day that President Reagan signed the Blitz Amendment into law.*

Nat Hentoff wrote, "In 1982, with the Blitz Amendment become law, we are moving again toward a Soviet-like standard for certain kinds of free speech in the United States. You don't suppose Dan Daniel is a mole, do you?"[69]

Opposition to the Blitz Amendment went into high gear, driven by the ener-gies of People United, that stalwart group of antifascists that met in the Red Vel-vet Club and Lounge in Greensboro after the Klan trial acquittals.

I visited the Blitzes in Martinsville again while Dori was waging her city council campaign. The new baby was securely cradled in a room in the ram-shackle country house, and Megan's older sister, Kendra, was just the right age to act out her maternal instincts. Dori was running on a platform that included a tax on corporations to finance a local hike in the minimum wage to $4.00 an hour, a ward system for city council elections, and attention to quality education. "This town," she told a reporter, "has been run too long by those whose only concept of social change is determined by gains and losses in their stock portfo-lios or whether they can fly to Europe in the spring."[70]

I must go back to the public record for the details on the outcome of the Blitz Amendment because, musing on it now, it appears to have slipped away like a thief in the night. Actually, it was the object of a lawsuit filed on behalf of Dori Blitz by the American Civil Liberties Union and the National Emergency Civil Liberties Committee. On May 14, 1982, Federal District Judge Barrington Parker declared that "the legislative history of the amendment left no doubt that it was specifically intended to exclude Mrs. Blitz from the CETA program because of her political beliefs and affiliations and because she expressed those beliefs in her community" and ruled it unconstitutional.

Dori Blitz earned her certificate in brick masonry. The Blitzes moved to New York late in 1982, and Dori became an organizer for the Federation for Progress, a coalition of progressive groups. Proud of the victory over the Blitz Amendment, and not terribly upset at having failed to win the Martinsville city council seat, Dori told a reporter, "we've made people think about who actually controls government. We've made people think what it means to organize."[71]

NOTES

1. Lanny Harward, Commissioner, "Position Statement: Subversive Groups," presented to the Durham Human Relations Commission, 9 September 1980.

2. William M. Smith, "Paper on CWP, Klan Rejected," *Durham Morning Herald*, 8 October 1980, 1C.

3. Amy O'Neal, "Two End Terms on Board," *Durham Sun*, 8 October 1980, 1C.

4. "Area Doctors Aid CWP Fund," *Durham Morning Herald*, 21 August 1980.

5. Dr. Neil Prose, letter to the *Durham Morning Herald*, 30 August 1980.

6. "Anger, Shock, Hopelessness, Fear Expressed; Some Distrust Justice," B2.

7. Martha Woodall, "Nazis to Attempt Establishment of Segregated Nation," *Greensboro Record*, 18 November 1980.

8. See "KKK Facing a Rising Tide of Protest," *Newsday*, 7 December 1980.

9. "Political Coalition Here Today," *Greensboro Daily News*, 5 December 1980, B1.

10. Bob Hiles, "Coalition Fears Rise of Fascism," *Greensboro Daily News*, 6 December 1980, B1.

11. Hiles, "Coalition Fears Rise of Fascism," B1.

12. "Klan Opponents Urge March in Washington on Inauguration Day," *New York Times*, 7 December 1980.

13. See Bob Hiles, "'60s Rebels' New Cause Fighting Racism?" *Greensboro Daily News*, 7 December 1980. See also Mark I. Pinsky, "A Leftist Strategy against Klan," *Newsday*, 7 December 1980.

14. For an example of this networking, see "U.S. Revokes Nazis' Visas; 4 Fly Home," *Greensboro Daily News*, 13 October 1980.

15. "Nazi Revival Threatens Munich," *Winston-Salem Journal*, 1 October 1980, 5.

16. Flora Lewis, "Does France Have a Nostalgia for Swastikas?" *Greensboro Daily News*, 8 October 1980.

17. Associated Press, "Bomb Rocks Paris Again; Tourist Hurt," *Durham Morning Herald*, 6 October 1980, 2A.

18. Associated Press, "Over 100,000 March against Anti-Semitism," *Durham Morning Herald*, 8 October 1980, 1A.

19. Associated Press, "Rocks, Eggs and Tomatoes Chase Nazi Demonstrators," *Durham Morning Herald*, 20 October 1980, 12A.

20. "The KKK Goes Military," *Newsweek*, 6 October 1980, 52.

21. See David L. Langford, "Klan: A Late Comer and Self-Made Imperial Wizard," second article in series of three, *Durham Morning Herald*, 30 December 1980, 9B.

22. See "No Paramilitary Training in State, Says Nazi Leader," *Greensboro Record*, 25 October 1980; and "KKK Leader Teaches White People Defense," (Thomasville, N.C.) *Times*, 21 March 1981.

23. David L. Langford, "Klan: Guerrillas Training for Race War," first article in series of three, *Durham Morning Herald*, 29 December 1980, 7B.

24. Associated Press, "Klansman, Felon Teaching Scouts Warfare Skills," *Greensboro Daily News*, 24 November 1980.

25. See "Other Klan Camps Claimed," *Durham Morning Herald*, 8 December 1980, 6B.

26. From the documentary *The Ku Klux Klan: A Secret History*, produced by Termite Art Productions in association with Bill Brummel for the History Channel, A&E Television Networks, videocassette, 1998.

27. David L. Langford, "Hooded Order: KKK's Racist Appeal Spreading in Discontented Nation," third article in series of three, *Durham Morning Herald*, 31 December 1980, 7B.

28. "Condemn Fascist Attacks," *Workers World*, 3 October 1980.

29. Langford, "Hooded Order: KKK's Racist Appeal."

30. Manning Marable, "The Red Year of 1980," syndicated column, *Carolina Peacemaker*, 31 January 1981.

31. Associated Press, "Blacks Urge Attorney General to Act," *Durham Sun*, 20 October 1980, 2A; and Manning Marable, "The Red Year of 1980," *Carolina Peacemaker*, 7 February 1981.

32. "Buffalo Confronts Nazi Rally," *Carolina Peacemaker*, 31 January 1980, 1.

33. "Caretaker Finds Body of 15th Slain Atlanta Child," *Greensboro Record*, 6 February 1981. See also "Atlanta Curfew Ordered," *Greensboro Record*, 28 January 1981; and "Atlanta Police Hunt for Another Child," *Greensboro Daily News*, 9 February 1981.

34. Associated Press, "Parents Blame Klan in Blast," *Durham Sun*, 14 October 1980, 2A.

35. "Two Gun-Carrying Members of Atlanta Patrol Arrested," (Thomasville, N.C.) *Times*, 21 March 1981.

36. Marable, "The Red Year," 7 February 1981.

37. Marable, "The Red Year," 7 February 1981. See also "KKK Leader Teaches White People Defense." Glenn Miller confirms what Marable says.

38. Kathryn Green, letter from the Anti-Klan Conference Coalition—North Carolina Task Force, inviting groups to attend a conference, 27 November 1980.

39. Southern Poverty Law Center, *Klanwatch*, 1981.

40. See Stan Swofford, "Wilmington 10 Convictions Overruled," *Greensboro Daily News*, 5 December 1980, A1.

41. Anne Braden, "What the Wilmington 10 Victory Means," *Southern Fight-Back*, January 1981.

42. Carol Hanner, "WSSU Students March in Rally," *Winston-Salem Journal*, 1 October 1980, 12.

43. "Group Forms to Expose Klan Activity," *Durham Morning Herald*, 11 December 1980, 14C.

44. See "Blacks Organize National Political Party," *Greensboro Daily News & Record*, 23 November 1980, A5.

45. See Winston Cavin, "Short-Time: 'It Hurts,'" *Greensboro Daily News*, 16 November 1980, A1.

46. Danny Barkin and Dennis Hartig, "Meeting Canceled, Union Fails to Oust Communist," *Martinsville Bulletin*, 11 November 1979, 1A, 2A.

47. "Dori Blitz to Continue Her 'Struggle,'" *Martinsville Bulletin*, 11 November 1979, 2A.

48. Carl Crothers, "Blitzes' Ouster from CETA Asked," *Martinsville Bulletin*, 12 November 1980, 1A.

49. Dori Blitz, Communist Workers Party press release, 11 November 1980.

50. "Daniel Offers CETA Changes," *Martinsville Bulletin*, 13 November 1980, 1A.

51. Danial D. Preston of Collinsville, letter, *Martinsville Bulletin*, 30 November 1980.

52. Quoted in Blaine Harden, "Red Hunting in Va.," *Washington Post*, 13 December 1980, A17.

53. John Hubner, "The Red Menace: Clear and Present Danger in Virginia," *Boston Phoenix*, 20 January 1981, 6.

54. Dorothy Blitz and Allen Blitz of Martinsville, letter, *Martinsville Bulletin*, 30 November 1980.

55. *Congressional Record*, Senate, 96th Congress, S16192, 11 December 1980.

56. *Congressional Record*, Senate, 96th Congress, S16192, 11 December 1980.

57. Virginia Senator John Warner took the floor in the closing hours of the 96th Congress and threatened to hold up adjournment until the Blitz Amendment was sent back to the House for a vote. He was only pacified when he was assured that the matter would be given priority in the 97th Congress. See Hubner, "The Red Menace," 6.

58. "Daniel's Bill to Be Revived," *Martinsville Bulletin*, 18 December 1980, 9A.

59. "Virginia CWP Supporter Wins Civil Rights Grievance against Local Government," CWP press release, Collinsville, Virginia, 10 October 1981.

60. Quoted in May Quan, "Courage contagious in Martinsville," *Workers Viewpoint*, 16–22 March 1981, 5.

61. Harden, "Red Hunting in Va."

62. Richard Cohen, "Want U.S. Job? Check Your Political Views," *Washington Post*, 23 December 1980.

63. "Item. Item. Item.," *The Nation*, 3–10 January 1981.

64. Hubner, "The Red Menace," 6.

65. Quoted in Hubner, "The Red Menace," 12.

66. Quoted in Hubner, "The Red Menace," 7.

67. Editorial, "The New McCarthyism," *Workers Viewpoint*, 12–18 January 1981, 2.

68. Victor Navasky, "McCarthy Time? Security and Terrorism," *The Nation*, 14 February 1981, 168.

69. Nat Hentoff, "They Starve Communists in Virginia, Don't They?" *The Village Voice*, 23 February 1982, 8.

70. "CWP Member Seeks City Council Seat," *Greensboro Daily News*, 3 March 1982.

71. Gregg Jones, "Activists Seek New Struggles in New York," *Greensboro Daily News*, 6 September 1982, B1.

A WINDING ROAD TO JUSTICE: BRINGING FEDERAL CHARGES

THE QUESTION OF FEDERAL CHARGES

After the Klan/Nazi acquittals, the cry to prosecute the November Third assailants under federal statutes for the criminal violation of people's civil rights was more insistent and widespread. There was no issue of double jeopardy: individuals could be tried on murder charges in state court and on civil rights violations in federal court. Since deaths had occurred, a federal conviction could mean life imprisonment. The Justice Department was capable of bringing federal charges for civil rights violations against our attackers. But since their hands were far from clean, they would have to be brought to the job kicking and screaming. So they were.

In Greensboro, in a letter to African American banker Alfred S. Webb on February 13, 1981, Nelson addressed the question of whether the federal government would bring charges of civil rights violations against the Klan and Nazis. He admitted that, after having met with Justice Department officials and with U.S. Attorney Michaux, he was discouraged by the apparent lack of serious work on the case. The civil rights violations on November 3, 1979, were of central importance to the black community and to workers' right to organize, Nelson wrote. His letter detailed federal statutes applicable to the situation:

One law (Section 241 of the Civil Rights Act) requires that there be a conspiracy to deprive persons of equal protection or equal privileges and immunities based on "racial or perhaps otherwise class based invidiously discriminatory animus." . . . The conspiratorial motive cannot just be against individuals as such. The object of the conspiracy has to be a legally recognizable class such as race, labor organizers, nationalities, religion, etc.

Another law (Section 242 of the Civil Rights Act) requires that the deprivation of rights take place "under the color of state law." As the memorandum states, "in seeking prosecution under the statute, the Justice Department need not prove that the actual crimes were committed by officers of the state. It is more than sufficient if the accused is a willful participant in joint activity with state agents or officials."

Nelson argued that there were at least four categories in which violations of civil rights could be charged: deprivation of the rights of black people, deprivation of the rights of militant labor organizers; involvement of local law officers (in the city and possibly the state) in crimes; and the involvement of federal officials in crimes.

The federal government was trying to say that the November 3 attack was a political and ideological dispute that had nothing to do with race. This supposition was ridiculous, Nelson said, like claiming water has no relationship to a flood.

Racial oppression and racist views are particular forms of politics and ideology. Yes, the Klan and the CWP have different political and ideological views. Ideologically the Klan believes in white superiority; the CWP believes in the equality of the races. Politically the CWP acts to promote its views by struggling to free the Wilmington 10 and exposing why they were locked up in the first place. Politically the Klan acts on its views by driving into the Black community and murdering people. There can be no discussion of abstract politics and ideology. If it exists, it has a form of expression and that's exactly where the race question comes in. . . .

There is an active and open process taking place now across the country of military preparation for "race war" by the KKK. Participants in the November 3rd murders have openly put forth their anti-Black views. But on November 3rd they acted on those views.

Part of the object of the November 3rd murders was to prevent Black people from assembling, speaking, and hearing political views. Those political views would have exposed both the basis (the economic system of exploitation) and the mechanism (the KKK working with the government) of racial oppression.

The parade permit for November 3rd stated the purpose as "political and educational: to educate and organize political opposition to the KKK and their secret supporters." The route of the march wound through four predominantly Black public housing communities (Morningside, Ray Warren, Hampton, and Smith). The entire route of the march was in the Black community. The government, the Klan, and Nazis knew this as Edward Dawson had picked up the parade permit with the entire march route mapped out. Posters and leaflets had been concentrated in the Black community. A & T State University was heavily leafleted. A site for the Conference had been secured in the Florida Street Shopping Center.

It was clear that a large number of Black people would be attracted to this event. . . . Black people organizing themselves, and being helped to organize by some who were not Black, to oppose the Klan and expose the government, was a grave concern of the local city officials and the Klan and Nazis.

The planned march and the conference at the end of the march were legally protected rights. There was a conspiracy to prevent this process from occurring. That is an attack on the rights of Black people for freedom of association, freedom of speech and freedom of assembly. That some people may disagree with the political views of the organizer (CWP) is not the point, except in so far as they resorted to conspiracy and murder to prevent the dissemination of those views.

The individuals in the WVO/CWP, who called for the November 3 anti-Klan rally (both black and white), had histories of working successfully with black people, Nelson pointed out. The fact that four out of the five people murdered were not black, he wrote, "does not in the least change the fact that there was a racial animus. As the Klan and Nazi newspapers have put it, they were 'commie nigger lovers.' . . . There is all the evidence in the world to file charges based on the deprivation of the rights of Black people."

The November 3 attack, Nelson said, "was a deprivation of the rights of militant labor organizers to organize industrial workers and engage in collective bargaining.

This labor organizing process included uniting Black and white in a common struggle for their mutual uplift. The Klan/Nazis, the companies and the government opposed this.

All five of the people murdered on November 3rd were active in labor. Four of the five—Sandy, Bill, Jim, and César—were skilled labor organizers. Their work particularly in the textile industry was well known to the company, the government, and the Klan. Jim Waller, for example, had been elected president of his union local. Numerous attempts were made to uproot these militant labor organizers out of the plant and/or break their influence.

Klan leader Joe Grady of Winston-Salem stated that there existed a hit list previous to November 3rd and that particular people were targeted to be murdered. These particular people turned out to be extremely successful trade union organizers. . . .

The interest of Black people and the need to organize strong fighting unions which fight against racial discrimination on the job and for the immediate and long

term welfare of all the workers are tightly linked. . . . Militant labor organizers, a
legally recognized class, were a conscious target of the November 3rd attacks.

Nelson goes on to review for Webb the facts pointing to official involvement,
beginning with the fact that Klansman and caravan leader Edward Dawson was
a paid informer for the Greensboro Police Department. Charges that local and
state officials participated in the murders and cover-up could not be dismissed
as "revolutionary rhetoric," as the attorney general put forward. There was
enough evidence to merit further investigation, that is, to convene a grand jury
to look into this matter. A grand jury needed to consider the involvement of the
federal government in the conspiracy, as indicated by the provocateur presence
of BATF agent Bernard Butkovich at Nazi planning meetings and many other
facts.

"I have made it unequivocally clear that I and the CWP will work with and
aid further investigative action by the Federal Government," Nelson wrote to
Webb. "But the Federal Government is still claiming publicly that it can't find ju-
risdictional grounds to bring charges. What's going on here is incredible."

Nelson expressed concern that the federal government might not only fail to
bring civil rights charges, but could try to throw out our civil rights suit as well,
thus blocking any further serious investigation. He invited Mr. A. S. Webb to sit
down and talk with him about these matters.

To be sure, we had our civil rights suit, filed on November 3, 1980, by the
Greensboro Justice Fund. In a forty-eight-page complaint, our suit charged that
a whole class of citizens—antiracist labor organizers—were deprived of their
constitutionally protected rights through a criminal conspiracy. Named as defendants were all of the fourteen originally indicted Klan and Nazis, BATF undercover agent Bernard Butkovich, Greensboro police informant and Klansman
Eddie Dawson, Governor Jim Hunt, State Secretary of Crime Control Burley
Mitchell, Mayor Jim Melvin, City Manager Tom Osborne, Police Chief William
Swing, District Attorney Michael Schlosser, several SBI and FBI officials, and
five U.S. attorney generals from John Mitchell to Benjamin Civiletti. The complaint traced a pattern as far back as 1968. It alleged that various levels of government used illegal undercover and surveillance techniques to interfere with
the legitimate organizing efforts of the plaintiffs in their civil rights activities and
organizing of textile workers. Initially, we asked for damages totaling $37 mil-
lion.[1] Aside from the civil suit, we still wanted a legal remedy in criminal court.
The struggle to compel the Justice Department to call a grand jury to investigate
civil rights violations on November 3, 1979, was a pivotal moment for the peoples' movement.

DANCING WITH MICHAUX

It was not always clear if the rich, handsome politician who was North Carolina's first black U.S. attorney was part of the problem or part of the solution. Alternately, we picketed H. M. "Mickey" Michaux and treated him as a valued ally. With a Republican election victory in November, Democrat Michaux was finishing up his work and making way for a Republican appointee. He called the Klan case "one of my top priorities."[2]

Michaux responded immediately to the Klan acquittal by announcing that his office was looking into the legal basis for federal charges. After several foot-dragging months, our lawyers expressed impatience with him.[3] We feared that a Reagan administration refusal to indict the Klan/Nazis on federal civil rights charges would undermine the separate proceeding of a civil suit. Michaux responded to our importuning by telling a reporter, "I'm the only thread these people have and the sooner they understand this the better off they're going to be."[4]

The Greensboro Justice Fund sought allies to help convince Michaux about the requisite jurisdiction. Attorneys Arthur Kinoy and Frank E. Deale of the Center for Constitutional Rights in New York sent Michaux a letter:

> We are firmly convinced that there is absolutely no jurisdictional barrier to prompt government action in this case. 18 U.S.C. 241, 242 and 245 were enacted for the very purpose of allowing the federal government to intervene in situations where, for one reason or another, the local courts have not been able to assure that the constitutional rights of political activists are fully respected. Our conclusion is based on an extensive analysis of the legislative history of these statutes which we conducted in preparation for our testimony before the Subcommittee on Crime of the House Judiciary Committee on December 9, 1980. As stated before the Committee, these statutes, "known historically as the 'KKK Statutes,' provide an immediate criminal remedy against conspiracies to use violence and threats of violence against citizens exercising their elementary constitutional rights." By failing to exercise the full prosecutorial authority of the federal government against those who violate the basic rights of citizens, the federal government negates its fundamental responsibility as the ultimate guarantor of those rights.
>
> We therefore support the Justice Fund in its demands upon the federal government. The Government should launch an investigation of the Greensboro shootings immediately. And, if the evidence warrants, prosecutions should be brought under these statutes.[5]

Greensboro Justice Fund attorney Gayle Korotkin thought that the Justice Department was stalling because "any investigation will lead to the door of the government, of the Greensboro police and of the state and city." About the question of jurisdiction, she said, "there is a legal question, but it doesn't take four months to resolve. You can send a law student to the library for an hour and find that out."[6]

Michaux, who was saying reassuring things in private while remaining publicly noncommittal, was considering running for Congress in 1982. We urged him to move soon or we would hire a private investigator to look into *his* office's suppression of information about a crime. The next word heard from Michaux—nearly six months after the verdict—was that he had indeed decided whether he would recommend filing federal charges in connection with November Third. He had notified the U.S. Justice Department of his decision but was honoring their request to not make his recommendation public just yet.[7] "Our hope is that the scope of the investigation will be broad enough to include inquiry of the alleged wrongdoing by federal as well as state and local officials and the Klan-Nazi participants," said GJF attorney Lewis Pitts.[8] Meanwhile, pressure from a justice-seeking grassroots continued, a noisy people's chorus audible all the way to Washington and beyond.

Six more weeks passed. During the last hour of his last day in office, Michaux held a press conference in his office at which he declared that he had recommended that the Justice Department begin a criminal investigation and seek indictments in connection with the November 3, 1979, anti-Klan rally. Five people were killed, he said, the people living in the community were innocent, and what happened was a signal to encourage other terrorist organizations to similar actions. In the middle of Michaux's press conference, Klansman Joe Grady telephoned and reporters got to hear Michaux's end of the conversation: "'I am sorry you feel disappointed. I really am, Joe. I am saying some civil rights were violated, and it could very well be those people living in the community who were innocent.'" Pause. "'You're going to tell me those kids running around that neighborhood playing are not innocent victims of this thing? And that those old people living in the community weren't victims? What was Jerry Paul Smith doing blazing away with those two six-shooters?'"[9]

Greensboro Justice Fund attorney Earle Tockman had praise for Michaux, saying, "It is extremely significant that a U.S. attorney after a lengthy investigation has recommended criminal prosecution for at least some of those responsible for the assassinations on Nov. 3."[10] Marty Nathan, declaring that we would cooperate with any good-faith prosecution attempt, admitted frankly, "we really don't have much confidence in the Justice Department, but we're willing to give them a whirl."[11]

U.S. Attorney Mickey Michaux was relaxed and in good spirits as he fielded questions about the contents of his May 5 memo. He even criticized the Justice

Department for not acting on his advice.[12] They urged him yesterday, he acknowledged, to *still* not divulge what he had recommended, but he felt that he had an obligation to the public.[13] You know, he joked with reporters after talking to Grady on the phone, "if I decide to run for Congress, Joe Grady said he won't support me."[14]

Michaux no sooner announced his recommendation to the Justice Department than the rumor/disinformation mill got to work with speculation that some CWP demonstrators might be targets of federal indictments: Nelson had to solicit a clear statement from Michaux that "demonstrators could not be prosecuted under the civil rights statutes and that it would be difficult, in his opinion, to prosecute them under any other federal statute."[15]

In late May 1981, the Justice Department asked to talk to some anti-Klan demonstrators as part of their continuing post–November 3 investigation. The FBI never publicized any of its reports on the CWP and kept its post–November 3 investigation a secret. After the acquittals in the state trial, the Justice Department claimed that it could not resolve the issue of jurisdiction in order to begin an investigation into a violation of federal laws. Yet in April 1980, shortly after the murders, the department was able, on the basis of reviewing the FBI's secret report, to clear local police of criminal wrongdoing—an action that implied jurisdiction to investigate and some sort of actual investigation. The Justice Department appeared to exclude the possibility of conspiracy charges against its own agents, despite the evidence. Since the Justice Department would be representing Butkovich and other federal defendants in our civil rights suit, they had a direct interest in not prosecuting federal agents. In the civil suit they would have all the opportunities of litigants to obtain information from us. Did they want information now to prosecute criminal violators of civil rights or to build a case for their own agents?

REMINISCING WITH MARTY, LEARNING
LESSON ABOUT ORGANIZING FROM MARTY

Michaux made it harder for his fellow feds to weasel out of their responsibility, but grassroots pressure nudged Michaux: *issues are decided at the grassroots.* The CWP and the GJF led public education campaigns to lay the facts before people and to counter government and media distortions. Church and civil rights organizations, prominent civic leaders, national human rights advocates, and celebrities all helped to reach and enlighten a wider public. Support for a federal prosecution grew as a result of these efforts until the Justice

Department was forced to proceed. It was the beginning of Ronald Reagan's administration. Greensboro was becoming a high-profile and embarrassing encumbrance. The White House needed to defend against the "misperception" that they were rolling back civil rights.[16] Again, I emphasize—*issues are decided at the grassroots!* Victories along the way, like the calling of a grand jury, are the result of organizers with passion who make them happen—like Marty Nathan.

Dr. Marty Nathan's father, Bill Arthur, was a Greyhound bus driver and union organizer, part of the CIO labor movement of the 1930s. Arthur organized eastern Greyhound workers into what became the Amalgamated Transit Workers union and was a union leader from the local to the international level. Marty grew up in a political, pro–civil rights household. "We knew we were working class, and we knew we had a social commitment," she told me in 1992 when I interviewed her. "We knew our family was not just our family: our family was all oppressed people. I knew from the time I was born that I had a responsibility to do things for the good of all humankind. I don't think most children are raised with that sense of commitment, but it shows that families can raise children that way."

After she was released from jail for denouncing the Klan trial as a sham, Marty assumed greater responsibilities in the Greensboro Justice Fund. The GJF—at first called the Legal Alliance for Greensboro Justice and later, when leading a larger coalition, called the Greensboro Civil Rights Fund—was formed to finance a civil suit on behalf of the November Third victims and their families. The organization also prepared to defend the anti-Klan demonstrators charged with felony riot and those illegally fired after November Third. The initial team of lawyers, Tockman, Korotkin, Laughinghouse, and Ono—a colorful enough blending of names—knew that public education, along with fundraising, was vital to any legal defense or legal offense that they might make. In New York, Buck Wong and Shelley Wong (unrelated) raised money for the Greensboro Justice Fund. Marty assisted the GJF legal team and fundraising effort from Durham, while raising Leah, then a toddler, and caring for her invalid mother-in-law. She described to me what that was like.

"We knocked on doors. Most people would have loved to have us go away. For a number of different, very valid reasons," she added, laughing. "But we knocked on doors until they had nothing they could do but keep them open. And that was the way we did our Greensboro Justice Fund work, by being absolutely persistent, unyielding, insisting that people had to take a stand. People were threatened, people who came on to our original grouping in Durham were threatened with the loss of jobs—these were professors at Duke."

I pointed out the article in the *Durham Morning Herald* listing people in an accusatory way for aligning themselves with the communists.

"Oh yes, Signe. That was very hard to face. You ask friends to help you out, and you see that you can potentially hurt them. It was a McCarthy-like state. But you know this."

"It makes you more determined," I said. "You are forced into a position where you either back down or you go full steam ahead."

Marty was thinking about what I said. "Well, yeah," she started slowly, "but when you're talking about going full steam ahead, the only way you can go full steam ahead is by getting other people to go with you. You have to develop a movement. If the very few people you manage to move into a movement are being attacked and losing their jobs, you can say that in theory you go full steam ahead, but how do you go full steam ahead?

"How am I going to ask someone to take over for a person who has just quit after being red-baited?" she continued. "It becomes much much more difficult. Theory is one thing, but in actual fact it's really hard. And these are friends."

She told me about a biology professor whose job was threatened but who stood by us, a pathology professor who quit and sent her a registered letter so that he would be able to prove he had indeed quit, and a local board member who was red-baited and barely able to hang on through rough times. "It's much more complicated than whether or not you go full steam ahead," she finished.

Marty's words challenged me. I felt as though I had been isolated, off in a corner waving my red flag. The same issue of justice absorbed both of our lives. But my work as a red correspondent and propagandist offered different sorts of encounters from Marty's. It was a moment of enlightenment, like my seeing November Third, years later, from my son's point of view—that of a traumatized adolescent, trapped, only partly comprehending.

"I know that the purpose of the attacks on us and our friends was to physically or morally disable us from going ahead," I said to her. "They can do it swiftly, or they can do it by degrees, by wearing people down."

"We faced so much all along the way," Marty recalled. "I remember an event we organized at Shaw University. The State Bureau of Investigation showed up the day we were to be there and convinced the Black Student Union that was supporting us not to have the event. They got the administration to pull the room. What did we do? We went out on the steps of the Student Union building and talked to anybody who passed our way. That happened a million times. We would set things up, and then the cops would appear, in whatever form—the SBI, who were most active, or the Greensboro or Durham or Raleigh police— and talk to people, turn them against us."

"You know, Marty," I said, "we never once had a public meeting *without* police intervention. And often their intervention either shut down the event or else had an intimidating effect on folks." I was struck anew with how pervasive that interference was. "So much for the right of free assembly, constitutionally protected," I added.

"It was just a routine thing," Marty said. "They would go around and say that we were violent people, and if people had us over, then violence would break out."

She paused and continued. "As if violence was some sort of natural thing that just 'breaks out.' It's not that way. People commit acts of violence. We had not committed an act of violence. The act of violence had been committed on us. We finally decided that we didn't want to stop the local organizing, but we had to somehow crack out of the box they had put us in. So we adopted this strategy we called 'going over the top.' We had to make it safe for people, locally and in the state. We weren't going to give up, even though this was the hardest turf of all. So we did this 'over the top' thing, which meant trying to get national support.

"That's when we got the endorsement for the civil rights suit from Hollywood stars, from the Congressional Black Caucus, from national church leaders, from the American Civil Liberties Union," Marty related. "The American Civil Liberties Union not only endorsed the civil rights suit, but their main lawyer became the chair of the Greensboro Civil Rights Fund board. Interestingly though, the North Carolina branch of the ACLU refused to ever endorse the suit or the call for a federal prosecution.

"We tried to get people who could step back from all the bickering and intimidation, people with some standing, to sign our petitions and so make it safer for others to sign, too," Marty said. "And we did—slowly, through incredible persistence and obnoxiousness," she added, laughing.

"We kept going back to people. I would spend the whole day—ten hours a day—on the telephone, or going around and talking to people, banging on doors and going in. Preacher after preacher, professor after professor, lawyer after lawyer, everyone we could go to. I have some great stories. There was a preacher in Winston-Salem who gave me a hundred dollars and asked me for a kiss. I said 'Thank you for the hundred dollars, see ya later.'"

"A real kiss?" I asked naively, making her laugh.

"Oh yeah—he shall go nameless. There was another one in Durham just like that. He shall go nameless, too," Marty said, enjoying this.

Elliot, who was within earshot, could not help entering the interview. "A kiss with the works," he said.

"Right. With the works," Marty echoed, again laughing. "I took their money and left."

She became a private investigator for the GJF. "There were no paid investigators early on," Marty explained. "I helped the lawyers investigate the suit. I went with Gayle or Lewis, whoever was available."

A woman named Daisy Crawford contacted the Greensboro Justice Fund. She was a black textile worker from the Kannapolis area and was a friend of Sandi Smith. She told the Justice Fund that a few days before November Third she was visited by a couple of men who identified themselves with credentials as FBI agents. They showed her several photographs and asked her to identify people in them. She immediately recognized the picture of Sandi, whom she knew personally. Later when she saw pictures of the five people killed in Greensboro and remembered the photos shown to her by the FBI agents, she thought photos of Bill, Jim, or Mike were among them. Daisy was willing to testify in court. She became a target of Klan harassment after she contacted the GJF.

"I went down with Gayle to talk to Daisy Crawford," Marty recounted. "She fixed us fried chicken and asked us where we'd been. The second time we went out there we saw 'KKK' spraypainted on the road fifteen feet from her house, and I reported it to the SBI."

"They knew she was talking to you," I said. "Were you aware of the surveillance?"

"We knew there was heavy surveillance," she told me. "Our phone was tapped. We had an informer in the police who said our house was circled four times a day, come rain or shine. This same informer had been asked to slap a bug on my car. I'm sure he did. I'm sure I ran around with a bug on my car the whole time I was organizing."

We talked about the red squad in Greensboro and Durham and swapped surveillance stories.

"I once went to Duke because somebody important was speaking at the university," Marty said, "and I thought I'd go over to visit one of our friends. As I passed one of the guards standing all around the Duke campus I heard coming over his walkie-talkie, 'She is walking toward Flowers Building,' and I said 'Thank you' as I walked up the steps of Flowers building. Another time—it was in 1984—I went down to Charlotte for an NAACP dinner that Carolyn Coleman had invited me to. I was exhausted after the drive. It had been a long day. I was alone and was walking in the underground parking lot of a fancy hotel. I passed an armed guard and heard coming over his electronic gear, 'she's parked her car and she'll be coming your way.'" Marty laughed heartily. And then there was the incident with her dog Bruno.

CHAPTER 16

"I used to only let Bruno run at night because he was really vicious. I loved him dearly. It's one o'clock in the morning and I hear this knock at the door and a cop's there. He says, 'Miss Nathan, I got your dog. I just hit him but he's okay. He put a dent in my car.' The cop's got Bruno with him. The dog had no tags. How did he know that's my dog? What was he doing out there? I said 'Thanks very much—you want to tell me about this?'"

Elliot joined in with the conjecture that part of the reason the police were there was that they didn't want anything bad to happen; they didn't want any trouble. Marty disagreed. "Oh, I don't think so," she said to him. "That was never my sense." Marty is convinced that the SBI and police, working in tandem, had political surveillance, not protection, as their mission. "They had whipped up such a furor about us provoking violence," she told Elliot, "that if anything ever had happened to us, they would have said these people brought it on themselves."

"You said to me at the time, 'Don't worry, I'm the last person the Klan would hit right now,'" Elliot reminded her. "That's true," Marty admitted. "But that was because of our own loud mouths. That was our protection. We were running our mouths constantly. And we said if anything happens to us the government is responsible. I think if anything *had* happened to us the police would have let it happen: we were a nuisance to them."

"Why the surveillance?" asked Elliot. "To find out who we knew, what we were doing," Marty answered. "If we had people coming to our house who were reputable, they would intervene. They would talk to them and warn them about us. I never made a contact who was not approached by the police," she said.

Marty's words recalled to me one particularly blatant act of surveillance on my house. I had a neighbor across the street, a single mom with two teenage daughters who were friends with my children. This neighbor came over one day to tell me about an amazing discovery she had made. The top story of the house where she rented the downstairs apartment was, as far as she knew, vacant. But once she heard footsteps on the stairway and surprised some police carrying equipment to the top floor. They had set up a station by the top floor window and were spying on my house. Years later, I met one of her daughters who, when I asked about it, confirmed the story. My next door neighbor in the other direction told me about the FBI visit he'd had. On days when rallies or other public assemblies were planned, helicopters flew over the school field across the street, presumably to monitor comings and goings around the Cypress Street house.

Such tactics did not deter the widows, the Greensboro Justice Fund, or the Communist Workers Party. We kept on organizing and pressing for federal prosecution of the November Third criminals, and we had help.

"We feel the only way the Justice Department will prosecute is if we pressure them to do so!" announced a flyer from People United, sponsors of a national petition drive. Two local groups in Greensboro embodied peoples' sentiments to see justice done. Citizens for Justice and Unity had at its core white liberals and pacifists: the Concerned Citizens of the November Third Incident had several influential black citizens in the lead. Both groups were racially mixed, and both welcomed members of the CWP and the GJF to work with them. They were people of fairness and good spirit who resisted the plague of red-baiting.

TELLING OUR STORY

We found ways to tell our story from the perspective of the victims of the November 3 attack. These efforts in the cultural realm were an important part of our struggle for justice.

The True Story of the Greensboro Massacre, by Dr. Paul C. Bermanzohn and Sally A. Bermanzohn, bears a 1980 copyright and was not updated or reprinted after an initial printing of five thousand copies. It ends with the acquittals of the Klan and Nazis in the state trial. The book was published in New York by the CWP's press, César Cauce Publishers and Distributors, Inc. Both the press and the organization are long gone, but both Bermanzohns have continued to tell the story of the Greensboro Massacre.[17] *The True Story of the Greensboro Massacre* was written under extraordinarily difficult conditions. The authors did not have the luxury of checking every fact and reference, and they did not. The strongly articulated ideology is daunting to some general readers. These caveats notwithstanding, a reader gets an accurate picture of what happened on November 3, and a sense of how and why it happened. How many people could produce a book within a year of being shot in the head?

I promoted the Bermanzohns' book. The work received favorable and thoughtful but not uncritical reviews from a couple of North Carolina journalists. Martha Woodall, who did a large portion of whatever little investigative reporting there was about Greensboro, wrote, "I doubt any reader can fail to be moved by the simple eloquence of the Bermanzohns' descriptions of those brief, terrible moments of Nov. 3, 1979."[18] She found "flaws" in some of the assertions about government conspiracy and saw these as detracting from the legitimacy of the questions raised in that regard. Reviewer William Smith in Durham approached the book from the point of view of the ideological challenge it offered its readers. "What sets the CWP apart," he wrote, "is its insistence on analyzing

American society and its conclusion that as a capitalist democracy, America has been poisoned by capitalism."[19]

People's amazement, Smith thought, that the widows "could shout party slogans even as they crouched beside their dead or dying husbands . . . or that they could carry rifles and shotguns at the head of a funeral march in Greensboro the week after the shootings" showed "our own lack of ideological grounding. Selflessness that astringent is chilling," he wrote, "and some of the women have bridled at their portrayal by press and newscasters as 'plastic ideologues,' a term Bermanzohn borrowed from Nathan's widow, Marty." Yet Smith did not feel that the Bermanzohns did justice to the complexity of the victims as human beings—either of the dead or of the survivors. The absence of complexity illustrated that "literary weaknesses inhere in an excess of ideology, just as political weaknesses do in a dearth of ideology." Nevertheless, Smith thought there was abundant value in a book that "causes some of us finally to take a look at the assumptions our society is built on." He wrote:

> Are capitalism and democracy inseparable? . . . Is American capitalism replaceable? . . . If it is, will capitalism go quietly or will it have to be trussed up and hauled off in a squad car? If capitalism fails, does democracy fail with it?
>
> Rather than trying to find comfort in the notion, vigorously disputed by the CWP, that Greensboro involved "a shootout among extremist groups" and that there is no reason to wake from our doze, we had better give some thought to such questions.[20]

Also from the perspective of the victims of the Greensboro Massacre was an eighty-minute color documentary, *Red November, Black November*, that premiered in Greensboro on March 1, 1981, in the Town Hall Auditorium at the coliseum. It was codirected and coproduced by Sally Alvarez and Carolyn Jung, friends of the victims and acquainted with their politics. (Eddie Dawson tried to buy a ticket at the box office and was firmly turned away by Sally, who told him, "You are not welcome here, Mr. Dawson.") The film powerfully affected all who saw it. Made with a near zero budget and inevitably a bit crude technically, it moved people with its directness and poignant biographical portrayals of the five people killed on November 3. Images of mass mobilizations back up optimistic, revolutionary political rhetoric. The documentary contains graphic television footage of the November 3 attack. Wounded CWP leader Nelson Johnson revisits the scene of the slaughter, describes the attack, and presents the evidence of official conspiracy.

The evening of the documentary's premier sticks in my memory as one of emotional ambush and personal anguish. I sat in the first or second row in front of

Burlington newspaper editor Ed Book and his wife. The huge screen occupied my entire field of vision. I was seeing the film for the first time. The documentary begins with the funeral march a week after the murders. I looked up and saw myself marching at the head of the procession, holding the rifle as if it were a newborn infant. Was I here—or *there*? During other sequences—kneeling over Jim's body, reminiscing with Dale, Marty, and Floris about our husbands, all our faces and gestures larger than life on the screen—I was almost confused about the locus of all these familiar personalities. Because everything was so intimately known to me beforehand, it was as if someone had sucked the anguished images from my head and projected them externally. They were *mine* in the most proprietary sense possible—was I sitting in a seat in the Town Hall of the Greensboro Coliseum or was I splattered on the screen? There was a nausea and dizziness associated with my spirit's dispersal. Parts of the film I could not watch at all. When a short clip came on suddenly of Jim giving a speech on African Liberation Day, I was completely wiped out by the sound of his voice. Observing us in the auditorium, a Greensboro reporter said that when Jim's image came on the screen, I hugged Dale and wept softly. "When police and an FBI agent appeared on the screen, the widows whispered angrily," he wrote.[21] The trauma of viewing the documentary for the first time was compounded by feelings of shame and remorse. A little more than a year after Jim's death, I became involved in an affair with another woman's husband. She was at the screening, and during the intermission I was assiduously trying to avoid bumping into her.

Red November, Black November, first made as a 35-mm film, was reproduced as a video. Along with the Bermanzohns' book, we used the video as an organizing tool to focus public opinion on the issue of federal charges for the perpetrators of the November Third crimes and to raise funds for the civil rights suit. Both book and video found their way into many living rooms in Greensboro, Durham, and elsewhere around the country.

A GREAT DIVIDE IN THE STRUGGLE
FOR HEARTS AND MINDS

In early October 1981, the Institute for Southern Studies (ISS), headed by Georgia state senator Julian Bond, issued a thirty-two-page report called "The Third of November." The ISS urged the U.S. Justice Department to act on Michaux's recommendation and to prosecute the Klan/Nazi attackers. For justice to be done, the report said, "we must have a public accounting of the extent of the intimate relationship between the police and KKK-Nazi caravan, and . . . we must know the degree to which local officials, the prosecutor and federal agents covered up and/or furthered the essential injustice of the November Third confrontation."[22]

The evening before the ISS released its report to the press, Justice Department lawyers contacted Paul Bermanzohn and Dale Sampson in New York and asked to interview them for its investigation into November Third. Dale and Paul were to be our pilot interviewees to see how the government behaved. They first held a press conference to discuss the ISS report.

A Greensboro press conference on October 5, 1981, brought together representatives of various grassroots groups that pointed to the ISS report and voiced support for our civil suit.[23] It was around this time, nearly two years after the murders, that we crossed a sort of divide in the struggle for justice. I remember one particular event very vividly. Even at that time, I felt that we had turned a corner—our cause had attained a critical mass. Formerly social pariahs, we were now official victims. As such we would be treated with solemn respect—in some quarters anyway, and notwithstanding perennial red-baiting.

On October 27, 1981, over 150 Greensboro citizens flocked to the Guilford County Courthouse for a program entitled "November 3rd: Perspectives on a Federal Investigation," sponsored by three local groups—the American Friends Service Committee, Citizens for Justice and Unity, and the Greensboro chapter of the American Civil Liberties Union.[24] Among the panelists were former U.S. attorney H. M. Michaux and Duke law professor William Van Alstyne. As I milled around talking to reporters, friends, and acquaintances, I was excited. Because so much had been done to deter people from pursuing justice, I was amazed that we had arrived at this point. It seemed to me that hoards of justice-hungry citizens were at the gates, invading the bastion of authority. I appreciated the moment.

During part of the program, while wandering through courthouse hallways, I found myself in a basement room full of TV screens—the subterranean electronic surveillance of everyone and everything. The entire meeting was video-taped. Maybe new FBI files of hitherto unmarked citizens were being generated. Nevertheless, I felt very happy. Our victory was at hand. We were in their house; we were on their video monitors; but Big Brother was impotent. We would overrun them. The issue would be decided at the grassroots after all. Weeks afterward I still felt a sense of triumph. The political scenery had shifted. The public pulse beat audibly. Justice was a steamroller and Big Brother would have to step aside. I was witnessing the transformation of public opinion.

The ISS report made a big difference. Michaux was unequivocal in backing Van Alstyne, who cited the statutes applicable to November Third and distributed the results of his legal research to forum attendees and the press. Van Alstyne was about to testify on civil rights statutes at Representative John Conyers' subcommittee hearing on criminal justice. He indicated that he would focus his testimony on Greensboro. In a nine-page memo he sent to Conyers' subcommittee giving a statute-by-statute review, he noted that the attack occurred on public streets during a parade for which the Communist Workers Party had a legal permit. "There is substantial reason to believe that the purpose of the Klan-Nazi engagement at the gathering spot was to intercept or disrupt or prevent the march from being held," he said. "Please bear in mind," Van Alstyne told Conyers' subcommittee, "that the very statutes we have been reviewing were adopted in the first place from an overriding congressional concern with the very kind of racial intimidation, the very kind of racist groups, and the very area of the nation involved here." The Ku Klux Klan Act was part of the South "with its history of unequal racial treatment. There is, here, a background of general intimidation linking race, unorganized labor, left-leaning ideological groups harassed as such and because they seem 'threatening' to antiunion and to antiblack groups."[25]

On November 3, 1981, Katie Greene was joined by the North Carolina National Lawyers Guild and several other organizations at a press conference in Raleigh. Green announced that North Carolina People United collected several thousand signatures on petitions demanding government action. On November 5, the National Council of Churches passed a resolution about Greensboro urging the Justice Department "to disclose fully the process of the investigation into the killings of the Greensboro 5 and its findings, including making a determination whether agents of the Bureau of Alcohol, Tobacco, and Firearms were involved in collusion as charged."[26]

The Concerned Citizens of the November 3 Incident, chaired by Charles Davis of the NAACP, announced plans to launch a petition drive to solicit signatures from Greensboro residents for federal prosecution of the Klan and Nazis.[27] Shortly after its formation, the Concerned Citizens succeeded in getting the Greensboro City Council to unanimously pass a resolution calling on the Justice Department to investigate, review, and take appropriate action with respect to individuals and groups involved in November Third.[28] Although cautiously worded, the resolution was positive. There were certain city politicians who would have preferred no resolution at all. In essence, the City of Greensboro was now on record denying that the case had closure with the state trial and calling for federal investigation to continue it. The Concerned Citizens later traveled to Washington and conducted a press conference. They met with Representative John Conyers and delivered to him their signed petitions, along with the official resolution from the City of Greensboro.[29]

Finally, a local reporter could write, "Amid growing community clamor for results, a federal Justice Department attorney came quietly to Greensboro Monday."[30] The press contacted me, and I said that the recent public criticism leveled at the government "is forcing them to do something" and called the public pressure "very helpful." Jumping to the government's defense and contradicting me was Greensboro Middle District U.S. Attorney Kenneth McAllister, Michaux's successor. "I'm sure the Justice Department is not going to be moved by political pressures," he said.[31]

I will stand by my assessment of the dynamics of power. If you are trying to make fundamental changes in the system, as was the CWP, then it is important not only to organize at the grassroots but to increase awareness that organizing at the grassroots is an effective political lever. The engine of democracy is supposed to be an enlightened and empowered citizenry: spontaneous sentiments elevated to informed strategy is its permanent possibility.

The posture of the Justice Department was that they were continuing an investigation that they claimed was ongoing since the attack. Heading the investigation for the Justice Department from the beginning was Michael Johnson of the Civil Rights Division. Nelson's six-hour interview in mid-November was preceded by a protest. The government showed bad faith, Nelson claimed, by including local FBI Special Agent Tom Brereton on the investigative team. Brereton testified at the Klan/Nazi trial that Dawson had done paid contracting work on his home.[32] He was present at interview sessions of some Klansmen and Nazis arrested on November 3 in which twenty-five minutes of a key defendant's taped statement was missing. Brereton was one of several governmental and law enforcement defendants in our civil suit. Despite the protest, Brereton continued to play a role in the investigation.

With good reason, we continued to be concerned about the Justice Department's handling of the Greensboro case and the negative effect it might have on the civil rights suit. In January 1982, the City of Greensboro filed a protective order blocking our depositions for the civil suit of Klansman Eddie Dawson and Nazi Raeford Caudle, two key figures in the November Third events. Neither had been called to testify in court at the state trial. The City's protective order was backed up by the Justice Department.[33]

Around the time of the City of Greensboro's motion to stay the depositions of Klan/Nazis for the civil suit, the United States government invited Salvadoran military officers and troops to train at Fort Bragg in North Carolina. The repression of the Greensboro Massacre was of a piece with U.S. sponsorship of repressive regimes abroad, we said at a local press conference called by the CWP on January 9, 1982. We pointed out that there were dozens of proposals for repressive legislation and new powers for domestic spying aimed at the growing resistance of people in the United States. While people here were struggling with inflation, unemployment, and massive budget cuts in social services, the government was spending $18 million to train Salvadoran troops that would be returning to their home country to wage war against their own people. In seeking justice for the Greensboro Massacre, we saw ourselves as challenging a repressive system whose quest for profit left a bloody trail from Greensboro to El Salvador and beyond. The government protected the same moneyed interests that stood behind U. S. imperialist policies abroad and the domestic right-wing terrorism of the Greensboro Massacre. The upshot of the struggle for justice in Greensboro would make it more or less safe for others fighting for social justice to proceed.

In the middle of February 1982, a U.S. district judge ordered a federal grand jury to meet in Winston-Salem. The following month it was confirmed that this grand jury would consider the violence that transpired on November 3.[34] A grand jury does not determine guilt or innocence. It hears the evidence and decides if there are grounds, or "probable cause," to file charges. That we reached the milestone of a federal grand jury investigation was due to the tenacious struggle of many concerned citizens. But we were not finished sparring with the Justice Department. The Justice Department, with its patent conflict of interest in the case, was in charge of the grand jury investigation.

A TERRORIST ATTACK THAT DIDN'T HAPPEN

The episode that follows bears a relationship to the Greensboro Massacre. I do not know, even today, what its precise relationship is. I can only present some of the facts, some hypotheses upon the facts, and the questions tugging at my mind. In March 1981 (while we were dancing with Michaux and raising our voices in protest throughout the land), federal agents arrested six North Carolina Nazis and charged them with plotting to blow up several areas in Greensboro and then to flee to South America.[35]

The Nazis were indicted based on information supplied by BATF undercover agents. Supposedly, they were planning to attack, with homemade explosives, downtown Greensboro (where government offices are located), a shopping mall, and a petroleum tank farm. Fortunately, this particular terrorist plot was never carried out. The conspiracy with which the Nazis were charged was said to have taken shape several months earlier, in the summer of 1980 during the trial in Greensboro. It was alleged that they were set to execute their plans if there had been convictions in the Klan/Nazi case. Presumably, the acquittal verdict led them to lay aside the vengeful plot.

The wired-up BATF agents who infiltrated the nest of Nazis reported many juicy bits of boastful conversation—remarks gruesome, shocking, and disgusting—and these were played to full advantage in the newspapers and at subsequent trials.[36] "If they had convicted them, Betty," Nazi Frank Braswell assures a friend in a secretly taped phone call, "we meant to make an example . . . we meant to kill as many damned people as we could kill."[37]

Among the indicted Nazis was Raeford Caudle, who was part of the murder caravan on November Third and owner of many of the weapons used and of the vehicle that brought them. It was Caudle against whom, mysteriously, Schlosser dropped all charges after initially charging him with conspiracy, and it was Caudle who told Grady about a person with a hit list. Another of the six indicted in the alleged plot to blow up Greensboro was Gorrell Pierce, prominent at China Grove. Though not in the caravan on November 3, Pierce was a party to the attackers' plans.

Beneath the surface of sensationalism and gory possibility, the Asheville bomb plot begs for closer examination. What was the precise relationship of federal agents and agencies with the Nazis? Why did the feds bring charges, why did they do so when they did, and why against those particular people and not others? If the government was rounding up loose cannons, why didn't they touch Harold Covington? (Braswell's phone tap revealed at least eighteen calls to Covington in a four-month period.)

At the time we supposed the Nazis were getting their wrists slapped for stepping out of line and fingering Butkovich. That may be true. Perhaps, too, the Nazis suspected that some of their members were playing a dual role: that was not necessarily an uncomfortable position either for the Nazis or the right-wing sector of government. They were ideologically compatible. In their collaboration, however, certain ground rules had to be obeyed, and it was not for the Nazis to set those rules. They were probably expected to keep quiet about their suspicions of government agents, their sometime allies capable of dispensing indulgences and providing resources beyond the means of mere downtrodden racists. Each party probably thought it was using the other. But the Nazis had to be kept in line and were forced to play the game by the feds' rules. The feds could and would lock them up, or do worse to them, if need be.

The Nazis argued in their defense in court that they were on to efforts to infiltrate them and were just stringing federal agents along with wild talk about blowing things up. They never intended to implement any of it, they said. The Braswells' boast of knowing all along that Swain was a BATF operative was perhaps not idle. The Nazis' real surprise may have been their indictment by turn-coat feds who were their ideological brethren.

It emerged in the course of several trials that the federal agents showed a reluctance to let the plot drop and instead encouraged the Nazis to proceed—a fact that gave some substance to an entrapment defense. Some of the Nazis' alleged plans were physically and logistically impossible, and there was no evidence that their plot was being carried out. The federal agents who testi-fied to the seriousness of the plot had not, nevertheless, investigated obvious details about it that might have determined whether a genuine terrorist plot was in the offing or there was just a lot of hateful, resentful talk. The lack of investigation on the agents' part gives the appearance that they were either unconcerned or already knowledgeable about whether they were dealing with a real plan of destruction or just a warped fantasy of one. For example, the BATF never obtained a search warrant to look for explosives where Braswell said they were hidden.

If the government was punishing the Nazis for betraying Butkovich, or mak-ing sure the Nazis knew their place in the scheme of things, a prosecution at-tempt, or the appearance of one, was a good scare tactic. It also made for good PR at a time when political criticism by the CWP and others was putting federal agencies on the defensive for supporting terrorists. I do not know whether the Nazi plot was truly intended, with the resultant loss of lives, or whether it was merely vile Nazi-speak. If the Nazis could not move fifty-five truckloads of ex-plosives into Greensboro and surreptitiously and remotely detonate a series of bombs at four different locations in the city, they were certainly capable of killing on a less ambitious scale—as they did to us. Fifteen years later, American right-wing terrorists, not unlike those encountered in North Carolina, carried out the kind of devastating attack that the Nazis talked about visiting on Greensboro by blowing up of the Murrah Federal Building in Oklahoma City.

In the early eighties, with the ascent of Reagan, terrorism was a buzzword em-anating from Washington. Then as today (after September 11, 2001), a double standard prevailed: maiming and killing innocent civilians for political purposes was only called terrorism when done by *other* nations or nationals. When the U.S. government carried out or supported similar acts resulting in the suffering and deaths of many human beings, in order to maintain political and economic hegemony, it *never* applied the term *terrorism* to itself. The use of terror and ter-rorist groups is a cornerstone of U.S. government policy both at home (when necessary) and abroad (routinely).

Returning to the 1980s, the trial of the six Nazis dragged on for several years, from a hung jury to a final acquittal with convictions and jail time in between.

Bernard Butkovich was never called to testify at these trials either, though he went to some sessions and hobnobbed with the Nazis.

From newspaper accounts, taken together, it appears that Butkovich was not a lone government agent in a plot to tame the communists. I counted a total of eleven agents in North Carolina who were dealing with individuals or groups with violent, racist histories or were in supervisory positions over such agents. I easily believe that there were agents swarming over the state for months and months, from Fayetteville in the east to Asheville in the west. I imagine that they explored various options for solving North Carolina's communist problem.

The BATF claimed their official investigation of the Nazis in the western part of the state began after November Third. But if Frank Braswell is to be believed on this point, BATF agent Michael Sweat, posing as a Nazi named Swain, contacted the Braswells much earlier—around the same time the BATF sent Butkovich to North Carolina in the summer of 1979, soon after China Grove. Agent Westra, in charge of the BATF for North Carolina, adamantly denied the Braswell bomb plot had anything to do with November Third and insisted the agents around Asheville were investigating an entirely different matter. But were Sweat and Butkovich's undercover operations really unconnected? It came out at the second trial of the Asheville Nazis that a BATF agent, Marshall Reese, who assisted Sweat, had also done surveillance work for Butkovich prior to November 3, 1979. And again, Butkovich, who was present and was photographed in the September 1979 gathering of Klan and Nazis in Louisburg, would have met many potential surrogates for a government strike against the communists. Perhaps Braswell as well as other Klan and Nazis were among the "almost ran's" of November Third. We learned, after November 3, 1979, that a weapons deal at Fort Bragg was negotiated prior to November 3. Was the report indicative of a government and right-wing alliance obsessed with stopping the communists in their tracks?

The government structure in the United States serves a corporate elite. This small elite, benefiting from the rapacious capitalist system, was disturbed by what the WVO was accomplishing (or would perhaps accomplish in the future) through its organizing of workplaces and communities. My view of the November Third attack is that it materialized out of a fishing expedition by the government and its corporate sponsors keen on stopping our organizing. The incident at China Grove, where the WVO and its friends confronted the Klan, yielded a promising avenue of attack on organizers. It was an option that we inadvertently made easier because of our boasting after China Grove. Without realizing it at the time, we gave our enemies an opening, that is, the cover story of the good 'ol boys seeking revenge for their hurt pride. But the pretext provided by China

Grove was not sufficient. The government needed a Dawson, or some other po-lice-instigated rogue, to rile up and organize the Klan. It needed a Butkovich, or someone similar, to penetrate the Nazis. Out of these elements an actual con-spiracy developed.

I can imagine an attack on us being attempted with a different cast of charac-ters as, for example, one including Nazi Frank Braswell. The federal government knew about and kept tabs on Braswell, a longtime Nazi activist in western North Carolina.[38] The indictments of Braswell and the other Nazis charged with plot-ting to bomb Greensboro were certainly not acts of pure, disinterested law en-forcement by the BATF. The interesting question in the Nazis' purported bomb plot, as in the actual assault of November 3, concerns the relationship of gov-ernment agencies to the violent right wing. Future investigators must establish more details of this collaborative interaction.

As the names of more and more agents surfaced, and as evidence suggestive of wider plotting around November Third appeared, our lawyers amended the civil rights suit, adding names of government agents who conspired to violate our civil rights. These are difficult matters to crack open. *Every judicial process following the Greensboro Massacre, including the civil rights suit that revealed much more of the truth than had previous criminal proceedings, barred disclosure about the role of federal agents and agencies in conspiring to bring about the No-vember Third attack and in the cover-up afterward.*

LEADING UP TO THE GRAND JURY

The "green-light-for terrorism" metaphor was turning out to be chillingly true. In April 1982 in Draper, North Carolina, an elderly black man was shot in the face and killed by a known Klansman for driving too slowly. In May in Durham, a young black man was threatened and then run over by a white man for walk-ing on the street with a white woman. In Butner and Creedmoor in the same month, KKK slogans were painted on the houses of interracial and black fami-lies.

From a right-wing perspective, the Klan and Nazis were "patriotic organi-zations," persecuted for their stand against communism. Glenn Miller of the Carolina Knights of the Ku Klux Klan thought the grand jury investigation was "an outrageous attempt to conjure up civil rights violations" against the Klan and Nazis.[39] Actually, the self-avowed patriots continued to enjoy their civil rights and even to bask obscenely in them. They held rallies where the acquitted murderers were exhibited as heroes, according to Randall Williams who directed the Klanwatch project for the Southern Poverty Law Center.[40] Typical was a small Klan rally in April 1982 in Rutherfordton, N.C., with Virgil Griffin and David Matthews presiding—the former a key organizer of the Greensboro Massacre and the latter the individual who killed most of those slain that day.

Leading up to the grand jury, the Greensboro Justice Fund put out a "Call for Justice in Greensboro." Signing it were notable church leaders of all denominations, civil rights lawyers, and well-known political and labor activists. The call was placed into mass circulation. Letters went out to William French Smith and William Bradford Reynolds in the Justice Department to inform them that people were watching, concerned "that *this* grand jury not be made a McCarthy-like witchhunt to harass, intimidate and indict the very victims of the attack simply for holding views that are unpopular with the present administration." North Carolina was "a testing ground for justice in the 1980's."[41]

The grand jury met over a period of thirteen months and spoke to approximately 150 witnesses. Based on the number of witnesses and sessions, it was the most extensive civil rights grand jury investigation in American history. In the course of the grand jury hearing, the Greensboro Justice Fund hosted several groups of fact finders. To prepare their distinguished guests for the fact-finding mission, the GJF outlined crucial questions that the grand jurors needed to address.[42] It was not a good bet that Justice Department attorneys Michael Johnson, Norajean Flanagan, and Kenneth McAllister would delve into these topics, much less come up with all the required indictments, but the GJF was certainly helping them do their homework. Each fact-finding group consisted of about six to ten observers, with rank in their own communities, who descended on Greensboro and Winston-Salem, mingled with citizens, asked questions, and talked to officials and to the media. After several days, the visitors returned home. Many thousands of people around the country learned about Greensboro through them.

NOTES

1. Martha Woodall, "CWP Sues for $37 Million," *Greensboro Record*, 3 November 1980, A1.
2. "Case Still Studied," *Greensboro Record*, 15 January 1981, C1.
3. Mark McDonald, "CWP Presses Michaux for Answer," *Greensboro Record*, 20 March 1981.

4. McDonald, "CWP Presses Michaux."

5. Attorney Arthur Kinoy and Attorney Frank E. Deale to Attorney H. M. Michaux, 23 March 1981.

6. Jon Rosenblum, "U.S. Agency Stalls Greensboro Investigation," (Duke University, Durham, N.C.) *Chronicle*, 7 April 1981, 4.

7. "Michaux Mum on Decision in CWP Case," *Greensboro Daily News*, 5 May 1981.

8. Mark McDonald, "Justice Department Reviewing Michaux's Nov. 3 Case Advice," *Greensboro Record*, 6 May 1981.

9. Ed Hatcher, "Nov. 3 Rally Indictments Are Asked," *Greensboro Daily News*, 25 June 1981, A12.

10. Hatcher, "Nov. 3 Rally Indictments," A12.

11. Associated Press, "Michaux Recommendation May Be Mulled for Months," *Durham Morning Herald*, 26 June 1981.

12. Jim Wicker, "Agent Says Mum CWP a Holdup," *Greensboro Record*, 25 June 1981.

13. Michael P. Massoglia, "Michaux Urges Charges," *Winston-Salem Journal*, 25 June 1981, 2.

14. Hatcher, "Nov. 3 Rally Indictments," A12.

15. "Federal Prosecution in the Case of the Greensboro Massacre," *Greensboro Justice Fund* press release, 26 June 1981.

16. See Ronald J. Ostrow, "Reagan Enforcer Cites Progress on Rights," *Las Vegas Times*, 13 February 1982.

17. See Dr. Sally Bermanzohn's forthcoming book, *The Greensboro Massacre through the Survivors' Eyes* (Vanderbilt University Press); and Dr. Paul Bermanzohn's brochure for the Greensboro Justice Fund, coauthored with Dr. Marty Nathan, "Justice and the Greensboro Massacre," 1999.

18. Martha Woodall, "Recounting Nov. 3, 1979: The Bermanzohns' Moving But Flawed Version," *Greensboro Daily News & Record*, 21 June 1981, G5.

19. William M. Smith, "The 'Massacre' and the Message," *Durham Morning Herald*, 5 April 1981, 3D.

20. Smith, "The 'Massacre' and the Message," 3D.

21. Larry King, "No Incidents Mar Showing of CWP Film," *Greensboro Daily News*, 2 March 1981.

22. Institute for Southern Studies, Durham, N.C., "The Third of November," 1981, 32.

23. See Bob Hiles, "Federal Probe Urged into Nov. 3 Killings," *Greensboro Daily News*, 6 October, 1981, B2.

24. See Larry King, "Panel Mulls Doubts from Nov. 3 Events," *Greensboro Daily News*, 28 October 1981, B1.

25. Martha Woodall, "Professor to Testify about Civil Rights," *Greensboro Record*, 26 October 1981.

26. People United against Government Repression and the Klan/Nazis, "Call for Justice in Greensboro," leaflet, n.d.

27. "Coalition Asks Prosecution of Klan-Nazis," *Greensboro Daily News*, 2 December 1981.

28. See "City Council Asks for Federal Probe of CWP Deaths," *Greensboro Record*, 8 December 1981, B2.

29. "Group Asks Probe of Justice Department," *Greensboro Daily News*, 28 January 1982.

30. Larry King, "Investigation into Nov. 3 Shootings Continue," *Greensboro Daily News*, 10 November 1981.

31. King, "Investigation into Nov. 3."

32. Jim Wicker, "Johnson Protests Agent's Inclusion," *Greensboro Record*, 6 November 1981.

33. Larry King, "Judge Closes CWP Interviews," *Greensboro Daily News*, 2 March 1982. See also Lewis Pitts, "Justice Department Handling of the 1979 Greensboro Klan-Nazi Attack and the Special Grand Jury," Christic Institute, Washington, D.C., March 1982.

34. Larry King, "Grand Jury to Probe CWP Deaths," *Greensboro Daily News*, 9 March 1982.

35. Larry King, "Nazis Arrested in Bombing Plot," *Greensboro Daily News*, 3 March 1981.

36. See, for example, Associated Press, "Jury Gets Nazi Tapes," *Durham Sun*, 24 June 1981, 2A.

37. "State Agents Testify on Plot against City," *Greensboro Daily News*, 24 June 1981, B2.

38. See Doug Smith, "The Nazis in North Carolina: A Mountain Base, Big Plans," *Charlotte News*, 17 October 1977, A1.

39. Glenn Miller, letter, *Greensboro Daily News*, 20 March 1982.

40. "Monitor: Klan-Nazi Verdicts Aid Racists," *Greensboro Daily News*, 13 April 1982. A significant victory over the official toleration of racist violence occurred around the same time as the opening of the November Third Grand Jury. Five black women who were injured in an attack by three Klan members in Chattanooga, Tennessee, were awarded $535,000 in damages in a class action suit filed on behalf of all black people in Chattanooga. It was the first civil rights damages verdict against a Klan group.

41. "A Call for Justice in Greensboro," Greensboro Justice Fund, March 1982, thirty signatories.

42. See "Greensboro Justice Fund Call for Grand Jury to Investigate Government's Role in Shootings," Greensboro Justice Fund, press release, 16 March 1982.

VICTORY AND A WHITEWASH: THE GRAND JURY IN 1982–1983

NOT YOUR TYPICAL GRAND JURY

It was a chilly, windy day in Winston-Salem on March 22, 1982, when the grand jury was impaneled. My hair whipped into my face as I stood on a street vigil with others holding picket signs, handing out flyers, and talking to reporters. The CWP had printed "Wanted for Five Murders" posters. One featured a large photograph of Dawson and another showed Butkovich, with their crimes listed below. Chants denounced U.S. intervention in El Salvador and pointed to parallels with Greensboro: death squads for the opponents of imperialism!

The first group of outsider fact finders brought by the Greensboro Justice Fund included representatives from the National Conference of Black Lawyers, the National Council of Churches, the National Lawyers Guild, the National Anti-Klan Network, the Christic Institute, the Unitarian Universalist Association, the Lutheran Church of America, the People United Coalition, and the United Church of Christ. They joined Greensboro's Concerned Citizens of the November 3 Incident in assuming a watchdog role over the grand jury. Some of the visitors met with Michael Johnson and elicited his assurance that the grand jury would examine "all allegations" pertinent to November 3, including those concerning the conduct of law enforcement officials.[1]

"All our civil liberties are at stake until justice is done," said Joyce Johnson, highlighting the importance of the grand jury.[2] She cited recent repressive measures, such as Executive Order 12333 expanding covert CIA operations at home and giving the president authority over "special activities" with no oversight by other branches of government. Despite a trend for repressive government and the Justice Department's control of the grand jury, we hoped that more of the truth would surface. We cooperated with the grand jury to that end.

***

Not long into the grand jury process, the Justice Department continued the interviews that began with Paul, Dale, and Nelson.[3] Of the fifteen anti-Klan demonstrators interviewed initially, every single one had been widowed, wounded, brought up on charges, or jailed in connection with November Third.

NOVEMBER THIRD SURVIVORS WIDOWED, WOUNDED, CHARGED OR JAILED FOR MORE THAN A DAY

	Widowed	Wounded	Charged	Jailed
Allen Blitz			X	
Dale Sampson	X		X	X
Don Pelles		X	X	
Dori Blitz			X	
Floris Cauce	X		X	X
Frankie Powell		X		
Jim Wrenn		X		
Lacie Russell			X	
Marty Nathan	X		X	X
Nelson Johnson		X	X	X
Paul Bermanzohn		X		
Rand Manzella		X	X	
Signe Waller	X		X	X
Tom Clark		X	X	X
Willena Cannon			X	

***

Grand juries normally proceed in secrecy. U.S. marshals guard the grand jury room. Jurors take an oath stating that they will not reveal the proceedings. The panel's subpoenas are secret and so is the final transcript. However, witnesses are not bound by oath or law to remain silent. In the Greensboro case, the extent to which the grand jury was made to exist in the public sphere floored people familiar with the usual operation of grand juries. One by one, demonstrators went into the grand jury room, answered the questions asked, and once outside repeated questions and answers for the edification of the press and public. The

CWP witnesses, exclaimed a reporter for the *Charlotte Observer*, "have side-stepped the cloak of secrecy that usually would shroud the grand jury. . . . And by doing so, they have accomplished something else: drawn attention, once again, to the CWP's nationally publicized charge that the shootings were the work of a government-directed conspiracy."[4]

Some of the media people who witnessed the attack also announced publicly what they were about to say, or had said, within the guarded chamber. Even many of the Klan, as if following our lead, took the opportunity to reveal their testimonies afterward to the press. No doubt, this was the least secret grand jury in American history. Of course, those police and government agents called to testify did not air their testimonies publicly.

Jurors first heard from Greensboro FBI agent Thomas Brereton, chosen to "orient" the grand jury. We found this choice repugnant and said so. Brereton's cozy relationship with Dawson, and the agent's presence at a police interrogation after the killings at which part of Klansman Jerry Paul Smith's taped interview was missing, aroused suspicion. Furthermore, Dori Blitz observed Brereton in the parking lot of the Budd Trailer Company in Ridgeway, Virginia, on November 10, 1979, when an important union meeting was canceled, preventing discussion among union members of Dori's threatened leadership status in the local. When the GJF amended the civil right complaint in May, Brereton was added as a defendant.

GRAND JURY TESTIMONIES

The two cameramen who shot the most revealing videotapes, Jim Waters of WFMY in Greensboro and Ed Boyd of WTVD in Durham, were among early witnesses heard by the grand jury. Both agreed on the essentials of this ambush: the Klan/Nazi vehicles "blocked a narrow stretch of Everitt Street, took weapons from the rearmost vehicles, fired and reloaded in a relaxed manner, and killed only CWP leaders."[5]

Nelson, asked by Michael Johnson about the five shooting victims, talked about their roles as union leaders at area textile mills and their other organizing activities. The anti-Klan rally on November 3 was a continuation of the antiracist programs that those killed had been involved in, Nelson emphasized, not some isolated, attention-getting demonstration.[6] In his testimony, Nelson also made a point of refuting the police claim of confusion about the march starting point. On October 19, 1979, Nelson told grand jurors, he met with Captain L. S. Gibson and penciled the route of the march onto a map. The map and the verbal description of the march route on the permit gave the starting point as Morningside Homes. "We worked out one arrangement with them and one only," Nelson said.[7] How could the police claim confusion when their own officer, Detective Cooper, followed the Klan caravan to Morningside?

Like Nelson, I gladly talked about the labor organizing in the mills. I told the jurors with pride about Jim's work in building his union local and the respect that he had from other workers, both black and white. As we testified, the range of questions asked and the liberty to answer led us to think that, at least on the parts of Michael Johnson and Nora Jean Flanigan, something of a good faith prosecution attempt was being made. Whether justice would be served, considering the waters in which even the well-intentioned had to swim, was another question.

The state trial established that some demonstrators fired back at the Klan. The grand jury testimonies added details but gave no new twist to the story. Some witnesses said that they saw Allen Blitz repeatedly try to fire a jammed derringer. A few people witnessed his wife, Dori, firing back at the Klan with a .38-caliber handgun. Dori testified that this gun was registered in my name. She had returned the gun to me after November Third. I handed it over to the Justice Department. Claire, who took cover with Sandi behind a building when the shooting started, told the grand jury that she fired one or two shots at a man aiming at her and Sandi. Rand admitted that he fired two shots in the midst of the gunfire, also. He recounted to the grand jury the sequence of events that day. He and Bill waved signs and chanted "Death to the Klan!" when the caravan drove up to the rally. They first ran to the front of the caravan, where a man fired into the air. They then turned and ran toward the stick fight. But the stick fight did not last long, and when more shots were fired, Bill and Rand ran for cover behind the WXII-TV car parked along Carver Drive. Bill fired back at the Klan with a handgun. Rand stood up briefly, saw the windows of the TV car shot out, and dove for cover. As he tried to shield himself, he was shot in the leg with birdshot. Bill told him, "I'm shot," and Rand responded, "Yeah, me too," thinking at the time that his friend was, like himself, only slightly wounded. That was the moment when Bill handed his gun to Rand who soon used it to try to stop "an older man with gray hair, sort of heavyset," charging at him from the side. He missed his attacker although the man was only two car length's away, he judged. The would-be assailant fled. Rand, in a state of shock, didn't even remember that he was still holding Bill's gun when the police arrested him, standing over César's body, some minutes later.[8]

Dale, testifying the same day as Rand, explained how Jack Fowler brushed her aside to get to Sandi. She saw Fowler club Sandi on the head. The blow fractured Sandi's skull. Dale also witnessed Jerry Paul Smith running up Everitt Street shooting pistols and Nazi Roland Wayne Wood firing a rifle or shotgun, although she didn't see who fell as a result of these shootings. When she spoke of finding Bill's body after the violence, Dale moved several of the jurors to tears.

Joyce Johnson bore witness to the conduct of the police. Prior to the anti-Klan march, police followed her as she put up posters. Rumors that the All Nations Pentecostal Holiness Church would be bombed—rumors traceable to the police department—caused the pastor and church members to reverse their decision to host the anti-Klan conference planned for the afternoon of November 3. She recounted Nelson's treatment at the hands of the police after he was wounded by a Klansman.

"My husband has been criminally indicted seven times in direct relation to November 3rd," Joyce said. "He was beaten by a deputy sheriff right in the courthouse. He still bears the scars. . . . He was jailed on numerous occasions and served twenty days for speaking out on his own behalf in court. Nelson was even placed under $100,000 bond and held overnight. This was done at District Attorney Schlosser's bidding, supposedly because my husband was a danger to himself and society. The total bond Nelson would have had to bear would have been $115,000, almost twice the bond of Klan and Nazis who were charged with murder. Though these efforts to jail him were not all successful, you should ask yourself why—why was he repeatedly harassed and thrown into jail while Klan and Nazis known to have killed our friends were receiving Class A treatment?"[9] Joyce called on the grand jury to look into the part played by District Attorney Schlosser in covering up facts surrounding the case.

Joyce spoke about her personal relationship to the people who were slain. "I knew, deeply respected, and loved all five people murdered on November 3rd, 1979," she said. "They were sensitive, self-sacrificing, and dedicated people who wanted to build a better life and a better world for us and our children to live in." Sandi was particularly special to her.

> Sandi Smith was my closest friend. We spent many, many hours together working, playing, and learning. Sandi's murder was a loss to all who love and respect justice and equality, but her death was also the loss of a personal friend to me. As a student at Bennett College, she lived with Nelson and me over the summer in the early 1970s. She came to be like a second mother to our two daughters. I was her matron of honor at her wedding. We worked together on many projects. In a sense we matured politically together as two Black women—as sisters in struggle. I am submitting to you a picture of Sandi Smith so that her strength and beauty which has been so terribly repressed and distorted over the last two years, can be better appreciated by you. I simply ache

every time I hear degrading comments about my "sister" who in actuality gave so much to so many others. I beseech you to thoroughly investigate this case and bring some form of justice against those who shot her down, even though she can never be returned to us.[10]

Hearing our stories evoked sympathy from the jurors. After her testimony, Marty sat in a foyer outside the grand jury room talking to reporters. Her nerves frazzled, she bummed a cigarette from a friend—the resolution to quit smoking would have to wait. When the grand jury room door swung open and the jurors filed out, a woman juror made a beeline for Marty, smiled at her, squeezed her shoulder, and whispered in her ear. Marty smiled back. "What did she say" a reporter asked when the juror left. "We love you," Marty replied.[11]

***

The grand jury finished hearing testimony from the demonstrators by the first week in May. When the twenty-one jurors returned from a recess in early June, they heard from Bernard Butkovich. It was the first time Butkovich was made to testify under oath about his activities with the Nazis. Also testifying were John Westra, agent in charge of the ATF in North Carolina; Glenn Fleming, head of the ATF regional office in Winston-Salem; and Winston-Salem ATF agent Fulton Dukes.[12] They were followed by an array of Klansmen and Nazis, many of whom recounted their testimonies afterward to reporters. Some of this testimony added significantly to a concrete picture of November Third and of the character and actions of the perpetrators of violence that day.

Imperial Wizard of the White Knights of Liberty, Joe Grady, told reporters that he testified mainly about the clash at China Grove. He told his followers not to go to Greensboro, he said to the jurors, and *he warned the FBI that there might be trouble in Greensboro.*[13] Grady met with two FBI agents in a Winston-Salem restaurant prior to November 3 to warn them of possible violence between the Communist Workers Party and the Klan.

The Greensboro Justice Fund called the new information by Grady "one of the most important public revelations to issue from the grand jury process so far" and said that it added to "a growing body of evidence linking the FBI to the killings." The GJF said Grady's disclosure revealed that the FBI *at least knew in advance* that the Klan and Nazis were planning to attack on November Third— something FBI officials denied. The GJF renewed a call for a special prosecutor to take over the grand jury.[14]

Gorrell Pierce appeared before the grand jury in his Nazi uniform—swastika armband and all. He told the grand jury that "the blood of these five people was on the government's hands." Since the police had an informant directing the caravan, they could have stopped it, he reasoned. He intended to go that morning, but he overslept.[15] Another Nazi, Raeford Caudle, did not oversleep. Caudle rode in the second car of the nine-car caravan, while the light blue Fairlane that he owned was driven by Jack Fowler and positioned at the rear, the eighth car in the line.[16]

Several months before their grand jury appearances, Caudle and Pierce were convicted in a federal court in Asheville for conspiring to blow up parts of Greensboro (as discussed in the previous chapter). They were free on bond pending the outcome of an appeal. One of their coconspirators in the alleged bombing plot, Frank Braswell, was not called but *asked* to appear before the grand jury. He afterward told reporters that he was investigated by the ATF in retaliation for the Nazi exposure of Butkovich's identity in July 1980.[17] A former Nazi, Roger Shannon, who earlier contributed to the exposure of Butkovich, repeated to the grand jury information that he had given at the state trial. Butkovich had called him within a few hours of the November 3 shootings and asked him to harbor fugitives and also to hide Butkovich's AR-15 rifle that Shannon thought had been converted illegally to an automatic weapon. During Nazi meetings prior to November 3, said Shannon, Butkovich suggested killing Klan leader Joe Grady, with whom the Nazis were then feuding. Shannon testified that Butkovich was "the most violent-talking person in the group" and that he urged the Nazis to purchase illegal automatic weapons.[18]

Testimonies presented to the grand jury confirmed several details about Dawson, his role as an agitator at a Lincolnton Klan gathering on October 20, 1979, and his relationship to the police. Moved by Dawson's urgings in Lincolnton, new Klan recruits went to Greensboro to confront the communists a few weeks later.[19] Speaking to the press before testifying to the grand jury, Dawson acknowledged his relationship with the police, and he blamed them for not preventing the shootings. He admitted that he was a "liaison" between the police and the Klan for a long time.

Later, at the conclusion of the grand jury, Dawson told a reporter that when he dropped into police headquarters in 1979, he already knew some Greensboro police officers and was friendly with them from his days as an FBI informant.[20] Dawson said that he was paid fifty dollars by the police to attend the Klan rally in October and to report back on how many Klansmen might attend the CWP rally.[21] During this period, he was in contact with Virgil Griffin, supposedly to better estimate the number of Klansmen expected at a confrontation with the CWP. He was also paid twenty-five dollars to attend a communist meeting, but apparently went to, or was sent to, the wrong group—the Revolutionary Communist Party (RCP). According to what Dawson told reporters (about what he said to the grand jury), police had no doubts concerning the origin of the march as they claimed. On November 1, 1979, when Dawson showed up for a meeting with the police, he was *asked* if he knew that the starting point of the march had been changed and was *told* to look at a copy of the parade permit.[22]

Dawson detailed two conversations that he'd had with his control agent, Detective Cooper, on the morning of November 3. Very early that morning, Dawson was at an all-night restaurant with Klansmen Griffin, Smith, and Pridmore. A few hours later, he called Cooper and reported on the guns that he had seen and the Klan's plan to head for a house on U.S. 220 South, where the caravan would assemble. He called Cooper again in midmorning to tell him that twelve to fourteen people had already gathered at the rendezvous house. Dawson questioned (to reporters and probably to the grand jury also) why Cooper did not notify other officers of the caravan's obvious destination and call for officers to go to the rally site. But Dawson's main concern in criticizing the police was to absolve himself rather than further the cause of justice. Dawson was totally devious about *his own* role in the set-up, portraying himself as innocent. He said that he told the police that the Klan was going to drive along with the march and that, at the end of the march, "there was gonna be heckling, maybe a fistfight or two."[23]

DAISY AND PICTURES

The Greensboro Justice Fund continued to receive fact-finding delegations at intervals throughout the grand jury hearing. In April and May, representatives from the Philadelphia Yearly Meeting, the North Carolina Lutheran Church, the Christian Church Disciples of Christ, Clergy and Laity Concerned, the Fund for Open Information and Accountability, the Southern Organizing Committee, the Southern Poverty Law Center, Sisters of Mercy, Those United to Fight Fascism, and Union Local 41 AFGE were in Greensboro.[24] The local NAACP, the North Carolina branch of the General Baptist Convention, and the United Presbyterian Church's northern organization held a press conference to declare that they, too, were monitoring the federal grand jury out of a concern for justice.[25]

Frequent press conferences were held at Trevi Fountain, a black-owned restaurant previously called Cosmos I. The restaurant was the site of a weekly meeting of the Concerned Citizens of the November 3 Incident. It was there that

I met Daisy Crawford. Daisy became acquainted with the WVO through labor organizing activities, befriended Sandi, and helped her procure a job at Cannon Mills, where Daisy worked. In July 1982, Daisy revealed that two FBI agents visited her trailer home in Salisbury a few days before November 3, 1979. "They showed me a picture of Sandi, which I identified for them," Daisy told a reporter. "They showed me pictures of men which I did not identify at the time, but I believe may have been members of the Workers Viewpoint Organization."[26]

When I talked with Daisy, she said to me, "yes, I'm sure one of the FBI pictures was your husband." She had by then seen pictures of all five people killed, and she felt almost as certain about Jim as about Sandi. She thought the blond man whose picture she was shown was Bill. The agents did not explain why they were showing her the photographs. When they left, Daisy said, she called Sandi and told her friend to warn the other organizers of the anti-Klan rally that something was wrong. Right after the FBI visit, she had a nightmare about the anti-Klan rally, she told me. Her foreboding made her scrap plans to go to Greensboro with her sons to take part in the rally and conference. Daisy told reporters that she felt the FBI had a lot to do with the killings of the five people. "Sandi was the only woman killed, and she was the only picture of a woman they showed me," she said.[27]

The FBI had retracted their initial hasty statement about a CWP investigation begun October 22, 1979, and concluded on November 2. They maintained that they never investigated our group and denied knowing about the November 3 attack in advance, or even being in a position to know. Their claims were contradicted by firsthand accounts rendered by very different individuals—Joe Grady and Daisy Crawford—who had nothing to gain in revealing their information. Daisy's story refuted the claim that there was no FBI investigation of the CWP prior to November 3. Grady's statement that he had tipped off the FBI about the threat of violence contradicted the agency's claim that they had no inkling of impending violence. Moreover, Ed Dawson admitted to the Institute for Southern Studies that he, too, spoke with the FBI during his preparation for the November 3 caravan. Dawson told the ISS that he shared his concern that the rally would be violent with his former control agent, Len Bogaty, in the FBI and that Bogaty urged him to stay away from it. Because of the generally tight relationship between the FBI and local police in matters of political surveillance, it is unimaginable that the information Dawson gave the police about the right-wing plan to confront the communists was not made available to the FBI. It is inconceivable that the violence on November 3 caught the FBI "completely by surprise," as agent Cecil Moses claimed in a television interview shortly afterward.

If the FBI, or the FBI and the BATF jointly, supplied photos to someone—Butkovich? Covington?—who did not go to the November 3 rally but knew who was to be hit (as Caudle had told Grady), if those pictures ended up in the hands of the Klan and Nazi sharpshooters who were positioned in the rear vehicles of the caravan, then there is some plausibility to the suspicion that particular people were being sought as targets. Some explanation of why one of the hit men (Fowler) nearly knocked Dale down in order to strike a blow to Sandi's head. Some accounting for why another assassin (Matthews) ignored Claire's head peering out from the corner of a building but put a hole through Sandi's the moment that she came within his view.

Thinking about all of the photographs in the "scrapbook" of Klan, Nazis, police, BATF, and FBI, I shudder. Before the killings, pictures of labor organizers were displayed by the FBI for identification. Detective Cooper and the police photographer riding with him trailed the Klan and photographed those same victims as they were shot. They took pictures of a murderous assault instead of preventing it. Afterward, a Klansman (Smith) brandished autopsy photos of the people killed at a Klan rally. The photographs are trophies of dead communists—a modern version of flaunting scalps. The flow of action is documented as each player does his part. Was not the production of dead communists, who are also dead labor organizers and dead antiracist activists, the point of this well-photographed collaborative mission?

Shortly after Daisy Crawford came forth, I helped to design and write a flyer for the GJF that featured a biographical sketch of Sandi beside her picture. The headline asked, "Will the Nov. 3rd Grand Jury Indict Sandi Smith's Murderers?" The GJF and the CWP presciently foresaw the outcome of the grand jury. As we stated on the flyer, we thought that only a few Klan and Nazis would be indicted, but not a single individual from among law enforcement and other government agencies that planned, carried out, and covered up the November 3 attack would be charged.

On July 23, 1982, as a militant picket took place in front of the FBI's regional headquarters in Charlotte, Marty, Lewis, and Nelson met with FBI agent Horace Beckwith in his office to confront the bureau with our latest proof that they were lying. An independent researcher in Santa Barbara, Murv Glass, had a letter from FBI Special Agent in Charge Robert L. Pence in which Pence responds to the researcher's request for information. Glass asked about the investigation of the CWP in Greensboro that began on or about October 11, 1979, and ended on November 2, 1979, and Pence wrote back that he should apply to the Washington headquarters of the FBI, where "this information had been previously reported." The still secret report of that investigation is at the FBI's national headquarters, and FBI officials lied when they denied investigating the CWP.

In Greensboro, Nelson told the press that "a planned assassination could not have occurred without substantial preparatory planning. This is the significance of the pre–November 3rd FBI work and the FBI's eagerness to cover it up. . . . How can the Justice Dept. claim that it is doing a full examination of all criminal activity in the case when *their* agents are themselves implicated in the crimes? . . . Having the Justice Dept. and FBI lead the Grand Jury process is like having the fox guard the chicken house."[28]

WE SEEK A SPECIAL PROSECUTOR

The call for an independent special prosecutor accelerated after July 1982. Greensboro Justice Fund lawyers prepared a paper summarizing the legal and factual basis for a special prosecutor in the Greensboro case, due to the Justice Department's conflict of interest.[29] According to legal ethics, the Justice Department was in an untenable position. The Ethics in Government Act, passed by Congress in 1978, addresses the institutional conflict-of-interest issue. It contains a provision for appointment of an independent temporary special prosecutor from outside the Justice Department to investigate allegations of criminal wrongdoing by high-level government officials and to prosecute them if necessary.

Greensboro Justice Fund lawyers moved the special prosecutor motion through appropriate legal channels.[30] By mid-September 1982, the call for a special prosecutor to take charge of the grand jury was supported by scores of prominent attorneys, politicians, religious and civil liberties leaders, academics, entertainers, and others across the land. Petitions signed by 1,175 Greensboro residents requesting a special prosecutor for the grand jury arrived in Washington, D.C., late in October.[31] The popular ground swell for justice *within* Greensboro must have been considerable to have extracted the concession from the local newspaper that the demand for a special prosecutor was "plausible." As expressed by one reporter, delicately, "questions about government complicity in the shootings, however far-fetched, have been aired—and not just by groups on the political fringes."[32] By then however, the grand jury appeared to be drawing to a close. Nearly finished, it recessed in September for five-and-a-half months.

The Ethics in Government Act[33] was applicable to several high-ranking officials who were among those named as defendants in our civil rights suit.

Among them were U.S. Attorney General William French Smith, FBI Director William Webster, and former BATF director G. R. Dickerson. In an October 7, 1982, press statement, the GJF explained that the special prosecutor issue was still legally alive despite obfuscating statements by the Justice Department.[34]

U.S. District Court Judge Gerhard Gesell heard the special prosecutor motion and issued a summons to the Justice Department, giving them sixty days to respond. At the end of that period, the Justice Department again tried to dismiss the GJF special prosecutor suit, to which were attached amicus briefs by legal and civil rights organizations.[35] The grand jury returned the second week of February 1983 and heard more Klan testimonies. But then it quickly recessed for another long period and did not reconvene until the middle of April.

Meanwhile Judge Gesell, having heard oral arguments on February 11, 1983, told the Justice Department bluntly that their interpretation of the Ethics in Government Act was wrong. *There was nothing in the law or in legislative history blocking us as private citizens from going to court to seek the remedy of a special prosecutor.* "Here are a bunch of people who got killed or wounded in a civil rights atrocity," the judge said. "If they haven't got a right to enforce it [the law permitting special prosecutors], who does?"[36] He scolded Attorney General William French Smith for not doing the preliminary investigation and report as required by law. We were encouraged by Judge Gesell's words. However, he deferred making a decision and later that month threw the ball back to the Justice Department, giving them more time to file their answer to our original request.[37] Had a special prosecutor been appointed, it would have been the first under the Ethics in Government Act to serve at citizens' request. Essentially, the Justice Department thumbed its nose at the law of the land.[38]

A DOCUMENTARY AND GRASSROOTS INITIATIVES

On January 24, 1983, a Public Broadcasting System (PBS) documentary, "88 Seconds in Greensboro," was aired on national television. It was one of the first programs in a new Frontline series and was narrated by Jessica Savitch. The documentary raised questions about possible police and government misconduct very clearly. Around Greensboro on the night of the program, groups of people gathered to watch and discuss the film together. Guilford College arranged a screening followed by a panel discussion with prominent local citizens.

Around this time, while the grand jury was still in recess, we mounted a campaign to get Greensboro Police Chief William Swing fired for his role in the November 3 crimes and cover-up. A letter by Nelson—actually a ten-page pamphlet with a comprehensive compilation and an analysis of the facts surrounding the massacre as known in 1983—was widely circulated.[39] The campaign to remove the chief, though it had many adherents, did not succeed against the powerful forces in the city. Swing retired a year or so later.

GETTING PAST THE FOX WITH NEW INFORMATION

Toward the end of the grand jury process, we obtained documented information that suggested pre–November 3 FBI planning and coordination of the role of Bernard Butkovich and pre–November 3 FBI knowledge of the pending assassinations. Nelson wanted to appear before the grand jury again—this time with only a court reporter present, not the federal prosecutors. (Jurors had the right to question witnesses *without* the presence of Justice Department lawyers, the U.S. attorney, the FBI, or any other federal official.) However, prosecutors insisted on controlling the information flow—how to get past the fox guarding the chicken house!

On April 13, 1983, Nelson held a press conference in the Trevi Fountain parking lot. A few months after he first testified before the grand jury, he told the media, Justice Department officials asked to meet with him, and he agreed to be interviewed again by Michael Johnson and FBI agent Brereton. He imagined that they would have a few specific questions about his testimony, but instead "an incredible line of questioning emerged which went into my background more than thirteen years ago . . . I now associate this whole line of questions with the FBI Counter-Intelligence program (COINTELPRO), used extensively in the sixties to slander, discredit, and/or assassinate Black leaders ranging from the members of the Black Panther Party to Dr. Martin Luther King."[40] Nelson thought that the COINTELPRO-type interrogation to which he had been subjected was relevant and should be made public.

His efforts to meet with the grand jury alone remained blocked, and, finally, the long grand jury hearing was about to end. At a press conference outside the Greensboro Federal Courthouse on April 20, 1983, Nelson publicized two significant pieces of information. One confirmed a report that CWP lawyers had received a short time before from Mordecai Levy, a leader in the militant Jewish Defense Organization. In 1979, Levy was a member of the larger Jewish Defense League (JDL). Through a network of informants, the JDL learned in advance of Nazi plans to commit violence at the CWP rally. On November 2, 1979, Levy made a telephone call to an FBI agent in Raleigh, who had a Jewish name, and told him about the Nazi plans and asked him to pass along the information. He was told by the agent that the FBI does not investigate Nazis and that it had no knowledge of any plans for violence.[41] The agent whom Levy thought was Jewish was not. The FBI did not use Levy's information to protect people's lives—not surprising, especially if Levy was telling the FBI something that it already knew.

Nelson also cited a five-page FBI memo describing the activities of a federal undercover agent who infiltrated the Forsyth County Nazis prior to November 3, 1979. This document indicated that Bernard Butkovich's activities were monitored by the FBI in North Carolina as well as by his ATF supervisors.[42] The FBI was kept apprised of developments leading to November 3, including the discussions at the Nazis' planning meeting on November 1. The memo showed that the two bureaus, the BATF and FBI, were pooling information and coordinating their investigations. The Levy document and the citation number for the other document were passed along by Nelson and Lewis to the federal prosecutors in Winston-Salem.

I was in Madison, Wisconsin, when the grand jury handed down its indictments. I stopped there on my way back to Greensboro from South Dakota where I had just attended an extremely moving ceremony as a guest of the American Indian Movement (AIM). I called home and Gayle gave me the news over the phone.

The federal grand jury in Winston-Salem issued a fourteen-count indictment of six Klansmen and three Nazis. They included Klansmen Virgil Griffin, Jerry Smith, Ed Dawson, David Matthews, Coleman Pridmore, and Roy Toney and Nazis Roland Wood, Raeford Caudle, and Jack Fowler. (Smith, Pridmore, Wood, Fowler, and Matthews had been among those tried and acquitted in the 1980 state trial.) All nine men were indicted for conspiring to violate the civil rights of participants in the anti-Klan rally. The demonstrators were participating in an authorized and legally protected activity by engaging in a rally "without discrimination on account of race," and the indicted willfully interfered by force. Their conspiracy to disrupt the rally caused death and bodily injury to rally participants. Specific actions of each conspirator, cited in the indictment, were in violation of Title 18, United States Code, Sections 245 (b) (2) (B) and (b) (4) (A). The conspiracy charge, if proved in court, carried a maximum five-year sentence. The grand jury charge summarized the planning activities of the Klan and Nazis in October and November of 1979 that constituted the conspiracy. The overt acts violated the U.S. Code Title 18, Section 371.

Counts of the indictment for willful injuries resulting in death were directed at Matthews and Wood for Jim, at Smith for César, at Matthews and Fowler for Mike, at Matthews for Sandi and Bill. If convicted, Matthews, Wood, Smith, and

Fowler could be sentenced to life imprisonment. There were counts against Wood for willfully injuring Frankie Powell (Chekesha), Don Pelles, Rand Manzella, Tom Clark, and David Dalton. Other counts charged Toney in connection with Paul's injuries and Matthews for Jim Wrenn's injuries. Those charged with inflicting injuries were subject to a maximum ten-year jail sentence if convicted. A final count named Griffin and Dawson for unlawfully conspiring with others to avoid arrest and to obstruct the investigation after November 3.[43] Made public when these nine indictments came out was the fact that Mark Sherer (who fired the signal shot on November 3) was charged as a coconspirator a month earlier in a separate indictment and pleaded guilty.[44]

By publicly airing the issues and organizing at the grassroots, we forced the Justice Department to at least acknowledge the criminality of the Klan and Nazis. But the grand jury was not set up for the thoroughgoing investigation needed to fully resolve culpability for November Third. *The indictments completely passed over all Greensboro police officers and all federal officials in relation to whom evidence of a criminal conspiracy and cover-up existed.* The comment of one of the indicted Nazis is revealing. "Why me?" Raeford Caudle said to a reporter. "Why not Harold Covington or Bernard Butkovich and the law dogs? If there was any conspiracy done, it was done by them. As far as it goes, I don't really know who set it up."[45]

Certainly, Caudle and the other eight men all amply deserved indictments for their violent and criminal actions. It is nevertheless true that the grand jury did not look very far beyond the trigger men and other surrogates like Caudle. "The omission of indictments for any government agents who have been implicated we find outrageous," declared Lewis Pitts.[46] To the world it may have looked like justice was done in Greensboro at last, however we knew that we had reached only another reference point in scaling a mountain of injustice. GJF Executive Director Marty Nathan's oxymoron was right on the mark—the grand jury yielded "a victory and a whitewash." Victory came in the form of nine grand jury indictments against Klansmen and Nazis who would later stand trial on federal charges of civil rights violations. Whitewash came in the form of a failure to indict even a single police or government agent who in fact conspired to violate citizens' civil rights.

NOTES

1. Stan Swofford and Larry King, "Grand Jury to Explore Conduct of Officers," *Greensboro Daily News*, 24 March 1982.

2. See Joyce Johnson, "A Great Deal Is at Stake: The Nov. 3 Grand Jury May Finally Answer the Questions," (Greensboro) *Northstate Reader*, April 1982.

3. See Larry King, "U.S. Attorneys to Interview 12 Witnesses," *Greensboro Daily News*, 7 April 1982.

4. Lee Weisbecker, "Communist Workers Party Revealing Secret Testimony on '79 Greensboro Killings," *Charlotte Observer*, 10 May 1982, 1A.

5. Larry King, "TV Men: CWP Killings Appeared Planned," *Greensboro Daily News*, 20 April 1982, A1, A2.

6. Larry King, "Federal Grand Jury Hears CWP Member," *Greensboro Daily News*, 22 April 1982, A11.

7. Larry King, "Police Knew Site, CWP Leader Says," *Greensboro Record*, 23 April, 1982.

8. Larry King, "CWP Member Says He Fired Gun," *Greensboro Daily News*, 24 April 1982, B1, B7.

9. Joyce Johnson to Special Federal Grand Jury, Winston-Salem, North Carolina, statement, 5 May 1982.

10. Johnson to Special Federal Grand Jury.

11. Larry King, "Nov. 3 Grand Jury Session Full of Quirks as CWP Talks," *Greensboro Daily News*, 2 May 1982, C1.

12. Larry King, "Grand Jury Hears More from Agent on Nov. 3," *Greensboro Record*, 4 June 1982.

13. Larry King, "Miller: Probe Besets White N.C. Patriots," *Greensboro Daily News*, 10 June 1982.

14. Larry King, "Grady An Informant—Justice Fund," *Greensboro Daily News*, 17 June 1982, B5.

15. Larry King, "Grand Jury Told Blood of CWP on Police Hands," *Greensboro Daily News*, 12 June 1982.

16. Larry King, "Nazi Dons Full Uniform to Meet Grand Jury," *Greensboro Daily News*, 11 June 1982, C11.

17. Larry King, "Agent Said Seeking Shelter for Suspects," *Greensboro Record*, 24 June 1982.

18. Larry King, "Ex-Nazi: I Wouldn't Hide 'Em," *Greensboro Daily News*, 24 June 1982.

19. See Larry King, "Three Testify to Grand Jury," *Greensboro Daily News*, 25 June 1982, C4; and "Jury Hears Klan Caravan Participant," *Greensboro Record*, 29 June 1982.

20. Gary Terpening, "Ex-Informer Says Indictments in KKK Shootings Unjust," *Winston-Salem Journal*, 24 April 1983.

21. Mark Wright, "Police Could Have Prevented Rally Shooting, Informant Says," (Winston-Salem) *Sentinel*, 15 July 1982, 1.

22. Larry King, "Dawson Tells of His Role under Oath," *Greensboro Daily News*, 16 July 1982, B2.

23. Wright, "Police Could Have Prevented," 13.

24. See Greensboro Justice Fund, newsletter, June/July 1982.

25. Leslie M. Allen, "Justice Fund Gets Backing of 3 Groups," *Greensboro Daily News*, 1 July 1982, C2.

26. Bruce Siceloff, "Woman Says FBI Tracked CWP Activist before Death," (Raleigh, N.C.) *News & Observer*, 9 July 1982, 6B.

27. Alex Charnes, "Pictures of 5 Slain Shown before Killings," (Burlington, N.C.) *Times-News*, 8 July 1982, 1A.

28. Communist Workers Party, "CWP Meets with FBI: Demands Special Prosecutor," press release, 23 July 1982.

29. Greensboro Justice Fund, "The Need and Basis for the Appointment of a Special Prosecutor in the November 3rd Case," paper by legal team, end of July 1982.

30. See "Unbiased Prosecutor Requested," (Winston-Salem) *Sentinel*, 4 August 1982. There were a few exceptions to the national media blackout of the Greensboro case. One was a column by Colman McCarthy, "Greensboro Trial Has National Importance," *Washington Post*, 22 August 1982, 5. Another was William K. Tabb and Martha Nathan, "Civil Rights, The Klan & Reagan Justice," in *The Nation*, 21 August 1982.

31. "More Signatures Mailed to Capital," *Greensboro Daily News*, 22 October 1982.

32. Editorial, "A Special Prosecutor?" *Greensboro Daily News*, 27 September 1982.

33. See 28 U.S.C. 591 & ff.

34. See also Gayle Korotkin, "Not Too Late for Prosecutor," *Greensboro Daily News*, 12 October 1982; and Larry King, "Justice Department Says No to Special Prosecutor," *Greensboro Daily News*, 5 October 1982, B9.

35. These included the Southern Poverty Law Center, the Black American Law Student Association, the Center for Constitutional Rights, the Constitutional Law Clinic at Rutgers University, the Southern Organizing Committee, the National Alliance against Racist and Political Repression, the National Lawyers Guild chapters at Harvard and Yale, the North Carolina Civil Liberties Union, and the North Carolina National Lawyers Guild.

36. Paul Clancy, "Justice Department Is Scolded," *Greensboro Daily News*, 17 February 1983.

37. "Federal Judge Rejects Denial of Prosecutor," *Greensboro Daily News*, 24 February 1983.

38. Larry King, "Need for Prosecutor Questioned in Document," *Greensboro Daily News*, 11 March 1983. See also "Justice Agency Files Last Response on Prosecutor for Nov. 3 Shooting," *Greensboro Daily News*, 12 April 1983, B5.

39. See "Letter from Nelson Johnson, Area Spokesperson for the CWP, to Mayor John Forbis, City Council Members and the City Manager concerning the November 3 Murders and Why Police Chief William Swing Should Be Fired," 1 February 1983.

40. Communist Workers Party, "Statement to the Press by Nelson Johnson, Regarding His Attempt to Provide New Information to the Grand Jury," 13 April 1983.

41. Larry King, "CWP Spokesman: Evidence on Nov. 3 Rally Touches FBI," *Greensboro Daily News*, 21 April 1983, B2.

42. King, "CWP Spokesman," B2. See also John Monk, "FBI Alleges Grand Jury Interference," *Charlotte Observer*, 21 April 1983, 1B.

43. See *United States of America v. Virgil L. Griffin, Edward Woodrow Dawson, David Wayne Matthews, Roland Wayne Wood, Jerry Paul Smith, Jack Wilson Fowler, Jr., Roy C. Toney, Coleman B. Pridmore, and Raeford Milano Caudle*, U.S. District Court for the Middle District of North Carolina, Greensboro Division, No. CR-83-53-01-G through CR-83-53-09-G, 21 April 1983.

44. *United States v. Mark J. Sherer*, U.S. District Court for the Middle District of North Carolina, Greensboro Division, No. CR-83-31-01-G, 24 March 1983.

45. Carl Briggs, "Officers Rounding Up 9 Indicted in Shootout," (Winston-Salem) *Sentinel*, 22 April 1983, 11.

46. Michael Massoglia and Gary Terpening, "Klan Defendants in Custody," *Winston-Salem Journal*, 23 April 1983, 2.

NO RACIAL ANIMUS? THE
FEDERAL TRIAL IN 1984

THE EARLY 1980s

From 1981, along with my party duties, I was very active in the movement to stop U.S. intervention in Central America. I joined the Triad Citizens Concerned for Central America, chaired by Father Henry Atkins and Professor Robert Williams. On February 27, 1982, we led a powerful and unprecedented demonstration inside of Fort Bragg. On one of the cruelest winter days, we took six or seven hundred people into that citadel of imperialist power to protest U.S. training of Salvadoran troops at the fort and our country's support for a regime that had killed thirty thousand Salvadorans in the preceding two years. However, my activities in the solidarity movement seemed to me of lesser importance than the struggles that related to the party and November Third. That was because I saw the party as a more comprehensive political endeavor. We were not just objecting to this or that imperialist foray—we would not stop until we brought about the socialist transformation that would end *all* imperialist forays.

In 1983, I went to South Dakota when the American Indian Movement (AIM) invited the CWP to send a representative to the tenth anniversary of the Siege of Wounded Knee. Jim set up and ran a medical clinic for AIM during the FBI siege in 1973. The Native American community included Jim Waller among those whom they honored in their spiritual ceremonies. I was very moved and gave AIM leaders Ted and Russell Means a copy of Paul and Sally's book, *The True Story of the Greensboro Massacre*, inscribing it with a message of solidarity.

In the early 1980s, my political activities included taking a strong public stand of condemnation toward Israel for its bombing and other barbaric attacks on Palestinian refugee camps in Lebanon. I joined others in press conferences, gave speeches, and was part of an active Raleigh-based statewide coalition of Jews and Arabs. I challenged myself to take the position that I knew was right against the weight of my cultural biases. I was raised to be, and everyone around me was, a cheerleader for Israel, but I had matured enough politically to understand the Palestinian struggle for liberation as no different from that of any oppressed people who struggle to be free.

In August 1983, my father died suddenly, shortly before my parents' fiftieth wedding anniversary. Fay and Ted were very close throughout their long marriage: they had permanently fused into one entity—FayTed. As in the creation story by Aristophanes, neither was a complete human being alone.

During a visit by my mother the following October, we took Antonia and Alex to the UNC campus at Chapel Hill, where Antonia would be a student after graduation from high school in the spring. We spread blankets, ate a picnic lunch, and I put the most positive spin I could on our quest for justice. The grand jury indictments had given us hope of making a breakthrough, I told my mother, perhaps at the upcoming federal trial. I told her about the benefit concert folk singer Pete Seeger gave for the GJF in Greensboro but omitted mentioning the Klan and Nazi threats that preceded it. My mother received the upbeat version of events as I tried to elevate her spirits. I wanted her to see that she still had a life to live, and I tried to persuade her that a woman in her mid-seventies was not too old to learn how to drive a car. However, she soon fell ill, and learning to drive ceased to be an option.

A week before Pete Seeger's benefit concert, Glen Miller, one of the state's most activist right wingers who boasted of his presence in the Klan caravan on November 3, announced that he would bring Klansmen to picket the concert.[1] Local citizens made the police announce publicly that they would assure the safety of concertgoers. On the day of the concert, October 9, 1983, the Klan announced that they had canceled their picket. That evening, squad cars lined the street in front of UNC-G's Aycock Auditorium as eight hundred people filed in for Seeger's uplifting performance.

It was a period of reaction: cross burnings, shooting attacks against blacks and interracial couples, and church burnings were occurring in counties throughout North Carolina and elsewhere in the South. Reverend Wilson Lee, a black minister and GJF supporter from Statesville, N.C., told the U.S. Commission on Civil Rights about a Klan attempt to lynch a black man, and a cross burning and shooting at his own home. In Greensboro at the end of October, Father Atkins, who was a vocal supporter of justice in the Greensboro Massacre case, was subjected to a cross burning in his yard and received death threats. At the same time, the tombstone of the CWP 5 was vandalized with red paint. Police called these incidents Halloween pranks.

THE FEDERAL CIVIL RIGHTS TRIAL—GAG 'EM!

The people of Greensboro want to forget about what happened at Morningside Homes, city officials maintained. Despite their muscular efforts to isolate those who did not want to forget, citizens' involvement in the fight for justice was not extinguished. We had wide support for our call to convict the criminal perpetrators of November Third. Around the fourth anniversary of the Greensboro Massacre, the widows, joined by Chekesha, summarized progress to date and thanked the people of Greensboro. Bennett College set up a scholarship fund in the name of its former student president, Sandi Smith. We wanted everyone to know that Sandi "led a movement for quality education for young black people. Later as a textile union organizer at Revolution Mill she was insistent and successful in securing for women workers freedom from sexual harassment by their male supervisors. Sandi believed in educational opportunity and in women's rights and worked hard for both." We affirmed that we were not through fighting because "the veil of cover-up has never been lifted."[2]

The federal trial of nine Klansmen and Nazis for civil rights violations did little to lift the veil of cover-up. The trial began on January 9, 1984, and resulted in an acquittal verdict on all fourteen counts on April 15, 1984.[3] With the cry to lift the "veil of cover-up" echoing in civic space, it must have been quite a challenge for the power structure to find ways to impose a cloak of secrecy instead—yet the latter is the more apt sartorial metaphor for what officialdom tried to do. One of the first acts of Judge Edward J. Devitt in preparation for the federal civil rights trial was to issue a gag order for attorneys, defendants, and witnesses in the case. It expressly forbade giving interviews to the mass media. The order was considered "rare, if not unprecedented in North Carolina litigation."[4] Ostensibly, it was to protect the defendants' rights to a fair trial, but some of the defendants' attorneys found it objectionable along with almost everyone else. Far more believable is that the gag order was an attempt to silence us.[5] If we obeyed the order, we would not only have to seal our lips about the upcoming federal trial but also about our civil rights suit. This order was challenged, but Judge Thomas A. Flannery, appointed to take over the case when Devitt became ill, retained it. Subsequently, the gag order was modified, permitting us to speak publicly about the related civil rights suit. My recollection of this ridiculous measure is that it was largely ignored. I cannot think of a single instance in which any of our group kept mum on account of the gag order—but of course that does not address the gravity and dubious constitutionality of such a broad order for the judicial system and civil rights.

After the grand jury had finished its work, the special prosecutor ball was still in play. In May 1983, Judge Gesell ordered the Justice Department to conclude the preliminary investigation within ninety days—something they should have done a year earlier. It was thought to be the first time a federal judge ever ordered the Justice Department to take such action. Judge Gesell's ruling implied that our conspiracy charges were sound enough to trigger a preliminary investigation and that the Justice Department was in violation of the Ethics in Government Act. However, the judge could have recommended a special prosecutor too, but he did not. By once again tossing the ball into their court, the judge, in effect, allowed the Justice Department to score. In the end, the Justice Department had its way, but we pushed the process as far as we could and created some openings for others seeking democratic reform of corrupt government.[6] (Also shortly after the conclusion of the grand jury, a U.S. Court of Appeals overturned, on a technicality, the conviction of the six Nazis around Asheville, N.C., for conspiring to bomb parts of Greensboro. In two previous trials, there had been a hung jury, then a conviction. The six Nazis would later be tried one more time and acquitted.)

Justice Department prosecutors in the federal civil rights trial were walking on eggshells. At the same time that federal prosecutors were preparing to conduct the federal civil rights trial, they were also arguing in court that the civil rights suit against their clients should be dismissed.[7] While convictions of some Klansmen and Nazis in criminal court would not necessarily have hurt the Justice Department, too much exposure concerning the entire conspiracy would have threatened the complicit agents and agencies that the department was bound to defend. It was this ever-present conflict of interest that the request for a special prosecutor was meant to resolve.

JURY SELECTION IN SECRET

Before the questioning of prospective jurors began on January 9, Judge Flannery cleared the courtroom of reporters and spectators, a move some said was unprecedented and perhaps unconstitutional. Turned away were representatives from the National Anti-Klan Network, the American Civil Liberties Union, and the National Council of Churches who had come at the invitation of the Greensboro Justice Fund to monitor the trial. Attorneys for the four

biggest newspapers in North Carolina, the *Charlotte Observer*, the *News &
Observer* in Raleigh, the *Winston-Salem Journal and Sentinel*, and the
Greensboro News & Record, filed a motion objecting to the secret jury selection.[8] The gag order and the closed jury selection were challenged in an appeals court.[9] Both were upheld.

Not surprisingly, the secret proceeding yielded another all-white jury that resembled the Klan and Nazis in race, educational level, and political orientation
far more than it resembled the demonstrators.[10] Writer Mab Segrest, who was
present at the trial's opening statements, described the atmosphere. "I have a
clear view of the jury, and they worry me. The jury pool, chosen from holders of
North Carolina drivers' licenses, contained a 'good mix' by race and age, according to a reporter who had been there to see. Now, by all appearances, 10 of
the 12 white jurors are over 50—the generation coming of age in the anticommunist fervor of the Cold War." Presiding Judge Flannery, wrote Segrest,
"screened the pool in secrecy. . . . I would feel more reassured that this all-white
Southern jury would not mean automatic acquittal if I could read the transcript
of their questioning, which the judge agreed to release after the selection. But it
will take one month to get a copy, at a cost of $3,400. I sit there fighting my voice:
This jury is rigged."[11]

Segrest was a member of North Carolinians against Racist and Religious Violence (NCARRV), a group born out of the protest of the Greensboro Massacre.
NCARRV tracked Klan activity and incidents of racist violence in the state. The
number of such incidents, she wrote, went from "15 in 1981, to 26 in 1982, to
more than 60 in 1983. Klan rallies increased three-fold in 1983. Crossburnings
rose from 5 to 15. Four black churches in Edgecombe County burned after KKK
graffiti were painted on them. Twenty-six Klansmen say they are running for
state office this year."[12]

Listening to opening statements by the defense, Segrest decided that the attorneys were making the same assumptions about the jury as she was, that as a
group the jury was far more sympathetic to the Klansmen and Nazis than to the
communists. "The lawyers hammer away at common themes from different angles: The defendants acted in self-defense and intended no harm. The men did
not come to the anti-Klan rally on account of race, but in opposition to communism. They are patriotic, white Christians, just like the jurors. . . . I am surprised
to learn that the Klan was *formerly* based on white superiority but is now a 'patriotic' organization that opposes communism."[13]

Segrest listened as Wood's lawyer, Roy Hall, praised the contributions to
this country by the German people—the largest ethnic group "after the Anglo-
Saxons"—thus encouraging the jury to identify with their roots. She heard

Hall laud the American Nazis as opponents of communism and call American and German Nazis patriotic. "No one rises in the courtroom to object to this definition of patriotism that includes the right of mass extermination. Some of the lawyers have said things they would never say looking into a black or Jewish face," wrote Segrest.[14]

As one might contend in a theater of the absurd, the defense argued that if the Klansmen and Nazis were really racist, they would have killed more blacks, but there was only one black person among the five killed. Defendants' attorneys continued to maintain that the Klan and Nazi posture was one of self-defense— as "proved" in the state trial—rather than aggression. And the stand-off at China Grove that took place four months before November Third was made much of, in spite of the fact that it was Klansmen who were flashing their weapons at apparently unarmed demonstrators. One defense attorney made creative use of testimonies (missing from the state trial) by demonstrators who fired retaliatory shots on November 3. He argued that since the communists had guns in violation of the stipulation on the parade permit, they were not entitled to the protection of the federal laws.

In a sentence, *the Klansmen and Nazis were acquitted because the jury was able to decide that they acted from patriotism, not from a racial animus.* The picture that comes into focus is this: a jury was questioned and picked in secret that inclined toward the racist philosophy and anticommunism of the defendants. This jury needed only the opportunity for an acquittal vote; it needed a legal fig leaf. Such was provided by the choice of civil rights statutes in the charges brought against the Klansmen and Nazis. Its reach went no further than violations of the law *from a racial animus.* To be proven guilty as charged, the jury needed proof that the violence was *racially motivated.* The Klan and Nazis' attorneys were able to argue successfully to that jury that their clients were *politically motivated* and acted out of patriotism, that is, out of a hatred of communism. Because of the patent difficulty of proving beyond a doubt that the Klan was more racially than politically motivated, the set-up practically assured an acquittal.

No attorneys from *either* side questioned the definition of patriotism as synonymous with violent anticommunism. They all assumed anticommunism *defines* patriotism. Thus, very specific legal decisions and actions led to the second round of acquittals for Klansmen and Nazis. Had the Justice Department chosen the broad "Reconstruction" statute under which to prosecute the Klansmen and Nazis, they would have been required to show only that the defendants intentionally interfered with a legally protected exercise of civil rights—proving motivation would not have been a key issue. The Justice Department chose instead a much narrower interpretation according to which culpability for interfering with others' civil rights must be indicative of racial motivation.

It is hard to believe that defense attorneys were able to talk their way around the Klan/Nazis' racism. But their case, that the Klan/Nazis did not act from a racial animus, was made to a credulous jury—one that had been questioned and selected outside of public scrutiny. This jury ignored a statement made by Virgil Griffin at a Klan rally preceding November Third: "If you love your children, you will shoot niggers." It overlooked the racial epithets hurled at the interracial group of demonstrators by the occupants of the caravan as it drove into the rally. It sloughed off Mark Sherer's exhortations to his fellow "patriots" to shoot the "niggers"—as was revealed in the course of the grand jury hearings when Sherer pled guilty to conspiracy charges.[15] The jury passed over posters that Ed Dawson tacked up before November 3 that showed a figure hanging from a noose with the caption, "Notice to traitors and race-mixers, it's time for old-time justice." And, apparently, David Matthews' blatantly racist language in his various testimonies—no less racist because three of the four victims in the killings he is linked to were white demonstrators—bore no connection to a racial animus, in jurors' minds. The only red flag that Matthews' frequent use of the n-word raised was that of communism. The jury must not have paid attention to Jerry Paul Smith's statement at the Klan/Nazi planning meeting on November 1. On seeing Nelson Johnson's picture on television, Smith pointed a gun at his television set and said, "I'm gonna shoot that nigger." Proof of a racial animus? Certainly not: Smith explained away the racism in his threat by telling the jury that he had said, "I ought to shoot the television for showing such stuff."[16]

It is highly probable that the credo of right-wing Christian fundamentalism played some role in the jury's decision to acquit. Perhaps not far from jurors' experience was Virgil Griffin's Whispering Pines Baptist Church in Dallas, N.C. The minister was a Klansman, and the church offered a congenial atmosphere for both racism and anticommunism.[17] In any case, the prosecution failed to persuade the jury of the obvious: that the Klan and Nazis were angered by the communists' embrace of racial equality, and that they indeed acted from racism in as much as they directed their actions at blacks and whites engaged in a racially integrated activity.[18] Chief Prosecutor Daniel Bell, Michael Johnson's replacement in the federal trial, had a lot to work with but did not make much of it.[19] The routing of justice was made easier by the prosecution's lackluster performance, according to some courtroom observers. For the more numerous and energized Klan/Nazi attorneys, the case was a real plum, not a nuisance or a threat.

ENLIGHTENING TESTIMONIES

The ballistics expert, whose testimony at the previous state trial was used by the Klan/Nazis to claim self-defense and hence to win an acquittal, changed his story in the federal trial. The expert now acknowledged that controversial shots three, four, and five might have come from the area toward the front of the caravan, where the Klan and Nazis were situated.[20] In fact, evidence and testimony indicated that Sherer fired the first, third, and fourth shots; Brent Fletcher the second; and Roy Toney the fifth (with the rifle he wrenched from Jim Waller). All three were Klansmen. From the ballistic evidence, it seemed certain that demonstrators only returned fire after at least eleven shots had been fired by the attackers and several people had fallen.

Mark Sherer was to be a key witness for the prosecution and to testify against his fellow Klansmen, but he changed his mind and tried to get out of his plea bargain. Scherer was no longer eager to talk about the "underground Klan." He had told the grand jury that he was with Jerry Paul Smith when Smith exploded a pipe bomb and asked him to make some more. When Butkovich testified, he quoted Smith as saying that the pipe bombs would "work very well thrown into a group of niggers."[21]

A few Klansmen who had been witnesses for the defense in the state trial became prosecution witnesses. Chris Benson testified that he first heard about the anti-Klan rally at the Whispering Pines Baptist Church when Virgil Griffin urged the congregation to go to Greensboro to oppose the communists. Benson testified that after the November 1 meeting at Wood's house, some Klansmen went to the A&T State University campus and tore down WVO/CWP posters announcing the anti-Klan rally. At Griffin's home the night before the rally, Smith, Pridmore, Benson, and Griffin "sat around and [Griffin] pointed out who we wanted to get when we got to Greensboro."[22] Benson, Sherer, and Griffin spent six days hiding out in a South Carolina swamp after the shootings.

In his first public testimony, ATF agent Bernard Butkovich admitted to attending two planning meetings where the November 3 confrontation was discussed—on September 22 and November 1. Butkovich had to account for why (supposedly) he never told the police what was afoot. He offered various reasons from which one can pick and choose: (1) He didn't believe that the Klan and Nazis would bring guns to the march; (2) He thought that the police already knew about the danger; and (3) It would have been up to his supervisor to take care of it.

Detective Jerry (Rooster) Cooper testified that he met and talked with Dawson *nine times* between October 11, when he registered Dawson as one of his "sources," and November 3. During these meetings, Dawson told Cooper about the Klan/Nazi plans to attend the WVO rally. Dawson was paid small sums, on October 15 and on November 1, for his information.[23] Cooper confirmed that Dawson called him on the morning of November 3 and told him that there were guns at Brent Fletcher's house, where Klansmen and Nazis had gathered, and that they planned to drive by Everitt and Carver where demonstrators were assembling. Cooper said that he went to a curb market across from Fletcher's house and copied down license plates, then he briefly returned to police headquarters to pass along the information. When he went back to Fletcher's house, most of the vehicles had left. He then went toward the parade route and caught up with the caravan at a ramp off of Interstate 85. As the photographer with Cooper took pictures, Cooper observed the Ford Fairlane join the caravan and get into position directly in front of the last vehicle in the procession, the yellow van. Although one can hardly imagine a more opportune or justifiable time for a weapons search— *before* known armed racists, heading toward a site with a racially mixed group, violated civil rights and took away lives—there was no weapons search.[24]

Cooper, in plainclothes and in an unmarked car that day, acknowledged that he was parked a block away from the intersection of Everitt and Carver. Cooper and his police photographer, John T. Matthews, were close enough to the gunfire to see what was happening. Photographer Matthews said that he saw defendant David Matthews firing from several positions. Cooper said that he stayed in the car and radioed for help after the shooting started.

Cooper's testimony and that of other police officers probably revealed much more than the police wanted to divulge. Art League was the officer who stopped the fleeing van. He and others were stationed at Dudley High School several blocks away from the gathering when they heard about the shooting over the police radio. League testified to the grand jury that police officers were told *not* to go to Everitt and Carver.[25] If the yellow van had not been tardy in leaving the crime scene, League would not have come upon it. If he had followed the order *not* to go to Everitt and Carver, he would not have made any arrests that day, and *all* the assailants would have gotten away. Tuned in to the same broadcast as League was Police Sergeant Tracy Burke with a group of officers at Biscuitville. The reader may recall that the police were given an early lunch break, from mid-morning until 11:30 A.M. Unlike League, Burke followed orders and did not go to Everitt and Carver. Instead he went to Gillespie Junior High several blocks away.[26] The police's orders were to travel *parallel to* the parade—in other words, to be somewhere else.

DEMONSTRATORS TAKE THE STAND

Demonstrators who were wounded on November 3, fired back, or whose testimony was otherwise deemed important were called to the stand: this time around we testified. Tom Clark said that he was singing and playing his guitar on November 3 to "create a spirit to get people to come to our march and the conference afterwards with the purpose of educating people about the Ku Klux Klan."[27] He told of running for cover, attending to a dying Bill Sampson, seeing Sandi and knowing that she was dead, finding Jim, thinking that Paul would either die or lose his eye, and finally discovering his best friend, César, "clearly dead." Tom Clark's wounds were charged to Roland Wood. Wood's lawyer quizzed Clark about the pro-communist lyrics of his songs and chants.[28]

Demonstrators who returned the Klan's fire gave an accounting of their actions, just as they did at the grand jury hearing. Rand Manzella testified that Bill returned the Klan's gunfire with one shot when he was hit and then passed the gun to him. Rand fired two shots back at the Klan and Nazis. It was clear from Dori Blitz's testimony that the Klan attack was well underway when she fired back. She saw Jerry Paul Smith with a pistol and fired five shots at him. She testified that Jim Waller gave her our .38-caliber gun that morning to use in case a sniper began firing at the marchers. He gave it to her, she said, because she had a cool head in a crisis. Jim also gave her a slicker with a big pocket in order to conceal the weapon. She had never used a gun before, and Jim gave her some quick pointers, she told jurors. Dori also described returning to my house afterward and searching Jim's papers. "We were so upset," she said. "I didn't even know what I was looking for. I burned some of Jim's love poems to Signe." A defense lawyer asked her if she burned some of his communist literature, too. "Probably," Dori replied.[29]

Paul Bermanzohn, on the stand for a long time, told of seeing César shot, of taking a few steps to help him, and of feeling "a terrific force in my head and arm and I could not get up. I kept trying to get up."[30] Paul acknowledged being a key planner of the rally and managed to say a great deal about our political organizing against racism. After Paul, Dale gave emotional testimony of her experience on November 3. She was followed by Jim Wrenn. Jim recounted how he tried to meet the Klan attack, then ran for cover. Jim told of seeing friends fall, of being wounded, and of wandering around once the gunfire stopped, trying to help the wounded until people realized that he was seriously hurt and attended to him.[31]

OFFICIAL STAMP OF APPROVAL FOR KLAN/NAZI VIOLENCE

Even these testimonies—absent in the state trial—coupled with the viewing of the videotapes did not overcome the jury's prejudices. In 1980, the state of North Carolina put its official stamp of approval on the Klan/Nazi violence of November Third. In the spring of 1984, the federal government did likewise. The government of the world's wealthiest and most powerful country, a country quick to spout self-righteous platitudes about democracy at other countries, aggressively sought the services of an immoral and reactionary element among its citizens to murder other citizens—critics, activists, and people's leaders working for real democracy and social equality. After the second acquittal verdict in the Greensboro case, only the likes of racist anti-Semite Glenn Miller were gloating over a "great victory for the Ku Klux Klan and for all patriotic anti-Communist, freedom-loving Christian people."[32] Decent people took to the streets in protest.

The early eighties were tumultuous times politically. There was vocal opposition to Reaganism and much protest activity around his administration's budget cuts that affected the very survival of poor people. At the same time, the military budget grew to obscene proportions under Reagan. The widespread government spying on political activists, particularly those involved in the Central America solidarity movement, engendered resistance. Many groups opposed the government's attempts to legalize domestic spying by giving special powers to the FBI, powers supposedly curtailed after Watergate. COINTELPRO, hardly a distant memory, had its critics even within government. Former U.S. senator Robert Morgan, who as a member of the Senate Select Committee on Intelligence investigated COINTELPRO in 1975 and 1976, was still concerned about the abuse of federal police power, and he cited specifically FBI agent Thomas J. Brereton.[33]

The antinuclear and peace movement attracted people from all walks of life. In Europe, the peace movement was a wide-ranging mass movement, and it was a force in the United States as well. On June 12, 1982, nearly a million people marched for peace and disarmament in New York City. They were also marching for new national priorities, for economic and social policies that would serve human needs, and for jobs with peace. Jesse Jackson's campaign for presidency in 1984 and the formation of his Rainbow Coalition, a noteworthy event in American political life, were possible because all this popular activity gave it impetus.

After the verdict in the federal trial, I joined the Triad Citizens Concerned for Central America for a silent protest vigil in front of Greensboro's federal building. The North Carolinians against Racist and Religious Violence held a vigil in

Durham. Statements of outrage came from Earl Jones, an African American Greensboro city councilman; from Lynn Wells, coordinator of the National Anti-Klan Network; and from many others. Phil Thompson, from the Central Committee of the CWP, came to Greensboro; he, Nelson, and I talked to the press.[34]

A couple of days later, the *Charlotte Observer*, in an editorial, declared that the results of the trial contradicted reality. "The charges were narrow," they wrote, "and difficult to prove. The evidence was voluminous. The defense team was skilled. The jury was once again all-white; little is known about how it was chosen because the judge had barred the press and the public from jury selection proceedings.

"It was unlikely that every defendant would be convicted of every charge against him. Yet the implicit message the system has sent forth—that no one was *really* murdered, that no one's rights were *really* violated—stands in shocking contrast to the bloody events recorded on videotape that day. Until the verdicts and reality are reconciled, justice has not been done."[35]

Democratic presidential candidate Jesse Jackson, in the Triad area to attend a Board of Trustees meeting at North Carolina A & T State University, called the acquittal verdict a "threat to justice everywhere."[36]

On May 5, 1984, several hundred people marched through downtown Greensboro protesting the latest acquittals of Klansmen and Nazis. The march was sponsored by the local group, Concerned Citizens of the November 3 Incident. Lewis Brandon, one of the march organizers, said that the rally was to assure the city, the state, and the world that "we will not be intimidated by Klan and Nazi hatred."[37] The president of the National Black Police Association, Ron Hampton, was there with fifteen other black police officers from Washington, D.C., expressing solidarity with the marchers and keeping an eye on the Greensboro Police Department. In a letter read aloud at the rally, U.S. Representative John Conyers said that the acquittals made "a mockery of our judicial system." And talking to the press about rally participants was Ed Whitfield. "We're men and women, black and white, Native American, Hispanic; we're from radical groups, we're from moderate, conservative groups, and we're from no group at all," he said.[38] Nelson, a key speaker on May 5, said that November Third had come to symbolize something much bigger than that day, something far beyond the conflict between two groups that clashed in the street. The event had become a lightening rod for people of many backgrounds fighting for justice.

The acquittals in the federal civil rights trial ended the possibility for justice within the criminal justice system. The civil suit, brought by citizens vic-

timized in the November 3 assault, was the last judicial recourse, the final opportunity to use the legal system to make the murderers liable for the damage
that they had done.

DEATH AND THE MEANING OF LIFE

Some weeks after the acquittals, Fay became ill and was diagnosed with liver
cancer. I went to New Jersey to live with my mother and care for her. I think
that I shed more tears and had greater daily fatigue than ever before in my life.
But beautiful Fay and I spent some precious moments together and grew
much closer. Once, when I had to return to North Carolina briefly, I went to
walk in Hagan Stone Park outside Greensboro, seeking some solace in the
lovely woods where I used to set up my tent and camp. I imagined that if I
could just get my mother to go camping with me, the woods, the fresh air, and
the natural and peaceful environment would heal her. She would recover, and
we would be companions forever. The only problem was how to get her to
want to go camping.

I left my mother's sick bed in July 1984 to be deposed for the civil suit by the
Klan/Nazi/government lawyers. Charles Nichols, an attorney for the City of
Greensboro, interviewed me for a grueling two days. I answered questions about
my personal background and political views. There were many questions about
Jim's role as a labor organizer. "Why had Jim decided to leave Duke University
and the practice of medicine?" The idealism and selfless dedication of the five
people killed did not fit the cynical stereotypes of the city lawyer. He seemed to
want me to say that Jim was on an ego trip and was out to subvert his union local.

Q: Did he want the labor union that was the textile union to become the CWP?
A: No.
Q: What did he want it to become? . . . What kind of union was he going to have?
. . .
A: He was trying . . . to strengthen the existing union, the ACTWU local at Haw
River. . . . That meant getting many more people to join and play an active role. . . .
That meant activating the whole system of shop stewards. That meant really utiliz-
ing a grievance procedure. It meant really bringing the contract to life. [The contract is] a book of past struggles, of what the workers had been able to get. But it
was all on paper. And the attempt was to bring it to life, to make the grievance procedure really work for the workers' grievances. . . . And you couldn't do that just
because it's written on paper that this is the procedure you go through. You have

to have a system of shop stewards and people's consciousness and organization to where you can actually file a grievance and people will support it and have it re-dressed. . . . When I say that he was building the union that's exactly what I mean. He wasn't trying to transform the union into the CWP or anything else. He was try-ing to build the union to be effective. . . .

Q: So in effect what your husband was doing was really trying to take that local union out of the system and make it his union; right?

A: No; that's not right. . . . He was trying to help the workers, himself, and all of us organize to a point where we had the power organized that we don't have dis-organized or unorganized—to make the changes that we need in order to lead happy and productive and reasonably decent lives. So you need to organize and he was helping to do that within the structure that existed. He was trying to fulfill those structures.[39]

On the ghastly return trip to Greensboro after Fay's death, I was so sick and nauseated with a vicious migraine that I could hardly see or walk. I had to call on one of my mother's friends to help me to the airport and put me on a plane. It was the trip from hell. My head was throbbing mercilessly, and I didn't try to cover up my tears. Grief, I think, made me look deranged as I slunk into the air-plane seat.

I buried Jim on November 11, 1979. Precisely five years later, on November 11, 1984, I buried my mother. Within that five-year interval, bounded by these two losses, my father died.

Back in Greensboro, preparations for the civil suit, in which I was one of the plaintiffs, were taking place. I was constantly participating in a variety of very meaningful political activities. Nevertheless, personal losses took their toll, and my mind was often on the large philosophical subject of human mortality.

NOTES

1. For information on some of Miller's racist activities, see Dawn DeCwikiel-Kane, "NCAE Chief: Keep Klan Away from School Vigilante Patrols," *Greensboro News & Record*, 13 April 1984, C4.

2. Dr. Martha A. Nathan, Dale Sampson, Signe Waller, Floris Cauce Weston, and Frankie Powell, letter, *Greensboro Daily News*, 16 November 1983.

3. See John Monk, "Klan-Nazi Defendants Acquitted," *Charlotte Observer*, 16 April 1984, 1A; and Rebecca Ragsdale, "All Klan-Nazi Defendants Acquitted," *Greensboro News & Record*, 16 April 1984, A1.

4. Larry King, "Gag Order in Trial Troubles Some Lawyers," *Greensboro News & Record*, 14 May 1983, A1.

5. The "Memorandum" from the U.S. District Court for the Middle District of North Carolina, Criminal No. 83-53-01-G through 83-53-09-G, 5 January 1984 (an amended gag order) bears out this view.

6. Our struggle gave impetus to the Center for Constitutional Rights, among others. Things took a different turn in the 1990s. It is hard to show that the appointment of a special prosecutor as employed against President Clinton was a usage of the Act consistent with the original intention of benefiting the least powerful citizens.

7. On December 3, 1983, in the first hearing on the Civil Rights Suit in a year and a half, a government motion to dismiss the suit was rejected by Judge Merhige.

8. Jim Schlosser, "Judge Clears Court in Nazi-Klan Trial," *Greensboro Daily News*, 10 January 1984, A1.

9. Jim Schlosser, "Klan-Nazi Trial Closure Challenged," *Greensboro Daily News*, 11 January 1984, B1.

10. Rebecca Ragsdale, "Klan Case Gets White Jury Again," *Greensboro Daily News*, 21 January 1984, A1; and Donald W. Patterson, "Except for Age, Two Klan-Nazi Juries Similar," *Greensboro News & Record*, 14 April 1984.

11. Mab Segrest, "The Nov. 3 Trial and the Klan Today: 'Racial Purity Is America's Security,'" *North Carolina Independent*, 3–16 February 1984, 22. About a month after jury selection, Judge Flannery was ordered by U.S. Middle District Court in Greensboro to place a transcript of the secret jury selection process in the public docket so that it would be available to the press and public.

12. Segrest, "The Nov. 3 Trial and the Klan Today."

13. Segrest, "The Nov. 3 Trial and the Klan Today."

14. Segrest, "The Nov. 3 Trial and the Klan Today."

15. Larry King, "Klan Link Didn't Fit Quiet Guy," *Greensboro Daily News*, 2 May 1983.

16. See Rebecca Ragsdale, "Defendant Relates Police Informant's 'Emotional' Speech," *Greensboro News & Record*, 31 March 1984, A8.

17. See Rebecca Ragsdale, "No Violence Planned, Klan Leader Tells Court," *Greensboro Daily News*, 27 March 1984, B3.

18. See Rebecca Ragsdale, "Klan Jury Will Consider Charges," *Greensboro News & Record*, 17 March 1984, D2. See also Rebecca Ragsdale, "Klan Jury Hears Final Arguments," *Greensboro News & Record*, 10 April 1984, B10.

19. See the indictment, "*United States of America v. Virgil L. Griffin et al.*," No. CR-83-53-01-G through CR-83-53-09-G, 19 December 1983. It is packed with information that lays out details of the Klan/Nazi conspiracy. In the aspects of the case that were not off-limits for him, Michael Johnson did a good job.

20. See Rebecca Ragsdale, "Expert: Klansmen May Have Fired Disputed Shots," *Greensboro Daily News*, 31 January 1984. It was well established that shots three, four, and five came from the Klan. The expert witness, Bruce Koenig, according to people present in the courtroom, explained his reversal by saying that he hadn't unfolded his map so as to consider a wider area when he first studied the origins of those three shots.

21. Rebecca Ragsdale, "Agent Tells of Role as Nazi," *Greensboro Daily News*, 10 February 1984.

22. Rebecca Ragsdale, "Delay Granted for Defense in Klan-Nazi Trial," *Greensboro Daily News*, 8 February 1984, B4.

23. Rebecca Ragsdale, "Detective Says He Saw Fight Begin at Rally," *Greensboro Daily News*, 11 February 1984, D1.

24. See Rebecca Ragsdale, "Police Wanted Low Profile, Klan Jury Told," *Greensboro Daily News*, 14 February 1984.

25. Ragsdale, "Police Wanted Low Profile."

26. Rebecca Ragsdale, "Officer Tells of Confusion on Day of Anti-Klan Rally," *Greensboro Daily News*, 28 February 1984.

27. Quoted here from Rebecca Ragsdale, "There May Have Been an Informant in CWP," *Greensboro Daily News*, 24 February 1984, D2.

28. Ragsdale, "There May Have Been an Informant," D2.

29. See Rebecca Ragsdale, "CWP Demonstrator Tells about Firing at Defendant," *Greensboro Daily News*, 1 March 1984, D2.

30. Rebecca Ragsdale, "Victim: CWP Rally Held to Fight Racism," *Greensboro Daily News*, 2 March 1984, D3.

31. See Rebecca Ragsdale, "'I Just Couldn't Believe He Was Dead,' CWP Widow Says," *Greensboro Daily News*, 6 March 1984, B1.

32. Quoted in Rebecca Ragsdale and Steve Berry, "Klan-Nazi Verdict Prompts Protests, Outrage in State," *Greensboro News & Record*, 17 April 1984, B2.

33. See Associated Press, "Morgan: FBI Tactics Still Questionable," *Greensboro News & Record*, 14 May 1984.

34. See Greg Brown, "Klan, CWP Have Varying Views," *Carolina Peacemaker*, 21 April 1984, A1.

35. Editorial, "Greensboro Killings: Justice Has Not Been Done," *Charlotte Observer*, 18 April 1984, 10A.

36. Jim Schlosser, "Jackson: Acquittals a 'Threat,'" *Greensboro News & Record*, 19 April 1984, A1.

37. Vincent Taylor, "250 Hold Greensboro March to Protest Klan-Nazi Acquittals," *Greensboro News & Record*, 6 May 1984, C2.

38. Taylor, "250 Hold Greensboro March," C2.

39. *Waller v. Butkovich*, Deposition of Signe Barbara Waller, U.S. District Court of the Middle District of North Carolina, Greensboro Division, 11–12 July 1984, 119–130.

ON NEW FOUNDATIONS

19

PARTNERS IN CRIME: THE CIVIL RIGHTS SUIT IN 1985

GETTING TO DISCOVERY

James Waller et al. v. Bernard Butkovich et al., the civil rights suit brought by the survivors and injured from the November 3, 1979, Klan/Nazi attack, was first filed on November 3, 1980. From that time until the end of the federal criminal trial in April 1984, the suit was in limbo, blocked by the defendants, the court, and our lack of funds. State and city officials denounced it as "revolutionary rhetoric," and in 1981, city, state, and federal defendants in the suit filed motions to have it dismissed. When our lawyers attempted to begin discovery by deposing two key defendants, Klansman/informant Dawson and Nazi Caudle, first the City of Greensboro, then the state of North Carolina and the Justice Department, blocked the depositions with a court order, granted without a hearing. The court sat on the defendants' motions to dismiss for three years: as long as the motions were pending, no discovery was permitted. The stay on discovery was not lifted until April 22, 1984. Soon after he was appointed to hear the civil suit, Judge Robert R. Merhige Jr. indicated that he would deny most parts of the motions to dismiss and allow the case to proceed against a majority of the defendants on most of the claims. Jury selection in the civil rights suit began on March 11, 1985, more than five years after the assault that occasioned the suit.

The second Klan/Nazi acquittal, in federal criminal court on April 15, 1984, was widely regarded as another green light for racist violence. People could be attacked and murdered for their political beliefs and labor activities with no federal response. Anticommunism was allowed to justify racist violence. Would the civil rights trial be different from the mockeries of justice that preceded it? For the first time, the victims' lawyers were in charge of presenting the evidence, not the lawyers of those with a stake in concealing or manipulating the evidence. *For the first time, some of the government officials who conspired to violate citizens' civil rights were defendants.* They had to stand in the docket alongside the Klan and Nazi gunmen with whom they had partnered in crime. The pretense that these officials were prosecuting and seeking to punish those gunmen was discarded. Right away this situation had a better likeness to reality than the previous judicial charades.

The civil rights suit was a steep uphill fight, with obstacles littering the path all the way. Some background will give the reader a better appreciation of what this struggle encompassed. The Greensboro Justice Fund was restructured in 1982, in conjunction with the Christic Institute, and became the Greensboro Civil Rights Fund (GCRF). Jack Novick, a director in the national American Civil Liberties Union, became the chair of the new Greensboro Civil Rights Fund Board, and ACLU joined the legal team. Greensboro Justice Fund (and later GCRF) members were part of a broader people's movement to safeguard civil liberties, and they worked in national coalitions.

We did not have money for the suit. Before providing grants, foundations needed to see broader representation on the GCRF Board and a trial date to show that the case was real. Once these conditions were met, Dale worked full time to raise foundation money for the civil suit. She was living in New York and editing a newsletter with updates on the Greensboro case. Shelley Wong reached out to major religious denominations to talk about Greensboro. Church organizations issued resolutions, sent representatives as court monitors, gave grants for the suit, and supported funding proposals to major foundations.

Because red-baiting was used to dismiss a civil rights atrocity, it was important to have literature that put November 3, 1979, in its rightful context, as part of the history of struggle for civil and human rights. Marty developed leaflets and brochures about the Greensboro Massacre. An impressive list of endorsers for the civil rights suit, which included Hollywood stars, Catholic Bishops, the Congressional Black Caucus, and respected civil rights leaders, resulted from her efforts. Marty brought William Kunstler, Arthur Kinoy, Frank Wilkinson, Father Dan Berrigan, and singer Pete Seeger, among others, to the state to publicly support the suit.

Gayle Korotkin researched and wrote much of the literature for the civil suit. FBI activities in relation to the Greensboro murders fit into the pattern of the FBI's Counterintelligence Program (COINTELPRO), Gayle pointed out. Black leaders (like Larry Little in the 1960s and Nelson Johnson in the 1970s) were targeted to be discredited, neutralized, or eliminated.[1] When the FBI heavily infiltrated the Klan in the sixties and seventies, Edward Dawson was one of its Klan informants. FBI agents and their informants literally organized forty-one Klan Klaverns, according to documents presented to Congress. FBI informant Gary Thomas Rowe was a central figure in acts of racist terror in the 1960s, done with the knowledge of the FBI and covered up by them.[2] The agency ignored the "Levi guidelines," designed to curb the FBI's infringement of civil rights. They circumvented the restrictions on them by shifting activities to the BATF and to local and state police agencies. Greensboro illustrates this pattern.

In contrast to most civil rights legal efforts, the preparations for our suit were largely done by women—the widows (particularly Marty and Dale) and women staffers and paralegals. A democratic process of discussion and decision making with regard to all political and legal issues brought forth a winning strategy. Lewis Pitts directed the legal team and was chief counsel in the demanding case.[3] Nelson and others injured on November 3 often attended strategy sessions with the legal team. To prepare the case, Marty and attorney Carolyn McAllaster commuted almost daily between Durham and Greensboro. A few weeks before the trial, Marty had a freak accident crossing the street, was tossed on top of a car hood, broke her leg, and wore a leg cast for the duration of the trial.

Gayle Korotkin described some of difficulties our lawyers faced in conducting the discovery phase of the case.

> The defendants fought discovery tooth and nail. The Justice Department and BATF limited the kinds of questions their agents could answer. FBI documents were dribbled in, with many of the most important delivered so late that follow up questions could not be asked in depositions, and there was inadequate time to digest them and follow up on the leads. One particularly important batch was delivered literally the Sunday before the trial was to begin on Monday. The City held back documents until discovery was over and nothing could be done to follow up. When the depositions were going badly for their clients, the federal lawyers would find an excuse to break them off.
>
> Judge Merhige . . . imposed "protective orders" on a vast amount of material— i.e., a gag order on the lawyers and plaintiffs . . . , thereby preventing them from using it to confirm the allegations which the defendants had denied all along.[4]

The suit charged Klansmen, Nazis, law enforcement, and government agents under various sections of civil rights law. We claimed that Klan and Nazi defendants violated plaintiffs' rights to assemble, to life, and to equal protection of the laws.[5] We charged that law enforcement and provocateur defendants encouraged and participated in the conspiracy[6] and conspired to cover up the incident.[7] We said that government officials initiated contact with the Klan/Nazis and used them willfully to carry out a physical attack on CWP leaders and anti-Klan demonstrators. Certain government agents and officials, although they did not plan and carry out the attack, were liable to conspiracy charges for participating in the continuing cover-up of what lay behind the crimes. The complaint charged the City with improperly controlling informants and with encouraging violations of equal protection of the laws.[8] Various wrongful death, conspiracy, and assault and battery claims were also part of the civil suit. The class of people against whom the conspiracy was directed was defined as "communists and/or labor organizers and/or civil rights activists who were organizing black and white workers equally into unions." A list of over eighty defendants (at one point) was whittled down considerably: deleted were Mayor Melvin, Greensboro FBI agent Brereton, and others with evident involvement in the conspiracy.[9]

Despite the roadblocks, discovery was fruitful, turning up missing pieces of the puzzle in the two government-conducted prosecutions. From the depositions of defendants, FBI reports and interview transcripts, BATF reports, diaries of BATF agents, and police intelligence and internal affairs reports came evidence supporting the claims that plaintiffs had made from the start: several law enforcement agencies had extensive prior knowledge of the planned attack; their informants and agents played a role in instigating the attack; law enforcement agencies deliberately failed to act to prevent the attack; the agencies involved tried to cover up their role; and the agencies involved had contact and communication with one another.

PIECES OF THE CONSPIRACY

The GPD

There were thirty-four city defendants in our civil suit—police officers, city officials, and the City of Greensboro itself. What the defendants knew before the attack and what they did after it are documented in numerous exhibits of interviews and reports that our lawyers filed in January 1985 in answer to the city's motion for summary judgment. The evidence presented in court of the police role came mostly from the defendants themselves.

Because I was personally involved in organizing the 1979 anti-Klan rally, I know that we were not apprised beforehand that a violent disruption of the rally was planned. It is clear, in reviewing what law enforcement agencies knew, that *we were the only ones who were not aware of it.*

On Thursday morning, November 1, 1979, Assistant Chief of Police Colonel Burch conducted a meeting to coordinate police activity for the November 3 march. Police received intelligence updates from Detective Cooper and Captain Thomas. They learned that several groups planned to attend the march, including North Carolina Klan members from Mt. Airy, Hickory, Greensboro, and Wilmington; members of Leroy Gibson's group, the Rights of White People, in Wilmington; and associates of Harold Covington, head of the Nazi Party in Raleigh. The ten police officers and the police attorney present at the meeting talked about the Klan's wanting to obtain the parade route of the anti-Klan march. They talked about Grand Dragon Virgil Griffin's intention to be in Greensboro early Saturday morning to ride the parade route in order to find a place for a confrontation with the marchers. Virgil Griffin was described to everyone present as a person with a very short fuse and a hot temper. They also discussed the clash between the WVO and the Klan at China Grove as the reason the Klan was coming to Greensboro, and they talked about a "rumor" that some Klansman had purchased a machine gun.

Colonel Burch recommended, and it was decided, that police assigned to the march would keep a "low profile." It was noted at this meeting that the starting point of the parade was listed on the permit as Everitt and Carver Drive. The police were told of the restrictions placed on the demonstrators' permit, namely, no arms open or concealed, and no posts larger than two-by-two inches or made of steel.

November 1 was a busy morning in downtown Greensboro. When Captain L. S. Gibson, commander of the Field Services Division, which included the tactical teams, left the meeting, he was told that Nelson Johnson was having a press conference. Gibson went to the main lobby and observed the conference for a while. (As I mentioned earlier, Dawson was on the sidelines of that press conference.) That morning, Dawson, *having been told by his control agent, Detective Cooper, to pick up a copy of the parade permit*, obtained a copy from Captain Gibson. Dawson told Gibson his name and that he was a Klan member. Gibson did not ask Dawson what the Klan planned to do with the permit.

As Nelson was in the building getting a copy of the permit for the WVO, he ran into Captain Trevor Hampton, who had been at the earlier police meeting. Hampton told Nelson that two police officers would meet him at Carver and Everitt at 11:30 A.M. on the day of the march, and Nelson agreed to the meeting. *Although fully aware of the danger to the marchers, Hampton did not mention anything about it to Nelson.*

About a week before the march, Sergeant Burke passed along a very critical intelligence report. The report indicated that "some members of the Klan living in the Winston-Salem area had obtained a machine gun and possibly other weapons" and that "these individuals planned to come to Greensboro on November 3, 1979, and shoot up the place."[10] Burke tried to call the BATF, but his call was not returned, and after two days he gave the information to Detective Cooper and Chief Swing and probably also to his superior, Captain Gibson. Gibson stated that this and other information he had prior to November 1 influenced his decision that additional manpower should be available for the march, including both tactical squads.[11]

Already by the middle of October, Gibson and other officers knew that the Klan was coming to Greensboro to confront the WVO. Gibson had the machine gun information by October 15—he said that was one of the reasons he put the "no weapons" restriction on the WVO parade permit. On October 19, the day Nelson applied for the permit, he was told of the unusual stipulation about weapons. That prompted Nelson to ask Captain Gibson pointedly if the police were expecting any problems. Blatantly lying, Gibson said no and told Nelson that the police would take care of security for the march. (Captain Gibson was the officer who, having helped to murder our husbands, arrested me and Dale and hauled us to jail for disrupting a city council meeting in 1980.)

A meeting to plan security in more detail took place on the afternoon of November 1, 1979. Officers from the tactical unit not present at the morning meeting were filled in about what was discussed there. The officers were told that Detective Cooper would supply intelligence information during the event to all officers assigned to the march. A deployment plan for two squads of the tactical unit was worked out consistent with the "low profile" strategy adopted. The tactical squads would be stationed at two locations *off the parade route*, one near the beginning and one in the middle, and would move roughly parallel to the parade. The tactical support section was to "go in between the marchers and any group causing problems should the need arise."[12] Captain Hampton, commander for the district where the march was starting, informed the commander of the tactical support unit, Lt. Daughtry, to have his men at their posts at 11:30 A.M. on November 3.

Thus, "low profile" was construed as *having no police at the march origin during the time the march was forming.* If this were the Easter Parade, the decision to keep a low profile and to send the police to lunch until 11:30 might have made sense. But what reason did the police have to expect the Klan to wait until 11:30? The police plan was made in full knowledge that "large numbers of right-wing forces from around the state, angry about China Grove, were planning to come to Greensboro, possibly armed, and were looking for revenge. They were sending a hot headed grand dragon early to survey the route, with a [police-provided] parade permit, to determine a confrontation site."[13] The plan remained unaltered Saturday morning, when the police were briefed that Klan and Nazis were actually assembling with their weapons. It remained in place without change even as Cooper monitored the unfolding of the attack.

The police did not discuss any conditions under which they might stop the Klan caravan. They did not deliberate on visibly accompanying the Klan vehicles wherever they went or on maintaining adequate surveillance. No mention was made of the need for command personnel to reassess the situation Saturday morning. The police plan failed to insure that those in command possessed all of the relevant information or that they were fully accessible. Officers were not given adequate and clear instructions about the conditions under which they were to move into the area of the march. No consideration was given to warning the demonstrators so that they might have a choice about what to do.

Another briefing, this one the day of the march, Saturday, November 3, 1979, at 10:00 A.M., was attended by the members of the tactical units and by Detective Cooper, Lt. Spoon, Lt. Daughtry, and police attorney Cawn. By 10:40 A.M., when the meeting concluded, the officers discussed the following: that a confrontation occurred between the Klan and the WVO/CWP in China Grove in July 1979; that a Klansman obtained a copy of the parade permit with the parade route; that the Klan, Nazis, and Rights of White People would attend the anti-Klan march and were in fact already gathering at a Klansman's house on Randleman Road; that several weapons were present at the house, including high caliber handguns; that volatile Virgil Griffin was among those assembled and was armed with a .44 caliber magnum or a .32 pistol; and that the Klan and Nazis planned to disrupt the march by heckling, throwing eggs or rocks, or fighting with demonstrators. At the end of the meeting, Lt. Daughtry sent the tactical squads to lunch until 11:30![14]

Among those with an active role in a conspiracy that resulted in deaths and injuries was Captain B. L. Thomas, commander of the Criminal Investigation Division of the GPD. Captain Thomas's intelligence duties included spying on the CWP, the RCP (another communist organization), and the Klan. He authorized the payments to Dawson and was involved in the "handling" of informant Dawson, whom he knew to be a Klan leader who met with other Klan leaders such as Virgil Griffin. (Dawson's business card given to Cooper described him as grand dragon.) When Detective Cooper and Lt. Talbott (Capt. Thomas's second-in-command) recruited Dawson as an informant, around October 11, Captain Thomas knew all about the China Grove stand-off that had nearly erupted into deadly violence. Thomas had seen many news photos taken at China Grove, showing heavily armed Klansmen. In fact, that information was generally known and must be viewed as the backdrop to police planning and decision making about November 3. Police knew that the counterdemonstrators were coming to Greensboro motivated not by some abstract dislike for communists, but by a desire for revenge at being humiliated in China Grove.

Throughout the GPD's use of Dawson as an informant, Thomas was briefed on all the information Cooper got from Dawson. For example, Thomas knew right after an October 20 Klan rally in Lincolnton that eighty to eighty-five Klansmen had volunteered to come to Greensboro to confront the anti-Klan marchers, and that Dawson answered questions about weapons. Captain Thomas claimed that he was concerned about Dawson's allegiance to the Klan, and he told Talbott or Cooper to contact the FBI to check on Dawson's reliability. However, Thomas's failure to properly supervise the use of police informant Dawson indicates a lack of concern about where Dawson's loyalties might lead. An incident revealed in an internal police document suggests that Thomas squashed attempts to follow up on Dawson and ignored the danger in the developing situation.

A retired GPD intelligence officer, Lieutenant S. N. Ford, who knew Dawson for fifteen years through Dawson's informant years with the FBI and Ford's own intelligence work, learned about the Klan's plans from Dawson about a week or so before the anti-Klan march. After hearing about the October 20 Lincolnton rally, Ford concluded that the anti-Klan rally "could be explosive, a dangerous situation."[15] The retired officer approached Assistant Chief of Police Colonel Burch, told him there were some real problems, and tried to set up a meeting between Dawson and police officials. Burch told him that there was no need to meet with Dawson, and Ford apparently dropped the matter. Meanwhile, Dawson reported his conversation with Ford to his control agent Cooper. Cooper told Thomas that Ford was trying to set up a meeting between Dawson and Chief Swing to allow Dawson to relay his information about the Klan's plans directly to the chief. Thomas nixed the meeting and told Cooper to instruct Dawson not to go to such a meeting. Thomas never asked Ford why he felt the meeting was necessary.[16]

The information, passed through Sgt. Burke about a Klansman in Winston-Salem having a machine gun and going to Greensboro to shoot up the place, was treated by Thomas, Talbott, and others as a "rumor" and, they said, never investigated.

In his deposition, Captain Thomas stated that he was told that Dawson saw the city attorney about getting an injunction to stop the march. But Thomas did not ask city attorney Jesse Warren why Dawson was doing this, nor did he instruct Cooper or Talbott to find out. On the morning of November 3, Thomas was Cooper's supervisor and was responsible for insuring that the intelligence function was carried out. Captain Thomas failed to properly supervise or even stay in touch with Cooper. Thomas certainly did not insure that all police involved appreciated the significance of the known intelligence facts in order to protect the community. On receiving notice from Cooper at 9:00 A.M. on November 3 about the gathering of men with guns at Brent Fletcher's home, Thomas did not remain in communication with Cooper but took his son for a haircut without taking a police radio.[17]

Captain Thomas met with Dawson and state prosecutors in June and October of 1980. Dawson threatened to blow the lid off of the police department if forced to testify at the state trial. Prosecutors were not eager for Dawson's testimony, and the defense was threatening to call him. Thomas began a phone conversation with Dawson with the comment, "I think you made a good decision." Dawson had not yet said that he would not testify, but Thomas was sending a clear message to Dawson to keep his mouth shut: the police would protect him if he protected them.[18]

Detective J. S. Cooper, regularly updated by Dawson, knew that the purpose of the October 20 Lincolnton rally was to discuss China Grove and the November 3 march. Cooper was told by Dawson on October 24 about the numbers expected from various right-wing groups and the discussion about bringing guns. Dawson, who claimed that he warned people against bringing concealed weapons, nevertheless concluded from the Lincolnton rally that the Klan intended to bring guns. Dawson said, "any time the Klan goes anywhere they always carry guns," an assertion any law enforcement person familiar with the Klan, like Cooper, could scarcely dispute. Captain Talbott admitted to the FBI during his pre–grand jury interview that Detective Cooper actually observed the Klan and Nazis loading their weapons into their trunks before heading to the site of the murders.[19]

Cooper had contact with Dawson on October 26, and Dawson told Cooper that he had learned from Virgil Griffin of a meeting scheduled for the next day to coalesce the Klan, Nazis, and Rights of White People. Cooper assumed that there was a concerted effort to assemble as many people as possible to go to Greensboro on November 3. By a week before the killings, Cooper received intelligence indicating at least 130 Klansmen and Nazis had vowed to go to Greensboro to counterdemonstrate. Cooper was told by Dawson about the staging area for the Klan and Nazis on Randleman Road, that Dawson was taking Klan members to survey the parade route, and that Griffin would be in Greensboro at 2:00 A.M. on November 3 to "see where a confrontation would take place between the WVO and the Klan groups."[20] Cooper didn't ask Dawson what he meant by "confrontation."

On November 1, Dawson met with Cooper, his control agent, and Talbott, Captain Thomas's subordinate in intelligence, to give them the final update on the Klan/Nazi plans. It was this information—that Virgil Griffin had a reputation as a "hot head" and that he wanted to survey the parade route—that Cooper brought to the police meeting that morning. That same morning, Cooper informed Dawson that the formation point of the march had been changed from Windsor Center (as per the posters) to the Morningside Homes Project at the Carver and Everitt intersection. Then *Cooper told Dawson* to get a copy of the parade permit. Also on November 1, Dawson told Cooper and Talbott about his contact with the city attorney to see if he could get an injunction to stop the parade, and his being told that there was no chance of stopping the parade through injunctive relief. Cooper did not ask Dawson why he tried to stop the November 3 parade.

Two days later, on November 3, Cooper presented his up-to-date, in fact, up-to-the-minute intelligence information at the 10:00 A.M. police briefing. Cooper reported that the Klan and other right-wing groups were assembled, had guns, and had a copy of the parade permit. Cooper had just received a phone call from Dawson, his information source.

A reasonable inference from the known facts is that this midmorning phone conversation with Dawson (the second one between them that morning) was the final go-ahead instruction from Cooper to Dawson. Dawson reports that things are in place, the men and their guns. Cooper tells Dawson to hustle it up. Cooper reminds Dawson that police will be in the area at 11:30 (back from lunch) and that the Klan/Nazis had better be out of there by then.

Earlier in the morning, Cooper and Sgt. Burke did surveillance on Fletcher's house and copied license plate numbers. Cooper admitted to Talbott that he saw guns loaded into the Klan/Nazi vehicles, but he lied about it under oath. When Cooper tried to deny in court having seen the guns loaded into a car trunk, plaintiffs' lawyers played the tape recording of Talbott's statement to the FBI. The excuse that police did not stop the caravan because they thought the Klan/Nazis may have left their weapons behind when they set out for Morningside Homes was exposed for the lie that it was.[21] After his phone contact with Dawson and the ten o'clock police briefing, Cooper drove back to Fletcher's house with GPD photographer John T. Matthews. Cooper and Matthews trailed the Klan caravan, taking pictures when the vehicles stopped briefly to regroup on the ramp of U.S. 220.

Other police officers give no better accounting of their actions. Several tactical squad officers sitting in restaurants heard Cooper's transmissions about the movement of the Klan caravan toward the rally site and continued eating their lunch. On hearing Cooper say that the Klan caravan was moving to the parade formation site, some officers left their eating places, headed to their assigned positions, and got stuck in traffic. They failed to engage their blue lights or sirens until they heard Cooper say that gunshots had been fired at Everitt and Carver.

Lieutenant Daughtry came away from Cooper's intelligence briefings on November 1 "with the feeling that it was a good possibility that the Klan and Nazis would show up."[22] Despite that feeling, and despite his responsibility to supervise the squads protecting the demonstrators, Daughtry was out of communication with Cooper, Spoon, and his men on the morning of November 3 until 11:15 A.M. Upon learning from Sgt. Burke at 11:16 that nine vehicles were already on their way to the starting point of the march and that tactical officers were still eating, Daughtry told Burke, "they've got fourteen more minutes according to my watch, rush 'em up." Two minutes later, Daughtry heard a transmission from Cooper that indicated the caravan's route was definitely to Morningside and not to Windsor Center, and that the Klan and Nazis were only three or four blocks away from Everitt and Carver. Daughtry still did not instruct his men to go to Everitt and Carver but sent them to their basic deployment positions—*out of sight of the march*. Daughtry did not call in his troops until Cooper reported a fight and requested the units. Daughtry, like other GPD officers, failed to take a single action from a whole range of possible actions to protect the demonstrators and the black community from a clear and looming threat of violence. Either the lieutenant wasn't implementing the November 1 plan to keep marchers and Klan apart, or that wasn't the real plan. Arriving on the scene shortly after the murders, Lt. Daughtry kicked a bleeding Nelson Johnson and assisted in his arrest.

Lieutenant Paul W. Spoon was the field commander for the march, appointed to this duty by Captain Hampton. He was the one in charge, and his job was to stay on top of all the intelligence information and act accordingly. However, between the end of the police briefing around 10:40 and the time that the Klan was parking at Morningside, Spoon neither contacted Cooper nor sought further intelligence on the Klan.

After the police briefing, Spoon claimed that he was caught up in a phone conversation with the preacher whose church, at one point, was to be the site for the afternoon conference. The preacher, as a consequence of police intimidation, wanted to back out of the arrangement, but that was a nonissue: Nelson had already announced in his November 1 press conference that the WVO would not use the church for the conference, and the police knew it. Spoon was killing time as a prelude to killing people. Since the lieutenant knew the tactical squads would not be on duty until 11:30, it was important to have someone in authority on top of the situation, but Spoon was incommunicado for much of the morning. Spoon knew that Officer Comer was at Windsor Center looking for Nelson. He instructed Comer to keep looking there, even though he also knew that Captain Hampton had set up the meeting between Comer and Nelson at Everitt and Carver. (These two locations are only a mile, or less, apart.) Spoon did not instruct Comer to check Morningside. He did not give Comer any specific instructions to enable an adequate police response to any problem. Division II officers were told to monitor their radios in case they needed to respond: there were no instructions about what they were to respond to.

In their answer to the City's attempt to dismiss the suit, plaintiffs' lawyers described Lt. Spoon's actions and attitudes: "It was not until the caravan was at the formation point of the march that Spoon acknowledges receiving Cooper's transmissions. At that point—*following notice of a fight* and *following Cooper's request for units*—Spoon did *not* call his troops in, neither District II nor tactical squads. It was only after Cooper said 'shots fired,' at 11:23:28 that Spoon ordered cars in. Spoon then twice advised the cars to move to Windsor Center instead of Morningside where the Klan was shooting—although stating he was sure the starting point was Carver and Everitt. In the face of gunfire, he wanted to check out the situation himself first, before calling in his men."[23] Spoon "failed to carry out his responsibilities and use the personnel at his command in even a minimal way to ensure the safety of the marchers. . . . He accepted a procedure that sent the tactical squads to lunch, and that seemed to require the Klan to actually show up and begin a confrontation before tactical units were called in. He failed to explore any measure to protect the marchers from such attack, from stopping the Klan vehicles, to surrounding the Klan with a show of force, to having the tactical squads available at the first sign from Cooper that the Klan was approaching the demonstrators."[24]

The inaction and conspiracy of silence by the police condemns them all, for *no police officer lacked the authority to intervene to prevent the planned violent attack on the demonstrators.*

First on the scene after the murders were Officers Bryant and League, in the tactical unit under Sgt. Hightower. League told the grand jury that he and other officers were told to be prepared for the presence of arms and to carry a bulletproof vest, but that there was no discussion about police authority to stop the Klan caravan or under what specific conditions the tactical unit would be called in.[25]

Officers Bryant and League left the restaurant where they were having lunch before 11:30 and went to the intersection of Everitt and Willow because they were curious to see the Klan. From there they observed the starting point of the march. They saw the sound truck and many people assembled. While on the way to Everitt Street, they heard Comer, who they knew was to accompany the march, say on the radio that he was at Windsor Center, not Everitt and Carver. They also heard Cooper's transmissions about the continuing movement of the Klan vehicles, and they realized that the caravan was close by and was headed in their general direction. They could see that the Everitt and Carver intersection was unprotected, yet they did not stay with the group of people assembled there. Nor did they try to contact Sgt. Comer, Sgt. Hightower, or any other commander to say that they had observed a group of people at Everitt and Carver with no police protecting that location. When the grand jury asked why not, League testified only that they were "supposed to stay out of the area" and were "told to go to Dudley High School for a low profile," but that curiosity took them too close.

Leaving Everitt and Carver unattended, the two officers went to their assignment at Dudley High School. At the school parking lot, they heard Cooper's transmission that the caravan had turned down Willow Road, making it absolutely clear that it was headed to Everitt and Carver. They then started to go to Everitt and Carver but did not proceed directly. Instead they stopped to talk to two other tactical officers arriving at Dudley. Finally, when they heard Cooper transmit that heckling was going on, they left for Everitt and Carver, putting on their bulletproof vests when they heard gunshots had been fired. *Officers League and Bryant were not ordered to go to Everitt and Carver*. Officer League could not recall being ordered to do anything. It was entirely fortuitous that some Klansmen and Nazis were arrested on November 3, 1979.

The real plan on the morning of November 3 was to keep officers *away* from Carver and Everitt until 11:30, as indicated by this additional evidence. GPD officer April Wise was responding to a routine call about a domestic disturbance near Carver and Everitt that morning. On her way to the area with Officer Cundiff, she saw the anti-Klan parade forming at Carver and Everitt. Several minutes before 11:00, Wise received a call from the dispatcher instructing her to "clear the area." She called back at 10:57 to say that she and the other officer were wrapping up their business at 801 Dunbar Street—right by Carver and Everitt. Wise's story was verified in sworn testimony by a Greensboro woman who made a hobby of listening to police frequencies and who heard and clearly remembered the instruction to clear the area. That memory was sealed by calls soon afterward for backup: the violence that followed the instruction to clear the area made her remember it.

In the November 19 police administrative report, the transcribed portions of the police radio tapes omit these transmissions to Wise and Cundiff. For one frequency, transmissions start at 10:50, but the transmissions from the frequency Wise used start at 11:00, thus concealing her 10:57 call confirming that she was clearing the area. Captain Williams rode to Morningside with Officer Wise a week after the killings. She pointed out to Williams where she and Officer Cundiff were on November 3 and told him that she had been advised to clear out.[26] Captain Williams did not include this information in the report. Commended and rewarded for the fine job he did on November 3, Williams was made head of a beefed up intelligence unit that harassed and illegally spied on me and other plaintiffs.

Everything happened, of course, with the knowledge and approval of Chief William Swing. He, in turn, was subordinate to Hewitt Lovelace, director of public safety for the city of Greensboro. Swing, Lovelace, and City Manager Osborne met on November 2 in a restaurant and discussed Nelson Johnson and the anti-Klan rally. Swing reported everything that he knew about the impending confrontation to these city officials. They, along with the mayor, authorized the police's plan for meeting what all knew was a dire threat.

Swing learned at an October 15 staff meeting that the WVO was planning an anti-Klan rally for November 3. At a meeting two days later, he was told that the Klan was probably coming. From the time Dawson was hired as an informant by the GPD onward, all important information Cooper received from Dawson about Klan/Nazi plans to attend and violently attack the November 3 rally was passed to Chief Swing through Col. Burch.[27]

After the murders, Swing lied to the media, pretending that he did not suspect trouble beforehand. He knew, however, that the Klan "had been put to shame in China Grove" and that they were coming to "generally get even" with the WVO.[28] When interviewed by the FBI on November 21, 1979, Swing admitted that he advised the police department that there could be heckling and possibly fighting with sticks if the Klan confronted the marchers.

On the morning of November 3, Chief Swing did not go to his office but went directly to the "Command Post," a communications center designed to allow commanding officers to reach everyone in the field and to control field operations in an emergency. From this communications center came the dispatch to Officers Wise and Cundiff to answer a minor disturbance call a block and a half from Carver and Everitt. Wise and Cundiff arrived in separate cars around 10:34. It was not their assigned zone: the zone containing Carver and Everitt was mysteriously without any of the normally assigned patrol cars or officers. While at the address near Carver and Everitt, the two officers got a call *from the communication center* asking how much longer they would be and telling them to "clear the area as soon as possible."[29] Officers Wise and Cundiff were surprised at the call, and Wise responded that they would be leaving in about five minutes. Police tapes show the calls dispatching Wise and Cundiff and their call at 10:57 announcing that they were clearing the area (some twenty minutes before the violent attack), but these transmissions were not included in the police report made available to the media and the public.

Around the time Officer Wise was told to clear the area, Dawson was rushing the Klan and Nazis out of Brent Fletcher's house (as per Klan testimonies in the course of the trials). A reasonable inference from the known facts is that the Everitt and Carver area was deliberately cleared of police by Chief Swing so that the violent assault could proceed unhindered.

With Swing's knowledge and approval, the police administrative report of November 19 was filed. Key data were left out of this report, and lies and innuendoes were included. The report blamed the communists for concealing their starting point and confusing the police even though the starting point was on the parade permit and every officer knew it. Dawson, previously convicted for acts of racial violence, went unnamed: his function as informant was totally absent from the report as were all of the known details of his role in instigating, organizing, and leading the Klan/Nazi caravan. Important facts discussed at police briefings (as shown in Internal Affairs Division documents) forming the basis for Swing's conclusion that there would be a violent attack with guns, rocks, eggs, and/or sticks were completely omitted.[30] The disingenuously labeled "rumor" of a machine gun—to which Chief Swing assigned a price of $280—was left out of the official report, along with many other facts. There is no mention that police officers were told to leave the area of Everitt and Carver moments before the death-dealing caravan entered the space of the unsuspecting and unprotected marchers. The police report made the victims the culprits. It was used to further lash out at the surviving demonstrators. This official cover-up was supported by Public Safety Director Lovelace, by Mayor Jim Melvin, and by City Manager Tom Osborne and peddled to the city council, the citizens, the media, and the Justice Department.

The BATF

Federal agencies hold pieces of the puzzle, too. Here is how the case against the BATF stood after discovery. Damning as the evidence is, it is probably just the tip of the iceberg. Bernard Butkovich was an agent provocateur among the Nazis. In looking at his conduct, it is important to remember that he represents the criminal complicity of a whole federal agency, the Bureau of Alcohol, Tobacco, and Firearms. Butkovich reported to his superiors, Agents Dukes,

Fleming, and Westra, and was expressly authorized and encouraged in his provocateur role. Agent Westra gave him permission to urge the Nazis to illegal acts.

Agents Dukes and Fleming told Bernard Butkovich to go to the Louisburg rally on September 22, 1979, where nearly two hundred people gathered to form a "United Racist Front." Butkovich wore a Nazi brown shirt. Butkovich and his "undercover" car were fully wired. Butkovich was wearing a body transmitter.[31] During the eight-hour meeting that day, Butkovich wore the transmitter, but he claimed in court that transmissions ceased after two hours because the batteries failed. He is contradicted by BATF agent Lazar, who testified, "I remember transmissions intermittently from the time we started until the time we ended."[32] Butkovich's transmissions were also monitored from the air by ATF Agent Reese who was flying over the Louisburg rally site as part of Butkovich's cover team. These agents were supposedly working on illegal gun running by the Nazis.

Roland Wood told Butkovich how bothered he was by China Grove and how he would get revenge against the communists. Agent Butkovich noted in his reports many violent racist and anti-Semitic statements by Wood. Nazi leader Harold Covington, deeply involved in the Greensboro plot, told Butkovich that there was a place in the party for people like Caudle and Wood because they were physically strong and potentially violent.[33] Butkovich urged the Nazis on, giving them support and encouragement in their attack plans. At Wood's house on October 29, Butkovich offered to train the Nazis in the use of explosives.[34] At various times, he offered to help obtain ammunition for Nazi Roger Shannon's illegal machine gun, he told the Nazis that he could get them selector switches to convert semiautomatic weapons into fully automatic ones, and he said that he would train them in hand-to-hand combat. At the November 1 meeting at Wood's house, where Klansmen and Nazis jointly made plans to go to Greensboro, Butkovich pushed for everyone to take weapons, saying that he would not go without one concealed on his person.

Butkovich denied that he suggested to the Nazis that they kill Klansman Joe Grady. However, an entry in the journal of ATF Agent Brown states that Butkovich was wired that day (October 31), which means there should be a transcript of what the agent said. Butkovich and Brown both denied that Butkovich was wired—covering up the trail.[35] Caudle called Grady to tell him what Butkovich said, and Grady called Agent Dukes for protection. Dukes went to Grady's house after the November 1 meeting and told him that he "wouldn't have to be worried about the Nazis much longer because they were going to Greensboro and the god damn Communists were gonna kill 'em."[36]

By November 1, the ATF knew from their own agents, from Grady, and from the Winston-Salem police that a confrontation was planned for November 3. Although they only acknowledge knowing about egg-throwing, they were well acquainted with Wood's, Covington's, and other Nazis' propensity for violence and knew the weapons would be much more lethal than eggs. They decided not to send Butkovich because, according to ATF Special Agent in Charge Westra, he might get hurt or injured and have to defend himself. The ATF made no plan to deal with the imminent confrontation. On the evening of November 2, Butkovich returned to Wood's house and again urged him to take a weapon to the November 3 rally.

The ATF claimed that they did not relay information to the Greensboro Police Department or to the FBI. A June 19, 1979, BATF memo about Butkovich's investigation of Wood says, "The FBI has been informed of this investigation and it is being coordinated with FBI and ATF at the SAC to SAC level."[37] That means the BATF and the FBI each knew what the other was doing.

After the November 1 planning meeting at Wood's house, Butkovich reported what had occurred to Dukes and to a Winston-Salem police officer who was part of Butkovich's cover team. Butkovich and Dukes also spoke to Westra. Yet official reports and statements by Butkovich and other ATF agents leave out all mention of Butkovich'provocateur role as well as crucial information shared by Butkovich with his superiors, for example, Jerry Paul Smith's boast about having made a pipe bomb to use on black people.[38] The ATF managed to conceal Butkovich's central role until Martha Woodall broke the story in the Greensboro paper in July 1980.

Butkovich gave several vague and conflicting accounts of his whereabouts on the morning of November 3. Marty Nathan, who was present at the GJF deposition of Butkovich, heard Butkovich say that he and another ATF agent were in the air, flying in the vicinity of Greensboro, but there is also some evidence indicating Butkovich may have been driving in the vicinity of Morningside Homes. Less questionable is where the Nazis aided and abetted by Butkovich were that morning.

On the morning of November 3rd, Wood left his home after putting his shotgun in his trunk. He was joined by Caudle, and his AR 180, Jack Fowler, and several other Nazis, who then drove to Greensboro where they met Virgil Griffin, Eddie Dawson, Jerry Paul Smith, David Wayne Matthews, and numerous other defendant Nazis and Klansmen at Brent Fletcher's house on Randleman Road. After mapping out the plan to attack under Dawson's leadership, they drove to Carver and Everitt Streets, where Wood, firing several shotgun blasts, and Jerry Paul Smith, firing his .357 Magnum handgun, commenced a deadly salvo of fire at the demonstrators, with three of Wood's blasts wounding five demonstrators and a TV cameraman.

Later in the massacre, Smith gunned down César Cauce, while Jack Fowler used Caudle's AR 180 to shoot plaintiff Paul Bermanzohn in the head.[39]

After November 3, ATF Agent Westra, fully aware of Butkovich's provocateur role, made public statements denying it. With regard to the November 3 assault, all the ATF defendants in the civil suit repeatedly met, communicated, and cooperated; in Westra's case, he also commanded. The evidence shows Butkovich "participated in the planning of the attack" and "encouraged the Nazis to purchase, carry," and, it can reasonably be inferred, "use weapons in the attack."[40] The BATF did not just know a violent attack was about to happen; they made it happen.

THE FBI

Shortly after the murders, I remember watching the WFMY-TV news broadcast in which FBI Agent Cecil Moses denied that the FBI had any advance warning about the violence on November 3. I knew in my gut that the FBI was lying: when our lawyers got through discovery, we could show they were lying.

In October 1979, Grady contacted the FBI and was interviewed by FBI special agents Alznauer and Schatzman, who worked under Agent Andrew Pelczar in the Greensboro office. Grady emphatically told the FBI agents that there was a potential for violence between the KKK and the WVO at the November 3 march because of the China Grove confrontation. There's "gonna be bloodshed," Grady told Pelczar.

Leading up to the march, Grady was also an informant for the BATF. At least they regarded him as such—in an ATF agent's diary, Grady is referred to as ATF agent J. J. Croswell's "profiled informant."[41] ATF Agent Dukes went to Grady's house to pacify his fears about possible violence by Wood and other Nazis against Grady himself. Wood was upset with Grady for kicking him out of the Klan, and Grady learned, via Nazi Raeford Caudle, that Butkovich was offering to help Wood get rid of Grady. I assume Grady thought Butkovich was just another Nazi and did not know at that point that he was an ATF agent and that Dukes was supervising Butkovich. To mollify Grady, Dukes assured him that his enemies (the Nazis and the Communists) would be dealt with because the communists were going to kill the Nazis.

Grady was not the FBI's only source of foreknowledge. Dawson informed for the FBI from 1969 to the fall of 1976, supplying them with information on the

Klan Klavern to which he, Virgil Griffin, and several others who later took part in the November 3 caravan, belonged. Dawson's information included plans for violent acts that he, Griffin, and Frank Braswell were hatching against leftist and labor organizations.[42]

Between 1971 and 1973, Len Bogaty, in charge of security matters in the Greensboro FBI office, was Dawson's control agent. In his deposition, Bogaty admitted that he also gathered information on Nelson and on me. When I arrived in Greensboro in 1971, committed to work for an end to the Vietnam War and a just peace, I didn't know where the road of social activism would lead, but I was determined to follow it. I recall the time that Nixon alit at the Greensboro airport, and we met him, bravely waving our protest signs his way. Then, later that day, our little antiwar group met in the shabby rented downtown store that housed the Greensboro Peace Center. An unsolicited visit by "plumbers" interrupted our meeting—this was at night, no one had complained about faulty plumbing, and it wasn't broken. At the time I figured that the FBI was on my case for nothing else but my being vocally and visibly against the Vietnam War. Now, after many years, I could personalize my suspicions: *Len Bogaty was on my case*. While Bogaty was keeping tabs on me and on Nelson (whom I'd just met but hardly knew) for Nelson's powerful organizing in the black community, he was getting reports from Dawson about the Klan.

In October 1979, Bogaty led "informal briefings" over coffee about Nelson Johnson. Pelczar, supervisory senior resident FBI agent in Greensboro from 1977 and Bogaty's supervisor, was present.[43] Bogaty, along with Bureau agents Pelczar, Moses, and Brereton, knew the November 3 anti-Klan march would most likely turn into a deadly fusillade. All three men could have prevented the violent, untimely deaths of five human beings. Instead, they helped end those lives, causing immense suffering to the spouses, parents, sisters, brothers, and friends of those killed.

After 1973, Dawson did carpentry work for his former FBI control agent, Bogaty, and he kept in touch with Bogaty during the period he informed for the GPD. When the GPD asked him to be an informant in the fall of 1979, Dawson visited Bogaty to check out Detective Cooper. Approached from the other side, Bogaty vouched for Dawson to Talbott and Cooper, even though Bogaty knew Dawson's history of violence against black people. Bogaty was aware that Dawson wanted to get an injunction to stop the march. He knew enough about the Klan's plans to "disrupt the WVO" to warn Dawson not to go to Greensboro—he reminded Dawson that he had hurt his back in an earlier confrontation with blacks at a Klan streetwalk.[44]

Bogaty tried to conceal the extent of his pre–November 3 knowledge by writing memos after the fact in which he mentioned meeting with Dawson but disclosed only a small and irrelevant portion of what was said. His superiors encouraged him to do this and also concealed *their* foreknowledge. Bogaty knew Dawson's prominent role in the preparations for the November 3 attack. Although Bogaty briefed agents Pelczar, Moses, and Beckwith, he asserted that he never told his supervisors, and that they never asked, what he knew about Dawson or plans for the attack.

A couple of days after the massacre, Bogaty was at the Greensboro police station and was led into an interview room where Dawson was sitting alone. Dawson told the grand jury, and also our lawyers in his deposition, that Bogaty was "pretty upset" with him, threw down his pad, and yelled, "I told you to stay away from the damn thing."[45] Bogaty then called Dawson and told him to come down to the FBI office for an interview. Dawson went and played a lengthy taped statement that he had previously recorded. Bogaty was in the FBI office, but claimed that he did not talk to Dawson. Dawson talked about his background and activities as an FBI informant, controlled by Bogaty and others, and about his involvement with Virgil Griffin in prior violent acts. Dawson said that Bogaty told him not be go with the caravan and recounted the angry discussion Bogaty had with him post–November 3 in which Bogaty castigated him for going. Dawson also mentioned that Bogaty knew that he had obtained the WVO parade permit. Bogaty's superiors in the FBI said that they did not follow up on any of these subjects or ask Bogaty about them. However, when the information about Dawson's interview with its references to Bogaty got around, Bogaty was asked to, and did, draft cover-up memos and letters to create a false, after-the-fact, and besides-the-fact paper trail. It is reasonable to infer, as plaintiffs' attorneys did, that "Bogaty, in the meeting at the police department, wired Dawson to his cover story—that he told Dawson not to go—as Bogaty realized that he and his co-conspirators were vulnerable for their roles before November 3rd and for Dawson's actions in planning and participating in the massacre on that day."[46]

Pelczar, Moses, and Beckwith all denied any knowledge of an impending confrontation and any concealment of vital information afterward. Pelczar saw pictures of China Grove, a number of which depicted armed Klansmen (one with what appeared to be an automatic weapon). He indicated in his deposition that he was amazed that violence was averted at China Grove. When Cecil Moses directed Agent Beckwith, in Charlotte, to investigate the WVO in mid-October, no correlative investigation of the Klan or Nazis was ordered. Beckwith opened the WVO investigation with a memo to the Greensboro FBI office.[47] The FBI visit to mill worker Daisy Crawford was certainly part of that investigation. Daisy was shown photographs of Sandi and Jim a few days before they were killed, as her affidavit presented at the civil trial stated. (The FBI denied this, and Daisy was deceased by then.)

Most damning to the FBI is this: a few days before November 3, agents Pelczar and Brereton went to Assistant U.S. Attorney H. M. Michaux to discuss the possibility of trouble at the coming rally. Michaux testified in his deposition that they talked about Dawson, and that Brereton told Michaux "how unreliable Dawson was" and that "maybe the Klan would seek some type of retaliation for the China Grove incident."[48] Michaux told them to keep their eyes on it: Brereton and Pelczar went golfing on November 3. The conversation with Michaux, and many other meetings and conversations concerning the impending confrontation, were not, according to the FBI defendants, reduced to writing before November 3, "despite the FBI's time-honored policy and practice of writing numerous reports about anything and everything."[49] Pelczar and Brereton "concealed their pre–November 3rd knowledge from the investigation, from their supervisors, from the Grand Jury investigators, from the Grand Jury, and, when questioned about it at their depositions, denied it under oath."[50] Their depositions were taken *before that of Michaux*, in which he revealed that Pelczar and Brereton met with him and shared their knowledge of the dangers brewing around November 3.

Moses, assistant SAC, was in charge of the FBI's post–November 3 investigation, and Pelczar and Beckwith also supervised the investigation. Instead of being investigated himself, Bogaty was one of the investigators. He conducted interviews with Greensboro Klansmen Fletcher and Buck, who had central roles in the assault and whom Bogaty knew as Klansmen through Dawson. (Fletcher used his home as the staging area for the attack and fired the second shot that day. Buck drove the lead vehicle, a pickup, with Dawson "riding shotgun.") In the closed-loop investigation of the agency investigating itself, Moses concluded that Bogaty acted in a prudent manner and did no wrong, that Dawson's previous violent activities were irrelevant, and that there was "nothing that would indicate any misconduct, any mishandling, any inappropriate action on the part of an FBI agent."[51] Taking over from Pelczar as SAC in March 1980 was Pence. He supervised the FBI's role in the criminal investigation and the federal grand jury and commended Moses for his "incident-free handling" of the investigation.[52]

More evidence substantiating an FBI cover-up was provided by Jewish activist Mordecai Levy. On November 2, Levy telephoned Special Agent Goldberg of the Raleigh FBI office. Goldberg acknowledges receiving the call from Levy and hearing that Harold Covington and the Nazis were training with weapons and "planned to attack and possibly kill people at the anti-Klan rally this week

CHAPTER 19

in North Carolina."⁵³ Goldberg (whom Levy mistakenly thought was Jewish) called the Greensboro FBI office to find out if a demonstration was planned for the weekend and learned that the word was all over town "that there was a 'Death to the Klan' rally taking place" in Greensboro.⁵⁴ Goldberg did nothing—at least nothing to prevent the violence. Our attorneys in the civil suit concluded that the FBI defendants engineered an "investigation" that covered up their true role and knowledge. They lied about their foreknowledge and destroyed the paper trail, creating scanty, after-the-fact documents.

MOMENTS IN THE CIVIL SUIT

Because our lawyers struggled over jury selection, we were able to get one black juror seated. He became the jury foreman. The legal team challenged the procedure for forming a jury pool as one that significantly underrepresented eligible blacks. There was a tit-for-tat struggle with the judge. Battles raged over challenges for cause. Attorney Flint Taylor summarized the results of the strategy of the plaintiffs' legal team.

> The judge became sensitized to the issues of race, prejudicial pretrial publicity, and anti-communism. Once all the prospective jurors were qualified, he employed a system of exercising peremptory challenges which prevented the defendants from removing every black person qualified by the court. The jury selected was comprised of a black man who had participated in civil rights demonstrations in the early 1960s, an older white woman who had moved south from New England in the late 1950s, and four southern whites who appeared to be less racist and anticommunist than most of the others questioned.⁵⁵

Over an eight-week period, our lawyers called to the stand seventy-five witnesses, starting with the testimonies of two cameramen who witnessed and filmed the November 3 assault. An unusual feature of the plaintiffs' case was that much of it was presented through adverse witnesses. "Plaintiffs used the defendants to tell the story, as only they could describe their conspiracy, since plaintiffs basically only knew what happened to them on November 3rd. . . . The defense called few witnesses, since plaintiffs had called so many of them."⁵⁶ The defense took just one week. Plaintiffs' lawyers interspersed their clients' testimonies with those of the Klan, Nazis, police, the BATF, and the FBI to highlight contrasts of character, action, and motive. When Nazi Roland Wood was sworn in, he put his hand out in a Hitler salute. In the course of testifying, he sang a virulently anti-Semitic song to the tune of *Jingle Bells*.

Plaintiffs' lawyers in *Waller v. Butkovich* documented the entrenchment of racist attitudes in the police department and a total lack of written policies or guidelines to determine or eradicate them. Cooper's and other officers' use of the word *nigger* was routinely tolerated. "Dawson was allowed to instigate and organize the Klan caravan and . . . to lead it unhindered into the Black community, with police knowledge that a violent attack was imminent, [demonstrating] a deliberate indifference to racism and Klan sympathy."[57] There was particular animosity by the police toward Nelson, who had exposed the city's endemic racism when he led students and the black community in the turbulent mass actions of the late sixties. Very strongly, racism fueled and motivated the conspiracy, as attorneys Lewis Pitts, Carolyn McAllaster, and Flint Taylor made abundantly clear in presenting the case in court.

Another key point for this case was the lack of adequate guidelines for informants. The failure to control informants was striking in the GPD's handling of Dawson. Chief Swing admitted in his deposition that there was no written policy about informants committing acts and engaging in conduct that would otherwise constitute a crime. Each division, or each officer, was at liberty to develop and guide its own informants, the chief said.[58] Detective Cooper, asked if informants were allowed to commit illegal acts, answered that they could if it were done with the knowledge of the police and if the police were there to observe it. Our lawyers argued that the city's poor or nonexistent policy about informants and the failure to train, supervise, or discipline officers as to the most basic prohibitions resulted in extreme injury to the plaintiffs. We were backed up by former Boston police superintendent Robert di Grazia, who condemned the police department's handling of Dawson and the failure to stop the attack.

EMOTIONS AROUND THE VERDICT

The verdict did not feel like a "victory" when it was announced on June 6, 1985. I was bitter, angry, and hurt at what seemed another miscarriage of justice.

The jury found Police Lieutenant Paul W. Spoon, Detective Jerry Cooper, police informant Edward Dawson, Klansmen Mark Sherer, David Matthews, Jerry Paul Smith, and Nazis Roland Wood and Jack Fowler jointly liable for the wrongful death of Dr. Michael Nathan.[59] State assault and battery charges against four Klansmen and Nazis were upheld for Mike and two surviving plaintiffs. The next day, $351,500 was awarded to the Nathan estate for Michael Nathan's wrongful death. Matthews, Wood, Smith, and Fowler were to pay assault and battery judgments of $3,500 to the Nathan estate for Michael and $38,358.55 to Paul Bermanzohn, while Matthews and Wood were assessed $1,500 for the wounding of Tom Clark.

No one was found liable for the deaths of Jim, César, Bill, and Sandi. The jury did not find violations of the plaintiffs' civil rights under federal civil rights law for any of the forty-five Klan, Nazi, police, or federal agent defendants and did not uphold conspiracy charges for any of these defendants— key points of our case.[60] Only one widow received any compensation. The injuries of Nelson, Chekesha, Jim Wrenn, Don, and Rand, as well as the unfair indictments and incarceration of various survivors, were ignored. No punitive damages were assessed on any of the defendants. The puny award was intended to compensate three plaintiffs, Marty, Paul, and Tom, for their loss.

A few days after the trial's end, Nelson made a statement for all the plaintiffs: "We ask our city leaders, including the mayor and councilpersons, our civic, political and religious organizations to join in a united effort for social, economic and racial justice. Together we can heal the scars and wounds of November 3. . . . Greensboro can become . . . a city which turns away from racism and inequality. Our city can represent jobs, peace and justice for all of its citizens. . . . We seek to work in harmony with all people who share this direction and vision."[61]

I went before the city council within a couple of weeks of the verdict to urge Mayor Forbis and the council members to have the city's lawyers pay the judgment and not appeal it. "We know of no precedent," I told the council, "where a civil jury has convicted Klan, Nazis and police officers for their concerted role in violence against private citizens." I expressed hope that we could end "a period of tenseness and acrimony in the city's history."[62]

I grappled with feelings about a verdict that fell far short of justice and was insulting. My emotions got in the way of appreciating its significance. In a letter to the plaintiffs, Marty and Dale put the outcome in perspective. "We have won a historic victory," they said. "Rarely have informants or police even been brought to court for the most outrageous criminal acts, let alone been found guilty of their crimes. The Liuzzo family lost their case though it was clear that Gary Thomas Rowe pulled the trigger against their mother in 1964. We faced almost insurmountable obstacles: two previous acquittals, years of anticommunist slander in the press, a deep-rooted bias on the part of many people in support of law enforcement, and the traditional and increasing racism and anticommunism of white southerners, especially those constantly exposed to Jesse Helms' reaction."

Other people could assess (better than we could) the deterrent power that the verdict had against official criminal behavior and the confidence it gave to those who fight official abuse. "They saw how effectively we had been able to put out the story through the media, independent of the verdict."[63] Anne Braden, who played a major role in organizing the peoples' movement that fought for justice with the massacre survivors, saw the fightback as "a major turning point in this nation's struggle against racism." The response to Greensboro, she wrote, "created a new unity among people's movements and touched off a decade of activism at a critical moment."[64]

Six years after the massacre, in November 1985, Marty received a check for $351,500 from the city's insurance company. *The City of Greensboro paid the fine for its two police officers and also for the six Klan and Nazis.* (A remaining $43,459.55 assessed against four Klan/Nazis for assault and battery was never paid to Marty, Paul, or Tom.) Spoon and Cooper were never disciplined: no police officer received so much as a reprimand. The City of Greensboro never apologized, nor even acknowledged its wrongdoing, although a court assessed it liable for a wrongful death. After paying the legal bills, Marty divided the award among the sixteen plaintiffs. A portion of the money was returned to the GJF, enabling it to become a grant-making organization that helps others fight injustice.

In a press conference held right after the settlement, plaintiffs declared that "the significance of this victory can only be fully appreciated when it is viewed against the mountain-like obstacles which had to be overcome to achieve it." The verdict in the civil suit was a "beacon of hope for victims of governmental abuse of power, police brutality and corruption across the nation" and "a contribution in the struggle for local official accountability and for the rights of all to speak, assemble, advocate change and organize for power in order to bring about positive change."[65]

But victory was not the same as full justice. By victory we meant that we overcame "extreme difficulties to prevail on essential legal, political and moral issues." Justice required all responsible for criminal acts to be held accountable for their actions and the victims to be reasonably compensated. "The verdict and settlement, by this measure, do not equal justice," we said.[66]

The verdict was a committee-type product embodying compromise and negotiation. Five human beings were killed by the same criminals on the same occasion and under the same circumstances, but only one was called a wrongful death. My flash of intuition on hearing the verdict was that anticommunist bias was so strong that only Mike's humanity counted, since he was not officially a WVO member when he was killed. This, crass as it is, is essentially what happened. Some jurors interviewed after the verdict touched upon the deep differences among them that may explain the bizarre, patchwork, inadequate outcome. As Flint Taylor has summarized:

> The black foreman and the white woman originally from New England strongly supported a verdict on the civil rights conspiracy charges in favor of most of the plaintiffs and against the BATF provocateur and several of the police and federal defendants. They also favored substantial damage awards.
>
> The southern white faction, however, wanted a narrow verdict or none at all. They were unable to put their anticommunism and racism aside. They feared the reaction in their communities to a verdict for the plaintiffs and focused on the plaintiffs' rhetoric and the alleged possession of a gun or the firing of one in self-defense as reasons to deny liability. As to Sandy Smith, an unarmed black woman who was shot between the eyes and killed, they refused to support liability because they disliked her former husband, a black doctor, who was the administrator of her estate, and did not want him to recover. They limited Dr. Paul Bermanzohn's recovery to his actual out-of-pocket expenses, despite permanent paralysis, because he was still a member of the CWP and they feared that any additional money would go to the party.[67]

When all is said and done, the imperfect jury in the Greensboro civil rights suit set a legal precedent. Never before in American jurisprudence had a jury ruled Klan, Nazis, and police officers jointly liable for a wrongful death.

NOTES

1. See Korotkin, "The Campaign for Justice," 82–83.
2. See Paul Wolf, with Robert Boyle, Bob Brown, Tom Burghardt, Noam Chomsky, Ward Churchill, Kathleen Cleaver, Bruce Ellison, Cynthia McKinney, Nkechi Taifa, Laura Whitehorn, Nicholas Wilson, and Howard Zinn, "COINTELPRO: The Untold American Story," paper presented to Mary Robinson at the World Conference against Racism in Durban, South Africa, by Congresswoman McKinney, 1 September 2001.
3. Attorneys Dan Sheehan of the Christic Institute, Flint Taylor of the Chicago People Law Office, and Durham lawyer Carolyn McAllaster joined the legal team with Pitts. Attorney Dan Siegal of Oakland, California, sent paralegal Jill Cahill. Victoria Osk, Pam DiStefano, Lin Delaney, and Curtis Pierce, all paralegals or law students, stayed in Greensboro much longer than they planned to and took on great responsibilities for little pay.
4. Korotkin, "The Campaign for Justice," 96–97.
5. Under 42 U.S.C. § 1983.
6. Under 42 U.S.C. §§ 1983 & 1986.

7. Under §§ 1983 & 1985.

8. Under *Monell v. Dept. of Social Services*, 436 U.S. 658, 1978.

9. Several lawyers who worked on aspects of the civil suit and also journalists familiar with the course of litigation that followed the massacre have written excellent summaries. Lewis Pitts' account for the Christic Institute is reflected in Mark Levey and Andrew Lang, "Greensboro Special Report: The Story of a Death Squad," *Convergence*, Fall 1985, 7–11. Flint Taylor wrote "*Waller v. Butkovich:* Lessons in Strategy and Tenacity for Civil Rights Litigators," *Police Misconduct and Civil Rights Law Report*, January/February 1986. Early in the course of litigation, Earle Tockman wrote "Tactic of Non-cooperation, Klan Trial," for the National Lawyers Guild, *Guild Notes*, November–December 1980. In 1982, in the middle of the various trials, Lewis Pitts wrote a special report for the Christic Institute entitled "Justice Department Handling of the 1979 Greensboro Klan-Nazi Attack and the Special Grand Jury." For a description of the suit, I have drawn on all of these.

10. Plaintiff's Exhibit City #15, Interview of Sgt. T. L. Burke by Capt. D. C. Williams, 3 June 1980.

11. "Plaintiffs' Answer to City Defendants' Motion for Summary Judgment," *Waller v. Butkovich*, U.S. District Court for the Middle District of North Carolina, Greensboro Division, No. 80-605-G, 30 January 1985, 42. This information from an Internal Affairs Division (IAD) report of 29 November 1979.

12. "Plaintiffs' Answer to City," 4.

13. "Plaintiffs' Answer to City," 52.

14. "Plaintiffs' Answer to City," 5.

15. "Plaintiffs' Answer to City," 27. This information from Exhibit 55, Ford Deposition.

16. "Plaintiffs' Answer to City," 27 and 34. See also interview of Lt. S. N. Ford by Capt. D. C. Williams, 21 November 1979.

17. "Plaintiffs' Answer to City," 38. This information from Exhibit 5, Thomas Deposition.

18. "Plaintiffs' Answer to City," 39.

19. Lewis Pitts, Carolyn McAllaster, Flint Taylor, Daniel Sheehan, and Victoria Osk to Malcolm Call of the University of Georgia Press, letter, 12 August 1986.

20. "Plaintiffs' Answer to City," 28. This information is from Exhibit 11, Cooper to FBI.

21. Korotkin, "The Campaign for Justice," 125.

22. "Plaintiffs' Answer to City," 63. This information is from Exhibit 47, Daughtry Deposition.

23. "Plaintiffs' Answer to City," 60. Emphasis in original.

24. "Plaintiffs' Answer to City," 60–61.

25. "Plaintiffs' Answer to City," 88ff.

26. "Plaintiffs' Answer to City," 16–17.

27. "Plaintiffs' Answer to City," 7.

28. "Plaintiffs' Answer to City," 9.

29. "Plaintiffs' Answer to City," 12. This information is from Exhibit 72, Wise Deposition.

30. "Plaintiffs' Answer to City," 15.

31. "Plaintiffs' Response to ATF Defendants Butkovich and Westra's Motion for Summary Judgment," *Waller v. Butkovich*, U.S. District Court for the Middle District of North Carolina, Greensboro Division, No. 80-605-G, 1 February 1985, 13. As in the previous section about the police and the subsequent one about the FBI, all claims in Plaintiffs' Response are backed up with exhibits that include depositions, interviews, and other documentation.

32. "Plaintiffs' Response to ATF," 14.

33. "Plaintiffs' Response to ATF," 16.

34. "Plaintiffs' Response to ATF," 16–17.

35. Lewis Pitts, "Draft of 'Pieces of the Greensboro Puzzle Obtained during Discovery,'" unpublished paper, 12 July 1991.

36. "Plaintiffs' Response to ATF," 23. This information is from Exhibit 32, Grady Deposition.

37. Pitts, "Draft of 'Pieces of the Greensboro Puzzle.'" SAC stands for Special Agent in Charge.

38. Taylor, "*Waller v. Butkovich:* Lessons in Strategy," 148.

39. "Plaintiffs' Response to ATF," 24–25.

40. "Plaintiffs' Response to ATF," 36.

41. "Plaintiffs' Opposition to Defendants Pelczar, Moses, and Pence's Motion for Summary Judgment," *Waller v. Butkovich*, U.S. District Court for the Middle District of North Carolina, Greensboro Division, No. 80-605-G, 14 December 1984, 4.

42. Plaintiffs' Opposition," 2–3.

43. Plaintiffs' Opposition," 4.

44. Plaintiffs' Opposition," 5.

45. Plaintiffs' Opposition," 19.

46. Plaintiffs' Opposition," 22.

47. Plaintiffs' Opposition," 6.

48. Plaintiffs' Opposition," 7.

49. Plaintiffs' Opposition," 7.

50. Plaintiffs' Opposition," 20.

51. Plaintiffs' Opposition," 14–15.

52. Plaintiffs' Opposition," 16.

53. Plaintiffs' Opposition," 6. Information is from Exhibit 2, Goldberg Deposition and Levy Affidavit.

54. Plaintiffs' Opposition," 6.

55. Taylor, "*Waller v. Butkovich*: Lessons in Strategy," 149.

56. Korotkin, "The Campaign for Justice," 124.

57. "Plaintiffs' Answer to City," 157.

58. "Plaintiffs' Answer to City," 146–151.

59. Stan Swofford, "8 Found Liable in Klan-Nazi Lawsuit," *Greensboro News & Record*, 8 June 1985, A1. The jury made bizarre use of the law in an effort to reach a compromise. The lumping of Klan and police together could only reflect conspiracy, but they did not cite conspiracy statutes.

60. See Meredith Barkley and Sharon Bond, "Plaintiffs Consider Verdict of Klan-Nazi Trial a 'Victory,'" *Greensboro News & Record*, 11 June 1985, B3.

61. Nelson Johnson, letter on behalf of all the plaintiffs, *Greensboro News & Record*, 15 June 1985.

62. Signe Waller, "Statement to the Greensboro City Council," 17 June 1985. See also "Bonds Authorized for Greensborough Court," *Greensboro News & Record*, 18 June 1985.

63. Marty Nathan and Dale Sampson, letter to the plaintiffs, undated but probably 12 June 1985.

64. Anne Braden, "The Cry Was Unity," *Southern Exposure*, Fall 1999.

65. Statement by the plaintiffs on the verdict in the civil rights suit. Also quoted in Meredith Barkley, "Greensboro to Pay Plaintiffs $351,500," *Greensboro News & Record*, 7 November 1985.

66. Greensboro Civil Rights Fund, "Statement by the Plaintiffs on the Verdict and Settlement of the Greensboro Civil Rights Suit," 6 November 1985, 2. Also see Barkley, "Greensboro to pay plaintiffs $351,500."

67. Taylor, "*Waller v. Butkovich:* Lessons in Strategy," 151–152.

20

CONVENED BY MARTYRS

The trumpet shall sound
And the dead shall be raised incorruptible
And we shall be changed.

—Händel, *Messiah*, Aria, no. 46

WHY DID THEY DO IT AND HOW COULD THEY NOT DO IT?

On the fifteenth anniversary of the Greensboro Massacre, I wander through the streets of downtown Greensboro. It is the ruling class' command center, with jails fortified by electronic security systems, insurance and brokerage firm high-rises, and small, landscaped enclaves of gentrification. I look at November Third from the bourgeoisie's perspective. Shaken by the civil rights movement and student uprisings at A & T State University in the 1960s, the local bourgeoisie did not want to take another beating. A civil rights steamroller was headed their way. Black power and labor power were joining forces! The same leader who had been a thorn in their side when he was at A & T, Nelson Johnson, was now influencing and leading *blacks and whites alike.*

Under the auspices of Workers Viewpoint, black and white workers confronted Cone Mills—in 1979, Guilford County's largest employer, a leader in the production of denim and corduroy, and one of the largest textile companies in the world—with fierce and sustained opposition. We challenged them with a united workers' movement in three key North Carolina mills. From the point of view of the business establishment, the WVO blighted the city. A bunch of communists running rampant does not create a favorable business climate. If you are unscrupulous enough, anything is possible, including murder. How could the ruling class *not* plan the Greensboro Massacre? How could they afford *not* to do it?

If you are united enough, anything is possible, even revolution. In every action or campaign, the WVO strove to connect the predominantly white working class with the movement of African Americans against racist oppression. We brought our white working-class friends to African Liberation Day and our black friends to workers' picket lines. In the course of building up the black liberation movement in the South, WVO was connecting with struggles of peoples of color around the world.

Workers Viewpoint leaders, like Jim, Bill, Mike, César, and Sandi, were good at integrating theory and practice. They helped others to understand, the better to act; and to act, the better to understand. Many workers and poor people, through their contact with WVO, were becoming better informed about economics, politics, and international events and were finding a voice for the first time. The lesson we *all* were learning was that fundamental social change can happen if we organize and unite to fight for it—a lesson still being learned.

The WVO taught people that the *class system* is the enemy grinding them down. The five people killed, and other WVO members and supporters, made people aware that there are alternatives to this system and that we can change things and improve our lives. After the murders, César's friend Ernestine, an African American woman, talked about what the work of the WVO meant to her. "I'm gonna fight until I can't fight no more," she said. "I want people to become clear and they are. They're becoming clear on what's really going down, why the party was attacked, why the people were attacked. They keep pressing us down and we keep rising up. And we're gonna keep rising up. They can't hold us down. People are becoming very clear. The party brings it out so that people can see it—'Look, it's not your next door neighbor, it's not your friend down the block, it's the system that's doin' it to you. It's the system.'"[1]

The WVO fought police and sheriff's departments on police brutality. It exposed sham reforms like the competency test that did nothing to satisfy the public demand for quality education for all children. In workplaces and communities, the WVO waged class struggle, keeping in mind the goal of going from a bourgeois state to a workers' state and, ultimately, to a society without classes. As we struggled, new vistas arose. It was an article of faith that the democratic, egalitarian values that motivated us would revolutionize all of society. We were doing what we set out to do—building a base of support for socialist revolution. *We were successfully contending for people power with the ruling elite.* In North Carolina, where the potential for popular empowerment was patent, the forces of repression were primed to strike back.

What is the yardstick of successful contending? Cone already had power; they did not have to contend for it. For Cone, success meant being able to conduct business as, or better than, usual; for workers, it meant being able to contend for power in a vigorous, sustained way. Workers were beginning to glimpse the possibility of breaking out of oppression in their daily lives. Many were becoming active participants in a movement for their own liberation. The specter of workers streaming forth to break the chains of wage slavery freaked out the capitalists and their allies in the police and local government. Mill owners, corrupted trade union officials, city and county potentates, and others used to making and enforcing the rules for society now had to contend *to hold on to their power.*

To successfully contend for power when you are the underdog may describe several degrees of motion short of actually taking power. A telling sign of *effectively* contending for power is that those holding power become very nervous and are constrained to act in ways in which they normally would not. Cone was forced to take more and more repressive actions to control their workforce. At the White Oak Plant, Cone tried to fire Bill Sampson and even had him arrested, without success. Militants took over the union and ran it. There was Bill—the shoe-in candidate for president of the union local—after more than two years of Cone's trying to get rid of him. Cone was only bailed out by the union bureaucrats who stepped in and put several Cone locals, including White Oak, into receivership. Had the election occurred, it would have fully authorized a militant rank-and-file led union local with Bill as its head.

Sandi Smith did not succeed in the *official* union drive at Cone's Revolution Plant. Labor bureaucrats were unwilling to have locals under radical leadership. But Sandi and other workers organized the plant anyway. Their strength and solidarity resulted in a de facto union that must have given mill owners and plant managers heartburn. ACTWU higher-ups had to acknowledge the powerful union sentiment and the workers' desire for autonomy. At her new job in Kannapolis, Sandi had little time to organize before she was killed.

Cone fired Jim Waller, but they did not stop the workers' movement. Surely there was no wholesale conversion to communism, but an anarchist spirit of fightback reigned at the Granite Finishing Plant. The workers there loved, respected, and trusted Jim. They elected him president of their local *in defiance of the receivership.* Though no longer on the plant floor, Jim kept on training workers so that they could continue to build the union without him. The July 1978 strike was a crucible of class struggle out of which was developing a worker-run local—to be sure, one existing uneasily within the larger union of which it was a part. It was a dangerous model (to the ruling elite)—*black and white workers were uniting and taking charge of their own destiny*. In the strike wave that swept the South that year, radical textile workers were linking up with workers in other industries for their mutual support.

From the perspective of their owners, the mills were getting out of hand. Capitalists were losing power and authority in proportion as workers were gaining it. Class society is a zero sum game.

Consider what the communist leaders in the mills did, what it led to, and what it meant. Through nonviolent direct actions, often very mundane ones, they helped workers file grievances, won most of the grievances filed, forced the company to back off from some of its repressive decisions, and strengthened the workers' movement by challenging—and overcoming to a degree—racist ideology. This led the bourgeoisie to react with desperate measures in an attempt to regain control over the workers. What all this means is that *workers were successfully contending for workers' power in the class struggle in the United States, in the South, in the 1970s.* As power relationships became more unstable, the outcome became less capable of being assured in advance. Into this instability crept even the possibility of ending wage slavery altogether. It did not come to pass, we know, but if not this time then the next. The path to every great achievement is strewn with past failures.

If mill owners and union bureaucrats were troubled by a small band of communist upstarts churning things up in the mills, the two mainstream political parties had no reason to look more kindly at the competition, puny now but potentially stronger. The reputedly more open and liberal of the two, the Democrats, rely on two main constituencies—workers and minorities. *WVO was contending for power by successfully organizing both of these constituencies,* and not necessarily to go to the polls to vote Democrat. And outside of North Carolina, other committed WVO organizers were also leading struggles against corporate power and sell-out unions.

Fifteen years later, Earl Jones, an African American Greensboro city councilman, tells an audience of blacks and whites who have come together to remember the Greensboro Massacre what his cousins, workers at Granite Finishing Plant in Haw River, told him. The workers there still talk about "Blackbeard," he says, and they insist that they have better working conditions, salary, and benefits because of "Blackbeard." It is gratifying to hear, and I am very moved. But I know that there is further to go on the road to worker and human liberation, and that Jim, Mike, Sandi, César, and Bill were heading further along that road when they were stopped in their tracks.

THE UNDERPINNINGS OF AMERICAN
DEMOCRACY OR DEATH SQUAD, U.S.A. STYLE

The mass media is a critical part of the big-money empire. Noam Chomsky, Ed Herman, and others have explored the topic of "manufacturing consent." What if the attempt to create a compliant, consenting public does not work, if dissidents cannot be pacified or bought off? If the stakes are high, the wealthy and powerful resort to violence. The class system of unequal wealth and power, a white supremacist system incorporating racism, sexism, and other caste discrimination, actually rests on violence and is guaranteed by violence. The Greensboro Massacre exposes the facade of capitalist democracy, showing *how American democracy works and how it has worked all along*. We must rightly name the attack on November 3, 1979—it was a U.S.A.-style death squad. The principle is the same as in death squads in Germany in the 1930s or in El Salvador in the 1980s. Greensboro bursts the illusion that government-sponsored death squads belong only to another time, another place, another government.

Certainly, the Greensboro Massacre was a *particular* incident, and we can emphasize its particularity. But the universal resides within the particular, the paradigm within the aberration. November Third was the paradigm of a police state, not a democratic one. The Greensboro Massacre was a triumph for death squads, U.S.A. style. Afterward, however, the fightback was resolute, broad, and sustained, thus making it more difficult for the evil forces that produced the attack to expand and intensify this sort of repressive tactic.

Hypocrisy gives the 1979 death squad its *American* flavor. Big-money people are in command of the squad, but they do not act directly. They use surrogates to keep hoi polloi in line so that they may pretend that their hands are clean. (In this matter, the best publicity is no publicity at all: a California-based media project, "Project Censored," declared what was going on in Greensboro was one of the two most censored "important stories" of 1981.) The bottom line is that the disproportionately wealthy and powerful want to continue enjoying, unchallenged, a largesse to which they are not entitled. Since raw power and violence is not the credo of democracy, when used it must be hypocritically disguised. Leaders and leading institutions in society must be shielded from being compromised by the resort to violence, or from exposure of their actual *might makes right* philosophy. In reality, the ruling class in the United States ranks among the most violent and abusive ever to walk the earth.

The Greensboro Massacre is an episode in the long history of class struggle. In Greensboro, the capitalists depended on their agents in city government, city law enforcement, and state and federal bureaus to remove a terrible inconvenience to their class. In using Klan and Nazis as shock troops, the capitalists and their defenders used the right (their lesser enemies) to zap the left (their real enemies).

We do not have all of the pieces to the puzzle. We do not have a smoking gun leading to the textile mills. That is not to say that it doesn't exist or will never be found. Pieces are missing of the solid links between the FBI and the BATF. Butkovich's investigation of Wood was, we know, coordinated on a SAC-to-SAC level by the BATF and FBI. Evidence for this conclusion was cited at the civil rights trial and an ATF agent acknowledged as much under cross-examination. A conceivable, even irresistible, surmise is that both agencies sat down with some high-up government officials to discuss what to do about us, that is, the new communist movement and specifically WVO. The attack in Greensboro was a massive intervention in that city that required preparation, voluminous communications, and real cooperation among many non-Klan/Nazi official parties, including the police in Greensboro, Durham, Winston-Salem, and other North Carolina cities; the FBI; and the BATF. Dawson and Butkovich were the links to the Klan/Nazi shock troops. Without doubt, there is more than, even now, meets the eye. Future investigators may find some of these missing pieces. That they are well concealed is not surprising.

For sure, "we're gonna keep rising up. They can't hold us down." Since the turn of the millennium, a worldwide anticapitalist movement in opposition to globalization, or the control of the world by a few profit-driven corporations, has made its presence felt in Seattle, Prague, Washington, Porto Alegre, Genoa, and elsewhere. If a brutal, racist, and undemocratic system that is destroying the ecology of the earth is to be replaced by sustainable, just, and humane practices, something like the WVO's organizing and political consciousness-raising is required—and it is happening under different contemporary banners. Ultimately, this is a battle of ideas, and your weapon is your mind. If you cannot imagine a better system than the predatory capitalism under which we exist today, then you are in trouble, otherwise not. For those who believe in TINA (there is no alternative), or, as Michael Albert of Z Magazine has called it, TINBA (there is no better alternative), capitalism is like the air we breathe—a necessary and inescapable part of the environment. Not only is capitalism not at all like the air we breathe, but capitalism is so befouling the planet that if it prevails much longer, even the air we breathe will be noxious.

MISTAKES, LESSONS, AND GOOD STUFF: A CRITICAL VIEW

It is important to identify mistakes if we and others are to learn from them. In retrospect, our rhetoric afforded a convenient launch pad for the conspiratorial moves of the police and government with Klan and Nazis. For example, our en-emies used the Open Letter to Grady and Pierce to extract, out of context, a pic-ture of two groups of crazies facing off—the Klan and the Communists. With that as a hook, the media could devote almost zero column inches, or sound bites, to more germane topics, like the Klan's terrorist history, or our history of uniting black and white workers, or the evidence of official complicity in the No-vember Third murders. I, and others, have come to realize that we unwittingly created an opening for the attack by failing to anticipate or imagine *what could be made of that rhetoric, and by whom.* Such mindlessness and lack of circum-spection made it *easier* for police, Klan, Nazis, and colluding government agen-cies to do what they did *and* to blame us for it. We did not do it to ourselves, as some people insinuated out of ignorance or malice, but we did *make it easier for them to do it to us.* All mistakes have consequences: a mistake, by definition, is what has unforeseen, unintended, or unwanted consequences.

Emily Mann and Marty Nathan, insightful and morally courageous women, have contributed to my enlightenment on this subject.

1996: Emily Mann did not know us in 1979. She met the survivors of the Greensboro Massacre more than a decade later. Her play, "Greensboro: A Re-quiem," premiered in Princeton, New Jersey, at the McCarter Theater in Febru-ary 1996.[2] I saw one of the final performances in its initial three-week run.

I felt small in my seat between my husband, Jim Rose, and my son, Alex Goldstein. Alex, approaching his twenty-eighth birthday, had not yet sloughed off the trauma of November 3. It took years for me to see that I had been on a dif-ferent wave length from his. I hadn't appreciated the difference between having experienced the trauma of November 3 and its aftermath as an adult and as a child, a child who had not thought the thoughts or acted the actions that pre-ceded that fateful day. Marty Nathan helped me to realize it, and Sally Berman-zohn, and finally Alex himself. "You don't listen to me," he would say, gently per-sisting. "You're not listening to me. Stop interrupting all the time." He was right. I needed to be a better listener, to him and to others. Here he was clasping my right hand tightly, and there sat Jim Rose allowing my left hand to grip his hand with supernatural force.

The actors are lined up on stage in Emily Mann's excellent documentary-style drama and, near the beginning of the play, that rhetoric is pitched back at me—the very words we wrote on leaflets, pronounced at rallies and press con-ferences, spoke to one another. Flash-ups on a screen behind the actors remind the audience that WORDS HAVE MEANING. Indeed. Now my vital circuits go numb as I sit and watch and hear, absorbing words that, after so many con-volutions through the air into the stratosphere around and beyond this planet and the next, carried on minute wave-like disturbances, loop back at me. For a fleeting moment, *I am the Klan, I am the public*, hearing the phrases that slap and insult, whether deserved or not, whether true or not, delivered with the force of conviction and righteousness, delivered unmindful of one-way transmission.

The playwright has performed a miracle. Only a few words and phrases are selected, staged, delivered with intensity—but the essence is captured, even concentrated. It is on stage as it was in reality, and the rendering renders me a temporary zombie. Transported in time to 1979, I see and feel the words begin their journey. Their strident militancy blares forth as from a marching band of all horns. The distant band approaches ever nearer; it jangles my sense organs. I squirm in my seat. The words are felt in the sudden surge of pressure to hands. Words have meaning.

1999: Around the twentieth anniversary commemoration of the Greensboro Massacre, Dr. Marty Nathan wrote a letter to a friend in which she shared her reflections about China Grove.

Although I wasn't at China Grove, I will trust Mike's opinion, and state that I don't think we were glorious, just youthfully arrogant and naive. And damn lucky. We were not so lucky in Greensboro—the Klan had gotten the clearance from the cops and knew they could do their thing with impunity.

We were not at all prepared either to be shot at or to shoot or fight with those sticks or guns. Yet we pretended we were. If the Klan had opened fire, scores of people could have been murdered. And that empty bravado, those pictures from China Grove, were used as the rallying and recruiting point for the Klan in coming months. We upped the ante to thugs.

We continued the mistake after China Grove by summing up that China Grove was "glorious" and that "we were ready to die in battle" or some such. No, we weren't. And the letter and other publicity were foolish—we were not ready for them to come to Greensboro, did not want them to come, did not know how to perform this so-called armed self-defense and abhorred the violence that followed, that was our first such experience. Our tactics had isolated us from much of the community. The officials were able to say, in a way that resonated (although by no means was true) that we "got what we deserved." Politically, we helped to set ourselves up for the coverup as well as the murders.

These are hard words, I know . . . China Grove is very difficult for me to talk about. I say that I would confront the Klan again (and have) when confronted by them. But, when people ask, I say that at that time we were very young, idealistic and inexperienced, and I would do it differently now, based on our experience. Our job as political leaders is to minimize violence, not promote it. Although I think that people do have a right to protect themselves when attacked, a far better approach is to force the cops and community politically to protect the people.

I believe what we did at China Grove was a mistake, not a crime. What the Klan and the police and the ATF and the FBI did were crimes. But we must be wise and understand and learn from our mistakes, not glorify them. I do not want Leah or any of our children to repeat what we did.

Difficult issues face the serious anticapitalist or antiglobalization forces of today that are seeking to gain the power necessary for instituting fundamental and liberating social change. Back in the 1970s and 1980s, the slogan *political offense, military defense* sounded reasonable to me. It may be a reasonable approach. However, much care must be taken in unpacking the meaning. I have, elsewhere in this book, been critical of the attitude adopted by many of us, myself included, that boldness will invariably win the day. To not admit the vulnerability of people in the face of overwhelming military odds strikes me now as sheer and dangerous idealism. It is foolish to think that the *attitude* of being staunch and bold will weigh in with the might of a military weapon—Jim pretending to be the invincible Hulk. If you survive, you learn circumspection.

There are times to incur voluntarily certain risks in daring to struggle for social justice, and there may be situations in which it is useful tactically to assume a military posture that is not backed up by the ability to follow through. But we assumed a military-like posture unaware that it was only a posture. This, again, goes to the issue of mindfulness and circumspection. Political offense is compatible with military defense, but it is not the same as military preparedness. Military posturing is not military preparedness. To say that you will respond if attacked does not mean that you are prepared to do so. I do not think the WVO/CWP's excellent political offense gained by posturing in a military manner, whether in China Grove, Greensboro, Kokomo, or New York.

Political exposure alone is quite powerful without the military accoutrements. WVO's willingness for bold, uncompromising truth-telling, even if sometimes done with a heavy rhetorical hand, makes me proud to have been associated with the organization. I am still of the mind that we understood the capitalist system very well by bringing into play, as we used to say, "the microscope and telescope of Marxism." We rooted ourselves in poor, minority, and working-class communities and helped to unite people in the fight against oppressive institutions. The CWP 5 represented the hallmark of the organization. Jim, Sandi, Mike, Bill, and César reached out to people, engaged them, struggled with their backward tendencies, led and trained them to be leaders, fought alongside them, and committed their lives to their fellow human beings on a daily and ongoing basis. There are no shortcuts to this method which, for want of a better phrase, I will call *existential engagement*.

The WVO/CWP attracted many people who were not only dedicated, but extremely bright, with great political and theoretical strengths. I think the quality of the analysis was very high, that we were right about many things. The general orientation of getting to the root of problems and changing what causes the problem to recur is an approach that still makes sense to me. Lest I depart from my purpose of constructive criticism, however, I want to turn to some limitations or errors.

A central thread in any critical reexamination of our experience as part of the New Communist Movement has to do with the Democratic Centralist structure of our organization. Though historically understandable, even compelling, it must not be exempt from criticism. I can do little more here than call attention to some issues in a general way, but I must do at least that for the sake of an honest critique. Democratic Centralism (DC) is a structural feature of most, if not all, actual Marxist-Leninist parties. My understanding of DC is this: you argue things out—that's the democratic part—but you have a hierarchical leadership structure that makes the final decree—that's the centralist part. In practice, you end up long on centralism and short on democracy. It works best in wartime, when decisions must be made quickly and under conditions of hardship. Democratic centralism gives you a "correct line" that people are committed to follow. Supposedly, everyone has had her say and all have struggled freely over the political position in question. More often than not, you end up with a view that is the leadership's view and that does not best reflect all viewpoints or is not the best collective product you could achieve. Figuring things out democratically is not as quick, clean, or uncontested, but it is much more desirable than a top-down, follow-the-leader approach. We had ample examples of both approaches in our organization. There was a lot of democratic debate. Nevertheless, the structure of the national organization, modeled by local chapters, was far too hierarchical and did not promote the fullest democratic participation.

Following the repressive example of some communist parties on the international scene, the WVO at its inception and for years afterward condemned homosexuality as a bourgeois deviation. WVO recruited some avowed homosexuals into its ranks, notwithstanding this bias, if they were seen also as strong working-class fighters. But gays and lesbians were made to feel that they needed to "reform themselves" with respect to their sexual orientation. Finally, around 1979, criticism of the WVO's homophobic position led to its abandonment. The dismissal of the Equal Rights Amendment as a meaningless bourgeois reform was another position that alienated people, particularly feminists. In fact there were many political questions, on foreign policy and other issues, where complexity was lost, people were left out, and positions were adopted that led to self-defeating results for the organization and its goals.

Closely related to this issue of DC is the issue of sectarianism. If the positions that people work off of have been narrowed to the point that there is one correct line, it is easy to dismiss all people who depart from that line, however slightly, as wrong. We were creatures of our time, perhaps no worse than the other creatures of our time with respect to a sectarianism that was rife in the New Communist Movement. Yet, there it is. If the goal is to unite people, to become more inclusive, and to get the benefit of diverse intellects and points of view, then DC is not your best method nor are other hierarchical structures.

An example of a democratic centralist and sectarian style hurting our work was our writing off big sections of trade union officialdom. We were quick to paint all (or nearly all) trade union officials and politicians with one brush as agents of the bourgeoisie. The brushstroke was too broad. The officials could not be expected to wade through our propaganda and see our many virtues through our denunciations of them. The sweeping generalizations that we made may have shut down possibilities for strategic alliances that would have empowered workers. We might have recognized that even "misleaders" are sometimes willing to change their tack. Our stiff-necked polemical stance made united fronts difficult and isolated us from potential allies in the mainstream. This was true not only of potential allies in the labor movement, but also of ministers, civil libertarians, and other left, progressive forces, including other communist organizations. We wrote off too many people all over the place due to sectarianism. After November Third, we reaped what we had sown before November Third, and we had to win people over or win back allies under difficult conditions.

Among those we tended to rebuff were other communists. For example, the WVO took pains to delineate its political differences with the Communist Party USA. Of course, at the time there was a split in the world communist movement: any self-respecting communist activist was expected to side either with the Soviet Union or with China. It seemed inconceivable on ideological and political grounds for rival communist organizations to join forces. There are indeed valid reasons to differentiate organizations. Certainly, there are differences of principle that cannot and should not be glossed over. However, today I would try to minimize what keeps us apart. The will to unite should take precedence over a smug sectarianism.

WHAT ABOUT COMMUNISM? MORE
RETROSPECTIVE AND CRITICAL VIEWS

Most of us can speak critically, and with the benefit of hindsight, about the political journey we experienced together. Rev. Nelson Johnson no longer sees communism as offering the ultimate solution for humankind. Christianity has filled that role in his own life. But "Marxist views are helpful in understanding the capitalist economic system and now the global economy," he said in 1999, "and there is much in Marxism that I embrace." Marxism taught him how, "under capitalism, people are polarized into classes and the momentum is created for certain elite outlooks, undergirded by the ownership of wealth."

"For me," Nelson explained, "the down side of it is a tendency to analyze people in the same way that one analyzes commodities. People are very complex and have within them many possibilities and capabilities. The direction each of us takes is dependent on a lot of factors. It's not set in stone. Therefore, while the tendency of a group of people to behave as a class is unquestionable, the rigid structures and boxes that we established as guidelines for our movement and for our behavior downplayed the possibility of change for the other. We were not as good or as dedicated or as right as we sometimes claimed to be, and the others were often not as bad or as wrong. I think that oversimplification in that regard led to some flaws and errors. But in the main it was a positive and very meaningful learning experience."

"All right, Nelson," I said. "We committed ourselves together, we studied how society works together, and we acted together. But did all that have to be wedded to a particular theory, such as Marxism-Leninism Mao tse-Tung Thought?" In putting these questions to Nelson many years later, I was remembering the countless times that workers, friends, or relatives said to me that *they really liked what we were doing, but did we have to call ourselves communists?* That word confused people terribly.

"Communism, as a worldview, does not express my outlook," Nelson frankly acknowledged. To explain why, he goes back to the biblical roots of the term. "In the second chapter of the Book of Acts, the first Christians sold all they had and shared all things in common. However, this root understanding of a community of shared beliefs and shared resources according to need is far from what the word *communism* has come to mean in popular culture.

"It has been almost impossible to convey any real understanding of what we were about by using the word *communism* to describe ourselves," he continued, "and so I see it as a mistake. It was thoroughly exploited by the powers-that-be to misrepresent us. I have been reluctant to express these criticisms publicly because the powers have elevated these mistakes to a primary role in explaining what happened on November 3rd and thereby tried to hide their own role. They have presented our language as the primary cause of what happened on November 3, 1979, and that is not true. They have used the basest presentation of communism to define and demonize us, and that also is not true to who we were in 1979 and who we are today."

The powerful indoctrination of anticommunism in American cultural life presented all of us in the New Communist Movement with a dilemma that had no perfect solution. I believe that if the WVO had executed the same actions under a banner other than communism, its members and friends still would have been castigated. Rev. Martin Luther King, a religious pacifist, was attacked and vilified as a communist anyway. If, as I argue above, we were successfully contending for power with the aim of transferring power from an elite ruling class to the people, we were vulnerable to attack no matter what we wrote on the banner under which we marched.

Our political activities, our study, our organizing, all took place in a brief span of time and were *due to the initiative of a handful of revolutionaries*. But a revolutionary handful, however good, could only make things happen because there was a *mass awakening* going on, to which the revolutionaries were related both as cause and effect. The amount and variety of grassroots activity in which the WVO/CWP and associated groups like ALSC were involved signified *thousands of people in motion*, trying to do something about their fate and effectively *supporting fundamental structural change* to address intolerable social and economic problems. Nelson and I have talked about how powerful the planned march and conference on November 3, 1979, would have been had it been allowed to take its course. We had many friends and supporters in Greensboro, and the struggle against the Klan and for workers' rights was truly becoming mass based. The potential was enormous.

The workers' potential to change the fundamental social relations of power was clear *to the bourgeoisie*. Perhaps it was not as clear to us, or we did not recognize that it was to them. I think that we had more power than we realized at the time, that we did not fully appreciate the people's power as it was developing through the work in the mills, hospitals, and communities; hence, we did not realize what a serious threat that power posed to the ruling elite.

We did not listen carefully to our own thoughts and pronouncements. In September 1979, in reading about the United Racist Front, I said that the Klan probably had our pictures and was doing target practice on them! Also in 1979, Jim said to me that the bourgeoisie would throw the Klan at us every time we were successful in organizing workers, that they would use the Klan to stop our drive for a worker-controlled trade union movement! And Nelson said, shortly before November Third, that the police were more dangerous than the Klan, because the police can murder us *legally*! It was all penetratingly true. Why weren't we listening to ourselves? Perhaps a more useful question for future activists is how do you continue to organize when you are likely to become a victim of your very success? The short answer is—you continue to organize.

The most impressive aspect of the WVO/CWP was the multinationality at the core of the organization. The WVO attracted people of every race, background, and religion, including a very significant proportion of people who came from the working class. The organization was started by Asian Americans, who continued to be well represented in it: in some areas of the country, an observer would conclude it was primarily Asian. Elsewhere, an observer generalizing from her perceptions would take the WVO to be primarily an African American organization. Still elsewhere, it was more white, or more Chicano or Latino than anything else. We were a rainbow before Jesse Jackson uttered the word. In this respect, the WVO/CWP is worth emulating today.

After all the kudos and criticisms, especially as they relate to the Greensboro Massacre of November 3, 1979, it must be said that in spite of our mistakes and shortcomings, it was right to take a stand and to struggle. As Nelson said, "the greatest mistake we could have made would have been to stand on the sideline and pretend that the exploitation and abuse of poor and working people and the rising racism reflected by the Klan and Nazis were insignificant and minor considerations."

I must apologize to those readers who have read this far in hopes of finding either my ultimate embrace or my ultimate rejection of communism. The issue is a complex one and, in any case, I would never presume to legislate for other people in their unique struggles, in their particular countries, at particular historical moments. A banner that did not fly in the United States in the last two decades of the twentieth century might fly elsewhere. On the other hand, *communism* is a term full of historical content, and that content includes, among other things, a hierarchical and centralized organizational structure and an attitude toward the environment that is no more forgiving than that under capitalism. It is not easy (as we learned) to say, "I don't mean *that* by communism, I mean *this*," and to define one's way into popular acceptance.

Today, people all over the world are facing historically unprecedented challenges; these are transformational times for the human race. War, racism and other institutional oppressions, and ecological devastation threaten all living organisms on the planet. What makes us think that humans will not be near the top of the endangered species list, if we are not already there? In order to survive, we will have to be fast learners, we will have to be far more radical than we were in the past, and we will surely need to break with centuries-old attitudes of domination toward nature and our fellow creatures. Some things will have to become sacred again. We will have to wean ourselves from a century-old oil-based economy. In the cultures of indigenous peoples, whose lives and livelihoods are today being destroyed so rapidly through the globalization of capital, I can see a path to future survival more clearly than I can see it either in the old-style communist state or the corporate capitalist one.

THINGS FALL APART, THE CENTER WILL NOT HOLD

The Communist Workers Party is no more. Even its successor organization, the New Democratic Movement, has disbanded. Shortly before the civil suit ended, the CWP met in New York City and agreed on a second major metamorphosis in its organizational life. The first was the transition from the Workers Viewpoint Organization to the Communist Workers Party. At the founding conference of the CWP in October 1979, Jim was elected to the organization's Central Committee. The CWP's North Carolina debut was to have been at the November 3 forum, in the afternoon, immediately following the anti-Klan rally. Murder most foul stopped that event. The transition to the New Democratic Movement (NDM) was completed in 1985, shortly after the verdict in the civil suit.

The New Democratic Movement's aim was a broad, progressive membership of both communists and noncommunists. Its goal was to bring people together around a program for a postindustrial, democratic society. In 1984 and 1985, CWP members recognized that great changes were taking place in communist bloc countries. We studied together and reassessed our own organization and the need to be more mass-based, especially if we expected to succeed in bringing about fundamental, positive social change. We started looking at local power models. Some NDM members contributed good theoretical work outlining the exciting possibilities of postindustrialism for realizing a genuinely democratic society. The improved reading diet now consisted not just of Marx, Lenin, and Mao, but also of Antonio Gramsci, Robert Reich, and many others. However, NDM floundered. The old habits of a communist-style, democratic-centralist organizational structure died hard and internal strife alienated some good people.

Adjusting to life outside the trenches was very rough for me and took years. In 1987, I left Greensboro and moved to the Midwest. I worked with the NDM for the duration and was among the last to leave the sinking ship in 1990.

THE LEGACY LIVES

The Greensboro Justice Fund is the living legacy of the Greensboro Massacre, born of that tragic and violent incident of national shame.[3] In 1985, when plaintiffs in the civil rights suit returned a portion of the jury's award to the GJF, the small endowment of $75,000 launched a nonprofit peoples' foundation that has been helping to sustain the movement for racial, social, and economic justice in the South ever since. I joined the GJF Board of Directors in 1991, one of several widows and survivors of November 3, 1979, on the board.

From first-year grants in 1986 totaling $1,200, by the turn of the millennium the GJF was giving away around $50,000 a year. As our guidelines state: "The Greensboro Justice Fund supports grassroots organizations and activists in the South that work for economic justice, workers' rights, political empowerment, and an end to racism, homophobic discrimination and violence, religious intolerance, police brutality, right-wing attacks, and environmental injustice. The GJF particularly supports groups that seek to address root causes of economic and social injustice and that develop links between issues and across diverse communities. We search for work that is a model for other communities and for the nation in the struggle against racism, bigotry, discrimination, and exploitation and that contributes to building a progressive social movement."

I returned to Greensboro for six months in 1999 to help the GJF organize and coordinate the Twentieth Anniversary Commemoration of the Greensboro Massacre. (By then I was a cancer survivor as well as a massacre survivor.) In the intervening years, I made many short trips back to the city, but in 1999, I was struck anew by how Greensboro had become a metropolis, with sprawling suburbs. Gone was the sleepy little mill city with a small-town feeling that I encountered in 1971. Haphazard, profit-driven city planning had built a city devoid of charm. I was bothered by the stark contrasts between the haves and the have-nots. Pockets of graceful, genteel culture and pleasant verdant tracts existed amid much larger splotches of urban decay—particularly where people of color resided, African Americans and Native Americans now joined by Southeast Asian and Latino immigrants. Poor service workers had replaced poor blue collar workers. The obscene gap between the few superwealthy and an impoverished many had continued to widen, just as it had in most American cities.

Since 1979, the Greensboro Massacre has been a reference point for all struggles involving race and labor relations in the city. In the mid 1990s, after years of struggle, predominantly black workers at a Kmart distribution center in Greensboro were able to obtain a union contract. Nelson Johnson's moral and strategic contribution to that effort was a poignant reminder of the thread connecting Kmart workers with the union organizers at Cone Mills who were murdered by the Klansmen and Nazis. Kmart workers organized under UNITE!—the Union of Needletrades and Industrial and Textile Employees. Ironically, that union is a descendent of ACTWU. Nelson helped Kmart workers build a strong labor–community coalition that had active support from area churches, civic leaders, students, and other citizens. At critical points, workers and their supporters engaged in civil disobedience. (Upon my return to Greensboro, I met an elderly church-going white lady who was proud of being arrested for the first time in her life, along with black ministers from the Pulpit Forum, at a sit-in for the Kmart workers.) Vital issues involved in the workers' struggle were discussed throughout the city and were aired at a large, televised town hall meeting. What were the working conditions at Kmart really like? Was the corporate bottom line the same as the community's bottom line? Did the community want to attract jobs *at any cost*? Were jobs that paid less than a living wage, that added to the ranks of the working poor, or that exacerbated race relations desirable? The Kmart Corporation was unable to marginalize union supporters because of the high degree of community solidarity with the workers.

Reverend Nelson Johnson's uninterrupted influence as a long-standing civil rights leader, a massacre survivor, and the city's moral conscience is enshrined in much of whatever uplift Greensboro has managed to achieve for over three decades. Between the Christian minister of today and the communist leader of yesterday, I see no vulgar denial or reversal, but rather the flowering and fulfillment of a great human destiny. Nelson's vision for humanity is demonstrated by the Beloved Community Center, a multiracial organization inspired by the dream of the Reverend Martin Luther King Jr. Nelson is joined by the retired Presbyterian minister Reverend Z. Holler and dozens of other Greensboro citizens from various walks of life. They are professionals, religious and community leaders, and business people, all with standing in the larger community as "movers and shakers," people with widespread respect who tend to get things done. They are the allies you want to have and need to have to transform a barren landscape of despair into a flourishing city of love and hope.

Other strong community organizing in which Nelson played a leading role freed Kwame Cannon after thirteen years in prison. Kwame, son of Willena Cannon, was ten years old when his mother took him to the anti-Klan rally at Morningside Homes in 1979. Eight years later, he was given two consecutive life sentences for unarmed burglaries that he committed when he was seventeen years old. The dual motives of racism and revenge against Kwame's mother must be assumed in accounting for the excessively harsh sentencing. He was a juvenile offender led to illegal acts by an older relative, and his petty theft crime of less than a thousand dollars involved no weapons or physical injuries. Willena, a tireless organizer of antiracist and antipolice brutality activities over many years, was well known as one of the organizers of the 1979 anti-Klan rally.

Kwame symbolized the plight of tens of thousands of oppressed and disproportionately incarcerated black youth. The Committee to Free Kwame Cannon persisted for years, sending thousands of letters to Governor Jim Hunt and other officials requesting Kwame's release. On the thirtieth anniversary of the assassination of Dr. Martin Luther King Jr. in April 1998, a large Greensboro contingent joined a demonstration in Raleigh, and over eight hundred people demanded Kwame's freedom. Kwame was freed on March 31, 1999.

When I returned to Greensboro in May 1999, Nelson and many others in the city were working to get a Citizen Police Review Board, one with subpoena powers to curb brutal or illegal actions by the police, which were still a problem. Nelson also designed and put together a visionary project, Jubilee 2000. It spoke to comprehensive reforms in the criminal justice system and to fostering humane communities to which incarcerated youth could return and be provided with education, compassionate nurturing, job skills, and employment.

The Greensboro Justice Fund and the Beloved Community Center cosponsored the Twentieth Anniversary Commemoration of the Greensboro Massacre. The theme was truth and reconciliation. The commemoration was a huge teach-in for the city that made a retreat to lies and ignorance more difficult and less acceptable than ever. Greensboro *did* turn a corner in coming to terms with its past. Various commemorative programs were held in Durham, New York, Washington, Los Angeles, and San Francisco, but Greensboro was the soul-wrenching hub of the prolonged activity. Months of education, argument, conversations, prayer, and organizing preceded the culminating weekend of November 5 through November 7. The Greensboro Massacre was commemorated in art, film, and theatrical production. Congregations, rich and poor, white and black, were involved. Hundreds of activists, artists, writers, theologians, teachers, political figures, and ordinary citizens contributed to an extraordinary project that did much more than reexamine the past; it insisted that history serve present life. The area's major colleges and universities—UNC, Guilford College, A & T State University in Greensboro, and Duke University in Durham—sponsored forums and lectures at which Professor Sally Bermanzohn, Professor Claude Barnes, Rev. Henry Atkins, Emily Mann, and Professor Bill Chafe, among others, spoke.

At one point, a group from the Beloved Community Center was invited to dialogue with editors of the local newspaper, and I went along. Nelson patiently reviewed the main facts about November Third and politely challenged the editors and managers to be self-critical and acknowledge that they contributed to a false and misleading picture of events. There was a discussion after which we felt very encouraged: the media people appeared to be listening. We felt that if they could be self-critical vis-à-vis coverage about November 3, 1979, they would be able to serve people better on *every* issue of the moment; it would be a real breakthrough. We thought that we were making some progress, but the small window of opportunity—during which the *News & Record* published a piece that I wrote several weeks before the main commemorative events—closed decisively.

The main event in the commemoration was a forum at Bennett College on November 6 called "Learning the Lessons: The Greensboro Massacre in Perspective." Hundreds of people packed into the Bennett College Chapel. One month after open-heart surgery, his gift of oratory undiminished, Nelson told the capacity audience, "In a strange way, the spirits of Bill Sampson, César Cauce, Jim Waller, Michael Nathan, and Sandi Smith have convened us. I want to report to those five spirits, wherever you are, 'a luta continua'—the struggle continues!" The forum was certainly a major event for Greensboro, with several distinguished speakers whose presence in the city could easily be tagged as front-page news. But the newspaper blacked it out. About a week before the major commemorative events, coverage of the commemoration dropped off the pages of the paper as from a cliff into an abyss. The local newspaper failed to cover Nelson's impassioned speech of November 6, 1999, and four other moving talks that evening as well. The paper ignored Professor Manning Marable, the director of the Institute for Research in African American Studies at Columbia University; Robert Meeropol, one of two sons of Julius and Ethel Rosenberg; law professor Lani Guinier of Harvard University; and veteran civil rights activist and codirector of the Southern Organizing Committee, Anne Braden. Each speaker was impressive in putting November Third into historical perspective and in drawing out lessons from his or her experience and wisdom for the continuing struggle. Many things will have to change before the mass media is transformed from the voice of corporate America to the people's voice.

HEALING BROKEN PLACES WHILE TRYING TO KEEP A REVOLUTIONARY EDGE IS HARD

I was in Greensboro to facilitate a collective experience, but gratefully accepted each opportunity to heal some broken places in my own heart. One peaceful interlude was a tree planting ceremony at Bennett College, one of several inspiring programs on that campus, led by Reverend Shirley Canty. Six trees were set in the ground, one for each of the five people killed in 1979, and one to honor the continuing dedication of Nelson Johnson.

When he was a divinity student in the mid-eighties, Nelson met several times with a group of Klansmen, including Virgil Griffin, in an effort to persuade the Klan to call off a planned march in Greensboro. The Klansmen even, at Nelson's initiative, knelt and prayed together with him. Maybe the very imperfect communication that took place, with the Klan quickly making a suspicious retreat, had some positive or moderating effect on people whose history has been one of extreme xenophobia and violence. And maybe it did not. Nelson was courageous to go, unarmed and unaccompanied, into that lair.

It was a different situation, and perhaps a more personal motivation, that led me to seek a meeting with Eddie Dawson when I returned to Greensboro in 1999. I met the old and ill ex-Klansman in a cafeteria in a mall, and we talked for about an hour and a half. I took a reporter whom I befriended from the *News & Record* along with me, for moral support. To persuade him to agree to the meeting, I told Dawson two things: I do not hate you, and I would like to learn more about how things happened on November Third. Both were true. I thought it unlikely, but possible, that I would learn something new. I think that I arranged to see Dawson out of feelings occasioned by past wounds, feelings that were leading me to a dead-end, but I'm not sure. The reporter and I did not learn anything new from a man who was very disabled, very old, very mediocre, but nevertheless a bearer of the human condition—keeping in mind that he was a bearer of the human condition helped me. Listening to Dawson was like hearing a broken record, its needle stuck in a groove of tired, familiar sounds. I reflected later that evil means *being stuck* and hope lies in *getting unstuck*. I talked to Nelson about the experience afterward. (He was supposed to go, too, but could not at the last minute.) Nelson reminded me that hatred destroys the soul of the hater, not the hated. (After November Third, I hated the Klan, the Nazis, and their government backers, such as Schlosser among others, so much that I had visions of being part of the firing squad after they were condemned to death.) I realized after I talked to Dawson, in a way that I had not realized before, that I cannot revisit November Third in terms of changing what anyone did at that time.

My partners in class struggle and I can never revisit a past that embodied so magnificently our passion for justice and our willingness for self-sacrifice. We struggled together for a collective dream, joyously, naively. Today, we are blessed with caring relationships with one another; our rainbow community of love and trust stood the test of time and distance and has grown to include many others. In the GJF of today, our immortal ideals have form and substance. Closure for

November Third comes from grasping that we chart our paths here and now. However we do it, that path must lead to loving human communities around the globe.

It took twenty years, but finally Kaddish (Jewish prayer for the dead) was said at Maplewood Cemetery for the five vicitms by Rabbi Guttman. A special engraving by world-famous artist Leonard Baskin was the logo for the commemoration program. A statuesque figure of Justice stands holding flowers; at the hem of her skirt are clustered the heads of five martyrs. Baskin, a close friend of Marty and Elliot, was terminally ill when he completed the drawing. He died not long afterward.

Emily Mann's "Greensboro: A Requiem," sensitively and powerfully directed by Marsha Paludan, associate professor of theatre at the University of North Carolina in Greensboro, was performed on the campus from November 3 through 7. Some two thousand people, most of them local Greensboro residents, came to see it. Watching it for the second time, I found its impact amplified many times by the venue. A public forum followed the opening night performance on November 3, and most of the audience remained in their seats to talk about the play and the events represented in it. Several people testified to the profound effect the play had on them. The play was the centerpiece of an interdepartmental curriculum that Marsha Paludan and others at the university made available to the larger community, a curriculum dedicated to eradicating racism.

Prior to rehearsals, I was invited to meet the student cast of the play. They were eager to hear a firsthand account of the situation and to meet the people whom they were about to portray. It was a wonderful experience for me. The students were open and naturally curious. Their questions were hard and honest. They really wanted to learn. It was a pleasure to talk to them. Later I had a similar reaction in talking to a group of Jewish youth at a local synagogue on the invitation of Rabbi Guttman.

Among the many new friends I made on returning to Greensboro was a young UNC-G faculty member, Michael Friarson, who did the technical, multimedia work on the production of Emily's play. The projection of images on stage was one of many superbly executed details in Paludan's direction of the play. Michael was the son of a retired local FBI agent. Not just any FBI agent—his father had been Eddie Dawson's control agent some years before the Greensboro Massacre occurred.

A thrilling finale to the commemoration was an ecumenical service at Nelson's church on November 7. Ministers representing various denominations participated, among them the rabbi. The church rocked and rolled. People left in a state of elation approaching intoxication, but none had imbibed any chemical substance—exposure to the normal workings of love, faith, and truth, experienced in community with others, created the high.

One of the most valuable things that I did with my time in Greensboro was to help organize and carry out the *Night of a Thousand Conversations*. The project was proposed by Lewis Brandon, Nelson, and Z and sponsored by the Beloved Community Center. This event took place all over the city on the evening of October 7, 1999. Groups large and small gathered in churches and private homes, at community centers and on campuses, to hold conversations about what happened twenty years before, what could be learned from it, and where we are today in the struggle against racism and economic injustice.

We held training sessions for people who volunteered to be facilitators. The facilitators received copies of a GJF brochure written by Marty and Paul, "Justice and the Greensboro Massacre." The brochure is useful in condensing the story of the Greensboro Massacre for both the informed and the uninitiated. Our trainees also received a one-page fact sheet. Each was given a short video essay, "The Guns of November Third," made by cameraman turned priest Jim Waters. An award-winning photo journalist who owned a couple of Emmys, Waters, as noted earlier, was on the scene in 1979 and recorded the assault as it took place. His life was profoundly changed by that experience. We used his dramatic, thought-provoking video essay as a conversation starter on October 7.

We managed to set up about two dozen gatherings with hundreds of people participating around the city. Afterward, everyone came together informally over refreshments at a downtown art gallery. The *Night of a Thousand Conversations* was a giant civics lesson for Greensboro.

The last month and a half of my Greensboro stay, I lived with Z (Rev. Holler) and his wife, Charlene. Z shared with me his experience about the Greensboro Massacre; he was then an active minister in Greensboro. There was no funeral parlor in town that was willing to bury our people. Indeed, I remembered this situation as Z recounted it—everyone was driven away from us, and we could not even bury our dead! Our status as *the enemy* was epic. In this hate-filled environment, Z interceded and persuaded a funeral parlor—as a white minister, he went to a black-owned business—to officiate at the funerals of Bill, Jim, César, and Mike. He did not do it out of a special love for the CWP. He did it because he felt that it was his Christian duty. At the time he accepted, as so many good people did, the pervasive propaganda the media was putting out about how November Third was a shootout between two extremist, violent groups—the Klan and the Communists. He remembers thinking—a plague on both your houses!

Z and Charlene hosted a group on the *Night of a Thousand Conversations*, but I did not go there. Instead, I dropped in at a couple of other gatherings. I was invited to a conversation in the home of a prominent Jewish family. Among some twenty people in attendance, there were a few there whom I had viewed previously as hostile to me—or maybe I was hostile toward them. The atmosphere was congenial, and we sat around a long table. I met a man who had been one of the managers at White Oak in the 1970s—he had regularly butted heads with Bill Sampson. Bill was usually right, he conceded, when he fought a grievance. An enlightening moment occurred that very same evening when the elderly former editor of the newspaper, under whose tenure the mythology of a shootout achieved the status of an official truth, whispered an aside into my ear. "It was a massacre, Signe," he said, "it wasn't a shootout, it was a massacre." Just what I needed—vindication twenty years after the fact and *sotto voce*.

At Maplewood Cemetery, where four of the five slain in 1979 are buried, markers are so placed that you might imagine that the spirits of the dead are having a meeting around a table (as in their lives they often did). Imagine them engaging in lively conversation, debating, arguing, laughing, drinking too much coffee. Of course their spirits are doing none of these things. It is for us, the living, to have lively conversations, argue, laugh, and drink too much coffee. There is work for us to do. Roll up your shirt-sleeves and begin. We are convened by martyrs.

NOTES

1. On-camera interview in Alvarez and Jung, *Red November, Black November*.

2. See Emily Mann, "Greensboro: A Requiem," in *Testimonies: Four Plays* (New York: Theatre Communications Group, 1997).

3. To visit the Greensboro Justice Fund on the internet, visit www.gjf.org.

APPENDIXES

APPENDIX A

**DIARY OF DR. JAMES WALLER
AT THE SIEGE OF WOUNDED KNEE**

April 30, 1973

Things sometimes move slowly. Things sometimes move fast. Rain falls over the Pine Ridge Reservation. We pack IV solutions and medicines that will be smuggled in. We engage in minor espionage with the puzzled druggists. There is a war going on and we are in the rear lines. We react to rumors, false alarms, try to imagine, but can't really.

I haven't prayed in years, but I prayed last night. We walked up a high hill in single file as the sun was setting, led by Henry Crow Dog and a nun. At the top of the hill was a small cedar tree, adorned with feathers, beads and indecipherable objects. At the base of the young tree was the sacred pipe. The pipe is very special. It's a living being. The bowl is red like blood and the smoke from it flows down the broad stream filling your spirit with power. The nun picked up the pipe and we all followed again down the hill. By this time it was dark. Henry Crow Dog assembled us about a hundred fifty in a large circle. He took the pipe and pointed it in all six directions and then began to chant. We prayed silently. Then I went to a sweat with Henry Crow Dog and five other men.

The sweat lodge is like a small hemisphere about 4 feet high and 5 feet in diameter. It is covered with layers of thick tarps and skins. There is a small slit to crawl through. Inside there is a pit 2 feet in diameter which is filled with glowing hot rocks. (This very faint glow is the only light since the slit is closed.) The seven naked men sit cross-legged around the pit silent in almost total darkness. The air outside is cold, but the rocks warm up the hut and we are comfortable. Then Henry Crow Dog ladles some water on to the rocks and steam hisses and the temperature rapidly rises to about 180 degrees Fahrenheit. My lungs and eyes are scalded. Salty warm liquid rolls down my face into my mouth. Breathing is almost impossible. Then he does it again and a third time. We sit silently like steamed clams.

Miraculously, Henry Crow Dog begins to chant. He ignites various leaves on the hot rocks. He prays to all his relations. He is a priest conducting a mass and after each part we respond with "Ho." The sweat continues to gush as Henry continues to pour the water on the hot rocks. We all pray silently for the victory of the brave warriors in Wounded Knee, for the restoration of harmony between man and the rest of the land, for liberation of all oppressed people. Crow Dog's chants continue as we labor to breathe. It takes great effort to say "Ho." Water and salt from my body mingle with the vapor of the rocks—the sweat of the other men and the water and salt of the earth. My head feels very light. Then Crow Dog stops chanting abruptly and opens the flap allowing the cool air to enter. He gives us each some water which we drink and pour over ourselves, gratefully proclaiming "to all my relations." The others say "Ho." When we have all finished he closes the flap, turns on the heat and begins chanting again. Another Indian also sings some songs.

The songs are very rhythmical with a wide range of tunes. They have a blowing quality of not really being produced by human effort, but more like wind blowing through the trees—Aolian harps. After awhile we (non-Indians) begin to join in. We generate power together forgetting the heat and the liquid rolling off our bodies. Henry opens up the slit a second time and brings in the sacred pipe. He touches both ends to the hot rocks and raises both ends to the sky. We pass the pipe around three times. After each one smokes he says "to all my relations." The others respond with "Ho." After each passage I realize my increasing relatedness to all things. This is why I'm here—because I am related to these people. I am related to the land they are trying to protect. I am related to the harmony which they maintain with nature.

After the pipe has circled three times, Crow Dog closes the slit a third time. He heats the lodge and begins to chant. And then finally the rocks have lost most of their heat. We leave saying "to all my relations" as we re-enter the cold night air. We stand naked around a fire and are cleansed.

***

It's hard to describe my activities as part of the medical team on the outside. We have organized the supplies and are assembling packs to go in each night. I have gone around to the various drug stores to buy narcotics and have seen people with feet aches and earaches, back aches and stomach aches and nerve aches. I have very little to offer but assurance. This is of no small value in this community. People are nervous and confused, waiting for something to happen. I too am waiting and help others wait.

This is a resistance movement. The people within Wounded Knee are fighting against a repeat of history. They are without sanitation, good food, pure water or electricity. Their main meeting place was burned down yesterday. They sleep in cramped quarters. Respiratory and diarrheal diseases are epidemic.

***

For me the most important aspect is feeling that I'm offering some support to my valiant relations at Wounded Knee. I'm assured by my comrades that I am and I believe it (for now).

May 3, 1973

Land on the Pine Ridge Reservation is never tiresome. There are multitudes of shapes and feelings. Gullies and gorges criss-cross with sometimes soft and sometimes hard intersections. On the rolling hills, cattle and horses graze and every so often a haystack protrudes, breaking the rhythm. Wind and rain have eroded the chalky sandstone into surprising sculptures. The telephone wires and fences of the large ranches hiss, but are drowned out by the soft and persistent murmur of the Black Hills.

The history of the people who inhabit this land goes back at least a thousand years and is unknown to me. In recent years, the tribes of the Sioux Nation have suffered genocide by the forces of U.S. imperialism and racism. Where once they lived in harmony with this awesome land and the other creatures inhabiting it, today they depend on the U.S. government for welfare checks. They are largely unemployed, malnourished, with a high rate of preventable diseases and prenatal mortality. The numerous white churches do nothing to improve the tar paper shacks.

The economy of the reservation is strictly exploitative and tourism dollars go to the whites. Rapid City contractors make money off new construction. The liquor stores do a booming business (even though there is to be no drinking on the reservation). And the white ranchers now own much of the reservation land and use it for fattening their herds.

The politics follows the rip-off economy. [Former South Dakota senator and 1972 Democratic presidential candidate] McGovern is supported by and financed by the ranchers. The BIA [Bureau of Indian Affairs] is the government agency to run the reservation and to implement the exploitation for a cut of the take.

You can't tell the players without a scorecard. The line-up is something like this:

For the government:
Helstrom, main negotiator
Frizell, Solicitor General for the Interior (the one doing the negotiating)
Coburn, Chief of Marshals
Wilson, Tribal Chief, Head of the BIA
CRS [Community Relations Service], "Third World troubleshooters," employed
    by the Justice Department to calm down third world people.
Lurking everywhere, the FBI.

For the Indians:
The traditional chiefs, Fools Crow, Bud Cobb, and Kills Enemy
Medicine men, Crow Dog and Black Elk
AIM [American Indian Movement], Dennis Banks and Carter Camp
Oglala leadership inside

Just what the substance of the negotiations are, I'm not sure, but basically it centers around the land and self-government, which has been stripped from the Indians.

In Wounded Knee, the struggle for regaining the land and self-government has been raised to armed struggle. However, at this moment, Pine Ridge has all the qualities of a bad Fellini movie. Enemies sit cordially with each other. Blue jump-suited marshals parade around with feathers in their hair. Bearded CBS newsmen lounge in the grass looking like FBI. There is a monosyllabic, anemic, deliberately non-committal doctor at the public health hospital. Beverly slouches over a chair. Ramon slumps back. People wait in silence for something to happen. Sometimes they are not sure why they are waiting. The goon squad lurks in the shadows.

An old Indian with yellow teeth and a face reflecting the land has a light of expectation in his eyes which cannot be dimmed by alcohol. He knows what's happening.

APPENDIX B

Haw River, North Carolina, 13 August 1978

Fellow Workers, Brothers and Sisters, We've said it before and we say it again today—The workers united will never be defeated. Just six weeks ago today we stood here on these steps. We stood up as human beings and said we were fed up. That's right, fed up with the slavery of Cone Mills, the starvation wages, dangerous working conditions, poor benefits and pay cuts that are called "wage adjustments." We said we were going to stick together and fight for a better life for ourselves and our families. We said we were going to build up our union as an organization to accomplish all these goals. And we unleashed a powerful strike that hurt Cone's profits and shook the foundation of Cone Mills. Management was scared and desperate, so they hit back at us through their control of the Sheriff's Department with arrests and their control of the court with an injunction. And we went about the difficult and important task of organizing our army and continued fighting. After twelve days of fighting we had the beginnings of a strong union. Seeing what we had accomplished, when we looked at the facts and saw we couldn't stop the drift, it was clear that our best move was to retreat in order to keep what we had built so we could return and fight again.

When we said we were retreating and not surrendering, we weren't kidding. And the company soon found that.... they had a real union on their hands. And they [tried to] bust the union by getting rid of me. They dug into my past and found out that I had falsified my application two years ago. But getting rid of me won't and can't bust the union. . . . We don't intend to go back to having a weak, small union that goes along with what the company wants.

Now some people are saying, "What are we going to do without Blackbeard? Woe is me." First of all, old Blackbeard isn't going anywhere. Instead of wasting eight hours a day making profits for Mr. Cone, I will now have eight more hours a day to work on building a union while I fight to get my job back. Second of all, let's say they did get rid of me completely. The union will continue to grow. There are other experienced leaders and many new leaders have stepped forward in the strike and are rapidly becoming seasoned veterans. What it comes down to is that the people is the union. Getting rid of one man will not and can not change that. So our future is bright. We are going forward to build our union.

We have no other choice. The struggle that we're in is inevitable under capitalism, because a small number of men like the Cones, R. J. Reynolds, the Dukes, and the Rockefellers own and control everything. They always try to reduce our wages, pay us as little as possible, because the less they give us the more profit they make. . . .

We saw in the strike how important organization is. . . . When we go as individuals or small groups it signifies our enslavement. But when we went out together as workers united we ceased to be slaves. We became masters of our own lives and saw that we, the producers, are the real masters. . . . This strikes fear in the hearts of the capitalists and undermines their rule. We also saw how the courts and the police are not neutral, even though they pretend to be. . . . We must [continue to] overcome divisions like black against white. These divisions only serve Cone.

We saw in the strike that we were not alone. Other union locals came and supported us, gave us money, words of encouragement and walked the picket line. We saw Cone workers from White Oak, Eno, Revolution and Tabadrey. And workers from Duke and L. & M., City workers, Western Electric, Traders Chevrolet all say the same thing. They knew what we were fighting because they were fighting it also. This is because our fight in Haw River is part of a fight of the entire working class. Right now, 30 miles on either side of us there are strikes. Traders is in its 8th week, Goldkist in its 4th. In the past month, there have been strikes from one end of North Carolina to the other, Wilmington to Asheville. . . . All of us are fighting attacks on our standard of living. And we in Haw River are part of this larger picture. It's this tiny bunch of bloodsucking capitalists that is our common enemy and we workers can only depend on ourselves and united action to fight them. . . .

Each time we take on the company we do it better because we understand just how this thing works. It's this understanding that is our powerful tool. . . . For example, it was correct to continue staying out on July 10th and correct to go back in on July 11th. Now what difference did twenty-four hours make? Well, it was being able to draw out the lessons of the previous strikes in 1951 and 1964, that they had been disastrous for the union because the people ended up thinking the union was no good. By fighting as hard as we could to stop the drift, the workers ourselves learned through our own experience what was correct and decided to go back together. We went back as a union determined to build it up, determined to return to fight again. And this is what we are about today, to continue the struggle to build our union, our fighting force. Cone tries to bust it, and we fight back.

Several workers have asked me, why would a doctor go to work in a cotton mill. The company has made a big deal about it and slandered me, saying I have "hidden motives." It wasn't as if I told them I could do a welding job. Then after three months they found out I couldn't weld, that I had lied on my application that I had the skill. No. As one worker said, as unsafe as the working conditions are, they should have been glad to have a doctor. They didn't fire me because I'm a doctor or because I lied. They only fired me because they thought they can destroy the union all of us are building. That's their motive. They're the ones trying to hide their motives.

But my motives were never hidden from the workers. When I first came down here I told people, and more importantly I showed them with my actions, what I stood for—organizing the workers, uniting the workers, educating the workers, building the union, fighting the company. . . . I came to work in a cotton mill, because I stand shoulder to shoulder with the workers in our fight against Cone and others of his kind. . . .

When I first came to North Carolina over three and a half years ago, I met textile workers while organizing the Carolina Brown Lung Association. Do you know what Brown Lung disease is? After you give 35 or 40 of your best years to make profits for the textile owners you become a cripple, unable to walk across the room without gasping for breath. And the only reason is that they care more about their profits than the health and safety of the workers. . . . I learned a lot through meeting workers [suffering from brown lung]. I no longer wanted to continue to make my living doctoring. I went to work in a textile mill to join this fight. That's my hidden motive.

Workers want to know how I'm going to get my job back. . . . We should have no illusions that Cone is going to give in easy. Before it's over we may well be fighting for other jobs back. It's going to be a long fight and a hard fight. And we must prepare ourselves for it. Are we going to give up? The answer to this question is not separate from the answer to the question what do we do to build the union. Whether I get my job back or not, . . . our main weapon is not the court, but the organization and unity of the people. We will continue to train shop stewards, file grievances, sign up new members, educate ourselves about what a trade union is and how it works, and raise money. At the right time, we'll hit the company again, this time many times harder than the last.

So, fellow workers, our future is bright. We are seeing how the slogan "The workers united will never be defeated" is not just words. We are putting it into practice. . . . We have already accomplished a great deal. Onward to further victories!

APPENDIX C

THE PERSONAL IS POLITICAL:
LETTERS, POEMS, AND SPEECHES

In the immediate aftermath of the November 3, 1979, attack, Jim Waller's friends burned many of his papers, thinking to protect those working with him in the event of further attacks. Inadvertently, they destroyed much of our personal correspondence. Below are some letters and poems that remained. (The last entry was written by my son after the Greensboro Massacre.)

Letter, 17 September 1977

Dear Jim,

September morning: This is the time of year when mornings get darker. Driving to the hospital parking lot, the asphalt is glistening with night rain and morning mist. It is five minutes to seven. Ten more minutes and the quality of light will change, from brown to light blue-gray. Morning freshness pervades everything.

I think how we struggle and how my love for you gives me more hope and confidence. So much is crying to be done. For centuries people have struggled against the oppression of class society. We will not achieve the liberation of mankind this minute. The tasks were handed to us in a certain shape. We will develop things, carry them further, carry them as far as we can. One day the oppressive and exploitative social relations in my workplace will change. One day the national question will be a problem of the past. The workers themselves will dictate the production policy in your plant. We, or perhaps our children, will be doing the tasks that objectively society needs and subjectively they need to do. Before you can heal, before I can teach, much work needs to be done. Here I am in a hospital, a place I never liked to be in, doing a minor technical job, for which I do not have the necessary background, training and inclination. There you are in a factory, lifting, sweeping, removing wheels and pushing trucks. What are we to make of this topsy-turvy state of affairs? We are doing these things because we have not yet overthrown the bourgeoisie. We are sped up, stretched out and oppressed, and must, under these conditions, where we are in an almost chronic state of fatigue, make revolution . . . and liberate the masses and ourselves. Signe

Letter for Jim's thirty-fifth birthday, 5 November 1977

Dear Jim,

In the words of the poet, we are "nel mezzo del camin di nostra vita." But unlike Dante we are not wandering "per una selva oscura." We are not "smarrito." No, not lost, my darling, but found. We have found our way and we stand in the light. Is this not a great accomplishment to have achieved by the first half of one's life?

The poem from my heart that I wanted to give you I cannot write. Poetry, images, flights of imagination fail me at this point. I can only speak to you directly, dearest love and truest comrade. I can only say to you everything our love is becoming, what its bright future is, what it means. I want so much to share with you what is in my heart, to sum up our experiences and all the changes we have been through about *love*, to concentrate our wisdom at this point in time, to give the impetus for the forward development of this positive force of attraction in us.

In the middle of the course of our life, I feel there is nothing more sublime than the struggle we are engaged in—to serve mankind through making revolution, to overthrow the rotten class society of the past and the present and to open the way for the bright future, for the noble cause of communism, grinding away like "rustless cogs"—this is what gives our lives and our love for each other meaning. . . . Our love pertains to the class of workers, toilers, oppressed people. It is only a particular manifestation of proletarian love. We can never make each other happy without plowing back nourishment into the ground where this love has taken root. . . .

Our love for each other is fusing with our course in life. This brings an excitement beyond anything we have known. Also, a sense of security and trust—an openness. What a relief to destroy all the old oppressive ways, to defiantly reject the petty power struggle, to consciously struggle against bourgeois ideology. . . . Our love for each other grows out of principled unity in our political viewpoint and working class stand. . . . Our love will be tested and tested again in the heat of class struggle. And in the dialectics of love that I sum up from my years of mistakes, errors, heartaches, struggles, etc. the way to strengthen the bond of love between two people lies in more and more complete dedication and service to the class.

Comrade, it is you whom I truly love. Your life is a shining example to me. You have made errors and have weaknesses, but you seek to overcome all obstacles to serving the class in a principled way. As a result, you are rapidly correcting the errors and turning the weaknesses into strengths. . . . At the plant, the workers are turning to you for leadership and you are providing real tactical leadership. In the personal sphere you are struggling every minute to uphold the correct line and the result has been great progress in helping to move me and yourself forward. And now, quite recently, the positive and powerful class effects of this struggle . . . are beginning to be evident. People are drawn and will be drawn to the example we set and we will win people over . . . and accumulate forces for the revolution. This is the power of our love we must unleash even more.

Because we are embarked on this course together, because you have overcome so much in order to take a stand with the working people, because you have given so much of yourself so unselfishly, and because your struggle to surge forth in this direction is a constant and genuine struggle—I love you and I deeply admire you. And so I open up to you and you alone the whole intimate part of my life, all my warmth, support, encouragement, tenderness—all my loving. I vow I will share those things with you. We are partners in class struggle.
Signe

New Year's greeting, 31 December 1977

Comrade husband,*

I do not think you are perfect. I see your strengths, I see your weaknesses, and I see your weaknesses developing into strengths. I see your high ideals, your genuine and persistent struggle, your solid commitment to working class revolution. These ideals, this struggle and commitment are the essence of manhood to me. You are better than all the men I have ever known and I love you with a love that is deeper, truer and more real. I feel as if I am loving in the real world for the first time; by comparison, all my notorious lovers and love affairs were chimeras, insubstantial apparitions in a wasteland of rotten romanticism. The basis, the be-all and end-all, was subjective need. But now that that is not the basis any more my needs are in fact being met on every level as never before. My need for a companion in class struggle who loves me is fulfilled. The happiness and joy that I feel in our love, the common dedication that we share is the most powerful stimulus making me struggle harder for the class every day. . . .

To me you are all men, you are the essence of manhood, you are noble, you are a fighter for the oppressed, you are a staunch communist, and you are developing all the time in a forward motion. . . . I know few people as unselfish as you are. You work cheerfully and wholeheartedly for others. Even when I'd like you to stay in bed and make love to me in the morning, I admire you even more for getting up, although it is cold, although you are not feeling well, at the crack of dawn to meet with your fellow workers, to build the trade unions and to make revolution. . . .

I wish in 1978 your struggles bear more and more fruit. May our love continue to grow and our love for each other reflect our love for the masses. Our love is beautiful because its essence is to make us better able to serve the people. Without doubt, we will have more rough times in 1978; there will always be some contradictions between us. We must never lose sight of the essence of our love—proletarian love.

Your comrade and wife

Signe

* We were not yet legally husband and wife. That would happen a month later.

Jim's wedding speech, 7 March 1978

In November 1977, Jim and I set up household together. We were married in Greensboro at the Guilford County Courthouse on January 27, 1978, but we did not get around to celebrating with friends and family until March.

I'd like to welcome you all and say how good it is to celebrate Signe's and my wedding among friends and family. Even though it seems crowded here there were many folks who weren't able to make it because of some important meeting this weekend. They are here in spirit and we have to party all the harder to take up the slack.

Signe and I were married by the state of North Carolina five weeks ago. We exchanged vows to stay with each other in sickness and health, for better or for worse, richer or poorer. Tonight among our friends and family we'd like to put some flesh on those vows.

Signe, guys at work when they heard the news came up and asked me why did I do it. My answer was simple—that I love you. Now there are a few folks here tonight who know me for a long time and they might say—I've heard that before. They know me for being quite a romantic. But I'm not talking about some misty mush—the April rose that only grows in the early spring. I'm talking about a love firmly based on a rocklike shared commitment and dedication to serving the people, and fighting to build a society in which the economic and political system serves the working class. My love for you and our love for each other is a reflection of our love for the people.

Signe, soon after I first met you, I commented I felt like we were members of the same family. It seems that we had similar backgrounds and experiences that led us to the same path. The attitudes and values we had in common bound us together with a thousand threads. In the time we've known each other we have woven these threads into a rich fabric of respect and personal closeness. This is really what a family is.

I promise to continue to build our family and to raise our two children, Alex and Antonia, and possible others, in the spirit of tenderness, cooperation, trust and respect—so that our family is a strong, stable unit best able to serve the people.

Early on in our relationship we began to struggle over differences. This is normal. Nothing exists without contradiction. It is contradiction that moves everything forward. I promise to not turn these differences into petty power struggles of who is right or wrong. I will start from the desire for unity, seek the truth from facts, and use methods of persuasion rather than coercion.

I am very thankful to have you as a loving companion and comrade in the class struggle. If we continue to encourage each other, using our strengths to overcome our weaknesses, we can serve the people better and we will have truly a bright future!

Jim's self-criticism, 30 June 1978

This was written on the eve of the strike at Cone Mill's Granite Finishing Plant in Haw River, N.C.
Signe,

Your criticism is correct. I was rude and arrogant. The basis of this was not lack of respect or lack of affection. In the past two days I have both appreciated your dedication and missed you. (If you don't believe me you can ask any of the guys at work with whom I've talked.)

I have worn myself to a frazzle. This is due to my individualism and self-importance (arrogance). The struggle is very demanding. The drive was very hot. I have gone a week with very little sleep.

I need to go now. I love you and hope to talk with you some tomorrow evening. I should be home by 5.
Jim

Letter, 24 July 1978

Dear Jim,

Marx was being interviewed by an American journalist as they were walking along the rough English coast, and was asked what he foresaw for the future. He answered in a deep, resonating voice—"Struggle!" We have plenty of struggle in store for us. . . . How much work needs to be done in class struggle before we reach the noble goal for which we are striving, before humanity is liberated! You could sit down and converse with Marx. He would have united with your leadership of the Haw River strike. You have an enormous capability for all-sided leadership of the masses. . . . Knowing you and loving you is the most enriching experience of my life.

Signe

Letter, 23 August 1978

Dear Jim,

You can live under the same roof with someone and talk to them all the time and still not be able to say it all. I have problems communicating. Last romantic stronghold—unquenchable need to communicate, to not be afraid to tell you everything. . . .

Darling, these days when I am unhappy, my happiness shines through it, if you understand what I mean. These days, if I do get a little depressed, it is a rare occurrence. It is mild, doesn't last long and is easily overcome. I have some personal fears and I struggle against them. I know they represent an aspect of the incorrect outlook and I feel certain they can be overcome. But sometimes this gnaws at me and I should tell you, instead of carrying it around in myself. I can't think of a delicate way to express it; bluntly, it is a fear of one or both of us being harmed, killed, separated.

In my imagination, it is very easy and very beautiful for us both to grow old together, to know each other and to use each other like an often read book with all the underlining, marginal notes, bent-back leaves and soiled appearance, so that at the end we know each and every wrinkle, each and every mood of the other in the most natural and thoroughgoing intimacy. But it is also easy to imagine the destruction of one or both of us. I cannot bear the thought of you being lost, either to me or to the struggle. In both cases you seem irreplaceable, infinitely valuable. Even the distinction is getting more and more blurred. You are a comrade to me. I see this aspect more and more. It is becoming more integrated with the family tie. I am beginning to understand things I didn't understand before—through living it. We used to talk about a proletarian relationship. Well, we have a long way to go on the road to building one with that character. But when I think how far along we have come in such a short time, from talking to beginning to practice (even if the practice has some flaws and inconsistencies), then I realize quite a bit more is possible. Why is it not possible to dare to go all the way? It is. As long as we are around. Do not be reckless. Don't give your enemies a chance, please.

This is a strange letter. Very hard to write. . . . Just, a little loneliness hit me, in the midst of having plenty of your company—loneliness in the midst of plenty. Aching for your arms and your physical closeness. It is never enough because we never know how long we will be together. . . . Whatever ways you would like me to show my love for you—my love and respect for what you stand for and support with your life—I will show it to you with my life.
Signe

Holiday greeting from workers at Granite Finishing Plant in Haw River to Jim, Christmas 1978

Every year at Christmas, one of the pick-up women or one of the fixers comes around and takes up a collection for the boss man's Christmas present. But what do the boss men do for us workers? Nothing! So this year the cutters on second shift decided to take up a collection for a Christmas present for you. Just to let you know that the cutters are behind you and the union. All the cutters on second shift gave but two and a few of the pick-up gave. All that gave for your present are not going to give the boss man anything. We wanted to let John and Jimmy know the way we feel about the way they do us workers. We thought this would be a good way to do it.
Merry Christmas.
Second Shift Cutting Department

Holiday greeting from Jim to second shift cutters and other Granite workers, Christmas 1978

Fellow workers and friends,
Thank you for a very beautiful card and useful gift! It was an honor to receive it and it serves as another very important lesson to me. This is what I am mainly grateful for—what you have taught me over the years. You said it all in the card. The line I especially liked was how the cutters are behind me *and the union*. It is through the union that we can best improve our lives and keep our self-respect. We've built a lot in a short period of time. Your Christmas message is another example of how we stick together as workers and the workers united will never be

defeated. I wish you all a Merry Christmas and Happy New Year. Before long I hope to be back in the plant to continue the struggle on the inside.
Jim Waller

Anniversary poem from Jim to Signe, 27 January 1979

HAPPY FIRST ANNIVERSARY COMRADE WIFE DARLING SIGNE
In a recess of today
A warm moment tucked away
I grasp my heart on the move
To express my richest love.
Comrade Wife Darling Signe
The year was full of joy for me,
Struggle is our cornerstone
And scaffold through which we've grown.
Struggling to serve the masses
Fighting to end all classes
Bringing the bourgeoisie low
Our love is built and will grow.
Jim

Anniversary poem from Alex (age 10) to Jim and Signe, 27 January 1979

THE MAN AND WOMAN WITH EVERY RIGHT TO LIVE
Once there was a man and woman,
They loved each other heart to heart,
They worked and struggled hard together,
For everything that they desired.
So with that, they have every right to live for.

Anniversary poem from Antonia (age 13) to Jim and Signe, 27 January 1979

ANNIVERSARY POEM TO MAMA AND JIM
Echoing steps in the hall,
The reining monarchs answer the call,
"Signe and Jim, Happy Anniversary!
Oops, we woke you up, didn't we!"

As Half Pint rubs against our legs
Antonia suggests we get a few kegs
(just for laughs, of course)
As gifts are showered on the pair,
Signe exclaims, "Look at this, Jimmy dear!"
Jim, being a little more dignified,
Just looks around quite surprised.
This is wedding anniversary number one,
So look out world 'cause we've just begun.
love,
Antonia

Anniversary letter from Signe to Jim, 27 January 1979

Dearest Jim,

All week long I have been in search of that quiet half hour in which to share my feelings with you and assess our first year together. Only now, at the end of a long, busy week is there a little time—as you are on the road returning from a meeting.

My darling, we have spent a glorious year together, rich in struggle and dedication. We both have struggled very hard to make our relationship have good class effects and that has meant overcoming romanticism, self-cultivation, swings of moods, subjectivity, etc., so that serving the class is always the stable basis on which our commitment to one another rests. Both of us have been pushed forward a great deal in our development as communists. This development has been greatly enhanced on both sides by the love and respect we feel for each other.

As we have developed in struggle and dedication to proletarian revolution, the focus both of us had early on, but especially me, on the relationship, has changed. The tone of our notes and letters to one another has changed somewhat and certainly the frequency. This is inevitable. It is a good thing. It reflects the strength and stability of our love for one another and, most of all, a new level of political maturity. . . .

This year conditions are rapidly ripening for proletarian revolution. The Party is getting in ever better shape. The masses are resisting and fighting back. The advanced and many others are wide open to socialism. I did not have time to write you a love letter this week because the masses are rising up to fight the contamination of our environment by capitalism, because the masses are fighting for our right to a decent and meaningful education and will become aware before long that this is not possible under capitalism. I didn't have time to write because the struggles of long-oppressed minorities are ripening. . . . But then you didn't have much time to read my letter either because of all the time and energy you must put into organizing, . . . because your experience, study and stand make you a good person to train future leaders and because you yourself are a leader to whom people go for advice on how to move their revolutionary work forward.

With so many fast-moving and exciting things happening in the world, with our class stand and desire to bring mankind closer to communism, we both find it hard at times to give our relationship its due. But instead of destroying the relationship, as it would if this were a bourgeois relationship, everything that happens only serves to strengthen it. When we get a chance to be with each other and talk, we give each other support, advice, criticism, encouragement—so that is good. But when we don't get a chance to be together and talk together, it is because we both value the struggle as the highest thing and we both understand it is the reason why we must go without the company of the other for an evening. . . . So that too is good, and when we finally come together we have increased love and respect for each other. I am not painting it ideal—there are still rough spots and will be. But, on the whole, what has happened between us this first year? You have become more sensitive and considerate of me, really trying to give me the personal support, love and reassurance I crave. At the same time, you have not become liberal. You encourage me to always take the hard road, persist in struggle, hold on to MLMTT. I have become much less demanding of you, subordinating my personal needs to the larger struggle as a result of developing a firmer stand and deeper grasp of . . . proletarian ideology. This has not been experienced as any martyrdom on my part. I experience it as the freedom that is the appreciation of necessity. It has resulted in love and security for me, which is truly based on reality, not a pipe dream. . . .

As we see people all over the world struggling, breaking the chains of ancient oppression, we can only feel rightly optimistic. We know the struggle will triumph, though times will get plenty hard, plenty painful. . . . One day it will happen in this country. We are part of this and are preparing the ground for it. What could we want better for our lives? For our children? For our class? For all mankind eventually? I love you, Jim. I treasure your companionship. I am intensely overjoyed by your love.
Happy Anniversary, dearest.
Signe

Letter, 17 February 1979

The ACTWU put all the Cone locals into receivership, canceling upcoming elections for local union officials. The workers at Granite Finishing defied the ban and elected Jim (a.k.a. Blackbeard) president of their local.

Dear Jim,

I was tempted to call and give you some news, but didn't want to make an unnecessary phone call. C called to say some guys on second shift are not going to put up with the mess [the receivership]. . . . They broke the lock off two bulletin boards where the receivership notice was posted, threw the lock in the trash and tore down the signs. The company vows it will get to the bottom of who did it— by taking fingerprints!

Jim, darling, I needed to write this little personal note to you at this time. It has been a very rough day because I am so sick to my stomach and my head that it has worn me down somewhat to have to struggle so hard every minute to meet necessary tasks and deadlines. I thought of not going to Warrenton tonight, but I'm afraid it would take more than pain to keep me back. I would have to be chained to the floor—at least. All during the day, the things that needed to be done that seemed to be overwhelming got added to, as Nelson came over and Dale showed me the stuff you left her. But we worked together and she ran the mimeo non-stop, so much of it did get done, though if there had been more time, the appearance of the work would have been neater. Dale is a real good friend and comrade and I treasure her.

I want to express my love for you, Jim, for our hearts and minds are forever united in the common struggle. Through pain and stress and sacrifice and whatever comes our way our hearts are a stronghold of joy and hope, for we are hastening the day when all mankind will be liberators and liberated by taking some giant steps toward working class revolution.

Really, it does get rough at times. The bourgeoisie strikes an unexpected blow, the masses remain unclear for a little while, we try to squeeze more hours out of each day, nights when we can't sleep, nights when we can't finish making love because the struggle leaves no energy in the reservoir, keeping on with the class struggle under difficult daily conditions in the midst of bourgeois decadence and decay, endeavoring to keep our bearings, keep strict scientific objectivity and follow MLMTT as our great guide and implement the Party's wise decisions. In each struggle there is so much outer wrapping to cut through to get to the essence. There is so much richness and depth to concrete reality.

This doesn't look much like a love letter. I wanted to hearten you some more in your struggles which I know are difficult. I know you feel the enormous weight of responsibility that truly rests on your and other comrades' shoulders. Our love is not separate from these struggles. When we help each other through stress, help each other with tasks, help guide, orient, criticize, teach, listen to each other, it is an expression of love, proletarian love. Therefore, I'm glad you are learning to take comfort in me and I am learning how to give it. . . .

I truly admire you and the way you struggle. We have helped each other a lot and are becoming more and more exemplary in the way of proletarian love. In this way, all the personal longings I ever had are fulfilled and I begin to have confidence I can make a small contribution to proletarian revolution.

I love you more deeply than words can say.

Signe

Letter from Jim to his father, Sidney Waller, 23 February 1979

Dear Sid,

Even to the casual observer, it's obvious that the world is in great disorder. The third world is throwing off the shackles of thousands of years of brutal oppression, e.g., Iran, Nicaragua, Afghanistan, Zimbabwe. At the same time, the two superpowers, U.S. Imperialism and Soviet Social Imperialism, circle around like hungry vultures moving swiftly to prepare for world war. At home here in the U.S., Carter tells us of growing inflation, unemployment, fuel shortages, cutbacks in health care and education. So you ask, what is there to be optimistic about?

And I am optimistic because perhaps as never before in the history of this country people are searching for answers—for solutions to what seem to be overwhelming problems. This takes many forms. For a lot of the youth it's getting lost in drugs, mindless sex and disco. For 900 oppressed people it's committing suicide in the jungles of South America. But these people are not crazy. People are seeking answers the best they can. But without the science of Marxism it is impossible to reach correct conclusions. Only when the masses of people have been made class conscious—conscious of the relations between the different classes and the historic tasks that fall on the shoulders of the working class to become the class to end all classes, all exploitation of man by man, can we see real hope for a bright future.

So I am doing my part, what I can in the course of actual struggles workers are carrying out, for unions, for better wages and benefits, for better schools and health care, to raise their level of class consciousness so that they themselves will carry out the struggle to a higher and higher level, learning from them, teaching and going forward to carry out the revolution to the end.

I'm sending you some of the newsletters we have been producing in our local and also a copy of two articles I helped write.

So in brief that's what I'm doing. Signe and I are very happy with each other. We struggle hard together to reach unity and our love for each other is a reflection of the love we share for the class—and it grows daily. Things with

Alex and Antonia have their ups and downs and it is truly a challenge to be a parent.

Which brings me to the most important point of this letter—how much I appreciate all you've done for me. Even when it was wrong, it was right! What I mean is that I have no doubt how much you love me and want the best for me. I do my best to return that love. Those weekly phone calls mean a lot to me. So keep them coming. Let me hear from you. Send my love to Jane.

Much love,

Jim

Note from Jim, mid-October 1979

Written before Jim left for the second session of the Founding Congress of the Communist Workers Party.

Dear Signe,

Saying goodbye by note doesn't come easy to my fatigued gray matter right now. I share your love for the Party and desire to serve the class struggle. And I too will miss you very much. I'll call Friday to see how things are going. Fight to carry out the Party's line. Have faith in the masses.

Jim

Letter from Alex Goldstein to Workers Viewpoint, December 1979

Thursday, November 29, 1979, K. [Kwame Cannon] and I went to a ladies campus in Durham. K. read a poem out loud by Langston Hughes called "Good Morning, Revolution." And I read a poem by Gil Scott Heron. K. got up and showed them his pants. He said he has holes and dirt spots in his pants and that people like Jimmy Carter can change their clothes even in suits three times a day. The teacher turned everything into a joke. It made K. so mad he just walked right out of the room. One of the ladies there said, "What are you going to do to my husband? He's a capitalist. Are you going to shoot him?" I said, "No, we're going to put a broom in his hand and make him work." Then she said, "I'm a capitalist, but I'm not rich." Then K. said, "Well, if you're not rich then you're not a capitalist." And they kept on talking like that for a while. And then I said, "You're either rich and a capitalist, or you're not rich and not a capitalist." One thing for sure is they hate the word communist. I said, "We are either going to have a world war or socialist revolution. And we are going to make revolution before world war!"

After that was over, K. and I went back in the room and said, "We're gonna make revolution no matter what y'all say!"

BIBLIOGRAPHY

Included under the heading "Books" are works cited in notes and a few other items relevant to my subject that I recommend. "Articles and Reports" lists those referenced in notes in this book and a few other relevant works. Since many primary sources for this book are in my personal archives, I have added an "Author's Archives" listing with a brief description of its contents. The archives include newspaper articles, unpublished material, legal documents, interview tapes, and videotapes, all important for documenting the information in this book. I have not listed individually the numerous newspaper articles used here as sources, but only the main newspapers and a range of dates. Video materials listed include those quoted in the book plus other relevant items.

BOOKS

Bermanzohn, Paul C., M.D., and Sally A. Bermanzohn. *The True Story of the Greensboro Massacre*. New York: Cesar Cauce Publishers & Distributors, 1980.

Bluestone, Barry, and Bennett Harrison. *The Great U-Turn: Corporate Restructuring and the Polarizing of America*. New York: Basic Books, 1998.

Boyd, Blanche McCrary. *The Redneck Way of Knowledge*. New York: Penguin Books, 1983.

Cameron, James. *A Time of Terror*. Baltimore: Black Classic Press, 1994.

Chafe, William. *Civilities and Civil Rights: Greensboro, North Carolina and the Black Struggle for Freedom*. New York: Oxford University Press, 1981.

Chomsky, Noam, and Edward Herman. *Manufacturing Consent: The Political Economy of the Mass Media*. New York: Pantheon Books, 1988.

Dees, Morris, with James Corcoran. *Gathering Storm: America's Militia Threat.* New York: HarperCollins Publishers, 1996.

Donner, Frank. *Protectors of Privilege: Red Squads and Police Repression in Urban America.* Berkeley: University of California Press, 1990.

Dooley, Mike. *Jim Waller M.D.* n.p.

Engels, Frederick. "The Origin of the Family, Private Property and the State." In *Karl Marx and Frederick Engels: Selected Works in One Volume.* New York: International Publishers, 1968.

Franklin, John Hope. *From Slavery to Freedom: A History of Negro Americans.* 4th edition. New York: Alfred A. Knopf, 1974.

———. *Race and History: Selected Essays 1938–1988.* Baton Rouge: Louisiana State University Press, 1989.

Gibbs, Jewelle Taylor. *Race and Justice.* San Francisco: Jossey-Bass Publishers, 1996.

Gornick, Vivian. *The Romance of American Communism.* New York: Basic Books, 1977.

Harrington, Michael. *The Other America: Poverty in the United States.* Revised edition. Baltimore: Penguin Books, 1971.

Hayden, Tom. *Reunion: A Memoir.* New York: Random House, 1988.

Kinoy, Arthur. *Rights on Trial: The Odyssey of a People's Lawyer.* Cambridge, Mass.: Harvard University Press, 1983.

Mann, Emily. "Greensboro: A Requiem." In *Testimonies: Four Plays.* New York: Theatre Communications Group, 1997.

Matthiessen, Peter. *In the Spirit of Crazy Horse.* New York: Viking Press, 1991.

Mullan, Fitzhugh, M.D. *White Coat Clenched Fist: The Political Education of an American Physician.* New York: Macmillan Publishing Company, 1976.

Navasky, Victor S. *Naming Names.* New York: Viking Press, 1980.

Novick, Michael. *White Lies White Power: The Fight against White Supremacy and Reactionary Violence.* Monroe, Maine: Common Courage Press, 1995.

Ridgeway, James. *Blood in the Face: The Ku Klux Klan, Aryan Nations, Nazi Skinheads, and the Rise of a New White Culture.* New York: Thunder's Mouth Press, 1991.

Segrest, Mab. *Memoir of a Race Traitor.* Boston: South End Press, 1994.

Wade, Wyn Craig. *The Fiery Cross: The Ku Klux Klan in America.* New York: Simon & Schuster, 1987.

FORTHCOMING BOOKS

Bermanzohn, Sally. *The Greensboro Massacre through Survivors' Eyes.* Vanderbilt University Press.

Elbaum, Max. *Revolution in the Air: Sixties Radicals Turn to Lenin, Mao and Che.* Verso Press.

ARTICLES AND REPORTS

Bermanzohn, Sally Avery. "The Greensboro Massacre: Political Biographies of Four Surviving Demonstrators." *New Political Science* 20, no. 1: 69–89

——. "Survivors of the 1979 Greensboro Massacre: A Study of the Long Term Impact of Protest Movements on the Political Socialization of Radical Activists." Ph.D. disseration. Graduate Center of the City University of New York, 1994.

Boyd, Blanche McCrary. "Ambush: An Inquiry into the Holy War in Greensboro." *The Village Voice* (26 May 1980).

Braden, Anne. "The Cry Was Unity." *Southern Exposure* (Fall 1999): 27–32.

Hubner, John. "The Red Menace: Clear and Present Danger in Virginia." *Boston Phoenix* 20 (January 1981).

Johnson, Nelson, Rev. "Deadly Betrayal . . . and a Return to Childhood Faith." *The Witness*, March 2001.

Levey, Mark, and Andrew Lang. "Greensboro Special Report: The Story of a Death Squad." *Convergence* (Fall 1985): 7–11

Lilley, Antonia. "The Personal Toll." *Independent Weekly*. Durham, North Carolina 20–26 October 1999.

Ludwig, Erik. "Closing In on the 'Plantation': Coalition Building and the Role of Black Women's Grievances in Duke University Labor Disputes, 1965–1969." *Feminist Studies* (Spring 1999).

McManis Associates, Inc. "Assessment of Planning and Operations of Greensboro, North Carolina Police Department for Demonstration of November 3, 1979." Washington, D.C., May 1980.

Nathan, Marty, M.D., and Paul C. Bermanzohn, M.D. "Justice and the Greensboro Massacre." Greensboro Justice Fund. Brochure. 1999.

Parenti, Michael, and Carolyn Kazdin. "The Untold Story of the Greensboro Massacre." *Monthly Review* 33 (November 1981): 42–50.

Pinsky, Mark. "KKK Victim: Remembering Sandi Smith." *Ms.* (April 1981).

Pitts, Lewis. "Justice Department Handling of the 1979 Greensboro Klan-Nazi Attack and the Special Grand Jury." *Christic Institute*. Washington, D.C., March 1982.

Potorti, David. "Five Dead in Greensboro." *Independent Weekly*. Durham, North Carolina, 20–26 October 1999.

Quant, Ted, and John Slaughter. "We Won't Go Back! The Rise of the Ku Klux Klan and the Southern Struggle for Equality." *Southern Equal Rights Congress*. Mobile, Alabama. 1980.

Swing, William E. "An Administrative Report of the Anti-Klan Rally, Greensboro, North Carolina, November 3, 1979." Greensboro Police Department, 19 November 1979.

Taylor, Flint. "*Waller v. Butkovich*: Lessons in Strategy and Tenacity for Civil Rights Litigators." *Police Misconduct and Civil Rights Law Report*, January/February 1986.

Tockman, Earle. "Tactic of Non-cooperation, Klan Trial." *Guild Notes*. National Lawyers Guild, November–December 1980.

Waller, Signe. "Five Alive: The Legacy of the Greensboro Massacre." *Z* magazine (September 1999): 45–49.

———. "Reconsidering Race and Nation." In *The American Constitutional Experiment*, edited by David M. Speak and Creighton Peden. New York: Edwin Mellen Press, 1991.

———. "We Are Convened by Martyrs." *Greensboro News & Record*, 24 October 1999.

Ward, Kurt C. "Who R We? Performance of Greensboro: A Requiem Gives City a Chance to Examine the 1979 Klan-Nazi Shooting." *UNCG Magazine* (Fall 1999): 17–20.

Wolf, Paul et al. "COINTELPRO: The Untold American Story." Paper presented at the World Conference against Racism in Durban, South Africa, 1 September 2001.

Wheaton, Elizabeth. "The Third of November." *Institute for Southern Studies*. Durham, North Carolina, 1981.

Wrenn, James. "The Greensboro Massacre." In *Encyclopedia of the American Left*, edited by M. J. Buehle et al., 280. Chicago: University of Illinois Press, 1992.

AUTHOR'S ARCHIVES

The archives consist of newspapers clippings filed by subject and date, leaflets, brochures, newsletters, press releases, legal documents, audiotapes, photographs, published and unpublished reports, and videotapes.

Main newspapers: 1977–1986
Greensboro Daily News, Greensboro Record, Durham Sun, Durham Morning Herald, Carolina Peacemaker, Winston-Salem Journal, Winston-Salem *Sentinel, Charlotte Observer,* Raleigh *News & Observer, New York Times, Washington Post, Workers Viewpoint.*

Unpublished material: 1976–1986
Leaflets and newsletters of union locals, national organizations, and grassroots organizations in North Carolina.
Press Releases from the Workers Viewpoint Organization/Communist Workers Party.
Reports from the legal team in the Greensboro case, most notably:
    Gayle Korotkin, "The Campaign for Justice in Greensboro," 1985; and Lewis Pitts, "Draft of 'Pieces of the Greensboro Puzzle,'" date unknown, probably around 1986.
Documents related to litigation in various cases connected with the Greensboro Massacre, including: Greensboro Justice Fund/Greensboro Civil Rights Fund letters, newsletters, and press releases.
Legal documents such as complaints, motions, exhibits, transcripts, and depositions including but not limited to:

United States of America v. Virgil L. Griffin, Edward Woodrow Dawson, David Wayne Matthews, Roland Wayne Wood, Jerry Paul Smith, Jack Wilson Fowler, Jr., Roy C. Toney, Coleman B. Pridmore, and Raeford Milano Caudle, U.S. District Court for the Middle District of North Carolina, Greensboro Division, No. CR-83-53-01-G through CR-83-53-09-G, 21 April 1983.

United States of America v. Virgil L. Griffin et al., No. CR-83-53-01-G through CR-83-53-09-G, 19 December 1983.

Waller v. Butkovich, Deposition of Signe Barbara Waller; U.S. District Court of the Middle District of North Carolina, Greensboro Division, 11–12 July 1984.

"Plaintiffs' Answer to City Defendants' Motion for Summary Judgment," *Waller v. Butkovich*, U.S. District Court for the Middle District of North Carolina, Greensboro Division, No. 80-605-G, 30 January 1985.

"Plaintiffs' Response to ATF Defendants Butkovich and Westra's Motion for Summary Judgment," *Waller v. Butkovich*, U.S. District Court for the Middle District of North Carolina, Greensboro Division, No. 80-605-G, 1 February 1985.

"Plaintiffs' Opposition to Defendants Pelczar, Moses, and Pence's Motion for Summary Judgment," *Waller v. Butkovich*, U.S. District Court for the Middle District of North Carolina, Greensboro Division, No. 80-605-G, 14 December 1984.

Taped interviews (some transcribed) with survivors of the Greensboro Massacre and others, including:

Sally Ann Alvarez, 1 July 1992; Paul Bermanzohn, 27 June 1990; Sally Bermanzohn, 27 June 1990; Willena Cannon, 3 March 1993; Yonni Chapman, 7 April 1990; Tom Clark, 29 June 1990; Elliot Fratkin, 2 November 1992; Alex Goldstein, 2 March 1993; Nelson Johnson, 2 March 1993; Dale Sampson Levin, 5 November 1992; Lucy Lewis, 29 June 1990; Pat and Ellyn Loy, 29 June 1992; Leah Nathan, 2 November 1992; Marty Nathan, 1 November 1992; Don Pelles, 1 July 1992; Roz Pelles, 3 July 1992; Lewis Pitts and Gayle Korotkin, 17 March 1994; Frankie Powell (Chekesha), 5 March 1993; Jane Waller, 19 November 1993; and Floris Cauce Weston, 15 December 1993.

Video productions:

Alvarez, Sally, and Carolyn Jung. *Red November, Black November*. 80 minutes, 1981.

Cran, Bill, and James Reston Jr. "88 Seconds in Greensboro." PBS, Frontline Series. 60 minutes, 1983.

New Jersey Channel. "Greensboro: A Public Dialogue." State of the Arts. 30 minutes, September 1996.

Waters, Jim. "The Guns of November Third." 10 minutes. Date unknown.

Brummel, Bill. "Lawbreakers: The Greensboro Massacre." In *The Ku Klux Klan: A Secret History*, prod. Termite Art Productions. The History Channel. 60 minutes, 2000.

INDEX

ABOUT THE AUTHOR

Signe Waller was born in Brooklyn, New York, on July 14, 1938, as Signe Barbara Burke. She received a bachelor's degree from Brooklyn College in 1960 and a doctorate in philosophy from Columbia University in 1969. With her first husband and their two children, she moved to Greensboro, North Carolina, in 1971. An antiwar activist, she continued a teaching career as an assistant professor of philosophy until 1975.

Politically radicalized in the decade of the 1970s, Signe fell in love with and married Dr. Jim Waller. Both were full-time revolutionaries and supporters of the Workers Viewpoint Organization. When her husband was one of five people killed in the Greensboro Massacre of November 3, 1979, Signe was part of a collective effort by the widows, massacre survivors, and others to bring those criminally culpable to justice. A member of the Board of Directors of the Greensboro Justice Fund for over ten years, Waller is currently involved in the Greensboro Massacre Truth and Reconciliation project.

Both of Signe Waller's children, Antonia Lilley and Alex Goldstein, and two of her four grandchildren reside in Durham, North Carolina. In 1991, Waller married Jim Rose, an Indiana farmer. Since 1992, Rose and Waller have operated a community supported agriculture project (CSA) on their certified organic farm, Earthcraft Farm. They are part of a growing rural/urban movement that is striving to build an alternative food system that is ecologically sustainable, community-based, and democratic. Sharing her time between farm labor and freelance writing, Waller has published many magazine and newspaper articles on a variety of social justice issues from the perspective of a critic of global capitalism.